P9-DNS-480

ALSO BY MARY BETH NORTON

Separated by Their Sex:
Women in Public and Private in the Colonial Atlantic World

In the Devil's Snare: The Salem Witchcraft Crisis of 1692

Founding Mothers & Fathers:
Gendered Power and the Forming of American Society

Liberty's Daughters:
The Revolutionary Experience of American Women, 1750–1800

A People and a Nation:
A History of the United States (co-author)

The British-Americans:
The Loyalist Exiles in England, 1774–1789

1774

1774

The Long Year
of
Revolution

Mary Beth Norton

Alfred A. Knopf
New York · 2020

DALTON FREE PUBLIC LIBRARY
DALTON, MASSACHUSETTS 01226

THIS IS A BORZOI BOOK
PUBLISHED BY ALFRED A. KNOPF

Copyright © 2020 by Mary Beth Norton

All rights reserved. Published in the United States by Alfred A. Knopf,
a division of Penguin Random House LLC, New York, and distributed
in Canada by Penguin Random House Canada Limited, Toronto.

www.aaknopf.com

Knopf, Borzoi Books, and the colophon are registered trademarks of
Penguin Random House LLC.

Library of Congress Cataloging-in-Publication Data

Names: Norton, Mary Beth, author.
Title: 1774 : the long year of Revolution / Mary Beth Norton.
Other titles: Long year of Revolution
Description: First edition. | New York : Alfred A. Knopf, 2020. |
"This is a Borzoi book" | Includes bibliographical references and index. |
Summary: "A book on the American Revolution that looks at the critical
'long year' of 1774, and the revolutionary change that took place
from December 1773 to mid-April 1775, from the Boston Tea
Party and the first Continental Congress to the Battles of Lexington
and Concord."—Provided by publisher.
Identifiers: LCCN 2019021556 (print) | LCCN 2019981577 (ebook) |
ISBN 9780385353366 (hardcover) | ISBN 9780385353373 (ebook)
Subjects: LCSH: United States—History—Revolution, 1775–1783. |
Boston Tea Party, Boston, Mass., 1773. | United States. Continental
Congress. | Lexington, Battle of, Lexington, Mass., 1775. | Concord,
Battle of, Concord, Mass., 1775. | American loyalists.
Classification: LCC E208 .N635 2020 (print) |
LCC E208 (ebook) | DDC 973.3—dc23
LC record available at https://lccn.loc.gov/2019021556
LC ebook record available at https://lccn.loc.gov/2019981577

Jacket images: (bottle) Boston Tea Party tea leaves, collected by
T. M. Harris, Dec. 1773. Massachusetts Historical Society, Boston,
Massachusetts, USA / Bridgeman Images; (background) Boston Tea
Party (detail). Bettmann / Getty Images
Jacket design by Jenny Carrow

Manufactured in the United States of America
First Edition

FEB 1 0 2020

For Martha Farnsworth
and
To the Memory of
Mary Elizabeth Lunny Norton

Come, come, my brave boys, from my song you shall hear,
That we'll crown Seventy-four, a most glorious year.

—*THE NEW-YORK JOURNAL*, AUGUST 18, 1774

———————

I almost wish to live to hear the triumphs of the Jubilee in the Year 1874, to see the medals, pictures, fragments of writings, &c., that shall be displayed to revive the memory of the proceedings of the Congress in the year 1774.

—*DUNLAP'S PENNSYLVANIA PACKET*, NOVEMBER 14, 1774

CONTENTS

ACKNOWLEDGMENTS

Any project that one has thought about for as long as I have thought about this book (since approximately 1972) has racked up the need for many acknowledgments. Over the years, students in my regularly taught undergraduate lecture course, Age of the American Revolution, helped to clarify my ideas, but special thanks are due to the enrollees, both graduate and undergraduate, in my 2012 seminar on the Revolution, and especially Tim Sorg, who generously shared research notes with me. A conversation with Holly Brewer as I began to think seriously about the shape of the book turned out to be crucial to its conceptualization. I also employed students as research assistants; thanks to the graduate students Molly Reed and Jacqueline Reynoso; and to the undergraduates Rachael Comunale, Caroline Estill (a Dartmouth student whose hometown is Ithaca), and Anne Powell. Rachael and Anne spent many hours transcribing innumerable political broadsides, a source that turned out to be more important than I anticipated; I am particularly grateful to them.

The audiences of talks based on my research supplied useful feedback; I thank attendees at St. Joseph's University, Drayton Hall, West Virginia University, the Omohundro Institute, and other participants in two conferences: Constitutional Convention: 225th Anniversary of the Ratification at the University of Georgia in 2013, and Propaganda, Persuasion, and the Press and the American Revolution, 1763–1783 at the University of Hong Kong in 2016, sponsored by the Thomas Jefferson Memorial Foundation. My longtime friend, the late Pauline

Maier, also participated in the Georgia conference. She strongly encouraged me to pursue this topic, and I had looked forward to receiving feedback from her as well, but her early death in August 2013 dashed those hopes.

As was true many years ago when I wrote my dissertation, I appreciated the wise counsel of Bernard Bailyn on an early draft of chapter 1. Special thanks go to my Cornell colleagues, who participated in a discussion of a draft of chapter 2 at our Comparative History Colloquium, where I benefited notably from the comments of Aaron Sachs, Robert Travers, and Rachel Weil. Michael McDonnell kindly read the entire penultimate manuscript. J. B. Heiser critiqued many of the chapters, identifying passages that needed clarification and amplification for readers who were not historians or specialists in the revolutionary period.

I could not have completed the extensive research required for this book without the assistance of librarians and archivists in many repositories. As always, I owe a great deal to Cornell's Olin and Kroch Libraries, where Virginia Cole, Katherine Reagan, and the now retired Peter Hirtle and Anne Kenney, along with the interlibrary loan staff, supplied help above and beyond what any historian could reasonably request or expect. I also appreciated the ability to consult the online databases America's Historical Newspapers (Readex) and Accessible Archives, to both of which Cornell subscribes. At Columbia University, I relied on Susan Hamson; at the New-York Historical Society, on Edward O'Reilly and Tammy Kiter; at William and Mary, on Amy Schindler; and on Mary Jo Fairchild at the South Carolina Historical Society. The staffs of the reading rooms of the Library of Virginia in Richmond, the Alderman Library at the University of Virginia, the Massachusetts Historical Society, the New England Historic Genealogical Society, the Boston Athenaeum, and the New York Public Library were unfailingly helpful, as were those at the Map Room of the National Archives at Kew and the Asia and Africa Room at the British Library, at both of which problems with inadequate indexes caused me to need additional assistance. At the Huntington Library, where I spent a month reading original pamphlets published between late 1773 and early 1775, Jaeda Snow and Alisa Monheim efficiently saw to it that I had access to multiple copies of the same publications, which proved eye-opening in their revelation of different printings, even if the pamphlets did not supply the marginalia I sought.

At other archives, I did not visit in person but nevertheless received copies of relevant documents from helpful staff members: Graham Duncan (South Caroliniana Library); Katherine Wilkins (Virginia Historical Society); Steve Rice (Connecticut State Library); Barbara Austen (Connecticut Historical Society); Sarah Bost (University of North Carolina–Chapel Hill); and Stephanie Fong (Newberry Library).

Apart from librarians and archivists, I thank James Fichter of the University of Hong Kong, with whom I have shared many conversations in person and online about tea controversies in 1773 and 1774; and the National Park Service staff at the Cape Cod National Seashore (George Price, the superintendent; Bill Burke, cultural resources program manager; and Chris Anderson, ranger), who ensured I was able to visit the probable site of the December 1773 wreck of the *William*. My friend Heather Huyck, retired from the Park Service, was essential in facilitating that visit.

My thanks too go to Victoria Wilson, my editor at Alfred A. Knopf, who offered guidance with a light hand; her assistant, Marc Jaffee; the designer, Betty Lew; and the meticulous copy editor, Ingrid Sterner.

Finally, this book is dedicated in part to my good friend Martha Farnsworth (Riche), a former director of the U.S. Census Bureau, who for years has joined me on travels to Caribbean islands and more recently to Italy. She and I bonded quickly when we first met in Ithaca years ago, especially after we learned we were both proud graduates of the University of Michigan. The other dedicatee is my mother, who died in August 2018 shortly before her 105th birthday. She too was a loyal University of Michigan graduate (class of 1935), and she inquired frequently about the progress of this book. Alas, she did not live to see it in print.

INTRODUCTION

The year 1774 dawned sixteen days after the Boston Tea Party, and by the time its twelve months ended, the royal provincial governments were in disarray, the First Continental Congress had convened and adjourned, and the battles at Lexington and Concord were just three and a half months in the future.

That sentence opened the first chapter of my first book, published in 1972. My research on Loyalist exiles during the Revolution convinced me that events in 1774 were critical to the development of the movement for independence, and I have remained convinced of that conclusion ever since. This book is the belated result of that conviction.

In 1774, the phenomenon known as loyalism first appeared, as did the term "Loyalist." The emergence of people who called themselves Loyalists signaled an important change in the colonial political climate, for their presence implied the existence of the opposite phenomenon: people who were openly *disloyal*. Before 1774, most politically aware Americans were united in criticizing policies about colonial taxation and governance that Parliament adopted after the end of the Seven Years' War in 1763. Conservatives and radicals debated methods of resistance, but well into the 1770s free colonists uniformly identified themselves as loyal subjects of King George III and gloried in their membership in the British Empire. For revolution to occur, that identification as loyal Britons had to change: some men and women had to start thinking differently about America's relationship with the empire, while others persisted in retaining their traditional loyalty to the Crown. I have come to term the period of dramatic change "the long 1774"—that is, the sixteen months between December 1773 and mid-April 1775. The unprecedented events that occurred in the English colonies in North America during those months are the subject of this book.

Almost all historians who study the Revolution as a whole have focused on the *revolutionaries*—the men who led resistance to Great Britain starting in the mid-1760s. For such scholars, developments in 1774 appear to be of a piece with previous occurrences. The Stamp Act riots of 1765, opposition to the Townshend Acts in 1767–1770, the Boston Massacre of 1770, the *Gaspee* incident of 1772: all seem to lead inexorably, if not almost inevitably, to the revolutionary war that followed. When historians have concentrated on events preceding the outbreak of fighting, they have devoted considerably more attention to Massachusetts than to the rest of eastern North America.

Yet a focus on those who remained loyal to the empire points up the significance of events in 1774 throughout the colonies, not just in Massachusetts. The evolving tactics pursued by colonial opponents of British policies began to cause new divisions in popular opinion, everywhere leading to increasing political polarization. Still, almost all scholars who have studied the Loyalists have confined their attention specifically to that subject, rather than venturing to approach the wider topic of the Revolution as a whole from the perspective of their previous work on those loyal to the Crown.

This book, by contrast, has been shaped by my long-standing interest in the Loyalists. Rather than viewing the months between December 1773 and April 1775 with the common implicit or explicit assumption that resistance leaders commanded a people largely unified around a radical agenda, it reveals the many debates, disagreements, and disruptions that characterized the period in all the colonies, from New Hampshire south to Georgia. Instead of privileging the viewpoints of men like Samuel Adams and focusing almost exclusively on his province of Massachusetts, it gives voice to such moderate colonists as Joseph Reed and John Dickinson of Pennsylvania and details the disputes that roiled New York throughout the year. It pays attention

to the opinions of colonial officials and others who sent regular reports
to London about political circumstances in their colonies. It also ana-
lyzes the writings of the Loyalist pamphleteers, who first published
their vehement dissents while the Continental Congress was in session
in September, and examines how more radical authors responded to
Loyalists' arguments.

I aim, in short, to include the views of all of those who participated
in formal political discourse in the colonies in 1774, regardless of their
gender, race, or place of residence. I sought evidence in a variety of
libraries, from the National Archives of the United Kingdom to the
Huntington Library in San Marino, California, and many universities
and state historical societies. The narrative has been constructed from
the published and unpublished correspondence of political leaders and
ordinary folk alike; from pamphlets and broadsides; from the official
records of colonial governments and their revolutionary successors;
and from newspapers with reports of local meetings and other activities, along with essays expressing a wide range of opinions. Because
of the emphasis on formal political discourse, it devotes less attention
to those who are often termed "the people out of doors," although it
does not exclude them entirely from consideration. As will be seen in
the following pages, people who did not leave written records of their
opinions nevertheless revealed their ideas through their actions.

The book's basic narrative is perhaps deceptively familiar. It begins
in October 1773, when seven ships carrying East India Company (EIC)
tea sailed from Great Britain to North America under the terms of the
recently adopted Tea Act, which for the first time allowed the EIC to
sell its tea directly to colonists. Five arrived in the ports of Boston,
Charleston, and Philadelphia in December, while another wrecked
on Cape Cod. The other vessel, blown far off course by an Atlantic
gale, did not reach New York until April after spending the winter in
Antigua. In Charleston, customs officers seized and stored the tea; in
Philadelphia and New York, the ships were not allowed to enter the
harbor; and in Boston, famously, men crudely disguised as Indians
destroyed the tea. Subsequently, colonists had to await Britain's reaction to the fate of the ships. News of that reaction first arrived in
mid-May, with further details trickling in over the next few months.
Americans learned that Parliament had closed the port of Boston until

the tea was paid for, then followed up with a series of punitive laws known as the Coercive Acts.

During the summer of 1774, Americans everywhere discussed the appropriate response to such parliamentary measures, leading to the convening of the (First) Continental Congress in September. Before adjourning in late October, the congressmen adopted resolutions on the controversy and, more important, called for the creation of a series of local committees to enforce a trade boycott of Great Britain. Throughout the rest of the year, the committees worked to establish their legitimacy and, in conjunction with newly elected provincial congresses, began to challenge the authority of the existing colonial governments. By the first months of 1775, many people were expressing the belief that war would begin in the spring, and those predictions proved correct when clashes occurred at Lexington and Concord in mid-April.

That story is well known to historians. The debates and disagreements that lay behind it have commonly been ignored, with the partial exception of some local and state-level studies.

Although the Bostonians' destruction of the tea is usually presented as unproblematic, it was not. Many colonists, including such prominent men as George Washington and Benjamin Franklin, believed that the destructive act was unwise.

The plan to elect a congress to coordinate opposition tactics came not from radical leaders but from conservatives who hoped for reconciliation with Britain. Then missteps by colonial governors obeying shortsighted directives from London helped to turn a body that could possibly have been the moderating force conservatives sought into one that went in a different direction.

Extralegal bodies formed by towns, counties, and provinces as directed by the congress encountered many obstacles to their exercise of authority, including doubts and hesitations from their own members.

The most vocal advocates of the freedom of the press and of the right to dissent in 1774—both key values for modern Americans— were not revolutionaries but Loyalists, who complained loudly and long about being denied the ability to publish their views freely.

Ordinary people did not always act in accordance with the wishes of their nominal leaders, sometimes pursuing more radical actions, sometimes rejecting what seemed to be the verities of the resistance movement, such as boycotting EIC tea.

In short, the standard narrative of events that focuses solely or primarily on revolutionary leaders, especially those in Massachusetts, and their opinions and publications omits or elides many key aspects of what happened during "the long 1774." Americans today tend to look back on the politics of those days and see unity in support of revolution. That vision is false. The population was divided politically then, as now.

Notes on citation practice: Some of the letters and documents cited here have been published numerous times, and some I read originally in manuscript. I have tried to cite them where they are most readily accessible—for example, in K. G. Davies, ed., *Documents of the American Revolution, 1770–1783* (here abbreviated as *DAR*); Paul H. Smith et al., eds., *Letters of Delegates to Congress, 1774–1789* (here *LOD*); or in the collected papers of revolutionary leaders. On occasion, most often when such materials appear both in modern collections and in Peter Force, ed., *American Archives,* series 4 (here *AA* 4), I have supplied duplicate citations. Because the great majority of citations in this book come from documents produced in the year 1774, in the interest of brevity I have omitted "1774" in footnotes when that date seems superfluous, in second and subsequent citations in the same notes. I have followed the same practice in chapter 1 ("1773") and chapters 7, 8, and 9 ("1775"), retaining the year only when there is some ambiguity.

A note on terminology: As will be seen in quotations in this book, people at the time sometimes adopted the British terms "Whig" and "Tory" to identify political allegiances—the latter commonly being a pejorative term for more conservative colonists, because Americans tended accurately to see their political beliefs as falling within the tradition of English Whigs. The text of this book primarily employs "supporters of resistance," "conservatives," or "moderates" to characterize its principal actors.

An explanation of format and dating: This book is firmly based on the North American continent. Accordingly, unlike some other works, its narrative does not move across the Atlantic to Britain to

explore parliamentary or ministerial debates over American policy in any depth. Rather, it uses the heading *Advices from London*
(occasionally elsewhere) to introduce information about crucial events
in England or to quote the contents of letters or, in one chapter,
a colonist's London journal. As readers of colonial newspapers will
recognize, the heading *Advices from* . . . commonly precedes articles
conveying news from other locations. In this book, the dates of the
sections titled *Advices from* . . . accord with the dates of the chapters
in which they appear. Still, readers should be aware that because sailing from England to America (and the reverse) usually took a month
to six weeks, or occasionally more, the news would arrive later, and
erratically. Therefore, because chronology is an essential component of
understanding developments in the colonies during 1774, the narrative
will identify with precision the timing of the arrival of key pieces of
news in various American ports.

1774

CHAPTER I

THAT CURSED TEA

During the stormy early morning hours of December 11, 1773, a vessel carrying tea and other cargo to Boston wrecked about two miles southeast of Race Point, the northern tip of Cape Cod. On board the *William* were fifty-eight chests of East India Company tea, fifty-five of which were successfully salvaged. The three damaged chests, each containing about 350 pounds of Bohea (black) tea, remained on the Cape when the other chests were transported later in the month to the safety of the British headquarters at Castle William, an island in Boston harbor. Responding to the sudden arrival of approximately 1,000 pounds of tea on their shores, Cape residents worked to earn it, bought and sold it, argued and fought over it, and destroyed some of it.

In so doing, they revealed what could well have happened elsewhere in Britain's North American colonies had six other vessels carrying the company's tea been able to offer their cargoes for sale. All seven ships had left England together in October with tea that the EIC was authorized to sell directly to colonists under the terms of a recently adopted law. Upon their arrival in Boston, Charleston, Philadelphia, and New York, the cargoes met different fates, most notoriously destruction at the hands of a large number of disguised Bostonians but also seizure by customs officials (Charleston) and exclusion (New York and Philadelphia).

The story of the so-called Boston Tea Party—it was not dubbed that until the early nineteenth century—is well known today, in large part because it has become an iconic event for Americans, and not just for those who align themselves with a political faction named the Tea Party. It has been the primary subject of two books and is discussed in many others. For most Americans, the "Tea Party" tale encompasses the beginning and end of colonists' reaction to EIC imports in December 1773. But Bostonians' violent response to East India Company tea constituted only one of the diverse reactions to Parliament's Tea Act. Residents of each of America's largest cities, along with those living on Cape Cod, had to confront directly the challenge posed by large amounts of tea sent by the East India Company.

TEA, LEGAL AND ILLEGAL

Neither American colonists nor Britons expected problems with tea as the year 1773 began. The colonists loved tea; a contemporary described them as "probably the greatest tea drinkers in the universe," for "even the very paupers" drank tea twice a day. Estimates of consumption varied widely, but all observers concurred that Americans drank "prodigious" amounts of the hot caffeinated beverage. Tea composed a regular part of daily meals. It also served as the basis for socializing in genteel households; families that aspired to gentility purchased teapots, tea tables, and other accessories as soon as they had sufficient income. Women proudly presided over domestic tea tables and over the conversations between women, and among women and men, that took place there, while men traditionally gathered in male-only groups at taverns and coffeehouses.

Calculating the quantity of tea sold in the colonies was and is difficult because so much of it was smuggled. All the tea originated in China, but the once-exotic commodity took various routes into North America. Legal tea came via the East India Company, the monopoly established by England in 1600. Before 1773, the law required the EIC to sell its tea at London auctions to wholesalers, who then vended it to retailers. Such tea was taxed when it entered Britain from Asia and again when exported to the colonies. Yet untaxed tea was smuggled into American ports in many ways, most notably from Holland and its colonies, especially the tiny island of St. Eustatius in the northern Caribbean. Thus smuggled tea was uniformly referred to as "Dutch,"

St. Eustatius, the tiny Dutch island in the northeastern Caribbean, was ideally situated for smugglers and their trade. Located in the Leewards and surrounded by other Dutch possessions, it offered easy access from the Atlantic. Few nearby islands belonging to other nations could threaten the clandestine commerce. The extinct volcanoes in the background of the print sheltered the ample anchorage on the eastern side of the island from prevailing winds.

regardless of its origins. But clandestine sources of tea also included ports in Germany, France, Portugal, Denmark, the Danish Caribbean, and Sweden. On the American side of the Atlantic, Rhode Island, Long Island, and Chesapeake Bay served as notorious smugglers' havens.

A rare surviving set of instructions for smuggling tea discloses how the surreptitious trade operated. In March 1774, Samuel and William Vernon of Newport, Rhode Island, addressed Captain William Tanner of their sloop *Dolphin,* directing him to sail to Charleston. He was to load the vessel there with rice, spending as little time as possible in port before formally clearing his cargo for Madeira at the customshouse. If he met other ships while at sea, he should tell them he was sailing to the English port of Hull. Instead of going to Madeira or Hull, though, he was to head to Hamburg, where he should sell the rice to a merchant the Vernons specified. He was to conceal his actual plans from that merchant, informing him that he was next sailing to Gothenburg,

Sweden, to buy herring, but when he arrived at Gothenburg he was to use the proceeds of the rice sale to purchase tea, again from a specific firm. He had to load the tea quickly, the Vernons warned Tanner, because authorities in London would soon learn why he was there and might try to prevent the next leg of his voyage. Then Captain Tanner was to sail back across the Atlantic to the Danish Caribbean island of St. Croix, where he was to sell the tea. Even though the letter did not reveal what the owners expected to happen to the tea after the captain disposed of it, a subsequent trip to North America, perhaps to Charleston or Newport, was obviously implied. The Vernons closed their letter by wishing Captain Tanner "a prosperous Voyage."

Among the most revealing aspects of the Vernons' instructions was the emphasis on the necessity for Tanner to conceal his plans, both from random ships he might encounter en route and from his associates. After he falsely cleared the vessel for Madeira, other vessels were to be told he was bound for an English port. The merchant in Hamburg could be informed truthfully that he was sailing to Sweden, but he was to hide his intention to purchase tea there. Only after leaving Gothenburg for St. Croix was he free to inform others, including his own crew, where he was going.

Such covert tactics continued when tea neared the North American mainland. New York authorities had a particularly difficult time controlling smugglers because of the complex local geography around Manhattan. Lieutenant Governor Cadwallader Colden reported that ships from St. Eustatius or Holland did not enter the harbor but instead "anchor at some distance in the numerous bays and creeks that our coast and rivers furnish, from whence the contraband goods are sent up in small boats." Henry Hulton, a customs commissioner stationed in Boston, explained that the same practice also occurred elsewhere along the Atlantic seaboard: the smugglers' ships "never come nigh their ports of discharge before they are cleared of all their illicit goods by small Vessels on the Coast." The only way to combat this trade, he advised, was for Britain to deploy many small ships for the purpose. He pointed out that "the Men of War may give protection to such Vessels, but never of themselves will suppress this illicit commerce."

The clandestine nature of such activities makes it hard to assess how much tea was furtively smuggled into the North American colonies in the eighteenth century. But that the surreptitious trade existed was evident to everyone; one historian has suggested that in some years just 25 percent of the tea consumed in the colonies had been imported legally, while another scholar estimated that the figure could have been as low as 10 percent. Colonial customs entries recorded only 128 pounds of East India Company tea imported into Philadelphia in 1772, yet a knowledgeable observer noted that city residents annually consumed about two thousand chests of Bohea tea. A Philadelphia customs officer's comment in early 1774 that "smuggling is become almost universal in this town" was supported by a local woman who about the same time remarked casually that what merchants "have done all along" was to "Run it from the Dutch." New York, similarly, registered just 530 pounds of imported tea in 1772, but the city was said to consume about 1,500 pounds each year.

Judging by customs records, Bostonians were somewhat more law-abiding than Philadelphians or New Yorkers. They imported more than 265,000 pounds of duty-paying tea in 1771 and over 107,000 the following year. But in 1771 Massachusetts residents also reputedly drank an additional 575,000 pounds of smuggled tea. Such illegal tea did not always find buyers, as James Rivington, a Manhattan printer and bookseller who also retailed tea on the side, learned to his likely dismay. In July 1774, he sent four chests of green Hyson tea, concealed in two large trunks conveyed by a British officer, to his Boston agent, the young bookseller Henry Knox. "This being a nice Affair I must intreat that the utmost Secrecy Vigilance and prudence be employed for the Security and early sale of this Article," he wrote, assuring Knox that the tea was "utterly free from duty"—that is, smuggled.

Knox responded that he, being unfamiliar with selling the commodity, consulted "the first Tea Dealers" in Boston, who explained that "this is the dullest time for it they ever knew" and that another type of tea, the smoky Souchong, would have been more attractive to potential purchasers. Knox noted that "the market was pretty overstock'd" and that "other large Quanti[ti]es" had also been imported from New York. He did not mention another possible reason for the relative lack of demand—a current boycott of tea in Boston (discussed in chapter 2). Knox assured Rivington that he would do his best to sell the tea, but as late as February 1775 he had managed to retail only one chest "to my particular friends." Smugglers, in short, had to confront the same problems of supply and demand as did legitimate merchants.

Colonists disagreed over the relative merits and quality of EIC and smuggled tea. But one point was clear: illegal tea was much cheaper than its legal alternative, about half or at most two-thirds the price. Enforcement of the customs laws was so lax that shipowners like the Vernons knew they rarely needed to worry about seizure of their cargoes in America; one contemporary hypothesized that only one in five hundred clandestine voyages ended in fines and confiscation. Thus, given the size of the colonial market, the risks were few and the potential profits "immense," one man remarked. Merchants and officials in the colonies and the home island alike accordingly strategized about how the EIC could capture the large share of the American market that smugglers dominated.

By early 1773, actions by Parliament and the ministry, coupled with colonial reactions, tended to increase rather than decrease the surreptitious trade in tea. The problem arose from the particular configuration of tea taxes developed as a part of the Townshend duties of 1767. The British government needed revenue to help pay off the huge debt run up to win the Seven Years' War against France, which ended in 1763.

Its first major attempt to raise money from the colonies, the Stamp Act of 1765, aroused extensive opposition, in part because colonists complained of having no voice in its passage. The law, mimicking one long in force in England, required tax stamps on legal and printed documents. No law could have been better designed to anger such influential colonists as printers, merchants, and lawyers. Protests occurred in many port cities; merchants were pressured to agree not to import British goods until the law was repealed; crowd actions eventually forced all the men appointed to distribute the tax stamps to resign; and the Stamp Act Congress met in New York to adopt resolutions against the act. Parliament repealed the law the following year.

But Great Britain still needed added revenue, and because colonists had routinely paid customs duties on items purchased from foreign countries, in 1767 Chancellor of the Exchequer Charles Townshend proposed, and Parliament adopted, a law that laid duties on tea and a few other imports into the colonies. The Townshend duties, though, taxed items originating within the British Empire; further, the money collected was designated to pay some colonial officials' salaries, previously controlled by (and thus a source of leverage for) provincial assemblies. Once more, colonists protested. In 1768 and 1769, many men and women signed nonimportation and nonconsumption agreements, promising to boycott British goods, especially tea, until the taxes were rescinded. Again, Parliament retreated, in 1770 repealing most of the duties but leaving the tea tax in force as a symbol of British authority. In the wake of repeal, the colonial boycott of tea largely collapsed, except in the middle colonies. Thus the minuscule importations of legally taxed tea into Philadelphia and New York during the early 1770s were explained not only by other factors but also by those jurisdictions' continuing adherence to the earlier boycott agreements. The young Philadelphia lawyer Joseph Reed, for instance, commented that relying on the "clandestine Trade [in tea] . . . has been deemed a Species of Patriotism" because following the law would surrender "an essential Principle of Liberty." By contrast, as was obvious from the record of their purchases of EIC tea, after 1770 many Bostonians abandoned the boycott and resumed paying the tea duty, which aroused considerable criticism from other colonists.

The retained tea tax became relevant in 1773 when Frederick, Lord North, First Lord of the Treasury, and Parliament tried to rescue the East India Company from a fiscal crisis. The Tea Act, passed in April and signed by King George III in May, was intended to allow the company to compete more effectively in the American market. The law freed the EIC from the requirement to vend all its tea at English auctions. That allowed the company to dispatch tea directly to American agents, called consignees, who could then better control the selling price. Although the Townshend duty of 3 pennies a pound was continued, the taxes paid by the company as the tea entered England were eliminated when the commodity was reexported. These provisions, it was thought, would make it possible for legally taxed tea to compete in price with smuggled varieties.

Although the ministry did not design the Tea Act of 1773 to force the colonies to accept Parliament's right to tax them, Americans of all political persuasions interpreted it that way. A Boston customs official, for example, commented that the act was "well calculated to Establish the Authority of Parliament in America." A frequently consumed, desirable, addictive commodity would now possibly be cheaper if Americans paid a tax laid by Parliament than if they did not. The partial breakdown of the tea boycott in 1770 after the repeal of the other Townshend duties suggested that Americans would readily purchase inexpensive tea, regardless of whether it was taxed. After all, Bostonians and others outside the middle colonies had already been buying the more expensive East India Company tea.

ADVICES FROM LONDON

August 1773. William Palmer, an employee of the East India Company, gives orders about what tea should be sent to America under the provisions of the Tea Act. "The Bohea tea to be taken out of what was refused by the buyers last sale: but particular care to be taken that none under the degree of middling or good middling, nor any damaged chests are sent," he tells the director of the EIC warehouse. As for better-quality tea, "a small assortment of about a dozen or twenty small chests of Hyson, Souchong, Congou, and each specie of Singlo tea, viz: Twanky, Skin, and First Sort" should also be dispatched to the colonies. Because Singlo spoils more easily than other tea varieties, he recommends trying to increase its sales, even if it has to be sold at the same price as the lower-quality black tea, Bohea. That will free the company from "the disagreeable alternative of selling it here under prime cost, or keeping a greater quantity unsold in their warehouses, until it is spoiled by age." In the end, the EIC sends to America 1,586 chests of Bohea, 70 chests of Congou, 290 chests of Singlo, 70 chests of Hyson, and 35 chests of Souchong, totaling nearly 600,000 pounds of tea. The chests are divided unevenly among seven ships—four sailing to Boston and one each to Philadelphia, New York, and Charleston.

OPPOSITION TO EIC TEA BEGINS

Even given the common delays of transatlantic communication during the late eighteenth century, an accurate description of the Tea Act's provisions took a remarkably long time to reach the colonies. One reason was that Lord North failed to inform the secretary of state for America, William Legge, Lord Dartmouth, that he should alert colonial governors to the EIC's plan to sell tea directly to North American consumers through merchants designated as consignees. Such neglect revealed both that North did not anticipate the EIC's encountering any unusual difficulties selling its tea under the terms of the new act and that he assumed the cheaper tea would readily attract North American customers.

Just as ocean voyages consumed from one to two months, so too the distribution of news up and down the Eastern Seaboard, most easily accomplished by sea, often required several weeks or a month. On this occasion, an act approved by the king in May was not described unofficially in an American newspaper until mid-August, when a Philadelphia paper published the following extract from a letter written in London in late May to a resident of that city:

> I take the first Opportunity of acquainting you that the East India Company have obtained Leave, by Act of Parliament, to export their Teas from England Duty free; and in a short Time, perhaps a Month, a Cargo will be sent by them to Boston (subject to the Duty payable in America) to be sold in that Place on their Account, and they mean to keep America so well supplied that the Trade to Holland for that Article must be greatly affected.

This paragraph was reprinted in newspapers from Portsmouth, New Hampshire (August 27), to Charleston, South Carolina (September 21). Frederick Pigou Jr., the letter's author, had some details correct, in particular the intent to foster more effective competition with smuggled "Dutch" tea, but he erred when asserting that EIC tea would be sent to Boston alone. Furthermore, he greatly underestimated the time that it would take to assemble such a cargo.

A New York newspaper published the Tea Act in full in early September, but that aroused little immediate comment. The statute's language was convoluted and its provisions difficult to understand, so early commentators sometimes misinterpreted its tangled prose. By mid-October, Americans in the North did know that EIC tea would be sent to Philadelphia, New York, and Charleston as well as to Boston, but Charleston residents themselves did not learn that a tea ship was headed there until November 15.

As the news arrived in bits and pieces, colonial governors and other residents of North America had to depend on the incomplete information found in local newspapers. Just as Lord Dartmouth, the man responsible for formal communications with colonial officials, had received no prior notice of the EIC's scheme, so too governors had little time to prepare for the EIC's shipments. Most did not even have verified copies of the act until after protests began. Officials everywhere were caught off guard by both the new statute and the colonists' reaction to it.

The adoption of the Tea Act and the EIC's decision to circumvent most of the American merchants who had previously sold its tea—only a few became the favored consignees—reenergized the opposition to the Townshend tea duty. Colonial officials later charged that smugglers in particular actively opposed the law, but all merchants who retailed one of the most commonly consumed commodities in America were potentially affected by the prospect that the EIC's new strategy could undercut that very profitable business. Additionally, colonists' hostility to the duty in the late 1760s had rested not only on its commercial effects but also on their resistance to taxes imposed by Parliament, as well as on the intended use of those taxes—paying the salaries of some colonial officials. Thus, in spite of the recent crumbling of boycotts of EIC tea, circumstances were ripe for renewed protests.

Americans' first published attacks on the direct importation of East India Company tea appeared almost simultaneously in New York, Philadelphia, and Boston between October 6 and 14, 1773. The authors, who could not have known what others were writing, took significantly different approaches to their mutual subject. Two Bostonians focused newspaper essays on the potential effects of the act

on commerce, whereas a New York merchant, Alexander McDougall, attacked the EIC itself in five broadsides collectively titled *The Alarm*. McDougall, a longtime political activist and member of the Sons of Liberty, an organization founded to oppose the Stamp Act, charged that the EIC was a corrupt monopoly and a brutal ruler of India. Only the last essay, published late in the month, suggested a means of resistance: he advocated rejuvenating the tea boycott.

Other tactical suggestions emerged from the nearly simultaneous publications of two Philadelphia authors. On October 9, Thomas Mifflin, a Philadelphia Quaker merchant and member of the Pennsylvania assembly writing as "Scaevola," published a broadside reminding readers of the recent history of colonial protests. Directly addressing the consignees, he compared them to the stamp distributors of 1765, all of whom had been forced to resign by crowd action. His threat to the tea agents was implicit but real. If they would not quit voluntarily, as he asked, the analogy to stamp distributors called to mind an effective alternative. Then, two days later, the physician Benjamin Rush recommended another approach. Writing as "Hamden," Rush warned that if the tea were landed, customers would surely buy it. After that, he lamented, "farewell American liberty! We are undone forever," because such purchases would admit Parliament's authority to tax the colonies. So, he urged, "let us with one heart and hand oppose the landing of it." In an emotional appeal that would later be echoed many times by others, he concluded, "Remember, my Countrymen, the present aera—perhaps the present struggle will fix the constitution of America forever.—think of your ancestors, and of your posterity."

Therefore by mid-October 1773, two Philadelphians and a New Yorker had already proposed three potentially effective tactics as a means of resisting the Tea Act: persuading—or, implicitly, forcing—consignees to resign; renewing the older nonimportation and nonconsumption agreements; and preventing the tea from landing in the first place. Yet not all Philadelphians agreed with such ideas. The moderate John Dickinson, the respected author of *Letters from a Farmer in Pennsylvania*, which had rallied opposition to the Townshend Acts, maintained silence on the Tea Act until October 30. Then he published a straightforward legal analysis of the statute's language. A month later, he suggested merely that Pennsylvanians not cooperate in the unloading or sale of EIC tea, a more passive response than those advocated by any of his fellow essayists.

But Philadelphians chose to follow the advice of Mifflin and Rush rather than Dickinson, becoming the first to mobilize in large numbers against the Tea Act. On October 16, a "very considerable meeting" at the statehouse, reportedly including many men "of the *first* rank," adopted several resolutions that, widely reprinted, were later to serve as the template for other such statements, including Boston's. The resolutions began with the principle that "the disposal of their own property is the inherent right of freemen [and] that there can be no property in that which another can, of right, take from us without our consent." The Philadelphians then asserted that the tea duty was a tax to which Americans had not consented; that its aim of paying the salaries of Crown officials undermined the authority of American assemblies; and that every American freeman had the responsibility to offer "a virtuous and steady opposition" to the "violent attack upon the liberties of America" represented by the East India Company's planned tea imports. Any man who aided and abetted that enterprise, the attendees declared, was "an enemy to his country."

A letter sent to England from Philadelphia early in October—before the essays appeared in print and prior to the local meeting—predicted that Americans' reaction to the impending tea shipments could not be foreseen. But the publications by Mifflin and Rush and the city's resolutions galvanized opposition to East India Company tea. Later that same month, a Philadelphian accurately anticipated a negative response, which he attributed to the "communication of sentiments" between New Yorkers and Philadelphians. Newspaper articles and broadsides were "most absolutely asserting the rights of the Americans," he warned a British correspondent, drawing comparisons between the Tea and Stamp Acts.

In Boston, by contrast, resistance lagged. The governor of Massachusetts, Thomas Hutchinson, initially thought that Boston opinion on EIC tea was sufficiently divided that the consignees, who included two of his sons and a family firm headed by Richard Clarke, would "meet with no great trouble" in receiving and disposing of the shipments. A consignee too wrote of his hope that "no obstacle" would be placed in the merchants' path. But then the reprinting of the Scaevola essay in *The Boston Gazette* on October 25 served as a crucial catalyst for local activists, and three days later "A Merchant" publicly lamented the absence of a local meeting comparable to that in Philadelphia. Clearly aroused by Mifflin's suggestive analogy between tea consignees and stamp distributors, on the evening of November 1 a group of men demanded that the consignees appear at the Liberty Tree two days later to resign their commissions—just as the Boston stamp distributor had done in 1765.

At the appointed hour on November 3, only a "trifling" group of protesters turned up at the Liberty Tree—so few, remarked one man, "that many were ashamed of it." Accordingly, the consignees did not even consider complying with the request to resign. Instead, they gathered with allies at Richard Clarke's warehouse, where the small but rowdy crowd came from the Liberty Tree to confront them before dispersing. Because "scarce any persons of note" were initially involved, the governor thought that the protests could be disregarded. But he quickly changed his mind, for on November 4 he commented that "the gentlemen of the town have shown more resolution upon this occasion than I have known before." The next day, Samuel Adams, founder of the town's official committee of correspondence, chaired a town meeting that proved the governor's second opinion correct. On November 5, Bostonians adopted the Philadelphia resolutions of the previous month with only minor changes, asserting that "the words of certain judicious resolves lately entered into by our worthy brethren the citizens of Philadelphia" perfectly expressed their own views. They also denounced the consignees' negative response to the resignation demands as "daringly effrontive." And they continued to urge the consignees to reject their commissions.

Thomas Hutchinson, the descendant of a Massachusetts family with roots in the province dating back to the early seventeenth century, had at the time recently been subjected to vehement attacks by Samuel Adams and other local political leaders. In personal correspondence with British officials the previous decade, Hutchinson had privately questioned whether Americans' claims of rights within the empire could be fully justified. Benjamin Franklin, Massachusetts's agent in London, had obtained the letters and sent them to Boston under injunctions of secrecy. The restrictions were not followed; the letters were published, and, in so many words, all hell had broken loose. Therefore, that Hutchinson—who could not doubt the Boston's leaders' commitment to resisting British policies they disliked—initially underestimated their reaction to EIC tea shipments reconfirms what the other sources also indicate: that Boston followed, not led, the opposition to the East India Company's tea shipments.

Philadelphians, who led the opposition that fall, also adopted the tactic Mifflin recommended. In early November, they pressured the local merchants designated as consignees to resign. The firms of Isaac & Thomas Wharton and James & Drinker, both owned by Quakers, initially gave ambiguous answers to committees deputed to speak with them. Thomas Wharton recorded that the committee behaved "with great decency" and accepted "with great satisfaction" the brothers' response that "we would do nothing to injure the property of the India Com[pan]y or enslave America," even though they did not formally reject the commission. The Whartons largely escaped further scrutiny, while James & Drinker bore the brunt of the city's anger as the residents awaited the tea ship everyone knew was coming. Finally, confronted in early December with what they termed "a very disagreeable & peremptory" ultimatum, James & Drinker formally declared that the firm would not act as an agent for EIC tea.

From New York, Governor William Tryon and Major General Frederick Haldimand, commander of the British troops stationed in Manhattan, both warned Dartmouth in early November that they anticipated significant opposition to the tea imports. The governor complained that he still did not have an official copy of the Tea Act and noted that residents were currently debating the meaning of its reported provisions. Tryon, like others then and later, explicitly identified smugglers as the principal opponents of EIC tea imports. He charged that the *Alarm* broadsides were "calculated to sow sedition" and to promote the smugglers' cause. To combat that sedition, though, Tryon and the consignees had an independent ally, an advantage officials and tea agents in the other northern ports lacked. Starting in mid-November, the Reverend John Vardill, a young American-born Anglican priest and professor at King's College, produced a series of broadsides and newspaper essays under the pseudonym "Poplicola."

In addition to defending the company (as a commercial enterprise performing a vital function for the British Empire) and its tea (as superior to the smuggled Dutch variety), Vardill contended that no true patriot would ever encourage smuggling and lawbreaking. Significantly, he warned his fellow New Yorkers about the "arbitrary incroachments" of men who without authorization were assuming the power to censure the actions of their fellow countrymen, the tea consignees. The "fluctuating and capricious decisions of a giddy cabal," Vardill charged, condemned men to "infamy and disgrace" without a trial. "Every friend to *liberty* must be alarmed at such procedures," he insisted, for they threatened even the perpetrators. "While we are watchful against *external* attacks on our freedom, let us be on our guard," he cautioned, "lest we become *enslaved by dangerous* tyrants within."

Vardill thus joined a dialogue about the appropriate exercise of political power that had begun during the Stamp Act crisis in 1765 and would persist for years to come. What was the source of legitimate authority in society? Did such power lie solely in formal governmental institutions? In Britain alone? In America alone? In some combination of the two? Or did it rather come directly from the people themselves? Who constituted "the people"? Qualified voters only? All free adult males? Did women, married or unmarried, have an appropriate role in political actions? How would opinion be determined? Through a majority vote? Through some sort of informal consensus? Last but not least, did any citizen have a right to dissent from such a majority, however it was determined?

One of the broadside replies to Poplicola addressed that last question directly. "A Mechanic" wrote,

When any Man, or Set of Men . . . set themselves in Opposition, to the general Interest of the Community, of which they are Members; and basely endeavour to overturn the Constitution of their Country; introduce Tyranny, and Oppression, and thereby deprive their Countrymen, and Fellow Citizens, of their just

Rights and Liberties; they tacitly declare themselves the Enemies
of the Community.

Having identified themselves as antithetical to the interests of their
fellow countrymen, any such individuals "must, therefore, disclaim all
Right to that Protection, and Security, which they otherwise, would
be justly intitled to," A Mechanic insisted. If they were "thrown overboard, to appease the Storm, which they themselves, have been the
Cause of raising," they had no right to complain. Because of their
support for tyranny, Poplicola and others like him would have to fend
for themselves and could not legitimately object to any ill treatment
they might have to endure.

The clergyman, by contrast, argued for the freedom to dissent and
for an orderly civil society not dominated by self-designated arbiters
who did not hold public office. Many other dissenters would echo his
critique in the months and years to come. Although modern Americans
celebrate the opponents of British authority as proponents of freedom
of speech and press, in the context of their own time they were more
often those who, like A Mechanic, rejected a right to dissent from a
community consensus. In responses to his critics, Vardill repeatedly
returned to his key assertion: "Can *they* be friends to liberty, who will
not allow any to think or speak differently from themselves, without
danger? . . . While they exclaim against tyranny, they are exercising
it over their fellow citizens." But many of those "fellow citizens" did
not find his arguments persuasive; a Philadelphia newspaper in early
December referred to him as "deceitful, lying, infamous Poplicola."

While the broadside wars raged in New York, residents of Charleston finally learned that a tea ship would soon arrive in their harbor.
Peter Timothy, the editor of one of the three local papers and soon
to be a vocal opponent of EIC tea, told his readers on November 15
that he was "well informed" that three hundred chests were on their
way to South Carolina. A week later, he revealed that the vessel carrying the tea was Captain Alexander Curling's *London*. Whereas previously the Charleston papers had largely ignored tea-related news from
the North, once it became clear that their port too would receive a
shipment, Timothy and two rival editors provided their readers with

a plethora of information and commentary on the subject, including locally produced accounts and stories reprinted from northern newspapers. Perhaps as a result, a Charleston resident wrote to a New Yorker on November 20 that "the tea affair makes a great noise here," even though "nothing is yet done." Still, he predicted, any tea would be prevented from landing. For the first time, northern papers began to carry tea-related news from Charleston, including that brief excerpt from the South Carolinian's letter.

On November 22, Timothy reported that South Carolinians "do not seem disposed, to *assist in the landing, or to receive cordially*" the *London*'s cargo. Rather, he asserted, local merchants were being asked not to import duty-paying tea. Because there had as yet been no meeting on the subject, Timothy was clearly speaking for himself. A week later, at the request of a reader signing himself "Junius Brutus," Timothy reprinted an incendiary essay by "Cassius," a Pennsylvanian who had promoted the meeting in Philadelphia the previous month. Cassius warned against being "cajoled by the cunning and artifice of ministerial policy," though it might promise cheaper tea, and insisted that "a Tax of the value of one penny levied upon us without our consent, as effectually takes away our liberty, as if the sum were a million. It is not the value of the Tax we object to, but the principle on which it was laid." Like Benjamin Rush, he summoned up an image of the future to help make his case: our children, he predicted, will "curse the folly of their fore-fathers" if we submit now and "tamely render up our rights." The Philadelphian's essay from six weeks earlier seemed to speak directly to Charleston's circumstances as the town awaited Captain Curling's imminent arrival.

Tensions rose in the three northern ports anticipating the tea imports, especially after ship captains began arriving from England with news that the tea ships had sailed. In Boston, an angry crowd attacked Richard Clarke's house and broke some of its windows on the night of November 17. Still, Clarke and the other consignees persisted in refusing to resign, which meant that when EIC tea arrived in Boston, they would be prepared to receive it. That contrasted with Philadelphia, where the agents had formally rejected the commission more than two weeks earlier. The consignees did make one concession to local opinion: they petitioned the governor and council, asking those officials to take charge of the tea temporarily until tempers cooled and it could be sold. The council refused to intervene.

In Philadelphia, the organizers of the anti-tea campaign published a broadside warning the Delaware River pilots—whose assistance would be needed to guide any tea ship into port—that they risked tarring and feathering if they accepted such an assignment. Even though Joseph Reed, a political moderate, derided those who produced the broadsides as "some inconsiderate [unimportant] Persons" and declared that their action was "generally disapproved of," the pilots heeded the threats.

In New York, the tea agents resigned on December 1. Subsequently, the governor and council declared that they would take charge of landing and securing the tea. At first, Alexander McDougall and his allies, known locally as the Liberty Boys, agreed to that plan, but then they changed their minds. They began to worry that people would want to purchase the tea once it had been brought ashore, just as Benjamin Rush had predicted in October. "We can't be sure it will not be vended," a delegation told William Smith Jr., a member of the council sympathetic to their cause, "& immense animosities may arise from it." Nevertheless, for several weeks the governor persevered with his plan.

In that context, an anonymous New Yorker penned "A Constitutional Catechism." After appearing simultaneously in two local newspapers in early December, the so-called catechism was reprinted in other colonies seven more times over the next two months. What attracted editors to the essay must have been its succinct and clearly expressed case for resistance to the tea duty.

"Why do the Americans refuse the Importation of English Tea at this Time?" the catechism began. The answer: "Because it is saddled with a *duty,* which is a *tax* for the Purpose of raising a Revenue from us, without our own consent, and such *tax,* or *duty,* is therefore *unconstitutional, cruel,* and *unjust.*" The catechism proceeded to explain why the duty was unconstitutional (it violated "a fundamental maxim of the British constitution," that taxation required consent); cruel (it treated Americans like enemies); and unjust (using parliamentary power to seize property without consent resembled "downright robbery"). The questions and answers moved on to assert that Americans should not submit to the claim that Parliament could tax them, for that would deny their "birthright," and insisted that Britons in general had no right to Americans' property.

Under such circumstances, the catechism asked next, "Is it not incumbent upon us to defend our common property, from all such impositions?" The response was the expected "yes," likening the actions of "the whole people" to those of individuals defending their property from robbers. And how should we defend ourselves? was the logical follow-up query. The answer, phrased vaguely, was nonetheless comprehensive: "By all such ways and means as we shall judge to be most likely to promote the important end of securing that property." Can the people judge what means to employ? Answer: yes, again; the people would be the best judges of the means to defend their property. Question: Should the people act lawfully? Reply: yes, when the laws offer sufficient means to achieve that goal. But in the end "the perpetual and universal binding law of *self defence*" should determine the outcome. That law "has been, and *ever will be,* the sole director of every people, when their rights and properties cannot be secured by the laws of their country."

The "Constitutional Catechism" thus moved quickly from explaining why the tea tax was unconstitutional, to declaring that it should be challenged, to providing a key, widely accepted rationale for resistance: the right of self-defense. No wonder the catechism was reprinted throughout the colonies. Unlike many contemporary publications—whether in pamphlets, newspapers, or broadsides—it eschewed turgid, precedent-strewn reasoning, replacing such arguments with statements that, if one accepted the premises (the tea duty was a tax; taxation required consent; America did not consent to parliamentary actions), led directly to the conclusion that the importation of EIC tea had to be resisted by whatever means seemed most likely to succeed. And the choice of those means soon confronted the residents of the four port cities to which EIC tea was dispatched.

On November 28, the first of the vessels—the *Dartmouth,* Captain James Hall—sailed into Boston harbor, followed on December 3 by the *Eleanor,* Captain James Bruce, and on December 7 by the *Beaver,* Captain Hezekiah Coffin. On December 2, the ship *London* tied up at a Charleston wharf after having reached the harbor entrance the previous day. Ironically, the vagaries of the Atlantic crossing meant that Philadelphia and New York, the cities that had taken the lead in the initial opposition to the tea, would not lead in dealing with its actual presence. The *Polly*, Captain Samuel Ayres, did not reach the Delaware until December 25; and the *Nancy*, bound for Manhattan under Captain Benjamin Lockyer, did not arrive at the entrance to New York harbor until mid-April 1774. Blown far off course by a North Atlantic gale—probably the same one that wrecked the *William* on Cape Cod on the night of December 10–11—the *Nancy* spent the winter at the Caribbean island of Antigua.

Because of the dates of the first vessels' arrival, events unfolded at almost the same time in Boston and Charleston. The slow transmission of information meant that neither city knew much about what was happening in the other. Yet the same legal imperative drove the residents of both towns. Under British customs law, duty had to be paid within twenty days of a ship's formal entry into a harbor, or officials would confiscate the cargo for nonpayment. Furthermore, once a ship had registered its presence at the customshouse, it could not leave without paying any duty owed on its cargo. In short, the confrontation between opponents of the tea imports and local authorities or tea consignees could not continue indefinitely in either city. There was a time limit. In Boston, the twenty days would be up on December 17; in Charleston, on December 22.

BOSTON AND CHARLESTON

The nearly simultaneous events in Boston and Charleston, when considered together, highlight the impact of local circumstances as American communities responded initially to the prospect of EIC tea imports. Both towns were, in effect, making it up as they went along. And they "made it up" in very different ways, each acting without reference to a precedent for action, although newspapers in both had reprinted the crucial publications by Thomas Mifflin and Benjamin Rush. Each city began with a meeting of the inhabitants, but there the similarities essentially ended. The contents of discussions at the meetings, decisions reached, actions of government officials, crowd responses, and outcomes all differed significantly.

The Immediate Reactions to the Dartmouth *and the* London

The *Dartmouth's* arrival in Boston on Sunday, November 28, triggered a call for an immediate meeting, which was announced in handbills posted all over town the next morning. "Friends! Brethren! Countrymen!" the notice read. "That worst of Plagues, the detested TEA . . . is now arrived in this Harbour; the Hour of Destruction or manly Opposition to the Machinations of Tyranny stares you in the Face." Residents were directed to assemble at Faneuil Hall when the bells rang at nine o'clock Monday morning. As it happened, so many people showed up that the meeting had to be moved to the largest space in town, the Old South Church.

Accounts of the ensuing two-day meeting of Bostonians and residents of nearby towns were widely republished in newspapers throughout the colonies during December. Participants voted unanimously to prevent the tea from landing and to ensure that it was sent back to England. Discussions focused less on whether to seek that goal and more on how best to achieve it. Both Francis Rotch, owner of the *Dartmouth,* and James Hall, its captain, attended on the second day; they were directed to carry out the town's wishes and not to try to land the tea. Fearing violence, both agreed to comply, although under protest. Men were recruited to keep a twenty-four-hour watch to make certain that tea chests were not removed from the ship. During the second day, Governor Hutchinson issued a proclamation declaring the meeting illegal and ordering it to disperse. The crowd predictably greeted the sheriff's official declaration with "a very loud and general hiss." The governor later observed that although most of the crowd came from "the lower ranks of the people," some "gentlemen of good fortune" had also attended. Accordingly, he told Lord Dartmouth, "I can scarcely think they will prosecute their mad resolves."

Likewise, as soon as Captain Curling arrived in Charleston on Thursday, December 2, with 257 chests of tea on the *London,* organizers posted handbills "at all the usual and most public places," asking "all the inhabitants, without exception, particularly the landholders" to gather the next day in midafternoon, at the large meeting room on the second floor of the mercantile exchange near the harbor. Reports in northern newspapers claimed so many people assembled that

Captain Curling of the *London* would have seen this view of Charleston's magnificent harbor as he entered it on December 2, 1773, with his cargo of East India Company tea.

The large building with the cupola in the right center (between the two churches) is the Exchange, where city residents met twice to discuss what to do about the tea ship and where the tea was stored after it was confiscated by customs officers.

"the main Beams" of the building began to give way. As unlikely as that observation appears, it suggests that the meeting was very well attended, perhaps especially because of the unusual nature of the summons to all residents, "without exception." (If free women or enslaved men or women were present, no one noted it.) One of the goals of the meeting, the editor Peter Timothy declared, was "to prevent any rash or violent proceedings" with respect to the tea.

Timothy, who had advance information about the tea ship and its captain, was also the Charleston printer known as a "conduit-pipe" to the local resistance movement. During the tea crisis in Charleston, his *Gazette* (the other two local papers confusingly used the same title) provided the most detailed accounts of current events in the city. But his reports were not entirely trustworthy, for his political commitments led him to describe a consensus in opposition to British policy, whereas other sources reveal considerable local dissension and confusion about possible options for dealing with the tea ship.

In the newspaper, Timothy described the many attendees at the December 3 meeting as engaging in "calm deliberation." He admitted that since 1770 Carolinians had patronized merchants who continued to sell taxed EIC tea in violation of the existing nonimportation agreement. Nevertheless, he insisted, because of the Tea Act Charlestonians "thought it would be *criminal* tamely to give up any of our essential rights as British subjects." Thus the citizens decided it was "high time to *contend, legally,* and to dispute the *assumed* power [of taxation]." Timothy recounted that the crowd readily agreed that the *London* should return to Britain without unloading its cargo and that all local merchants should now be asked formally not to import or sell duty-paying tea.

But his was not the only contemporary account. Other witnesses' statements and subsequent events disclosed that the partisan Timothy suppressed the information that a significant number of participants failed to support the agenda of the meeting's organizers. According to a Captain Hunt, Charleston residents vigorously debated—rather than "calmly deliberated"—the issues raised by the *London*'s arrival. Some contended that the East India Company had the same right as all British subjects to send items for sale to the colony. Proponents of that position, the council member William Henry Drayton later recalled, even included many "friends to liberty" who generally opposed the ministry. Other attendees argued that duty-paying EIC tea ordered by individual retailers should be sold as usual, although the tea sent directly by the company should be rejected. In the wake of the meeting, participants described considerable disagreement to those who had not attended. For instance, William Bull, the lieutenant governor heading the colony at the time, was told—perhaps by Drayton, his nephew—that although "the warmth of some was great[,] many were cool and some differed in the reasonableness and utility [of opposing the landing of the tea]."

The meeting did achieve consensus on one point: using "threats and flattery" to persuade the Charleston tea agents to resign. Roger Smith, Peter Leger, and William Greenwood, like the New Yorkers and

Philadelphians and unlike the Bostonians, publicly declared that they would not accept the tea, a statement greeted with applause. Captain Curling, who attended the meeting along with the consignees, asked how he could deal with the problem posed by the agents' refusal to receive the shipment. He was directed to return to England with his cargo. No one at the meeting appears to have proposed forcefully resisting the landing of the chests, nor did attendees seek to involve either Lieutenant Governor Bull or customs officials in the dispute. A committee of notables was selected to approach merchants who had not attended the meeting to urge them to sign a nonimportation agreement covering duty-paying tea. By December 6, when Timothy published his account, "upwards of Fifty respectable names" had reportedly been appended to the document. Moreover, the editor indicated, the "principal planters and landholders" also drafted a statement in which they pledged not to buy dutied tea or to purchase any items from tea importers. They reasoned that to do so would be to admit Parliament's right to tax them without their consent.

Junius Brutus, who inveighed against the tea before its arrival, revealed in an essay in Timothy's *Gazette* that he had attended the December 3 meeting. He praised the consignees for their "truly noble" conduct and thanked the merchants who had agreed not to import tea until the duty was repealed. But he also suggested that they could have gone further, for tea on hand could have been collected and publicly burned and any tea currently on order could be dealt with similarly after it arrived. He introduced another innovation into the conversation by addressing himself to "*dear ladies*" as well as to men and contending that tea drinking contributed to women's "*nervous disorders.*" Not only did women accordingly have good reason to boycott tea, he proclaimed; women and men both should agree to "*not, either directly or indirectly, import, buy, sell, or countenance*" the purchase of not just tea but any and all dutied items, thereby considerably broadening the reach of the proposed nonimportation agreement.

Thus the immediate reactions in the two cities resulted in contrasting strategies. In Boston, where the consignees remained ready to receive the tea, residents voted to prevent it from being brought onshore (as Benjamin Rush had advised) and to enforce that decision by posting a guard on the wharf so that it could not be landed in secret.

The Charleston meeting chose a different course of action. There, the consignees had resigned and were not available to market the tea, but individual merchants might conceivably still purchase it if the chests were landed. So the Carolina opponents of EIC tea sought two goals: persuading the captain to sail back to England with his cargo intact, and gaining merchants' formal consent not to sell duty-paying tea.

Boston, Early December

On November 29, while their fellow townsmen met at the Old South Church, most of the tea consignees fled for protection to the British army's headquarters at Castle William in the harbor. One Boston merchant commented that "the Fury of the People" toward the agents "exceeds all Conception." Yet the artist John Singleton Copley, whose wife was the daughter of Richard Clarke, hoped to negotiate a settlement. In early December, he carried messages back and forth between the Clarkes and such local leaders as the wealthy merchant John Hancock and the physician Dr. Joseph Warren, even while he simultaneously "warmly expostulated with som of those violent Sons of Liberty against their proceedings." Because the consignees persisted in refusing to resign, several newspapers commented that "their obstinacy has rendered them infinitely more obnoxious to their countrymen than even the stamp masters were." During the period before the ominous deadline of December 17, Bostonians kept trying various tactics to induce the tea ships to leave the harbor, repeatedly approaching customs officers, the consignees, the shipowners, the British navy, and the governor to have the vessels depart without either paying the duty or unloading their cargoes. But Thomas Hutchinson stood firm, insisting on enforcing the law that after a ship had entered the harbor it could not legally depart without paying duties and being formally cleared to leave.

While the governor and the Bostonians engaged in a standoff, individuals and entire towns offered their opinions on the matter. Abigail Adams, for one, was thrilled by the opposition to what she termed "this weed of Slavery," praising the "United, Spirited and firm" resistance to landing the tea. "The flame is kindled and like Lightning it catches from Soul to Soul," she exclaimed to her friend Mercy Otis

Warren on December 5. Five days later the town of Lexington not only adopted vigorous resolves supporting Boston's efforts to thwart the consignees but also promised not to consume "Bohea tea of all sorts, Dutch or English."

But not everyone agreed with such sentiments. A week after Plymouth on December 7 adopted resolutions praising Boston's efforts, a substantial minority of the town's male residents formally filed a protest. They decried the way in which their fellow townsmen had been "deceived by the cunning stratagems of men who under the specious masque of patriotism have attempted to delude an innocent and loyal people" and declared that the town's resolves were "repugnant to our ideas of Liberty, law and reason." In their opinion, the Boston meetings were not "lawful or regular," not "necessary or laudable," and the consignees did not deserve the treatment they had received. More outspoken in his criticism of conditions in Boston was the customs officer Benjamin Hallowell. "All Authority for the present is at an End except the Authority of the Mob," he informed a British correspondent early in December. Yet at the same time he predicted that order could easily be restored when Britain took the proper steps, because "almost all ranks of people" would support that effort and "the factious party [would] shrink into their hole & Corners." If Bostonians "once can but see that the Lion was roused they would tremble," for they are "mightily Valliant" only when no one opposes them.

Hallowell's confidence that American protesters would "tremble" and "shrink into their hole & Corners" if Britain were to exert its authority was to be a constant refrain voiced by many supporters of colonial governments in the months to come. But, evidently without fully realizing it, he contradicted himself when he also referred to "the Authority of the Mob." If large crowds resisted tea imports and squelched all dissent, what would be the source—or the fate—of those from "almost all ranks of people" whom he predicted would step forward to support British authority?

Charleston, Mid-December

Despite Timothy's apparently definitive narrative of the decisions reached at the December 3 meeting, Charleston residents found themselves confused in its aftermath because of the dissension the editor had not acknowledged. According to William Henry Drayton, some men "alleged that what had been taken as the determination of the Meeting, was actually against the sense of the majority then present." What had Charlestonians decided, other than accepting the resignation of the consignees and instructing Curling to return to England with his cargo? The nonimportation agreement being circulated to merchants targeted duty-paying tea regardless of ownership; many attendees, though, had advocated boycotting only direct shipments like the *London*'s, rather than all EIC tea. In addition, what of tea imported clandestinely? The (former) consignees informed the East India Company that, hoping to "Wink at every Pound smuggled in upon Us," the meeting's participants had deliberately omitted discussing that question. But the issue was one of consistency and fairness. If imports directly from the EIC were alone prohibited, then retailers of EIC tea purchased from wholesalers would benefit, or if illegal tea was not boycotted, sellers of the smuggled commodity could dominate the local market.

According to the ex-consignees, Charleston merchants soon concurred that the discussions on December 3 lacked "Solidity." Many refused to sign the nonimportation agreement, vowing to continue to import chests from the EIC unless the proposed boycott encompassed all dutied and illegal tea alike. Consequently, on December 9 local merchants, seeking to foster unanimity in their ranks, founded the Charleston Chamber of Commerce, the stated goal of which was to "extend Commerce, encourage Industry, and adjust Disputes relative to Trade and Navigation." The current dispute desperately needing "adjustment" then sat visibly at a wharf in the harbor in the form of the cargo of the ship *London*.

Brief notices published in December issues of Peter Timothy's *Gazette* indicated that the seeming consensus of the earlier meeting had collapsed, if one ever truly existed. Another "General Meeting" was scheduled for the fourteenth, but postponed. On the fifteenth, a "very numerous" gathering of "the most respectable *Planters* and *Landholders*" and a separate meeting of "Mechanick[s]" took place. On the sixteenth, the newly organized Chamber of Commerce met for the second time. What happened at those sessions went unrecorded by anyone, but opinion in Charleston had obviously fragmented. A customs official wrote that the merchants and planters who attended the smaller gatherings "came to no determination."

The residents of Charleston, unlike Bostonians, could not draw on a long tradition of town meetings at which citizens repeatedly discussed and debated controversial topics before arriving publicly at a local consensus. Possibly Carolinians' unfamiliarity with such gatherings and with the mechanisms of achieving agreement among diverse interests caused the difficulties at the December 3 meeting. But regardless of what was, or was not, accomplished that day, the subsequent lack of accord about the outcome only added to the confusion.

Boston, December 16

In Benjamin Hallowell's Boston, unlike Peter Timothy's Charleston, there was no doubt about consensus: a large majority of New Englanders agreed that any attempt to land the tea should be resisted. Once it was onshore, no one could predict what would happen, in large part because the consignees still refused to resign. On December 16, about five thousand Bostonians and others again gathered at Old South Church. When final negotiations with Governor Hutchinson failed, a peaceful solution seemed impossible to achieve. The next day, customs officers would presumably try to seize and land the cargoes of the tea ships for nonpayment of duties. If Bostonians then forcefully opposed that effort, they would be resisting the king's officers, with unforeseeable but surely negative consequences. So, in the early evening, a large group of men crudely disguised as Indians—called "Mohawks" at the time—boarded the three vessels at Griffin's wharf. They destroyed 342 chests containing more than forty-six tons of tea worth more than £9,000, or approximately $180,000 in 2015 dollars. The men broke open the containers, tossing them and their contents overboard, while being careful to preserve the ships' other cargoes.

Despite the protection of those other cargoes, the assault on the vessels was the most destructive event in Boston's recent history. The only roughly comparable episode during the previous decade had been an attack that demolished Thomas Hutchinson's mansion in Boston's North End during riots over the Stamp Act, an act triggered in part because he was erroneously thought to favor the law. In the aftermath of that incident, Hutchinson requested and received substantial compensation for his lost property from the provincial government.

Before many weeks had passed, the topic of compensation for the EIC's losses would likewise be raised on both sides of the Atlantic, but that possibility was far from people's minds as Bostonians expressed a variety of opinions about the Mohawks' act. One man remarked that Hutchinson and his allies seemed "struck with a Pannic"; the governor himself exclaimed, "Such barbarity none of the Aborginals were ever guilty of," but he also acknowledged that "there is no pity for so great a body as the East India Company." The Massachusetts assembly's committee of correspondence ultimately blamed the consignees and their abettors, who refused to compromise and who had possibly intended "to irritate and inflame the minds of an injured oppressed People to measures of violence." Hannah Winthrop, wife of a Harvard professor, exulted in the "Virtuous & Noble resolution of America's sons in defiance of threatned desolation & misery from arbitrary Despots." A local merchant offered one common observation: "The who[le] Affair was conducted with the greatest dispatch, Regularity & Management, so as to evidence that there were People of Sense & of more discernment than the Vulgar among the Actors." Barbarous aboriginals? Men of sense and discernment? Which interpretation would prevail was not immediately evident.

Charleston, December 17–22

In Charleston, a second general meeting of the city's inhabitants seemed to be required to restore or establish a consensus, so men again convened at the mercantile exchange on December 17. The chairman, George Gabriel Powell (who had also chaired the previous gathering), began by "strongly recommending Temper and Moderation throughout their Proceedings" to the participants. Peter Timothy remarked that "the greatest Order and Regularity was accordingly observed; and no Gentleman, that had an Inclination to speak, suffered the least Interruption, but was heard with the greatest Attention.—Each Side of the Question had its Advocates; the unpopular one *very few*." Unsurprisingly, Timothy failed to identify "the unpopular one"; perhaps some attendees continued to advocate allowing the *London*'s tea to be landed and sold.

This time the gathering could not avoid addressing all tea imports, legal or illegal. After several hours of debate, the attendees resolved first that the East India Company's tea in the *London* "ought not to be landed, received, or vended in this Province" as long as the duty remained in force. In a second resolution, they expanded that prohibition to include all past and future imports of duty-paying tea and in a third declared that "it is the Sense of this Body, that *no Teas* ought to be imported from any Place whatsoever, while the offensive Act remains unrepealed." Furthermore, "that every Person [may] be put on the same footing," those present decided that all tea currently on hand in the city had to be bought and consumed in the next six months or forgone completely until the duty was repealed. In one sense, tying all tea imports and consumption to the duty laid on legal EIC tea alone was irrational, but at the same time doing so was essential to achieving the necessary consensus. The new Chamber of Commerce preferred that all tea be treated alike to prevent dissension among the merchants, and that position had now apparently prevailed.

The ex-consignees' report to the EIC about the debates at the December 17 meeting make it clear that participants fully recognized the looming deadline of December 22 imposed by customs law. Smith, Leger, and Greenwood told the company that they unsuccessfully sought to persuade attendees to allow them to take and store the tea until they received the company's instructions. Participants instead voted that if the customs collector seized the tea for nonpayment of duty, "all Persons whatever was forbid to purchase [it], on pain of forfeiting the Resentment of the people of this Province." Once more, no one seems to have publicly advocated destroying the tea or otherwise attempting to forestall a seizure. Taken together, the resolution against buying confiscated tea, the attendees' obvious awareness of the December 22 deadline, and the failure to propose decisive action against the *London* all suggested that Carolinians expected customs officers to take possession of the tea. As John Adams learned months later, many residents silently colluded in that outcome.

Lieutenant Governor William Bull remained on the sidelines of the dispute until December 21. Determined to facilitate the unloading and

storage of the tea the next day and also responding to anonymous letters vaguely threatening "great damages" to the ship and the wharf if
the tea were landed, he summoned Captain Curling and the customs
collector, Robert Haliday, to a meeting of his council. Questioned,
Curling and Haliday expressed no fears for their personal safety but
stressed their concern for the tea. Bull ordered the sheriff to provide
protection, if requested, when the collector confiscated the tea, and
the council voted its approval. That was the sole direct involvement of
the colony's political officials with East India Company tea. At sunrise
on December 22, customs officers and the crew began to unload the
257 chests from the *London*.

Peter Timothy, having not revealed in print that such a result was anticipated by those at the recent meeting, claimed that customs officers
worked so rapidly that "the whole was completed" before most people
realized that the process had started. The officers, he declared, quickly
stored the tea in the cellar of the Exchange building. Yet the very
quantity of tea that had to be moved (about ninety thousand pounds)
rendered that report questionable even without another contemporary
account explicitly contradicting it. A customs supervisor disclosed that
by noon on December 22 only about half the tea had been stored and
the rest was still sitting on the dock. In spite of the anonymous threats,
"there was not the least disturbance," he noted; "the gentlemen that
came on the wharf behaved with their usual complaisance and good
nature to me." After all the tea was stored, Timothy reported that
people "Confidently rely, upon its remaining locked up, in the Cellar
Where it is now lodged," either until the company ordered it reshipped
to England or until the duty was repealed. It must have appeared to
Timothy and his allies that they had successfully resolved the problem
confronting them, thanks to the cooperation of the authorities, but
more trouble still lay ahead.

Between November 28 and December 22, 1773, Boston and Charleston thus considered each of the three ways to resist East India Company tea advocated by the New York and Philadelphia essayists in
October. Targeting the consignees led to resignations in Charleston
but not in Boston. Reviving the nonimportation and nonconsumption agreements caused confusion in Charleston and was rejected in
Boston, as Samuel Adams declared publicly at Old South Church that

"he could not trust the private Virtue of his Countrymen in refraining from the Use of [tea]." Preventing the tea from landing could not work in either city, for the inexorable twenty-day deadline in customs law led to violent destruction in the northern city and to a collusive customs seizure in the southern one. But Philadelphians (partially) and New Yorkers (wholly) learned from the experiences of the other cities and were able to craft an effective response that avoided both extremes.

PHILADELPHIA

On the morning of December 17, the Boston committee of correspondence dispatched its messenger, Paul Revere, south to New York City and then on to Philadelphia, with the electrifying news of the tea destruction the previous evening. The Bostonians jubilantly reported that "every ounce of the teas . . . was immersed in the Bay, without the least injury to private property. The Spirit of the People on this

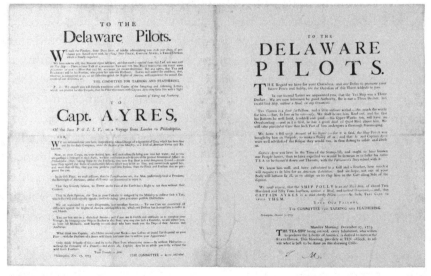

After Philadelphians learned the identity of the ship transporting EIC tea to their community, the "committee for tarring and feathering" produced new broadsides directed to the pilots on the Delaware River who guided ships into port, describing the vessel *Polly* and its "short fat" captain, Samuel Ayres, warning them not to help him approach the harbor or to land any tea.

occasion surprised all parties who view'd the Scene." Revere arrived in New York on December 21, and in Philadelphia on December 24—fortuitously, shortly before the tea ship *Polly* appeared near the city in the Delaware River. By the time Philadelphians gathered to discuss what to do about the *Polly* and its cargo, they knew that New Englanders had destroyed the tea sent to them. They also were aware that the Carolina tea agents had resigned and that Charleston residents had voted to send the ship *London* back to England with its cargo intact, but they did not know that the customs collector had seized the tea five days earlier.

Before the *Polly* sailed into the Delaware, "a great Number of respectable Inhabitants" had already decided that they could not allow the captain to enter the cargo at the customshouse. That simple step would avoid the difficulties with the customs laws encountered in both Charleston and Boston, because the twenty-day deadline would not be activated. So when the anti-tea leaders in early December obtained a physical description of the *Polly* and Captain Samuel Ayres, they addressed another broadside to the Delaware River pilots, enjoining them against assisting that vessel in any way, on pain of tar and feathers. The city then waited for weeks with "Anxiety and Suspence" before the ship appeared. Even as early as the end of November, Thomas Wharton observed that "to such a pitch of zeal are some people rais'd that I fear the worst." Many rumors preceded the confirmed news that on Saturday, December 25, the *Polly* had made its way upriver without a pilot as far as Chester (about eighteen miles below Philadelphia). The next day, Gilbert Barkley, a consignee and passenger, disembarked to make his way by land into the city. A committee greeted him and persuaded him to resign his commission.

Other committee members intercepted the *Polly* as it was proceeding upriver on the morning of December 27, explaining to Captain Ayres (in the words of a frequently reprinted account) "the general Sentiments, together with the Danger and Difficulties, that would attend his Refusal to comply with the Wishes of the Inhabitants." The contents of that conversation were surely not quite that unemotional. The committeemen took Ayres "in a kind of Custody" into Philadelphia, where he was quickly convinced of the "Truth and Propriety" of what he had been told and agreed to cooperate with the citizens. In the street, a few boys showed him "some small Rudeness" (probably by throwing snowballs at him), but "several Gentlemen interposed, and suppressed it before he received the least Injury."

The men then made their way to a general meeting held outside the statehouse. This gathering, the recorder stressed, "is allowed by all to be the most respectable, both in the Numbers and Rank of those who attended it, that has been known in this City." The large crowd—estimated at eight thousand—then adopted a series of resolutions, directing the captain not to land the tea, not to enter the cargo at the customshouse, and to remain in town only long enough to obtain supplies for his voyage back to England. The account noted that "the whole Business was conducted with a Decorum and Order worthy the Importance of the Cause" and praised the "glorious . . . Exertion of public Virtue and Spirit" evident on the occasion. After less than forty-eight hours in town, Ayres and Barkley left to return to the *Polly*, "attended to the Wharf by a Concourse of People, who wished them a good Voyage."

The meeting also approved Boston's "Spirited Conduct in destroy-ing their Tea rather than suffering it to be landed," a vote that Phil-adelphia activists proudly reported to Samuel Adams. But Thomas Wharton later disclosed that the statement commending Bostonians' actions was drafted by just two members of a twelve-man committee. The other ten "absolutely refused to have it inserted with the other resolves," but the dissenters carried the day in the meeting by linking the "salutary" decision to reject the tea with their resolution lauding what Wharton termed "the unjustifiable conduct of the Bostonians." He claimed that subsequently the resolution praising Boston was rec-ognized as "very inconsistent with the sentiments of the substantial thinking part of our inhabitants," and recorded that his acquaintances thought that Boston should reimburse the company for the tea. His account, in short, recounted disagreement among leading Philadel-phians amid what seemed to be general public acclaim for the Bos-tonians' act. Such dissension revealed in private correspondence thus belied the newspaper accounts that left readers elsewhere with a false impression of Philadelphians' unanimity.

Some commentators applauded Philadelphia's restraint rather than Boston's rash act. Joseph Reed, for example, boasted of the city's "peaceable & regular Demeanor," drawing an implicit contrast to Boston events by reporting that "there has been no Mob, no Insult to Individuals or Injury to private Property." More explicitly critical of Boston was the twenty-two-year-old James Madison, who wrote from Virginia to his friend the printer William Bradford, "I congratulate you on your heroic proceedings in Philad[elphi]a with regard to the Tea. I wish Boston may conduct matters with as much discretion as they seem to do with boldness." Madison clearly had his doubts about the New Englanders' method of opposing the tea shipments, and events would prove that he was not the only colonist to think so.

What, one might ask, was Pennsylvania's deputy governor John Penn's role with respect to the tea ship? A month earlier, Wharton had accurately seen in Penn no inclination to intervene to protect the East India Company's property. Unlike Thomas Hutchinson, William Tryon, or William Bull, the risk-averse Penn did absolutely nothing as the events in Philadelphia unfolded. Penn later explained his passivity by remarking that he had received no instructions in the matter and that no one had asked for his involvement. Thus Philadelphians dealt with the tea without the interference of anyone in authority. Lord Dartmouth was not pleased and later chided Penn for neglecting his duty.

NEW YORK

New Yorkers as well as Philadelphians waited anxiously for a tea ship's arrival, and they had had months to consider how to respond by the time the *Nancy* finally approached their harbor in April 1774. When they acted, they knew that tea had been destroyed in Boston and landed and stored without incident in Charleston, as well as having been excluded in Philadelphia.

Unsurprisingly, they imitated Philadelphia, but not until other options had been considered and discarded. After the city's consignees resigned and Governor Tryon decided to land and store the tea, he predicted to Lord Dartmouth that his plan could be carried out "without obstruction," despite "the general voice [being] No Sales, No Consumption." On December 17, four days before they learned what had happened in Boston the previous evening, two thousand men reportedly attended a meeting at city hall to debate proposals roughly congruent with Tryon's plan, offered by a group calling itself the Committee of Associates. The resolutions asserted that no EIC tea would be sold or purchased until the duty was repealed but that citizens would also agree not to "hazard the peace of the city, *by opposing the landing or storing the said tea with force.*"

Governor Tryon sent the mayor to the meeting as his emissary to explain that he believed it his duty to protect the tea from destruction; that he would land the tea openly, without using force; and that "not an Ounce of it" would be distributed without the council's consent or an order from the king. The mayor delivered Tryon's message but reported that the attendees nevertheless seemed to oppose allowing the tea to land. The opponents, though, were not confident enough in their majority to call for a tallied vote. In retrospect, William Smith thought that not requesting a formal vote constituted "an egregious Error." Proponents of the governor's plan had given Alexander McDougall and his anti-tea allies "an immense Advantage," Smith remarked, by failing to underscore the extent of disagreement at the meeting. Thus, as happened in Charleston and Philadelphia, the existence of significant dissension at large community meetings ended up being suppressed.

But then news of the tea destruction arrived from Boston, as well as the information that Philadelphia and Charleston had voted not to allow EIC tea to be landed. Smith recorded that the reports had a significant impact in the city and that the plan to land and store the tea simply "vanished" as "every moderate Sentiment was extinguished." New York's former consignees informed the EIC directors that the question is "not being viewed now as Local or Provincial, but Continental." The governor prudently backed down, admitting to Lord Dartmouth that the tea could be landed and stored only "under the Protection of the Point of the Bayonet and the Muzzle of the Cannon" and that even then he did not see how it could ever be sold safely. New Yorkers thus concurred that when Captain Benjamin Lockyer arrived, they would "assuredly follow the Example of Philadelphia. Not a Box of the Tea will be landed here." The ship would not be allowed to enter the harbor.

Throughout January, colonial newspapers regularly recounted rumors about the *Nancy*. Finally, in early March, New Yorkers learned from a Caribbean vessel that the *Nancy* had spent the winter in Antigua. About the time that news arrived, according to William Smith, the Liberty Boys and the ex-consignees agreed to resupply the ship and send it back to London. Later that month, a letter arrived from Captain Lockyer, revealing that having learned of the tea's reception in Boston and Philadelphia, he had no intention of attempting to land his cargo but would instead anchor at Sandy Hook, arrange to be resupplied, and return immediately to England. He explained that he wanted everyone to know his plans so he would not encounter "personal insults."

The hard-luck *Nancy* finally reached Sandy Hook on April 19, 1774, having suffered significant damage in yet another gale early in the month. Captain Lockyer came ashore on the pilot boat, being greeted at the wharf by a large group of men eager to demonstrate their opposition to the cargo he carried. He was entirely cooperative and was later pronounced "a sensible, discreet, and very well bred man" by the demonstrators. When he left two days later, having secured the supplies he needed (and having had the ship hastily repaired), he was sent off with "loud huzzas" and the firing of "many guns." Thus, declared an account in one of the newspapers, "to the great mortification of the secret and open enemies of America, and the joy of all the friends of liberty and human nature, the union of these Colonies is maintained in a contest of the utmost importance to their safety and felicity."

THE SEVENTH TEA SHIP

Narratives of the East India Company tea ships usually end with the story of the *Nancy*, if indeed they include more than the tale of the destruction in Boston harbor. But without an account of the seventh vessel—the *William,* which wrecked on Cape Cod in mid-December—the chronicle of the tea ships is incomplete. The story of the *William,* in brief, supplies persuasive evidence that colonial anti-tea organizers chose well when they decided to try to prevent EIC tea from being brought onshore and marketed to colonial customers. It also allows historians to consider the sort of hypothetical question that is usually unanswerable: How would colonists have responded if the East India Company's tea had actually been landed and offered for sale? The sudden appearance of a large quantity of tea on a New England shore led to disorderly and occasionally chaotic scenes that could well have been replicated in many other American locales had the resistance not succeeded as well as it did.

The news of the *William*'s wreck on the Cape appeared first in a Boston newspaper on December 16—the very day of the meeting at Old South Church that ended with "Mohawks" destroying the tea on the three ships that had made it safely into the harbor. Commentary in newspapers and correspondence then reflected knowledge of what happened that night. One New England editor wrote, "'Tis expected the Cape Indians will give us a good Account of the Tea," and a Boston merchant predicted that "if the Tea escapes Destruction from the Sea," it would not escape from the people. John Adams put his own spin on the theme by declaring that he expected "Vineyard, Mashpee, Metapoiset Indians" to take charge of the tea "and protect it from Violence, I mean from the Hands of Tyrants and oppressors who want to do Violence with it, to the Laws and Constitution."

Yet such confidence turned out to be misplaced. The first official on the scene was John Greenough, a Barnstable County justice of the peace based in Wellfleet, about fifteen miles from the site of the wreck. Greenough, a merchant, had business dealings with Richard Clarke & Sons, which owned the *William*. Greenough was also a personal friend of Jonathan Clarke, one of the firm's "sons." Soon, in the absence of the owners, Greenough supervised the unloading of the cargo by the crew and local workers, who carted the salvaged items to Provincetown, at the tip of the Cape. Some contents had been damaged, including four of the fifty-eight tea chests, although one of the four was reloaded into a barrel. Greenough used the tea in one of the other three damaged chests of Bohea to pay the workers he had hired.

Shortly after the unloading was completed, Jonathan Clarke joined John Greenough at Provincetown, and together the two friends took charge of the salvaged cargo. Jonathan had left his refuge at Castle William on the sixteenth, soon after news of the shipwreck arrived. He then rode the 119 miles to Provincetown, Samuel Adams later lamented, without encountering "a single Instance of Contempt" from the people along his route. Indeed, Adams angrily charged, because the surviving tea was then held at Provincetown for some time, the "Marshpee Tribe" had been "sick at the knees."

Clarke and Greenough knew that they had to deal separately with the two parts of the vessel's contents: on the one hand, the regular cargo bound for Boston; and, on the other, the tea, which they decided had to be sent to Castle William. They had no difficulty finding two sloops to carry the other commodities, but the company's tea posed a significant challenge, because some residents had already refused to help unload and move the cargo. Captains whose vessels lay idle in Provincetown harbor rejected requests to carry the tea, but fortunately for Clarke and Greenough a Salem fishing schooner, the *Eunice,* had taken shelter there from the winter storm. Its captain, John Cook, agreed to take the salvaged tea to Castle William.

After the fifty-four chests and one barrel had been off-loaded at the Castle in early January 1774 and Cook returned to Salem, he was called before the town meeting and charged with carrying the tea intentionally. He responded that his vessel was blown into Provincetown harbor by contrary winds, where "through mere inadvertence" and "ignorance" he hired his ship out to Clarke and Greenough. Cook also defended George Bickford, the *Eunice*'s owner, declaring that Bickford had not sent him there to transport the tea. Nevertheless, several newspapers reported, a group of men, "dressed in the Indian manner," set out to punish Bickford in some unspecified way for the offense. Conveniently for him, although inconveniently for his attackers, he was at the time ensconced in the new Salem smallpox hospital, undergoing inoculation—a dangerous procedure that could infect those who had never had the virus. Accordingly, the story commented without elaboration, the potential attackers "deferred proceeding to extremities." Even though the widely reprinted tale implied that the postponement of punishment was temporary, both Cook and Bickford appear to have escaped unscathed.

Probably close to a thousand pounds of tea—though an unknown quantity was lost in the wreck—remained on the Cape to ignite disputes that persisted through the rest of the winter and, indeed, were not resolved until May. Cape Cod residents were, it turned out, just as sharply divided about tea as were South Carolinians, and unlike their counterparts in other colonies they had the opportunity to act on their opinions. The populace seemingly divided into three factions: those who would sell or purchase any tea; those who would sell, earn, or purchase EIC tea from the wreck, on which no duty had been paid; and those who opposed the buying and selling of all EIC tea, regardless of its taxed status. Smuggled tea was not involved in the Cape contests, but the divisions would likely have been even more complex had it been.

Initially, disputes centered on those workmen who had been paid in tea. Some sold parts of their shares to others, seeking to turn the desirable commodity into cash. In nearby Truro, those who ended up with even small quantities of the company tea were forced to acknowledge their error at a town meeting, during which they adopted the same excuse as John Cook: they had acquired the tea through "ignorance and inadvertence." An unnamed "elderly gentleman" from another town purchased two or three pounds from one of the Provincetown workers; while en route home, he was accosted in the Wellfleet woods by three men in disguise. They searched his saddlebags, found the tea, and threw it out along the road. Near the end of January, a group of disguised men (the same?) reportedly searched every house in Provincetown, confiscating whatever tea they found. Unless the laborers Greenough hired had managed to dispose of the tea they earned before then, they therefore subsequently had little to show for their effort in salvaging goods from the vessel.

Another raid in Provincetown targeted a man named Stephen Atwood, who in early January purchased one of the two remaining chests from Greenough. Toward the end of the month, seven local "Incendiaries," as Greenough termed them, confronted Atwood. They found a large quantity of tea in his house and burned it publicly. The raiders might not have located all that Atwood had acquired, though, because by then it had been in his hands for several weeks and part could already have been sold. Some months later, a peddler from Martha's Vineyard turned up in Lyme, Connecticut, with a hundred pounds of tea to sell. People there concluded it had probably come from the wreck of the *William*. The chest Greenough turned over to

Atwood would indeed seem to have been the most likely source for such a large amount of tea.

That left one damaged chest in John Greenough's custody, a chest that ended up causing even more dissension than the other two. While John was still in Provincetown, a letter from his brother in Wellfleet warned him about "that Cursed Tea." David Greenough begged John to have nothing to do with the tea, "as you Value your own Interest, Credit & the Credit of our Family." He did not want it reported "that a Brother of mine a son of our Honourable Father ever bought or Sold any of the detestable Stuff." John's neighbors in Wellfleet had threatened to destroy not only the tea but also John's house and his other property if he brought the tea there. When that occurred, "no body [will] pity you," David predicted, signing himself, "Your Loveing Brother (if you don't consern with any Tea)."

But John ignored the well-intentioned warning. He sold somewhat more than half of the good tea in the remaining chest of Bohea (about 190 pounds) to Colonel Willard Knowles, one of the leading residents of Eastham, the town within which Wellfleet composed a separate district. Knowles then started to market the tea, which set off confrontations in both Eastham and Wellfleet between supporters and opponents of the two elite men.

The presence of EIC tea in Eastham led to competing town meetings and later to standoffs between angry crowds and the local militia. At the first town meeting, on January 21, the town voted to allow Knowles to continue to sell the tea and expressed no concern about the sales of any tea, taxed or untaxed. But the second meeting, a month later, reached a very different conclusion. In February, the summons to the meeting explicitly included residents who were not qualified as voters; conversely, wealthier men regarded that session as irregular and failed to attend. Those present excoriated Knowles for buying and selling the tea obtained from Greenough and deliberately insulted the militia leader by ordering the selectmen to remove the town's store of ammunition from his custody. When the selectmen refused to do so, in early March a disguised crowd threatened one of them with tarring and feathering before desisting after he announced that he recognized some of the men—thus potentially opening them to subsequent pros-

ecution. On two later occasions, crowds gathered again to try to attack Knowles himself, but the local militia mustered to defend him and the attackers reluctantly ended their campaign.

Finally, in late March, at still a third meeting, Eastham townsmen formally reversed the February vote, declaring its criticisms of Knowles "false & scandalous & defamatory." They insisted that the previous meeting had been "a Violation & breach of the good & wholesome Laws of this Country" and that such gatherings would "never have any Tendency to restore the Liberties of America." Furthermore, they resolved that the buying and selling of untaxed EIC tea should not be interpreted as endorsing the Tea Act or the right of Parliament to tax America. They publicly defended the honor and character of Colonel Knowles, asserting that the insults to him were "a gross reflection on his unshaken Fidelity to his King & Country." Thus the meeting ordered the town clerk to "erase deface obliterate & blot out" the record left by its February predecessor. And then, having for a second time formally approved the sales, the residents of Eastham presumably continued to purchase salvaged and non-duty-paying EIC tea from Willard Knowles.

John Greenough did not have to confront mobs, but he did have to defend himself verbally against his fellow townsmen. In a formal statement to the other residents of Wellfleet drafted in late January, he supported taking "all lawful & prudent" steps to prevent the importation and sale of tea taxed by a law to which Americans had not consented. But that did not apply to the tea in his possession, on which no duty had been, or would ever be, paid. Greenough criticized the "Ruffains" who had raided houses in Provincetown, terming them "Plunderers & Assassins." He asserted that they showed "a malicious & invidious Disposition," a "Curse that . . . [is] as destructive to Society as the most cruel Tyranny." If such men gained power, the people of Massachusetts would be worse off than under the current regime, he insisted, because anyone who did not agree with them would be sacrificed to "cruel Vengeance." John Vardill as Poplicola would surely have approved the language had he read that statement.

Wellfleet men voted to place the tea remaining in Greenough's hands (probably about a hundred pounds) into the custody of the local committee while they sought advice from Boston. They wrote to the com-

mittee of correspondence there on January 25 to inquire whether tea could be sold in Wellfleet from the damaged chest. Then they had to wait two months for an answer. When it came, the Bostonians shifted the responsibility back to the Cape, for they told the inquirers to rely on "your own good sense." And what was Wellfleet men's best judgment? The same as Eastham's: they allowed Greenough to market the tea, which he proceeded to do, despite some persistent opposition from those he termed "factious Persons." He had sold it all by early May.

The events on Cape Cod following the wreck of the *William* therefore illuminate aspects of the tea crisis of late 1773 to early 1774 that would otherwise be obscured by the success of the Americans' effort to prevent the tea from being sold in the four cities to which it had been sent. Two key conclusions can be drawn from the narrative of the wreck's aftermath.

First, and most obviously: the ubiquitous demand for tea. The colonists loved tea and were eager to acquire it cheaply. Thus the Tea Act confronted them with a dilemma. Many already relied heavily on smuggled Dutch tea, but some, especially New Englanders, had proved willing to purchase East India Company tea even when it was assessed a duty, despite what that duty represented. When hundreds of pounds of untaxed tea unexpectedly washed up on their shores, many residents of the Cape proved willing to work to earn it; to purchase it in large or small quantities; and to adopt formal resolutions contending that buying or selling undutied tea was a politically neutral activity. Although there were "Cape Indians," such as those in Eastham, who took a more hard-line stance against purchases of EIC tea, they were outnumbered by those reluctant to give up their favorite beverage. Colonists found tea so alluring that it was difficult for those who opposed parliamentary taxation to know how best to combat its consumption and the resulting symbolic payment of a duty imposed by Britain. They were to continue to experiment with different methods in the months to come.

Second: the pervasive dissension. Although residents of the Boston area might have been more or less of one mind about tea shipments, that was not true elsewhere in the colonies or even in all Massachusetts towns. The debates in Charleston revealed wide-ranging disagreements, and both New York and Philadelphia chose to exclude the tea ships at least in part because that solution avoided issues the ships' presence in port would have raised. The sorts of conflicts that could arise over tea were vividly illustrated on Cape Cod. Ordinary laborers and sailors were divided between those who would assist in landing or transporting the tea and those who would not. In Provincetown, men in disguise raided their neighbors' houses and attacked travelers on the road, seeking and destroying tea. Eastham residents engaged in competing town meetings; angry crowds there challenged the selectmen and Colonel Knowles, to the dismay of many. John Greenough's family was divided, as were his Wellfleet neighbors. Surely not only Greenough found the circumstances chaotic and unsettling. Were towns on the Cape to be ruled by men he called "Indian Liberty Sons" and by a government he termed the "Indian Constitution"?

Moreover, the ultimate resolution of the disputes in both Eastham and Wellfleet—allowing the sale of undutied EIC tea from the wreck of the *William*—was certainly not a satisfactory outcome from the standpoint of the colonial opponents of the Tea Act. No wonder far-sighted Americans did not want the tea landed. Correctly predicting the possible divisive consequences, they chose the most effective course of action, the one recommended by Dr. Benjamin Rush in October 1773: preventing the tea from landing in the first place. Over the next months, colonists on all sides of the issues raised by British policy would find disagreements less easy to resolve.

CHAPTER 2

DIVIDED SENTIMENTS

Eleven days after the disguised "Mohawks" destroyed the tea in Boston harbor, the Reverend Israel Holly of Suffield, Connecticut, preached a sermon on 1 Kings 12:15: "Wherefore the King hearkened not unto the people, for the cause was from the Lord." After explicating the story told about King Solomon in that Old Testament passage and offering his interpretation of it—God uses men's sins for his own wise purposes—Holly turned to current affairs. If God allows "arbitrary and tyrannical edicts" from the ministry to abridge the colonists' "natural and constitutional liberties," and the king will not respond to our petitions, Holly declared, "the cause is from the Lord."

Given his strong language, one might think that Holly would have gone on to echo John Adams in declaring Bostonians' action against the tea ships "magnificent," amounting to "an Epocha in History." Adams had no doubt that the EIC tea deserved its watery fate. To him, Bostonians had committed "but an Attack upon Property," one that was "absolutely and indispensably" necessary, and he calmly contemplated an even more violent future. "Many Persons wish," he wrote bloodthirstily in his diary, "that as many dead Carcasses were floating in the Harbour as there are Chests of Tea"; among those he singled out as appropriate victims were the tea consignees, customs officers, and Governor Thomas Hutchinson.

But Israel Holly's reaction to the events in Boston was instead tentative and uncertain. Holly advocated sacrificing "private interest" to "public good" in combating British policy, yet he expressed concern about the destruction of private property, which could be justified only by "pure necessity." Americans could anticipate retaliation for such an act. Should they continue to resist Britain, even "unto blood"? Or should they submit? "All who are not stupidly blind," he concluded, knew that the colonies faced "a sad and woful" future, whichever option they chose. Making matters worse were "the divided sentiments among us concerning what is right, and best for us to do, while some take one side the question, and some the other."

Holly's congregation seems to have been even less certain than he was. When the clergyman published his sermon a few months after he delivered it, "with some Enlargements," he added a footnote to his statement that only "pure necessity" could warrant the destruction of the East India Company's tea. Surely responding to one or more members of his congregation who had questioned him on that point, he elaborated and backtracked. "I mean not absolutely to determine whether there was a real necessity for it or no," he explained. The perpetrators might have been "too hasty and rash, as it is natural to run into extremes, even in the defence of a just cause." Still, he contended that "English liberties are valuable and precious" and should not be "tamely" surrendered, for that would show "more baseness than true loyalty of spirit."

Holly called on his listeners to repent, to humble themselves before God in such a time of trouble. Explaining that he would leave political solutions to others, he identified what religion required: submission to God's will. He aligned himself with the protesters but admitted that Americans were divided about what Bostonians had done and were further divided about submitting to parliamentary claims. In the end, he refused to reach a judgment about whether the destruction of the tea had been justified by "pure necessity," even as he expressed firm opposition to British policy.

In that he was not alone. Other Americans too were less convinced than John Adams that Bostonians had acted properly. During the winter and early spring of 1774, many Americans expressed concern about the destruction of the EIC's property, fearing that anarchy and mob rule might follow. But most commentators maintained a tactful silence about Bostonians' actions while nonetheless endorsing resistance to taxation by Parliament. Colonists everywhere began to consider whether to symbolize their opposition to British policy not only by forgoing purchases of EIC tea but also by declining to buy the smuggled variety too. Some even went so far as to argue that Americans should stop drinking the beverage altogether, including tea they had already purchased and had on hand in their larders. From Maine south to Georgia, residents of the colonies discussed the events of December 1773, prominently voicing the "divided sentiments" that Israel Holly identified in his sermon.

INITIAL RESPONSES

News of the destruction of the tea, which reached New York on December 21 and Philadelphia three days later, was published in Annapolis, Williamsburg, and Charleston by mid-January. On January 20, the same information reached Savannah and London. A week after that, the empire's capital learned about Philadelphia's rejection of the *Polly* from the tea ship's captain himself. Reports of the seizure of the tea in Charleston also spread through the colonies and to the home country, and by the end of January most places in North America and the authorities in London had been informed of the fate of the six tea ships that had by then reached American shores.

As soon as they learned the news, Americans living on both sides of the Atlantic began to offer their opinions on what had happened. Bostonians weighed in quickly on reports from Philadelphia and Charleston. On January 13, *The Massachusetts Spy* carried a long story about the *Polly* and praised "the united spirit" of Americans in all four ports in combating the "subtle design" of the ministry to use the EIC to establish the right of taxation. Contrasting the "obstinacy" of the Boston consignees with the tea agents elsewhere, who had all resigned, the author decried the "disagreeable alternative" Bostonians had faced: either destroying the company's property or in the long run endangering the security of their own. When, four days later, Bostonians learned about the customs seizure in Charleston, one essayist used the story to confirm the wisdom of the Mohawks' action. If the tea had not been destroyed locally before the twenty-day deadline expired, "A Countryman" argued in *The Boston Gazette*, "bloodshed" would probably have resulted. Customs officers attempting to seize the tea would have been supported by troops stationed in the city, and men guarding the wharves would not readily have given way.

Across the ocean in London, Benjamin Franklin and Henry Laurens, two colonists who later became prominent supporters of the Revolution, also offered their opinions on the tea incidents. A Philadelphian and ex-Bostonian, Franklin had for fourteen years served as the agent in Britain for several colonies, whereas Laurens, a wealthy South Carolina planter, had temporarily relocated to London while his younger sons were being educated there. Franklin at first and Laurens on reflection concurred that the Mohawks' act had been a mistake; both believed that the East India Company deserved compensation for its loss. Franklin termed the destruction "an Act of violent Injustice" because a dispute over "Publick Rights" should not require attacks on private property. Calling for "a speedy Reparation," he assured the Massachusetts assembly's committee of correspondence that "Making voluntarily such Reparation can be no Dishonour to us or Prejudice to our Claim of Rights."

Laurens, who on initially hearing the Boston news praised the "wily Cromwellians" who attacked the ships, changed his mind less than a month later. In mid-February, he remarked that he wished the Bostonians would be "So wise & So honest as to pay for the Tea." Possibly, he averred, all the colonies could contribute funds to reimburse the company. Laurens, unlike Franklin, also commented on events in Philadelphia and Charleston. In January, he lauded the "peaceable crafty Quakers" who had managed to turn the *Polly* away, but once he learned what had happened in Charleston, he observed, "I commend the proceeding at Charles Town in preference to all the rest," predicting that the conduct of his fellow Carolinians would be "approved of by every true English man."

In that assessment, though, Laurens erred badly, because many colonists criticized the ambiguous outcome in Charleston. The first news of the customs officers' actions arrived in New York in early January, carried by a Captain Mason. Before that, other colonists had relied on Peter Timothy's deceptive narrative of the December 3 meeting, with its account of unanimous opposition to the tea ship. Accordingly, Mason's report of the customs seizure shocked northern readers, and the January 6 issue of John Holt's *New-York Journal,* the paper aligned with Alexander McDougall and the local Sons of Liberty, contained not just Mason's news but also critical commentaries. "Tacitus" wondered how Carolinians' "patriotic designs" had been defeated, reporting rumors that "a difference had arisen between the merchants and the planters, and that through private animosity, public duty was neglected." Even more sharply censorious was Holt's own statement, which accused South Carolina of thwarting "the grand and important interest of all America" and speculated that "some secret Enemies" had connived to effect the landing of the tea, thereby eventually enabling its sale.

By the time he prepared the January 17 issue of his paper, Peter Timothy had learned about the destruction of the tea in Boston and the rejection of the tea ship in Philadelphia, along with the Cape Cod shipwreck and the nonappearance of the vessel sent to New York. Anticipating the criticism that was even then appearing in the other colonies, he defended his city by insisting that although the EIC tea had been landed, "it will be found an article *equally unsaleable*, as if it had been destroyed—without the Company's having their private property taken from them." A vigorous defense was indeed required. Just two weeks later, one of Timothy's competitors printed a New Yorker's expression of dismay at the Charleston events. The author told a Carolina friend that "the Ardour of our Rejoicing for the first Intelligence was scarce over" when Mason arrived with news of the seizure. He commented that the news "was an Evil Hour for America." Charleston's having landed the tea could well delay repeal of the duty, for it "Manifests a Disunion among the Colonies." Even if the tea would not be sold, he predicted, "the Ministry will be encouraged by your receiving it."

The story New Yorkers heard oversimplified the complex disagreements in the southern city. The dissension in Charleston involved deep divisions within the mercantile community, in addition to merchants' reputed differences with planters. Issues that seemingly had been resolved at the second citywide meeting in mid-December quickly reemerged after the seizure to cause more controversy. Some Carolinians continued to advocate boycotting only duty-paying tea. Others preferred to proscribe all purchases and sales of tea, so that smugglers could not control the local market. Further complicating the matter were those tea merchants who had substantial quantities already on hand or who had ordered chests from overseas suppliers before December 3. Such men wanted to ensure that they could sell the tea that arrived in the colony during the next few months, even if they had signed the December agreement not to import or retail tea until repeal of the duty.

So Charlestonians moved once more to try to achieve consensus despite the splintered opinions, this time by preparing in advance for another general meeting. In an unusually opaque report, Timothy revealed that on January 20 an unspecified number of residents of the city gathered at an unspecified place. The unidentified men, he disclosed, wanted to ensure that the business of a third meeting was "conducted, and completed with the greater Regularity, Ease and Dispatch, to more general Satisfaction" than the other two and to ensure that it would lead to a hitherto elusive "final and conclusive" result. The attendees appointed a large standing committee to draft resolutions and organize the meeting, which then took place in mid-March, chaired once more by George Gabriel Powell. The committee's resolutions, adopted at the gathering, allowed retailers the desired exemption for tea ordered or currently owned but forbade importing or marketing any other legal or smuggled tea until after the duty was rescinded. Responding to the criticism of their collusive tactics, participants promised to prevent the seized tea from being sold or moved, except to be reloaded on a ship leaving the colony. Furthermore, they pledged not to do business with anyone who imported, bought, or sold tea, whether legal or smuggled.

Despite the seeming unanimity, Christopher Gadsden, a local resistance leader, revealed two months later to Samuel Adams that divisions in the community persisted even after the third meeting, because many merchants refused to sign the compact not to retail any tea except for that already in their shops or on order. Instead, they contended disingenuously that an effective nonimportation agreement should encompass wine, coffee, and other duty-paying goods as well as tea. The tea boycott's backers saw through the arguments of "these *overvirtuous* Gentry," Gadsden explained, recognizing that such men advocated extending the reach of the agreement only so as to ensure its demise. Charleston accordingly remained divided, primarily over the question of vending and consuming tea other than that which had been seized from the *London* by customs officers. On the tea dispatched directly by the East India Company, the town could agree: it could not be sold. Everything else still appeared potentially open to dispute.

Commentary in places outside those to which the EIC ships had been sent tended to focus on Boston and Philadelphia but also occasionally mentioned Charleston. In Virginia, for example, Philip Vickers Fithian, a recent graduate of the College of New Jersey (Princeton) employed as a tutor on a Virginia plantation, recorded on January 24, "great Professions of Liberty expressed in Songs Toasts &c" the day after news arrived from Boston and Philadelphia, adding, "Gentlemen here in general applaud & honour our Northern Colonies for so manly, & patriotic Resistance!" Yet that opinion was not universally held in the colony. A wealthy Virginia planter termed the Bostonians' action "Injustice," for "I never could think so violent a Transaction was the Effect of Patriotism." A Fredericksburg merchant rendered a similar verdict. He expressed doubts about whether the Bostonians had acted ethically, indicating that he preferred Charleston's solution. Bostonians should have stored the tea and then "let it lie in the publick Warehouses & Rott" by refusing to purchase it. A Bermudian offered a comparable observation to his brother, who had recently relocated to Virginia. The Bostonians had taken an unnecessary step, he declared; "they have exposed themselves to Hazard without Reason & furnished the Enemies to the Liberties of America with Arguments against them." They and the other mainland colonists should simply have agreed not to consume taxed tea. That would have made their point and would not have "aggravate[d rather] than conciliate[d] Measures."

Virginia newspapers echoed the differences of opinion expressed in private correspondence. In February, "A Virginian" asserted that he saw no difference between tea sent directly by the EIC and other taxed tea, which had long been imported. He expressed concern about the possible "hasty inconsiderate determination of the populace to the northward," which could lead to "alarming consequences." Another writer, "L.H.," criticized the "Sons of Riot and Confusion" who had destroyed the tea in Boston, and asked, "Is there no Danger to Liberty when every Merchant is liable to have his House, Property, and even Life, invaded or threatened by a Mob, who may be assembled at any Time?" A reply to L.H. by "Thousands" insisted that the tea tax had been intended as a precedent for "the farther unlimited Expansion of Taxes on America by the British Parliament" and, adopting an argument from the "Constitutional Catechism," contended that "the great Law of Nature and Reason" allowed every society "to defend itself from Ruin."

In New England, such political opinions appeared in the resolutions adopted by town meetings. Whereas it is impossible to know whether other Virginians shared the ideas voiced in correspondence or in print, the northern town meeting resolutions nominally represented the views of ordinary residents as well as the towns' leaders, even though selectmen might have drafted and presented the statements for approval. During the late winter and early spring of 1774, few such resolutions applauded the Mohawks. Two Massachusetts towns—Marshfield and Freetown—even formally expressed abhorrence of "the late tumultuous, and as we think illegal proceedings" (Marshfield) or termed the Mohawks' action "very contrary to the Spirit of our Laws and the Liberty of the People" (Freetown). We "renounce all methods of imposition, violence and persecution," declared Marshfield; we "fear there is a Spirit of Anarchy, Disorder and Confusion prevailing in some Parts of this Province," avowed Freetown.

Other towns in the region supported Boston tepidly at best. For example, *The New-Hampshire Gazette* published eight sets of town resolves between early January and early March, only one of which (from Falmouth, Maine) explicitly praised the Bostonians' "intrepid behaviour upon the late TEA-*Ships* arrival." All the other statements confined themselves to asserting American rights in general terms, promised to boycott EIC tea in the future, or tellingly advocated using only "lawful" or "rational" methods to prevent taxed tea from landing in America. Of eight town meetings in Rhode Island between mid-January and late March, not one went as far as Falmouth. Even those that adopted strongly worded affirmations of American rights also referred specifically to using "due and legal means" to oppose dutied tea.

The silences were significant. Although most Americans appeared committed to opposing Parliament's claims to taxation, in the winter and spring of 1774 most also seemed unwilling to support the Bostonians' action publicly. Judging by the contents of individual and collective statements, many colonists worried about the threats to private property and the potential dangers of mob rule implied by the Mohawks' violent destruction of the EIC tea. The town of Bristol, Rhode Island, addressed such apprehensions explicitly in resolutions adopted on February 28. Some might be afraid that all protests would lead to "anarchy and confusion" and thus establish "tyranny and arbitrary power, as one extreme leads to another," the townsmen declared. But, they insisted, we "are as firm for the support of government, agreeable to our excellent constitution, as for the defence of our own rights and privileges."

Still, the questions remained: If violent protests defending "our own rights and privileges" became commonplace, could order be maintained? Could anarchy leading to tyranny be avoided? Those questions arose especially pointedly on Cape Cod, because John Greenough, the primary purveyor of the untaxed EIC tea from the wreck of the *William,* faced ideological challenges from his own father as well as the physical ones from his neighbors already discussed in the first chapter.

In February, Thomas Greenough, an activist allied with the Boston committee of correspondence, wrote several letters criticizing his son. In reply, John vigorously defended himself and his plans to retail the salvaged tea. How could his father think that he could "sell the Libertys of my Country" for financial gain? John asked. Lost freedoms would come not from the actions of men such as himself but rather from the failings of civil officials. How could they allow "private Persons and Societys" to decide "what is lawfull prudent just and right for a Man to say and do and what is not"? he inquired. Charging that a "Court of Indians" now ruled in Boston, he exclaimed,

> Thus is our Liberties destroyd, so far as such Men who have no lawfull Power and Right, do govern and controul our private lawful Actions, or the Publick Acts of Government, and our Properties are become precarious and uncertain being at the disposal of these Indian Liberty Sons—can we imagine [a] more absolute state of Tyrany and outragious Cruelty than when every pri-

vate gang of Plunderers & Assassins may wreek their Vengeance
against any Person or their Property unpunish'd.

Yet some Bostonians, John added, surely with his father in mind,
"countenance protect and encourage such Violations of the Laws of
God and this Country."

John questioned by "what right power or Authority" he could be
prevented from selling tea that had paid no duty. "Is Tea the Cause of
the Dispute between this and the Mother State or the Duty on Tea?
If not Tea consider'd in itself why ought we now to curse or call that
detestible, that on which we have so often asked the Divine Blessing?"
He contended that the actions of "your Indians" were "more dangerous than any Act of the British Parliament" in that they constituted
"a greater infring[e]ment of our Rights and Liberties." On the whole,
he concluded, this is "a dark and melancholy Day."

Thomas Greenough did not let his son's letter go unanswered. "I
find you differ with me in Sentaments as to the Authority," he began
in response. When officials acted as they should, he averred, opposing
them was a political and religious sin. But men were obliged to obey
magistrates only insofar as officials ruled according to law. "When
Magestrats . . . play the Tyrant," and when petitions have failed to
resolve grievances, he insisted, "I think wee have Just reason to rouse
up and try to brake the Yoke of Tyrany, & releve Ourselves from the
Thretened Servitude." Admitting that he did not approve all mob
actions in Boston because of the threat the crowds posed to private
property, Thomas nevertheless defended the committee of correspondence, because its members were "striving all in their power to save us
from Ruin & distruction." Moreover, he asserted, "when our libertys
are invaided, and wee cant be heard, a Mobb is as requisite to the body
Politick as a portion of ficick [physic] is to a fowle Stomick."

The Greenoughs ended their written exchange at an impasse. To
John, the crowds in Boston and on the Cape were composed of "Savage
Barbarians" who had "treasonably usurped" governmental authority
and threatened the social order. To his father, Thomas, who acknowledged those dangers, the ordinary folk who constituted the mobs nevertheless played essential roles in the struggle against Britain. Although
father and son both claimed to support the cause of American liberty

and both opposed any attempt by Parliament to tax the colonies, they disagreed sharply on the methods of that opposition and the dangers (or lack thereof) involved in the conflict.

Such disagreements were to perplex colonists during the months to come. People elsewhere, as on the Cape, had to confront the questions raised by crowd actions: By what authority did the members act? How could they acquire legitimacy? Why should anyone comply with what "private" men sought violently to achieve, other than through fear of the consequences for one's person, family, or property? Could the destruction of private property ever be justified by an appeal to the greater good? Thomas Greenough offered one possible answer to those queries: the crowds constituted necessary medicine applied to a sick body politic, and they should be viewed as a dose of unpleasant physic that could lead to a cure of the disease. But such medicine was to be endured, not welcomed.

Furthermore, the Greenoughs' correspondence raised the topic of tea consumption itself. If one accepted John's position that the issue was the duty, not the tea, it was difficult to contend that people should not drink untaxed tea, whether that commodity was salvaged from the shipwreck or smuggled from the Caribbean or Europe. Thus Cape residents collectively decided in town meetings that untaxed tea from the *William* could be freely sold and consumed without violating colonial political unity. In Charleston, though, the Chamber of Commerce wanted to forbid all tea sales because its primary concern was equalizing competition rather than opposition to the EIC. The merchants collectively voiced their opinion that those who usually purchased tea from smugglers should not be able to profit while the nonimportation agreement damaged the trade of those who had retailed legal tea. Even if colonists concurred in opposing the EIC's tea shipments, many significant and potentially divisive questions remained unresolved in the months after December 1773.

TEA, REAL AND SYMBOLIC

In the spring of 1774, Americans realized that stopping the ships with tea dispatched directly to four cities by the East India Company was easier than stopping the importation of all EIC tea to every American port. Some vessels carrying tea ordered by individual merchants left England before news of the (non)reception of the EIC's tea arrived there in late January. Furthermore, some English merchants appear to have assumed that colonial opposition would be confined only to tea shipped by the company itself or that chests bound for other ports would be welcomed. Consequently, shipments of duty-paying tea continued to arrive throughout 1774 and even into early 1775, to meet with predictably negative receptions, because opposition to the tea duty soon became nearly universal.

The first vessel with new consignments of tea that arrived at an American port in 1774 was Captain Benjamin Gorham's brig *Fortune,* which had left England in early January and entered Boston harbor on March 6, with a cargo including twenty-eight and a half chests of EIC tea directed to four local merchants. The owners of the tea and the vessel readily agreed to send both back to London, but because other items on the ship were needed in Boston, they proposed unloading the rest of the cargo first. Customs officers refused to approve that plan, insisting that duty had to be paid on everything before the vessel could leave. So, on the night of March 7, about sixty disguised "Indians" gathered, hauled out the chests, broke them open, and tossed the contents into the harbor. Governor Hutchinson, reporting the incident to Lord Dartmouth, indicated that even if the owners of the tea were able to discover the identity of the perpetrators, they would almost certainly not be charged with a crime. "If [the owners] had attempted to land it," he declared, "it's probable they would have shared in the fate of the consignees of the Company's tea," who had not been able to return to town since late November.

The next new shipment of tea came to New York in April, coincidentally just one day after the EIC tea ship *Nancy* appeared at Sandy Hook. Without the knowledge of his ship's owners, Captain Chambers carried with him eighteen chests of Hyson tea, which he personally owned and intended to sell in the city. When the local committee appointed to deal with tea imports asked for the ship's records, Chambers sought to conceal that part of his cargo. Unfortunately for him, New Yorkers had already learned that Chambers intended to bring tea into the colony, so they refused to accept his denials. He eventually admitted the truth.

The shipowners then publicly revealed the presence of tea on board in hopes of avoiding "the most imminent danger" to the vessel and its cargo. That led to a farcical result, because two competing crowds of men, one of which gathered spontaneously upon hearing that news and another disguised group that arrived later, both planned to destroy the tea. The first crowd successfully effected its aim, purportedly with the assistance of "persons of reputation." In the midst of the confusion and despite the wrath of the rival mobs, Chambers managed to slip away. He made his way onto the *Nancy* and returned to England with Captain Lockyer and the EIC's tea. Lieutenant Governor Cadwallader Colden, in charge of the colony because Governor Tryon had left for England shortly before, informed Dartmouth that Chambers had attracted "the particular resentment of the people . . . by the duplicity of his conduct," since he had been publicly thanked in the fall for a decision not to carry EIC tea to New York.

The Boston-style destruction of Chambers's tea chests provoked extensive commentary in New York. *Rivington's New-York Gazetteer* published essays both supporting and criticizing the action. An unsigned and untitled article observed that it was common for captains to bring tea from London on their own accounts, and asked that the so-called "*persons* of REPUTATION" involved in the events be publicly identified so that their "*pretensions*" could be confirmed. Making clear his contrary assessment of the low social standing of the participants, he declared himself "a sworn foe to *Coblers* and *Taylors,* so long as they take upon their everlasting and unmeasurable shoulders, the power of directing the loyal and sensible inhabitants of the CITY and PROVINCE OF NEW-YORK." Several weeks later, "Brutus" replied in a series of bombastic rhetorical queries, one of which advocated continued smuggling: "Is it not a public virtue, while this badge of slavery is held over us, to supply the wants of our inhabitants at the risk of a seizure, and by that means to elude the payment of the odious tax?" He mocked the reference to cobblers and tailors: Does anyone intend us to walk "barefooted, or in rags"? In a more serious vein, he insisted that "there was no alternative left between the destruction of the tea at Boston and New York, and a submission to the odious duty."

Yet others who contemplated the colonists' opposition to EIC tea imports could well have reached different conclusions. The *Nancy* had been successfully prevented from discharging its cargo. The recent destructive acts in Boston and New York could be seen as exceptional: the first because of the intransigence of customs officers, who refused to agree to what seemed an appropriate compromise; the second because of local anger at Captain Chambers for his apparent about-face on EIC tea and his personal attempt to profit from tea sales. Did those exceptional circumstances excuse the renewed destruction of merchants' property? Colonists openly expressed concerns about mob violence in the future, which suggested that the answer to that question might be no. At the same time, the attacks on tea in the spring of 1774 seemed to set a new precedent. The Philadelphian Joseph Reed, for example, predicted that if more company tea arrived in his city, "it is my opinion that it would be immediately destroyed," despite the success of the earlier, more cautious approach.

In the midst of such discussions, public opinion in the colonies started to turn against purchasing or consuming any tea. Stopping imports of taxed EIC tea inadequately addressed the significant symbol that imbibing tea quickly became, because everyone realized that ending legal shipments left smuggled tea untouched. A New England editor referred to such tea discreetly as that "sent here from the neighbouring colonies, subject to no duty." One of the few authors who forthrightly addressed issues raised by Dutch tea was a Rhode Islander, "Mentor." He argued that because one could never be certain one was drinking untaxed tea, the beverage should be avoided completely. As many understood, preventing further imports also did not solve the problem of what to do with tea already in colonial homes and stores. So "A Batchelor" asked in *The Norwich Packet,* "What Good, either of a moral or political Nature, will arise to this much injured Continent, from burning or otherwise destroying those *Teas* which private Persons have now in their Custody, and for which they have paid Duty?"

So the commodity, duty paying or not, became the synecdoche representing British taxation in general, acquiring a symbolic significance extending far beyond the specifics of the Townshend or Tea Acts. Perhaps Mentor's argument that all tea should be regarded as suspect was echoed by and persuaded others. Certainly the actions of some northerners in Virginia suggested the need for caution in consumption decisions, for James Parker, a Norfolk merchant, informed a friend that "New England men have bought a great deal of [EIC] tea here, intending to introduce it as tea from St. Eustatius." But more likely the formal rejection of tea drinking was soon recognized as a convenient means of displaying one's support for resistance to British policies. Announcing a decision not to drink tea became a key symbol of one's opposition to Great Britain. The town of Falmouth forbade consuming the beverage within its boundaries, so an innkeeper there refused John Adams's request for tea that had been "honestly smuggled." Instead, he had to drink coffee, which he reported to his wife having "borne . . . very well," adding that he had to be "weaned" from tea because it "must be universally renounced."

Essayists and clergymen tried various means to persuade Americans to forgo all tea. A Massachusetts minister sermonized against the beverage, describing it as a "*needless* luxury" that led "all orders, ranks and ages of people" into "excesses of wickedness." Authors promoted local herbal alternatives or advocated growing tea bushes in America; a diarist noted his "fine dish of funn" when he was served a purported substitute, "Monongoheley Balsam," which turned out to be Hyson. One New York mercantile family paid no attention to such reasoning. Thomas Ellison Jr. informed his father in early June 1774 that tea (presumably smuggled) had arrived in the city and that he would try to purchase some. A week later, he reported that he had acquired a chest, which he was dividing among himself, his father, and his brother.

Newspaper editors frequently described public performances of opposition to tea. For example, in Charlestown, Massachusetts, witnesses reported that men collected all the tea in town and burned it in front of a thousand people, including Bostonians who came to see the spectacle and were served "Punch and wine" at Charlestown's expense. At Lexington, similarly, "every ounce" of legal and illegal tea was thrown into "one common bonfire." Students and teachers at Princeton and "ladies" from Boston alike publicly forswore the use of tea, as did an "affluent" Newport woman, who was said to have decided "to have no India tea drank in her Family" until the duty was removed. Many reprinted notices reportedly originated in Newport, perhaps because it was such a well-known center for clandestine trade that people would conclude that the tea being forgone had been smuggled. Fifty, sixty, or three hundred Newport families—the numbers varied—were described in colonial newspapers as no longer consuming that "noxious weed" or "pernicious herb."

Because women were especially associated with socializing over tea in eighteenth-century American culture, published essays and such reports of public performances were often aimed explicitly at a female audience. A Fredericksburg merchant observed that "the Newspapers abound with the heroick behaviour of ye Females," who were giving up "the only Liberty which they are posses'd of (Drinking Tea)." But he added cynically that women were still consuming smuggled tea "with more pleasure & in greater quantities than ever"; if he was correct, the anti-tea campaign failed in its aim of persuading women to forgo all tea. That campaign focused primarily on essays alerting women to the purported dangers of drinking tea. For instance, a New Yorker warned about the "Train of Disorders" that tea would cause in women with "delicate Constitutions," even sometimes proving fatal. The South Carolinian Junius Brutus quoted "the learned and very eminent Dr. TISSOT," calling tea "most pernicious" and charging that for women it "first DESTROYS the strength of the stomach and, if not soon laid aside, equally destroys that of the VISCERA, the BLOOD, the NERVES, and the whole body," increasing the prevalence of nervous disorders among them.

The anonymous author of *A Sermon on Tea* also cited Dr. Tissot and other medical authorities, contending that "Tea rendered habitual, gradually saps the constitution." The beverage's impact was "slow but sure," a "slow consuming poison." A "Pandora's Box" that affected both sexes, tea made Europeans shorter and weaker after its introduction to the Continent a century earlier. Indeed, the beverage has "reduced the robust masculine habit of men, to a feminine softness," thus turning men into women and "women into—God knows what." Directing his attention specifically to younger women, he informed them that drinking tea would leave them less attractive to men. It will "either suffuse your faces with a deadly paleness, or what is worse, with a sallow hue," making a regular consumer into a "ghost-like pale faced spectre." And every mother needed to be concerned about her "unborn posterity," for he predicted that the child of a tea drinker would die young, "a speedy martyr to her ill judged diet."

Such "scare crow stories" did not impress "A Woman," who wrote to

The Massachusetts Spy, expressing skepticism and inquiring, "Why were not these arguments used against the use of it in former times, before it was thought a political evil?" She suggested that if men would write about "all the political reasons for discarding the use of Tea," women would find their narratives more persuasive. In response, Dr. Thomas Young, one of the leaders of the Boston committee of correspondence, refused to back down. He declared that the political tale had been published repeatedly, whereas the medical one still needed telling. Likening tea to "its sister opium," he contended that drinking tea made one unable to digest food properly. If people moved on from Bohea to finer sorts of tea, the problem worsened, until "at length [imbibers] arrived at so extreme a delicacy of stomach, that nothing but the very finest [foods] can be borne." And that in turn led to a "general weakness," to a "proneness to every disease of the low nervous, flatulent, corbutic, hypochondriac kind." Like the author of the *Sermon,* he thought that worst of all was the potential effect on "hapless posterity," because the "feeble, lax, effeminate constitution" was inheritable. "I presume, Madam," he concluded with a flourish, "you would hardly wish to be the mother of such a puny race."

Probably A Woman would have found two anti-tea essays purportedly penned by southern women more to her liking, had she come across them. Both "A Planter's Wife" and "Margaret Homespun" took a political approach to the issue of tea consumption. "Surely, my Sisters," wrote A Planter's Wife, "we cannot be tame Spectators. . . . By our persisting hitherto, in the Use of the East-India TEA, we have opposed our Friends, and greatly assisted the Enemies of America, to enslave ourselves and Posterity." Margaret Homespun saw that "the principal bone of contention (to wit the article of tea) lies altogether between the Parliament of Great-Britain and the Women of America," because women held "the undoubted sovereignty of the Tea-Table." In such circumstances, "silence in our sex" was "unpardonable." Both authors exhorted women to do their part by forgoing tea and other "East-India Goods" as well. "Whatever may be the event of the present struggle," Margaret Homespun concluded, "let it never be said our sex were accessory to the death of AMERICAN LIBERTY."

In the same vein were two versions of a poem titled "A Lady's Adieu to Her Tea Table," which appeared in both northern and southern newspapers and revealed a regional intellectual exchange among women. The poem of New England origin rhymed; the other (the earliest, first published in Williamsburg) did not. It seems likely that a female reader in Newburyport, Massachusetts, the location of the northern paper that initially printed the rhymed version, was dissatisfied with the unrhymed poem. She therefore turned it into verse, perhaps for the amusement of her friends as well as herself. The first began, "Farewell the Tea Board, with its gaudy Equipage, / Of Cups and Saucers, Cream Bucket, Sugar Tongs." The second transformed those lines into "Farewell the Tea-board, with your gaudy attire; / Ye cups and ye saucers, that I did admire." Both gave the same reason for abstaining from tea: "Because I'm taught (and I believe it true) / Its Use will *fasten slavish Chains upon my Country*," which became, in the rhymed version, "Because I am taught (and believe it is fact) / That our ruin is aim'd at in a late act." And both closed with a paean to an image of the goddess liberty: "And LIBERTY'S the Goddess I would choose / To reign triumphant in AMERICA"; "LIBERTY'S the goddess that I do adore / And I'll maintain her right until my last hour, / Before she shall part I will die in the cause, / For I'll never be govern'd by tyranny's laws."

Women's prominence in the anti-tea literature created a climate in which satires flourished. For example, one article noted that "the fair Daughters of Liberty" in Hartford had resolved that because the aiders and abettors of the tea trade had committed high treason, they had decided to meet at each other's houses "to HANG the Tea Kettle, DRAW the Tea, and QUARTER the Toast." A New Hampshire author, "Susanna Spindle," went further, drafting a series of resolves resembling those adopted by various New England towns in early 1774. The first read, "That the Women in America are entitled to all the Liberties which the Women in Great Britain enjoy, and particularly to drink Tea," and the second, that women would never have entered into a marriage covenant if their husbands had not promised to supply them with tea. The most famous satire took as its visual subject a meeting of women in Edenton, North Carolina, to support resistance to Britain, transforming it into a grotesque tea party. The gathering itself had little directly to do with tea, but the cultural association of women with the beverage was so strong that the English cartoonist chose tea as the exclusive vehicle for his satire.

What some women—for example, Margaret Homespun and the poets—saw as a powerful weapon in women's hands thus became a satirical tool for American and English men alike. (Surely Susanna

The association of women and tea drinking was so strong that when the British cartoonist Philip Dawe sought to satirize the involvement of women in the colonial resistance movement, he portrayed grotesque women in Edenton, North Carolina, as not only signing a protest about the "pernicious custom" of tea drinking but also (in the left rear) emptying their tea canisters. Note the neglected child under the table in front and the dog urinating on another tea canister. The women's actual statement said nothing about tea.

Spindle was male, just like Philip Dawe, the English cartoonist.) That from the early decades of the eighteenth century women and tea were linked in Anglo-Americans' minds meant that when tea became the focal point for colonial resistance to Britain from late 1773 through the first months of 1774, women's consumption decisions acquired symbolic significance. Yet men were unwilling to grant women much cultural authority. Even as they recognized that if the boycott of legal tea (and perhaps the illegal variety, too) was to succeed, women's involvement would be essential, men did not acknowledge that women would respond positively to political arguments based on calls to pay attention to the common good. Instead, they used stereotyped and explicitly feminized scare tactics, contending that tea was physically debilitating and that drinking it would lead to the birth of sickly children.

Given the paucity of evidence beyond the exempla in the newspapers, it is impossible to know which arguments, if any, succeeded. More than one merchant continued to stock and advertise tea for sale; a Worcester man, for instance, reported to his brother in early 1774 that he had easily sold "Very poor" tea and that in spite of any agreements to the contrary "was I disposed I Could then Sell more Tea than ever I did." And, like a Pennsylvania family, others who supported resistance and thought "the name of tory . . . opprobrious" nevertheless drank tea "by stealth."

ADVICES FROM LONDON

January 29, 1774. Benjamin Franklin attends a Privy Council meeting to present a petition from Massachusetts asking for the removal of Governor Thomas Hutchinson. Franklin has already admitted publicly that he obtained and sent to Boston private letters written by Hutchinson and others in the 1760s to a London official. The furor caused by their publication in America has engulfed both Hutchinson and Franklin. In the Whitehall room known as the Cockpit, the solicitor general, Alexander Wedderburn, subjects Franklin to a vicious hour-long inquisition and diatribe, thoroughly humiliating him. In addition, Wedderburn excoriates Massachusetts for the colony's opposition to British authority and its destruction of the tea, of which Londoners learned nine days earlier. The Privy Council rejects the Massachusetts petition and several days later deprives Franklin of his longtime position as deputy postmaster general of the colonies.

January 31. Gilbert Barkley, the Philadelphia consignee who had traveled on the tea ship *Polly,* having had the voyage back from America to consider what to do about the rejected tea, approaches the Court of Directors of the East India Company shortly after he returns to London. He has a proposal: he will take the *Polly*'s entire cargo of tea off their hands, if they will give him a year's credit and sell it to him at a discount. He presents detailed figures showing that the company would make only about £2,000 less by selling to him than it would have been projected to earn from sales in Philadelphia, considering all the costs it would have incurred there. He explains that he plans to export the tea to St. Eustatius. Left unstated, but understood by all, is his next step: he will smuggle it back into North America disguised as Dutch tea. On February 2, the EIC rejects his offer. The company then futilely petitions the Treasury for compensation for the costs it sustained because the *Polly* could not land.

February 5. Lord Dartmouth, having received detailed information from Boston about events from early November to the tea destruction on December 16, summarizes those incidents and asks the Law Lords, "Do the acts and proceedings stated in the foregoing case or any of them amount to the crime of high treason?" And: "If they do, who are the persons chargeable with such crime, and what will be the proper and legal method of proceeding against them?" That same day, Dartmouth writes to William Bull, declaring that although Charleston's actions do not "equal in criminality" what happened in Boston and Philadelphia, they constitute "a most unwarrantable Insult to the Authority of this Kingdom." Six days later, the Law Lords reply: some of the acts, including the resolutions of the Boston meeting on November

29–30, do constitute "high treason, . . . the levying of war against His Majesty." But, alas, with only one witness (a ship captain) currently available in England to attest to the truth of the written statements, the evidence "is scarce sufficient to affect any person with the crime of high treason" unless the resolutions in question can be securely linked to specific individuals by additional sworn testimony. Before receiving their response, Dartmouth already signals a different approach to the dispute by addressing a series of letters to the governors of six provinces, all with the same message: he and the king have decided that America's dependence on Britain is to be secured. But he does not reveal how they intend to achieve that goal.

March 14 and 31. Lord North rises in the House of Commons to describe how the ministry has decided to respond to the Mohawks' destruction of the tea. The Boston customshouse and the colony's capital will be moved to Salem. The port will be closed to all but commerce in essential food and fuel until the tea has been paid for, and until the governor certifies that the people are fully complying with the rule of law. North declares that his aim is not only to punish Boston but also to dissuade other colonies from following the New Englanders' lead further than they already have. Drawing on reports sent by Lieutenant Governor Bull of South Carolina and Governor Tryon of New York, he contends that Boston's "outrages, acts of violence," have already been "guilty of setting that example from one end of the continent to the other." Americans resident in London, among them Henry Laurens, present petitions to Parliament and the king against the bill, but according to one colonial agent the petitions do more harm than good because the small number of signatories convinces some MPs that the petitions lack sufficient support. The king signs the Boston Port Act on March 31, but the colonists will not have confirmation of its provisions until over a month later, in early May.

April 9. Lord Dartmouth drafts instructions to General Thomas Gage, soon to depart for Boston as the new governor of Massachusetts, serving in both military and civilian capacities and replacing Thomas Hutchinson, who has been asking for months to be relieved of his post. Dartmouth informs Gage that he and the king do not expect Bostonians to resist the Port Act, but if they do, he can employ troops against the populace. Even though the Law Lords have told him that the leaders of the disturbances in late 1773 cannot be prosecuted in England, such men have "a deep degree of Guilt" and their punishment would serve as "a very necessary and essential Example to others." Gage should attempt to persuade local authorities in the Bay Colony to bring them to trial, but if he thinks such an effort will fail, he should avoid creating such a "Triumph to the Faction," which would be "disgraceful to Government." If men allied to the resistance movement are selected as council members in an upcoming election, Gage is to veto them. Despite the latest dispatches from Boston, which leave "little room to hope, that order and obedience are soon likely to take the place of Anarchy and Usurpation," George III trusts that Gage's "fortitude and discretion" will succeed in managing whatever situation he encounters.

A "CLOUD RISING IN OUR POLITICAL HEMISPHERE"

In early April, Joseph Reed, a Philadelphia lawyer who was then thirty-two, took up his pen to write at length to Lord Dartmouth. He had twice addressed Dartmouth in late 1773, offering comments about local politics. But this letter differed from the other two. His brother-in-law Dennis DeBerdt Jr., he disclosed, had told him that Dartmouth was interested in receiving information from him about American "publick affairs," and he was pleased to comply with the request. He acknowledged the honor that Dartmouth was paying him, promising to try to send useful news. A few weeks later, Reed told DeBerdt that "Lord Dartmouth's acceptance of my letters is a sufficient inducement to continue them, as I hope they may be of some use to him, and not prejudice the real interests of my country."

Reed, a graduate of the College of New Jersey, studied law at the Middle Temple in London in the mid-1760s. While there, he became acquainted with Dennys DeBerdt, a colonial agent for Massachusetts, and his daughter, Esther, whom he married in 1770. Presumably in London, Reed met Lord Dartmouth, a close friend of DeBerdt's, because in his first letter he did not formally introduce himself. Reed was well connected in Philadelphia and active in the resistance movement. Although politically moderate, he was unashamedly a colonial partisan.

The colonists had detested Dartmouth's predecessor, Lord Hillsborough, a hard-liner who antagonized Americans by his heavy-handed response in 1769 to a call from the Massachusetts assembly for resistance to the Townshend Acts. By contrast, they regarded Dartmouth as a potential or actual ally within the North administration, largely because Dartmouth, unlike most English peers, was an evangelical Christian, as were many Americans. Colonists welcomed the news when Dartmouth, Lord North's friend and stepbrother, replaced Hillsborough as secretary of state for America in 1772, and many continued to hold positive views of him throughout 1774.

So in April, having been specifically invited to correspond with the American secretary, Reed was surely flattered and must have chosen his words carefully. Assuring Dartmouth that he was regarded with "Affection & Esteem," Reed reported that since the departure of the tea ship "nothing of Importance has occurr'd." Nevertheless, he thought Dartmouth should be informed about some plans under way, because he believed that previous administrations responded too tardily to colonial developments, having had no advance warning of "Schemes . . . in Embryo." He told Dartmouth about two such "schemes." The first was to establish a new colonial post office network that would not be controlled by the British; the second was "to distress & harass the Admiralty Courts, so as to make all the offices in them odious & disgraceful." Other than these, he commented, "I know of no Cloud rising in our political Hemisphere, unless our Conduct respecting the Tea should produce any," for "we hope & trust we have not forfeited your Lordships Favour & Protection." As it happened, nothing came of either scheme, in part, perhaps, because the Americans' "Conduct respecting the Tea" did produce just such a "Cloud" that quickly spread over the colonies and swallowed up other concerns.

No Bostonian actively involved in resisting British policy would have written such a letter to Lord Dartmouth in April 1774. There Samuel Adams, the leader of the committee of correspondence, saw the minister as weak and ineffective; Adams remarked that he placed a higher priority on promoting unity among the colonies than on winning "the friendship or patronage" of an English nobleman. In Boston, writing in private to alert Dartmouth in advance to what colonists might be planning would have been seen as a betrayal comparable to that contained in the private letters written by Thomas Hutchinson

A New Method of MACARONY MAKING, as practised at BOSTON.

The attacks on John Malcom in Falmouth and Boston aroused intense interest and anger in London. A British cartoonist portrayed Malcom after he had been tarred and feathered and taken to the gallows. He is being threatened by a man with a teapot; the number 45 on the man's hat links him visually to supporters of the English radical John Wilkes, who had been penalized for an essay in number 45 of *The North Briton*. A "macaroni" was a London gentleman who dressed in the height of fashion, a frequent target for satire.

and others in the late 1760s, the publication of which had led to the humiliation of Franklin in the Cockpit. Even though a customs officer described Boston as "tollerable quiet" late in April, that observation was accurate only by comparison to the agitation that preceded the destruction of the tea.

Since mid-December 1773, Boston and Massachusetts as a whole had experienced a series of disturbing events, in addition to the March incident in which the tea on the *Fortune* was destroyed.

In January, John Malcom, a customs officer from Falmouth, arrived in Boston seeking assistance from Governor Hutchinson. By seizing a ship for lack of proper paperwork, Malcom had angered his fellow townsmen, who tarred and feathered him in retaliation. He wanted Hutchinson—for Maine was part of Massachusetts—to arrange to have the perpetrators prosecuted. But on a Boston street he was harassed by a crowd of boys. Malcom, whom Hutchinson described as "passionate," struck out with his cane, badly injuring a Boston tradesman who was trying to protect one of the boys. A justice of the peace issued a warrant for Malcom's arrest, but he managed to evade the authorities. One night, though, he could not evade a large, riotous crowd, which removed him from his house, stripped him to his underclothes, tarred and feathered him again, carried him to the Liberty Tree, and ordered him to resign. He refused, so the men took him to the gallows, hung a noose around his neck, beat him with the end of a rope, and threatened to cut off his ears. Finally he complied. John Rowe, a local merchant, commented in his diary that he and "every Sober man" viewed the incident as "an act of outrageous Violence."

The next month, the Massachusetts assembly began an unsuccessful but prolonged attempt to impeach the chief justice, Peter Oliver, because he insisted on receiving his salary from Townshend Act revenues, rather than from the colony's funds. Then, when Lieutenant Governor Andrew Oliver, the chief justice's brother, died in March, an unseemly scene ensued at his funeral. Members of the assembly refused to process properly to the grave, causing "promiscuous Confusion." Further, "a large Mob . . . huzzaed," cheering when the coffin was lowered into the grave, and finally a man declared within Thomas Hutchinson's hearing that he hoped the governor would be next. For his own safety,

Peter Oliver decided to attend neither his brother's deathbed nor the funeral. *"Could Infernals do worse?"* he later exclaimed.

The brutal treatment of John Malcom and the disrespect shown to Andrew Oliver's body after his death did not appear to concern Samuel Adams, who commented on neither, but another incident raised for him the same issue that troubled John Greenough: Could crowds with nominal public purposes go too far in destroying private property? In late March, that property was the Marblehead smallpox hospital, owned by the town's leaders, who also composed the local committee of correspondence. An angry mob, afraid that inoculated individuals would spread the deadly pox in the town, attacked and demolished the hospital. The proprietors, who all immediately resigned their public positions, arranged for the arrest and confinement of two suspected ringleaders, but another huge crowd gathered and forcibly freed the men from the Salem jail, despite attempts to muster the militia to thwart them. Learning the news, Adams observed, "The tumult of the people is very properly compared to the raging of the sea. When the passions of a multitude become headstrong, they generally will have their course."

Urging his allies to try to direct the people's fury in the right direction, Adams lamented conservatives' triumphant realization that "the friends of liberty themselves, were obliged to have recourse even to military aid, to protect them from the fury of an ungoverned mob." He asserted that such conservatives failed to distinguish appropriately between "a lawless attack upon property" (like that which targeted the hospital) and "the people's rising in the necessary defence of their liberties, and . . . rationally destroying property, after trying every method to preserve it" (like the Mohawks' actions). Many other New Englanders, though, might not have perceived that distinction with such clarity. After all, the vast majority of town meeting resolutions failed to celebrate the Mohawks' destruction of the tea, which Adams placed in his "necessary defence" category. Others in addition to John Greenough regularly voiced concerns about mobs that damaged private property. Following the crowd action that freed the suspects, the Boston committee of correspondence encouraged the Marblehead men to do their public duty and resume their posts, but they refused to do so for another six months.

Referring to the attempts to impeach the chief justice, Cambridge's Hannah Winthrop asked a friend in early April, "Dont you think our hardy sons of Freedom have taken many resolute steps which will be applauded by future generations?" Some of her Boston contemporaries thought otherwise, at a time when one commented that "little else is done" in the town but politics. The merchant Richard Lechmere declared that "no body dare speak their sentiments, for fear of being Tarr'd & feather'd, or perhaps worse Treated." Indeed, he insisted, the town was in a "shocking," "miserable" situation, because "there is not the smallest degree of Government" remaining. The Reverend Henry Caner of the Anglican King's Chapel lamented what he saw as earlier leniency on the part of Britain and the governor, which had brought Massachusetts "to the very brink of ruin." If Hutchinson had acted sooner and more vigorously, Caner averred, he could have "humbled the disturbers of the public peace." He compared Boston to the fleeting glory of Troy and declared that "we have every thing to [fear] from the increasing violence of the people."

In that context, the merchant John Hancock, one of the wealthiest residents of Boston, was selected to deliver the annual address commemorating the Boston Massacre, which had occurred on March 5, 1770, when British soldiers guarding the customshouse shot and killed five colonists who were harassing them. According to Samuel Adams, the annual speeches were intended "to preserve in the Minds of the People a lively Sense of the Danger of standing Armies," and to his mind Hancock succeeded in that aim. "A vast Croud" attended at the Old South Church, recorded John Adams in his diary, so vast that John Rowe could not push his way in, although he commented that others spoke of the speech with "Great Applause." John Adams pronounced it "an elegant, a pathetic, a Spirited Performance" that produced "rainy Eyes," adding that it exceeded his own expectations. Hannah Winthrop, who was there too, observed that Hancock spoke with "Ciceronian Eloquence" and "a gracefull dignity."

Hancock drew such praise from his large audience by reminding them in emotional language of the distressing eighteen-month British occupation of Boston that preceded the confrontation four years earlier. He reached his rhetorical high point with a description of the massacre itself, "when Satan with his chosen band open'd the sluices

Paul Revere, better known today as a messenger and silversmith, was also an artist and engraver. He regularly contributed images to the short-lived Boston publication *The Royal American Magazine,* which published his portrait of Hancock as the frontispiece to its issue of March 1774, recognizing Hancock's role as the annual Boston Massacre orator that month. A scroll with "Magna Charta" is in the foreground, Liberty with a cap on a pole on the right, and a soldier in armor on the left.

of New-England's blood, and sacrilegiously polluted our land with the dead bodies of our guiltless sons." No wonder there were "rainy eyes"! Hancock then expressed regret that the perpetrators had not received justice on earth—John Adams, one of the attorneys who successfully defended the soldiers, did not record his reaction to that part of the address—but assured his listeners that heaven would judge the miscreants.

Having fulfilled the responsibility to discuss the past, Hancock moved to the present. He lauded the fact that "the dark deeds of a treacherous Cabal" (Hutchinson and his allies) had been exposed to

the public (via the publication of the private letters, everyone understood). The ministry, he warned, was trying to make the governor and judges independent of the people by paying them from the Townshend Act funds, "but this people will never be enslaved with their eyes open." Had EIC tea been successfully imported, "we should soon have found our trade in the hands of foreigners, and taxes imposed on every thing which we consumed." Instead, the tea had been rejected, and "the total disuse of TEA in this country" would likely follow, to everyone's benefit.

But, Hancock cautioned, Americans needed to fear the "restless malice, and disappointed ambition" of "our inveterate *enemies*." The colonies should unite to face that threat, and although the committees of correspondence established by colonial assemblies had accomplished much good, more was required. Thus he recommended "a general Congress of Deputies from the several Houses of Assembly on the Continent." At such a meeting, he declared, "a firm foundation may be laid for the security of our Rights and Liberties; [and] a system may be formed for our common safety." The congress would help to "restore peace and harmony to America, and secure honor and wealth to Great-Britain, even against the inclinations of her ministers."

Hancock thereby became the first colonist in 1774 to publicly propose the establishment of an intercolonial congress, but the idea was not unprecedented. Prior congresses had met in 1754 and 1765, although neither had a lasting impact. The assembly-level committees of correspondence to which Hancock referred had been suggested initially by the Virginia House of Burgesses in 1773, but few colonies responded immediately in the absence of compelling arguments to establish such bodies. In March 1774, when Hancock spoke, most coordination among the colonies was informal and based on the personal ties of individuals. Further, the primary precedent for Hancock's proposal had met nearly a decade earlier, for the sole purpose of protest.

Probably he was advocating another singular meeting, but one with a dual aim: to lay a foundation for American rights and to create a system of defense, possibly one along the lines suggested by Franklin two decades earlier. That Hancock did so about two months before Britain's response to the tea incidents was known is telling and suggests

a considerable degree of foresight on his part. In the event, though, the leaders of Boston's resistance did not immediately seize upon his idea.

Before the tea was destroyed in Boston harbor, a correspondent warned Samuel Adams that doing so would "give ye Eneimys a thousand Opportunitys against this Town." But as they waited to learn how the North administration would respond to the way in which the ports—especially Boston—greeted EIC tea, colonists did not appear to be overly worried. In the immediate aftermath of the Mohawks' action, a Boston merchant speculated that occupying troops might again be sent but that such a move could have been anticipated in any event to protect the tea if it had been landed. John Adams foresaw "Threats, Phantoms, Bugbears, by the million." There would be talk of "Armies and Navies," of "Charters annull'd," of "Treason, Tryals in England and all that." But, he predicted, "these Terrors are all but Imaginations." The worst that could happen, he thought, would be that Massachusetts would have to pay for the tea. For his part, the New York lawyer Peter Van Schaack concluded that Parliament would probably think "conciliatory Methods" were best, even when dealing with Boston.

Late in March, when ships that had left England in late January started to land in the colonies, Americans began to hear rumors about the British response to the tea incidents. The destroyed tea would have to be paid for "by Somebody," declared one account; other reports said that three, or possibly six, warships with troops were being dispatched to Boston. In early April, John Adams predicted that there would probably be no "compleat Decision" in the immediate future. "We shall oscilate like a Pendulum and fluctuate like the Ocean, for many Years to come," not achieving redress for grievances and also not fully submitting to Parliament. But later in the month, more ships came with letters dating from mid-February and even early March. Such missives spoke ominously of likely "Coercive measures" aimed at Boston and even of "blocking up all your ports." They revealed that the ministry was about to place the matter before Parliament and hinted that the Massachusetts government might be "metamorphosed." Still, on April 30, Thomas Hutchinson wrote to one of his sons that he did not know what measures Parliament had adopted.

All that changed the next day, when the *Minerva* arrived in Boston with London newspapers dated March 15, carrying brief accounts of North's speech in Parliament the previous day. Boston papers on May 2 included the report, which Hutchinson told a friend left people "much alarmed" because of its stated plan to close the port of Boston. Three days later, a ship arrived in Newport with information that the Commons had passed the bill; news of final passage reached Boston on May 10 and New York a day later. Then, on May 12, copies of the act closing the port arrived in both cities; Isaiah Thomas, publisher of *The Massachusetts Spy,* immediately printed it as a supplement to his current issue, and Hugh Gaine of *The New-York Gazette* included the full text in his paper four days later. John Adams, as Boston faced dire consequences he had not anticipated, nevertheless assured his wife, Abigail, that he was not "in the Dumps." Rather, "I look upon this as the last Effort of Lord Norths Despair. And he will as surely be defeated in it, as he was in the Project of the Tea."

On May 12, the Boston committee of correspondence asked the selectmen to convene a town meeting the next day, and the committee conferred that very afternoon with committees from nearby towns. The group drafted and approved language for the town meeting to adopt, proposing that the resolutions be distributed via circular letters to all Massachusetts towns and to other colonies north of Pennsylvania, while asking Philadelphians to forward the dispatches farther south, because Bostonians had not previously communicated directly with those colonies. The committee declared that it could not fully describe "the Art, Injustice, and cruelty" of the act nominally aimed solely at Boston but actually at all the colonies. Parliament has "accused tried and condemned said Town unheard, contrary to natural Justice and the laws of all civilised States even supposing they had competent Jurisdiction." In conjunction with the other committees, it published a broadside summarizing the act's provisions and asserting that "we cannot entertain a Thought so dishonorable to our Friends, that in this Crisis *we* shall be left to struggle *alone.*"

Stressing Bostonians' unity in the face of such a threat to their town's existence, the committee informed other colonies that even residents who had previously favored British measures regarded this move as "barbarous." It issued a clarion call for joint resistance: "Now

A broadside dated May 12 announced the adoption of the Boston Port Act. The signature of William Cooper, the committee's secretary, attested to the accuracy of its information. The Bostonians stressed the concurrence of eight other towns in their call for an immediate trade boycott of Great Britain.

therefore is the time when *All* should be united in Opposition to this violation of the Liberties of *All*. Their grand Object is to divide the Colonies." If, the committee declared, "*you* consider Boston as now suffering in the common cause," then other provinces should immediately suspend all commerce with Great Britain. That would be "a great, but necessary sacrifice, to the Cause of Liberty, and will effectually defeat the design of their Act of Revenge." It would lead other places to endure voluntarily what Boston would soon experience from "the immediate hand of Tyranny," for the act was to go into effect on June 1.

Instead of calling for the intercolonial congress that Hancock had suggested in early March, the Boston committeemen thus opted for requesting an immediate colonies-wide boycott of all trade with Britain. They chose that strategy based on their interpretation of events of the previous decade and on their awareness that imports of British goods into the colonies had risen dramatically in recent years. Recognizing that the colonies were purchasing increasing quantities of textiles and other commodities from Britain, Americans assumed that the colonial market was crucial for British manufacturers. They concluded that the British economy would suffer significantly if Americans suddenly stopped buying those goods and ceased sending to Britain key exports such as tobacco. They also believed that previous nonimportation and nonconsumption agreements, originated during the crises over the Stamp and Townshend Acts, had helped to bring about the total repeal of the first in 1766 and the partial repeal of the second in 1770. They reasoned that British merchants and manufacturers wielded influence in and over Parliament and that such people—often long-standing business associates of colonial merchants and planters—had in the past and would in the future successfully pressure Parliament to repeal laws the colonies regarded as obnoxious. The same logic, as shall be seen, informed actions of the First Continental Congress later in the year. Yet the reasoning was faulty in many respects, although accurate in its observation that North America had become an important market for British goods. But the commercial relationship did not create the sequence of cause and effect on which Americans based their decision making.

Men crowded into the town meeting at Faneuil Hall on Friday, May 13; hundreds who wanted to attend were reportedly excluded by the limited space available. Samuel Adams was chosen to moderate the session, at which participants voted to support the committee's proposal that Boston ask other colonies to immediately halt all trade with Britain and expanded that appeal to include the West Indies as well. If other colonies continued such commerce, the town predicted in melodramatic prose, "Fraud, Power, and the most odious Oppression will Rise Triumphant over Right, Justice, social Happiness and Freedom." Then participants discussed "several judicious, spirited and manly Proposals," reported *The Boston Gazette,* "with a Candor, Moderation and Firmness of Mind becoming a People resolved to preserve their Liberty," but reached no conclusions. The attendees named a committee of ten, including Samuel and John Adams, the lawyer Josiah Quincy Jr., Thomas Cushing (a merchant and Speaker of the assembly), and Dr. Joseph Warren, to consider the proposals and report to the next town meeting on Wednesday, May 18. Meanwhile, the committee of correspondence was to convey the town meeting's resolutions to other towns and colonies. The *Gazette*'s account appended a participant's comment that "there was never more *unanimity* than appeared in Faneuil Hall last Friday; and . . . it was as perfect as human society can admit of."

Dr. Thomas Young, who attended the meeting, described it as "very large and respectable." He concurred that men who had previously been "very cool in the common cause" now joined in zealous support for it, and he declared that participants had pronounced the act "in every principle repugnant to Law, religion, and common sense." Significantly, he revealed that the inclusion of the West Indies in the final resolution calling for a general trade embargo was intended to encompass the French, Dutch, and Danish islands as well as British possessions, so as to keep everyone "as much on a level as may be" and to prevent "avaricious and inconsiderate individuals" from profiting by smuggling. In short, Bostonians in May 1774 were becoming concerned about the same issues that had roiled Charleston for months.

The May 13 meeting might indeed have lacked contention, but that which followed on May 18 did not. True, the official minutes recorded that participants unanimously asserted that Boston was "an essential Link in that vast Chain of Commerce" that had produced the "Opulence, Power, Pride and Splendor" of the British Empire, and that they accordingly decried the "Impolicy, Injustice, Inhumanity and Cruelty" of the act closing the port. But other sources reveal that dissension emerged at the meeting, most notably around the question of whether the town—or some of its wealthier residents—should pay for the EIC tea. One man offered to contribute £2,000 to the effort, and a prominent merchant "urged the matter much" to his fellow citizens at the gathering, according to an attendee, John Andrews.

Harrison Gray, the colony's treasurer under the royal government and an ally of Thomas Hutchinson's, later described in detail what he said were deliberations in May over whether and how to pay for the EIC tea, a prerequisite for reopening the port. He claimed that "most who were then present" thought that the act should be complied with, a dubious assertion. But Gray also summarized the terms of a likely debate. Various speakers proposed ways the town could raise funds to pay for the tea, but others then "artfully" objected to each of the suggested methods. Such critics admitted "the justice and equity" of compensating the company but argued that Boston should not act without hearing from the other colonies first. Such reasoning seemed "very plausible" to the participants, Gray recounted, and so the town did not accept any of the ideas.

While the town was meeting on May 13, the prominent young lawyer Josiah Quincy Jr. must have been writing furiously, because the preface to his pamphlet *Observations on the Act of Parliament Commonly Called the Boston Port-Bill* was dated just one day later, May 14. Thirty years old in 1774, Quincy had worked with John Adams to defend the soldiers in the Boston Massacre trial. The previous year, he had voyaged to South Carolina, primarily for his health, but also to make contact with such like-minded men as Christopher Gadsden and Peter Timothy. The trip did little to repair his health—he would die of tuberculosis less than a year after his pamphlet was published— but it did help him establish a network of acquaintances on which he would draw when he undertook a quixotic trip to London late in 1774.

The pamphlet's contents revealed its hurried composition, for which Quincy explicitly apologized. *Observations* was in part a legal argument about the nature and details of the Port Act, in part an emotional appeal on the need to oppose tyranny, and in part an essay on standing armies and civil society that Quincy had written earlier but had not published.

With respect to the "astonishing" statute, Quincy set out in lawyerly fashion to challenge purported statements of fact in the Port Act. Did the town of Boston itself bear responsibility for the destruction of the tea? Had it been more lawless than other colonial ports? How could Parliament adopt such an ex post facto statute, penalizing the "*acknowledged innocent,*" as well as the "*supposed guilty*"? He asserted that all the residents of Boston had been "accused, prosecuted by they know not *whom;* tried they know not *when;* proved guilty they know not *how.*" But after reviewing such matters of law, he switched his tone and began exhorting Americans (his term) to unite; we have "ONE

COMMON INTEREST," he emphasized through his use of capital letters, urging his fellows "TO STAND OR FALL TOGETHER." He insisted that "submission to the yoke of bondage is the worst that can befall a people after the most fierce and unsuccessful resistance." Therefore, even if they failed, resisting Britain would not worsen their circumstances. "Nothing glorious is accomplished, nothing great is attained, nothing valuable is secured without magnanimity of mind and *devotion of heart to the service*," he intoned, ending with a final call for "*courage*."

It is hard to know what Bostonians or other colonists thought of Quincy's production. Unlike Hancock's much-admired oration two months earlier, the pamphlet seems to have aroused no comments. The legal arguments would have appealed only to a few, but the emotional language reflected and amplified that of the Boston committee of correspondence, with which Quincy was closely allied. In the immediate aftermath of the "astonishing" Port Act, which indeed seems to have astonished residents of Massachusetts Bay with the severity, swiftness, and inescapable nature of its punishment, the Boston committee acted quickly to try to rally other colonists to help the soon-to-be-blockaded town. Quincy's heartfelt call for all Americans to stand together was of a piece with the committee's assertion that an attack on Boston was an attack on all the colonies. But the other American provinces had been less than enthusiastic about Boston's destruction of the East India Company's tea. How would they respond to the urgent pleas for an immediate colonies-wide trade boycott of Britain and the West Indies carried south on May 14 by Paul Revere, the committee's messenger?

CHAPTER 3

THIS BARBAROUS EDICT

According to Richard Henry Lee, the arrival in mid-May of the news of "the Tyrannic Boston Port Bill" brought a "shock of Electricity" to the Virginia body politic, "suddenly and universally" arousing "Astonishment, indignation, and concern" in all his acquaintances. Even his associate Colonel George Washington, offering an opinion on the imperial controversy for the first time in his diary or letters, asserted to a friend that "the cause of Boston . . . now is and ever will be considerd as the cause of America," although he added parenthetically, "Not that we approve their cond[uc]t in destroy[in]g the Tea." In early June the wealthy Marylander Charles Carroll of Carrollton similarly thought that "the Colonies will consider the case of Boston as their own." He predicted that Americans would create "some well concerted Plan," but expressed his uncertainty about its possible details, explaining to a British correspondent that "a variety of Interests, of opinions, the distance, and the local Situations and peculiar Circumstances of each Colony will create many obstructions and some delay."

Carroll was correct on all counts. The weeks after mid-May were filled with action in response to the news of the Port Act as colonial jurisdictions employed committees of correspondence to establish regular lines of communication from Massachusetts to South Carolina, but those committees often disagreed about what should be done. Only a few colonists thought that Boston should be left alone to deal with the Port Act by itself. Americans concurred that the colonies needed to achieve consensus on how to react to Britain's coercion, but just as they had differed over Boston's destruction of the East India Company tea, so too they now disagreed about the proper course to take with respect to Boston's punishment. Should they adopt the proposal for an immediate, comprehensive cessation of commerce with Britain and the West Indies? Should they suggest that Boston submit to the terms of the statute, at least to the extent of paying for the destroyed tea? Or should they convene an intercolonial congress, as they had in 1765, when Parliament adopted the Stamp Act?

RESPONDING TO THE BOSTON PORT ACT

In addition to sending messages to other colonies and Massachusetts towns asking for assistance in combating what Samuel Adams termed "this barbarous edict," the Boston town meeting and the committee of correspondence quickly took steps to implement the boycott they proposed. A formal agreement to countermand or withhold current orders for British goods (at least until other colonies replied to Boston's request) was quickly drafted and circulated for merchants' signatures. The town also asked that "every Gentleman, who has Friends and Correspondents in the other Sea-Port Towns and the Colonies," write personal letters to their acquaintances seeking support. And it dispatched several men to Salem and Marblehead, the ports with the most to gain from the closing of Boston's harbor, asking that they agree to a trade embargo. The immediate response was encouraging; local merchants began to agree to cancel existing orders or forgo new ones, and the messengers returned to report that they had been cordially received. Both Salem and Marblehead offered help "in the present Struggle for our invaded Rights."

At first, positive responses poured in from elsewhere as well. Town meetings in Providence and Newport, as well as those in Salem and Gloucester, formally adopted the plan for a quick cessation of trade with Britain and the West Indies. Merchants in Newburyport and local committees in Portsmouth, New Hampshire, and Westerly, Rhode Island, soon declared support for the idea. Reporting such promising results to a friend in Manhattan, Dr. Thomas Young nevertheless noted a crucial qualification appearing in some of the statements: the ports in question would join a boycott if all "maritime towns" would do the same. Even though other towns made a point of expressing deep sympathy for Boston's plight, such caveats supplied the first hints that the city would not find it easy to win undisputed adherence to its strategy for opposing the Port Act.

That also became evident in correspondence exchanged between the Boston committee and Marblehead's Elbridge Gerry. In late May, Gerry detailed his efforts to advocate on Boston's behalf while outlining the machinations of "ye Tory party" in opposition to "ye Whigs." At a key town meeting, the "Tories" were defeated, he exulted, and Marblehead adopted a call for an embargo on all trade with Britain, but nevertheless rejected Boston's proposed inclusion of the West Indies. Attendees feared that Canadians could supply the islands with fish and wheat, with potential long-term negative effects on New England's commerce. As an alternative, he proposed ending commerce with the Caribbean only in lumber, which could not be so readily replaced by products from elsewhere. Again, specific objections from an ally portended additional protestations in the future.

Despite the majority votes in the Boston town meetings on behalf of an immediate boycott, difficulties arose in the city as well. Some conservative residents welcomed the Port Act in spite of its likely impact on their own finances. A distiller, for example, insisted that although he would be "no inconsiderable sufferer," he would readily submit to the law, "in hopes that hereafter, when the people by suffering, are brought to their senses, we shall enjoy a peaceable and Regular Government." In a similar vein, two customs officers initially expressed optimism about the statute's likely positive impact. Nathaniel Coffin observed in late May that "the Physick begins to operate," for "the Spirit of the Party which has for so many years reigned triumphant here, begins to break." And the commissioner Henry Hulton predicted that the town would agree to compensate the East India Company, "profess a disposition to be peaceable and obedient," and ask the governor to intercede on its behalf with the ministry, thus restoring order in the community.

Those statements appeared in private correspondence, but such men also repeated them publicly when they signed formal addresses to the departing governor, Thomas Hutchinson, or to his successor, Thomas Gage, who arrived in Boston on the ship that brought the Port Act.

The able Doctor, or America Swallowing the Bitter Draught.

A copy of a British cartoon, engraved by Revere for *The Royal American Magazine,* June 1774. America is portrayed as a partly clothed Indian woman, being held down by Lord Mansfield, the chief justice, while Lord Sandwich looks up her skirt. Lord North, the Boston Port Bill sticking out of his pocket, pours tea down her throat. In the background, Boston is (inaccurately) shown being "cannonaded," while Britannia weeps; at left, France and Spain discuss the situation; and in the foreground lies a torn Boston petition, presumably that criticizing Thomas Hutchinson.

Even when the statements did not explicitly support that act, they made it clear that the signers were aligning themselves with past and present colonial officials and their policies. Large groups of Massachusetts citizens—among them 133 Boston "Merchants and Traders," 24 attorneys, and 31 Middlesex County magistrates—commended Hutchinson's long service and bade him a formal farewell as he sailed for London. "Several Gentlemen of the Law," for instance, affirmed Hutchinson's "distinguished abilities," marked by "a uniform purity of principle and integrity of conduct," and expressed the expectation that in Britain he would use his influence to help relieve the province from the burden of the Port Act.

Other similar, overlapping groups warmly greeted Thomas Gage, promising to help him "promote peace and good order." The largest such assemblage—128 merchants, all but 18 of whom had also signed the merchants' and traders' farewell address to Hutchinson—declared that reimbursing the company would be "quite equitable" and voiced their individual willingness "to pay our proportions whenever the same can be assertained." The statements were published in newspapers and broadsides, commonly with the men's signatures attached.

Collectively, the men who thus publicly proclaimed their support for Hutchinson and Gage became known as "Addressers," and as Henry Hulton noted, soon "great murmurs arose" against them. One broadside appeared quickly, charging that the "merchants and traders" had "clandestinely" circulated their address and had refused to show the text to a formally convened merchants' meeting when asked to do so. "We hereby utterly disclaim said address," the broadside's authors asserted, insisting that it was "injurious in its tendency." Another, later broadside publicized the names of Addressers by listing them alphabetically with attached identifying phrases, clearly in the hope that Bostonians would retaliate against them. The broadside described specific signers as related to tea consignees, customs officers, or government officials; as violators of earlier nonimportation agreements; as recent immigrants; or with such phrases as "a Scotch Trader, and as such almost of Course inimical to the Liberties of the People," "a staunch Courtier in the present reign," or "a high-flying Tory by principle." But the public opprobrium directed at the Addressers did not initially deter them. Hulton, who signed none of the addresses, observed that the signers "buoyed themselves up, and seemed to make head[way] against the faction of the people."

Because even Bostonians expressed varying opinions about the city's punishment, the urgent call for a quick end to all commerce with the rest of the British Empire unsurprisingly met with a mixed response in other colonies. While explicitly sympathizing with Boston's plight, other provinces voiced considerable hesitation about the strategy the city proposed for winning repeal of the act. Most forthrightly condemned Parliament's action, but instead of quickly affirming the plan for immediate adoption of nonimportation and nonexportation, colonies outside New England urged caution, calling for the careful consideration of alternatives. One of those alternatives was finding some means to pay for the tea; another was calling an intercolonial congress to discuss matters. As the news spread southward along the Atlantic coast, carried by express messengers, by official mail, and by vessels from Britain, Americans responded in diverse ways to the news of Boston's punishment.

New York, May 11–23

Residents of Manhattan first learned about the passage of the Port Act on May 11; then copies of it arrived from London the next day. Three days after that, when New Yorkers still had not heard from Boston, they sent an express rider north with the act and a supportive letter, fearing that the news had been delayed in reaching Massachusetts. But two days later, on May 17, Paul Revere arrived with the messages dispatched by the Boston committee of correspondence after the town meeting of May 13.

New Yorkers thus knew about the statute for six days before they were informed of Boston's reaction to it. During that period, General Frederick Haldimand, commander of British forces, reported to Dartmouth that many people believed that the Bostonians would

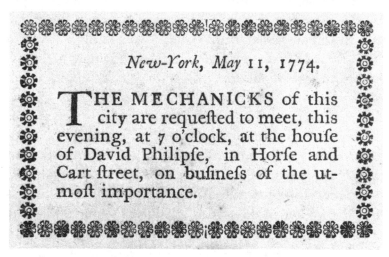

The date on this brief, hastily produced broadside summoning New York's mechanics (workingmen) to a meeting reveals that the topic of "utmost importance" requiring immediate action was the arrival in New York that day of news that the Boston Port Act had been passed by Parliament, even though the contents of the act were not yet fully known. It is hard to imagine that anything else could have demanded such urgency.

acknowledge their offense, pay for the tea, and "endeavour to reinstate themselves into His Majesty's favour." Those with whom the attorney Peter Van Schaack conversed appeared less convinced of such an outcome. He observed that "some think the Bostonians will submit, others that they will not." As for New York, "it is difficult to say what the Temper of the People is." In such uncertainty, the Sons of Liberty and local merchants soon concurred on the need to convene a meeting that could discuss a possible nonimportation agreement, plan a new citywide committee, and "try to bring about a Congress."

On May 14, John Holt published and distributed a free broadside copy of the Port Act, with "Extracts of private Letters from London" dated in early April on the reverse side. The "Extracts" complained about the ministry's "plan of despotism and arbitrary power," described the act's passage in conspiratorial terms, claimed that "thinking people" in Britain opposed it, and predicted that other colonies could expect similar penalties in future if they did not unite to resist the law in its entirety. But an essayist in Hugh Gaine's *New-York Gazette,* describing himself as "a British American, who is a lover of peace, as well as a hater of every species of tyranny," recommended limited compliance. He suggested that Bostonians voluntarily collect a fund to reimburse the EIC yet also vigorously assert the right to dispose of their property as they wished.

At the scheduled meeting of "merchants and others" on Monday, May 16, participants clashed publicly. McDougall recorded that many attendees advocated paying for the tea and opposed developing a nonimportation agreement until New York could learn whether other colonies would join too. Further arguments arose over the size of the proposed new city committee: Would it have twenty-five members or fifty? The workingmen preferred the smaller number, whereas the larger was sought by those whom Lieutenant Governor Cadwallader Colden termed "the most prudent and considerate People." According to Colden, wealthier men who had not previously taken part in large political gatherings appeared in force and dominated the proceedings, even though they thought the assembly "illegal." The larger option prevailed, reportedly by a "great Majority."

After a citywide meeting was announced for Thursday, May 19, to confirm the names of the proposed fifty appointees, Revere arrived.

The letters he brought were publicly read at the coffeehouse, seemingly galvanizing the workingmen into action. They chose a list of twenty-five "Friends to Liberty," whom they claimed had been nominated by both "respectable Merchants and the Body of Mechanics." Dueling broadsides soon appeared on the streets supporting the two slates of candidates. One simply listed the twenty-five names, while the other, signed "A Citizen," argued that the larger group comprised "men of honour, probity and understanding" who could distinguish between "the calm resolute purposes of liberty and the unjustifiable violences of lawless licentiousness." The councillor William Smith Jr. revealed the motive behind the high-minded rhetoric: "Many People of Property" preferred the larger committee because they "dread[ed] the Violence of the lower Sort." Consulted by McDougall, Smith promoted "Prudence," advocating a congress rather than an immediate boycott of Britain.

Many merchants attended the contentious meeting on Thursday, the nineteenth, afraid that the abrupt adoption of nonimportation would "irreparably" injure the local economy, and they, along with other participants they influenced, won the vote for the larger committee, which was increased to fifty-one by the addition of a member favored by the mechanics. The merchant Isaac Low, a leader of the moderate faction, had chaired the May 16 meeting and perhaps authored the Citizen broadside, judging by the resemblance between its contents and his recorded remarks on the nineteenth. He urged participants to display "calm reason" and "to banish from our hearts all little party distinctions, feuds and animosities." McDougall's workingmen allies subsequently complied with the plea, agreeing that it was important to avoid dissension in the present circumstances. Although pleased with the defeat of those he termed "violent enthusiasts," General Haldimand warned Dartmouth that "it is to be feared that the fire is only smothered at present, and might break out anew."

Outvoted and outmaneuvered, the proponents of an immediate nonimportation agreement receded into the background as the committee of fifty-one began its work, adopting formal procedures, choosing leaders and subcommittees, and deciding how to reply to Boston. The crucial first meeting occurred at intervals during the day on May 23 as the committee convened; elected Low as chairman and

John Alsop, another moderate merchant, as his deputy; named a sub-committee to draft the answer to Boston; and then adjourned until the evening, when the subcommittee—McDougall, Low, and the attorneys John Jay and James Duane—submitted its report, which was accepted with only one minor modification. The letter's language was temperate, declining to give "a decisive opinion" on nonimportation, while nonetheless offering "inexpressible concern" to Bostonians. The New Yorkers explained that because "the cause is general and concerns a whole Continent," they thought that "no remedy can be of avail unless it proceeds from the joint act and approbation of all." Thus it was "premature" to adopt nonimportation. The letter also included a call for "a Congress of Deputies from the Colonies in general."

The day before that meeting Revere returned from Philadelphia, whence he had traveled after bringing the Port Act to Manhattan, and the following day (May 24) he departed to take the New York committee's message back to Massachusetts. The missive Revere carried surely disappointed the committee of correspondence. Brief minutes reveal that the Boston committee's members took three days and several drafts to craft an acceptable answer, which was approved on May 30. They updated the New Yorkers on recent events and agreed that in the long run a general congress would be needed, but continued to call for an immediate nonimportation agreement. Yet in further exchanges the committee of fifty-one remained adamant, insisting that such a tactic be discussed by a congress before being implemented.

Philadelphia, May 14–June 1

In Philadelphia too, information about the Port Act arrived before Boston's messenger, this time by post from New York on May 14. Esther DeBerdt Reed, characterizing the political situation as "threatening," remarked that the act "distresses every thinking person." A customs officer reported the next day that at first the news "caused great heat" but that soon "the sober part" of the people decided it would be appropriate for the colonies to pay not only for the destroyed tea but also for the costs incurred by the EIC in shipping tea back from New York and Philadelphia. Asserting that the act "seems to make every man feel very sensibly the Power of the Mother Country," he described it as "a very wise and manly measure." The former tea consignee Thomas Wharton predicted that with Hutchinson removed from office, Boston would acquiesce and reimburse the company.

And then Revere rode into town with the messages from the Boston committee, along with personal letters written by Samuel Adams, John Hancock, and Thomas Cushing to Joseph Reed and Thomas Mifflin. Philadelphians accordingly scheduled a meeting at the City Tavern for the evening of May 20. Between two hundred and three hundred men of "all ranks and interests" crowded into the room to listen to the reading of the official Boston letters and debate what to do. But unknown to the other attendees, Mifflin, Reed, and their associate Charles Thomson had secretly hatched a clever plan to determine the outcome of the meeting by recruiting John Dickinson as their ally.

In 1767–1768, Dickinson authored the renowned and widely re-printed *Letters from a Farmer in Pennsylvania,* which established the chief rationale for the colonies' opposition to the Townshend duties: that they were not an acceptable regulation of trade but instead a tax laid on unconsenting Americans. Known as a moderate but also, in Thomson's words, as "the first champion for American liberty," the wealthy Dickinson was characterized by Reed as "cautious and timid," a man of "weak" nerves. In December 1773, perhaps because of that timidity, he had not involved himself in the rejection of the tea ship *Polly.* Married to a Quaker, he had important ties to the pacifist Pennsylvania community. Consequently, Reed, Mifflin, and Thomson thought it essential that Dickinson not only attend the meeting at the City Tavern but also play a prominent role in the discussions.

The three men went to visit Dickinson at his home on the morning of May 20, finding him initially "very distant, cool and cautious." They nevertheless returned later for dinner and, deliberately "circulating the glass briskly," insisted that his reputation would be ruined unless he conducted himself in accordance with that outstanding record of patri-otism. They thus won his reluctant acquiescence in a scheme to fore-stall opposition to supporting Boston. At the meeting, Reed, Mifflin, and Thomson would advocate "the most vigorous measures," and then Dickinson would suggest a more moderate approach, which in that context and because of Dickinson's "great weight" would carry the day.

That night, the plan worked perfectly. After the three others spoke heatedly, Dickinson's proposal seemed such a "great relief" that it was adopted despite some lingering objections. In the crowd was Thomas Wharton, who aligned himself with Dickinson's position and counted its success a victory, unaware of the behind-the-scenes plot. The participants, as Dickinson advised, voted to appoint a committee of correspondence to send a "friendly and affectionate answer" to Boston and to communicate with the southern colonies. They also asked the governor to convene the assembly and recommended summoning an intercolonial congress.

The three plotters correctly predicted that John Penn would refuse to call the assembly into session, but that was not their aim. They rather sought two primary goals: delaying decisive action, and demonstrating to the province at large that the city did not intend to act without broad support from the countryside. The City Tavern meeting, Reed recalled later, significantly "gave birth to a Public Body in appearance," and thus "by prudent management led to other open actions."

The Philadelphia committee's letter to Boston was, if anything, even more measured than that drafted by its New York counterpart. The committee disclaimed any ability "to judge or act for this populous Province" on the subject of the Port Act. Philadelphians needed time to deliberate. They also had to consult Pennsylvanians in general, and the other colonies as well, before taking any action. If compensating the company for the tea would resolve the matter, they expressed certainty that Bostonians would agree to doing so, but that step alone clearly would not suffice. A "weighty Question" faced them all: Should they choose a commercial boycott, or a congress to state American rights and petition the king? Pennsylvanians, they averred, would prefer the latter, with a boycott as a last resort. They closed by offering Bostonians only "sincere fellow feelings for your Sufferings" and "great Regard to your Persons." Paul Revere left immediately to carry the message back north.

Several days later, a Philadelphian characterized the city committee's anemic letter to Boston as "a moderate one, yet *warm* and *firm* enough," while a Marylander more accurately termed it "very cool indeed" and tinged with "insulting pity." Thomson was reduced to writing privately to assure Samuel Adams that despite the lukewarm prose Philadelphians would support Boston and that they truly believed that an intercolonial congress would be "the most effectual way of uniting *all*." He reminded Adams that although the city's residents had delayed entering the 1768 nonimportation agreement, "none were more steady when once they engaged."

Also writing a private letter in the aftermath of the City Tavern meeting was Joseph Reed, who again addressed Lord Dartmouth. Reed alluded to the "almost incredible" change "in the Prospects & Tempers of the People of this City & Country" in reaction to the Port Act, admitting that he had assumed a local leadership role in the resistance movement. "I cannot think myself a Rebel, or a Traytor," Reed explained, insisting that "I love my King, revere the Parliament & have the highest Veneration & Regard for the Mother Country." He predicted that other colonies would come to Boston's assistance, warning of "the most dreadful Consequences" if Britain adopted additional coercive measures. Beyond expecting Americans to call "a Congress of Deputies," though, he could not foresee what would happen. He ended with the assurance that he intended to continue to supply Dartmouth with useful information. (Months later, Dartmouth replied, thanking Reed for his candor, insisting on enforcing Parliament's authority over the colonies, and observing that if Americans would not submit to British laws, "they say in effect that they will no longer be a part of the British Empire"—a point that Reed was not yet ready to concede.)

If Philadelphia balked at signing on to a nonimportation agreement, the city nevertheless proved willing to go further in expressing collective sympathy for Boston than did New York. On June 1, the day the Port Act went into effect, many Philadelphians closed their shops, lowered ships' flags to half-mast, held special church services, and solemnly tolled muffled church bells at regular intervals throughout the day—although, the rector of the Anglican Christ Church later made certain to point out, not the bells at his church, nor were any services held there. A broadside printed in German ensured that the large immigrant population of the city was informed of the planned observance.

Virginia, May 16–30

The Philadelphia committeemen also followed up on Boston's request that they communicate with the colonies farther south, soon dispatching to Maryland and Virginia by several different routes copies of the documents from Boston, along with Philadelphia's own letter. Before those materials reached their intended destinations, though, two copies of the Port Act had already arrived in Norfolk from England on May 16. The addressees quickly sent copies of the statute to Williamsburg, where burgesses had convened on May 4 for their annual session.

On May 19, Alexander Purdie and John Dixon's *Virginia Gazette* noted the existence of the act but admitted that the printers had not yet acquired a copy of the complete text. Within a few days, though, the burgesses had seen and were responding to its provisions. Richard Henry Lee quickly drafted resolutions declaring that punitively closing the port of Boston was "a most violent and dangerous attempt to destroy the constitutional liberty of and rights of all North America," and proposing that Virginia elect delegates to an intercolonial congress. Lee thought that a majority of the burgesses would have favored the resolutions, but some suggested a different approach. Those members anticipated that such strong language would cause the governor, the Earl of Dunmore, to dissolve the house, so they prevented Lee from introducing his resolves in hopes of finishing regular business first. On May 24, the burgesses voted to declare June 1 a day of fasting and prayer in the colony, "devoutly to implore the divine Interposition for averting the heavy Calamity, which threatens Destruction to our civil Rights," and to ask that God inspire the king and Parliament to act with "Wisdom, Moderation, and Justice."

Their caution went for naught, for Dunmore, taking offense at the fast-day designation and the implied insult to the king, issued a decree two days later ending the burgesses' session. That left key pieces of legislation in limbo and, in effect, closed the colony's courts for lack of a bill establishing court fees. The day after the dissolution, eighty-nine members and several other Virginians signed a statement calling for an annual congress of the colonies and insisting that tea "ought not to be used by any person who wishes well to the constitutional rights and liberty of British America." They also pledged to avoid purchasing any goods from the East India Company other than spices and saltpeter. Then many left to return home. The burgesses' committee of correspondence next drafted and sent letters to their counterparts in other colonies to ask their opinion of creating an annual congress.

Two days later, on May 29, the packet of documents from Boston via Philadelphia finally reached the hands of Peyton Randolph, Speaker of the House of Burgesses. By then, just twenty-five burgesses remained in town. "Legally assembled" the next day (though what made the meeting "legal" is not clear), that small rump session expressed support for nonimportation while reaching no consensus about the efficacy of nonexportation. The small group agreed to ask all the ex-burgesses to reconvene on August 1. Like Charles Thomson, Richard Henry Lee wrote to Samuel Adams to assure him that Massachusetts would "most certainly be supported by the other Colonies," despite Virginia's current inaction. He expressed the hope that Bostonians would not be "dispirited" by their situation.

Maryland, May 25–31

Marylanders acted more decisively than Virginians in response to the punishment of Boston, although with some notable dissenters. After the packet from Philadelphia reached the colony on the morning of May 25, separate meetings, first in Annapolis and then a week later in Baltimore, finally supplied Bostonians with some of the support they sought. A hastily convened group of Annapolis residents met later on May 25 to advocate a trade embargo against Britain and also against any colony that refused to join a coalition to that end. The attendees further resolved, controversially, that until the Port Act was repealed, Maryland attorneys should not file lawsuits against colonists on behalf of English creditors. An essay appearing the next day in the *Maryland Gazette* challenged those votes and called for dissenters to attend another meeting on the twenty-seventh. But at that gathering, despite some vocal opposition, all the earlier resolutions were reaffirmed, reportedly by a tally of 47 to 31. A subsequent printed "Protest" signed by 161 men focused specifically on the resolution about lawsuits, claiming that such a measure was "founded in treachery and rashness," for it would bring "bankruptcy and ruin" to innocent Britons who had relied on their American debtors' "good faith and integrity."

A Baltimore meeting held at the courthouse on May 31 appears to have been equally contentious, although the organizers did not offer the same proposal to interdict lawsuits. Their resolutions—adopted with a few acknowledged dissenters—supported a trade embargo comprising the West Indies as well as Britain and called for both a Maryland and an intercolonial congress. One participant, the attorney and future Loyalist George Chalmers, later claimed that he attended the Baltimore meeting "to counteract the inflammatory harangues of the Seditious." But after one of his allies was physically attacked and rendered "bloody and dishevelled" in the "Tumult" of the meeting, Chalmers and his associates decided to leave and to ignore any similar gatherings in the future. After the Revolution, Chalmers dated the origins of "the unhappy Epoch . . . of civil discord, and domestic Warfare" in Maryland to the meeting on May 31.

What Virginians and Marylanders who were not directly involved in politics thought about such developments is not always easy to determine. In the spring of 1774, their newspapers printed fewer opinion essays than did those in the major port towns, perhaps because without direct involvement in the EIC tea controversies of the preceding months residents of the Chesapeake colonies did not have to come to terms with the issues raised until they, like George Washington, first became aware of the Port Act. Some merchants occasionally added political comments to their business correspondence, as when, for example, a Scotsman in Maryland reported in late May that "the most thinking part of the People with whom I have had any conversation" thought that Maryland "ought not to have taken the Lead," but instead should have waited to learn what the larger and more important colonies would do. One Norfolk resident remarked that the Bostonians "are highly blameable & that Virg[ini]a Should take no part in the Quarrel," while another observed, "let the Yankie fight their own Battles." A Scot in Virginia warned his Glasgow correspondent that "the worst is to be dreaded, as moderate men are not listened to in the present ferment," and both he and a Yorktown merchant revealed their fears about the closure of the courts in the wake of the assembly's dissolution, for that left merchants without the ability to sue to recover debts.

Most, though not all, such merchants were Scots representing British tobacco firms. Virginia planters' comments in diaries differed considerably from that commercial correspondence. Even though the irascible Landon Carter, like George Washington, did not mention the budding imperial conflict in his diary until he learned of the Boston Port Act, he thereafter aligned himself wholeheartedly with resistance to parliamentary authority. He termed the Port Act a declaration of war against Boston, recording that at a county court session in early June he attempted to persuade others that "the case of the Bostonians was the case of all America." Diaries also described political exchanges in plantation households that resembled what must have been said at Carter's Sabine Hall. For example, Nicholas Cresswell, an Englishman on an unfortunately timed colonial tour, commented after a dinner he attended in Nanjemoy, Maryland, on May 30, "Nothing talked of but the Blockade of Boston Harbor the people seem much exasperated at the proceedings of the Ministry and talk as if they were determined to dispute the matter with the Sword." Likewise, Philip Fithian, the Virginia tutor, noted that a dinner conversation on May 29 focused on politics. "The Gentlemen seemed warm," he remarked, observing that afterward they drank coffee, being "now too patriotic to use tea." Two days later, he recorded that "the lower Class of People here are in a tumult on the account of Reports from Boston, many of them expect to be press'd & compell'd to go and fight the Britains!" Even so, in early June he reported that Virginians generally agreed "to unite with the people of Boston and the other northern trading Cities," by adopting nonimportation and nonexportation.

Charleston and Savannah, May 23–June 8

On May 23, the first news of the Port Act appeared in print in South Carolina when Peter Timothy published a summary of the law's provisions. About a week later, a ship brought the packet of documents from Philadelphia, and on June 3 Timothy published the act in full in a black-bordered "extraordinary" issue. In his next regular edition, he predicted that the act would be "the very means to perfect that

Union in America, which it was intended to destroy." By June 8, after *The Georgia Gazette* printed the statute on its front page, at least some residents of all the mainland colonies had learned of the penalties imposed on Boston.

Immediate reactions in South Carolina (none were recorded in Georgia) resembled those in the colonies to the north. Using the same word as Richard Henry Lee, Henry Laurens's brother James declared himself "shock'd to the very soul," and he pronounced the act the work of a "Despotic power," deeming those who supported it "wicked tools." Likewise, Christopher Gadsden termed the law "diabolical," expressing deep sympathy for Boston and proclaiming his confidence that Boston would not pay for "One Ounce of the Tea." Even though supporting that city, however, one anonymous Charlestonian never-theless voiced the wish that Bostonians had adopted his city's strategy for dealing with the EIC tea, which remained in storage and which he thought would likely be soon shipped back to England.

Carolinians (and Georgians as well) failed to pursue collective action in immediate response to the Port Act. Instead of organizing a citywide meeting, Charleston residents decided to wait before taking any significant steps. Perhaps they were influenced by the Philadel-phians, who had adopted a similar course, albeit after the gathering at the City Tavern. Still, Gadsden explained to Samuel Adams, Caro-linians had an added dual rationale for inactivity. Theirs was "a weak Colony," he observed, citing both "the Number of Negroes we have amongst us" and the many "Ministerial men" who opposed himself and his Charleston associates. Planters were "hearty and spirited" but rarely willing to attend meetings in the city. Thus a small group that met at a Charleston tavern in mid-June to discuss possible options decided to summon men from throughout the province to a gathering on July 6. The plans were "imperfect," William Henry Drayton later recalled, because "this was the first attempt, to collect a meeting of the people, on so constitutional a principle." Despite the delay, Gadsden assured Adams, Carolinians could eventually be depended upon to join in any common measures "to the utmost of our Power."

The first month after news of the Boston Port Act arrived in North America, then, brought little satisfaction to those Bostonians who had urgently asked other colonies to retaliate against Britain by quickly adopting a policy of nonimportation and nonexportation. Only a few scattered jurisdictions outside New England—most notably Annapolis and Baltimore—replied positively to that call. Charleston and Savannah did nothing; action in Virginia was thwarted for at least two months by Dunmore's dissolution of the burgesses; New York and Philadelphia offered only sympathy and lukewarm support. Further, a growing consensus and swelling numbers of replies to Boston's messages advocated summoning an intercolonial congress, a tactic that the beleaguered New Englanders feared would take too long to be effective. Nathaniel Coffin accordingly reported that Bostonians found the answers to their plea "very discouraging."

ADVICES FROM LONDON

April 15, 1774. In the House of Commons, Lord North introduces the Massachusetts Government Act, altering the 1691 charter of the Bay Colony in several ways. Most notably, it forbids more than one meeting each year in every town without permission from the governor; empowers the governor to name and remove judges and other officers on his own authority; and changes the composition of the council by providing that its members will be appointed by the king (as is the case in most other colonies), rather than being elected by the lower house. For years, Massachusetts governors have complained that the council's dependence on the representatives for their positions has meant that councillors in the colony do not serve as a counterweight to the lower house or as a governor's independent advisers.

April 21. Just six days later, the ministry proposes the Administration of Justice Act, authorizing English trials for any civilian, military, or customs officials charged with killing colonists in the course of their duties to keep the peace. Americans in London (and later in the colonies) dub it the Murder Act.

April 16–May 11. "Forlorn" Americans in London have no hope of stopping the passage of these acts, writes Henry Laurens on April 16, but nevertheless want to show other colonists that they are not "Idle unfeeling Compatriots." A despairing Benjamin Franklin reports the same day that Americans have "very few friends in Parliament at present." Yet thirty colonists resident in the capital, including Laurens and Franklin, petition the House of Lords on May 11, declaring that the two laws "will be fatal to the rights, Liberties, and peace of all America." The Massachusetts Government Act will remove the "Chartered Rights" of a province without a proper hearing, an unprecedented move rendering all charters in Britain or America "utterly insecure." The other act freeing marauding soldiers from the prospect of prosecution in the colonies, they contend, will bring on "the horrid Outrages of Military Oppression, followed by the desolation of Civil Commotions." They foresee in the two acts "a direct Tendency to reduce their Countrymen to the dreadful Alternative, of being totally enslaved, or compelled into a Contest the most shocking and unnatural, with a Parent State, which has ever been the Object of their Veneration and their Love."

May 7. Henry Laurens writes to his brother James in Charleston, blaming Americans' "rash impolitick proceedings" for the North ministry's recent actions. "Surely some Judas has been at work among you," he observes. Our English friends are "tongue tied" because of how badly the colonists have been behaving; he cites among other offenses the mistreatment of John Malcom and the destruction or rejection of EIC tea. Yet that does not mean "we are wrong in the main point of our dispute," he adds, urging Americans to act with "Speed & Manliness" to adopt "Constitutional measures" of resistance (which he does not specify). Then, he predicts, "we shall undoubtedly succeed."

May 20. The king formally approves both the Massachusetts Government Act and the Administration of Justice Act.

June 3. Lord Dartmouth writes to Thomas Gage, enclosing the two recently adopted laws and commenting that they "close the consideration of what relates to the state of your government." He expresses the hope that they will strengthen civil authority sufficiently to prevent "those unwarrantable assemblings of the people for factious purposes which have been the source of so much mischief," and sends a list of men appointed to the reconstituted council (soon to be known as the Mandamus Council). Dartmouth recognizes that some of them will probably be intimidated into refusing to serve, but predicts that those should be few in number. He repeats several times that his most recent information about Massachusetts dates from early April and that he has no idea how the people have responded to the Port Act. He stresses, "Whatever violences are committed must be resisted with firmness, the constitutional authority of this kingdom over its colonies must be vindicated, and its laws obeyed. . . . It is not the mere claim of exemption from the authority of Parliament in a particular case that has brought on the present crisis; it is actual disobedience and open resistance that have compelled coercive measures."

THE SOLEMN LEAGUE AND COVENANT

By mid-May, Bostonians had heard rumors about possible changes in their 1691 charter but knew nothing specific. Instead, they focused on the impending implementation of the Port Act and on their new governor. They greeted Thomas Gage with formally correct ceremonies that included a militia muster and an "elegant entertainment," at which one attendee nonetheless noted that toasts to the departing governor, Hutchinson, elicited "a general hiss." Gage reported to Dartmouth on May 19 that the act had "staggered the most Presumptuous" and that consequently he intended to give Bostonians time to recover from the shock they had received, in the hope that in a few weeks the colony's political leaders would be more likely to comply with the terms of the act than if he pressed them immediately.

After a newly elected assembly met on May 25, Gage followed instructions and vetoed some of the councillors the assembly selected, including John Adams. He announced that after June 1 the legislature would move to Salem, in accordance with the provisions of the Port Act, and adjourned the session until June 7 there. And then he was expected to participate in a Massachusetts ritual dating back to the seventeenth century, listening to the annual election sermon, delivered that year by the Reverend Gad Hitchcock of Pembroke. With the new governor in the audience, Hitchcock spoke bluntly. The clergyman, known for his wit, later remarked, "To judge by the number of people who got up and walked out while he was preaching, this must have been a moving sermon."

Hitchcock's provocations began with his text, Proverbs 29:2: "When the righteous are in authority, the people rejoice: but when the wicked beareth rule, the people mourn." He then returned repeatedly to the assertion that people were the proper judges of their rulers. A clever reference to history helped to prove his point. Britons judged their rulers when they deposed a king (James II) who was violating the constitution. "If they meddled with that which did not belong to them," then the Hanoverian succession was illegal, and the Stuarts accordingly remained "the only just, and lawful claimants to the British throne." But, he averred, no loyal Briton or American should accept that doctrine.

Turning explicitly to current events, Hitchcock insisted that "our danger is not visionary, but real. Our contention is not about trifles, but about liberty and property, and not ours only, but those of posterity." Although he referred at the end to the need to "respect and honor our civil rulers" and to obey the law, the clergyman's overall message presented an unmistakable and direct challenge to the new governor and his authority to rule the colony. Governor Gage would have squirmed uneasily in his seat if he remained throughout the sermon, but he had probably left with others long before Hitchcock reached that conclusion.

The merchant John Rowe, who attended the event, observed in his diary that Hitchcock's sermon was a "high Discourse suitable to his Party," but made no other comment about its contents. About two weeks later, though, a similar "high Discourse" offered by a Massachusetts cleric on another public occasion clearly aroused negative reactions from some who heard it. When the Reverend John Lathrop of Boston's Second Church published the sermon he delivered at the annual election of officers for the local artillery company, another ritual the governor would have been expected to attend had he still been in town, the clergyman added a long footnote defending his right to take a political stand.

In that note, Lathrop observed that those who favored tyranny sometimes complained that clerics were inappropriately preaching about politics if they discussed rulers' duties to the people or inferred that "there is a design to deprive them of their just rights and liberties." But, Lathrop proclaimed, a minister could not fulfill his responsibilities "if he is *ignorant* or *silent* as to these matters." He contended that "injustice, oppression, and tyranny" were as much "moral evils" as were "riots, tumults, and licentiousness." He concluded, "When I hear people *gravely* pretending that the minister of religion should never meddle with political matters, I cannot help suspecting that they are engaged in some bad cause which they wish to carry without opposition."

The theme of the sermon itself was the need to resist tyranny and to prepare for "unavoidable war." Like Hitchcock, Lathrop alluded approvingly to the Glorious Revolution and the Hanoverian succession. Then he engaged in speculative history, describing how historians fifty years hence would assess current events. Would the colonists hold a congress and embark on "a quiet and peaceable suspension of trade" that would lead to union and eventually to "opulence and strength"? Or would "unhappy divisions" and "fatal jealousies" make a unified response to Britain impossible, so that people would fail to oppose subsequent parliamentary revenue acts? Then, he foresaw, Americans would begin "to lose their virtue, their love of freedom, and their religion," and so would become "the most ignorant, stupid and abject creatures, in the world, fit only for slaves to domineering masters." In a footnote to that passage, he commented that some of his listeners wanted him to omit such a disheartening vision from the published sermon. But, he explained, he decided to contrast the two predictions "because he fully thinks that *life* and *death* in a political sense are *now* set before us; and that the fate of America, for many generations, depends on the virtue of her sons and daughters at the *present day*."

John Lathrop and Gad Hitchcock thus boldly aligned themselves with resistance to the Port Act and the new governor's administration. The election and artillery company sermons were both important annual public events, with resonance resembling that of the regular Boston Massacre orations. Hitchcock publicly confronted Gage and his aides in the audacious election sermon, and Lathrop made it clear that he would have done the same had Gage and the members of the council and assembly not already moved to Salem by the time he delivered his address.

Such strong opposition to British policy prominently voiced before what must have been large crowds could well have been decisive in leading the usually sure-footed Samuel Adams and the Boston committee of correspondence to make a major misstep at about the same time that Lathrop spoke.

The Reverend Charles Chauncy, an Adams ally and the author of an anti–Port Act pamphlet, identified the key problem Boston's resistance leaders faced in attempting to implement a boycott of trade with Britain. "We have found by experience," he wrote, "that no dependance can be had upon *merchants,* either at *home,* or in *America,*" because many of them are too "mercenary." Thus instead of asking merchants not to import goods, the colonists needed to move to "an agreement among the freeholders and yeamonry of all the Colonies, not to purchase of the merchants any goods from England," perhaps with a few exceptions for necessities. "We can in America live within ourselves," Chauncy predicted, "and it would be much for our interest not to import a great deal from England."

Thwarted in their efforts to win a quick colonies-wide nonimportation and nonexportation agreement, in short, Adams and the Boston committee decided to focus first on the people of the Bay Colony and to persuade them to subscribe to a nonconsumption agreement. The committee made its reasoning explicit in a letter to the inland town of Colrain. "If there are no Purchasers of British Goods there will be no Importers," the committee asserted. So a nonconsumption agreement could resolve the problem posed by uncooperative merchants. Although Adams himself had explicitly rejected such a strategy when confronted by EIC tea in December 1773, the prospects for success

This copy of the nonconsumption agreement known as the Solemn League and Covenant circulated for signatures in Charlton, Massachusetts, in June 1774. Most signers were men, but the first two were "Rev. Caleb Curtis" and "Mrs. Charity his wife."

now appeared better, in the context of the seemingly universal negative local reaction to the Port Act.

The apparent need to act swiftly and locally was underscored when on June 2 a vessel arriving at Marblehead brought news of the proposed Massachusetts Government and Administration of Justice Acts. Even though there was as yet no confirmation of the statutes' enactment, the committee of correspondence of the Massachusetts assembly immediately drafted messages to the other provinces, warning them that the entire continent would soon similarly be targeted by Parliament.

At a town meeting on May 30, Bostonians had already voted for limited nonconsumption, binding themselves not to purchase imported items if the same could be manufactured locally. But facing the prospect of the two proposed acts and in light of rumors that "five gentlemen, in their private capacity," had begun to discuss with Gage the prospect of paying for the tea, the committee of correspondence "in a private clandestine manner" (according to Nathaniel Coffin) drafted and approved a nonconsumption agreement titled "The Solemn League and Covenant," a name reminiscent of the English Civil War in the 1640s. Not seeking approval from the town meeting, which was not scheduled to reconvene for another two weeks, on June 8 the committee began distributing the Covenant outside Boston, accompanied by an explanatory circular letter, and requesting signatures of men and women alike. Bostonians first learned of these activities from a brief statement published the next day in *The Massachusetts Spy*, but the full details of the Covenant and the cover letter would not become known in the port until late in the month.

The Covenant itself described current circumstances in terms that verged on the apocalyptic, referring to "no alternative between the horrors of slavery, or the carnage and desolation of a civil war, but a suspension of all commercial intercourse with the island of Great Britain." It asked subscribers to pledge not to purchase any goods imported from Great Britain after August 31, and also to promise that they would not deal with anyone who did so, for those people clearly preferred "their own private interest to the salvation of their now perishing country." It furthermore declared that the names of those who refused to accept the Covenant should be published as "enimical to, or criminally negligent of, the common safety." The cover letter added details of the proposed laws and assured potential subscribers that such a universal effort would succeed in fending off Britain's "oppressive hand." It asked that the Covenant be circulated for signatures as soon as possible so that opponents could not block the effort.

Most Bay Colony towns at first reacted negatively to the Covenant. Local committees questioned its details, so the Boston committeemen hastily drafted a second circular letter, softening their language. The document need not be taken literally, they explained; rather, towns could retain its "spirit" and concur in nonimportation, along with suspending dealings with nonsigners. Bostonians too did not seem eager to sign. Still, the Boston committee's flexibility might in the end have led some colonists to subscribe to an agreement. In early July, Nathaniel Coffin reported that the Covenant "has made great progress in many parts of the Province having been signed by whole parishes & towns," but in other areas "the interposition of some Men of Influence" had halted its advance.

One such "man of influence" was the Reverend Jeremy Belknap of Dover, New Hampshire, who penned a long explanation of his refusal to subscribe to the Covenant. The clergyman began with his major objection: "Tyranny in one shape is as odious to me as Tyranny in another." The Covenant qualified as tyrannical, because it had been promulgated by a committee not selected for that task, nor had the drafters consulted their constituents. They were "imposing their own private opinions upon other people under the penalty of being looked upon as 'inimical to & criminally negligent of the common safety.'" The notion that "private men," unauthorized by anyone, could demand that others adhere to such agreements constituted "a most dangerous precedent," Belknap argued. If men and women's "private judgment" led them to refuse to sign, they would be "stigmatized as Enemies to their Country." That was just as tyrannical as any act of Parliament. He accordingly viewed the Covenant as "the very first beginnings of such a spirit of lawless Imposition & Restraint [that] ought to be checked & discountenanced by every consistent Son of Liberty and every true friend to his Country." The decision to adopt such an agreement should be made by all the colonies collectively, and a congress would be required to endorse and enact it.

Shortly after Belknap drafted and submitted this statement, the Dover committee decided to stop circulating the Covenant within its jurisdiction, thereby seemingly signaling their agreement with his position. The cleric's was the fullest and most extensive recorded individual objection to signing the Covenant, but reasoning about practical problems of enforcement appeared in fragmentary form in various towns' replies to the Boston committee. Further, his comments about tyranny echoed John Vardill's Poplicola essays, as well as John Greenough's complaints about opponents of tea sales on Cape Cod. Vardill, Greenough, and Belknap forcefully expressed their concerns about the "private men" who were intruding themselves and their opinions into public affairs without authorization. All three saw potential for tyranny in such activities and warned their fellow colonists about that danger.

At the same time as the Covenant was arousing controversy throughout the colony and beyond, the Massachusetts House of Representatives created controversy of its own after it convened in Salem on June 7. Although its address welcomed Thomas Gage with formulaic greetings and contrasted him favorably with his detested predecessor, Thomas Hutchinson, the house protested the move out of Boston forced on it by the Port Act. Gage rejected the house's address as a "libel," declaring its critical tone about the past administration "an insult upon his Majesty and the Lords of the privy Council and an affront to myself." Still, the governor's immediate concerns were assuaged when the assembly took care of some routine business, then named a nine-member committee that purportedly discussed "moderate and conciliating measures" for the next three days.

But that description of the committee's intentions was deliberately deceptive. Years later, Robert Treat Paine of Taunton explained how he and the other committee members concealed their goals from both the governor and colonial opponents of bold action. Among the nine men was Daniel Leonard, "a Gentleman of natural good sence & Eloquence," Taunton's senior representative in the house. His election to the committee could not be blocked, Paine recalled, but the other members knew that he supported the governor. Therefore, in his presence the committeemen discussed "very favourably" the option of paying for the tea, with Samuel Adams stressing the need to act "Cautiously" and to reach a compromise. Unknown to Leonard, however, after the committee adjourned each day, the other members reconvened in a different room with additional allies to debate "freely & fully on all the Subjects of Grievances."

Doubtless those debates in the secret legislative committee focused in part on whether to accede to the proposals for a congress that were flooding in from other colonies by mid-June. Among the most insistent were some composed by Connecticut's Silas Deane, who dispatched numerous such missives on behalf of his colony's assembly. In private, Deane described the Covenant as "very wrong, totally and absolutely so," largely because the Boston committee had failed to consult anyone else before issuing it. Replying directly and publicly to Boston, though, he merely advised avoiding "any one step of a Partial, or Private Nature"—that is, the Covenant. Instead, "the greatest Union, and most general Consultation" were required, for any act by a single province could never have the impact of a congress filled with "respectable Characters" from all the colonies. In mid-June, Deane busied himself writing individualized letters to other colonies' committees, advocating a congress to meet as soon as possible.

Whether Deane's multiple missives to the Bay Colony or responses from elsewhere were dispositive, when the Massachusetts House on June 17 went into a marathon closed-door session to consider the secret committee's report, it approved the idea of a colonial congress to meet in Philadelphia on September 1; chose five delegates to attend that gathering; and voted an appropriation to pay their expenses. Daniel Leonard was absent, for Paine had lured him away from Salem on a pretense. The representatives also asked Bay Colony towns to contribute funds to the relief of Boston and its neighbor Charlestown, both beginning to suffer under the strictures of the Port Act, and asked that residents of the province forgo drinking all tea. They in addition called for nonconsumption of British and East India goods in general; declared a preference for American manufactures; and announced a colony-wide fast day for July 15.

The flurry of resolutions came as a surprise to the governor. As soon as Gage learned what was happening in the secret session, he sent the colony's secretary with an official message dissolving the legislature. The members would not open the locked door for him, so the secretary humiliatingly read the governor's proclamation while standing on the stairs outside the meeting room.

Boston, meanwhile, was dealing with the initial impact of the Port Act. Residents lamented "the Distressed Situation of this Poor Town," observing that "our wharfs are intirely deserted; not a topsail vessel to be seen." Nathaniel Coffin commented that "the Harbor was quite emptied" and that "every day wore the appearance of one of our Sabbaths." According to one clergyman, the town "looks very melancholy, people are every day removing." Those who were not abandoning the city were trying to cope with changes wrought by the act: shippers rushed to finish loading their vessels, which were allowed to leave until June 14; wharf owners requested the navy's business to replace civilian commerce; customs officials tried to work out the logistical details of how to enforce the act; and the town established a special committee to distribute relief to the poor, on which Thomas Greenough served.

DEBATES IN BOSTON

Debates roiled the blockaded town. Two separate but linked issues dominated political discussions there for the remainder of June: First, should Boston arrange to pay for the tea? And second, how should its citizens respond to the committee of correspondence's rash decision to distribute the Solemn League and Covenant without consulting the town meeting? John Andrews remarked on June 12 that after Bostonians learned that other colonies would not adopt immediate nonimportation, merchants like himself anticipated that the city would soon comply with the act's terms. Instead, though, he charged that "the authors of all our evils" became "more obstinate than ever." Mercy Otis Warren, visiting Boston that day from Plymouth, added that because "the wisest among the other sex are much divided in opinion" on current issues, offering an opinion of her own would be "impertinent."

Many Bostonians took the possibility of compensating the East India Company more seriously than did the members of the secret legislative committee. In Nathaniel Coffin's opinion, after Boston received such mixed replies to its urgent pleas for assistance, "most of the considerate part of the Community began to think of nothing else than paying for the Tea and Complying with the other Requisitions of the Act." Tradesmen and ordinary folk wanted steps taken to reopen the port, he observed. For instance, a Yale student heard in New Haven that "almost all the People of Boston are willing to pay for the Tea, only they could not agree upon the method how it should be done."

So on June 15, two days before the next scheduled town meeting, hundreds of tradesmen characterized by Coffin as "the midling & lowest Classes of the People" met at Faneuil Hall to discuss alternatives. Dr. Young reported that a supporter of compensation introduced the possibility of paying the company but could not win sufficient backing for his position. After heated debates, the session ended with "Altercations." According to John Rowe, the tradesmen did nothing because they were "much Divided in Sentiment." Dr. Joseph Warren worked to persuade the participants that it would be a mistake to surrender to any of Parliament's demands. Harrison Gray later charged that Warren and his allies warned the tradesmen as they entered the meeting that if they supported compensating the company, the town would be "undone" and that the attendees had been so "terrified" that they decided to take the "prudent" course of no action.

Newspapers were filled with debates, even as one author, "Cincinnatus," denied the claim of another, "Mercator," that Boston was sharply divided over whether to pay for the tea. Any quarrel split the many from the few, Cincinnatus asserted; those favoring payment were merely a "*little host* of unthinking merchants, unprincipled traders, eager dependants, and riotous spoilers." Although he denied the prevalence of significant disagreements, Cincinnatus nevertheless replied to Mercator's contention that *"the principles of equity"* required compensating the company. How would it be equitable for Bostonians who did not participate in the destruction of the tea to contribute to paying for it? Cincinnatus inquired. Why should innocent residents be liable for "an action they never committed"? The proper solution would be to identify the perpetrators and then to consider methods of reimbursement.

Other authors acknowledged the existence of the disputes that Mercy Warren noticed and Cincinnatus denied. "K.D.," in an essay published on June 16, began by commenting, "Various as the Colours in the Rainbow are the Opinions of Gentlemen in this Town." He went on to illustrate that point by advancing a unique argument supporting both paying for the tea and summoning an intercolonial congress. Because the tea was private property and the town had not prevented its destruction, K.D. declared, Boston should reimburse the company. Compensating the EIC was the necessary prerequisite that would make colonial unity in a congress possible. The same issue of the paper also contained a more consistent "tory performance," an essay by "X" with thoughts about local merchants, the committee of correspondence, and the Covenant. Boston merchants should not be "proscribed and ruined" because traders in other ports would not join in nonimportation, he argued. Nonconsumption adopted in Boston alone would be worse than useless; and he proclaimed with Jeremy Belknap, *"I have no notion that freedom can be established by opposing arbitrary principles in one instance, and tamely submitting to them in another."*

The June 17 town meeting thus took place in what Thomas Young characterized as a context of "much talk out of doors, as well as writing in the papers concerning payment for the Tea." Even though the populace was obviously divided and "very serious Debates" (about unidentified topics) reportedly occurred at the crowded meeting, no one seemed prepared that day to publicly advocate paying for the tea. Only one voter was recorded as dissenting from an innocuous resolution that authorized the committee of correspondence to write to the other colonies with an update on Boston's "Public Affairs." It explained that a nonconsumption agreement was being circulated in the province and that the town now "chearfully" awaited the results of a continent-wide congress. The meeting also voted its thanks to the other jurisdictions that had expressed sympathy for Boston and promised future aid, and to the committee of correspondence for its "faithfulness." Dr. Young derided the presumed dissenters (who had remained silent) as those who supported "propositions fit only to be whispered in the conclaves of our addressers, composed of a *few men* who deserve better company, than the fry of Scotch pedlars, Sandemaneans, and importers to which they have unluckily joined themselves."

After the meeting, though, the committee's opponents, many of them said to be merchants with large stocks of goods on hand, girded themselves for battle, and so did the committee's defenders. Reporting on the "desperate" opposition, rumored to have recruited allies among lawyers who had never previously attended a town meeting, Dr. Young declared, "We may have a trial, but we are prepared for the Combat." The primary focus of the debate then shifted from whether to pay for the tea to challenging or defending the committee and its Covenant. Perhaps local merchants were discouraged by the failure of anyone to speak out for compensating the company on June 17 or concluded from the recent meetings that theirs was a minority position. Perhaps they simply changed tactics, deciding that the committee was vulnerable because of its precipitate and much-criticized act of distributing the Covenant without prior consultation and that if they could successfully challenge its authority, they could return later to the subject of compensation.

The newspaper debates continued, beginning with a long essay by "Y.Z.," a self-identified merchant. He asserted that the committee had acted in a way *truly contemptuous to the Town"* and indeed to the *"collective Wisdom of the Province in General Assembly."* The committee had proceeded hastily, Y.Z. charged, thereby directing the people of the Bay Colony "into a Step the most tyrannical and oppressive, as well as dangerous to their Peace, Morals and Happiness." His essay was soon followed by two others, untitled and unsigned. Both asked a series of pointed questions about the Covenant. One set of queries emphasized the damage it would cause Boston merchants if fully implemented. The author concluded that only a congress could draft an appropriate nonconsumption agreement, drawing on "the united Wisdom of the whole Continent." The other essay added cautions about the divisive impact of the Covenant on families and communities. Both articles included explicit attacks on the committee, which had acted "a most extraordinary Part" by not consulting the town and by adopting an "arbitrary, unjust, impolitic" document that did not aid "the grand Cause of Freedom."

Samuel Adams, writing as "Candidus," quickly leaped to the defense of the committee he chaired. On June 27, the very day the town meeting would reconvene, his response to the recent articles appeared in *The Boston Gazette,* the newspaper allied to the committee. Most important, he cleverly turned the other colonies' reluctance to adopt nonimportation back onto Massachusetts. Is it not the case, he inquired, that the "actually suffering" Bay Colony's failure to adopt the

As Samuel Adams's role as head of the Boston committee of correspondence became crucial, Revere memorialized him in a portrait engraving as frontispiece for *The Royal American Magazine,* April 1774. The female figure on the left has a liberty cap on a staff and tramples "laws to enslave America"; that on the right has the head of George III underfoot. A scroll with "Magna Charta" is prominent in the foreground.

Covenant, "the only peaceful Measure that remains for our Extrication from Slavery," would "naturally excuse every other Province from taking one Step for the common Salvation?" Massachusetts, he insisted, needed to step forward to serve as an example for the other colonies in order to win their backing for a boycott of British goods. Moreover, he asked, when "the Beneficence of the whole Continent" was soon expected to come to the relief of Boston, was it not "utterly unbecoming" to contend that importers elsewhere would usurp the city's trade? Adams ended by insisting that any errors in the Covenant could be corrected by a congress, and by belittling the expressed concerns of merchants about goods already on order that would arrive after the deadline and so could not be sold. "No Gentleman Trader," he proclaimed grandly, "need distress himself so mightily about the Profits of one Fall-Importation." Samuel Adams thus held firm. He would backtrack neither on the need for the Covenant nor on the circumstances of its distribution.

The town meeting convened on the morning of the twenty-seventh in Faneuil Hall with Adams in the chair. Committeemen started to read aloud the correspondence exchanged with other colonies over the past months, none of which had previously been disclosed publicly. It then became evident that the committee's letters to New York and Philadelphia had singled out the Addressers for harsh criticism, terming them "worthless wretches" willing to prostitute themselves for personal gain and to protect their "tottering hero," Thomas Hutchinson. One attendee reported that the day was very warm, and the room soon became uncomfortably hot and so crowded that people in the back complained that they could not hear what was being said. Josiah Quincy Jr. then suggested that the meeting move that afternoon to the larger space of Old South Church. There the public reading of documents included the Covenant and the cover letter that had accompanied it. Knowledge of the committee's comments about the Addressers, John Andrews reported, "rais'd such warm emotions in their breasts, that nothing less than the committee's being annihilated would satisfy 'em." So the merchant Thomas Amory, an Addresser, moved that the committee of correspondence be "Censure[d] and annihilate[d]," a proposal "seconded by many Voices." At that point, Adams stepped down from the chair so he could participate in the deliberations. Thomas Cushing replaced him.

The debate raged on until dark, continuing into the next day. John Adams's law clerk, who participated only on the twenty-seventh, termed the meeting "very respectable," with nearly equal numbers of "torys" and "Wigs" in attendance. He remarked that "there was a liberal flow of Sentiments and much Severity from the Tories upon the Committee." John Rowe recorded that both days the debates were "very warm on both sides." Those who spoke on behalf of the committee included Samuel Adams, Dr. Warren, Josiah Quincy Jr., and

Dr. Young. On the other side were lined up, among others, Thomas Amory and his brother John, George Erving (an Addresser and an organizer of the committee's opponents), and Harrison Gray.

On one of the two days, wrote John Andrews proudly, his brother-in-law, Samuel Eliot, also a merchant, "display'd his eloquence in a long speech upon the subject, deliver'd in so masterly a stile and manner as to gain ye plaudits of perhaps the largest assembly ever conven'd here, by an almost universal clap." Eliot, Andrews explained, described his circumstances, which resembled Andrews's own: John initially signed on to nonimportation in response to the Port Act and countermanded his current orders for British goods. But when he learned that other colonies had not joined the agreement, he canceled the countermand and "re-ordered about one fourth part of such goods as I thought would be most in demand." Then he learned a few weeks later about the Covenant, which would halt any sales of the reordered items. In addition to causing such confusion, he declared, that document "has serv'd rather to create dissentions among ourselves than to answer any valuable purpose."

When the debate finally ended on June 28, the committee's opponents lost by what the town record termed "a great Majority," which participants reported as approximately four to one. That majority then formally voted to approve the committee's conduct, praising its members' "honest Zeal" and urging them to continue "stedfast" in their "usual Activity and Firmness." Andrews commented in retrospect that he had expected his fellow merchants to propose merely that the committee be directed to suspend distributing the Covenant until a congress could meet, but that the content of the committee's letters had infuriated them. Andrews implied that he thought the Addressers erred in their overly zealous attempt to censure and destroy the committee. Nathaniel Coffin was certain that the minority made an "unfortunate" mistake after the vote by leaving the town meeting en masse, accompanied by "a general Hissing." Had they remained, he thought, they could have offered a motion to establish a committee to consider how to pay for the tea. That would probably have failed, he predicted, but the motion would have at least given them "an opportunity of protesting against [the town's] proceedings in this important perticular."

The mercantile minority nevertheless found other means of publicizing their position, drafting what an Addresser described as "a flaming Protest." The day after their defeat, 129 men signed a complaint against the committee, the Covenant, and the town meeting. They declared that the Covenant was "a base, wicked, and illegal measure, calculated to distress and ruin many merchants, shopkeepers, and others, in this metropolis, and affect the whole commercial interest of this Province." It would in effect stop all exports from the colony as well as imports, because exports were primarily traded for the imports. The signers questioned the principles set forth in the Covenant, claiming that they caused more difficulties than they resolved. Further, they expressed their anger (as Andrews had indicated) at the contents of the committee's letters to other colonies, which "falsely, maliciously, and scandalously, vilified and abused the characters of many of us, only for dissenting from them in opinion; a right which we shall claim as long as we hold any claim to freedom or liberty." But, retreating from their position at the town meeting, they did not challenge the existence of the committee itself.

Eight other dissidents, including the Amory brothers and Andrews and his brother-in-law, Samuel Eliot, published a statement that went further toward fundamentally questioning the legitimacy of the committee. They explained that such a body, "constitutionally appointed," could be useful if it were properly instructed by the town. But the current committee, set up in November 1772, had completed its assignment by the end of 1773 at the latest. No new committee had been appointed. Moreover, the committee showed a "dangerous Tendency" because it exercised "such extensive Powers" and acted secretly in sending out the Covenant. They assured readers that they had "no private Pique" against any committee members, but in light of the calumnies contained in the letters, they wanted "to defend the Character of our Neighbours."

Fifty-two residents of Worcester, a town that produced its own version of the Covenant and followed Boston's lead by circulating it for signatures, even more forcefully challenged its local committee's legitimacy in late June. In the course of criticizing the papers being distributed by the town, the so-called Protestors termed all committees of correspondence "creatures of modern invention," with no "legal foundation." They declared that committeemen were "enemies of our King and country, violators of all law and civil liberty, the malevolent disturbers of the peace of society, subverters of the established constitution, and enemies of all mankind."

Governor Thomas Gage outdid even the Worcester Protestors with his enraged, though delayed, reaction to the Solemn League and Covenant. He probably waited to learn the results of the Boston town meeting, because on June 29, the day after the proposed censure failed, he issued a proclamation against the "unlawful" Covenant and the "scandalous, traiterous, and seditious Letter" accompanying it. Those who considered signing the document were toying with "high Criminality, and dangerous Consequences," he warned. Such "unprecedented Combinations" opened their adherents to being designated "the declared and open Enemies of the King, Parliament and Kingdom of Great Britain." Accordingly, the governor ordered all Massachusetts magistrates and other officials to arrest and hold for trial anyone who circulated or signed such an agreement or who was involved in "aiding, abetting, advising, or assisting" in such an endeavor. When he forwarded the proclamation to London, he enclosed copies of the dissenters' statements from Boston and Worcester, the Covenant, and the committee's letter, explaining that he wanted "to prevent the ill effects of it [the Covenant] as much as possible."

No one ever seems to have been arrested under the terms of the proclamation, but a few accounts attested to its impact. For example, a Maine resident recounted the story of a young clergyman who had signed the Covenant but who then was informed of Gage's action and the promised "Ill Consequence" of subscribing to it. "Ignorant People, who ware miseleed and Deceived and Drawn in by Designing men, might be forgiven," he was told, but not an educated person, who should know better. Accordingly, the minister asked to see the Covenant again, "and when he gott it, he run off with it, and Distroyed it." James Warren of Plymouth, Mercy's husband, similarly wrote to Samuel Adams that at a local town meeting some "Insignificant Tories," including his own cousin, "played their Game by holding up the Terrors of the governors Proclamation." But that, Warren added without further explanation, "rather served us than themselves." In a similar vein, Nathaniel Coffin reported in early July that "it is said [the proclamation] rather accelerates than retards [the Covenant's] progress," implying that the governor's action energized the opponents of British policy.

Whatever the cause, the Covenant failed to achieve anything close to universal acceptance or approbation in the Bay Colony or its neighbors. It never made much headway in Boston itself, despite the town meeting's vote of confidence for its promulgators. Even when smaller towns generally approved it, they added modifications or exceptions that lessened its impact. In communications to Boston, they expressed concern that it would "create discord and confusion," predicted that it would "Exasperate our Parent Country," declared a preference for seeking reforms through "some more Resgular Stream," or simply pledged to wait for a decision from a congress.

Just as the circulation of the Covenant continued despite the governor's proclamation, so too the debates in Boston persisted after the town meeting. Some newspaper essays still defended the destruction of the tea; some advocated reimbursing the company; others kept on attacking the Covenant. A new element was disparagement of John Andrews and his seven associates for their criticism of the committee of correspondence. For instance, an essay by "B" in *The Boston Evening-Post* defended the committee as properly authorized and asserted that the only people hurt by nonconsumption would be "selfish Merchants and other Enemies of our Country." B termed the Covenant "a Scheme which the Arts and Bribery of the Tools of Power cannot break or overturn." Ominously, he accused Andrews and the others of "promot[ing] Divisions," concluding that "you must be considered as such kind of Men and Politicians as ought not to have the Ear of their Fellow Citizens; and whom the wise and good would wish to see excluded from our publick Counsels forever."

Newspaper coverage elsewhere in the colonies of these Boston events in late June was highly selective. Roughly speaking, the farther away a town was located from Boston, the less likely a newspaper was to publish an account revealing the full extent of the dissent expressed at the meeting and in its aftermath. Only four editors reprinted the statement signed by the 129 protesters, and none republished the one submitted by John Andrews and his associates, whereas many reprinted the Solemn League and Covenant, with some claiming inaccurately that it was being readily adopted in most Bay Colony towns. Some added comments in favor of the Covenant and a paragraph disparaging the "virulent abuse" directed at committee members during the meeting. Accounts stressed how few were the Addressers and other dissenters. Only three mentioned Gage's proclamation.

All in all, the message conveyed to other colonies in the press about Bostonians in these weeks amounted to reassurance that although some dissent had been voiced at the late June town meeting, the city—and indeed all of Massachusetts—was essentially united in opposition to Britain and that many inhabitants had already pledged to adhere to nonconsumption after August 31. Remaining questions, then, seemingly revolved around the other colonies. Boston's resistance leaders had reluctantly acknowledged that a congress would be required before additional American jurisdictions would do more than express sympathy for their situation, and the assembly had elected delegates to it. But whether other colonies could follow that lead, much less how such an important gathering could be coordinated and organized, was uncertain.

CHAPTER 4

TIMES OF PERPLEXITY, DANGER, AND DISTRESS

From late June through mid-July 1774, John Adams left his home in Braintree and his usual legal base in Boston to appear on behalf of clients in several court cases in Maine. His letters to his wife, Abigail, reveal that there he encountered many people who criticized the destruction of the tea as "Mischief and Wickedness," refused to endorse the Solemn League and Covenant, and denied that the tea duty was a tax. Adams reported participating in or overhearing a number of political conversations during his journey. A common topic was mobs, their causes and results. One older man explained that he believed "the Judgments of God upon the Land, were in Consequence of the Mobbs and Riots, which had prevailed in the Country." Others complained that crowd actions "render the Populace, the Rabble, the scum of the Earth, insolent, and disorderly, impudent, and abusive." Such a picture, he told Abigail, was "drawn from the Tory Pencil," but he admitted that he thought it contained some truth. Still, like Thomas Greenough, he also believed that some mob actions could be justified by current circumstances. "Is not the Killing of a Child by R[ichardson] and the slaughter of half a Dozen Citizens by a Party of Soldiers as bad as pulling down a House, or drowning a Cargo of Tea? even if both should be allowed to be unlawful."

Yet John Adams's attitude toward mobs was more conflicted than it seemed. In early July, he appeared as an attorney on behalf of Richard King, a supporter of the 1765 Stamp Act whose house had been vandalized by a mob in March 1766. King sued the trespassers, claiming damages of £2,000; Adams was involved in an appellate phase of the complex proceedings. "These private Mobs, I do and will detest," John informed Abigail. "Popular Commotions" could only be justified "when Fundamentals are invaded," and only "for absolute Necessity and with great Caution." By contrast, "these breaking open Houses by rude and insolent Rabbles . . . cannot be even excused upon any Principle which can be entertained by a good Citizen."

For Adams, as for others, the key was the distinction between a *public* purpose (such as the tea destruction) and a *personal* one (such as the "Resentment for private Wrongs" that he believed had motivated the rioters who attacked King's house, terrorized his family, and caused "outragious Injuries"). The difficulty, of course, was differentiating between the two. Surely the members of the crowd that attacked King's house would have cited his approval of the Stamp Act when explaining their motives.

While on his journey during what he termed "these Times of Perplexity, Danger and Distress," Adams also began to look ahead to the congress, to which he had already been elected as a Massachusetts delegate and which was expected to meet on September 1 in Philadelphia, as proposed by the Massachusetts assembly. "What Measures are practicable, and expedient?" he asked a friend, detailing diverse "Sentiments of the People" as he understood them. Some preferred petitions to the king or Parliament; some advocated negotiations; some proposed "bold and Spirited Resolutions"; some wanted nonimportation, perhaps in conjunction with nonconsumption; some promoted "building new Government," even an annual congress. To Abigail he wrote, "I dread the thought of the Congress's falling short of the Expectations of the Continent, but especially of the People of this Province." And he articulated what seemed to him to be the central point at issue: "Whether the american Colonies are to be considered, as a distinct Community so far as to have a Right to judge for themselves, when the fundamentals of their Government are destroyed or invaded?"

John Adams's reports of his experiences on the legal circuit in the summer of 1774, and his reflections on his coming responsibilities as a member of what would come to be called the First Continental Congress, mirrored other Americans' conversations and concerns during those months. Throughout the colonies, discussions similar to those Adams witnessed and participated in dominated both private and public discourse. Authors of newspaper essays, broadsides, and pamphlets joined the debates, which also arose at local meetings and, eventually, at extralegal gatherings that elected delegates to the congress. Unlike Massachusetts, in which the assembly acted quickly and clandestinely in late June, few colonies found it possible to choose congressional delegates through official actions of their elected representatives. Instead, they had to adopt informal and ad hoc ways of proceeding, methods that came to be termed unconstitutional.

THE MYSTICAL WORD *"UNCONSTITUTIONAL"*

"We have been almost stunn'd with the Noise of the word *Unconstitutional*," wrote "Observator" in an essay in *The Massachusetts Gazette and the Boston News-Letter* in February 1773; "our News-Prints and some of our Towns Resolves ring with the Noise of it as if something were in the Word very mystical." Even if thousands of "private Men" declared that such a law was "unjust," that would not matter, because "private Men have no Right of Judging the Equity of the Laws."

Observator accurately pointed up both the rise of a neologism in American political discourse in his own day and its most common usage at the time he wrote. The term had appeared only rarely in American newspapers before 1765, almost exclusively in items reprinted from the British press. But during the controversies over the Stamp Act in 1765 and the Townshend Acts in 1768–1770, some Americans began to deem those statutes "unconstitutional," which they defined as did *The Oxford English Dictionary* for the mid-eighteenth century: "not in harmony with, or authorized by, the political constitution; at variance with the recognized principles of the state." Colonial authors, in other words, viewed 1760s parliamentary legislation not only as bad policy but also as diverging from their basic understanding of appropriate imperial political arrangements. That early in 1773, eight years after it initially appeared in American parlance, a writer still expressed unfamiliarity with the term "unconstitutional" suggested that by then its use had not yet become commonplace. But that would soon change, for in 1774 Americans started to employ it regularly, although in sharply varying contexts.

Those who wanted to resist the Tea Act and Parliament's 1774 statutes continued to use "unconstitutional" in the same way it was first utilized by colonists, as a characterization of British actions, often coupled with a term such as "unjust," "cruel," "oppressive," "unwarrantable," or "arbitrary." But the locution also turned out to be useful for the opponents of colonial resistance, because in 1774 they increasingly charged that local and provincial committees, along with later conventions and congresses, were themselves "unconstitutional," unauthorized by the government and at odds with Britain's political principles. The "mystical" neologism of early 1773, in sum, became during the following year a designation applied not only to British policy but also to Americans' primary means of organization. Even colonial supporters of resistance pondered the implications of their actions in the context of widely accepted assumptions about governmental legitimacy. A Pennsylvania pamphleteer, for example, mused about the validity of actions not "authorized by any law, or constitutional usage." Would they not be "very pernicious . . . and big with dangerous consequences"? he asked.

The dilemma arose because of the colonies' consensus that a general congress was required to determine the best strategy to further their resistance to British policy. They accordingly needed to address a key question: How could they establish the legitimacy of the novel body they proposed to create?

Colonial representatives had previously come together twice to discuss topics of mutual concern. A meeting at Albany instigated by British officials in the summer of 1754 aimed to forge an agreement for both defense against the French and a possible alliance with the Mohawks. Seven provincial legislatures sent official delegates, thus clearly establishing the body's legitimacy, although no assemblies later adopted its recommendations. In October 1765 at New York, representatives from nine colonies gathered for the Stamp Act Congress to draft a protest petition to Great Britain. Most governors opposed that effort, and some managed to thwart assemblies' selection of delegates during formal sessions. Assemblymen convening informally then chose their colonies' representatives to the congress, potentially providing a precedent for how to proceed in 1774.

Colonial assemblies had established committees of correspondence to communicate with each other or with their agents in London, but when royal governors prorogued or dissolved the assemblies, many assumed that neither the committees nor their assemblies could act legitimately. As chapter 3 noted, some "late burgesses" of Virginia, members of the assembly dissolved by Lord Dunmore, gathered in early June to sign a nonimportation and nonconsumption agreement and to issue a call for another meeting two months later. But the Virginians' action was both ad hoc and of questionable public validity, because after the dissolution of the assembly the burgesses recognized that they had reverted to their roles as "private men." Thus the agreement they signed was explicitly identified as personal and voluntary, without applicability to the colony as a whole.

Still, could that same tactic of an informal gathering of current or former assemblymen be adopted as a means of electing delegates to the planned congress, as it had been employed in some colonies to choose men to protest the Stamp Act in 1765? Such a move could possibly backfire. Like some Pennsylvanians, would representatives chosen irregularly be derided as "Tavern Declaimers" who had tried "in an informal Way, to enter upon any public Business"? Would colonists in general accede to actions by unauthorized gatherings of "private men," former assemblymen or not? Or would gubernatorial obstructionism such as that employed by Dunmore or by Thomas Gage put an effective halt to America's collective resistance to parliamentary measures by preventing the official selection of delegates to the congress?

Early in the summer of 1774, governors clearly understood the political circumstances in those terms. For example, when Governor William Franklin of New Jersey—Benjamin's son—initially informed Lord Dartmouth about the proposals for a congress, he commented that the idea was "very absurd, if not unconstitutional," for a governor could prorogue or dissolve an assembly, and then "the power of its committee is of course annihilated." Likewise, Governor John Wentworth of New Hampshire explained to Dartmouth that his dissolution of the assembly "precluded any meeting of those persons to contrive undesirable measures," which had "extremely disconcerted" the assemblymen. Cadwallader Colden recorded, though, that some New Yorkers "deny that [such assemblies] are unconstitutional when a national grievance cannot otherwise be removed."

The novel issue forced colonists of all political persuasions to confront basic questions of governance. The author of a Georgia broadside, for instance, lamented the "unconstitutional measures" being adopted in his province. He pointed out that even the advocates of an unauthorized meeting of the inhabitants admitted that it was not "strictly legal or constitutional," although they thought it justified by the "extraordinary" circumstances. A New York essayist proposed that because "we talk much of the CONSTITUTION," they should act "constitutionally." He predicted that any resolutions adopted by an irregularly chosen congress would have no influence on British policy, because by being "unconstitutional" itself, the congress would have no "existence in *law*." To him, the only possible constitutional strategy required each colonial assembly to address the king separately.

So the question arose: Would Americans participate in extralegal gatherings, even in circumstances deemed "extraordinary"? Many colonists showed considerable reluctance to abandon regular political procedures, thereby exposing their concerns about the legitimacy both of a congress and of various methods for selecting delegates in the event assemblies could not act formally. Events in Philadelphia provide an instructive example, illustrating Pennsylvanians' hesitancy to pursue means they feared were unconstitutional.

In early June, pressed into action by a request from New York's artisans to join them in aiding Bostonians, Philadelphia tradesmen began planning an inclusive "great assembly" of the city's residents. Soon sixty or so "respectable Inhabitants," comprising representatives from "all [religious] Societies in Town," took over the process. That group met for two days at the headquarters of the American Philosophical Society to discuss resolutions and possible methods for selecting Pennsylvania's congressional delegation.

The June 11 broadside announcing the results of the men's deliberations revealed Philadelphians' concerns about the politico-constitutional dilemma they confronted. Because John Penn rejected a request to summon the assembly, that body could not elect delegates to the congress, the means they preferred. So the self-appointed group instead asked the assembly's Speaker, Joseph Galloway, to convene it. Perhaps assuming correctly that the conservative Galloway would refuse that unprecedented request (as he soon did), the group then attempted to legitimize its efforts by announcing that only men *"quali-fied to vote for Representatives"* could participate in the planned city meeting, thus significantly restricting its scope. If Pennsylvania's prop-erly elected assemblymen could not act officially, at least the voters who had selected them could be consulted. Excluding the unqualified would lend an air of regularity to the otherwise informal proceedings.

On June 18, Thomas Willing and John Dickinson chaired the "very large and respectable Meeting of the Freeholders and Freemen" of the city. At the outset, the Reverend William Smith, provost of the College of Philadelphia, cautioned participants to observe "order and deco-rum" in their discussions and to recognize that "matters of the highest consequence" were on the agenda. They were considering nothing less than how to identify "ways and means, upon constitutional ground," to close the breach with Britain. Perhaps his speech had the desired impact, because the resolutions adopted by the meeting were mod-erate, with the exception of the first, which declared the Port Act "unconstitutional" and "oppressive." The other resolutions initiated a fund for the relief of poor Bostonians and called for a congress but failed to designate Philadelphia's delegates. Instead, attendees estab-lished a committee with forty-four members to determine "on mature deliberation" the best method of naming deputies.

The committee of forty-four decided that a provincial convention could select congressional delegates and began to consider how to organize unofficial colony-wide elections for such a convention. But then Deputy Governor Penn, confronted by the threat of an Indian war on the western frontier in territory disputed between Pennsylvania and Virginia, felt forced to call a new assembly to meet in mid-July. The committee quickly took advantage of the unanticipated opportu-nity by scheduling their (irregular) elections in conjunction with the (regular) assembly elections. Delegates and assemblymen would be chosen at the same local meetings, at the same time, and might well be the same people. The provincial congress was summoned for July 15, the assembly for three days later. Thus the charge of unconstitutional-ity could be rendered essentially moot—or so it was hoped.

Questions about the legitimacy of local and provincial gatherings continued to resurface in various jurisdictions (especially New York and Georgia) during the summer of 1774 but tended to be overlooked in part because of such clever maneuvers as that in Pennsylvania and in part because of repeated emphases on the "respectability" of those involved in the meetings. The congress, after all, was proposed as a moderate alternative to Boston's call for quick action, and most Americans, despite diverse political opinions, ultimately proved willing to set aside concerns about the appropriate processes for the election of delegates and to wait to see what happened when the congress met. The neologism "unconstitutional" would eventually be employed by all concerned, but in different ways. During the summer months, the most common use applied the term to detested parliamentary statutes. After the congress published its resolves in the autumn, critics used it to define the congress itself.

ADVICES FROM LONDON

June 22, 1774. George III signs the Quebec Act, a law expanding the boundaries of the province won from France in the Seven Years' War south to the Ohio River, thus encompassing the western region disputed by Virginia and Pennsylvania. Catholics are given new religious freedoms, and previous forms of civil government under French rule are restored. Then Parliament is dissolved and new elections called for the fall.

July 6. Lord Dartmouth writes to General Gage, in response to a letter from him carried to London by Thomas Hutchinson. "The state in which you found things at your arrival at Boston was better than I expected, and from what has passed since I am inclined to hope that the tranquillity of the province and the authority of government in it will speedily be restored." He praises Gage's actions so far, and adds, "There is room to hope that the other colonies will not consent to the propositions suggested to them

by the factious leaders at Boston. Many have I understand actually refused."

July 25. William Lee, a Virginian resident in London, addresses
his ally Samuel Adams in Boston. The recent statutes "are the
fruits of the seeds that have been sowing since 1764." The congress should "specify every oppressive Act of Parliamt since that
period . . . with decency & manly firmness." But he foresees a
problem: "Was the Congress composed of Deputies regularly
authorized by the Assemblies of each province, it might be proper
to have it presented to the King, by a Deputy, as an Ambassador,
from every Colony, but as the Congress will not be so constituted,
your Bill will not be received thro' such a medium, therefore suppose it must go thro' the old Channel of the Agents."

August 3. After receiving dispatches from Boston containing news
from late June, Dartmouth expresses optimism to Gage: "The
false holds held out to the Inhabitants of Boston, of assistance
from the other Colonies, may for a whole keep up the Spirit of
the Mob, but the Hour of distress must soon come that will, I
hope, awaken the People to a right sense of their situation." After
the Boston committee of correspondence was challenged in the
town meeting, "and their Duplicity detected," he avers, it is surprising that people retain any confidence in its members. Even
though he thinks it unlikely that the people will be "misled into
Measures of Violence, yet it is certainly prudent to guard against
every possible Event." No "Relaxation" from the recent statutes
can be anticipated, he affirms, until "Submission is satisfactorily
obtained."

A SUMMER OF LOCAL MEETINGS AND DEBATES

As chapter 3 showed, many colonists condemned the vengeful Boston Port Act while still maintaining a studied silence about the city's
destruction of the East India Company tea. So at the same time other

Americans sympathized with Bostonians, they also saw New England-ers' fate as unique. Philadelphians, New Yorkers, and Charlestonians angered the ministry by how they greeted EIC tea, but in no case did that anger cause similar retaliation, not even after crowds in sev-eral cities demolished additional chests of EIC tea belonging to or consigned to local merchants. Americans in other colonies, in short, could interpret the Port Act as irrelevant to their circumstances while simultaneously lamenting its dire effects on Boston and Massachusetts as a whole.

But the two additional statutes debated by Parliament in April and accepted by the king in late May appeared to many Americans to pre-sent a greater threat to the other colonies than did the Boston Port Act. Even though the Massachusetts Government Act and the Administra-tion of Justice Act technically applied only to the Bay Colony, politi-cally cognizant Americans foresaw that if Parliament could claim the power to change the Massachusetts charter, it could likely do the same for their own, and that the statute some dubbed the Murder Act had significant implications for the future enforcement of criminal justice in other provinces as well. (The two laws, along with the Port Act, will henceforth be referred to collectively as the Coercive Acts.)

Information about the two statutes' provisions became known in June and July from newspapers and unofficial copies, which dispersed rapidly through the continent. So in the middle of June, the Baltimore committee of correspondence wrote to a Virginia counterpart,

> However alarming the Boston Port Bill may be in its native ten-dency, what is it compar'd to the effects of the two other Bills for altering & changing the Constitution of their Govermt and for the trial of Persons concern'd in Shedding the Blood of our fellow Subjects who may be removed else where or even to England for trial as if intended to protect them from the Justice of the Laws. If we can tamely submit to these things what security remains for Life, Liberty, or Property.

Similarly, a Harvard professor commented that the Port Act was "swal-lowed up" by the Government Act, which "mutilated the Charter, so as to leave only an empty phantom remaining; and, by depriv-

In early July, Isaiah Thomas, a strong supporter of resistance to Great Britain, changed the masthead of his newspaper, perhaps in reaction to the news of the two additional Coercive Acts. For four years, he had used a version of Benjamin Franklin's famous segmented snake cartoon from 1754, with the exhortation "Join or Die," but in July 1774 he added the image of the griffon (Great Britain) at the right, under attack by the snake. On the left, the female figure holds a staff with a liberty cap; on the right, the two figures represent an allegory of American commerce.

ing the people of every privilege, has erected an absolute despotism." And he added that the "manifest design" of the Justice Act was "to empower the military to kill the inhabitants without danger or fear of punishment."

Colonial opinion reached a negative consensus on the acts long before official confirmation of their provisions arrived in August. For example, in Newport in mid-June, the Reverend Ezra Stiles recorded in his diary that the acts caused "amazing Alarm"; a Philadelphian opined to Josiah Quincy Jr. that they "give us a greater certainty of approaching tyranny" than ever before; and a future Loyalist in New York concluded that the Justice Act "amounted to an Act to cut our

Throats with Impunity." Likewise, an Alexandria, Virginia, merchant explained to an English correspondent that "the two last [laws] are much worse than the first." Another Virginian gave a very personal reason why: "Can we be said to enjoy Liberty if the Villain who Ravishes our Wives, deflowers our Daughters or Murders our Sons can Evade punishment by being tryed in Britain, where no Evidence can pursue him?" Governor Gage underscored the impact of the two statutes when he observed in retrospect that he had anticipated making progress in strengthening governmental authority in Massachusetts—until news of the acts arrived. That "overset the whole," he informed Lord Dartmouth, "and the flame blazed out in all parts at once beyond the conception of everybody."

When the New Castle, Delaware, committeemen summoned local residents to a meeting in mid-June, they briefly summarized the laws' reputed contents and commented, "These are no mere phantoms arising from a heated brain, but real facts, not exaggerations." One possible participant in that meeting was nonetheless led to fantasize about the acts' effects. Francis Hopkinson, who lived in New Castle for part of 1774, created and published a family fable set one thousand years in the future. In his telling, an elderly gentleman sends his sons to settle another farm, where they prosper, and then punishes one for objecting to a tax. His brothers sympathize, but their meetings to discuss helping him are deemed "treasonable, traiterous [*sic*], and rebellious." The "harsh and unconstitutional proceedings irritated *Jack* and the other inhabitants of the new farm to such a degree that *********": thus Hopkinson ended his tale, in mid-sentence, noting that the rest of the purported manuscript was missing. Neither he nor anyone else could predict what would happen next.

What did occur, primarily from mid-June through late August, were local meetings convened in colonies from New England south to North Carolina that adopted resolutions expressing opinions on the dispute with Britain and promising to send food and financial aid to besieged Boston. Most, though not all, supported nonimportation, and some also advocated the more controversial nonexportation. As it became clear that governors would try to prevent assemblies from electing delegates to the planned intercolonial congress, the gatherings chose representatives to provincial conventions that would select those delegates.

Although the meetings' resolves differed sufficiently from each other to make clear their local origins, they contained a mix of common elements. Some began with a statement of principle, affirming loyalty to the king or Britain generally. Next (or sometimes first), they declared that Americans had the right to tax themselves, explicitly denying Parliament's authority to do so. Most then described the Coercive Acts as unconstitutional and oppressive. Attendees declared their sympathy for Boston and vowed to send aid, often placing local men in charge of collecting donations. The greatest variations came when participants considered possible courses of action or described nonimportation or nonexportation agreements. Some exempted certain items; others proposed universal applicability. A few added resolutions on other topics. Finally, once the plans for the congress became widely known, participants usually pledged to follow its decisions.

Nearly one-third of all the recorded meetings took place in Virginia, in part because the ex-burgesses had called for a convention on August 1 and in part because Lord Dunmore, confronting the same frontier threats as John Penn, summoned a new assembly for August 11 in hopes of replacing an expired law authorizing expenditures for the militia. Thus Virginians, like Pennsylvanians, needed to elect new members of the legislature, and the conjunction of meeting times would mean that they could also choose delegates to the provincial convention—almost always the same men. One Philadelphian, relying only on those two examples, predicted to his brother in early July that therefore "the Deputies [to the congress] will be mostly appointed in a Constitutional way by the Assemblys." But he was incorrect, for—as will be seen in this chapter—most delegates were instead chosen in other ways. In the end, the Virginia burgesses did not meet as planned, and Dunmore headed to the frontier on July 10 without the militia funding he sought.

A focus on the resolves adopted in those Virginia meetings and on related correspondence helps to highlight the contents of such documents with greater specificity. Of twenty-nine sets of resolutions approved in Virginia counties between June 8 and July 28, twenty included a pledge of loyalty to Britain or the king personally; all but two insisted that only colonial legislatures could tax Americans; and all but five explicitly referred to the Coercive Acts as unconstitutional, unjust, arbitrary, or the like. All lamented the state of affairs in their "sister colony" Massachusetts Bay, and all but one promised assistance to Boston. But when the counties considered remedies, the consensus dissipated. Although all but two counties advocated some sort of commercial boycott of Britain, ten favored only nonimportation, whereas seventeen were willing to consider nonexportation as well. The seeming consensus collapsed further when some counties listed exceptions to nonimportation. For example, Prince George County excluded "negroes, clothing, and tools, Irish linen, medicines, and paper" from any agreement. Chesterfield County enumerated, among other items, books, needles, gunpowder, blankets, steel, "and implements necessary for the manufacturing of woollens and linens." Even the best-known resolves, those from Fairfax County, included a long list of such exceptions to a potential nonimportation agreement.

In early July, the youthful but politically savvy James Madison explained counties' preferences for different commercial strategies by citing a combination of economic motives and the ethnicity of local residents. Most native-born Virginians, he claimed, resolutely supported a complete embargo on trade with Britain, but Scotsmen and "some interested Merchants among the natives" resisted adding nonexportation to nonimportation. Those men advanced their position at county meetings by disingenuously advocating the need to repay debts to British creditors. According to Madison, "some honest moderate folks" therefore decided not to support nonexportation, fearing that Americans would be dishonorably unable to fulfill existing financial obligations. That kind of covert opposition could indeed have influenced the ten Virginia counties that preferred nonimportation alone.

Even more fundamental disagreements emerged when the topic was Boston's destruction of the tea. Most of the summer meetings resolutely remained silent on that topic. In Virginia, only five offered an opinion. Essex County alone firmly praised Boston's "spirited conduct," which attendees insisted had aided "the cause of freedom." By contrast, Middlesex County declared bluntly, "We do not approve of the conduct of the people of Boston in destroying the tea," because "we apprehend violence cannot justify violence." Other counties fell somewhere in the middle. Hanover freeholders declared that they did not have enough information to decide whether the Bostonians' action was justified, but they did know that Parliament's punishment of the city was excessively severe. Dinwiddie residents called the destruction of the tea an "outrage," yet decried penalizing the entire city for "a trespass committed by a few." Norfolk failed to offer an opinion on the destruction but after a meeting that, according to James Parker, was filled with "incoherent Stupid" comments, recommended that all the colonies help Boston pay for the EIC tea.

A Scots schoolteacher in Westmoreland County observed that such local meetings were intended "to feel how the pulse of the common people beat," but he and others noted that local leaders wanted to do more than collect public opinion; they also hoped to influence it. In Westmoreland, he reported, "some of the greatest men in the Colony" harangued "the common people" about the importance of unanimity in opposing Britain. One approving participant in another meeting pronounced it "very uscfull" because many attendees had learned the truth of the colonies' political circumstances, after arriving with "an Opinion, too common among the Vulgar that the Law affecting Tea alone did not concern them, because they used none of it." Stress on the significance of unanimity led to the suppression of dissenting opinions. For instance, James Parker commented that some Scots factors were elected to the Norfolk committee despite not having been consulted in advance. He explained that "some consented through fear, & others to temporise," but he thought that all were "ashamed" of being involved with the committee. Only a few men in Norfolk, it seemed, were as adamant as one John Saunders, who as late as January 1775 absolutely refused to assent to the county's resolutions, although he continued to attend most of the meetings.

In two instances, surviving letters supply detailed information about alternatives presented to or suggested for discussion at the local meetings. Robert Beverley, a politically moderate Virginia planter and son-in-law of Landon Carter, proposed resolutions to the Essex County meeting on July 9 that suggested sending a combined colonial delegation to meet with the king as a prelude to taking any other action. Essex voters rejected his argument that before "instantaneous & violent Measures" could be justified, "every other honorable Method" to effect reconciliation with Britain should be attempted. He thus told his father-in-law that he could not vote for the resolutions the county meeting adopted, in part because they included a "cruel & unjust" nonexportation agreement harming debtors on both sides of the Atlantic.

Likewise, a mid-July exchange of letters between George Washington and his friend and neighbor Bryan Fairfax provides insight into debates over the Fairfax Resolves, the most elaborate collective expression of Virginians' opinion. The resolves, drafted by a committee on which both Washington and George Mason served, were discussed and adopted at a county meeting in Alexandria on July 18. They began with an unusual historical statement observing that Virginia was founded by men entitled to rights "by the Laws of Nature and Nations." They then asserted that only Virginians could tax themselves and that Parliament's current actions were motivated by "a premeditated Design and System . . . to introduce an arbitrary Government" into America. If their grievances were redressed, the Fairfax residents promised, they would seriously consider contributing to compensation for the East India Company. They supported a congress to defend American rights and to create a "just, lenient, permanent, and constitutional Form of Government" to link the colonies to Great Britain. After a series of detailed statements about nonimportation and nonexportation, almost as an afterthought the resolves concluded with a recommendation that the congress address a petition to the king, assuring him of their affection "in the strongest terms."

Bryan Fairfax could not attend the gathering, but he sent Washington comments on the draft resolutions that he hoped his friend would read publicly at the meeting and was later disappointed to learn that Washington had not done so. Like Beverley, Fairfax recommended a petition to the king as an initial step, warning that passing "hasty Resolutions" would foreclose conciliatory options. He strongly opposed a resolution denying Parliament's general authority over the colonies, rather than rejecting its right of taxation alone (a claim with which he agreed). The more comprehensive position was "unreasonable," he insisted, because "it becomes good Subjects to submit to the Constitution of their Country."

In response to Fairfax's complaint about his not conveying these ideas to the freeholders, Washington insisted that "no person present seem'd in the least disposed to adopt your sentiments." Indeed, some of the men to whom he had shown Fairfax's letter thought it "repugnant . . . to the very principle we were contending for." Washington acknowledged and regretted his significant political disagreements with his friend. He explained that he was personally convinced that "Government is pursuing a regular Plan at the expence of Law & Justice, to overthrow our Constitutional Rights & liberties," as evidenced by the Coercive Acts. Two weeks later, Fairfax disclaimed any desire to thwart the will of a "large Majority" but reported that since the meeting a dissenter had told him that "there were a great many of his opinion in the Court House who did not care to speak because they thought it would be to no Purpose." Furthermore, another attendee revealed that he "did secretly object to some of the Resolves but could not speak his Mind." In short, in Fairfax County as elsewhere in Virginia, hints of suppressed dissension surfaced in the aftermath of meetings that had seemingly reached unanimous (or nearly unanimous) conclusions about current politics.

Not all the dissidents at such gatherings adopted more moderate positions. At the Albemarle County meeting, a man evidently suggested that "the people should go into the Merchts. stores, and take what goods they wanted, and pay for them when it suited them at their own price," because local traders had been overcharging customers for years. "Now it was their turn and they would take them at what [price] they thought proper," the man concluded, reportedly to "applause." No trace of such ideas appeared in the resolutions the county adopted, which fit the standard Virginia pattern.

The collective resolutions adopted throughout the colonies thus placed a veneer of unanimity over a vigorous debate that filled newspapers, pamphlets, and personal correspondence during the summer of 1774. According to one South Carolinian, "The Talk upon the Situation of American Affairs and Politics here seems to drown all other." In Charleston, "The Gentleman & Mechanic, those of high, and low life, the learned & illiterate in their several Clubs and as they casually meet harrangue upon the same Subjects." Like Bryan Fairfax, nearly all colonists by then accepted the premise that Parliament, which Americans now commonly referred to as the "British" Parliament, had no right to tax them. But on other topics, disputes persisted.

Most notably, opinions continued to differ about whether Boston's destruction of the tea had been justified, whether the EIC deserved compensation, and, if so, how reimbursement should be arranged. William Franklin told his father in early July that he thought "strict Justice" required Boston or Massachusetts to pay for the tea, but although Benjamin had once said the same, by the time he received that letter, he had changed his mind, insisting in reply that the Port Act was so ambiguous that it gave Bostonians "no surety" that commerce would be restarted even if the company were compensated. The debate appeared in print as well as in private correspondence. A moderate Pennsylvania pamphleteer concurred with the son that "equity and justice" required that the company be reimbursed for its losses; he went so far as to volunteer to pay a share of the expenses the EIC sustained because of the cargo turned away from Philadelphia. Anticipating such demands from the company led another essayist to counter that Boston should not accept responsibility for the destroyed tea, because that would open Philadelphia and New York to requests for freight charges. A third author proposed that the British government compensate the company.

In Virginia, a major debate erupted over the destruction of the tea and the Port Act. The first to weigh in on the subject was Virginia's conservative attorney general, John Randolph. In *Considerations on the Present State of Virginia,* Randolph averred that "even the most zealous *American* whatsoever" should admit that Bostonians' destructive actions were indefensible. Characterizing the Port Act as a necessary response to "that growing Disorder which appeared to [the ministry] to be Licentiousness instead of Freedom," he urged Virginians to publicly criticize New Englanders. Like Bryan Fairfax and Robert Beverley, he advocated petitioning the king for redress, assuring his fellow Virginians that their monarch would surely respond positively to their plea. The colony's treasurer, Robert Carter Nicholas, replying in a pamphlet of his own, admitted that he would not try to justify the Bostonians' "Acts of Violence or Intemperance." But he declared himself an agnostic on the question of their guilt: he needed to have "a thorough Knowledge of the Motives of their Conduct" before reaching a judgment. By contrast, he did not hesitate to attack the motives of both the EIC and the ministry. He pronounced the Port Act "*unconstitutional*" in that it was "entirely *ex post facto*," identifying and penalizing a crime after it had been committed.

The seemingly endless debate over Boston's response to the EIC tea was not purely theoretical, because tea shipments continued to arrive in the colonies and Americans had to decide how to deal with them. Three options had emerged in late 1773—destruction, confiscation by customs officers, and rejection. In the spring of 1774, a fourth was employed on the Cape in the case of John Greenough's remaining tea chest—sequestration under the control of a local committee. Later in 1774, all those tactics would continue to be used.

For example, when the brig *Mary and Jane* arrived in Maryland in early August with a total of eleven chests of tea dispatched to area merchants, everyone involved agreed to supervision of the tea by the local committee if it proved impossible to send the chests back to Britain; the same decision was reached a month later when thirty-three chests of EIC tea arrived in Salem. In late June, though, that outcome was not considered when the *Magna Charta,* captained by Richard Maitland, brought one full and two half chests of tea to Charleston. Although Maitland assured the local committee that he would personally destroy the tea in front of witnesses, he failed to act before the twenty-day period for paying duty expired, and so customs officers confiscated and stored the chests. Angered by Maitland's failure to live up to his promises, "several hundred" men boarded his vessel intending to tar and feather him, but (reported William Bull) "as they entered his ship on one side he went off from the other," taking refuge in a royal naval vessel in the harbor. In the end, the Charleston committee decided that the tea's fate was appropriate, because it mimicked that of the EIC chests in December 1773, and that the planned destruction had been "prudently prevented," thus resolving a "delicate situation."

Richard Maitland's difficulties troubled James Laurens. Referring to Maitland as "a poor Old Greyheaded Ratling Captain," Laurens attributed his problems not only to the detested chests but also to the captain's "few unguarded Expressions." James told his brother Henry, at the time still in London, "I *love Liberty,* Liberty of Sentiment, Liberty of Speech. . . . I would have others Enjoy it as freely as I do, &

by Suppressing it they may make Hypocrites but not Converts." He explained that he thought "the most judicious & Moderate part of our Community" concurred with his negative opinion of how Maitland was treated.

Laurens thus pointed to a development that also affected participants in the published debates in the summer. Like the attendees at local meetings who afterward described disagreements that they hesitated to express freely during those public gatherings, so too men who supported Britain's punitive measures began to complain about obstacles they confronted when trying to publish their ideas. Americans could argue openly about what tactics to employ—for example, whether to add nonexportation to nonimportation—but essayists who wanted to critique resistance in general found it difficult to publish their views.

Only in Georgia did the summer debates range freely enough to include attempts to defend not just the Port Act but also the other two Coercive Acts. In Savannah, James Johnston, a royalist-leaning printer, opened his newspaper and the sole press in the colony to multiple anonymous authors, who publicly debated all three statutes. The dispute began in *The Georgia Gazette* in late July with an unattributed essay, "The Case Stated." The author presented an argument against the Port Act ("a sentence unparalleled in British annals") and what he viewed as excessive power granted to the governor in all three of the statutes. He contended that the "plain and single question" was this: "Has the British Parliament a right to levy what sums of money on the Americans they [can], and in what manner they please?" To that he answered, no. In the same issue of *The Georgia Gazette,* "A Georgian" asserted that the Coercive Acts could readily be extended to other colonies. "As members of the same community," he inquired, "are we all not equally affected by every attempt which is made to deprive that community of those established rights which constitute the very being of it?"

In early August came a flurry of responses. A "Religious and Faithful Friend of Georgia" admitted that the recent laws were *"too severe"* but nevertheless pronounced them *"necessary to force these people into a proper sense of justice and moderation."* For his part, "A True Friend to Georgia" termed it a "dreadful Phantom" of an "overheated imagination" to think that the Administration of Justice Act applied to their colony. In one broadside, "A Friend to Moderation" charged that the Bostonians' destruction of the tea was "a most daring contempt of Government," claiming that the Port Act left open the prospect of "a dutiful submission" that could lead to an "equitable" solution. An unnamed author chimed in, declaring that "every impartial man" would conclude that destroying the tea deserved to be "severely punished," and defending the Massachusetts Government and Administration of Justice Acts as appropriate measures under the circumstances. Both this author and A Friend to Moderation contended that Georgia, which needed the protection of British troops against the Indians, should not involve itself in disputes they characterized as pertinent only to the northern colonies. An essayist in the *Gazette,* though, observed that Britain had not sent assistance to Georgia to counter Indian threats in the recent past and most likely would not do so in the future.

In mid-August, the one contributor to the debate whose identity is known, the Reverend Haddon Smith, an Anglican clergyman, added his voice to the mix. Writing as "Mercurius," Smith declared that the "Case Stated" author had misidentified the key question. It was not whether the colonies could be taxed by Parliament but rather *whether the Americans have a right to destroy private property with impunity.*" He joined others in contending that the destruction of the tea was "highly criminal" and argued that Boston had the ability to make reparations by reimbursing the East India Company. He also thought that the Massachusetts Government and Administration of Justice Acts were irrelevant to Georgia; accordingly, it was "unseasonable (not to say preposterous) . . . to fly in the face of lawful authority" and adopt resolutions "provoking the Mother Country to desert us." The following week the dialogue continued, with "A Freeholder" revealing himself as the author of "The Case Stated." While denigrating the "Boston mob," he lamented that innocent Bostonians were now suffering "punishments inflicted without a trial." He challenged Mercurius's assertion that compensating the company was a viable option, pointing out that the act did not make clear that repayment would suffice to lift the blockade. But in the same issue of the *Gazette,* Mercurius continued his defense of Parliament's statutes, particularly the Massachusetts

Government Act. It was "absurd," he contended, to think that colonial charters could not be amended, and the changes in the Massachusetts political structure were entirely warranted, with the complaints of the other writers being "frivolous and ill grounded."

After Haddon Smith was revealed as the author of those Mercurius essays, he was forced to leave Georgia. A similar fate befell two other Church of England clergymen whose statements angered their parishes and neighbors at almost exactly the same time in mid-August 1774, thus foreshadowing what would happen to many other outspoken conservatives in the months to come. One, the Reverend John Bullman, was an Englishman who had served as assistant rector of St. Michael's Church in Charleston, South Carolina, since 1769; the other, the American-born Samuel Peters, graduated from Yale and was appointed rector of St. Peter's Church, in his birthplace, Hebron, Connecticut, in 1757.

Bullman's offense was not a published essay but a sermon he delivered on August 14. In it, he decried men's "needless intruding our selves to meddle with, and to pass our censures upon other Men's Bussiness." In particular, he complained about men who thought themselves capable of assessing "the Fitness or Unfitness of all persons in power and Authority." A man "who cannot perhaps govern his own houshold, or pay the Debts of his own contracting," Bullman proclaimed, nevertheless "presumes he is qualified to dictate how the State should be governed, and to point out means of paying the Debts of a Nation." And then he reached the climax that affronted many who attended church that morning:

> Hence too it is, that every silly Clown, and illeterate Mechanic, will take upon him to censure the conduct of his Prince or Governor, and contribute as much as in him lies to create and foment those Misunderstandings, which being breeded by Discontent and Diffused through great Multitudes, come at last to end in Schisms in the Church, and sedition and Rebellion in the State. . . . There is no greater Instrument or Ornament of Peace, than for every Man to keep his own Rank, and to do his Duty in his own station, without . . . pretending to censure his Superiors in Matter wherein he is not himself immediately aggrieved.

At those words, William Henry Drayton recalled, "the greatest part of the congregation took fire; scarcely continuing quiet, during the service." The vestry's minutes noted that Bullman's sermon "exasperated" many St. Michael's parishioners; moreover, Drayton observed, "a report ran through the town, that the preacher had inculcated passive obedience; and had censured the popular proceedings."

In hopes of learning more and calming the waters, the parish vestrymen asked the cleric to supply them with a copy of his remarks. According to Drayton, the vestrymen did not find anything especially offensive in the sermon, a fact that revealed much about their own status and attitudes. But after they explained to Bullman the "Impropriety" and poor timing of his political remarks from the pulpit, the clergyman stubbornly refused to retreat or apologize. He declared resolutely that "he wou'd not be dictated to by the Vestry or Parishioners" and immediately offered his resignation if the vestry failed to approve his message. Reportedly his disrespectful behavior upset them more than did the contents of the sermon. Perhaps he expected to call their bluff (for he had previously been regarded as "an edifying preacher"), but the opposite happened.

The vestrymen quickly summoned a parish meeting and asked the attendees if they approved Bullman's conduct. Some regretted his having delivered the sermon, but nevertheless attested to his good "general character." After a reputed "sharp altercation," some of his supporters left the meeting, and in the end the parish voted against him. Drayton commented that the outcome was seen as a "triumph on the side of the people in favour of the American cause" and that when announced in church, the decision was received with an unseemly shout of joy. The vestrymen ordered that Bullman be paid his back salary in full, and he was formally dismissed from his position.

The controversy did not end there. John Bullman had numerous supporters who charged that the clergyman had been handled with "unreasonable severity" and that the vestry had acted illegally. First seventy-four and then eighty-six Charleston residents (not all of them parish members) eventually signed petitions on his behalf, futilely appealing his dismissal first to the vestrymen and then to higher authorities. Drayton commented that "the affair grew so serious, that if prosecuted, it was feared blows would ensue," so commissioners appointed by the governor to look into the dispute found repeated pretexts to postpone making a final decision. In the end, Bullman gave up and departed for London in late March 1775, carrying a letter of introduction from William Bull to Lord Dartmouth. Bull described the cleric as "a firm friend to Government in Church and State, tho no inflammatory Zealot," who had been mistreated by "Demagogues."

In Hebron, Connecticut, Samuel Peters's problems began with gossip rather than with a sermon and continued with publications, both authorized and unauthorized. First, word spread that Peters had written letters to England criticizing the actions of Connecticut's popularly elected government. Before dawn on the morning of August 15, about three hundred unarmed men from Hebron and nearby towns surrounded his house to ask about the truth of the rumors. Peters denied any wrongdoing and showed the letters in question to a committee chosen by the crowd. Some men objected to his having "to lay open to publick view his private letters," but the committee and most of the "tumultuous people" appeared satisfied by Peters's protestations of innocence. About twenty men remained for another hour or so, threatening the clergyman with tar and feathers, until some of his supporters arrived, and then they too left the scene.

Peters apparently survived the confrontation with little damage to himself or his reputation, but he gave the committee permission to publish satirical "resolves" he had drafted and readied for the press. Those resolutions purported to represent the views of several Hebron residents; they denied that the tea duty was a tax on the colonies, because the EIC could not force Americans to buy tea. "If we will live without teas, as our fathers did in the purity of this country," the seventh resolution read, "the tax will not hurt us." That same argument was advanced by others, and perhaps in and of itself would not have caused more trouble for Peters, but the final resolution declared that the town of Farmington had committed treason by publicly burning the Port Act.

After the resolves appeared in print, men again gathered at the clergyman's house on September 6 to charge him with "making and publishing sentiments and principles incompatible with our civil liberties, subversive of our Constitution, and tending to make discord." Peters engaged in an extended dialogue with the men, attempting to convince them that by purchasing tea, they in effect consented to pay the tax. The crowd pushed into his house, damaged it and his clothing, and placed him on a horse to carry him to the Hebron common, where—surrounded by another huge crowd—he was forced to sign a document renouncing his resolves as having "justly offended the People." The statement also expressed support for "the present Measures now taking in the American Colonies, to obtain Redress of our Grievances."

Two days after this second confrontation, Peters sought assistance from Governor Jonathan Trumbull, who ordered the Hebron justice of the peace to use his authority to maintain order and to try to convince other local residents that "while they contend for Liberty they do not destroy it, and by causing divisions to hurt their own designs." But Peters did not trust Trumbull, later charging that the governor himself had instigated the crowds that attacked his house. So he fled to safety in Boston.

Once in the garrisoned city, he was in "high spirits" and wrote exuberantly to his mother that as soon as a new contingent of troops and men-of-war arrived from England, "hanging work will go on, and destruction will first attend the sea-port towns; the lintel sprinkled on the side posts will preserve the faithful." Unfortunately for him, that letter was intercepted and widely reprinted in northern newspapers, as was an equally damning letter to a fellow Anglican clergyman in New York, the Reverend Samuel Auchmuty. To him Peters exclaimed, "Their rebellion is obvious; treason is common; and robbery is their daily diversion; the Lord deliver us from anarchy." His letter to Auchmuty insisted that all the Church of England clerics in Connecticut were under attack from "the rage of the puritan mobility." That accusation led other Anglican clergymen to sign public statements disavowing him and declaring their support for American resistance to Britain. The Reverend Ezra Stiles of Newport, characterizing Peters as "full of Malice & Venom against his Country," rejected their disavowal, declaring instead that Peters "speaks the Hearts of Nine Tenths of the Episcopalians throughout the Territory North of Maryland."

Samuel Peters's departure from the colonies for England in late October was not as smooth as John Bullman's from Charleston several months later. Because of the closure of the port of Boston, he sailed from Portsmouth, New Hampshire, and had to take shelter in the fort there before he left because of an unspecified "insult" planned for him. Further, he was preceded not by a positive letter to Dartmouth but by its reverse: a missive terming him an untrustworthy "Lump of Vanity." As a final embarrassment, another of his letters to Auchmuty (written after Peters arrived in London) was intercepted and published in Connecticut. Ironically, it begged Auchmuty's pardon for the "foolishness" and "folly" of the contents of the earlier epistle.

ELECTING DELEGATES TO THE CONGRESS

The summer's debates and such crowd actions in local communities overlapped in part with colony-wide meetings, which were often called into session by assemblymen or former assemblymen. Timing and election arrangements differed from colony to colony, but by late August provincial-level gatherings had taken place in almost all the colonies from New England south to Georgia. At them, representatives adopted resolutions, selected delegates for the congress, and occasionally drafted instructions to those delegates. In retrospect, Thomas Gage observed to Lord Dartmouth that when the summer meetings were held, the "popular fever" was at its height, and therefore most colonies chose "the greatest incendiaries." Yet he erred in that assessment. True, prominent leaders of the resistance movement, such as Samuel Adams, Richard Henry Lee, and Christopher Gadsden, numbered among the members of the First Continental Congress, but the ranks of delegates also included conservatives like Joseph Galloway and moderates like Isaac Low, John Jay, and John Dickinson. In addition, surviving accounts suggest that the attendees at about half the provincial conventions held diverse opinions not only about which men should be selected to attend the intercolonial congress but also about what options the colonies should pursue in the crisis they confronted.

What became the defining characteristic of the Continental Congress, though, was not the range of opinions among its members but instead the constitutionally irregular manner in which most of the delegates were selected. In only a few colonies—including, ironically, Massachusetts, where assemblymen had acted swiftly in mid-June before the governor could dissolve them—were delegates chosen by votes of legally elected legislatures. In most jurisdictions, governors could not thwart the meetings of provincial bodies composed of men chosen by some variant of a popular vote. In early August, Lord Dartmouth ordered governors to prevent such "unlawful assemblies," but by the time he issued that directive, the matter was long since moot. Even had the order been given and transmitted in timely fashion, it could not have been enforced: that was the uniform opinion of colonial officials.

At five of the conventions, all elected "unconstitutionally"—Maryland, Delaware, New Jersey, New Hampshire, and North Carolina—consensus seemingly prevailed among the members from the outset. In the latter two, the only reported conflicts involved frustrated governors, not the conventions' participants. In New Hampshire, John Wentworth issued a proclamation in early July against the "rash and ill-advised" men who had summoned others to "a new, illegal and dangerous Assembly," ordering them "forthwith to disperse" and warning them against continuing, "at your Peril." No one apparently paid any attention; the convention selected two men to attend the congress. In North Carolina, assemblymen successfully concealed their plans to call a convention from Governor Josiah Martin until he saw a notice in a newspaper. He then took what action he could, issuing a proclamation in mid-August against such an "unlawful and indecent" gathering. He was astonished to learn that his councillors "abetted and encouraged" the convention, thus "flagrantly insult[ing]" the king's government. Members of the convention elected three delegates, expressed support for Boston, excoriated the Coercive Acts, pledged not to drink tea after September 1, and vowed to oppose "all unconstitutional encroachments whatsoever."

In the colonies of Rhode Island and Connecticut, which elected their own governors, the process of delegate selection differed from that in the other provinces. At its regular meeting in mid-June, the Rhode Island assembly simply approved the idea of a congress (not yet more than an idea) and named two delegates. Connecticut held no convention or assembly session; rather, the colony's committee of correspondence met in mid-July to name its delegates. Of the five men they initially chose, three declined the nomination, two for health reasons. The third, William Samuel Johnson, cited a conflicting prior obligation but revealed his true reason to a friend: he was afraid that the congress would only "widen the Breach already much too great betw[ee]n the Parent State & her Colonies," and he preferred seeking "Reconciliation" by other means. "Little room I fear will be found in that Assembly for Moderate Men or Moderate Measures," Johnson wrote, averring that "in every light the prospect is Melancholy."

In five other colonies—Virginia, South Carolina, Pennsylvania, Georgia, and especially New York—complex disputes erupted as Americans met to adopt resolutions and elect representatives to the congress. Virginia delegates reportedly arrived in Williamsburg on August 1 with "a great variety of different opinions with respect to the means of redress," although all agreed on opposing parliamentary taxation and Britain's exercise of "arbitrary power." Perhaps because of such disagreement or perhaps because of their uncertainty about their own constitutional status, the more than one hundred participants drafted an association they signed as individuals, leaving those who had elected them to decide for themselves whether to join. In that association, they affirmed their loyalty to the king; blamed the current troubles on "several unconstitutional Acts of the British Parliament"; agreed to nonimportation of all items from Britain or the West Indies, including slaves and excepting only medicines; pledged not to drink any tea, including what they currently owned; and postponed any nonexportation pact for a year. Covertly, without a public announcement, they concurred on keeping the courts closed. Through an unknown process, they also elected seven delegates to the congress, including George Washington, Richard Henry Lee, Patrick Henry, and Peyton Randolph.

When about one hundred South Carolinians convened in Charleston for three days in early July, they faced significant disagreements over commercial strategies. The dispute centered on whether to add nonexportation to nonimportation as a preferred economic tactic. After nearly two days of "warmly contested" debates, the convention chose a compromise proposed by the brothers John and Edward Rutledge, who argued that congressional unanimity would be required, and so definitive resolutions might constrain the decision-making process. The Carolinians thus gave their congressional delegates "full and absolute power to agree to, or propose, whatever they should think would redress the grievances complained of." Yet the attendees were also concerned about being outvoted by northerners, so they decreed that South Carolina would be bound only by those congressional resolutions their own representatives approved—a proviso that would have major consequences at the Philadelphia meeting.

Accordingly, what would otherwise have been even longer debates over economic tactics were deflected onto the question of which men should be chosen for South Carolina's congressional delegation. The Charleston Chamber of Commerce staunchly opposed nonexportation, putting forward a slate of five candidates who concurred with that position. But voting was opened to "every free white person" in the colony, and in the end only two of the chamber's preferred candidates (John Rutledge and Henry Middleton) were selected. The other three, including the resistance leader Christopher Gadsden, came from the ranks of planters and their allies. Despite the open balloting, published accounts of the meeting stressed that it constituted "the largest body of the most respectable inhabitants" ever convened in the colony, having been filled with "gentlemen of the greatest property and character." To assure others that it was not "the meeting of a rabble, and the election of a mob," the organizers explicitly noted that many current and former assemblymen had participated in and voted at the meeting.

The Carolinians took two additional steps. First, they appointed a committee of ninety-nine to serve as a continuing authority until another general meeting could be held. Thirty representatives were named for Charleston (half merchants, half mechanics) and sixty-nine for the rest of the colony—a procedure that William Henry Drayton admitted was "rather unconstitutional," because the outlying parishes did not choose the men designated to represent them. But, he commented, because of "the urgency of the occasion," those involved acquiesced in the irregular arrangement.

Second, the assemblymen moved in early August to legitimize the appointment of congressional delegates through a subterfuge. Lieutenant Governor Bull had prorogued the assembly until August 2. Knowing that he intended to prorogue them again when they convened that day at their regular time of 10:00 a.m., the assemblymen instead met at 8:00. Before Bull could stop them, they swiftly approved resolutions supporting Boston and condemning the Coercive Acts, appointed the designated representatives to the congress, and voted to fund the delegation's expenses. The next day Bull fumed to Dartmouth, "Your lordship will see by this instance with what perseverance, secrecy and unanimity they form and conduct their designs." Thus the South Carolinians managed to make theirs one of the few colonies that appointed their congressional delegates by legislative procedures that at least purported to be regular.

Another was Pennsylvania. As already indicated, the convention in that province was scheduled to meet on July 15, with the assembly convening three days later. Joseph Reed, who was one of about sixty members of the convention but was not an assemblyman, reported that, as was true elsewhere, although the delegates agreed on principles, "warm Debates" developed about the methods of implementing those principles. The Pennsylvania convention criticized the "unconstitutional, oppressive" Coercive Acts but voiced some doubts about nonimportation and nonexportation as immediate tactics. They expressed the hope that "our just remonstrances will, at length, reach the ears of our gracious Sovereign"; therefore, they wanted the congress to "first try the gentler mode of stating our grievances, and making a firm and decent claim of redress." In short, they preferred an initial petition to the king before a commercial boycott was announced, the very strategy favored by Robert Beverley and Bryan Fairfax. But they also voted "by a great majority" (that is, not unanimously) to support a boycott if the congress approved one.

The convention members established a committee to present their resolutions to the assembly and to propose instructions for the colony's delegates to the congress. Those instructions, drafted by John Dickinson, included a willingness to grant specific concessions to Britain: to obey the Navigation Acts; to provide the kingdom voluntarily with necessary revenues; and "to satisfy all damages done to the East India Company." In return, they asked for repeal of the Coercive Acts and the abandonment of Parliament's claims to legislate for and tax the colonies. Any less than that, they insisted, would be "inadmissible." If such negotiations were unsuccessful and the congress opted for a commercial boycott of Britain, the Pennsylvanians unanimously agreed that such an agreement had to be binding and comprehensive, with no exceptions. In the end, though, they declared that the most important goal was unanimity, so the congressional delegates should not feel constrained by the instructions.

When Joseph Reed wrote to Dartmouth to fill him in on the convention's deliberations, he explained that the resolutions on the Coercive Acts "will sound strangely from this Province, which has hitherto been distinguished for its Moderation." He had opposed those resolves in the meeting, he revealed, because he thought them insufficiently conciliatory. By contrast, James Madison—while praising the "elegance and cogency" of Dickinson's prose—believed that the convention's position relied too heavily on the king's benevolence. Rejecting the plan to petition the king first, he asserted that "Delay on our part emboldens our adversaries" and "affords opportunity to our secret enemies to disseminate discord & disunion."

One of the potential enemies who worried Madison distributed an essay to members of the Pennsylvania assembly on the evening of July 21, after the convention's committee had presented the suggested resolutions and instructions earlier that same day. Signing himself "A Freeman," the anonymous author, probably Joseph Galloway, fundamentally challenged the legitimacy of the convention.

He reminded assemblymen that they were meeting "in a *legislative capacity*"; the issue before them was "whether the people of this province shall assert their rights and privileges on *constitutional grounds;* or, deviating from the long known, and securely trodden paths of prudence and regularity, wander into the maizy labyrinths of perplexity and disorder." What, he asked, was the "*legal* authority" for the convention? That body included many respectable gentlemen, but nonetheless its existence relied only on "the authority of the committees." Thus it represented "THE BEGINNING OF REPUBLICANISM." Indeed, "gigantic strides" had now placed "the resolves of the populace above the law, and above the constitution." He admonished his fellow Pennsylvanians, "Deliver down to posterity 'the laws, the rights, the generous plan of power' which your ancestors have delivered to you," and do not open yourselves to criticism for your actions from your descendants. That closing echoed, no doubt deliberately, the perorations found at the end of many statements from men on the other side, such as John Hancock and Dr. Benjamin Rush.

The Freeman essay's argument about the importance of acting constitutionally might well have influenced the assemblymen, because instead of adopting the convention's lengthy resolutions and instructions, they declared unanimously and succinctly that the congress should attempt to obtain redress of America's grievances "upon the most solid constitutional principles" in order to reestablish "union and harmony" between Britain and the colonies. Declining to choose as delegates the men the convention preferred (John Dickinson among them), the assembly selected representatives solely from its own ranks, including Galloway and Thomas Mifflin.

In New York too, extended debates developed over the choice of delegates and the contents of resolutions, but those debates took place primarily in Manhattan, because no colony-wide convention was summoned. Silas Deane and James Rivington both remarked on the "virulence" of political struggles in the city during 1774; the persistence, complexity, and vehemence of the conflicts confirmed the accuracy of their shared observation.

The disputes began in late June when the New York assembly's elected committee of correspondence declined to participate in the choice of congressional delegates. The committee of fifty-one then proposed to act in its place. Yet Peter Van Schaack, a committee member, questioned its authority to name delegates, for that was "not within the Purposes for wh[ich] this Committee was appointed." Despite his objections, the committee on July 4 moved ahead with a plan to appoint five men to a congressional delegation. It considered two competing slates, one proposed by Alexander McDougall and his allies, representing the mechanics, and another supported by more moderate committee members. The latter prevailed; the committee voted for Philip Livingston, James Duane, John Alsop, Isaac Low, and John Jay and called for a citywide vote a few days later to approve them. If the committee members thought that the plan for such a vote would assuage the mechanics, they were seriously mistaken, because their action led to a split in the committee and a monthlong debate involving multiple meetings and competing broadsides.

Once the nominees had been announced, a group of mechanics summoned residents to a meeting chaired by McDougall on the evening of July 6 in "the fields," a large outdoor space, to consider other nominations and adopt resolutions. The men in the fields voiced support for Bostonians, criticized the Port Act, advocated a nonimportation agreement, and pledged to follow the congress's lead. The next day the committee of fifty-one formally censured McDougall for his role in the proceedings. But it also named a subcommittee to draft resolutions on the same topics as those considered by the residents in the fields, "to quiet the minds of the People," as McDougall and his ally Isaac Sears explained to Samuel Adams.

Attendees at a wider city meeting then rejected the committee of fifty-one's slate of nominees. Disagreements over that slate led McDougall and ten of his allies to withdraw from the committee, which nevertheless printed and distributed the resolutions prepared by its subcommittee. Those promised aid to Boston but also contained "an indirect Censure" on that city's destruction of the tea and insisted that only "dire Necessity" should lead to nonimportation. Even the future Loyalist William Smith Jr. pronounced them "pusillanimous," and they were firmly rejected at a meeting at the coffeehouse on July 19.

That presented the committeemen with a dilemma. According to Sears and McDougall, the members were "mortify'd" by the rejections of both their nominees and their proposed resolutions. The committee reacted by appointing another subcommittee (this time including McDougall and Sears) to draft amended resolves. The new version dropped the offensive language about the tea destruction and openly advocated a nonimportation agreement. Perhaps influenced by a July 25 broadside asserting that "the Resolves are not material," the committee then ignored the disputes over the wording of resolutions and scheduled a citywide poll for July 28 to elect delegates. After potential dissidents were satisfied by assurances from the committee's original slate that they would support a nonimportation agreement at the congress, the five men (Low, Alsop, Jay, Livingston, and Duane) were finally chosen as the city's representatives. And the debate over the resolutions was apparently forgotten. Once the election was at last completed, the committee of fifty-one turned to additional matters, such as organizing relief efforts for Boston and addressing letters to other counties in New York, offering the opportunity to name their own congressional delegates.

Cadwallader Colden wrote three times to Dartmouth to keep him informed about these complex events, expressing his disappointment that the "considerable merchants and men of cool temper" on the committee of fifty-one were unable to resist the pressure to name delegates. But he could not have prevented the election had he tried, he explained, and the effort itself would have exposed his weakness, with the result that "the most violent men would have gained great advantage." As it was, the New York delegation consisted of "moderate men," and he had some hope that the congress would adopt "such prudent measures as are calculated to remove the destructive dissensions which subsist between Great Britain and her colonies." In September, he wrote to add that he was now optimistic about the trajectory of the city's politics. The "former Demagogues" had lost their influence; "Gentlemen of Property, and principal Merchants" had begun taking the lead in local meetings. "The licentious Spirit" that had dominated the city was waning, so "we have no more burning of Effigies." Newspapers had also started publishing statements supporting the government.

In Georgia, the governor, Sir James Wright, was less sanguine about current events. He informed Lord Dartmouth in late July that South Carolina's resistance leaders were trying to recruit men in his colony, but admitted that Georgia too had its resident "Male Contents & Violent Liberty People." When men assembled in Savannah on July 27 to discuss what the governor termed "imaginary Grievances" and called for a subsequent, larger meeting "by their own Authority," Wright issued a proclamation to disabuse his fellow Georgians of the belief that such sessions were allowed. On the contrary, he insisted, such gatherings were "unconstitutional, illegal, and punishable by Law." Mimicking New Hampshire's John Wentworth, he ordered residents of the colony to heed his warning or risk the consequences.

Disregarding Wright's proclamation, a group of men gathered at a Savannah tavern on August 10. They adopted resolutions declaring that Americans had all the rights of British subjects, including the right of taxing themselves, and criticized each of the Coercive Acts in turn. But they also voted against sending representatives to the congress. Dissidents later charged that fewer than thirty men had taken part in this meeting. Furthermore, the dissenters maintained, they attempted to enter the inn, but the door was barred against them.

Could a gathering composed of "a few persons in a Tavern, with doors shut," they asked in *The Georgia Gazette,* truly be termed a "General Meeting," as the participants had claimed?

In the aftermath of that session at the tavern, the Reverend Haddon Smith, writing as Mercurius, characterized it as *"unconstitutional."* No "private person," he asserted, could summon others to a meeting "upon any *publick* occasion whatever." Georgians, he contended, should obey only formal acts of their government; "we have nothing to do with resolves illegally entered into without doors." If real grievances were at issue, they should pursue redress in a proper way. But instead the so-called grievances were "creatures of the imagination, mere *non-entities,* that have no shadow of existence."

For his part, Wright took steps to prove that the August 10 resolutions did not represent Georgians' views but had rather been "unfairly and Insolently" drafted by a small "Junto." Unlike any other governor, he called a counter meeting, apparently attended by at least a hundred men from Savannah and environs, who signed a statement disavowing the resolutions. Moreover, he elicited other, similar statements from outlying areas, which were then published in the *Gazette* and which he forwarded to the Colonial Office in London. For example, men from St. Matthew Parish explained that they had been deceived into thinking that the meeting would draft a petition to the king begging relief for the Bostonians; men from St. George Parish declared that they disagreed with the resolutions; and men from St. Paul Parish sought to dissociate themselves from New Englanders altogether. Because Georgians "had no hand in destroying any teas" and did not share in the Bostonians' guilt, they averred, "they can have no business to make themselves partakers of the ill consequences resulting from such a conduct."

Summing up his efforts for Dartmouth, Governor Wright declared that he had done all he could to thwart the designs of Georgia resistance leaders. Even so, he predicted, the future would bring "nothing but cabals and combinations," with Georgians' minds being "continually heated, disturbed and distracted." His proclamation against the August 10 meeting had been deemed "arbitrary and oppressive and an attempt to debar them of their natural and lawful rights and privileges." Like Colden, he revealed that he did not have enough power to stop the multiple "illegal and improper" gatherings. He urged Dartmouth to consider seeking a permanent settlement of the disputes, because now the colonies were characterized by "nothing but jealousies, rancour and ill blood, law and no law, government and no government, dependence and independence, and everything is unhinged and running into confusion." Circumstances were "most disagreeable," he concluded, for anyone like himself who sought "to support law, government and good order and to discharge his duty with honour and integrity."

"DARK DAYS" IN MASSACHUSETTS

Before the Massachusetts House of Representatives was dissolved by Governor Thomas Gage on June 17, it had issued a call for clergymen to designate a colony-wide fast day. The date selected was Thursday, July 14. Remarkably, six sermons delivered that day were later published, thus providing a snapshot of clerical opinion at a crucial moment for the colony. By then, swirling rumors predicted the possible arrest of resistance leaders and their transportation to Britain for trial, and even though there was yet no confirmation that the king had approved the Massachusetts Government Act, the Administration of Justice Act, and the Quebec Act, their provisions had been widely publicized. Accordingly, as the Reverend Peter Whitney of Northborough observed in his fast-day sermon, "this country seems to be in a most alarming and critical situation. So dark a day perhaps North America never saw."

The six ministers lamented conditions in the colony and addressed their origins in religious as well as political terms, blaming the province's woes in part on God's punishment of the people for past misbehavior. Three specified sins directly connected to current events. For Peter Whitney, the fundamental problem was overindulgence in tea, a "*needless* luxury," which had led colonists into "excesses of wickedness." Women especially had engaged in slanderous talk, in "idle, vain and sinful conversation," while imbibing the beverage. Thus the Port Act was perhaps "a just frown of heaven upon the town and country, for their . . . amazing extravagance in the consumption of foreign commodities." To the Reverend Nathan Fiske of Brookfield, Americans' sins originated in oppression, including the ways in which Americans oppressed each other. He argued that even when men did not join "lawless riots," they could still combine to intimidate their fellows and reveal themselves to be "as tyrannical, imperious and oppressive, as arbitrary rulers."

The Reverend John Allen of Salem identified another sin entirely as the source of the colonists' difficulties: "your iniquitous and disgraceful practice of keeping *African* slaves," which contradicted "the natural and unalienable rights of mankind." The claim that slave owners were Christianizing their human chattel, he asserted, was simply a pretense. Becoming one of the first Anglo-American colonists to remark in print on the hypocrisy of those who nominally promoted liberty but ignored "the sacred natural rights and privileges of the *Africans*," he accused slaveholders of perpetuating "this lawless, cruel, inhuman, and abominable practice" while at the same time "fasting, praying, non-importing, non-exporting, remonstrating, resolving, and pleading for a restoration of your charter rights." He asked pointedly, "What is a trifling three penny duty on tea in comparison to the inestimable blessing of liberty to one captive?" Although other Anglo-Americans later similarly remarked on the colonists' hypocrisy, few matched Allen's passion and clarity, which echoed and underscored that of self-identified African authors who published such sentiments in New England newspapers in 1774.

The Massachusetts clergymen who preached on July 14 of course blamed Great Britain as well as divine judgment for their colony's circumstances. Thaddeus Maccarty lamented Parliament's imposition of taxes on America as "contrary to the principles of sound policy." Timothy Hilliard focused on the injustice of the Coercive Acts, especially the Port Act, which left "thousands of innocent persons . . . to perish with hunger, if not relieved by the charity of their friends." The other four emphasized Britain's attempt to seize Americans' property without their consent. "Is it just or usual for one nation to tax the private properties of another nation or province, and oblige them under penalties of death to pay the tax?" inquired Allen dramatically. Samuel Webster charged that the British "threaten to take away all our *liberty* and *property,* and to reduce us to *slavery* and *beggary.*" Yet Fiske stressed that Americans needed to oppose British policies lawfully.

Remember, he told his congregation, "the respect and submission we owe to those who are cloathed with authority." For his part, Whitney cited John Locke as he insisted that people were required not to obey oppressive rulers but instead to "resist them as public robbers and the destroyers of mankind and of human happiness." Still, Whitney, like Fiske, counseled his congregants against lawless behavior. Averring that "a factious, licentious, and tumultuous spirit" prevailed among some New Englanders, he warned that liberty "may be as much abused as government and power, leading into measures equally tyrannical and oppressive."

Peter Whitney and Nathan Fiske thus explicitly joined John Greenough in questioning the tactic that one historian has termed "patriotic terror"—that is, the use of mobbing and other coercive measures to intimidate those who publicly aligned themselves with Great Britain. Those two clerics could well have been reacting in part to news of

An unsigned illustration by Paul Revere from the first issue of *The Royal American Magazine,* January 1774. At center is the Long Wharf. Although the view dates from an earlier period, Boston harbor must have resembled this during the British blockade under the Port Act. Letters identified harbor landmarks.

a recent incident in Connecticut involving Francis Green, a prominent Boston merchant who had been one of the Addressers of Thomas Hutchinson.

On July 11, a Boston newspaper reprinted a story from *The Norwich Packet* about what had happened to Green a few days earlier while he was on a business trip to Windham and Norwich; the same narrative also appeared in another Boston paper on the fast day, July 14. Green was staying at a tavern in Windham when local residents realized that he was "one of the insiduous [*sic*] crew who fabricated and subscribed the adulatory address" to the departing governor of the neighboring colony. They gathered at the tavern and told him to leave town immediately. He resisted and remained overnight, but early the next morning a large group threatened "exalting him upon a cart," which (reported the newspapers) "operated so powerfully that he decamped with precipitation." He then traveled to Norwich, where the news of his journey had preceded him. When he entered town, he was greeted by "*the grave digger* . . . ringing the meeting-house bell." A "numerous and respectable" crowd assembled, ordering him out of town. He again proved reluctant to leave, the *Packet* noted, but "a horse and cart was provided, so that he had no other alternative, but to mount the cart or his own carriage; he chose the latter, and set out properly attended, with drums beating, horns blowing, &c." Francis Green later deposed that he thought his life was in danger and that the Norwich crowd "pelted me with great rage and violence, and thus obstructed me in my business, to my great injury," as townspeople followed him out of town for almost half a mile.

Although these crowd actions occurred in Connecticut, they were directed at a wealthy Bostonian and undoubtedly shocked not only the other Addressers but also all who regarded themselves as "friends to government." In early July, Governor Gage alerted Dartmouth to "the usurpation and tyranny established here by edicts of town meetings enforced by mobs" and admitted that he was finding it difficult to "spirit up every friend to government, and . . . encourage many to speak and act publicly." Some attributed the troubles in Boston specifically to Samuel Adams, "a poor man with very powerful wrangling abilities." Those called "Tories," Henry Hulton's sister Ann told a friend, were "intimidated and overpowered by the Numbers, and the Arts, and Machinations of the Leader [Adams], who Governs absolutely, the Minds and the Passions of the People."

Whether or not Adams as an individual had the influence in Boston that such contemporary observers accorded him, after the victory in the late June town meeting the committee of correspondence cooperated effectively with the selectmen in coping with the difficult conditions caused by the blockade. Even though the Port Act allowed local coastal trade in food and fuel, customs officers ruled that foodstuffs shipped from other colonies had to travel overland to Boston from Salem, the only legal port of entry, which slowed the flow of goods. Despite that obstacle, assistance from other colonies began to arrive in July. The committee on which Thomas Greenough served distributed cash, food, and wood to the needy, especially widows and children, and the selectmen began to use donated funds to employ both skilled and unskilled laborers on public works projects. Such practices seem to have fueled wildly contradictory rumors that circulated around town. One claimed that the arriving aid was minimal, its amount misrepresented by the authorities; another that, on the contrary, the city and its wealthiest residents were growing rich from the many generous contributions; and a third that the other provinces would support Boston only until they had taken control of all the commerce with Britain, and then that they would abandon the city to its unenviable fate.

Still, the presence of so many troops unexpectedly helped to support the people of Boston and vicinity, because the soldiers had to be supplied with food and other necessities. Officers and their families occupied local housing, with increased demand raising rents and providing a crucial source of income for anyone who owned suitable buildings. Shipyard owners exploited what emerged as the Port Act's major loophole: it did not forbid the operation of Boston's active ship construction and repair business. Vessels had to arrive or leave without cargoes, but no provision of the act prevented work from being done on ships in the port. In early August, Admiral Samuel Graves lamented that a "great number of handicrafts and other people" were still working in Boston's shipyards, thereby preventing the "general distress" that he assumed the Port Act was intended to cause.

Several Boston residents commented that during the blockade the poor were employed; the wealthy shifted their businesses to other locations; and the middling sort suffered the most serious financial consequences. One such family was Richard and Mary Cranch; Mary told her sister Abigail Adams in August that she and her husband were discussing moving out of town because of the "unnumberd distresses" they were suffering. Ironically, noted Nathaniel Coffin, particularly hard hit were the Addressers, "against whom such a Spirit prevails as cuts them off from reaping any part of the benefit of the Trade we have left[,] for no body will deal with them."

For the last half of July and the first week of August, Bostonians apprehensively awaited the arrival of the *Scarborough* man-of-war with copies of the Massachusetts Government and Administration of Justice Acts. Even though their purported texts had been published in the colonies months earlier, the statutes could not be implemented until Gage received the official documents. On August 6, about a month after the ship was first expected, it finally sailed into the harbor. Gage moved quickly to swear in the newly appointed members to the reconstituted council, but the astute Nathaniel Coffin had already accurately predicted the outcome. The new councillors, he warned, would be "scattered all over the Province" and locally well known as "friends to government." When their appointments became public, "every art will be made use of to intimidate and prevent their acceptance of a mandamus, and if any of them should notwithstanding be hardy enough to accept, they will be exposed to every species of Indignity & affront." Which of them "in his Senses" would accept a position that would expose them to "all these Evils"? He knew that he certainly would not. For her part, Mercy Otis Warren pronounced the establishment of the council "the last comic scene we shall see Exhibite'd in the state Farce which has for several years been playing off," foreseeing a "Tragic Part of the Drama" still to come.

On August 8, Governor Gage tendered the oath of office to eleven mandamus councillors, and on the sixteenth, to thirteen more, but at the first official meeting of the council on August 31 only thirteen attendees were recorded. Some appointees declined from the outset and others named in the law were unavailable for one reason or another, but the primary reason for the low participation was intimidation, just as Coffin had foreseen. To quote Thomas Young, "The rage of the people against these traitorous villains who have thus easily sided with a foreign usurpation, is not easily described." The men accepted office as a group, but one by one many were forced to resign by crowds that gathered to threaten them, their families, or their property with physical harm. It was the first use in 1774 of systematic, rather than isolated, instances of patriotic terror. The details differed, but the results were the same. Only a few men resisted the pressure; some who initially refused to resign later did so. All those who continued in office fled to Boston for safety, regardless of where in Massachusetts they lived.

For example, when Timothy Ruggles of Hardwick headed to Boston to assume his post on the council, he was met on the road by fifty men armed with clubs, who did not stop him but warned him never to return home. After Daniel Leonard likewise left for Boston to join the council, "sundry Muskets" fired on his house in Taunton in the night, breaking windows and frightening his pregnant wife. Abijah Willard of Lancaster, caught like Francis Green while on a business trip in Connecticut, was threatened with imprisonment until he agreed to resign; and Joshua Loring, whose house was attacked on two successive nights, "thought it most prudent to leave" on the second, abandoning his son and the rest of his family to face the mob without him. Seeking, in effect, a two-for-one impact, a crowd in the Worcester area pursued two local councillors in succession, first Timothy Paine (who resigned under pressure) and later John Murray (whose son warned him to stay in Boston, whence he had already fled). Among those who quickly resigned their commissions were Thomas Hutchinson Jr. and his relative Andrew Oliver; among those who did not were Daniel Leonard, Joshua Loring, and Timothy Ruggles.

On September 2, Gage informed Dartmouth of these events, enclosing narratives by Leonard, Loring, and Paine, along with written resignations of other putative councillors. He explained that for safety reasons the Mandamus Council had been forced to meet in Boston rather than Salem, contrary to the requirements of the Port Act. At its first meeting, the council advised Gage against sending troops out of Boston, concluding that the disturbances were so widespread that it was unclear where such troops could usefully go. The frightened councillors, concerned primarily about their own defense, told him that "the first and only step now to take was to secure the friends of Government in Boston and to reinforce the troops here with as many more as could possibly be collected." Accordingly, he had already asked General Haldimand to send soldiers from New York, where "the people in general [are] moderate and well affected to all measures but taxation." But in Massachusetts, by contrast, he told Dartmouth, "civil government is near its end."

The attacks on the mandamus councillors, as widespread and effective as they were, would not by themselves have served as an adequate justification for the governor's judgment about the end of "civil government" in the Bay Colony. But Gage's long report to Dartmouth revealed that courts too could no longer function. The Massachusetts Government Act had changed the method of selecting jurors and made justices of the peace and inferior court judges liable to removal by the governor. Consequently, people throughout the province were refusing to participate in court sessions, and in some jurisdictions large crowds gathered to stop the courts from meeting. Dr. Joseph Warren asserted that because people now thought the courts were "unconstitutional," any judicial decisions could be ignored. The judges of the Superior Court, who had on September 1 experienced the unanimous rejection of service by grand and petit jurors summoned for a scheduled session, were cautioning Gage about "the impossibility of carrying on the business of their court in any part of the province." The governor pledged to try to avoid "any bloody crisis" for as long as he could but stressed that "conciliating, moderation, reasoning is over; nothing can be done but by forcible means." The people were "numerous, worked up to a fury, and not a Boston rabble but the freeholders and farmers of the country." Nothing decisive should be undertaken without a firm foundation, he concluded, but he still thought order could be restored, though he did not specify how.

Massachusetts citizens also brazenly refused to obey other provisions of the law. In both Salem and Boston, town meetings were summoned without the authorization from Gage the act required. In Boston, town leaders claimed that the meetings in question were merely adjourned from a previous date; in Salem, the governor ordered the arrest of local committeemen for "unlawfully and seditiously causing the people to assemble." Even so, they posted bail and were soon released from custody.

Various ad hoc bodies, quickly convened during the month of August after the official texts of the acts arrived, adopted resolves that mirrored those drafted in other colonies earlier in the summer, but also went beyond them in the strength of their opposition to British authority. The Middlesex County convention, for instance, declared that submitting to the acts would "annihilate the last Vestiges of Liberty in this Province," insisting that disobedience was justified "by God and the World." The Boston committee, meeting with counterparts from several nearby counties, like Joseph Warren proclaimed the "unconstitutionality" of the courts under the amended charter, simultaneously calling for the establishment of "Referree Committees" as replacements. And nearly as notably, the Worcester County convention recommended not only that towns in the county not submit to laws "altering our free constitution" but also that they "retain in their own hands, what moneys may be due from them severally to the province treasury, till public tranquility be restored."

The implications of the statements from Boston and Worcester were striking: one called for establishing novel judicial bodies, and the other recommended withholding funds owed to the colony's government. Both presaged independence, as did a stunning argument from a member of one town committee: "If there is any force in the Late acts of Parlament, they have Sett us, a float, that is have thrown us into a State of Nature; we Now have a fair Oppertunity of Choosing what form of Goverment."

One Bostonian predicted in late August that only a "few days will elapse before the Province is declared in open rebellion." And so some Massachusetts residents began to underscore the need for caution. In June, John Dickinson had written to Josiah Quincy Jr. to warn that no colony should engage in "breaking the line of opposition, by advancing too hastily before the rest. The one which dares to betray the common cause, by rushing forward, . . . will inevitably and utterly perish." In the midst of the turmoil of late August, Quincy replied, noting that Dickinson's comments were "no doubt just" but adding that behaving cautiously was difficult "under the scourge of publick oppression." Still, others in Massachusetts echoed Dickinson's warning; members of the Marblehead committee of correspondence, for instance, told their Boston counterpart that they "apprehend great

Danger of Hostilities commencing in the province, unless the people can be dissuaded from acting too much on their own Judgments." The committee predicted that "once the Sword is drawn, We must expect a long and bloody War," but insisted that "the greatest Care is to be taken to avoid it while good prospects remain of it being unnecessary." Therefore, they urged "Discipline" for the populace.

By the time the new councillors were attacked and the court sessions halted, the Massachusetts delegation to the Continental Congress had already left for Philadelphia. John Andrews did not witness their departure, but on August 10 he learned from others that "they made a very respectable parade" that morning in a coach and four, "preceded by two white servants well mounted and arm'd, with four blacks behind in livery, two on horseback and two footmen." He expressed the hope that "their joint deliberations will effect something for our relief; more particularly to concert such measures as may be adopted by the *Mother Country,* so as to settle a friendship between us that may be lasting and permanent." Abigail Adams too hoped for a peaceful settlement, but a letter she addressed to her husband, John, on August 19 while he was en route was dominated by her anxiety. "The Rocks and quick Sands appear upon every Side. What course you can or will take is all wrapt up in the Bosom of futurity," she wrote. "Uncertainty and expectation leave the mind great Scope." She and many other Americans awaited the news from Philadelphia with combined hope and fear.

CHAPTER 5

EXPECTING GREAT THINGS

In late August 1774, Nathaniel Coffin disdained the Massachusetts men sent to Philadelphia as "worth nothing." The wealthy James Bowdoin, the only exception in Coffin's mind, refused election, citing his wife's poor health. Coffin deemed that "a very frivolous reason," attributing Bowdoin's refusal instead to his desire not to risk his fortune by participating in the extralegal gathering. The customs officer remarked sarcastically that "great things are expected" from the congress, with Bostonians predicting that any measures the congress adopted would "soon bring Great Britain upon her Knees," even though no one knew what the congress would recommend. Coffin himself thought that "this matter will end in nothing more than a humble remonstrance & Petition to the King in his parliament." But Coffin's cynical attitude was not shared by those with opposing political views. Using almost the same language as Coffin but with very different import, Joseph Greenleaf wrote in anticipation to his brother-in-law, the delegate Robert Treat Paine, "We expect great things from your councils."

The respectful attention the Massachusetts delegation attracted as it journeyed to Philadelphia revealed that many other colonists concurred with Greenleaf. John Adams recorded in his diary that as the delegates approached New Haven, Connecticut, on August 16, they were met by a large number of horsemen, and "all the Bells in Town were sett to ringing, and the People Men, Women and Children, were crouding at the Dorrs and Windows as if it was to see a Coronation."

The next day they dined with a group of men and women, and "were very genteelly entertained, and spent the whole Afternoon in Politicks, the Depths of Politicks." When they arrived in New York on the twentieth, Alexander McDougall gave them a city tour, ending at the coffeehouse, where Adams caught up with newspapers from Virginia that had not yet reached Boston. There too they were entertained at meals, and they met the "Liberty Printer" of *The New-York Journal*, John Holt. At Princeton, they toured the college campus and were introduced to its president, the Scots Presbyterian clergyman John Witherspoon, whom Adams described as a "high" Son of Liberty. And finally, when they reached Philadelphia on August 29, "dirty, dusty, and fatigued," they were greeted outside the city by a sizable group of men, including delegates who had arrived earlier. Despite their exhaustion, they immediately repaired to the City Tavern, "the most genteel one in America," where they encountered still more delegates and prominent Philadelphians.

On or soon after their arrival, Adams, Paine, and the others would have been able to read letters from New England dispatched to them while they were en route. Such correspondence could only have heightened their sense of impending crisis, for the letters openly discussed the possibility of war and bloodshed. Thomas Cushing's wife, Deborah, declared that she hoped "in this Diffacult Day [you] have the presence of God with you & his spirit leading you . . . & may the Blessing of many thousend reddy to perish fall upon you." Dr. Joseph Warren wrote twice to Samuel Adams during the last weeks of August, reporting mandamus councillors' resignations and expressing fears of "Bloodshed" to come. John Adams heard from Joseph Hawley of Northampton, who predicted that the Massachusetts Government Act "will soon annihilate every thing of value in the charter, [and] introduce perfect despotism." In Hawley's opinion, the congress needed to develop "a certain clear plan" for accumulating sufficient arms and ammunition to supply those who were prepared to resist British authority and to provide the means to enforce a new government's decrees.

More than two months earlier, John Adams had remarked in his diary about how daunting he found the prospect of being a delegate to the congress. "I feel myself unequal to this Business," he wrote;

the "new . . . grand scene open before me" suggested many questions. "What can be done?" Should the congress draft a petition, but if so, to what person or body? "What will such Consultations avail? Deliberations alone will not do." He concluded his June ruminations, "In every Thing I feel unutterable Anxiety—God grant us Wisdom, and Fortitude!" Surely Adams had not changed his mind by the time he reached Philadelphia, and undoubtedly many other delegates echoed such thoughts but did not record them.

ADVISING THE CONGRESS

As the summer weeks passed and Americans' attention turned increasingly toward the Continental Congress, colonial printers began to receive submissions for newspaper essays and pamphlets that not only commented on the current political scene but also aimed their advice squarely at the men who were to convene in Philadelphia. For example, Thomson Mason penned a series of nine essays published in Clementina Rind's *Virginia Gazette,* reviewing the political and legal history of the British colonies, questioning any plan to have Americans reimburse the East India Company, and arguing against choosing nonimportation as a tactic. "Juba," from Connecticut, opposed nonimportation alone, contending that nonexportation too was necessary. An anonymous author from New Jersey proposed that the congress admit Parliament's power to tax trade goods, including tea, yet reject other British levies. Another New Jersey resident listed a series of questions he thought the congress should consider: Because we declare that Parliament cannot tax us, but admit that we owe our fair share of imperial expenses, how should we pay? Should we compensate the EIC? If we adopt economic tactics, do we boycott trade with Ireland or the West Indies as well as with England? And should sessions of the congress be closed, or open to the public?

As the publications multiplied, so too did the complaints of would-be authors who had difficulty publishing their views. Uniformly, such writers had submitted pieces that questioned the dominant narrative of resistance to British policies. For instance, in the late summer of 1774, when John Drinker Jr. published his *Observations on the Late Popular Measures,* he disclosed that he had offered part of it to two different printers before William and Thomas Bradford accepted that essay. Presumably, the trouble arose because Drinker condemned "those ambitious spirits who are fond of *any* opportunity of giving themselves consequence with the populace." He charged that the "sinister zeal" of such men had led to "many well meaning persons [being] duped," so that "the traiterous fire of false spirits" had begun to prevail over "the true strength of a real and virtuous patriotism."

The Bradfords published the first of the two essays that made up Drinker's *Observations* in a supplement to their *Pennsylvania Journal* on August 17, but not the second, internally dated August 20. No publisher was listed on the pamphlet's title page; thus *Observations* became the first of numerous publications with a conservative bent that failed to publicly identify their printers. Furthermore, the Bradfords added a note after the essay in their newspaper, explaining that they had published it in part to disprove Drinker's complaint about his lack of access to the press. He either was "misinformed or means to abuse the public" with such an assertion, they insisted. They would uphold the ideal of freedom of the press, "but will any say that this requires the publishing in a news-paper every peice that may be sent to a printer?" They opened their *Journal* to political discussions and debates, but that did not mean they should publish an "inflammatory declamation." They would continue to reject any essay, "from whatever quarter it may come, which, without throwing light on the subject, is only calculated to inflame and divide."

In his pamphlet, Drinker commented on the Bradfords' note, claiming that he spoke as well for other "respectable inhabitants" who had expressed "uneasiness" to him about press bias "as a publick evil, and grievous hardship." He was particularly concerned about complaints he had heard from people outside Philadelphia who had access to publications on only one side, even though "the safety of their lives and fortunes" depended on the outcome of the political debates.

This dialogue between Drinker and the Bradfords exposed the tensions that confronted colonial printers in 1774. A scholar has characterized the struggle as one between an "open press," impartial and open to all submissions, regardless of political viewpoint, and a "free press," dedicated to defending American liberty. Traditionally, printers had adopted the former model, because they had difficulty generating enough income and could not afford to alienate potential customers by taking positions on controversial issues. But in the heated political atmosphere in 1765 and thereafter such practices became increasingly hard to sustain. Printers started to line up on one side or the other, most of them supporting American resistance to Britain. The Bradfords fell into that category but clearly remained sufficiently committed to the other model as late as mid-August 1774 that they were willing to publish Drinker's first essay, although not without adding a disclaimer. One prominent colonial printer who publicly proclaimed his commitment to impartiality in 1774 was James Rivington, whose masthead for *Rivington's New-York Gazetteer* included the phrase "printed at his ever open and uninfluenced press" after early May. But Rivington became less and less able to maintain that position as the months passed.

Between late July and early September, four Americans wrote pamphlets offering advice to or commenting on the congress that was to convene in Philadelphia. The first to appear in print, Thomas Jefferson's *Summary View of the Rights of British America,* constituted his draft of instructions for the Virginia delegates to the congress, published not by him but through the intervention of his political allies, probably in late July. William Henry Drayton's *Letter from Freeman of South-Carolina* carried an internal date of August 10, so it was composed shortly after the South Carolina assembly officially designated congressional delegates. The other two criticized the resistance movement but not the congress. The Reverend Jonathan Boucher of Maryland, later an outspoken Loyalist, almost certainly penned the anonymous *Letter from a Virginian, to the Members of the Congress to Be Held at Philadelphia.* The fourth pamphlet, *The American Querist,* was at the time attributed to others, but is now known to have been written by the Reverend Thomas Bradbury Chandler, a New Jersey Anglican cleric. An internal reference reveals that at least some of it was composed after August 18.

Jefferson's *Summary View* began by describing Parliament as "the legislature of one part of an empire" and the king as "no more than the chief officer of the people, . . . and consequently subject to their superintendance." He followed that with his version of Virginia's history, contending that the emigrants had voluntarily submitted to British laws and to the monarch, "who was thereby made the central

link connecting the several parts of the empire." Having thus questioned Parliament's right to rule the colonies, Jefferson argued that "a
series of oppressions, . . . pursued unalterably," revealed Parliament's
"deliberate and systematical plan of reducing us to slavery." He then
methodically analyzed statutes adopted since 1763, with special attention to the Coercive Acts, before moving on to other, longer-standing
grievances, such as the monarch's delays in approving colonial statutes.
He advocated a congressional address to the king, composed "with
that freedom of language and sentiment which becomes a free people
claiming their rights, as derived from the laws of nature, and not as
the gift of their chief magistrate."

Jefferson ended his proposed instructions by speaking to the king
directly in the voice of the congress. "No longer persevere in sacrificing the rights of one part of the empire to the inordinate desires
of another," he exhorted George III, "but deal out to all equal and
impartial right. Let no act be passed by any one legislature which
may infringe on the rights and liberties of another." Such an arrangement, he concluded, would ensure a continuing connection between
America and Britain.

Jefferson's radical statement of colonial equality in the empire was
unique in the summer of 1774. William Henry Drayton's *Letter from
Freeman* concerned itself rather with a series of specific grievances he
thought the congress should emphasize—the Coercive Acts, the Quebec Act, and the monarch's supervisory role in colonial government
generally. With more stress on legal history and fewer ringing phrases
than Jefferson's, Drayton's pamphlet insisted firmly that the issue was
not taxation without consent but rather whether Britain—he did not
distinguish between the monarch and Parliament—"has a constitutional right to exercise *Despotism* over America." Even so, the remedy
he proposed dealt primarily with taxation: he urged the creation of
an American assembly that would determine the colonies' appropriate
monetary contributions to the empire. He exclaimed in conclusion,
"The Eyes and Attention of America, nay of Europe, are fixed upon
the American Congress—O Deputies! I doubt not, that you will act
worthy of such an expectation."

Boucher's *Letter from a Virginian* began as Drayton ended, by praising the members of the congress. They had been "chosen as freely

as the Circumstances of the Times would admit," involving fewer machinations than for "a Seat in many of our legal Provincial Assemblies." The word "legal" implied that the congress was *illegal,* but no matter: the congressmen's "Opinions will have the Effect of Laws, on the Minds of the People, and your Resolves may decide the Fate of America." The clergyman accordingly urged the congressmen to think carefully about their actions. Then he embarked on an analysis that he claimed would uncover "whether the present Discontents are founded on Truth or Ignorance."

Like Jefferson and Drayton, Boucher turned to history for answers, but he interpreted that history differently. Charters, he argued, rendered the colonies subordinate to Parliament as well as to the king, so congressmen should not claim any exemption from parliamentary authority. He focused particularly on the futility of opposition to the "trifling" tea duty, levied "on a Luxury, . . . unknown to our Ancestors," and downplayed the importance of the Boston Port Act ("little more than a temporary Suspension, of the Trade, of that City, until Restitution, which God, and Man calls aloud for, be made"). Commercial retaliation against Britain would not work, he insisted; instead, congressmen had to devise a means of paying America's fair share of imperial costs while reconciling that method with their definition of "the peculiar and inestimable Rights of an Englishman." Because "the best and the wisest Men, the Friends, as well as the Enemies of America, differ in their Opinions," achieving a consensus might be difficult. Crucially, they needed to warn their fellow Americans against "wantonly draw[ing] their Swords," for "the uncertain events of a War" might result.

The other pamphlet published just prior to the meeting of the Continental Congress took a unique approach: Thomas Bradbury Chandler's *American Querist* asked a series of one hundred rhetorical questions. The publication history of Chandler's clever production suggests its significance, for it went through at least five printings and seemingly aroused special enmity. Two editions published by James Rivington appeared in New York; a third, probably also from New York and perhaps by Rivington, lacked publication information on the title page; a fourth was printed in Boston; and a fifth came out in London in 1775. The two attributed to Rivington, one labeled "tenth edition" and one "eleventh edition" (though no prior designated "editions" have been found), carried a dramatic note on the title page: "This Pamphlet, on the 8th Day of September last, was, in full Conclave of the Sons of Liberty in New-York, committed to the Flames by the Hands of their Common Executioner; as it contains some Queries they cannot, and others they will not answer!"

A brief comment by John Holt in the September 8 issue of his *New-York Journal* linked Poplicola's publications from the previous year to Boucher's and Chandler's, all with known New York printers but unidentified authors. He described the *Querist's* one hundred ques-

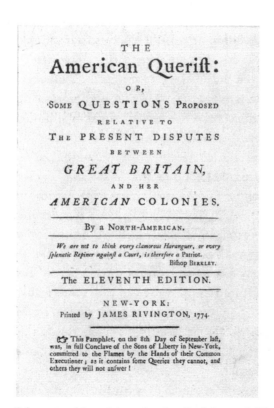

This printing of the pamphlet claimed to be the "eleventh," but other than one similarly labeled the "tenth," no other printings have been identified. Because it is said to have been publicly burned in "September last," it must have been printed no earlier than October 1774, and perhaps later. Rivington was still identifying himself as the printer on the title page, a practice he abandoned for conservative publications later in the fall.

tions as "trifling and impertinent." The pamphlet contained "ground-less and invidious reflections," and so "deserve[d] to be treated with the greatest contempt by every lover of American freedom," Holt asserted. Assuming that the title page of the so-called tenth and eleventh editions of *The American Querist* correctly described the events on September 8 after the newspaper appeared, Holt's call for treating the pamphlet with "the greatest contempt" could well have led to its public destruction.

Chandler's initial seven queries complained, as John Drinker Jr. did, of a lack of access to the press, starting with the very first: "Whether *Americans* have not a right to speak their sentiments on subjects of government; and whether all attempts to check and discourage freedom of speech . . . are not to be considered as unwarrantable usurpations?" Then Chandler drew analogies between the colonies' "political body" and human bodies sickened by fever and inflammation, and between parent and child. Number 13 asked, "Whether some degree of respect be not always due from inferiors to superiors, and especially from children to parents," and number 15, should a parent "put up with such disrespectful and abusive treatment from children, as *Great Britain* has lately received from her colonies"?

The clergyman next posed a set of political questions about the colonies' position in the empire: Can there be "any medium between being subjects and not subjects" (18); have the colonies any "*direct* evidence" of an exemption from parliamentary taxation (22); if the colonists are not subjects, how can they claim the protection of British laws (28)? After a series of inquiries pointing out that Americans had repeatedly altered their positions on parliamentary taxation, he asked in number 60, was it not obvious that "nothing less will satisfy the colonies, than an absolute renunciation of all claims of authority or jurisdiction, in the *British* parliament"?

Query 74 echoed the theme of John Bullman's Charleston sermon: "Whether interested, designing men . . . or ignorant men, bred to the lowest occupations—are any of them qualified for the direction of political affairs, or ought to be trusted with it?" Query 76 mirrored concerns voiced in Massachusetts: Have not the colonies been ruled by "unprincipled *mobs*" for the last decade, creating "an iniquitous and tyranical government"? Then, nearing the end, Chandler turned to the congress. In query 91, he revealed his reliance on that new source of authority in America, regardless of its unconstitutional origins: "Whether full confidence ought not to be reposed in the wisdom, the prudence, and patriotic spirit of our representatives at the congress, who are generally men of property, and have much more to risque than most of their constituents?" He followed up with number 92: "Whether it be not time for our farmers and mechanics, and labourers, to return to their business, and the care of their families; and all serious Christians to a sense of their duty?" The remaining queries focused on religious principles of subjection to proper authority, with the concluding number 100 driving the point home: "Whether it be not a matter both of worldly wisdom, and of indispensible Christian Duty, in every *American,* to *fear the Lord and the King, and to meddle not with them that are GIVEN TO CHANGE?"*

After his many strongly worded criticisms of the ideas and actions of the resistance movement, Chandler's remarks about the Continental Congress were therefore framed so as to reflect an underlying optimism about the possibility of a positive outcome from the congress's deliberations. His comments supply an important reminder of the congress's origins in May and June 1774: as a moderate alternative to Boston's call for an immediate commercial boycott of British goods. Chandler and others, including Jonathan Boucher, hoped that the congress, irregularly chosen though it was, could become the vehicle for the reconciliation with Britain they desired. Unlike Nathaniel Coffin, Chandler emphasized the relatively high social and economic status of the congressmen, which accorded with his denigration of farmers, mechanics, and laborers, who he thought were currently showing inadequate deference to superiors. In early September, the course the congress would take was as yet unknown and uncertain. But events in Massachusetts would soon have a major impact on the intercolonial meeting.

"LIKE A SHIP IN A GRATE STORM"

Most of the congressmen gathering in Philadelphia had not met before, and many of them, like John Adams, had never previously journeyed to the city on the Delaware. Adams, for one, filled his diary with first impressions of his new colleagues. William Livingston (New Jersey) was not "elegant or genteel" but was reported to be "very sensible, and learned"; the Virginians Peyton Randolph ("large, well looking") and Richard Bland ("learned, bookish") were part of the delegation Adams deemed "the most spirited and consistent, of any." As for the brothers Rutledge from South Carolina, John—the older—showed "nothing of the profound, sagacious, brilliant, or sparkling" and seemed "Cunning," whereas Edward was "sprightly but not deep" and "good natured, though conceited." (In late October, after weeks of acquaintance with "Young Ned Rutledge," Adams would write much more critically of him: he was "a Peacock—excessively vain, excessively weak, and excessively variable and unsteady—jejune, inane, and puerile.")

Regardless of how they assessed each other as individuals, the congressmen immediately confronted two collective responsibilities: selecting a place to convene and defining the rules that would guide their deliberations. Because some delegates from the twelve participating colonies arrived late, they officially assembled first on Monday, September 5. They agreed to survey two possible meeting sites: Carpenters' Hall, offered by the local tradesmen's society, and the assembly chamber of the Pennsylvania State House, offered by Joseph Galloway, Speaker of the assembly and the most prominent Pennsylvania delegate. They went first to Carpenters' Hall and, at the suggestion of a South Carolinian, decided to look no further, because the venue was "in all respects suitable." One attribute that might have attracted delegates to the hall was the city library's location in a room of the same building, for the librarian later commented that congressmen made "great & constant use" of the books during their sessions.

But the choice of Carpenters' Hall, especially without assessing the assembly chamber as an alternative, constituted a significant rebuke to Galloway. Another rebuke followed: the delegates chose as their secretary one of his adversaries in Pennsylvania politics, Charles Thomson. Galloway observed about the two selections that "the New Yorkers and myself and a few others finding a great majority [in favor] did not think it prudent to oppose [them]." Galloway concluded that other delegates had reached both decisions privately before the meeting.

Congressional rules, though, had to be decided by consensus after an open debate. Because they could not agree on another method, the delegates on September 6 determined that each colony would have one vote. No one could speak more than twice on any one topic without permission. They established two committees, each of which would have members from every province. One would "state the rights of the Colonies in general," explain how those rights had been "violated or infringed," and identify "the means most proper" to restore them. The second would focus on "the several Statutes, which affect the trade and Manufactures of the colonies." Significantly, the delegates decided that their deliberations would be secret, the doors would be shut against outsiders, and they swore not to reveal details until after the proceedings had been published at the end of the meeting. Finally, in a deliberately inclusive gesture, they named as their chaplain a local Anglican cleric, Jacob Duché.

The decision to keep the content of congressional debates confidential, when coupled with the secretary's minimal notes and sketchy eventual publications, meant that both contemporaries and historians have found it difficult to unearth the details of delegates' discussions and disagreements. Delegates tended not to write comprehensively about how they reached their decisions to outsiders, even their relatives. John Adams and James Duane both kept personal notes of important debates, and others, like Silas Deane, did the same occasionally. Still, accounts of the proceedings must be pieced together from fragments.

Two of the three most informative surviving contemporary narratives of congressional discussions preceded the adoption of the secrecy rule. Galloway wrote to his friend William Franklin on September 3 and 5, fully describing the initial organizing process, but he then evidently ceased similar communications until after the congress adjourned and the rule of confidentiality adopted on the sixth no longer applied. Franklin forwarded those letters to Lord Dartmouth without Galloway's knowledge, and Dartmouth failed to follow the New Jersey governor's injunction to keep the letters "entirely secret."

By late February 1775, Benjamin Franklin and others in London heard it "whisper'd" that Galloway had supplied the ministry with "private Intelligence" about congressional proceedings, and rumors claimed that John Jay served as a similar source. Jay could well have been the (unknown) author of a third extant letter, filled with leaked information about the debates over commercial policy, which will be discussed later in this chapter. The rumors in London revealed the significance and staying power of gossip about leaks from the congress, and the later missive to Cadwallader Colden, if not from Jay, surely came from another member of the New York delegation. But even the leaks supplied only incomplete information.

The first session on September 6 began with the routine business already noted but also moved into a substantive discussion recorded in part by John Adams. Patrick Henry, he noted, declared that "all Government is at an End. . . . All America is thrown into one Mass." John Jay disagreed. Government has not ceased, he observed; a "new Constitution" was not yet required. Henry's and Jay's remarks appear to have been provoked by a pamphlet penned by the Reverend John Witherspoon, which was distributed to the delegates at the outset of their meeting. In contrast to colonists who expressed concern about the irregularity of congressional elections, Witherspoon contended that the votes of legal assemblies were not required to select delegates, whose legitimacy rested instead on "the great law of reason, the first principles of the social union, and the multitude collectively." Rather than worrying about legal forms, the congress should "unite the colonies, and make them one body," Witherspoon argued. After such a stunning reinterpretation of the congress's extralegal standing, though, the college president followed up with conventional recommendations, including declaring loyalty to the king while nonetheless denying Parliament's authority to tax the colonies.

The congress's deliberations had not proceeded very far that day before they were interrupted by an express rider with a shocking report relayed from Boston: six men had been killed opposing redcoat troops confiscating gunpowder from a local arsenal, and the British had begun bombarding the city with cannon from men-of-war in the harbor. In Philadelphia, rumors quickly spread that "All New England was in Arms." John Adams found the report "confused" and "alarming," adding in his diary, "God grant it may not be found true." The city responded by muffling church bells, as if for mourning, and ringing them continually the rest of the day. Before the story reached Pennsylvania, it had already triggered an uproar in New England and frightened New Yorkers too.

A congressman later recounted that although the story was "much doubted" from the beginning, the congress considered becoming "a Council of War" and moving to Rhode Island to be closer to Boston, so "We might be at Hand to give any necessary Advice." Still, the delegates waited for confirmation and further information before taking any precipitate action. The next day they proceeded with regular business, appointing members to the two committees. Then, on September 8, they learned that the tale was false, as many had already surmised. *"No Blood had been spill'd,"* a relieved Adams wrote in his diary.

In the aftermath of what has come to be called the powder alarm, Deborah Cushing wrote from Boston to her delegate husband, Thomas, "We seem to be like a ship in a grate storm the winds blowing and waves riseing high and we in grate Distress." What had happened, and why did the erroneous report of the "grate storm" spread so quickly through the colonies that by September 17 it had reached as far as Robert Carter's Virginia plantation, not being contradicted there for another five days?

The powder alarm began with the August 29 publication and distribution in Boston of a purloined letter written two days earlier to Governor Gage by General William Brattle of the Massachusetts militia. In it, Brattle expressed concerns about the state of the militia, and he revealed that the Medford selectmen had just removed their town's supply of gunpowder from the collective arsenal on Quarry Hill in Charlestown. (Gunpowder is volatile and potentially explosive, so publicly and privately owned powder was commonly held in arsenals like that in Charlestown, regardless of ownership.) Although Brattle did not recommend any action on Gage's part, the governor reacted to his letter by ordering the removal of the colony's gunpowder from the same arsenal and its transportation to Castle William.

That move, undertaken by a large number of soldiers early in the morning on August 31, alarmed local people who feared that it presaged military action. Soon an erroneous rumor spread that the troops had also seized locally owned gunpowder stored there. The next day, September 1, large numbers of men gathered at the Charlestown arsenal, then moved into Cambridge, where they surrounded the homes of General Brattle and Attorney General Jonathan Sewall. At the latter's house, some "boys and negroes" in the crowd broke a few windows, partly in frustration because both men had already left to seek safety in Boston. Another rumor alleged that six men had been killed the previous day by the soldiers who moved the gunpowder.

The Reverend Ezra Stiles of Newport, who was sufficiently intrigued by the powder alarm to investigate its origins carefully several months later, could not ascertain who first spread that false tale, but he did learn that by the evening of September 1 the account of the supposed deaths had reached Shrewsbury, forty miles west of Boston. Messengers urgently carried the story through the countryside to the north and south as well. But the key to its subsequent widespread dispersal, Stiles learned, came when the purported news arrived at the home of Colonel Israel Putnam in Pomfret, Connecticut, on the morning of Saturday, September 3. Either Putnam or his source, a Captain Keyes, appears to have been responsible for expanding the narrative to include the bombardment of Boston.

In a letter Putnam dispatched to others, which was printed and distributed widely as a handbill, he wrote that "the Men of War and Troops, began to fire upon the people last Night [the second] at sunset at Boston." By the time Putnam learned on Sunday, September 4, that the story was incorrect, his letter was already en route to New York and Philadelphia. Putnam's version spread rapidly through Massachusetts, Connecticut, New Hampshire, and New York. As many as twenty thousand men reportedly mobilized to march to Boston's defense before they learned that the information was false. Afterward, Boston committeemen cautioned Putnam that in the future he should wait for "authentick intelligence" by express messenger from them before taking any action.

Meanwhile, in Cambridge on September 2 more than a thousand men from nearby towns gathered on the common, attracted in part by the rumor of the six deaths. According to one observer, the crowd contained many "Landholders, led by Captains of the Towns, Representatives, Committee Men &c." The people forced the resignation of two local mandamus councillors. The newly appointed lieutenant governor, Thomas Oliver, rode to Boston to inform Gage about the crowd and to win his assurance that no military action was planned. Oliver returned to Cambridge, reported Gage's response, and resigned his post, to the crowd's satisfaction. Boston committeemen, notified by their

Cambridge counterparts, arrived on the scene to make certain there would be no violence. They informed those present that Gage had removed only the colony's gunpowder and that there had been no deaths.

All seemed likely to end without further incident, when Customs Commissioner Benjamin Hallowell appeared in Cambridge in his chaise, en route to Boston. Hallowell later described the crowd as so large (he estimated it at two thousand) that the chaise could not easily make its way through the streets, but even so he was nearly out of town when some horsemen started to chase him, and he ordered the driver of his chaise to accelerate. Hallowell eventually pointed his pistol at a persistent pursuer, and someone shouted, "Stop the Murderer the Tory Murderer he has killed a man," which led others along the road to try to impede his progress. The terrified Hallowell switched to his servant's mount and continued alone on horseback until he reached safety in Boston. After detailing the incident for an English friend, he observed that "justice and all civil power is now at an end over all this province," because "Dominion is the principle upon which they now act." No neutrality was allowed; "those who are not for them, they say are against them."

Colonists who favored resistance too thought that a significant change occurred because of the powder alarm. Abigail Adams wrote to her husband on September 2 that "there is great apprehension of an immediate rupture." Paul Revere celebrated the fact that "the Spirit of Liberty never was higher than at present." To Dr. Joseph Warren, the men assembled in Cambridge on the second were "a fine Body of Respectable Freemen," who showed "Patience Temperance and Fortitude." He exulted to Samuel Adams, "I never saw a more glorious Prospect than the present. The generous Spirit of our Ancestors seems to have revived beyond our most sanguine Expectations." Massachusetts citizens, he reported, "say they have a Right to determine for themselves under what Government they will live hereafter." Ezra Stiles, certainly one among many, concluded that "New England[ers] are ready to fight for their Liberties."

Henry Hulton and Nathaniel Coffin, both in the customs service, experienced the same events but interpreted the consequences very differently. A few days after the powder alarm, Hulton told a correspondent that "appearances here grow every day more hostile." Both men reported that colonists began to arm themselves, while militia troops started having regular musters. "The Country is in a state of Anarchy, and distraction," Hulton wrote, and Coffin concurred. "The Whole Country is now in as high a State of Frenzy as can be conceived," he commented in late September. They both remarked that Boston was "now the only Asylum" for any friend of government, which to Elizabeth Adams, Samuel's wife, turned the town into "a den of thi[e]ves." Hulton recalled later that after the powder alarm "all civil Officers were either silenced, and intimidated, or parties in the forwarding Anarchy, and rebellion."

Such observations implied that no one in Massachusetts attempted to maintain order after the powder alarm, but evidence from western Massachusetts suggests that the concerns about impending anarchy were overblown, greatly inflected by their own positions in the hierarchy of British colonial administration. The seemingly frenzied, disorderly crowds usually had specific aims and did not lack internal direction or what might be termed a moral compass, nor were local leaders unaware of the potential challenges such crowds posed. A good example is provided by a September 6 crowd action in Hatfield, the investigation of which unearthed unusually detailed information. Combined with information from a diary kept by a relative of one of the targets, the statements gathered from participants in the crowd provide considerable insight into the recruitment, goals, and activities of a group of men contemporaries deemed a "Mobb."

Talk about attacking certain elite men in Hatfield on September 6 began two days earlier, after the Hampshire County militia mustered in connection with the powder alarm. Hatfield men urged others from elsewhere in the county to come to their town to target five "Toryes." Questioned as to why Hatfield residents did not act themselves, one man responded that "it would Brake Neighbourhood"—that is, set neighbors publicly against one another—and that he thought a crowd composed of "stran[g]ers" would be more effective. If those from other towns took the initiative, a second man commented, "he believd a great Part of ye town would joyn them." It was important, remarked a third, to distinguish "our Friends from our Foes," and a fourth added, "it would not be safe to go to battle and leave a Mess of Torymen behind to Destroy the People at Home."

The potential recruits sought further information about the intended goals of the crowd action. An emissary from Williamsburg's militia asked, were the Hatfield men trying to "rectifi privet Dameges"? He was told no, the complaint was a public one, against "acorupt vicious . . . crew" in Hatfield, including Colonel Israel Williams, who with his family had reportedly had "a Feast" with a fiddler on the July fast day, "by which it was suppos'd they were against Liberty." So, one man insisted, "they the Tories deserv'd it." The inquiring militiaman nevertheless declared that "we was comeing in Regular order and that we Did not Desire to Damage any person['s] property." With that understanding, the men from Williamsburg and two other neighboring towns agreed to target Williams and a Colonel Partridge, along with others the Hatfield men identified.

Early on the morning of the sixth, Williams's relatives and friends were awakened by a messenger with the news that "all the Western World were coming in to Mobb Colo [Israel] W[illiams] and others for Private Pique"—in contrast to what the recruits had been told. To combat the oncoming mob, men gathered from Hadley, Deerfield, Amherst, and Hatfield itself. They chose a committee that met with representatives of the crowd to discuss the charges against Williams and Partridge. But both men "satisfied" the intruders about their political stance, Williams's nephew Elihu Ashley wrote in his journal. "This Mobb was sent for by some Hatfd People which the Mobb declared themselves," commented Ashley, who then set to work over the next few days to persuade men in the vicinity to agree to sign a covenant "in order to prevent Mobbs &c." Men in Hatfield voted to accept it and decided to give copies to "every Town" involved.

The recorded exchanges among members of the crowd revealed much about their goals and motives. The men from Hatfield made a point of informing the potential recruits, apparently deceptively, that they were not seeking "privet" revenge but rather had a public purpose—attacking a man who had openly violated the fast day by feasting and celebrating with music. They characterized their targets as corrupt, vicious "Toryes," warning that such men could not be left behind to cause trouble while the militia marched to the defense of Boston. The men from other towns expressed some skepticism and, although they agreed to come to Hatfield, nevertheless insisted on having local allies (who evidently did not appear), asserted that they would not damage anyone's property, and declared that they would act only "in Regular order." That so many other men mustered from nearby towns to challenge the crowd, and that men appear to have readily signed the covenant against mobs that Elihu Ashley initiated and circulated, suggest that the Hatfield recruiters had indeed acted from motives others regarded as illegitimate and that local people in western Massachusetts feared unrestrained mob action for personal motives just as much as did John Adams, John Greenough, and the civil authorities in Boston.

Even so, conditions throughout the Bay Colony were unsettled in the aftermath of the "grate storm" of the powder alarm, raising many concerns among local resistance leaders. How could order be maintained when crowds gathered so quickly, sometimes based on what turned out to be falsehoods such as the one spread by a trusted source like Colonel Putnam? With the colonial government paralyzed by New Englanders' refusal to accept the newly amended charter, and with the assembly having been dissolved by Gage's order, Massachusetts's local leaders thus moved to create new political institutions.

Unlike most other American jurisdictions, the Bay Colony had not elected a provincial congress. The primary motive for creating such "unconstitutional" congresses was to select representatives to the meeting in Philadelphia, but in Massachusetts the legally constituted assembly had succeeded in choosing delegates in June. Yet in August, and more urgently following the powder alarm in early September, resistance leaders recognized the need for coordination above the level of individual towns. And so local committees issued calls for county conventions, which soon assembled in such locations as Ipswich, Concord, and Worcester. Their resolves sought to maintain a semblance of civil authority while nonetheless ensuring people's continuing resistance to the Massachusetts Government Act. The county congresses also unanimously proposed holding a provincial-level convention. Writing from Philadelphia, though, Samuel Adams recommended against electing a provincial congress, reminding Dr. Warren, "There is a charm in the word 'constitutional.'" Operating against his advice and without fanfare, the Massachusetts county conventions of early and mid-September 1774 nevertheless moved subtly from protesting British authority to beginning to replace it.

The most important convention was that held for Suffolk County, which began a three-day meeting on September 6. An appointed committee presented draft resolves to the delegates from throughout the county, which were revised and accepted "UNANIMOUSLY," according to the official record.

The document began with a historical account told in passionate prose and italicized for emphasis. The Suffolk Resolves charged that *"our fugitive Parents"* had been *"persecuted, scourged and exiled"* from the mother country. Those ancestors had provided New Englanders with a *"dear bought Inheritance,"* which they were obliged to transmit to their *"innocent and beloved Offspring."* On them now depended *"the Fate of this New World, and of unborn Millions."* If they were to surrender to *"the arbitrary Will of a licentious Minister,"* they would be enslaved. But if instead they successfully resisted *"the unparalleled Usurpation of unconstitutional Power"* embodied in the Coercive Acts, they would enjoy *"Rewards and Blessings."*

The over-the-top language of the preamble became only slightly less impassioned in the nineteen resolves that followed. Although some similar elements appeared in the resolutions that other counties adopted that same week, the Suffolk Resolves stood out for their fervor and comprehensive reach. The convention first acknowledged loyalty to the king but then quickly asserted "an indispensable Duty" to defend "those civil and religious Rights and Liberties" their ancestors had fought to establish. In addition to resolutions attacking the Quebec Act, promoting domestic manufactures, and pledging support for boycotts of British goods, including tea, the resolves highlighted grievances specific to Massachusetts.

The Coercive Acts violated their rights under the British constitution, the provincial charter, and "the Laws of Nature," the delegates asserted, deeming those acts "the Attempts of a wicked Administration to enslave America." They insisted that judges holding office under the Massachusetts Government Act were "unconstitutional" and "disqualified" and suggested employing arbitration as an alternative to the courts. They called for the immediate resignation of all mandamus councillors. They recommended that current militia officers be replaced unless they were "inflexible Friends to the Rights of the People." Townsmen should muster at least once a week under appropriate commanders, but for "Defensive" purposes only. If resistance leaders were arrested, "every Servant of the present tyrannical and unconstitutional government" should be taken into custody and held hostage until the arrestees were released. The delegates joined the call for a provincial congress, promised "all due Respect and Submission" to whatever the Continental Congress recommended, and proposed a publicly funded system through which they could contact other jurisdictions for assistance should "our Enemies" engage in "sudden Maneuvers." The delegates also advised tax collectors to halt payments to the Massachusetts treasury until the government was "placed on a constitutional Foundation."

Meeting just a week after the powder alarm, attendees at the convention also expressed considerable concern about the maintenance of social order, referring to *"the universal Uneasiness"* then prevailing, which might *"influence some unthinking Persons to commit Outrage upon private Property."* The italics emphasized the importance of the point, as had the same typographical device used in the prologue. "We would heartily recommend to all Persons of this Community not to engage in any Routs, Riots or licentious Attacks upon the Properties of any Person whatsoever, as being subversive of all Order and Government." Instead, people should show "by a steady, manly, uniform and persevering Opposition" to Britain that they deserved "the Approbation of the Wise, and the Admiration of the brave and free of every Age and of every Country."

Employing the word "manly" to describe the manner in which New Englanders should oppose British measures echoed similar language then being used elsewhere in the colonies. Americans came to utilize "manly" to mean opposition behavior that was steadfast and determined yet never disorderly or uncontrolled. So Eunice Paine told her brother, Robert, in mid-September that Bristol County men had "annihilated" a recent court session with "no rioting, no Licentiousness," but rather with "a manly resolution." Ironically, such locutions excluded her and other women from those who were viewed as struggling against Britain, a far different circumstance from what had been true when the earlier opposition centered on tea.

The fervent prose of the Suffolk Resolves tended to deflect attention away from the understated, nearly covert elements in the county's
resolutions that looked beyond protest and pointed toward a possibly
independent future. Going beyond other colonies in which the regular
courts were not operating, the Suffolk delegates proposed to replace
civil lawsuits with a new system of arbitration unconnected to the
regular judiciary. The procedure they laid out for warning others of
military action by the British called not for volunteer riders of the sort
who had spread the word of the purported British attack on Boston
but for designated couriers who would be dispatched by selectmen or
committees of correspondence and compensated by the government.
And most tellingly of all, the convention directed local tax collectors
to withhold funds from the colonial treasury, funds that presumably
would pay those couriers. Thus the convention in effect authorized the
first appropriation of public funds for the cause of colonial resistance.

The leaders of the Suffolk convention sent Paul Revere as an express
rider to the congress in Philadelphia with a copy of the resolves and a
letter seeking advice. The delegates wanted to know if they were striking the right balance: Were they going too far? Or, in their "defensive"
mode, perhaps not far enough? Revere arrived on Friday, September
16. Congressmen were at the time meeting in committees, so the full
body did not formally address the resolves until the next day, but
surely informal discussions began as soon as the text of the document
was known. After what Galloway later described as "long and warm
debates," the congress adopted a resolution approving "the Wisdom
& Fortitude" of the people of Massachusetts. It then recommended to
Bay Colony citizens a continuation of their previous "firm and temperate" conduct—in short, that they should remain in their "defensive" posture for the time being.

Charles Thomson immediately released the Suffolk Resolves and the
congressional statement expressing sympathy for the plight of "their
countrymen" in Massachusetts to John Dunlap's *Pennsylvania Packet,*
which published the texts two days later. (The use of "countrymen"
was significant, because it usually applied only to residents of one's
colony.) The statement's wording, probably the subject of the debates
Galloway described, referred to "the late unjust, cruel and oppressive
acts of the British parliament" and to the "unwise, unjust and ruin-

ous policy of the present administration." Perhaps most congressmen focused on their advice to the Suffolk convention to remain calm and not to provoke retaliation from Gage. That, at least, was reported by one congressman, who later argued that the congress had not uncritically accepted the resolves but had rather recommended "moderate and pacific" conduct to residents of Suffolk County. Still, the delegates' language aroused an emotional response and garnered more attention than did their cautionary advice. John Adams pronounced September 17 "one of the happiest Days of my Life." To Nathaniel Coffin, though, the congress's action implicitly ratifying the resolves constituted "a declaration of War." Other future Loyalists would later concur.

ADVICES FROM LONDON

September 10, 1774. William Lee writes to his brother Richard Henry, arguing that it will be "totally wrong" if the congress agrees to compensate the East India Company. He warns his brother against Lord Dartmouth, "who will whine, preach and cry, while he is preparing privately a dagger to stab you to the heart." The congress should form "a Federal Union with all the Colonies" including Quebec if possible, which should be modeled on the Dutch confederation or that of ancient Greek cities. It is essential for the congress to "engage the Body of the people," a task that will require "infinite perseverance, address and assiduity."

September 15. John Vardill addresses James Duane, conveying advice he has recently elicited from Lord Dartmouth "in the confidence of private conversation" about how the congress could win favor in London. "If the Congress recommended to their several Assemblies, to present a Petition stating with precision what you would concede & the limits of your claims, & if (after a compensation made by the People of Boston for the Teas destroyed) your Assemblies would unanimously present such a Petition, it would be candidly attended to, & some measures for future harmony adopted."

September 24. Thomas Hutchinson writes to Israel Williams, remarking, "The Ministry say let the fire alone and it will burn out in America as it has done in England. . . . But, I tell them, there is more fewel in proportion in America than there is in England."

October 8. Dennis DeBerdt responds to Joseph Reed, who has asked whether he should continue to correspond privately with Lord Dartmouth. Facts are always useful to ministers, DeBerdt replies; if the government had been accurately informed about American affairs, the current crisis might have been averted. Still, "as Party runs so very high wth you I shld th[in]k you cannot be too cautious in giving your Opinion . . . least your L[etter]s shld ever come to light."

October 17. Lord Dartmouth, who has just received Gage's news of the Bay Colony's reaction to the Massachusetts Government Act, declares that the province is in "a very dangerous and critical situation." Without a functioning court system, there will be "the greatest anarchy and confusion." He has to rely on Gage's "fortitude and discretion" because the distance between London and Boston makes it impossible for him to offer timely instructions, especially "should the madness of the People urge them to a continuance of the violences they have committed or lead them to more desperate measures." Even so, he avers, Massachusetts must still contain "many friends to the constitution," and he names new mandamus councillors to replace those who have resigned.

October 29. Henry Laurens prepares to leave London to return to South Carolina. "I am going to a Country which in all appearance will be with all other the American Colonies involved in Deep Distress," he tells one friend; and to another he writes of the "dismal Gloom" he perceives at home. Yet his "Duty to my Family and my Country" compels him to "participate [in] the Calamities, as I have shared in the Felicitie of Carolina, and Submit in all things to the overuling Providence of God."

THE FIRST CONTINENTAL CONGRESS

On September 8, delegates to the congress began extensive exchanges about the nature of colonial rights and America's appropriate position within the empire, especially the colonies' relationship to Parliament. All the representatives in Philadelphia must have participated in conversations on such subjects previously in the context of their own colonies; thus the disagreement between Patrick Henry and John Jay recorded by John Adams on September 6 before congressmen learned about the powder alarm surely replicated points familiar to all. For the rest of September and well into October, the delegates argued about the wording of the documents they finally produced: a petition to the king, separate statements directed to their fellow Americans and to Britons, the Continental Association, and an address to residents of the province of Quebec that sought to recruit them to the cause of resistance. Significantly and deliberately, the congressmen neglected petitioning Parliament, an omission grounded in their rejection of that body's authority.

In the course of their discussions, they considered myriad familiar topics, along with some unfamiliar ones. Should they challenge all parliamentary oversight of their commerce, including the acts that predated 1763, or should they instead confine their complaints to post-1763 measures? (They chose the latter.) Should they offer compensation for the destroyed tea? (After a vigorous debate recorded by Silas Deane, the congress voted no, and thus finally laid to rest what had been a contentious subject for ten months.) Should they advise Massachusetts to reopen its courts under the provisions of the 1691 charter, or, more dramatically, should they suggest reverting to the original 1629 charter, or concur with some residents that the province was now in a "State of Nature" and could establish an entirely new government? (All three ideas seemed too radical; the congress continued to counsel patience and forbearance instead.) Should they adopt Richard Henry Lee's proposal, seconded by Patrick Henry, to ask each colony to raise and arm a militia? (That also went too far for the delegates.) On such contentious issues except for reimbursing the EIC, in other words, congressional majorities selected the more moderate option. Therefore the delegates in effect met colonists' initial expectations.

John Jay succinctly laid out the congress's three major choices: "Negotiation, suspension of Commerce, and War." The first promised little immediate effect. As for the third, John Adams observed that his fellow delegates' opinions were "fixed against Hostilities and Ruptures, except they should become absolutely necessary, and this Necessity they do not yet See." Accordingly, in their attempt to avoid a military conflict, the congressmen devoted a great deal of time after their mid-September debate about the Suffolk Resolves to discussing nonimportation and nonexportation, which had previously dominated the agendas of the provincial conventions. Echoing the delegates to those conventions, they more readily agreed to the former than the latter. On September 22, they signaled their intent by issuing a public statement advising merchants not to order any goods from Great Britain and to retract orders already sent. Five days later, they formally adopted such a policy, providing that no items should be imported from the British Isles after December 1. Not until nearly a month after that did they also reach consensus on a threat to institute nonexportation if their grievances were not swiftly resolved.

The congress's deliberations over commercial policy repeated in many respects the debates of the previous summer as congressmen argued over the starting dates for nonimportation and nonexportation and discussed at length whether a prohibition on trade should contain exceptions. According to confidential information obtained by Cadwallader Colden, New Englanders initially advocated an end to both imports from and exports to Britain, coupled with nonconsumption to give more force to the agreement. But no other delegations, not even the radical southerners, at first supported any tactic other than nonimportation, and everyone, including New Englanders, sought exemptions as well. "The Virginians & Carolinians contended for an exception of Goods for the Indians & the Negroes," Colden's source disclosed, whereas New Englanders wanted fishing gear excluded, so that Nova Scotia could not take over the lucrative fishery trade. New Yorkers, who opposed nonimportation and hoped to create divisions among its proponents, proposed that "the Resolution should be general and extend to all commodities & all places," so that merchants would all be treated equally. Their formulation, intended to divide the majority that favored nonimportation with (different) exceptions, instead provided the solution to the congress's dilemma. Like Charlestonians dealing with legal and smuggled tea months earlier, the congress found it easier to treat all commerce alike than to try to make distinctions.

The debates over nonexportation involved both specific commodities and dates on which the policy might commence. Tobacco, remarked Richard Henry Lee, was sold the year after it was harvested, so timing had to be taken into account in any agreement. Wood products, including naval stores like pitch and tar, aroused considerable comment because, said a Marylander, "the Importance of the Trade of the West Indies to G. Britain almost exceeds Calculation," and North American timber was essential to the mother country and the islands both, although for different reasons. The South Carolina delegates, in a move that would cause controversy after they returned home, insisted on an exception from nonexportation for the rice trade to Europe. Because the Carolinians' instructions provided that the colony would adopt only those measures their representatives approved, other congressmen reluctantly agreed to the exemption, for their primary goal was unanimity. As the Connecticut delegates observed in a report to Governor Trumbull, unanimity was "of the last importance," so "every one must be heard" on every topic. "It often happens," they added, "that what is of little or no Consequence to one Colony, is of the last To another."

Joseph Reed, who was not a delegate, had only the partial information he gleaned from "private Conversation" with such congressmen as John Adams to convey to Lord Dartmouth. Nevertheless, in late September he once again wrote to the secretary of state for America, updating him on recent news, including the powder alarm, the Suffolk Resolves, and the advice to merchants that the congress promulgated on September 22. He stressed the "great Unanimity of Sentiment" in the congress and warned Dartmouth that what once had seemed to be an extinguishable "Spark" had become "a Flame that threatens Ruin to both Parent & Child." Attributing the escalation of tensions to colonists' reaction to the Quebec Act and fears that attacks from "Canadians & Savages" might be imminent, Reed cautioned that unless "healing Measures" were adopted, "we are upon the Verge of a Civil War." Admitting that Parliament was supreme in the empire, he nevertheless suggested that such supremacy be "expressly defined, & its Operations limited by some certain Bounds."

In their sessions, congressmen wrestled with the same question: How could they simultaneously allow for imperial power and protect what they viewed as essential American liberties? Before the First Congress, few if any Americans had thought systematically about possible ways to reorganize the governance of the empire to provide more colonial autonomy. But in the aftermath of the Coercive Acts and the claims of "unconstitutionality" on all sides, circumstances seemed to require thinking about new constitutional arrangements. The man who made such a proposal was Joseph Galloway, who offered his fellow delegates the scheme that has come to be called the Galloway Plan of Union. His idea led to a crucial daylong debate.

Galloway, the experienced Pennsylvania lawyer and legislator, had long been allied with Benjamin Franklin as influential proponents of royal status for the colony, opposing John Dickinson and other supporters of the Penn family proprietorship. Forty-four in 1774, he had married a wealthy woman in the early 1750s and had been elected Speaker of the assembly in 1768. His commitment to making Pennsylvania a royal colony led him to take conservative stances in the Stamp Act and Townshend Act crises, and unlike other colonial political leaders at the time he failed to voice significant criticisms of those laws. From late 1773 until midsummer 1774, Galloway was ill and suffering from depression, remaining cloistered at his estate outside Philadelphia. Accordingly, he was not involved with the city's efforts to deal with the tea ship or the initial local reactions to the Boston Port Act. He thus missed a time of major political turmoil, which could have led to his later misjudgments about the colonies' political mood. He only reentered Pennsylvania public life in July, when the assembly and the provincial convention both met to discuss resolves and the election of delegates to the First Continental Congress.

In early August, Galloway informed a British acquaintance that after "an impartial Examination" of many relevant volumes, he had become convinced that a "solid political Union" of Britain and the colonies had to rest on a new foundation. On the one hand, to argue that Parliament had appropriate jurisdiction over millions of people with no means of communicating their "Desires, Wants, and Necessities" to that body did not accord with "Reason or Common Sense," or indeed with the principles of the British constitution. On the other hand, the Americans were denying Parliament's constitutional authority yet refusing to consider the option of representation in that body. Galloway advocated compromise. He contended that the conflict could be resolved by establishing a formal "constitutional Mode" through which the colonies could affect British policy. In a pamphlet he wrote in August (but decided not to distribute), Galloway eschewed setting forth a specific proposal for that "mode." He attributed the current conflict to the fact that Britain had never adequately incorporated its colonies into imperial governance. In particular, he argued that representation in any legislature rested on landownership and that the constitution had not been modified to allow American landowners a voice in the empire.

Galloway later explained that before proposing his own solution to the congress he waited to see if his fellow congressmen would adopt "any rational scheme of union." He complained, though, that the other delegates were "bewildered, perpetually changing their ground, taking up principles one day, and shifting them the next." So he decided to put his own ideas forward. He presented only an outline, he declared, noting that he had "several propositions of lesser consequence" in mind to add if that outline had been accepted.

After the nonimportation vote on September 26, the Pennsylvanian introduced his plan with resolves calling for the congress to ask George III to redress American grievances while assuring him of the colonies' commitment to the British Empire. Because Americans could not be represented in Parliament, they were proposing a plan to advance "the Interest of both Countries" and to preserve "the Rights and Liberties of America." Galloway's language was telling, not only in his reference to the colonies and Britain as separate "Countries," but also in a version he considered but did not use. That draft referred to "a manifest Defect in the Constitution of the British Empire," which repeated a point from his pamphlet: colonization had not been properly accounted for in the British constitution. Presumably, he decided that language about a "manifest Defect" was impolitic, because he intended the resolves to be formally adopted and dispatched to the ministry.

His Plan of Union applied to the British mainland colonies other than Quebec, Nova Scotia, or Florida, providing that each province should retain authority over its own internal matters "in all Cases whatsoever." A government to regulate America in general would be headed by a president-general appointed by the king and a "Grand Council" elected triennially by colonial legislatures, with unspecified proportional representation. The grand council would meet at least once a year, could choose its own Speaker, and would enjoy the same rights and privileges as the House of Commons. The president-general would serve at the king's pleasure; his assent as well as the king's would be required for all laws pertaining to the colonies. This government would have jurisdiction over civil, commercial, or criminal matters involving more than one colony. It would be regarded as "an inferior and distinct Branch of the British Legislature united and incorporated with it," and the consent of both Parliament and the American council would be required before statutes relating to the colonies could go into effect. The only exception would come in the event of war; in such an emergency, colonial actions would not require Parliament's concurrence.

According to John Adams's notes of the subsequent debate, Galloway asserted at the outset that nonimportation would be "too gradual" in its effects to aid Boston, and the next step, nonexportation, would be unacceptable to most colonists. He reviewed recent history and contended that in 1765 or 1766 Britain should have proposed a plan to renegotiate imperial arrangements, but did not, so the congress needed to take the initiative. He denied that the colonies were legitimate subjects of parliamentary rule, although they needed Britain's protection. To resolve that dilemma, he laid out his scheme for shared governance. James Duane then seconded Galloway's motion. John Jay too approved, as did Edward Rutledge. But Virginians raised objections: Richard Henry Lee insisted that he would have to consult his constituents before acceding to the plan, and Patrick Henry charged that members of the grand council could be corrupted by Britons. Galloway then defended the plan by pointing out that every government had to have "a Supream Legislature" but that individual colonies were "totally independent of each other." Accordingly, where would the supreme power be placed? We need an American legislature, he argued, or else "we should give the Power to Parliament or King."

Other delegates reportedly seconded Lee's and Henry's objections and claimed that the scheme "deprived the colony legislatures of a part of their rights." Galloway had a ready response: the jurisdiction of the council would not reduce but rather extend the power of individual provinces, because they would now be involved in establishing policies for the entire continent. A later exchange of letters between James Duane and Samuel Chase, a Maryland delegate, further revealed what must have been the content of some of the debates, as Duane forcefully reiterated Galloway's rationale and Chase contended that the elaborate scheme would be unnecessary if the colonies, as he and other Marylanders preferred, simply acknowledged parliamentary power to regulate American commerce, "bona fide" (that is, not taxation in disguise).

In retrospect, Galloway on several occasions offered an interpretation of the disagreements at the congress that distinguished between the delegates elected by "lawful Assemblies" and those chosen by "lawless conventions." Men in the latter group, he averred, had "secret and treasonable designs" and were implacably opposed to himself and his moderate allies, whom he described as "gentlemen of abilities, fortune, and influence." Members of the other faction, Galloway insisted, wanted "to throw off all subordination and connexion to Great-Britain" and were "determined to precipitate the people into a civil War." But he never reconciled his interpretation with the troublesome facts that among his opponents were the Massachusetts delegates, who were selected legally by an assembly, or that among his staunchest supporters were New Yorkers, whose election had been irregular and confined only to city dwellers.

John Dickinson and Charles Thomson later misrepresented the reception of Galloway's plan, claiming that its "merits" had not been "regularly debated in Congress." The amount of surviving detail about the discussions suggests that delegates took the plan seriously, although they ultimately rejected it. Nor was it likely, as Dickinson and Thomson also asserted, that the delegates "heard it with horror—as an idle, dangerous, whimsical, ministerial plan." All the contemporary evidence suggests the contrary. James Duane, one of its supporters, lamented after the congress adjourned that he now had no idea "what System will content a Majority of the Colonies." At the end of the day, the vote was reported as 6 to 5 against the plan, with one colony divided. Galloway subsequently argued that the vote merely postponed further discussion to a later date rather than being a final verdict on his scheme. As the congress neared the end of its session in late October, he charged, his opponents, citing lack of time, then mustered a larger majority against him.

Once the congressmen chose not to adopt the Galloway plan as a basis for negotiation, and instead to pursue John Jay's second option of utilizing commercial weapons in the conflict against Britain, they had to address another crucial question: How were nonimportation and nonexportation or nonconsumption (if implemented) to be enforced? They had two prior models from the 1760s—coercion or persuasion of merchants through informal public opinion or direct action, and non-consumption pacts signed by individual colonists. But, although both had already been used in 1774 with respect to EIC tea, neither had wholly satisfactory outcomes. Recent and past experience suggested that both were insufficiently comprehensive, relying too heavily on the initiative of "private" persons. Even though colonists believed that those earlier, incomplete boycotts had helped to bring about repeal of the Stamp Act and most of the Townshend duties—a conclusion many historians today would question—the methods used to effectuate those tactics would surely be inadequate to the larger task in 1774.

The decision they made was probably the most consequential of the entire session, but it is poorly documented, perhaps because, as Silas Deane informed Governor Trumbull, important matters, "being the most critical and requiring the greatest attention," were left to be considered at the end of the meeting and suffered because of "the hurry of the Members." In the event, no delegate recorded the debates over the provisions of the Continental Association, formally adopted on October 20 but based on a committee draft presented to the congress eight days earlier and subsequently amended numerous times over a three-day period, according to Charles Thomson's sparse minutes. In a report to Trumbull, the Connecticut delegates commented that implementing the commercial agreements required that "every possible precaution should Now be taken, on the one hand to prevent wicked, & desperate Men, from breaking through, & defeating it either by Fraud, or Force, and on the other to remove as farr as possible

JOURNAL

OF THE

PROCEEDINGS

OF THE

CONGRESS,

Held at PHILADELPHIA,

September 5, 1774.

PHILADELPHIA:
Printed by WILLIAM and THOMAS BRADFORD,
at the *London Coffee-House.*
DCC,LXXIV.

William and Thomas Bradford published the official journal kept by Charles Thomson, the congressional secretary, after the First Continental Congress adjourned in late October 1774. The title promises more than the pamphlet delivered; the notes were sparse, formal, and not very informative. But it did supply curious Americans with the precise language of the Continental Association.

every Temptation to, or Necessity for the Violation thereof." After the New Hampshire delegates had seen the draft document, they reported merely that "we have agreed upon Methods to prevent the violation" of the accord. But neither delegation specified either those methods or the rationale behind them.

The Association itself, adopted and signed by all the delegates—according to Galloway, he agreed to sign under some duress and regarded the measures as "too warm & indiscreet"—contained fourteen provisions, most of them outlining the details of the nonimportation, nonexportation, and nonconsumption agreements. For example, the congressmen promised for themselves and their constituents that starting immediately they would not "purchase or use" any EIC tea, whether duty paying or not, and would not consume any they already owned after March 1, 1775. They declared that they would begin nonexportation on September 1, 1775, if their demands had not been met. They directed merchants to countermand any orders already sent to Britain, and they stated their wish to encourage "frugality, economy, and promote agriculture, arts and the manufactures of this country," while discouraging "every species of extravagance and dissipation." But the key clause subsequently turned out to be the eleventh:

> That a committee be chosen in every county, city, and town, by those who are qualified to vote for representatives in the legislature, whose business it shall be attentively to observe the conduct of all persons touching this association; and when it shall be made to appear, to the satisfaction of a majority of any such committee, that any person within the limits of their appointment has violated this association, that such majority do forthwith cause the truth of the case to be published in the gazette; to the end, that all such foes to the rights of British-America may be publicly known, and universally contemned as the enemies of American liberty; and thenceforth we respectively will break off all dealings with him or her.

So to enforce the Association, the congress turned to local committees, which came to be termed "committees of observation and inspection." Committees had already been appointed or elected in some areas, charged with managing correspondence and collecting and disbursing funds or goods for the relief of Boston. After late October, those groups, or other bodies that supplanted them, were legitimized by the congressional mandate in three ways. First, they were to be elected solely by qualified voters, thereby avoiding irregularities. Second, they were given an explicit but limited assignment: investigating and adjudicating alleged violations of the Association. Finally, the only penalty they were authorized to impose for noncompliance was publication of the miscreant's name, to be followed (it was hoped) by social and economic ostracism. The primary punishment for dissenters would be community pressure to conform. Clearly, the congressmen intended to prevent the impulsive destruction of dissenters' property or the physical attacks that had been occurring during the reign of patriotic terror in New England.

Of the three provisions, the first was arguably the most crucial. By defining the voters who would choose committee members as those already legally qualified, congressmen intended to prevent, or at least to mute, renewed charges of unconstitutionality. Like Philadelphians in June or New Yorkers in July, they opted for excluding from the voting population men who did not meet local property requirements for the franchise. Women, even property-holding widows, it should go without saying, were not included either. As a Pennsylvanian had contended in June, if legal assemblies could not meet to discuss current politics, the best alternative was to revert for decision making to the voters who had originally selected the members of those assemblies.

The congressmen probably did not know about the controversies over the salvaged EIC tea that had rocked Eastham, Massachusetts, the previous winter. But had they known the story of the three successive town meetings and the resulting disputes, they would have seen those events as fully justifying their decision to specify voting qualifications for choosing committee members. Town meetings in January and March, both populated by regular voters, had defended Colonel Willard Knowles; their February counterpart, attended by many unqualified townsmen, had not only derided him but had also instigated crowd actions that almost caused violent confrontations with the local militia. The threatened attacks on Knowles and John Greenough, the earlier raids in Provincetown, and indeed the mobbing of Samuel Peters and the mandamus councillors in August all represented outcomes the congressmen hoped to avoid in the future.

Their specification of a social and economic punishment—not a physical or destructive one—for violations of the Association aimed at the same goal: creating a process for continued resistance to Britain that nevertheless maintained order and even a measure of civility. It laid out a limited role for ordinary folk: boycotting both those merchants who ignored the Association and any colonists who did business with them. That role was simultaneously passive and important: the punishment would not be effective unless colonists generally observed the Association's prohibitions, but what it required was more the absence of action rather than any positive steps. In short, upholding the Association required doing so in an orderly fashion.

Coda: *The Destruction of the* Peggy Stewart

Just as the congress was finishing its work and finalizing the Continental Association and addresses to the king and other audiences, a confrontation in Annapolis brought home to the congressmen and many other Americans the dangers of the mob action the Association hoped to prevent. Once again the flash point was East India Company tea and the tea duty.

The brig *Peggy Stewart,* owned by Anthony Stewart and his father-in-law, James Dick, arrived in Annapolis on October 14. The ship carried fifty-three servants indentured to Stewart, British goods ordered by Chesapeake merchants hoping to beat the November 1 deadline for nonimportation as set forth in the June Virginia Association, and more than two thousand pounds of EIC tea. Stewart did not own the tea, which had been sent to the Annapolis firm of Williams & Company, nor had his captain, Richard Jackson, learned that the tea was on board until after the voyage was well under way. The Williams brothers of Annapolis admitted that they had ordered the tea in May, assuming that all imports would be allowed before the Virginia Association's November 1 deadline. When the ship arrived, the firm directed Stewart not to pay duty on the tea and to turn it over to the local committee for disposition. Stewart tried to follow those instructions and to pay duty on all the cargo except the tea, but the customs collector rejected that option. Faced with a leaky ship holding fifty-three persons who had already been on board for three months, and with the prospect of having the entire ship and cargo seized for nonpayment, he decided for the sake of "humanity and prudence" to pay all the duty owed and then to let the local committee decide what to do.

That turned out to be a disastrous mistake. The local committee summoned a town meeting for that evening, at which people debated possible solutions but came to no conclusions except to set a watch to ensure the tea was not landed, and to call another meeting that would include Marylanders from the surrounding county as well as the town of Annapolis. Next the committee, meeting separately and having heard Stewart's explanation, decided, at the suggestion of one of its members, Charles Carroll, Barrister, that the tea should be brought onshore to be burned and that Stewart and the merchants should be forced to apologize publicly. But Matthias Hammond, another committee member, rejected Carroll's idea and distributed handbills throughout the region, summoning "disorderly People under different Ringleaders," to adopt Stewart's characterization. At a larger gathering on October 19, which included men from outside Annapolis, Carroll and Hammond debated the matter. Some of the participants insisted that the entire vessel be set ablaze. The matter was put to a vote, and according to several accounts a substantial majority supported Carroll's proposal, deciding that an apology and burning the tea would be sufficient to resolve the controversy.

Yet those who wanted to destroy the ship remained "clamorous," declaring that they would do greater damage to Stewart and his possessions if the vessel were not burned. They threatened to tar and feather him and to set his house afire with his pregnant wife inside. Because she was about to give birth, Stewart and Dick agreed to personally burn the ship and the tea, for the other cargo had already been unloaded. Stewart and the Williams brothers signed and read a humiliating statement, acknowledging that they had "committed a most daring insult, and act of the most pernicious tendency to the liberties of America," and had "deservedly incurred the displeasure of the people now convened." Set fire by Stewart, the vessel along with all its sails, tackle, and rigging, "colours flying," burned to the waterline, a complete loss. Publicly, it was announced that Stewart acted voluntarily to set fire to his vessel, but with good reason he later declared that he had feared "the Fury of a lawless Mob."

He was not the only one. In the aftermath of the destruction of the *Peggy Stewart,* John Galloway, distantly related to Joseph and a participant in the meetings, described his dismay in a long letter to his father in Philadelphia. "I think Sir I went to Annapolis yesterday to see my Liberty destroyed which was done when the fire was put to the brigg," he wrote. Everyone knew that Stewart had erred in paying the duty, but after he had agreed to burn the tea and apologize, "it was monstrous to destroy his vessel." Another man had owned a third of the ship; he was entirely innocent. "If this is Justice they certainly must have found a new code of Laws." Moreover, John and others concluded that it was a "Scandal" to act "against the sense of the majority of the people," and so they tried to prevent the ship's destruction but desisted after being warned by James Dick not to intervene, because Stewart's losses could have been still worse.

Galloway assumed that the Annapolis committee would find it difficult to publicize the incident, "as they cannot say it was with the consent of the major part of the people that the vessel was burned." But the committee finessed that troublesome fact by omitting it entirely from an authorized published account. A broadside, dated October 20 and widely reprinted in newspapers, merely stated that the committee's recommendation for destroying the tea and requiring an apology from Stewart and the Williams brothers was found "not satisfactory" by the large gathering. "Mr. Stewart then voluntarily offered to burn the vessel and the tea in her," the broadside continued, thus eliding the formal vote and the majority that favored Carroll's less drastic solution. The Annapolis committee lost Galloway's respect by its failure to stand by its own decision. "For the future I would not give a copper for all that their committee can say or do," he told his father. Describing the destruction of the *Peggy Stewart* as "infamous and rascally," he averred that in its wake "all men of property reflect with horror on their present situation to have their lives and propertys at the disposal & mercy of a mob is shocking." He claimed that "the whole Province are crying out against the proceedings and the Ring-leaders begin to be ass[h]amed of it themselves."

Indeed, a Maryland merchant, after inveighing against the "Desperadoes" who had caused the problem, opined that the fate of the *Peggy Stewart* was "Generally exclaimed against by every prudent man, and particularly by the Committee & Inhabitants of Annarundel County, whose province alone, it was to Judge of this Matter." A Scotsman from Bladensburg informed his brother in Glasgow that after the ship was burned, "the common sort seem to think they may now commit any outrage they please." Yet Americans' opinion appeared divided. Joseph Reed commended "the spirit of the people" evident in the fate of the vessel, which would show Britons that "opposition to parliamentary tyranny is not local or partial"; Charles Carroll of Annapolis declared that he hoped other "Enemies of America" would now be deterred from "impudent Endeavours"; and William Lee told Anthony Stewart himself that he was "well pleased at the whole transaction." Writing from London, Lee, assuming that Stewart would be compensated for the loss of the ship, insisted that the incident would make the British public recognize the seriousness of the crisis in the colonies.

It is unclear what message Americans elsewhere took away from the destruction of the *Peggy Stewart*. Those who knew the details knew that the Annapolis committee had lost control of the situation, and that gave many pause. Even those who only read the incomplete newspaper stories recognized the violence of the incident and the potential for disorder it represented despite its emotional heft. Some accounts exaggerated the threats to Stewart and his family, reporting erroneously that a gallows had been erected outside his house to frighten his wife. Many colonists other than congressmen surely hoped that the fury expressed about the *Peggy Stewart* in Annapolis and during the powder alarm in New England could be contained and channeled to Americans' benefit.

Thus Samuel Webb wrote from New Haven to his stepfather, Silas Deane, reporting the view held by "our warmest friends" that "mobs, which I fancy you judge ruinous to all good government, will be opposed by every true Son of Liberty in this Colony. . . . [I]f mobs are allowed to take hold of persons and private proper[t]y, dissensions will follow, and we should be, instead of a United, a broken Body." He accordingly advised that "all such riots should be stop'd in their first growth," because Connecticut, like other colonies, faced the prospect of being "as destitute of all Law and Civil Government" as Massachusetts was. Maintaining order while nevertheless resisting Great Britain appeared essential, but how to accomplish that goal remained a challenge.

CHAPTER 6

A FERMENT THROUGHOUT
THE CONTINENT

Americans had few reliable sources of information about the First Continental Congress while it was in session between September 5 and October 26. Yet they were eager to learn about the proceedings; the congressmen were, as one of Thomas Cushing's friends informed him, "the topick of all conversation." In fact, Joseph Warren explained to Samuel Adams in late September, "people were so rapacious for the intelligence brot from the Congress by Mr. Revere" that he had published part of the delegates' most recent letter to him without asking permission from Adams or Cushing. Intense interest and comments about lack of information were not confined to Boston. Correspondents throughout the mainland colonies filled their letters with similar remarks: a Charleston resident commented that he was waiting "with impatience" for the results; in Norfolk, James Parker reported that "nothing transfers from the Congress, all is done with doors Shut"; and a relative told Silas Deane that people "are continually inquiring what the Congress have done, . . . they are very anxious to be inform'd, and wonder at their being kept so long in suspense." A Philadelphian was as much in the dark as other Americans. He wrote to a nephew, "I don't know what they have done," so "why should I trouble you with guesses."

Governors, too, knew little of what was happening in Philadelphia, or at least if they had information, they did not convey it to London. Their letters to Dartmouth during those two months reported only routine business, such as describing boundary disputes with neighboring colonies, rather than expressing anxiety about the congress. For example, William Bull wrote from South Carolina to inform Lord Dartmouth that he had no news from Philadelphia and that in the interim "nothing new hath arisen lately in this province."

After the congress ended with published resolves, including the Continental Association, and with the announcement of another meeting scheduled for May 1775, the uncertainty finally ended. Some colonists reported the results jubilantly, like a Philadelphian who exclaimed, "It is wonderful to see so thorough an union of all America!" Others lamented that their hopes for a moderate outcome had been dashed. According to Peter Van Schaack, New Yorkers like himself felt "very great Dissatisfaction"; they had anticipated that the congressmen would have been "the Mediators of Peace," but instead they were "the Heralds of War." The anonymous New Jersey author who signed himself "Z" insisted that the congressmen "deliberately have made bad worse, left us no retreat, nor the mother country any opening to advance to reconciliation." They had demonstrated "sovereign contempt" by ignoring Parliament, and the committees that would enforce the Association amounted to an "inquisition." The congressmen, he charged, had not truly sought compromise, because they wanted to retain their "new and unconstitutional" power.

To Lord Dartmouth, Joseph Reed stressed "the utmost Unanimity" of support for the Continental Association, emphasizing that "many Judicious Persons, Friends to order & good Government," hoped that the ministry would now propose "some Plan of Union and Authority founded upon Reason and the Constitution." One of the most important sources of the colonists' dissatisfaction with Britain, he underscored, was the "Contempt" with which their petitions had been received previously. Change that reaction, and he predicted that Americans would "cheerfully" submit to the "general Superintendance of the Mother Country."

But if in the rest of the colonies little of significance occurred while the congress met, circumstances differed dramatically in Massachusetts. There, General Thomas Gage's reaction to the powder alarm in early September initiated a major escalation of tensions. Although New Englanders were curious about the outcome of the congress, local events soon consumed more of their attention and concern.

MASSACHUSETTS AFTER THE POWDER ALARM

Unnerved by the crowd action in Cambridge and by Benjamin Hallowell's tale of a headlong flight from his pursuers, Gage moved swiftly to fortify Boston Neck, the sole land route into the city, by creating new defensive positions and stationing cannon at the strategic location. Guards carefully examined people and their possessions as residents traveled in and out, confiscating gunpowder and arms being carried in either direction. Because the Port Act interdicted all traffic by water, the measures had the immediate effect of restricting New Englanders' movements. Still, in an exchange of letters with the Boston selectmen, Gage denied acting with hostile intent, declaring that his aim was rather "to protect his Majesty's Subjects and his Majesty's Troops in this Town."

With winter approaching, Gage took steps to build more permanent housing for the soldiers, who through the summer had been living in tents pitched on the Common and in repurposed buildings, including a distillery. Probably anticipating local opposition, he sought to hire workmen and obtain supplies from New York and Philadelphia as well as from Boston and environs. In the occupied city, a diarist on September 18 recorded that "most of our town carpenters, with a number from the country," were busily constructing barracks for the army.

Bostonians probably welcomed the prospect of well-paid employment for tradesmen who had been thrown out of work by the closing of the port. But Medford and other nearby towns expressed "uneasiness" over the city dwellers' willingness to assist in providing convenient housing for the troops. Boston officials reacted to such concerns by directing contractors to cease involvement with the barrack construction project. John Andrews's detailed accounts make it clear that the city's leaders were responding to outside pressure and that they acted primarily in order to avoid offending "their country brethren," so as not to endanger the relief supplies the town needed. Once committed to the cause, though, Bostonians (along with neighboring committees) forbade supplying the troops with "Lumber, Joice [joists], Spars, Pickets, Straw, Bricks or any Materials whatsoever" that could help the occupiers, with the sole exception of "what Humanity requires" for their subsistence.

The directive had immediate consequences. On September 26, all two hundred or so carpenters working on the barracks abandoned their jobs, leaving the buildings unfinished. The governor offered "extravagant" wages in ensuing weeks. Bostonians remained adamant and uncooperative, but carpenters from New York and Portsmouth, New Hampshire, arrived to earn unusually good wages, leading Andrews to decry the fact that their Boston counterparts were "starving" to avoid ostracism as enemies of America. Finally, in mid-November, the buildings were completed and the troops moved in, leaving their tents and transport ships behind. Still, the hastily built barracks were of poor quality. Andrews noted that the "spirited behaviour of the Eastward people [from Maine]" prevented sufficient supplies of firewood from reaching the barrack master. The inferior housing conditions promoted the spread of disease, and a smallpox epidemic (which would persist for the rest of the occupation of the city) broke out among the troops.

While he was confronting difficulties housing the soldiers, Gage wrote regularly to Dartmouth but did not trouble the American secretary with that tale. Instead, he described the situation more generally, revealing that New Englanders were acquiring arms and ammunition and mustering militia units in the countryside. Although the Port Act required the government to be located in Salem, Gage explained that the councillors had fled to Boston and that they could not safely leave the city. Likewise, although he summoned a new assembly to meet in Salem in early October, he realized that holding such a session would be impossible, so he dissolved it preemptively. Appearing overwhelmed, Gage told the minister in late September that the problems were now "so universal there is no knowing where to apply a remedy." When he wrote again a month later, Gage admitted he was "not a little chagrined" at his lack of success as governor. But, he rationalized, "nobody here or at home could have conceived that the Acts made for the Massachusetts Bay could have created such a ferment throughout the continent and united the whole in one common cause." He disclosed that he was deliberately behaving cautiously, "lest all the continent should unite in hostile proceedings against us, which would bring on a crisis which I apprehend his Majesty would by all means wish to avoid."

As Gage was writing to Dartmouth, friends and relatives of the

The BOSTONIANS in DISTRESS.

A British cartoonist produced this image that appears to sympathize with the Bostonians in the blockaded port. They are suspended in a cage on the Liberty Tree, fed by fishermen from what seem to be collection boxes used in churches. On some occasions, enslaved prisoners were punished thus in the colonies, so the image resonates with the claim that Britain was attempting to "enslave" America. In the cage a clergyman preaches to the prisoners, a man holds out a bundle (possibly wheat) labeled "promises," and two men are fighting. The lower right contains a depiction of cannon and British troops.

Massachusetts delegation in Philadelphia were conveying similar information to them. In such correspondence and in other letters during September and October, New England's women took an unusually prominent role, as both subject and object.

For instance, Dr. Thomas Young revealed that his wife was so distressed by the fortifications on Boston Neck that "she took bed and appeared as inanimate as a corpse." He felt obliged to "seek an asylum for her," and so he moved to Newport, abandoning his membership in the Boston committee while ironically commending "the manly behavior of the Citizens" he had left behind. Other women showed more fortitude than Mary Young. Deborah Cushing gleefully described to her husband, Thomas, how "slie" Americans had carried away cannon the British thought they had safely sequestered. She reported that while riding near the Boston Neck military encampment, she was depressed by encountering smiling "tories" but expressed hope that "their triumphing will be but short," adding that colonists should rather wear "sheps and goats skins than bye English goods of a peopel that have insulted them in such a scandelous mannor." Thomas Cushing was so proud of her letter, misspelled though much of it was, that he showed it to leading Philadelphians. He subsequently reported to her that John Dickinson, Charles Thomson, Thomas Mifflin, and their wives admired her "patriotic, calm & undaunted" tone. Dickinson had even commented that "if it was Customary to cho[o]se Women into the Assembly, he should be heartily for choosing you Speaker of the House."

Deborah Cushing was not alone in her adherence to the cause of resistance. The Massachusetts delegates' wives were joined in their fervor by the delegates' other female relatives—Robert Treat Paine's sister Eunice and his niece Abigail Greenleaf, Abigail Adams's sisters, Elizabeth Smith and Mary Smith Cranch, or friends like Hannah Winthrop and Mercy Otis Warren. Yet in offering comments on public affairs, all the women knew they were transgressing a norm firmly established in Anglo-America since the early eighteenth century, which dictated that women not discuss politics—not even when a culturally feminine topic like tea drinking was involved. Essayists such as Richard Steele and Joseph Addison, in their influential British periodical *The Spectator*, ridiculed and derided women who dared to venture into the public realm, contending that they thereby abandoned their proper domestic sphere and rendered themselves unattractive to men. And so these Massachusetts women often apologized for introducing the topic, but they nevertheless persisted because, as Abigail Greenleaf told her uncle, "tis the most animating Subject to me at Presant; as it Concerns us all."

Women related to congressmen might have been expected to write to their menfolk about political subjects, but that they should include such commentaries in letters to each other was nearly unprecedented. Yet that was what Mercy Otis Warren and Hannah Winthrop did when they exchanged political observations in September and October. They expressed fear of "the Horrors of Civil War," yet belief that "our Cause is righteous" (Winthrop), or confidence that America was producing "a glorious race of Patriots & Heroes" (Warren). When Hannah lamented that people equally committed to "the glorious cause of liberty" were "perplext" and could not agree on a course of action, Mercy reassured her: "It is not at all strange that persons of equal firmness in the support of Liberty & Virtue, should yet vary in sentiment in regard to some particular measures." In fact, she argued, it was "best . . . that every point may be more accurately discussed & that no step may be taken in this important crisis without due deliberation & the most critical survey of future consequences." No experienced male politician could have said it better.

Remarkably, Mary Smith Cranch even went so far as to instruct her younger cousin the Reverend Isaac Smith Jr. about politics. Writing from Boston to Cambridge, where Isaac was a Harvard tutor, she informed him in late October that many people had critiqued the content of his recent sermons. A year ago, people "heard you with admiration and talk'd of you with applause," she remarked, but now she knew of two occasions when listeners walked out of Boston churches to protest his preaching. She was finding it difficult to defend him, because Isaac, who was searching for a parish, had made "imprudent" statements. Mary warned him that "Orthodoxy in Politicks is full as necessary a quallification for Settling a minister at the present Day as orthodoxy in divinity was forme[r]ly." He should avoid being perceived as "unfriendly to the country and constitution and a difender of the unjust, cruil and arbitrary measures that have been taken by the ministry." She concluded, "It is not my province to enter into politicks, but sure I am that it is not your Duty to do or say any thing that shall tend to distroy your usefulness." He would only hurt himself and his parents if he persisted, and she was certain he would not willingly do that.

Isaac resisted Mary's message. Although acknowledging his cousin's "benevolent intentions," he asserted that he could not help it if he was seen as a "heretic" in politics or religion. He was not "indifferent" to what others thought, but he could not surrender "the independance of my own mind." He inquired, "Into what times are we fallen, when the least degree of moderation, the least inclination to peace and order, . . . is accounted a crime?" Isaac cited John Dickinson as his political model and admitted that he disliked the Coercive Acts. Yet he still averred that—in line with many other conservative colonists—"I had rather calmly acquiesce in these, and an hundred other acts, proceeding from a British Legislature, . . . than be subject to the capricious, unlimited despotism of a few of my own countrymen."

Isaac Smith's concerns about the possible "capricious, unlimited despotism" of some of his fellow Americans were shared by others, including his cousin Elizabeth Smith, Mary's youngest sister. She, a Weymouth resident, reported that when carpenters from her town were building the barracks in Boston, other residents planned to demolish their houses. But after the Boston committee ordered them to cease work, the carpenters returned home. Thus the town's "Spirit" was instead embodied in the erection of two tall liberty poles, an outcome Elizabeth pronounced satisfactory. She insisted on the importance of "suppress[ing] our turbulent Passions"; colonists should be "checked and guided by Reason, and Prudence." Abigail Greenleaf expressed similar sentiments while informing her uncle Robert Treat Paine about the August attack on the mandamus councillor Daniel Leonard's house in their hometown of Taunton. She had feared that the participants in the crowd would take an unjustified "rash step," she wrote, "but they behaved *like men,* with a resolution, & firmness which becomes *free men.*" When the crowd wanted to honor Paine with "a flag of Liberty" on his house, she commented approvingly, his brother-in-law told them that "the greatest honor they could do *you* would be, by their good *behaviour.*"

Elizabeth Smith and Abigail Greenleaf thus expressed their concerns about potential mob violence not as Isaac Smith Jr. did—by advocating submission to the Coercive Acts—but rather by praising orderly resistance to the British. In that, they resembled others, including members of Massachusetts county conventions who thought a provincial congress could provide a source of legitimate authority. The signal for the creation of such a body was Governor Gage's order dissolving the legislative session summoned for early October. Those elected to the assembly traveled to Salem despite his order. Many towns, including Boston, had provided that if the assembly did not meet as scheduled, delegates were to regard themselves as a provincial congress. After an initial gathering at Salem, during which they adopted resolutions criticizing Gage, the representatives moved to Concord, then Cambridge, reconstituting themselves as the Massachusetts Provincial Congress and electing John Hancock as their presiding officer.

The new congress then had to confront circumstances that Dr. Benjamin Church, a member of the Boston committee, summarized for Samuel Adams: "A prevailing Discontent, a threat'ned Insurrection, no Government except a contracted Military One." The "Country is very uneasy, long they cannot be restrained," he observed. In the same vein, John Andrews recorded one of Gage's comments: "He can do very well with the Boston selectmen, but the damn'd country committees plague his soul out, as they are very obstinate and hard to be satisfied." In such counties as Plymouth and Barnstable, large crowds prevented judges from holding court sessions, contending that they were unconstitutional. Among the most obstinate were the residents of Worcester, town and county. Strikingly, Worcester in effect declared independence in its October 4 instructions to its representative to the Provincial Congress, insisting that if the Coercive Acts were not immediately repealed, he was to think of the colony as in "a State of Nature" because of "the Dissolution of the Old Constitution." He was to help create a new government, "wherein all officers Shall be Dependent on the Suffrages of the People for their Existence." This goal Worcester residents saw as the only alternative to "a State of Anarchy or Slavery."

Most members of the Provincial Congress were not willing to go so far. Concerned lest they should anger either the Continental Congress or other colonies by moving too fast, they remained in a sort of limbo, beginning to try to govern the colony but without the means to accomplish that end nor even a consensus that they should do so. James Warren explained to John Adams in mid-October that the delegates "dare not Attempt to Form A Civil Constitution or redress our Inconveniencies," because they feared the Continental Congress would disapprove. He described the Provincial Congress as being "in perfect Leading strings," like children learning to walk, dependent on the Philadelphia meeting "for Motion if not for Being." In an attempt to regularize their role, the congressmen invited the councillors displaced by the Massachusetts Government Act to join them when they reconvened after a short adjournment.

The Massachusetts congress focused initially on a limited agenda on which they were certain all would agree: criticizing Gage for the fortifications on Boston Neck and trying (futilely) to persuade him to remove them. They adopted a formal address to the general, which their representatives presented to him in person. As he later explained to Dartmouth, Gage found that accepting and responding to the address confronted him with a dilemma. "I cannot consider them as a legal Assembly," but if he refused to receive their communication, "a handle would have been made of it." Moreover, he needed to order them "to desist from such unconstitutional proceedings." So, when he rejected the appeal, he replied as though to a committee of gentlemen, whom he named individually, rather than to the congress as a whole. He told those who addressed him that they were "subverting" the colony's charter and "acting in direct violation of your own Constitution." Their response, delayed for ten days and apparently much amended, turned the tables on Gage, charging *him* with undermining the constitution; it focused on the "great grievance" of having an army stationed in Boston.

The delegates to the Provincial Congress could not avoid addressing pressing issues that had been raised by the county conventions and town meetings held during September and early October. Their minutes from late October show that they were systematically working their way down a long list of agenda items, not all of which they were able to resolve. They readily concurred on a resolution against "the unnecessary and extravagant Consumption of East India Teas," asking all residents to forgo the beverage. Yet a proposal that apparently would have ratified the Solemn League and Covenant was significantly modified before being adopted, and another dealing with supplying straw to British troops in Boston was dropped altogether. Likewise, they seemed unable to agree on how to direct local authorities to handle imprisoned criminal suspects while the courts were closed, so that subject remained open when the session ended. Too, the congress voted not to act when a member asked about the "propriety" of attempting to "preserve our Selves from Slavery" while not also considering "the State and Circumstances of the Negro Slaves in this Province."

The congressmen chose a receiver general of taxes, Henry Gardner, to whom they asked towns to remit tax payments, rather than to Harrison Gray, the colony's treasurer. Although numerous towns subsequently refused to send levies to Gray, many also withheld them from Gardner, instead ordering them held in the towns until further notice. Their reluctance might have arisen because Gray quickly issued a notice to sheriffs and constables, directing them to ignore orders from "*any* Bodies of Men, *who cannot legally controul them, however numerous or respectable they may be.*" Gray warned tax collectors that they would be held personally liable for failure to comply. Gage then underscored Gray's order with a proclamation declaring that any persons paying Gardner would open themselves to legal action.

Along with that decision to name a receiver general of taxes, the delegates boldly considered "what is Necessary to be now done for the Defence and Safety of the Province." On October 20, they appointed a committee with representatives from every county to recommend a course of action. The resulting report was debated at length and amended repeatedly, but after six days the congressmen accepted the final version "almost unanimously." That document insisted that Massachusetts residents had "not the most distant Design of Attacking, annoying or molesting" the king's troops. Resolutions then established a committee of safety with the power to "Alarm, Muster and cause to be Assembled" the colony's militia whenever the committee deemed that necessary and directed officers to obey such a call to duty. Such forces were to be supplied, armed, and paid with provincial funds that had been collected but not remitted to Harrison Gray. All militia companies were to choose their own officers and should try to improve their "Military Skill." The following day, the congressmen named nine men to the committee of safety, including Joseph Warren, John Hancock, and Benjamin Church, and elected five commissaries and three generals, not all of whom agreed to serve.

And of course such troops would need arms and ammunition. The congress began the process of trying to acquire guns, bayonets, gunpowder, cannon, and shot. Even though the Provincial Congress had copied the Continental Congress in providing that its meetings would be closed to the public, it directed its members to use special care to keep this particular discussion secret from nonmembers. Elbridge Gerry advised Samuel Adams that "from every province Vessals should be dispatched for Arms & Ammunition." He thought it crucial to recruit merchants who would maintain secrecy about all aspects of the essential clandestine maritime trade. After the meeting, Gerry himself worked to acquire gunpowder, but by land, not sea. He directed an emissary to try to buy some in Providence or New York and to send those purchases to Worcester, "keeping the matter as Secret as possible for New York abounds with Tories who would be glad to give General Gage intelligence to have it intercepted on the road." Indeed, Lord Dartmouth in November received a warning from New York that New Englanders "have bought up a *great q[uanti]ty of pow[d]er* and arms in these Parts and carried them to the Eastward."

After the congress adjourned for two weeks in late October, the governor informed Dartmouth perceptively that the congressmen seemed "a good deal puzzled to determine to what lengths they should go," revealing that he recognized the body's hesitancy about assuming full governmental authority. Despite characterizing the people of the colony as "so besotted" that they would not consider evidence contradicting their beliefs, he asserted that they would likely "cool" if they were not continually encouraged in their opposition to Britain. The general described adopting measures he considered "prudent," such as arranging to buy essential supplies in other colonies, in case Boston stopped all sales to the troops, and ordering the keeper of the colony's powder magazine not to deliver any privately owned gunpowder to local merchants. Gage assured the American secretary that with the recent arrival of two more regiments he was amply prepared to defend Castle William and that if war came, he had sufficient men to save Britain "blood and treasure." Still, he concluded, the colonists are "violent everywhere," and "no decency is observed in any place but New York."

The adoption of the Continental Association had little immediate impact in Boston, where problems stemming from the continuing occupation by the army were of much greater concern than nonimportation or other policies the Association recommended. Everyone agreed that conditions in the city were bad. Letters in November recounted tales of frequent confrontations between troops and civilians, often fueled by alcohol; "there is hardly four and twenty hours Pases without some fray" involving soldiers, Jane Mecom reported to her brother Benjamin Franklin. John Andrews noted that prices were already high because of the cost of transporting goods overland from Salem. The large number of refugees from the countryside in the city only increased the demand and the cost of living. Thus the Association's provision that forbade raising prices when nonimportation was implemented was essentially meaningless.

The outlook appeared bleak to most Bostonians, although one supporter of resistance did exult in the "Multiplication of Committees *out* of the Sea-Ports." One man who had sought shelter in Boston informed a friend in London that Bay Colony residents "neither are or will be sensible of their own Weakness till they try their Strength with Discipline Troops." Accordingly, people had started to predict a clash in the spring, "before the Rubbish of their old Constitutions can be clear[e]d to the foundation." As such talk of a possible armed confrontation spread, a local clergyman prayed "that Heaven will prevent the Horrors of a civil War. Shall Brethren go to War with Brethren! Forbid it Reason, forbid it Reason!" he exclaimed.

THE NEW YORK ORIGINS
OF LOYALIST PUBLICATIONS

All observers concurred that New Yorkers were more "moderate" politically than New Englanders. "They think the dispute with Great Britain is carried far enough," reported Cadwallader Colden in early October, "and abhor the thoughts of pushing it to desperate lengths." Even in the city, he informed Dartmouth, "a large majority of the people" opposed nonimportation. Another of Dartmouth's sources, though, anticipated New York's reluctant adherence to nonimportation because the colony would not want to be "Singular" and because city merchants active in clandestine commerce would look forward to "making their fortunes" if legal trade with Britain ended. But he predicted that New Yorkers would never agree to nonexportation: "Self interested Motives will operate to defeat that Measure effectually."

Dr. Thomas Young, commenting from his new base in Rhode Island, also viewed New Yorkers as politically moderate, but to him that was reprehensible. He lamented to one of Alexander McDougall's allies that a group of "those perfidious scoundrels the enemies of our common Rights" still "cursed" New York by their presence, although they had been defeated elsewhere in the colonies. "For Gods sake my brethren," he urged his friends in the city, "destroy that malignant party spirit that so predominates among you," and he offered suggestions for proselytizing their opponents.

New York's seeming moderation, though, obscured the nearly constant political battles that continued to roil the city. In early September, some New Yorkers agreed not to transport troops and supplies to Boston. But Gage's persistent attempts to recruit laborers in the city set off a war waged in competing meetings and broadsides. Isaac Sears became the head of a committee composed either of "very respectable Citizens" or of "the lower class of people," depending on whom one believed, which set out to interrogate merchants they suspected of complicity with Gage and the army. Complex political alignments soon emerged, for John Holt published a broadside criticizing the Sears committee's tactics and urging patience until the congress offered its guidance. "Humanus" pointed out that "we have delegated our Authority, with Respect to American Measures, to the Continental Congress," and thus should not act without its approval. He feared that depriving the troops in Boston of necessary supplies might lead them to sally forth, setting off "Skirmishes, and then general Hostilities." Sears, never one to be shy, defended himself in a broadside of his own.

Other groups intervened as well. A "Number of the Citizens" headed by the merchant Joseph Totten called on the city committee—which no longer had fifty-one members, because McDougall, Sears, and others had resigned in July—to take control of the situation. The "citizens" challenged the Sears group's legitimacy by questioning its "presum[ing] to call themselves a Committee from the Body of the Inhabitants of the City," while the "citizens" nevertheless ironically claimed to act by the "unanimous Desire" of a similarly unauthorized committee. At the end of September, the remaining members of the city committee responded, formally disapproving Sears's actions and decrying "all such irregular Proceedings." Colden pronounced that statement a victory for "the principal people," who had managed to silence "the turbulent factious few who are never easy when the people are quiet and orderly." He told Dartmouth that "the merchants now go on completing their orders [for Boston] without farther interruption."

The victory of the rump committee ended the public meetings but not the publications. In mid-October, "Philo-Libertas" thanked "the worthy Merchants and Citizens of New-York" for combating "the unwarrantable and bold attempts of those persons who use the prostituted name of liberty, only to infringe that of others." He charged that those who would deny the king's troops necessary supplies were "children of mischief, tumult and riot." Similarly, an anonymous wit published a satire of "Isaac Sheer-off" and "Alexander McDoubtful" that ended with a brief verse:

> QUOTH Demagogue S[ears], that spruce son of Faction,
> In order to promote our cheef ame, distraction,
> Nor biskits, nor blankits, nor skillits, nor Flour,
> Shall be shypt to the troups, from this very oure.
> The rogues, if their bellys they want to have cramd,
> Don't sel them a morsil—theil die, and be damd.

In this contentious context, New York City became the progenitor of public Loyalism. The first lengthy publications that can accurately be termed "Loyalist" appeared in the city during the fall of 1774 while the First Continental Congress met in Philadelphia and arguments raged over whether Manhattan's merchants and tradesmen should aid the British troops in Boston. Before the congress convened, conservative colonists had reluctantly been willing to give that body the benefit of the doubt. As was seen in chapter 4, the idea of a congress was presented as a moderate option during the summer. Even the pamphlets published in August by the future Loyalists Jonathan Boucher and Thomas Bradbury Chandler allowed for the possibility that the congress might succeed in sketching a plan for conciliation.

During and especially after the congress, though, conservatives' opinions changed. In September, some New Yorkers produced more extended critiques of the resistance movement, even though no one knew for certain what the congressmen were thinking or doing. Such critiques increased in intensity after the congress publicly supported the Suffolk Resolves on September 19 and three days later warned merchants not to place new orders for British goods, thereby signaling a probable nonimportation agreement. Decisions that to congressmen could seem unexceptionable and measured acquired a dramatically different resonance in New York. The contentious atmosphere in the city, caused in part by the spillover of events from occupied Boston, provided the impetus for the earliest Loyalist pamphlets and newspaper essays.

In his memorial to the Loyalist Claims Commission in London after the war, the Reverend Charles Inglis explained that "observing a restless and seditious spirit" around him, he and two friends, Chandler and the Reverend Samuel Seabury, decided to respond quickly to "all publications that were disrespectful to Government or the parent State." The three clergymen not only reacted to others' writings but also initiated public political dialogues that persisted for months. Two printers willing to open their presses to conservatives made possible the initial outpouring of Loyalist publications: Hugh Gaine of *The New-York Gazette and the Weekly Mercury* and James Rivington, who was to become especially notorious as the "Tory printer."

Gaine, Irish-born and trained as a printer there, immigrated to the colonies in 1744. In 1752, he opened his own business in New York and founded his paper, which—following traditional practice—kept its pages open to all sides of the political spectrum throughout the 1760s and early 1770s. His chief competitor until 1773 was John Holt, of *The New-York Journal,* who unabashedly aligned himself with Sears, McDougall, and their allies. But then James Rivington began to publish his *Rivington's New-York Gazetteer; or, The Connecticut, New-Jersey, Hudson's-River, and Quebec Advertiser.* Rivington, who had gone bankrupt in London and was the son of a family of British printers and booksellers, immigrated to Philadelphia in 1760 and moved to New York two years later. He focused solely on selling and publishing books until starting his newspaper in 1773.

In late 1774 and early 1775, Rivington published numerous Loyalist pamphlets, sometimes with incomplete title pages that failed to identify the printer. In early December, he described himself as "A Free

PRINTER, approved such, by both PARTIES," and advertised accurately in his *Gazetteer* that he had published eight pamphlets *"written on the* Whig *and* Tory *Side of the Question,"* with a ninth currently in press. A few weeks later, his list of titles for sale had ballooned to thirteen, some of which responded to others he had also published. That some of these publications supported resistance to Britain did not prevent him from becoming a special target for radical colonists, perhaps because he had quickly become very successful. In October 1774, after just eighteen months as a newspaper publisher, he boasted that he had thirty-six hundred subscribers, drawn from all the North American colonies, the West Indies, and some European countries. Even if he exaggerated, it is clear his press had a very wide geographic reach.

In the fall of 1774, New Yorkers eagerly snapped up publications by both supporters and opponents of colonial resistance. One of the most popular in the former category, in New York and elsewhere, originated in Britain but was reprinted many times in America: *A Speech Intended to Have Been Spoken on the Bill for Altering the Charters of the Colony of Massachusetts Bay,* by Jonathan Shipley, bishop of St. Asaph, who was a member of the House of Lords. Abigail Adams and the congressman Caesar Rodney of Delaware both commented on it approvingly in mid-September, as did Charity Clarke, a teenage girl in New York. "Oh that all your Bishops were like ye Bishop of St. Asaph," she wrote to an English cousin on September 10; if so, "America might have cause to revere [Britain] as a parent, assist her commerce & continue to flourish under her protection, but alas! her wise men are not listened to." She proclaimed her allegiance firmly: "You cannot deprive us, the Arms that supports my family shall defend it. though this body is not clad with silken Garments, these limbs are armed with strength, the soul is fortified by Virtue, and the love of Liberty is cherished within this bosom."

Although Rivington probably did not reprint Shipley's *Speech,* he seems to have sold copies of it in his store. That he sought to purchase similar works from other printers is evidenced by a letter he wrote to Thomas and William Bradford in early November, ordering twenty-five copies each of two pamphlets they had recently published in Philadelphia: John Dickinson's *Essay on the Constitutional Power of Great-Britain* and James Wilson's *Considerations on the Nature and the Extent of the Legislative Authority of the British Parliament.* And, he added, "if you have lately printed any other pamphlets on the Dispute with G B pray send me 25 & if any thing is in the press let them come to me when finished without delay." The previous month he had likewise addressed Henry Knox in Boston with a request for a *"well written"* pamphlet on the current dispute that he could reprint "whilst it shall be quite new to our readers in this province."

As a businessman, Rivington wanted to attract all potential customers, regardless of their views on the current conflict. But by the time he directed the order to the Bradfords, he had already been stereotyped by Silas Deane as an "incendiary" who printed "false, & scandalous" political news. Rivington was detested everywhere south of New York, Deane asserted; he was compared to "whatever is mean, base, servile, & treacherous." The printer had possibly cemented his reputation as a Loyalist sympathizer, despite the wide range of pamphlets he printed, by his August publication in the *Gazetteer* of an all-out attack on John Holt. "Mercator" (who later revealed his identity as Benjamin Booth, one of the New York tea consignees) directed a lengthy vituperative tirade at Holt and the *Journal*. He accused Holt not only of serving as "a receptacle for every inflammatory piece that is published throughout the continent" but also of publishing articles by authors "of the lowest class" who wrote with poor grammar and a lack of "propriety and elegance of stile." Holt was outraged. He defended himself and his contributors vigorously in not one but two issues of his own newspaper, concluding that he would always be ready "to repel any Attack upon my Person."

When Joseph Reed referred to "the vilest collection of invectives upon the cause and every private character that appears in support of it" in the New York newspapers, he therefore surely had both Gaine and Rivington in mind, particularly the latter. In fact, he insisted, the New York papers were so "replete with falsehoods" that he was certain the editors had been corrupted by "some Agent of Administration."

The articles to which Reed referred undoubtedly included those in Gaine's *New-York Gazette* by Charles Inglis, writing as "A New York Freeholder." Inglis explained in his claims memorial that he began to write "when many were in suspense concerning the designs and views of the American Congress" and that he ceased after that body commended the Suffolk Resolves, which confirmed his suspicion that "the Congress really aimed at Revolt and independ[enc]y." In the essays, published from mid-September to mid-October, he laid out "the probable Consequences that would attend violent Measures on our Part, and the ruinous Effects of a Civil War." Citing the powder alarm to show that his fears of war were realistic, he described the death and destruction that would inevitably ensue if Americans continued on their present course. And what had led them into such peril? The "rash Action" of the Bostonians in destroying the EIC's tea. If only the tea ships had been greeted as one was at Charleston, all would have been well. He averred that he too opposed parliamentary taxation, but what was needed was an American constitution, not a nonimportation agreement. His final essay closed with the hope that the "*Constitutional Line*" the congressmen were defining would end the "unhappy Disputes"—but, although those words were published later, he had drafted them before learning of the congress's decision on the Suffolk Resolves.

The most extended and influential response to the events of September and October 1774 written prior to the conclusion of the congress came from Thomas Bradbury Chandler. The author of *The American Querist* reentered the ranks of political polemicists with *A Friendly Address to All Reasonable Americans on the Subject of Our Political Confusions*. Rivington published the pamphlet, but without identifying himself as the printer on the title page, perhaps rendered wary by the negative reaction to Chandler's previous work. Even so, that he printed it was widely known. Rivington jocularly described a public immolation of the pamphlet in the city shortly after its publication, along with a warning he received from a "Waggish Correspondent": "Keep *yourself* out of the *fire*, Mr. Printer." Still, the "inflammatory" reception underscored the significance of Chandler's effort and the importance of the negative response it elicited. Although his identity as the author was unknown, the *Friendly Address* was publicly burned in Chandler's native Elizabethtown, New Jersey, as well as in Maryland and rural New York, and it was reputedly banned from sale in Philadelphia and Norfolk.

The contents of the *Friendly Address* showed that the New Jersey clergyman started writing the pamphlet after September 19 and finished it before the congress's resolutions were revealed in late October, but the text was not published until November 10, the very day it was publicly burned in Manhattan. Some supporters of resistance who commented on the pamphlet argued that it should simply be ignored—that, as the congressman William Hooper remarked, the anonymous author should "speak in obscurity"—but James Madison, who heard it described as "the best performance on that Side of the dispute," wanted to read it, and George Washington eventually owned two copies. The *Friendly Address* could thus well have been the unnamed Loyalist pamphlet a correspondent dispatched to Lord Dartmouth in mid-January 1775, with the explanation that among recent publications it "has been of the most essential Service, as it is calculated for People of middling Capacities, and great Pains were taken by the Friends of government, to disperse them privately through the different Colonies." In short, surviving evidence points to its significance and widespread distribution.

Chandler began his *Friendly Address* by reiterating many of the points he had made in *The American Querist,* but in the form of statements rather than rhetorical questions. For example, he stressed the need for Americans to show "reverence, respect, and obedience" to proper authority, and he argued that Boston's quarrel with Britain need not involve all America. Like Inglis, he contended that Charleston had selected a better solution than Boston to the problem presented by the EIC's tea shipment. He challenged negative interpretations of the Massachusetts Government Act and the Quebec Act, pointing out that the former did nothing more than amend the Bay Colony charter to make it conform to practices in other colonies and claiming that the latter had been mischaracterized by its opponents as establishing (rather than simply tolerating) Catholicism. Americans' only actual complaint was the tea duty, which, he asserted, they could easily avoid by not purchasing tea. It was "truly astonishing" that "such an indecent and violent opposition to government" had been based on "so slight a provocation."

After the congress ended, Chandler abridged the *Friendly Address,* halving its length by omitting the pages just summarized. In effect, he produced a second edition acknowledging that re-litigating the debates of the previous months would no longer carry much weight with his intended audience of "reasonable Americans." He signaled decisively his recognition that the summer's arguments had been superseded and that future discussions would not emphasize complaints about Parliament. Rather, the contentious issues would be resistance tactics, the Continental Association, and the possibility of war. By removing what had been the first half of his pamphlet, he newly emphasized relevant themes of his original text: in the event of war, Americans had no chance against British forces; a nonimportation agreement would not accomplish Americans' goals; and, perhaps most significantly because of its novelty, New Englanders had now disclosed that they were "thorough-paced *Republicans.*" In approving the Suffolk Resolves, the congressmen had joined them. Warning his readers that they were in danger of being "hurried into a state of rebellion before you are aware of it," he urged them to "resume the liberty of thinking, and speaking, and acting for ourselves." In other words, they had to abandon the habit of deference to authority he had previously promoted in *The American Querist.*

So what did Chandler recommend to his "reasonable" compatriots? Americans should do what the congress should have done: make "a candid acknowledgment of our political errors and offences—a formal allowance of the rightful supremacy in general, of *Great Britain* over the American Colonies—a declaration of our aversion to a state of independency . . . an assurance of our willingness to contribute, in some equitable proportion, towards defraying the public expences—and the proposal of a reasonable plan for a general American constitution." That last was key. A "*general American Constitution,* on a free and generous Plan," would be in the interest of both Britain and America. Chandler thus advocated a solution much like Joseph Galloway's, but the same difficulty loomed ahead: how to persuade both Americans and Britons that such an outcome was either possible or desirable.

A key indication of the contemporary importance of Chandler's pamphlet was the number of refutations it elicited, all of which attempted to address the full version. John Adams began, but failed to finish, an essay challenging the clergyman's adherence to "the absurd and exploded Doctrine of Passive obedience and Non Resistance." Charles Lee, a retired British army officer, questioned at length Chandler's insistence that the colonies could not win a war with England. He expressed confidence that America's "active, vigorous yeomanry," expert users of firearms, could readily defeat an army of Britons, "the refuse of an exhausted nation." And the New York congressman Philip Livingston undertook a comprehensive attack on the pamphlet. He spent multiple pages addressing the tea duty, Boston's destruction of the tea, and Britain's response in the Coercive Acts; predicted the success of nonimportation; and contended that no one need worry about the possibility of war. He concurred that an American constitution was desirable, but averred that it would have been "presumptuous" for the congress to propose one. Livingston ended by criticizing the Administration of Justice Act—a law Chandler had not mentioned, probably because few Americans were willing to defend it.

An anonymous "Friend to his Country" also replied at length to the *Friendly Address,* but in *Dunlap's Pennsylvania Packet* rather than a pamphlet. His was perhaps the most convincing of all the critiques, in large part because he fundamentally challenged much of Chandler's reasoning rather than questioning details. For example, he charged that the major problem with the Massachusetts Government Act was not the specific changes to the provincial charter but rather Parliament's "daring usurpation" in enacting them. He too cited the Administration of Justice Act and asked, could not everyone understand "how easy the victory over all America would be, if once the people of Boston could be brought to a submission"? He further drew a positive analogy between Americans' current situation and that of the Dutch when they won independence from Spain, and with respect to the likely outcome of nonimportation he asserted (as did others) that the colonies were far better able to live without British manufactures than were Britons able to forgo American agricultural products.

While Chandler's abridged edition was being typeset in Rivington's print shop, New Yorkers were preparing to elect a committee of observation and inspection to enforce the Association. The remaining members of the committee of fifty-one, including the returned delegates from Philadelphia, took charge of the electoral process. To avoid the friction that had developed in July, the rump committee consulted the committee of mechanics and worked out a mutually acceptable arrangement: the committees would together propose one hundred names, and sixty would be elected. After that election on November 22, the rump committee of fifty-one was dissolved and the committee of sixty took over.

Despite the consensus that led to the election of the new committee, New Yorkers remained less enthusiastic about resistance than did other colonists. That became evident in the muted reaction in the city to the First Continental Congress, compared with events elsewhere. For instance, Joseph Reed stressed that Philadelphia contained "a band of staunch, chosen sons of liberty, among some of our best families, who are backed by the body of the people." There, a newly elected city committee moved swiftly to enforce provisions of the Association against price gouging and in favor of conserving sheep, whereas New York showed "a strange delinquency and backwardness," and the new committee there took little immediate action. Likewise, the return of South Carolina's delegates to Charleston quickly led to the choice of a new general committee that soon announced an election for a provincial congress to meet in mid-January. To such actions, William Henry Drayton later recalled, "we may date, the strengthening of the popular branch of our Government."

By contrast, in New York the burst of Loyalist pamphlets continued, primarily from James Rivington's press. After the congress adjourned, Rivington published a satirical poem by "Mary V. V.," *A Dialogue, Between a Southern Delegate, and His Spouse, on His Return from the Grand Continental Congress,* which William Bradford thought "grossly scurrilous." In the poem, the wife is the voice of reason, telling her husband that he will regret having participated in the congress. He responds that she should "Mind thy Houshold-Affairs, teach thy Children to read, / And never, Dear, with Politics, trouble thy Head," which she answers by challenging men's primacy in public affairs:

> *Because Men are Males, are they all Politicians?*
> *Why then I presume they're Divines and Physicians.*

> *And born all with Talents every Station to fill,*
> *Noble Proofs you've given! no doubt of your Skill:*
> *Wou'd instead of Delegates, they sent Delegates Wives;*
> *Heavens! we cou'dn't have bungled it so for our Lives!*

As the poem continues, she warns him, "This will at last end in Blood," because defying "the high sovereign Power," for whatever reason, is "deem'd, little short, of High Treason." She asserts, "Your Non-Imports, and Exports, are full fraught with Ruin, / Of Thousands, and thousands, to the utter Undoing," and moves on to the Association, "big with rank Tyranny."

> *You have read a great deal,—with patient Reflection,*
> *Consider one Moment, your Courts of Inspection:*
> *Could the Inquisition,* Venice, Rome, *or* Japan,
> *Have devised so horrid, so wicked a Plan? . . .*
> *Let Fools, Pedants, and Husbands, continue to hate*
> *The Advice of us Women, and call it all Prate: . . .*
> *Oh! my Country! Remember, that a Woman unknown,*
> *Cry'd aloud,—like* Cassandra, *in Oracular Tone,*
> *Repent! Or you are forever, forever undone.*

Whatever Mary V. V.'s identity, she or he was well acquainted with conventional thinking on the relationship of women and public life. As has been seen, in the eighteenth century women were expected to focus on household and family, not on politics, and both men and women regarded it as surprising, perhaps even shocking, if they ventured into the public realm. The author of the *Dialogue* effectively combined a conservative critique of the congress with the use of rhetorical femininity, or the adoption of a female pseudonym, in order to comment on politics. The satire's content presented a direct challenge to British authority and to the creation of committees of observation and inspection. Mary V. V. adopted the stance of an outsider who could view the congress and its actions with clarity precisely because she was female. She used congressional actions she regarded as misguided to puncture men's belief in their superior wisdom. She tells her husband pointedly,

> *Instead of Addresses, fram'd on Truth, and on Reason,*
> *They breathe nothing, but Insult, Rebellion, and Treason;*
> *Instead of attempting, our Interests to further,*
> *You bring down, on our Heads, Perdition, and Murder.*

That the nature of the debate had changed was shown by the fact that the poem, ostensibly by a woman, never mentioned that quintessentially feminine topic, tea, or the tea duty. Rather than Americans' earlier focus on measures adopted by Parliament, their attention had now shifted to congressional actions and their implications, for good or ill.

The new emphasis continued in two pamphlets drafted and published in November by the Reverend Samuel Seabury, the third member of the group of Anglican clergymen who had vowed to support British authority publicly. His *Free Thoughts, on the Proceedings of the Continental Congress* had a final internal date of November 16 and was advertised by James Rivington on November 24; *The Congress Canvassed; or, An Examination into the Conduct of the Delegates at Their Grand Convention* had an internal date of November 28 and was advertised by Rivington on December 15, although Seabury added a postscript on December 16. Seabury addressed *Free Thoughts* explicitly to New York farmers, and *Congress Canvassed* to New York merchants. He signed both "A. W. Farmer."

In *Free Thoughts,* Seabury focused on the difficulties that he claimed the nonexportation provision of the Continental Association would cause for farmers. When exports from New York were halted, he argued, the colony's farmers would be ruined. Without exports such as flaxseed sent to Ireland, they would earn nothing, would not be able to pay their debts, and therefore would lose their farms to creditors. "This cursed scheme," he contended, betrayed New York's agriculturalists. Meanwhile, "the proud merchants, and the forsworn smuggler, riot in their ill-gotten wealth." Moreover, the committees enforcing the Association would "examine your tea-canisters, and molasses jugs, and your wives and daughters petty-coats," but not A. W. Farmer's: "Before *I* submit, I will die: live *you,* and be slaves." Seabury urged farmers to "renounce all dependence on Congresses, and Committees," and instead turn for guidance to "your *constitutional* representatives," the members of the assembly. They would use their "wisdom and prudence" to find the best way to restore peace to the empire.

Seabury's message in his second November pamphlet, *Congress Canvassed,* differed in large part from that in *Free Thoughts.* For obvious reasons, he did not accuse his imagined audience of city merchants of "riot[ing] in their ill-gotten wealth." Rather, he attacked the congress at length (terming it a *"foreign* power"), raised questions about New York's electoral process, and criticized the congressmen's weeks of silence about their deliberations. Showing his intended urban readers that he was familiar with a recently published account of Captain James Cook's first voyage to the South Pacific, he satirized the congressmen by comparing them to the natives of New Zealand, who before confronting their enemies "animate themselves by singing their war song, exercising their lances, and brandishing their patoo-patoos" to "work themselves up into such a state of frenzy." Like Mary V. V., Seabury compared the committees to the *"papish Inquisition,"* with the accused having no chance to present a defense. "Your liberties and properties are now at the mercy of a body of men unchecked, uncontrouled by the civil power," he cautioned. Are you certain, he asked his readers, that "you are not nourishing and bringing to maturity, a grand American Republic"? Should the colonies declare independence, he predicted that "a horrid scene of war and bloodshed" would follow, ending with "CONFISCATIONS and EXECUTIONS."

Just as *Congress Canvassed* was being published, Seabury's *Free Thoughts* drew a response from a newcomer to political polemics and indeed to the American mainland itself: Alexander Hamilton, then a nineteen-year-old student at King's College in New York, had arrived from St. Croix in 1772. He studied first at an academy in New Jersey and entered the college in the fall of 1773. Rivington, true to his pledge to publish pamphlets with differing political approaches, printed Hamilton's effort, as he had Philip Livingston's, this time identifying himself on the title page. *A Full Vindication of the Measures of the Congress, from the Calumnies of Their Enemies, in Answer to a Letter, Under the Signature of A. W. Farmer,* appeared in mid-December, attributed to "A Friend to America."

Hamilton began by asking how anyone could be so "presumptuous" as to question the acts of the Continental Congress, a "truly

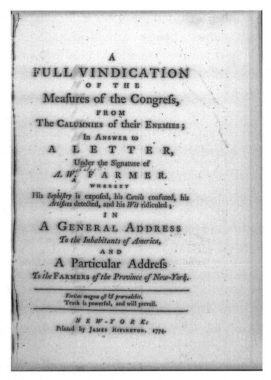

A

FULL VINDICATION
OF THE
Meaſures of the Congreſs,
FROM
The CALUMNIES of their ENEMIES;
In ANSWER to
A LETTER,
Under the Signature of
A. W. FARMER.
WHEREBY
His *Sophiſtry* is expoſed, his *Cavils* confuted, his
Artifices detected, and his *Wit* ridiculed;
IN
A GENERAL ADDRESS
To the Inhabitants of America,
AND
A Particular Addreſs
To the FARMERS *of the Province of New-York.*

Veritas magna eſt & prævalebit.
Truth is powerful, and will prevail.

NEW-YORK:
Printed by JAMES RIVINGTON. 1774.

Title page of the young Alexander Hamilton's initial contribution to public political discourse, a response to Samuel Seabury's *Free Thoughts, on the Proceedings of the Continental Congress*. The dialogue would continue in another pamphlet by Hamilton and two by Seabury, all published by James Rivington.

respectable" group of men who had "devised and recommended the only effectual means to secure the freedom, and establish the future prosperity of America upon a solid basis." Americans, he argued, had not given Parliament authority to rule them. Rather, they owed allegiance to the congress—the body they had elected—and should regard its resolutions as "binding." How could anyone oppose "the united counsels of men, in whom America has reposed so high a confidence"? Referring to the failure of recent American petitions to Parliament, he contended that only the congress's commercial tactics had a chance of succeeding. If the colonists submitted to British demands, the outcome would amount to enslavement. On the other hand, the British so depended on trade with America that they would soon change their policies. Indeed, the British would never risk going to war, for "the conquest of so numerous a people, armed in the animating cause of liberty could not be accomplished without an inconceivable expence of blood and treasure."

Hamilton devoted several pages to responding to Seabury's specific arguments to farmers, for example contending that the impact of stopping colonial exports would be far greater elsewhere in the British Empire, especially the West Indies, than in North America. Admitting that he was not an agriculturalist and voicing his suspicion that neither was A. W. Farmer, he asked his own readers, "Will you give up your freedom, or, which is the same thing, will you resign all security for your life and property, rather than endure some small present inconveniencies?" He informed his imagined audience of farmers that he had heard them denigrated as "ignorant and mean-spirited," concerned only with their own welfare, and he exhorted them to join other Americans "in the same common measure." Otherwise, he warned, you would "fall a prey to your enemies, and repent your folly as long as you live."

Seabury replied to Hamilton in a third pamphlet, titled *A View of the Controversy Between Great-Britain and Her Colonies*. In addition to specifics and expressions of contempt for his rival—with such snarky comments about youth that he must have learned Hamilton's identity from Rivington—Seabury reemphasized his major points in the other pamphlets: first, that colonies needed to remain subordinate to the mother country; and second, that accepting the authority of the congress meant establishing an American republic. When the Second Congress met in May 1775, he predicted, "*then* our whole constitution is to be finally destroyed; . . . our legislatures rendered useless; our laws overturned;—in order to make room for an American republic, on a true democratical plan." Hamilton's lengthy response to that pamphlet, *The Farmer Refuted,* analyzed examples from American and British history to support his assertion that the colonies should not be subject to Parliament and attacked Seabury's arguments with terms as disdainful and dismissive as Seabury had used about his (for example, "puerile and fallacious," "illiterate, trifling, and absurd"). He did not address Seabury's contention that a republic was in the offing.

Yet an anonymous Philadelphia author implicitly advocated what Seabury and Chandler most feared. Although the essay, "Political Observations, Without Order, Addressed to the People of America," did not overtly call for the establishment of a republic, readers had no problem discerning the thrust of the essay, which aroused considerable commentary, including by John Adams. The author began by praising the Continental Congress as "founded upon the principles of the most perfect liberty," contending that "a more august, and a more equitable Legislative body never existed in any quarter of the globe." The foundations of "an American Constitution" were being laid, a constitution that would be freer and less corrupt than the earlier constitutions of Greece, Rome, and Britain. Predicting that the colonies would "dissolve our connexion with Great Britain," he made clear that he foresaw a glorious independent future. "I almost wish to live to hear the triumphs of the Jubilee in the year 1874," he wrote; "to see the medals, pictures, fragments of writings, &c., that shall be displayed to revive the memory of the proceedings of the Congress in the year 1774."

Commentators employed terms like "extraordinary" and "audacious" to refer to "Political Observations." One New Yorker accused the author of being "an open, an avowed Republican," devoted to tearing down "a fabrick that is the work of ages, that has long been the admiration of the whole world." Another indicated that he had recently been in "several companies" that discussed and condemned the essay as "a vile, inflammatory, and treasonable publication." He had not joined in the condemnations, though, because he welcomed the open revelation of the republican schemers, who had hidden their intentions for so long. Now the author had *"let the cat out of the bag"* and appeared "in all the terrible pomp of his own horrid visage."

The author of "Political Observations" ended his essay with "to be continued," but no continuation has been located. Perhaps the negative reactions silenced him, at least for a time. To a reader today, his comments about a celebration in 1874 evoke the actual centennial celebration of independence in Philadelphia in 1876. In the context of his own day, he was indeed audacious, but he also put into "extraordinary" words what some Americans had begun to think—and on which they had started to act.

ADVICES FROM THE HAGUE, LONDON, BATH, AND HAMBURG

October 11, 1774. Sir Joseph Yorke, British ambassador to the Dutch Republic, writes from The Hague to Lord Suffolk, one of the secretaries of state in London, informing him that American smugglers have started to purchase arms and ammunition, not just tea or other traditional contraband items. A vessel from Rhode Island has come to Amsterdam seeking "different sorts of Fire Arms." Reportedly, the *Smack* "(or some such name)," captained by one Benjamin Page, has already taken on board forty "small Pieces of Cannon."

October 14 (Hamburg). Emanuel Mathias addresses Suffolk from Hamburg, with news that the sloop *John* has arrived in the Elbe River with a clandestine cargo of rice and logwood from America. Instead of entering the port of Hamburg, the ship unloaded in the Elbe, and he has learned that chests of tea and "a Number of Chests and Barrels, supposed to contain Ammunition," will soon be taken on board the vessel. The *John* is headed to New York but will have "Bills of Lading, as if bound for St. Eustatia," to show any British ships it might encounter. He has heard that such ships off-load their smuggled cargo on Long Island, away from the customshouse, and then proceed to New York in ballast.

October 14 (Bath). Lord Barrington writes from Bath to inform Dartmouth that when he was recently in Plymouth the customs collector there told him that "a very large quantity of Gunpowder was on board a ship in that port, bound for N. America."

October 17. Lord Suffolk addresses two urgent letters to Sir Joseph Yorke in The Hague about the *Smack* "by Messenger & Extraordinary Packet." He suggests that Yorke ask the Dutch authorities to adopt an "Expedient to check & controul such improper Exportations to our Colonies," although he recognizes that it is a "delicate Point." To prove their "Friendly Dispositions towards us," perhaps the Dutch can find a pretext to search the ship without giving a reason.

October 18. Dartmouth encloses Yorke's October 11 letter to Suffolk in a missive to the Lords of the Admiralty, asking them to dispatch a cutter to Amsterdam immediately to investigate the report and, if possible, stop the *Smack* from leaving port. He urges "the greatest caution and secrecy" and directs the commander of the British ship to be "very circumspect" so as to conceal "the object and intention of his voyage."

October 19. King George III issues an order in council prohibiting the exporting of any arms and ammunition from Great Britain for the next six months.

October 21–November 18. In a series of detailed letters dispatched every few days, Yorke reports to Lord Suffolk on his efforts—and those of the British coast guard cutter *Wells,* which arrived on the evening of October 19—first to ascertain whether the rumors about the cargo of the *Smack* are correct, and then to prevent Captain Page's departure with that cargo while still not alerting Amsterdam's mercantile houses to Britain's efforts. He also futilely requests assistance from Dutch authorities, winning expressions of sympathy but little else. Yorke's confidential sources inform him that Page has added gunpowder to cannon in the hold and has concealed it under other items. The two ships maneuver in a game of cat and mouse in the extensive waterways surrounding Amsterdam, until finally Page decides to unload his vessel and to winter there rather than to risk sailing into the North Sea and confronting the *Wells* directly.

November 1, 22. Emanuel Mathias continues his reports to Lord Suffolk from Hamburg. The *John* has sailed, with a cargo of "Fire Arms and gunpowder." Three weeks later, he reports that another American vessel, the *Flora*, has now been loaded with a similar cargo on the Elbe outside Hamburg in the same clandestine manner and has sailed to the head of the river, ready to go to sea.

November 2. Lord Dartmouth writes to Lieutenant Governor Cadwallader Colden, urging him to pay more attention than usual to smuggling in and around Manhattan, "as every day almost furnishes some fresh Intelligence of the Americans purchasing large Quantities of Arms and Ammunition in the different Ports of Europe."

November 22, 25, December 2. In missives to Suffolk, Yorke celebrates his success in dealing with the *Smack*. He has learned that the merchants trading in contraband to America "have been a little check'd," and he has let all the merchants know that "we will not suffer that Trade [to continue]." He adds on December 2, "The Loss the Owners of the *Smack* & their Associates will have undergone, will I hope serve as an Example to deter others from the like illicit & unjustifiable Proceedings."

December 9. Suffolk informs Yorke that he has learned, to his chagrin—he does not say how—that the *Smack*'s cargo has been reshipped on a Dutch vessel, which, along with two other Dutch ships, is preparing to depart for St. Eustatius, carrying tea, gunpowder, and "25 pieces of Canon." He remarks that the Dutch should be warned that the British could station ships between the Dutch Caribbean islands and the North American mainland to interdict trade and that Yorke should make it clear that such an "unpleasant" outcome can be avoided if the Dutch cooperate to ensure that "the little Selfishness of private Shopkeeping" is not allowed to interfere with "great National Systems." On December 20, Yorke reports that the gunpowder, at least, has not been reshipped and will remain in the Netherlands. But is that information accurate?

(When Peter Oliver pens his acerbic account of the American Revolution while living in exile in Birmingham, England, in the 1780s, he recalls that in late 1774 New Englanders began sailing to St. Eustatius for gunpowder.)

CHAPTER 7

THE BRINK OF A PRECIPICE

On December 15, 1774, many Massachusetts churches observed a day of thanksgiving proclaimed by the Provincial Congress, to thank God for a good harvest and the good health of the populace, and in addition for "the union which so remarkably prevails not only in this Province, but through the Continent, at this alarming Crisis." Yet the message the Provincial Congress conveyed to New Englanders was not entirely positive: the proclamation called on people to humble themselves before God, recognizing that the current calamitous dispute with Great Britain had resulted from his "Righteous Judgment." People should pray for God's blessing and reform their behavior. Then, the congressmen declared, "we may again rejoice in the Smiles of our Sovereign."

Just as sermons delivered on the colony's fast day the previous July 14 provided a snapshot of ministerial opinion in midsummer, so too did four sermons on December 15, along with a fifth delivered a week later at a commemoration of the Pilgrims' 1620 landing. As was seen in chapter 4, the earlier sermons focused in large part on identifying Americans' sins that had provoked God's anger and on Parliament's attempts to tax the colonies. The themes of the December sermons were very different: love of country, defined more broadly than simply one's colony, and paeans to patriotism filled the sermons, along with detailed dissections of British policy and praise for America and Americans. One clergyman declared of the Continental Congress that "*Heaven directed their Councils*"; another asserted, "If the British legislature is the constitution, or superior to the constitution, *Magna Charta, the bill of rights, and the protestant succession,* these boasts of Britons, are . . . not *solid securities.*"

Of particular significance were two sermons preached by clergymen who had published the sermons they gave on Boston's ritual occasions six months earlier: Gad Hitchcock, who had delivered the election sermon, and John Lathrop, who had spoken to the Artillery Company. In June, Hitchcock stressed the need for people to judge their rulers; in December, he made it clear that he had judged those rulers and the Americans who called themselves "friends to government" and found them wanting. He likened the so-called friends to "the grand apostate spirit himself" who worked to "accomplish the baneful designs of the kingdom of darkness." Above all, Hitchcock lauded liberty, which he defined as a key component of Americans' experiences, from the first settlers of Plymouth to contemporary colonists. Although he acknowledged briefly the need for "humiliating reflections" about Americans' sins, he insisted that Americans could always rely on the assistance of God, "the mighty avenger of wrongs." Hitchcock closed with a poetic vision of the future that, while not explicitly advocating independence, omitted any reference to a link with Great Britain: "The American desert rejoices and blossoms as a rose, cities and empires rise, arts and sciences flourish, and the solitary places are glad."

And Lathrop, a man who in June had drafted a long footnote defending his right to take a political stand, clearly found no such passage necessary in December. Instead, a footnote listed all the British regiments and warships stationed in Boston, with the obvious aim of publicizing the extent of the occupation of the city to those outside it. "This whole community has been condemned, without trial, and is this day suffering in a manner that can scarcely be parallelled in the history of the world," he proclaimed. To Lathrop, the resolutions of the Continental Congress "*will,* as they most certainly *ought to,* have *the force of laws,*" for those resolves represented "the wisdom and strength of this amazing continent." Rather than the Bible, the sermon quoted extensively from John Dickinson, the bishop of St. Asaph, the Massachusetts Provincial Congress, the Continental Congress, John Locke, William Pitt, and other sources from both sides of the Atlantic. Even though Lathrop asserted his loyalty to the king, he indicated that rebellion could be a last resort, if "*absolutely* necessary to our own defence."

By December 1774, in short, Gad Hitchcock and John Lathrop, along with the others who preached on the Thanksgiving Day, constituted excellent examples of clergymen who had, in Chief Justice Peter Oliver's words, converted their pulpits into "Gutters of Sedition." Such men "had quite unlearned the Gospel, & substituted Politicks in its Stead," he charged in the memoir he wrote in exile in England.

Such obvious politicization of the clergy was yet another confirmation of the significant polarization of the population as a whole that followed the adjournment of the First Continental Congress. Americans increasingly aligned themselves for or against a continuing connection to Great Britain. Even though few spoke or wrote openly of independence, like the Reverend Gad Hitchcock many colonists, a plurality if not a majority, began to contemplate the prospect of severing their transatlantic ties, some more openly than others. As one North Carolina critic of the trend observed to a friend in early February 1775, "Such there are, and can it be believed, who seem to have nought but independancy in view. . . . Good God! is there not a Political wisdom as necessary in the Conduct of public Life as prudence is in private manners."

LORD DUNMORE AND OTHERS
WRITE TO ENGLAND

John Murray, Lord Dunmore, had left Williamsburg for the western frontier in mid-July without any appropriation of funds. The governor returned in early December, having dealt with threats to Virginia from Native Americans, primarily Shawnees, and from another British colony—Pennsylvania. Both provinces laid claim to the land around the forks of the Ohio, the site of Pittsburg, and frontier settlers there clashed with local Native peoples while the two colonial governments and their representatives clashed with each other. Dunmore's presence on the frontier in the autumn of 1774 ensured his primacy in that struggle at the time, even though Pennsylvania's boundaries, not Virginia's, would eventually encompass the area.

During his absence, Virginians resident in the tidewater expressed skepticism about Dunmore's mission to the frontier. In August, James Madison reported that men familiar with Indian affairs expected Dunmore to encounter only "a few old squaws & superannuated warriors." In late September, James Parker thought that the governor would "find it very difficult to do any thing to purpose with the Indians." A month later, though, Parker knew that Virginia militiamen led by one of Dunmore's subordinates had successfully defeated Native forces on October 10 at the Battle of Point Pleasant. Dunmore "is much admired by the frontier people," Parker reported, but "how he is to be reimbursed I cannot tell." Richard Henry Lee, better acquainted than Madison or Parker with provincial politics, concurred with their opinions. He remarked in mid-December that at the next meeting of the burgesses, "it is expected much dislike will be taken at the Indian manoeuvres of Lord Dunmore. . . . [Wher]e the money is to come from heaven only knows."

Despite such doubts, on Dunmore's return with a victory over the Shawnees and with four Native hostages to ensure that the Indians would henceforth stay north and west of the Ohio River, Virginians greeted him warmly with formal addresses of thanks. The city of Williamsburg congratulated the governor on defeating the "Designs of a cruel and insidious Enemy," while the faculty of the College of William & Mary exclaimed that they hoped he would be "ever crowned with victory!" Dunmore responded to both, thanking them for their good wishes and declaring that the victory itself had been his primary reward. Somewhat tardily, the colony's councillors chimed in with their own address two weeks later, but compensated for their sloth with an effusive statement lauding Dunmore's "vigorous Opposition to the Incursions and Ravages of an Indian Enemy." But at the burgesses' meeting, Richard Henry Lee voted against thanking Dunmore, for he regarded frontier settlers as responsible for the hostilities and believed the war should have been avoided.

Dunmore waited for almost three weeks before describing his successes on the frontier to Lord Dartmouth. In the lengthy missive he sent then he defended himself against accusations of misconduct from John Penn and others; traced Virginia's experience with Native Americans since the end of the Seven Years' War; explained why he had felt compelled to take personal charge of frontier defenses; and exulted in his victory, in spite of the loss of forty-six men killed and eighty wounded. He did not recount the warm reception accorded him in Williamsburg. Instead, he revealed that affairs in the colony had deteriorated significantly during the five months he had been away. Perhaps the governor postponed dispatching the account of his victory in the west so he could inform himself about what had been happening in the tidewater in his absence. In any event, he ended with a lengthy assessment of current conditions in the colony.

Dunmore revealed that county committees had now been established throughout Virginia. They not only examined merchants' records but also "watch[ed] the conduct of every inhabitant without distinction"; questioned those they suspected; and "stigmatize[d]" anyone who violated "what they are now hardy enough to call the laws of the Congress." Further, each county had an independent militia company pledged to obey the orders of its local committee. Even though Dartmouth had ordered governors to thwart such "dangerous measures," Dunmore explained that implementing that directive would be impossible. The authority of the Virginia government was "entirely disregarded if not wholly overturned." Courts were not operating, and attorneys were refusing to do any work. The committees and militia companies, empowered by the congress, had "set themselves up superior to all other authority." Virginians referred to congressional resolutions respectfully and "with marks of reverence which they never bestowed on their legal government or the laws proceeding from it." In short, his government was "feeble" and to attempt to exert any power would lead only to disappointment and "disgrace," thus animating his opponents and adding to their influence.

Yet the governor still voiced optimism that "every step which has been taken by these infatuated people must inevitably defeat its own purpose." He foresaw that defeat as the consequence of the Americans' economic tactics. Whereas wealthy provincials and their slaves could survive without commercial connections for two or three years, middling and poorer folk could not. They would realize that "they have been duped by the richer sort, who for their part elude the whole effects of the Association." Committees' "arbitrary proceedings" would cause "quarrels and dissensions" that would soon lead Virginians to prefer to live under British authority instead. He recommended accelerating that process by blockading American ports and ceasing all governmental functions under the Crown. That would persuade Americans to "prostrate themselves before the power which they had so lately considered as inimical and treated with contempt."

Dunmore was alone in proposing such a drastic solution to the problems then facing imperial authority, but during December other governors too described to Lord Dartmouth their inability to deal with the colonists' "heighth of Frenzy," as Sir James Wright put it. "Our Liberty Folks are really very active in Fomenting a Flame throughout the Province," he explained, promising that he would do all he could to oppose them but indicating that he had found little local support for his efforts. Far to the north, Governor John Wentworth of New Hampshire told a similar tale: an "inflammatory spirit" was spreading through his formerly quiet province. Those who promoted "a cry about liberty will captivate and bear sway with the populace . . . as there is no power to restrain their impetuosity." Congressional resolutions, Wentworth complained, were readily obeyed. And in New Jersey, William Franklin faced analogous circumstances. Few people were courageous enough to challenge the congress publicly. "They well know, if they do not conform, they are in Danger of becoming Objects of popular Resentment, from which it is not in the Power of Government here to protect them," he told Dartmouth. Officials throughout the colonies except for those in Boston had "but little or no Protection for themselves." Still, Franklin retained some hope that reconciliation could be achieved. He enclosed Joseph Galloway's Plan of Union in his early December missive to Dartmouth, commenting that "it has been much handed about at New York, and greatly approved of by some of the most sensible Men in that City."

In December 1774 and January 1775, others joined the governors in providing correspondents in Britain with their assessments of current political circumstances. Joseph Reed wrote twice in December to inform Dartmouth that Pennsylvanians were readily obeying the Continental Association and that the assembly voted to approve other congressional resolutions. Even Quaker assemblymen favored those measures, he noted, although members of that sect had previously "acted a passive Part" in the disputes with Britain. He reported that militia companies had begun to muster and that the province had an ample supply of gunpowder. Despite the dire implications of the news he conveyed, Reed ended with the hope that Dartmouth would be "happily instrumental in restoring Peace & Harmony." Simultaneously, Reed informed his brother-in-law that if Dartmouth did not like the information he supplied, "it tells him what he ought to know."

Reed was proceeding as he had for more than a year, but a note of hesitation entered his exchange with Dennis DeBerdt, as he referred to the need for "a due degree of caution" if he were to continue the correspondence. Clearly, he recognized that the political situation had become more polarized and that his regular communications with the American secretary could be seen as betraying the American cause. Yet Reed remained optimistic about the potential benefits of that correspondence—at least until late January, when he received a long missive from Dartmouth (now lost). What Dartmouth wrote in that letter troubled him deeply and made him lose hope that his epistolary efforts had had a positive impact. He nonetheless consoled himself with the thought that "at least I shall have the Satisfaction of having done my Country some Service by removing some Aspersions & Prejudices."

Joseph Reed's correspondence with Dartmouth was both remarkable and unusual. But many other Americans also dispatched urgent missives across the Atlantic during the few weeks around the end of 1774 and the beginning of 1775. Such letters make it clear that colonists up and down the coast had separately concluded that the empire was confronting what could be a final crisis. Americans' message to their acquaintances in Britain was nearly unanimous: the colonies would continue to resist parliamentary taxation and the Coercive Acts. They would not submit to rule by Parliament, even if they retained their loyalty to the king and to what they deemed the principles of the British constitution. If a solution were to be found, compromise would have to be initiated in the home island, not in North America. Although a few, like William Franklin, expressed the hope that both sides would make concessions, most letters dispatched across the Atlantic in these two months focused instead on Americans' determined resistance and on the need for Britain to yield on some of its claims. Not all writers saw war as the sole alternative if Britain did not respond positively to the resolutions of the First Continental Congress, but most did, especially those from New England or Virginia.

John Adams, for instance, declared that the empire was on "the Brink of a Precipice," indeed a "civil War," because of the colonists' rejection of Parliament's authority. His wife, Abigail, too insisted (to the English historian Catharine Macaulay) that the only options were "an ample redress of our Grievances—or a redress by the Sword," in which she was seconded by the Adams's friend Mercy Otis Warren, who likewise told Macaulay that the "unshaken" colonial union awaited a response from Britain "with the sword half Drawn from the scabard." Similarly, the Virginian William Reynolds assured a friend that "the whole Continent of America are unanimously determined to oppose the execution of those [Coercive] Acts by any means whatever." This is, he asserted, "the last Struggle for American liberty, if we give up we are a ruined People."

Some letter writers held out hope that the new Parliament (elected after its predecessor had been dissolved by George III on June 22) would be open to repealing the Coercive Acts. Others, among them Charles Carroll of Annapolis, believed that "Blood shed & a Civil War" could be avoided if Britain would revert to the trade regulations that predated 1763. After Henry Laurens returned to Charleston from London, he reported in letters to Britain that although Americans from north to south were united in "a firm & steady opposition to the Measures adopted by Administration," they were divided about "the proper means for obtaining a redress of grievances" if the congress's petition to the king proved unsuccessful. He declared that "Men of Wealth & consideration," among whom he numbered himself, rejected both the "Red-hot" people who "foolishly talk of Arms" and the others who advocated "implicit obedience." Instead, he preferred "the interposition of a mediating power," which he assumed would come from Britain.

CROWD ACTIONS IN NEW YORK AND NEW ENGLAND

On December 8, news of George III's October order in council prohibiting the exportation of arms and ammunition from Great Britain arrived in North America. That order had an effect opposite of its intent, for it galvanized colonial military preparations. *The Providence*

Gazette quickly published the order, along with Lord Dartmouth's accompanying directive that governors take "the most effectual Measures for arresting, detaining, and securing" any armaments that colonists attempted to import. What motivated such an order? Governor Jonathan Trumbull asked an acquaintance, rhetorically. Some Americans' dramatic actions soon revealed their own answer to Trumbull's question. As Thomas Cushing observed, they believed the order "forbodes the most vigorous exertions of martial force." Colonists took immediate steps to curb the impending aggression they both feared and anticipated.

The arrival of a vessel carrying guns and ammunition from England then set off a firestorm of protest and mob action in New York. That ship, the *Lady Gage,* had sailed just before the king's order was issued. Cadwallader Colden moved to implement Dartmouth's order after a customs officer discovered that part of the cargo, labeled "Hardware" on the ship's manifest, consisted of ten chests of arms, three boxes of lead, and a barrel of gunpowder, all consigned to Walter Franklin, a New York merchant, but designated for reshipment to Rhode Island. The customs collector, Andrew Elliot, ordered the seizure of the so-called hardware. A crowd led by men whom a witness termed "3 or 4 of our very tip top Sons of Liberty" overpowered the officer who was taking the gunpowder to the powder house for storage, commandeering it from him. But then Manhattan merchants responded to Elliot's request that they intervene on behalf of the customs service. The gunpowder was retrieved and placed in the powder house, and the other confiscated items were taken for safekeeping to a naval vessel in the harbor.

The seizure of the disputed cargo led to a proliferation of broadsides about the *Lady Gage.* Anonymous authors argued that the arms had been legally exported before the royal order was issued, and hinted darkly that the items could now be sent to Boston to be used against Americans. The customs collector, Elliot, received a threatening letter; in response, he again reached out to prominent local merchants, with whom he had a good relationship. At a town meeting summoned to deal with the controversy, Elliot was backed by twenty or thirty of them, most notably the congressman Isaac Low, the former chair of the committee of fifty-one. When he supported Low's Loyalist claim after the war, Elliot praised Low's "haranguing address" at the meeting, which caused divisions among the attendees, and so "the tumult was quelled." Replying to Colden's report on the incident, Dartmouth later observed with satisfaction, "A few instances of such a Determined resolution not to submit to the tyranny of Mobs, would soon I am persuaded, overcome their violence, and restore vigour & tranquillity to Government."

In Rhode Island, Connecticut, and New Hampshire, a different flash point emerged: not ships carrying guns and ammunition, but rather cannon and other armaments already housed in coastal forts. The stunning news of the order in council led crowds in Newport, New London, and Portsmouth to move quickly to take control of such arms, fearing the British would employ them against Americans in a coming conflict.

The Rhode Island General Assembly was in regular session on December 8, having convened in Providence early in the month. Upon learning of the order even before its publication, and anticipating that Gage would send a man-of-war to seize the cannon from Newport's Fort George, the assembly directed several ships to sail there immediately to collect the arms. The vessels arrived at ten o'clock that evening. Their crews, augmented by local volunteers and working through the night and for the next two days, loaded and carried off to Providence forty-four cannon by nightfall on the tenth.

The following day, the *Rose* man-of-war arrived in Newport, having sailed from its regular station in New London. Finding the cannon gone, Captain James Wallace of the *Rose* confronted Governor Joseph Wanton about the "extraordinary" seizure. "He very frankly told me," Wallace reported to Admiral Samuel Graves, that "they had done it to prevent their falling into the hands of the King, or any of his Servants; and that they meant to make use of them, to defend themselves against any power that shall offer to molest them." One Rhode Island critic of the Newport action exclaimed about the "black ingratitude" shown to Britain. "What can these things indicate but a civil war? Horrid reflection!"

While the *Rose* was in Newport, New London residents took advantage of the ship's absence to gain control of cannon in their own harbor's battery. On December 14, they moved most of the cannon four miles inland, storing them in three widely separated locations. They planned to transport fourteen additional cannon and "the other war-like stores" the next day, reported a local committeeman, who recommended to Governor Trumbull that the colony immediately take steps to obtain an adequate supply of gunpowder. Just a few days later, committeemen from another Connecticut town suggested that a ship be sent from New London to the West Indies, where they were "credibly informed . . . that a plentifull Supply" of gunpowder could be found.

Unlike Rhode Island and Connecticut, New Hampshire had a royal governor who was determined to thwart any attack on Fort William and Mary, also known as the Castle, which was located near Portsmouth on Great Island at the mouth of the Piscataqua River. On December 13, Paul Revere rode from Boston with information about the recent events in Newport. Rumors swept through Portsmouth that General Gage was sending troops to take over the Castle, later leading to a charge that Revere had deliberately spread the false tale. The talk so alarmed the populace that even though Governor Wentworth did not expect an attack on the Castle, he ordered the fort's defenders to be prepared.

The local committee met after Revere's arrival to discuss what to do but postponed a decision for lack of sufficient attendance. Nevertheless, according to a Portsmouth resident, "two or three warm zealous members" of the committee decided to act on their own and recruited men to remove the fort's gunpowder supply. Wentworth learned of their plans around noon on December 14. He sent an emissary to tell the gathering crowd that what they were planning was "not short of rebellion," but to no avail. Three or four hundred men from Portsmouth and nearby communities overran the fort and its six resident soldiers. They held the captain and his men prisoner while they confiscated about a hundred barrels of gunpowder and hauled down the fort's flag, then freed the soldiers and gave three cheers.

Describing the assault to General Gage later the same day, Wentworth attributed the "mischief" to the publication in Rhode Island of the order in council and Dartmouth's allied directive and to the news of the attack on the fort in Newport. "This event too plainly proves the imbecility of this Government to carry into execution his Majesty's

Order," Wentworth told Gage. The accuracy of that prediction was confirmed the next day, when a large contingent of men "of the best property and note in the Province" arrived from the countryside to threaten the fort once more. Led by one of New Hampshire's congressional delegates, John Sullivan, the men chose a committee to speak to the governor. Wentworth denied that troops were en route from Boston but failed to dissuade the men from their goal. A local militia captain, attempting to muster men to defend the Castle, "Paraded the streets, caused the Drums to be beat, & Proclamation to be made at all the Publick corners," but no Portsmouth militiamen heeded the summons. The crowd accordingly met no resistance when that evening they carried sixteen cannon and about sixty muskets away from the fort, caching them on the outskirts of town, where they were guarded by another group led by the colony's other congressman, Nathaniel Folsom. On the sixteenth, the raiders took advantage of a favorable tide to load everything on barges and move the arms away from the coast.

That day, the town was still full of "armed men, who refuse to disperse," Wentworth told Gage; he feared they would return to the fort to carry off the seventy remaining cannon. He urgently requested assistance from Boston, which arrived in the form of two naval vessels dispatched by Admiral Graves. That prevented further attacks on the Castle and allowed the governor and others some time for reflection.

"A Watchman" from New Hampshire defended the crowd action. "When we are by an arbitrary decree prohibited the having Arms and Ammunition by importation," he asked, does not "the law of self-preservation" give us "a right to seize upon those within our power"? A Bostonian, though, blamed "a few flaming demagogues" for "a most outrageous overt act of treason and rebellion." He observed, "No history, I believe will furnish us with an instance of a King's Fort being taken and his colours struck by his own subjects in a time of peace, and without any cause or provocation." Worse, the province's own congressional delegates were involved in the lawbreaking, yet the Continental Congress had urged Americans to be peaceful and to obey current law. "Can it be expected that the inhabitants of these Colonies will be prevailed upon to abide by the Resolves of that body when its own Members are the first to break through and violate them?" he asked.

For his part, Governor Wentworth decried not only the attack on Fort William and Mary but also the lack of support he received when trying to stop it. "The springs of government failed me," he lamented to Dartmouth. Many magistrates and militia officers who should have aided him instead openly encouraged the assault, and others were afraid to act. Those responsible could not be punished, for "no jail would hold them long and no jury would find them guilty." Yet perhaps because he was affected by his grief at "the insult on the British flag, hall'd down with ignominy," as he put it to a friend, or because he simply did not want to surrender to "the mad intemperance of a few indiscreet zealots," Wentworth on December 26 issued a proclamation against those who assaulted the Castle. He urged other New Hampshire residents to help identify and arrest the perpetrators and to return the king's armaments, because otherwise they would face "dreadful but most certain Consequences . . . [for] yourselves and Posterity."

The attacks on forts in Newport, New London, and Portsmouth alarmed ordinary colonists as well as government officials. A Philadelphian remarked in mid-January that "Many of those whoe are real Friend[s] to Liberty and Zealous in the Cause" feared that such aggressive acts would divide the colonies. Perhaps counterintuitively, he explained, some "Toreys" applauded the assaults, thinking that the rebellious actions "would most likley produce a civil War" among Americans themselves. James Duane too doubted the wisdom of the crowd actions, phrasing his remarks circumspectly in a letter to his fellow congressman the Marylander Thomas Johnson. Duane commented that some New Yorkers found the raid on Fort William and Mary "a strong Indication of the Impetuosity of our Eastern Brethren" and "repugnant to the Spirit" of the congressional resolution recommending against violence. Such men—Duane implicitly included himself—were afraid that the ministry would now have an excuse to declare the colonies "in a State of actual Hostility," which would end all hopes of reconciliation. And New Yorkers believed as well that it would be "impolitic to inflame [New Englanders'] Ardour or stimulate them to Action by military preparations in other Colonies."

CONTROVERSIES IN MARYLAND
AND MASSACHUSETTS

Although he did not mention it to Johnson, Duane had already been unnerved by actions of the Maryland Provincial Convention in early December. The convention adopted a series of resolutions, most of them endorsing the resolves of the First Continental Congress. But, controversially, the representatives also called for the organization of a colony-wide militia. All men between the ages of sixteen and fifty would be enrolled, and funding would be "voluntary," collected at the county level. Duane protested that action vehemently to Samuel Chase, another Maryland delegate. "The Step you have taken which will be called an Assumption of the Militia into your own hands is certainly of a very serious nature and here it produces great Anxiety," he exclaimed, for it was "the first publick Act out of the pale of New England which indicates a preparation for war." Maryland's action would "inflame" the Bostonians, divide the colonies, and give "a vindictive Ministry" a reason to start a war. He advocated acting "with wisdom and Temper, [to] avoid the Imputation of commencing hostilities." Americans should instead "persevere with Virtue and Fortitude in our Association."

Duane's caution had little or no impact on his correspondents; Johnson and Chase remained staunch supporters of the efforts to raise and arm the militia in their colony. But the purportedly "voluntary" plan for funding—an obvious means of circumventing the problematic issue of whether the convention could impose taxes on the populace—aroused vocal opposition throughout Maryland. In both Baltimore and Annapolis, contentious meetings addressed the questions of how to raise the money and how to penalize men who failed to contribute. Controversies developed over schemes to solicit funds privately, to post public subscription lists for signatures, or to publicize the names of those who failed to comply.

Some, like the Baltimore attorney George Chalmers, not only refused to give any money but also tried to persuade friends to do the same. Others, like some of Johnson's acquaintances, were so angered by "cursed Hand Bills" threatening public shaming for delinquents that they either declined subscribing or refused to pay after they had

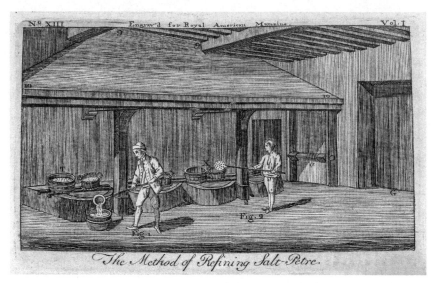

The August issue of *The Royal American Magazine* included this illustration (copied by Revere from *The Universal Magazine* for 1773, a British publication), showing the various steps (labeled and explained) in producing saltpeter, a key ingredient in gunpowder. Like the vessels that must have begun to leave the colonies that month to seek arms and ammunition in Europe—if they were in the Netherlands in October—the production of this picture suggests the escalating tensions in the relationship of colonies and mother country.

initially signed up. The *Maryland Gazette* published a series of rhetorical questions, including "Is it consistent with liberty—the distinguishing characteristick of British subjects—to condemn, with a partial fury, those who dissent from any popular opinion?" And another: "Is it wise, is it politick, to ferment and create divisions among ourselves?" The answers were clearly no but were nonetheless offered explicitly: "Let us not . . . commit violences greater than those of which we complain."

To the New Yorker Peter Van Schaack, the events in New Hampshire and Maryland were of a piece with Rhode Island's nearly simultaneous move to revive its militia. "Under a situation like this Men of Property begin to tremble for the Consequences," Van Schaack wrote to his friend John Vardill in early January after mentioning the three examples. All the "Committees, Remonstrances, Addresses to the People, pretended Danger of impending Slavery civil & religious" reminded him of the English Civil War. "In short my dear Sir the Situation of many Parts of this Country is just now such that either they are in actual . . . [a blank: 'rebellion' was implied] or in a State of Nature absolved from their Subjection to Government by the Abuses of their Superiors." The Marylander William Fitzhugh did not make the same analogy, but adduced another list just three days later: "We hear of Nothing now, but Raising Companys, Military Exercise, Meetings of Committees, Seising Goods, Advertising *Delinquents,* &c &c." Both brief summaries conveyed a sense of the rapid developments overtaking residents in several parts of the colonies, especially those who, like Van Schaack and Fitzhugh, were skeptical and potentially dissident observers.

Yet Maryland and Rhode Island were unusual in December or early January in their attention to organizing and funding militia troops and gathering weapons at the colony-wide level. The Connecticut assembly had authorized occasional militia musters in late October, but when asked in January to reconvene the assembly to take additional steps, Governor Trumbull declined, declaring that he wanted to await further information. He did, however, begin to appoint officers for county militia units and reportedly dispatched a ship to Holland to buy gunpowder and ammunition. In Virginia, individual counties took the initiative while the House of Burgesses was not in session. For example, several counties recruited George Washington to lead their local troops, and in mid-January Fairfax County, explicitly endorsing the language of the Maryland Provincial Convention, ordered a similar collection of funds to purchase ammunition. But, George Mason later reported to Washington, "very few pay, tho' every body promises."

Notable for its absence from such efforts was the Massachusetts Provincial Congress, which convened for a second session from November 29 to December 10. During the meeting, the congress reelected the colony's congressional delegates, designating them to attend the Second Continental Congress in May. Before announcing an election for another provincial congress to meet in early February, representatives also adopted detailed policies to enforce the Continental Association, called on Massachusetts towns to send financial and food aid to block-aded Boston, refused to consider a petition from Baptists complaining of religious discrimination in the province, responded to a report of opposition, and attempted to deal with the failure of most locales to pay taxes to the receiver general, Henry Gardner. But they failed to agree on further military preparations in addition to those previously approved.

Because the representatives met behind closed doors and surviving official records do not disclose any discussions of military or governance matters, the primary evidence that such topics were debated at the meeting comes from information that reached Thomas Oliver, Thomas Flucker, and Nathaniel Coffin. All three heard essentially the same tale, which the first two transmitted to Thomas Hutchinson in London, who then passed the story on to Lord Dartmouth. There were "great Divisions" at the meeting, Oliver learned, caused by proposals to raise and pay an army at the provincial level and to "erect a Form of Government." The first failed for lack of funds and the second because of disputes over what that government should be.

Recounting "what has leaked out," Coffin produced the most detailed narrative of events. He reported that Samuel Adams and "other desparadoes" met with unaccustomed opposition from Adams's fellow congressional delegate Thomas Cushing, who successfully argued that recruiting a provincial army violated the September resolutions of the Continental Congress, which had urged the Bay Colony to act cautiously. Attempts to revive the former council were also rejected, as were proposals to choose a new governor and other civil officers. According to another account, though, John Hancock came close to being elected governor. Coffin thought he knew the reason for the abrupt end to the session after just twelve days: "Adams Hancock &c found there was among them some prudent sensible men who were in their Way." They therefore "artfully" engineered the dissolution and a new election in order to gain the opportunity to rid the congress of their opponents. Adams and his allies hoped, he heard, to influence voting for a second provincial congress, thus winning the election of delegates who supported them rather than Cushing.

A brief notice of the heated discussions at the Massachusetts Provincial Congress appeared in *Rivington's New-York Gazetteer*, where it was read by Samuel Purviance, chair of the Baltimore committee. Alarmed, he wrote to Thomas Cushing, whom he had never met, warning him

that Massachusetts should not name a governor—ironically, because
Purviance praised the militia resolutions that James Duane and others
cautioned Marylanders against. Purviance alerted Cushing to what
he saw as "ye fatal tendency of such a Wild Measure," arguing that it
would prove "ruinous" to both Massachusetts and the colonies as a
whole. Because the very idea was so dangerous, he deliberately had not
mentioned it to others, hoping that if the news spread, people would
think it false because of its inclusion in the notoriously "malicious"
Gazetteer.

So if he had never met Cushing, why did Purviance address him?
He reported that he had also received a personal letter from a friend
in the Bay Colony, who disclosed the identity of the congress mem-
ber who challenged Samuel Adams, information not published by
Rivington. Purviance told Cushing that the content of the debates
frightened him. He predicted that if Massachusetts proceeded to elect
a governor, "it woud detach every Prov[in]ce in America from your
Interest," alienating "your warmest Advocates & Friends in all the
South[er]n Colonies." The move would confirm the allegations that
Massachusetts sought independence, thus causing a loss of support in
Britain as well. The Bay Colony would be sacrificed to the vengeance
of the ministry, which would lead to the submission of the other
colonies, "and all Attempts for ye preservat[io]n of Liberty [would]
cease." He urged Cushing to do all he could "to extinguish this dangerous Flame" and to maintain the moderate conduct that had thus far
brought honor to Massachusetts. Purviance indicated that he was so
concerned about what the Bay Colony might do that he had written
to John Dickinson, Thomas Mifflin, and Thomas Johnson to ask them
to contact Cushing as well.

Dickinson quickly followed up Purviance's request with his own
letter to Cushing, noting that the news from the Massachusetts congress had given him "inexpressible Pain of Mind." He too thought that
naming a governor would anger Americans' British allies and "break
the present Harmony of the Colonies." Why would New Englanders
adopt such a course of action? he asked. "Will it add a single Man
to our Cause? Will it not take off many from it?" Terming the idea
a "pernicious Scheme," he explained that Pennsylvanians "cannot *yet*
bear the Thoughts of arming for Fear of Dissensions." The impact of

a move by Massachusetts was incalculable. Do not, he warned, throw "fresh Fuel . . . into a Fire already sufficiently raging."

Johnson also drafted a letter to Cushing, but instead of sending it to Boston, he enclosed it in one to Purviance, with directions that it should be dispatched if Purviance approved. Perhaps he did not approve, or perhaps the letter has been lost, for there is no evidence that it reached Cushing. But Johnson's reply to Purviance made it clear that the Baltimorean's request left him of two minds. He concurred with Purviance's choice of addressee: the two of them and Cushing "could very nearly say our political prayers together," Johnson observed, commenting that he believed he could influence Cushing more readily than the other Massachusetts congressmen he had met in Philadelphia. Yet Johnson wondered whether advice from him would be useful in the current ambiguous circumstances. If bad news came from Britain, the Bay Colony would have to "settle an internal Governm[en]t," and Maryland should do the same. If the news was good, the issue was moot.

Cushing replied to Dickinson and Purviance in nearly identical terms, stressing his agreement with them and assuring them that electing a governor had been rejected. The plan would not be revived at the Second Provincial Congress, which by then was in session. Moreover, he explained that he had "strenuously" opposed the idea because it portended "the most fatal Consequences." Even so, he emphasized the difficult circumstances in which Massachusetts residents found themselves: "We are without Law, without Courts, without the administration of Justice, which is Essentially necessary in Society." Still, people were surviving hardships with a "calm temperate & fixed Spirit." Not unless the ministry tried to enforce the Coercive Acts militarily and made it "*absolutely necessary* for our Defence & preservation" would the colony establish a new government. And if they did, he assumed that "the Whole Continent" would join them.

The members of the First Massachusetts Provincial Congress thought they were being careful not to move too far, too fast, whatever their motives and internal disagreements. They had no way of knowing that in January Lord Dartmouth forwarded the record of their first session, during which they had named militia officers and appointed Henry Gardner to receive tax payments, to the solicitor

The family of Josiah Quincy commissioned Gilbert Stuart to paint this posthumous portrait of the patriot, who famously died in April 1775 just off the American coast as he was returning from England and fighting began. It was considered an excellent likeness; a family member posed for it, and Stuart portrayed Quincy's cross-eyed gaze.

general and attorney general, asking if those were acts of rebellion and treason. Nor did they know that the answer to that query was yes.

ADVICES FROM LONDON

September 28, 1774. The young Boston lawyer and pamphleteer Josiah Quincy Jr. sails to England on a "clandestine" mission that arouses considerable speculation about his purpose: some say he is an emissary from the Continental Congress, others that he is going to Holland or France, still others that he is traveling to restore his health, which has been poor. Jonathan Sewall, the Massachusetts attorney general, bets that he will be arrested and jailed as soon as he arrives. He takes with him letters of introduction from many Americans to their acquaintances in London and keeps a journal describing his experiences.

November 17. After landing in Falmouth ten days earlier and making his way to London, Quincy goes to see Benjamin Franklin. "Drank tea with him. He appears in good health and spirits, and seems warm in our Cause, and confident of our ultimate success. I find many friends to Liberty and America rejoiced on notice of my arrival. . . . My *Observations* have been reprinted here with approbation, as I hear."

November 19. Quincy receives an invitation to call on Lord North, which of course he accepts. "His reception was polite and with a cheerful affability. His Lordship soon enquired into the state in which I left American affairs. I gave him my sentiments upon them together with what I took to be the causes of most of our political evils—gross misrepresentation and falsehood. His Lordship replied he did not doubt there had been much, but added that very honest [men] frequently gave a wrong state of matters through mistake, prejudice, prepossessions and biasses of one kind or other. . . . We spoke considerably upon the sentiments of Americans of the right claimed by Parliament to tax, and of the destruction of the tea and the justice of payment for it. His Lordship went largely and repeatedly into an exculpation of the ministry. He said they were obliged to do what they did; that it was the most lenient measure that was proposed. . . . Upon this topick I made many remarks with much freedom and explicitness. . . . In the course of near two hours conversation many things more passed between us."

November 22. Quincy dines with a customs commissioner, Corbyn Morris. "I observed a remarkable conformity of sentiments between him and Lord North." The ministry, Morris says, "have no inclination to injure, much less to oppress the Colonies. . . .

You must be sensible of the right of Parliament to legislate for the Colonies, and of the power of the nation to enforce their laws.... You must know your countrymen must fail in a contest with this great and powerful people."

November 29. At the House of Lords, Quincy sees "the Grand Procession of the King, his reception [of] the New House of Commons in his robes and Diadem, surrounded with his nobles and great officers. I was not awe-struck with the pomp.... The Trappings of a Monarchy will set up a Commonwealth."

December 12. Richard Price, one of those to whom Quincy brought letters of introduction, tells him that Lord Shelburne, a member of the opposition, wishes to meet with him. "His Lordship appeared a very warm friend to the Americans:—approved much of their Conduct and spirit, and said if they continued united, they must have all they ask. He said the Ministry would not be able to carry on a Civil War against America; that they began to hesitate and would be obliged to give way."

December 17. Quincy pens a long letter to Joseph Reed, reporting what he has seen and heard. He concludes, "I can not forbear telling you, that I look to my country with the feelings of One, who verily beleives they must yet seal their faith & constancy to their liberties with Blood. This is a distressing witness indeed! But hath not this ever been the lot of humanity? hath not blood & treasure ever been the price of civil liberty?"

ASSEMBLIES, PROVINCIAL CONGRESSES, AND CONTESTED AUTHORITY

In December 1774 and thereafter, the regularly constituted assemblies in Rhode Island and Connecticut could meet without challenges to their authority because the members held office under their mid-seventeenth-century charters, along with popularly elected governors and councillors. In neighboring Massachusetts, the unique circumstances of the blockade and the military occupation of Boston meant that even though the Provincial Congress declined to take steps to establish an army formally or to choose government officials other than a receiver general of taxes, that congress became the de facto ruler of the colony outside the city and its immediate environs. Nearly everywhere else in the mainland colonies, with the exception of New York, contests of one sort or another developed among governors, assemblies, and newly elected representative bodies variously designated as congresses or conventions, along with their allied local committees. The specifics varied, but the outcomes were similar. As William Henry Drayton later described the situation in South Carolina in early 1775, "An independent authority virtually arose; while the Royal Government retained little else, than public officers without power; and a show of government, without the means of supporting it."

In New Hampshire, for example, Governor Wentworth, who had dissolved the assembly, proved powerless to prevent a provincial convention from meeting at Exeter in late January. That convention elected delegates to the Second Continental Congress and unanimously approved the actions of the first. It adopted various measures designed to implement congressional recommendations, including urging residents to avoid lawsuits and pay their debts voluntarily; to obey existing provincial laws; to comply with directives from local committees of inspection; to avoid extravagance and engage in manufactures; and to forgo drinking East India tea, "whenever, or by whatever means it has or may be imported." Wentworth learned that the proceedings at the convention were "very warm and exceedingly irregular," with "ev'ry moderate man . . . silenced." When one participant raised the issue of the meeting's appropriate scope and legitimacy, John Sullivan reportedly responded "that their whole meeting was unlawful, and therefore might do one thing as well as another. They were the people, & their powers unlimited; that the Continental Congress was unlawful, yet they acted." The governor's attempt to counter what he termed "an uncontrouled dictatorial power" by convening a new assembly in March failed when the leaders of the attack on the fort were elected to it. He then postponed its session until May, when he hoped that moderates might have more influence.

Even when assemblies were able to meet, the results resembled those in New Hampshire. In New Jersey—where no extralegal convention met until May—William Franklin tried without success to persuade the assembly's January session to vote against approving the Continental Congress's resolutions and against electing delegates to the Second Congress. He explained to Lord Dartmouth that the "artful Management" of the province's congressional delegates had won the assembly's endorsement of their work in Philadelphia. The delegates argued successfully that the impact of the congress would be "entirely frustrated" unless the assembly participated in "preserving an Appearance of Unanimity throughout the Colonies." Although at Franklin's urging the assembly did agree to submit a separate petition to the king, its contents were not to his liking, and he told Dartmouth that he did not think it would be helpful.

In other colonies, assemblies and provincial congresses roughly coincided or met in chronological proximity to each other, with similar outcomes. The Pennsylvania assembly session in December was followed by a provincial convention the next month. Both approved the First Congress's resolutions and elected representatives to the next. In accordance with his caution to Massachusetts, John Dickinson supported acting prudently and at least "keep[ing] up the appearance of an unbroken Harmony in public measures." In both bodies, many leading members opposed arming the province, and so Pennsylvania, unlike Rhode Island or Maryland, made no move to revive the militia, although its resolves did allude to the importance of manufacturing gunpowder. Both Dickinson and Charles Thomson would have preferred working through the assembly alone to maintain "the legal forms of government" and thus to have "more weight and authority among the people," but they lost that argument to Joseph Reed and his allies, who wanted to have a convention as well. In retrospect, Thomas Wharton attributed the assembly's measures both to Dickinson's able politicking and to John Penn's failings.

Likewise, in South Carolina a provincial congress, chosen by freeholders explicitly defined as those qualified to vote for the assembly, met in mid-January. William Bull informed Dartmouth in advance about the scheduled meeting but evidently did nothing to impede it. Instead, he called an assembly session two weeks later. The laconic official record of the convention noted approval of the resolutions of

the First Continental Congress, along with policies designed to implement them, and also chronicled the election of delegates to the second.
The assembly, the membership of which substantially overlapped with
that of the congress, then formally aligned itself with the votes of the
other body, in addition to adopting some legislation needed to keep
the government operating. Charles Pinckney, chair of the colony's
general committee, later indicated that the convention and the assembly carefully coordinated their actions so as to avoid interference by
royal officials. On February 17, led by the Speaker, assembly members
"with their mace before them," solemnly attended church together
and observed a day of fasting and prayer decreed by the congress.
Because the assembly thus formally acknowledged an act of the convention, wrote Drayton in his memoir, "the staff of Government was
virtually transferred." Among those attending the "very good patriotic
and Xtian like discourse" was Charles Pinckney's mother, the wealthy
widow Eliza Lucas Pinckney, whose comment on the occasion marked
the first time she offered an opinion on the dispute with Britain.

Still, the official record of the Provincial Congress concealed deep
divisions and acrimonious exchanges that were exposed both in Drayton's later memoir and in Henry Laurens's contemporary correspondence. Before the congress met, Laurens, like Drayton a delegate,
predicted "dissentions" about the role played by South Carolina's representatives at the First Congress and specifically about the exemption
they had won in the Continental Association allowing the exportation
of rice after September 1775. The delegates' reelection was threatened,
he told his son, and "censure" would be proposed.

Precisely as Laurens foresaw, many participants in the convention
expressed "great offence" at their congressmen's actions—actions for
which the congressmen had surely expected to be lauded. Not only
were Carolinians embarrassed by the provision that made their colony
appear unwilling to join others in sacrificing for the common good,
but the clause also exposed divisions among the congressmen and
within the convention as well. Representatives learned that Christopher Gadsden alone of the Philadelphia delegation had initially
opposed the exception for rice, but that he had given in to the others
under pressure. Attempting to defend his equivocation to the congress,
Gadsden ended up pleasing no one. His statement "fell little short of

an impeachment of that of his Colleagues who are much displeased with him," Laurens observed. During a debate that lasted almost three days, Thomas Lynch and the Rutledge brothers vigorously championed the exemption they had advocated in Philadelphia. Attendees eventually supported them narrowly, with Gadsden voting on the losing side, and all the congressmen, including Gadsden, were reelected. But then the convention had to confront complaints by those who grew indigo and tobacco or others who dealt in lumber products, all of whom claimed they were injured by preferential treatment given to rice. The upshot was an elaborate scheme, opposed by Laurens as ineffective, in which rice planters were directed to compensate those Carolinians who were forbidden by the Association from exporting their products.

In addition to dealing with the controversy over the exclusion of rice exportation from the proscriptions of the Continental Association, the Provincial Congress had to address an issue that also confronted their counterparts elsewhere in the colonies: how to handle the closure of the civil courts and the consequent question of how people could sue to recover debts. Whereas most provinces (like New Hampshire) simply exhorted debtors to satisfy their creditors voluntarily, the South Carolina congress established a committee described by Laurens as composed of "certain persons who are themselves Great Debtors & Some who have no visible Estates," with the responsibility of hearing petitions from creditors. Although dubious about the enterprise, Laurens agreed to serve on the committee. He pronounced its functions "a Melancholy Droll" because it required "Men of property Rank & respectable Character, Standing up uncovered [without a hat] humbly requesting . . . permission to Act according to Law & justice." In his opinion, the committee usurped the authority of judges and juries. Laurens contended that "Erecting a new Court unknown to the Constitution" meant that "we have taken the Reins of Government into our own hands," a development he deeply regretted. In short, Laurens believed, the South Carolina Provincial Congress had taken a step the Massachusetts congress did not: it in effect constituted itself as the governing authority in the colony.

Georgia sent no delegates to Philadelphia, so the colony faced complicated political circumstances after the end of the First Congress. A clause of the Association provided that any nonparticipating colony would be boycotted; consequently, the entire province faced being cut off from trade with the rest of mainland America, most notably its nearest neighbor, South Carolina. That prospect frightened leading Georgians, who moved in early December to correct the situation by calling for a provincial convention to meet in Savannah on January 18. But only five of the twelve parishes sent delegates to the meeting, and Sir James Wright maneuvered to forestall it entirely by announcing a legislative session to start on the same day.

As was standard, that official meeting began with an exchange of formal addresses between the governor and the assembly and council. Wright congratulated the legislators for having hitherto avoided involvement in the "Alarming" affairs of the provinces to the north, and he warned them, "Be not led away by the voices and opinions of Men of overheated Ideas, consider coolly and sensibly of the terrible consequences which may Attend adopting measures expressly contrary to Law; and hostile to the Mother Country." They needed to remember that "where there is no Law there can be no liberty," for only the law could secure their lives and property. The assemblymen responded briefly, referring to Americans' "Numerous Grievances" while insisting that they would act in ways "Strictly Consonant with our Duty to his Majesty." The council's reply caused the governor greater concern. Although the councillors indicated their disapproval of "all violent and Intemperate measures," they also declared that it was "highly necessary that the Constitutional Rights of [the king's] American Subjects may be Clearly defined and firmly established." When he forwarded the documents to Dartmouth, Wright described the council's address as "not so carefully penned as it might have been."

The assembly and the convention met simultaneously for a week, and then the convention dissolved after its members drafted and signed an association resembling but not identical to the Continental Association. They also directed local areas to establish committees. Meanwhile, the assembly thanked the members of the First Continental Congress, adopted resolutions decrying laws passed by Parliament since 1763, and elected delegates to the Second Congress (who did not, however, attend). According to Wright, South Carolinians employed "every method" to influence Georgians, including threatening them with "blood and devastation" if they did not approve the Continental Congress's actions.

Despite taking steps that seemingly aligned Georgia with the other colonies, neither the assembly nor the convention formally approved the Continental Association; the convention's association varied from it in detail and effective date. One Georgian termed the resolutions "mock" and the association "lukewarm." Colonies following the dictates of the Association could thus ostracize Georgia. Consequently, a group of planters from St. John's Parish drafted a letter to the general committee of South Carolina, declaring their support for congressional resolutions and asking that they be deemed "detached" from the rest of their province so that they could continue to trade with other colonies. The St. John's planters insisted that the Savannah meeting represented too few parishes to be considered a proper provincial convention, and therefore that they were not bound by its decisions. Although the Carolina committee in February made an exception to the rule of no commercial contact for Carolinians who owned property in Georgia, it refused the planters' request, ruling that they could not be recognized as a separate entity.

Some residents of St. Andrew's Parish also sought to act independently of the province as a whole, meeting at Darien in mid-January to endorse congressional resolutions and, remarkably, to align themselves with those few northerners who were starting to criticize the institution of slavery. Explaining that they wanted to prove to others that they were motivated by "a general philanthropy for all mankind, of whatever climate, language or complexion," they expressed "abhorrence" of enslavement, "a practice founded in injustice and cruelty" and contrary to the ideals of liberty Americans were propounding. They promised to work for the manumission of enslaved Georgians, "upon the most safe and equitable footing for the masters and themselves." The surprising statement had no concrete effect but has been attributed by one historian both to the Highland Scots origins of the St. Andrew's settlers and to their desire to quell thoughts of revolt among their enslaved chattel by appearing to promise a future of freedom.

Whether because of Georgians' reluctance to become involved in the quarrels roiling colonies to the north, the disagreements among parishes, or his own efforts, Sir James Wright could claim greater success in obstructing the efforts of resistance leaders than all but one other governor—Cadwallader Colden of New York. In Colden's sharply divided province, the assembly then sitting had been elected years earlier, in 1769, giving that legislative body a relatively conservative cast in the context of 1774–1775. That fact handed Colden a major advantage.

As he explained to Dartmouth in early December, Colden summoned the assembly to meet on January 10, hoping that it would adopt "conciliatory measures" and offer the ministry proposals that might "possibly avert the calamity which hangs over this country." He expressed the hope that Chandler's and Seabury's pamphlets, which had disclosed "the extravagant and dangerous proceedings of the Congress," augmented by a more recent publication, would lead New Yorkers to choose "the most reasonable and constitutional means" of resolving the current dispute.

The brief, newly published pamphlet to which Colden referred, written by the assemblyman Isaac Wilkins, focused on counseling New Yorkers to depend on their legislature rather than the Continental Congress. Trust the assemblymen you legally elected, Wilkins recommended; do not let "*Republicans, disaffected persons, smugglers, men of no character,* and *desperate fortunes*" take control of the government. Samuel Seabury himself then reinforced Wilkins's message in mid-January in *An Alarm to the Legislature of the Province of New-York.* Whereas Wilkins targeted voters, Seabury directly addressed the legislators. He charged that "their *dignity* has been *trampled upon* and their *authority contravened*" by local committees. Referring explicitly to the events in Rhode Island, Maryland, and New Hampshire, as well as to the threats to Andrew Elliot, Seabury argued that the Second Continental Congress would destroy the current "happy constitution," replacing it with a republic. But New York's assemblymen could halt that process by pursuing "*moderate measures,*" in particular "a solid *American Constitution,* such as *we* can *accept* with *safety,* and *Great Britain* can *grant* with *dignity.*"

Whether the admonitions from Seabury and Wilkins had any effect is unknown, yet the two pamphleteers and the lieutenant governor had reason to celebrate the outcome. By small margins but in repeated votes, the New York assembly refused to endorse the Continental Association or other congressional resolutions, or to name delegates to the Second Congress. One New Yorker explained to Silas Deane that the Whigs in the assembly deliberately designed multiple requests for votes "to extract their [opponents'] political creed," which could then be publicized in the newspapers. The session continued for months, with the addition of tardy members from the countryside, but the negative majority remained constant. Conservatives rejoiced. Prompted by Colden, the assembly proceeded to draft its own petitions to Britain, which in the end listed many of the same grievances as had the congress, although the New York petitions diverged in tone and specificity and addressed Lords and Commons as well as the king. Alexander McDougall insisted that the differences constituted "a mere nullity" and that the ministry would be "egregiously mistaken" if it thought that New Yorkers disagreed with other colonists, despite the negative votes on the Association and the election for the Second Congress.

In the colonies as a whole, therefore, claims of authority at the provincial level varied significantly in early 1775. In New York, New Jersey, Rhode Island, and Connecticut, governors and officially elected assemblies remained in control. In Massachusetts, New Hampshire, and Maryland, provincial congresses had taken over the government de facto if not yet de jure, whereas in Pennsylvania, South Carolina, and Georgia the concurrent existence of assemblies and congresses (with significant overlaps in membership) raised serious questions about which body was truly in charge. In Virginia and North Carolina, such issues had not yet arisen only because assemblies were not scheduled to meet until later in the spring. Commentators throughout the colonies addressed controversies about provincial authority: What was its appropriate source? How should it be wielded? How could conflicting claims be resolved?

COMMITTEES OF OBSERVATION
AND INSPECTION ASSUME LOCAL POWER

At the local level, though, there was little doubt: the First Congress had recommended the appointment of committees to enforce the Continental Association, and cities, towns, and counties moved quickly to comply, regardless of whether a provincial congress or an assembly recommended such a move. "The most resolute Determinations are made here as well as in the other Colonies to execute the Grand Association Plan," observed a Bostonian in early December, even though citizens there could not fully implement the Association because of the British occupation. Not every locality voted positively for a committee, but qualified voters gathered in most areas to do so, with the result that local political power began to be wielded by groups of men whose authority rested only on their selection by other freeholders. It was bottom-up, not top-down, governance. Many committee members had never held office before; indeed, many localities outside New England had never previously experienced such elections. Frequently, the primary local officials in the colonies had been justices of the peace or sheriffs who owed their appointments to men higher up in the hierarchy than they.

Under the eleventh clause of the Continental Association, the members of such committees had a vague and potentially wide-ranging assignment: "attentively to observe the conduct of all persons touching this Association." They were directed to assess that conduct and to identify violations by majority vote and, as indicated in chapter 5, to publicize the names of those deemed to have contravened the Association, so that "all such foes to the rights of British America may be publickly known, and universally contemned as the enemies of American Liberty." Then "all dealings with him or her" could be ended.

Other clauses laid out the complexities of the conduct that committees were to observe "attentively." After December 1, 1774, no one was to import goods from Britain or Ireland into the colonies, nor "any East India Tea from any part of the World," nor molasses or unrefined sugar from the British Caribbean, nor Madeira wines, and a few other items. If goods did arrive after that date but before February 1, 1775, they were to be returned to their original port, turned over to a local committee to be stored until nonimportation ceased, or auctioned off. If the items were sold, the owners would be reimbursed from the proceeds, and any profits would be sent to Boston to relieve the suffering poor. Any goods arriving after February 1 would automatically be returned unopened to their senders. To provide "effectual security" for nonimportation, the Association went on to provide for nonconsumption as well. Once again, tea was a major source of concern: the Associators (congressmen and their constituents) were not to buy or consume any duty-paying tea after October 20, nor consume any tea at all after March 1, 1775, nor any other items imported after December 1, 1774, except those properly auctioned by a committee.

Further, all involvement in the slave trade was to cease, whether by Americans or in colonial vessels. Among those things to be discouraged were the slaughter of sheep; extravagant gifts at funerals; and such entertainments as horse racing, cockfighting, plays, and dances. Conversely, frugality would be encouraged, along with "Agriculture, Arts, and the Manufactures of this Country, especially that of Wool." Finally, merchants were directed not to raise the price of goods when the items became scarce because of nonimportation. Violators of that injunction were to be ostracized, and even though the committees were not mentioned as the enforcement mechanism for that order, they provided the only possible means of oversight.

Even before December 1, when the Continental Association's ban on imports from Britain took effect, Virginia committees began to enforce the Association that their Provincial Congress had adopted in early August, with its November 1 starting date for nonimportation. Virginia's efforts at implementation thus presaged those in the other colonies a month later.

Shortly after the November deadline, the ship *Virginia,* belonging to John Norton & Sons of London, sailed into the York River carrying in its hold two half chests of tea consigned to Prentis & Company of Williamsburg. The way that cargo was greeted revealed the continuing explosive symbolism of EIC tea. Some men wanted to mimic the recent fate of the *Peggy Stewart* by burning the ship, but they could not accomplish that aim because of the *Virginia's* inconvenient anchorage. They nevertheless quickly disposed of the tea by throwing it overboard. But the dispute did not end with that destruction. The Gloucester County committee declared that John Prentis, who ordered the tea, should be made a "publick example" (he soon offered an abject apology) and that the captain had acted "imprudently," deserving Virginians' censure. The major target of local wrath, though, was John Norton, declared by the committees of York and Gloucester Counties to have "forfeited all title to the confidence" of Virginians. The committees urged planters not to ship tobacco on Norton's vessels "until satisfactory concessions are made."

That recommendation, potentially devastating to the business of one of the wealthiest London mercantile firms dealing with Virginia, initiated months of correspondence from both sides of the Atlantic. Representatives of the company, including John Norton himself, offered a variety of excuses for their lack of attention to the commercial regulations Virginians had promulgated in June and August. Virginians greeted such explanations skeptically. One of Norton's correspondents, William Reynolds, wrote repeatedly to the firm and to George Norton, John's son, expressing his dismay about the decision to send the tea and the damaging aftermath. In retrospect, he commented to George, "it amazes me that your Father after receiving the Resolves enter'd into by our Burgesses (immediately after their dissolution) against useing Tea, should ship any in the *Virginia.*" As a member of the York committee, Reynolds disclosed that he had tried to defend John Norton from "unjust reports," but as a result the committee dropped him from its ranks. Reynolds added emphatically and unsurprisingly, "I hate the name of tea." In the end, Norton's vessel was able to return to England filled with barrel staves, so the voyage was not a total loss, even though that cargo was far less valuable than tobacco would have been.

Another incident in Virginia before the Continental Association went into effect, reported to a Londoner, inspired a British cartoon, "The Alternative of Williams-burg." James Parker recounted the story: Colonel Archibald Cary ordered the erection of a pole opposite the Raleigh Tavern in Williamsburg; on it was hung a bag of feathers and below that a barrel of tar. A young man "spoke very Violently" against two merchants who had imported small amounts of tea, asking how "they durst insult the Majesty of the People." Some residents planned to treat the two badly, presumably by tarring and feathering, but local leaders intervened. A militia colonel insisted that "such proceedings were more arbit[r]ary than any the Americans were complaining of, & tended to destroy their Cause," because the tea in question had been imported before December 1 and thus was allowed by the Continental

THE ALTERNATIVE OF WILLIAMS-BURG.

Plate IV.

The incident depicted in this British cartoon seems to be based on a description James Parker sent to Charles Steuart from Virginia in November 1774. Local planters are being required to sign the Continental Association, with the implicit threat of tar and feathers if they refuse to comply. The label on the gibbet reads "A cure for the refractory"; that on the barrel refers to the English radical John Wilkes. Women and children are among the spectators.

Association. Ultimately, the local committee took control of the tea, and residents removed the pole, blaming Cary for a disruptive act.

In Norfolk, James Parker tried to avoid trouble by failing to attend local meetings (despite the threat of a fine) and refusing to sign the Association, which was, however, "signed by almost every body." Some dissidents, he reported, came as far as the building where the local committee was to be elected, but would not enter the door. Accordingly, one of the organizers—whom he dubbed "a Vile incendiary"—took a list of nominees outside and asked the crowd if they had any objections to the names on the ballot. When no one replied, "it was declared to be an Unanimous election." Parker marveled that "the resolves of the Congress are Called the American Constitution," although the congress had not done what he expected; that is, formulated a "respectfull & reasonable" petition to the king and "fabricated something like a Constitution as a grand work for the different assemblys to go by." Instead, he saw only "a determined enmity against the Supremacy of G Britain" and observed that it was dangerous to speak in favor of George III. When formally asked by the committee why he refused to sign the Association, Parker responded that he held a government post in the customs service and had taken an oath to the king, which he could not break. Because he had not signed the Association, the Norfolk committee decided that he did not "come under the Congress law," and accordingly the Norfolk committee had ignored a few items he imported from Glasgow.

Yet Parker nevertheless complained of the committee's bullying tactics. He remarked, "Every thing is Managed by Committee, Selling & pricing goods, inspecting books, forcing some to Sign Scandalous Concessions." Other colonists also complained about the committees and their extensive regulatory reach. In New York, a lawyer caviled at being "Subject to A Set of commite men, to examine into what we eat, and what we Drink, and what we are cloathed withall; is not this A curious Specimen of American LIBERTY, who would not prefer the Grand Turks Goverment, to A republican one." So too a Philadelphia merchant wryly quoted a friend's comment about "our Lords and Masters, the high and mighty Committee Men": "instead of being devour'd by a Lion, we are to be gnawed by rats and Vermin."

Local committees had remarkably full agendas, and different committees focused on varying aspects of their tasks. A New Hampshire committee, for example, worried about the "Hawkers, Pedlars, and Petty-Chapmen . . . tempting women, girls, and boys with their unnecessary fineries," whereas the Philadelphia committee adopted detailed rules for butchering sheep and conducting sales of items arriving after December 1. Virginia committees dealt with complaints about overpriced goods, which led them to insist on access to merchants' accounts for as long as the past year. They also tried to govern behavior. Local committees banned "publick Balls and Entertainments," along with gambling, horse racing, and other diversions; urged farmers to plant hemp and flax; and warned them against killing lambs, because of the need for wool. Commenting on the impact of the commercial restrictions, an Annapolis woman wrote to an English friend, "I cannot tell how we shall dress: I have cloaths enough for some time, but have no pins to put them on." Americans were now drinking "very good coffee" rather than tea, she reported.

Some committees policed speech. For example, in Hanover County, Virginia, the local committee forced two men to apologize and to express publicly their "Hearty Sorrow," offering "candid" confessions about statements they had made. One had openly complained against the "many respectable Gentlemen" who questioned him about his possible violation of the Association; the other had remarked that "a little gold, properly distributed," would lead Virginians to support the British. In addition, a Scots schoolteacher in Westmoreland County was called to account for the "false, scandalous, and inimical" content of a letter he had sent to a friend in June, which (unfortunately for him) was published in a Glasgow newspaper two months later and then made its way back to Virginia. On his knees virtually or in actuality, he publicly implored forgiveness for his statements, which constituted "so ungrateful a return for the advantages [he had] received." He pleaded to be allowed to remain "amongst the people I greatly esteem."

Committees handling cargoes that arrived after December 1 but before February 1 developed what seems to have become a standard practice, adopting the option of auctioning the goods. But the consequences were a "farce," declared James Parker, because the owners were commonly the only bidders. John Penn informed Lord Dartmouth that the price in Philadelphia was just "one pr Cent above their first Cost and Charges," so assistance to the poor in Boston might be minimal. Henry Laurens described such an auction in Charleston, involving "even Polly's little Wax Toys," as a "mere ceremony," because "no person bids beyond the Cost & charges therefore the purchase is made of each parcel by the Proprietor."

Perhaps there was nevertheless an influx of cash into Boston, because rumors spread in January that the managers of relief (like Thomas Greenough) were profiting from the contributions by keeping a share for themselves and by using donations to hire workmen for their own businesses. The Boston committee issued a broadside denying the "slanderous Report raised by evil minded Persons," insisting that it was "groundless and false" and declaring that their books were open for inspection, as "advertiz'd [to] the Publick some Months ago." That forceful response seems to have been persuasive, because the rumors soon dissipated.

The need to interpret the Association's complex clauses led to intricate decisions. According to the Baltimore committee, salt imports were covered by the Association, but brick and coal imports were not. According to the Norfolk committee, medicines that arrived in November, an allowable exception to the Virginia Association, could not be distributed after December 1, because the Continental Association did not include the same exemption. According to the New York committee, a ship that took on a pilot off Perth Amboy before sunset on February 1, but did not land in New York harbor until the next day, could not unload its cargo, because the placement of a pilot on the ship did not mean it had arrived in port. Within the New York committee, a dispute arose between James Duane, who said that no tea of any sort could be imported after December 1, and Alexander McDougall, who maintained that "Foreign [smuggled] Tea" could be imported until February 1 and that it would be unfair to merchants who expected shipments of it to ask them to "sacrifice their property, without advanceing the Public Cause." Duane contended in response that if large quantities of tea were landed as late as the beginning of February, merchants would be tempted to sell what remained in their stock after March 1, thus violating the nonconsumption agreement, but a majority of the committee supported McDougall's position and allowed smuggled tea to be imported until February 1.

In early December, Cadwallader Colden correctly predicted that exemption in the city, because, he wrote, "the smugglers expect large quantities of Dutch tea" to arrive soon. He anticipated that the Association would be observed only nominally because of the smugglers' influence and found it "shocking" that "smuggling is such a business among us as to be publicly espoused by numbers and more strenuously advocated than the legal trade." According to a Bostonian, the same attitude prevailed on Cape Cod, where twelve chests of tea were going to be destroyed until people learned it was smuggled; they subsequently helped the owner conceal the chests. And some tea landed clandestinely at Greenwich, New Jersey, was burned in mid-December by "persons unknown" disguised as Indians before the local committeemen could determine its origin. They and others then condemned the hasty action, because the tea might have been smuggled.

Clearly, regardless of the rules set forth by the Continental Association, tea, most likely the Dutch variety, kept arriving in the colonies long after all imports of it were to cease and even after its consumption was forbidden. At first, the populace seemed to support, or at least comply with, nonconsumption. Even Peter Van Schaack, a prominent critic of the resistance movement, told his brother in late February that he would stop drinking tea on March 1 and would advise members of his household not to challenge the restriction publicly, because he regarded the measure as "innocent" and thought that "much worse consequences" might result from opposing it. On February 28, Nicholas Cresswell, visiting in Alexandria, commented that "The Lady's seem to be very sad" about being forbidden to drink tea starting the next day. In Providence in early March, a large bonfire consumed about three hundred pounds of tea gathered from merchants, along with small quantities of the "hurtful trash" contributed by "many worthy women, from a conviction of the evil tendency of continuing the habit of Tea drinking." Newspapers published by James Rivington and Mills & Hicks were added to the conflagration. And in Wilmington, North Carolina, women "burnt their tea in a solemn procession."

But the same female English visitor who witnessed that procession also recorded being served "a dish of tea" on a proper tea table just a few days earlier. A Philadelphia diarist penned an "obituary" for tea on March 1: "Early this morning, departed these parts, universally lamented by the friends of slavery, but to the joy and satisfaction of the lovers of freedom, that baneful and detested weed, East India TEA, whose return is never desired or wished for by the true sons of American liberty." Yet that his obituary was premature quickly became evident, for people continued to purchase and drink tea despite the prohibition. Indeed, Dartmouth learned that merchants redoubled their efforts to obtain tea from "Holland, Gothenburgh, & L'Orient" after Americans vowed not to buy the commodity from the EIC. Peddlers in Massachusetts bedeviled committees with their ability to evade surveillance as they traveled from town to town with their packs filled with "East India Goods and Teas and Various sorts of European manufactures." In Newport in mid-March, a traveler reported that "tea is commonly & publickly drank"; in Boston, a Marblehead merchant surreptitiously purchased tea for his own use from a store, defending himself by pledging that he would not sell it to someone else.

The problems of enforcement extended beyond New England and even to officeholders who might be expected to obey the prohibition. A committee member in New Jersey admitted that his family consumed tea at home after March 1 and asserted that he would "persist in the same practice," which he presumably did until formally expressing regret two months later. A merchant in Kingston, New York, ignoring "friendly admonitions and entreaties to the contrary," declared in April that he "had, and would sell Tea," just as he always had; he was designated "an enemy to the rights and liberties of America" by the local committee. A militia officer's insistence on drinking tea caused a division in a local committee in western Massachusetts in March. "They Could not agree about Censuring him," reported the young doctor Elihu Ashley. "Three thot he ought first to be chastised, four on the Contrary." So, after hours of debate, the committee decided to refer the matter to the town meeting. The following month, Ashley was invited to drink tea at the home of another militia officer. He recorded that he thought the offer "in jest" but then when he accepted "found it to be Tea in reality. I drank none of it," Ashley recorded, but noted that the captain enjoyed imbibing it and revealed himself by his conversation to be "a High Torey."

A story that made its way to a London newspaper recounted the experience in April of an impoverished New York woman. Members of the local committee found tea in her house and seized it to carry outside, planning to set fire publicly to what must have been a commodity she valued highly. Furious, she took a kettle of boiling water and threw it on the committeemen. An amused bystander suggested that the men would probably behave more cautiously in the future.

The woman's anger highlighted the type of opposition committees faced when trying to apply the Association's strictures at the household level. No wonder, then, that Baltimore committeemen were reduced to exhorting compliance from the people they called "their Constituents" rather than effectively enforcing the ban on consuming tea. Recognizing that it would be difficult for people to stop using "any article which custom has rendered familiar, and to many almost necessary," the committee urged women in particular to "cheerfully acquiesce in this self-denial, and thereby evince to the world a love of their friends, posterity, and Country."

As was revealed in surviving scraps of paper from Wethersfield, Connecticut, committees that controlled stored tea could make exceptions to the prohibition on its use. Several brief notes contain requests for distributions of tea to the sick. Edward Pattison "desires I would consent to his having some Tea, he being in a very poor state of Health," Elisha Williams, a committee member, told Leonard Chester, who controlled the stored commodity. Even though the supplicant did not have a certificate from his doctor, Elisha averred, "if you will please to let him have half a pound, I think it will not be contrary to our Association." Or, wrote Williams, "Mrs. Bartes has applied to us for Liberty to buy a Quarter of a pound of Bohea Tea, I think by her account of her age and bodily Infirmities," she should be allowed to have it. Or again: "My neighbor Seaman Riley informs me that one of his Children is very sick and the Doctor advises to the use of Tea."

The persistent problems that tea consumption in particular posed for the local committees of observation in the colonies underscored the wide range of responsibilities the small groups of men had assumed— responsibilities that in many respects were entirely novel. No previous governmental entity in America had attempted to control people's consumption of any item. In the 1760s, compliance with nonimportation agreements had been voluntary or enforced informally by ad hoc bodies. But the committees established under the eleventh article of the Association, and thus under the authority of the First Continental Congress, differed significantly: they, most colonists seemed to concur, were enforcing *laws*. As Samuel Adams put it in early March, "The Laws of [the Continental Congress] are more observd throughout this Continent than any human Laws whatever." Accordingly, the committees' reach was increasingly wide and the opposition their actions aroused increasingly intense and determined.

Crucially, all committee actions involved men's supervision of the populace at large. The Association's emphasis on governance in local areas by elected committees ensured the primacy of men as actors and decision makers. The congressional resolutions targeted merchants primarily as importers of British goods, not as retailers of them, despite the provision that forbade price gouging during the presumed scarcity to come. Had the Association instead followed the model of the Solemn League and Covenant by enlisting the participation of all consumers as active boycotters of British products, women's cooperation would have been essential. As it was, women participated only implicitly in the commercial policies established by the Virginia and Continental Associations. If merchants were successfully coerced, the agreements would prevent forbidden British goods from reaching store shelves in the first place. The one frequently consumed item that still required women's involvement was the ubiquitous tea, so efficiently smuggled from the Dutch Caribbean and elsewhere that embargoes on EIC products would have only a slight impact. Women were the presumed and probable primary purchasers and consumers of tea; accordingly, the anonymous Maryland woman who drank coffee rather than tea was fulfilling the one role publicly left to her.

Did men intend to achieve that result, deliberately preventing women from playing as active a role in resistance to Britain in 1774–1775 as had been the case during the consumer boycotts of 1768–1769? No one said so, but male leaders both implicitly and explicitly preferred approaches that did not require the mobilization of the entire population, including women. During the crises involving tea imports in late 1773, it will be recalled that Samuel Adams specifically rejected relying on colonists to forgo purchasing tea, opting rather for destroying the cargoes of the three ships in Boston harbor. The lingering confusions that resulted when some of the *William*'s tea ended up on Cape Cod, or when Charleston tried futilely to implement consumer boycotts, revealed the effectiveness of his approach, as did the eventual lack of success of the Solemn League and Covenant. It was far easier, male leaders realized, to intimidate a relatively few merchants—even though peddlers might elude the authorities—than it was to enlist all colonists in the cause. Many showed reluctance to participate in a tea boycott, for reasons ranging from a love for or addiction to the beverage, to opposition to the cause itself. For people like the "high Torey" militia captain in Massachusetts, drinking tea became as easy a way to demonstrate disapproval of resistance as forgoing it publicly served to proclaim a person's patriotic commitment.

CHAPTER 8

A CONSTANT STATE OF HOT DEBATE

The activities of committees and congresses provoked diverse reactions from conservative colonists in late 1774 and early 1775. Some wrote newspaper essays and pamphlets to question the Continental Congress's resolutions and the actions of "unconstitutional" bodies at all levels of governance, predicting a dire future if the colonies continued to resist Great Britain. Some individuals openly challenged the committees' authority, and a few colonists formed associations to support continued imperial rule and to protect themselves from retaliation for their political views. For the first time, those people termed themselves "American Loyalists." In Marshfield, Massachusetts, such Loyalists dominated local politics, leaving a revealing record of local contentions, on-the-ground organizing, and recruitment efforts. The "Whig" versus "Tory" phraseology of previous months did not disappear, but the introduction of the locution "Loyalist" signaled movement to a new phase of the conflict. The opposite of "loyal," after all, had to be "disloyal," which meant that despite resistance leaders' claims to the contrary, they were now being perceived by others (even if not yet by themselves) as traitors to the British Empire, as those who sought independence for the colonies.

OPPOSITION TO RULE
BY COMMITTEES AND CONGRESSES

A few brave, or possibly foolhardy, individuals chose to stand alone, or nearly so, against local committees. Three notable instances in Virginia, for example, involved more than the outbursts or noncompliance with committee directives discussed in the last chapter. In Nansemond County, the Reverend John Agnew persisted in delivering sermons that "abused" the Continental Association and its adherents. Confronted by parishioners who told him that message was "disagreeable," he refused to back down. He termed all associations "detestable" and declared that congressmen were rebels. Accordingly, the local committee deemed him a violator of the Association and subject to ostracism. Likewise, in King George County, the planter Austin Brockenbrough, who had signed the Association, was charged with violating it. When committee members accused him of contempt for their authority, he replied, "That I have, and always shall." When they ordered him to attend a meeting to defend himself, he defiantly answered, "I shall not." He too was declared an enemy of America.

Less directly confrontational was a group of about twenty Scots traders in the small community of Falmouth, also in King George County. The men adopted what must have seemed a clever strategy to avoid difficulties with their county committee. Because the Continental Association directed "every county, city, and town" to elect committees, their "trifling village" held what Richard Henry Lee termed "their own private and partial election" for a committee. By establishing an official body under the terms of the Association, the Scots must have expected to prevent excessive scrutiny of their activities, commercial or otherwise.

Yet Lee challenged them formally. The word "town," he argued in a legal opinion, did not apply to "small knots or collections of interested Traders" who depended on the very commerce in question. Rather, the term referred to "very populous large Towns," such as those in the North. A Falmouth committee's decisions, he averred, could possibly cause "the utter destruction of the Association" and "endless confusion" by differing from the edicts of the freeholder-elected committee of King George County. He concluded that because the Scots merchants would be "Judges in their own Causes," they would thwart the intention of the Association, which was to put "disinterested persons" in a supervisory role. So he advised the county committee to pay careful attention to the Falmouth traders. The Scots themselves, interrogated one by one about their strategy, decided in advance to answer all questions with simple yeses or noes, thus frustrating the committeemen's broader inquiries about their intentions. But one of their number reported that after they were threatened with violence, they "thought it expedient, not from any conviction, but from motives of self preservation," to sign a document acknowledging bluntly that "we was wrong."

Like the Falmouth merchants, colonists who rejected rule by committees and congresses could occasionally find allies. In the northern and middle colonies, a few dissident communities adopted resolves in the fall of 1774 lamenting the direction of affairs; in the spring of 1775, some groups signed statements pledging fealty to the king. The grand jury and magistrates of Tryon County, New York, for instance, declared in March 1775 their opposition to "the specious illusion, independency," and vowed to "bear faith, and true allegiance to their lawful Sovereign King George the Third." Hundreds of residents of four North Carolina counties that same month expressed their "abhorrence of the many lawless combinations and unwarrantable practices actually carrying on by a gross tribe of infatuated anti-monarchists," protesting the "enthusiastick transgressions" of "a most profligate and abandoned Republican faction."

But those who signed such statements did not go as far as the Loyalists who began to form counter-associations in December and January. After the December votes in the Maryland Provincial Convention to establish and arm militia units, George Chalmers decided "to introduce new modes of Safety by an Application of the Ancient principles of Law to the New State of things." Having realized that local magistrates could not be depended on to protect dissenters or to maintain order, he established "a private association" to act as a "posse Comitatus" that would aid the local sheriff whenever called upon for help. He was authorized by his fellows to ask the governor, Robert Eden, for some of the colony's arms. The governor promised assistance but failed to follow through. Chalmers later speculated that Eden feared that if it became known he had furnished Chalmers's men with guns, the action would have made him unpopular. Why Chalmers's efforts had failed, indeed "why all measures proved unsuccessfull," he told the Loyalist Claims Commission after the war, "future historians will tell," and Chalmers himself became one of those historians.

George Chalmers's doomed "posse comitatus" in Maryland predicted the fate of similar associations, although most of the others did not involve loyal local officials. Rather, they resembled or exactly imitated the one that drew attention as far away as Virginia and that had arguably the greatest success: an attempt by a Massachusetts brigadier general of militia, Timothy Ruggles, to rally others for mutual support. Ruggles, a mandamus councillor, had fled to Boston but distributed a proposed defensive association to several Bay Colony towns in early December. He submitted the text for publication in Boston newspapers, insisting that he intended to distinguish the king's loyal subjects from men who pretended to be "friends to liberty" but were instead "banditti, whose cruelties surpass those of savages." Loyalists, he declared, needed to identify themselves so they could be protected from subsequent charges of involvement in the resistance movement.

After a preface stating that the subscribers understood "the blessings of good Government" and knew as well "the evils and calamities attending on tyranny," the association document moved to a mutual pledge of assistance. The signers would defend each other's lives, liberty, or property "whenever the same shall be attacked or endangered by any bodies of men, riotously assembled, upon any pretence, or under any authority not warranted by the laws of the land." They would support each other's right to engage in "eating, drinking, buying, selling, communing, and acting what, with whom, and as we please." They would not acknowledge the authority of a congress, committee, or "any other unconstitutional assemblies of men," but would rather oppose such bodies, even at the risk of their lives. And they vowed to uphold the authority of George III to "the utmost of our power."

The Massachusetts Provincial Congress took the threat posed by Ruggles and his proposed association seriously, recommending that all local committees be alert to the possibility of such groups being organized in their vicinity. A man rumored to have carried to Gage such a signed association from the town of Montague protested in print in mid-January that the tale was "false, groundless, and scandalous." If that story was untrue, one about Petersham was not. A number of residents of that town publicly admitted joining Ruggles's association. When almost all of the signers then refused to appear before the Petersham committee to explain themselves, the committee deemed them "incorrigible enemies of America" and pronounced them "traitorous parricides." A later newspaper account claimed that the men in question were imprisoned in a fortified house until they agreed to behave "peaceably" and not to "act against their country for the future."

The news of Ruggles's association heartened many conservative colonists, including Nathaniel Coffin. He told a London correspondent,

> The bold steps taken by their Associators, must evince to you what I have before told you, that when ever they can meet with a support there will in every part of this province be a great defection from our seditious Leaders. Great numbers from principle, & much greater thro' fear of loosing their property & Lives will list on the side of Government whenever it acts with vigor.

But in the same letter, Coffin acknowledged that another association, formed in Weston, Massachusetts, by Colonel Elisha Jones, "a staunch friend to Government," had met with significant opposition and that the associators had been threatened with death. Whether that threat caused most of the signers of the Weston covenant to offer retractions is unclear, but about a month later that is exactly what they did. The Weston committee formally declared the few remaining adherents of the original statement to be enemies. Colonel Israel Williams's attempt to raise troops in Hatfield to support the king was likewise quashed. The fate all these efforts shared suggested that men like Coffin were grasping at straws when they predicted that Loyalists would readily rally to the support of the imperial government.

A case in point is the fate of Colonel Thomas Gilbert of Freetown, in Bristol County. In early April, the Massachusetts Provincial Congress praised people there for opposing Gilbert, whom it described as "an inveterate enemy to his Country, to reason, justice and the common rights of mankind." In mid-March, he and his "abandon'd knot of

Tories" had begun mustering and training with guns and ammunition supplied by General Gage. But men from nearby communities gathered to stop the "deluded wretches" who had signed on with Gilbert, and within a month Gilbert and some of his men took shelter in the man-of-war *Rose* in Newport harbor. Others were captured and threatened with imprisonment. Most of the captives, though, were "sufficiently humble" to admit their error, an observer commented, so they were allowed to return to Freetown.

In one Massachusetts community, Loyalists dominated the town government, even if they perhaps did not constitute a majority of the population. The Ruggles association began circulating in Marshfield, on the south shore near Plymouth, in late December, and new recruits were still signing it on January 20. Reputedly, between 100 and 150 men added their names before a backlash began in nearby towns; associators were threatened with unspecified harm and future retaliation by a mob of 1,500 or more men unless they recanted.

On January 10, a crowd confronted several Marshfield residents at an auction held near the Plymouth lighthouse. Elisha Foord of Marshfield bid on some hemp, but one attendee insisted, "No Damned Tory Should bid there." Another added, the hemp was "very Good to make halters for the Torys," and Foord should have "sum of it abo[u]t his neck." One of the crowd challenged Foord to fight with swords or pistols; Foord replied mildly that no such weapons were available, and, regardless, he did not know how to use them. The crowd then set a guard on the Marshfield men's horses so they could not leave. The Plymouth residents formed themselves into a committee and questioned each of the men from Marshfield about whether he had signed an association sent by Gage, which they all evidently denied. Because the document originated with Ruggles, not Gage, the men from Marshfield could easily have justified responding as they did, even if they had signed it. To end the conflict, the auction attendees from Marshfield were forced to accede to statements withdrawing from the association in order to avoid being taken to Plymouth to appear before the committee there.

The debate over the Ruggles association in Marshfield generated a paper trail that exposed the involvement of women as well as men in the political dispute. Elizabeth White, for example, deposed that "after the Association paper came Down, a brother of mine from Hanover came to se me. He being a Whig and I a Tory, Did not agree in our Sentiments." Her brother told her, "I pitty you," because "the Torys will be taken care of soon." She asked, will you shoot me, your only sister? He replied, no, "but Don't say that I Did not give you timely warning." That, she admitted, "alarm'd me and my Husband . . . and thought that It was time to take care of our selves." Ruth Baker, wife of one of the men who were accosted at the auction, swore that "a near Relation" had "in a friendly manner" transmitted a rumor that some men were soon going to march to Marshfield and that "the Damned Torys hands would be all off within five Days." Huldah Wright reported that she heard another woman declare that "She wish'd som Jud[g]ment might be sent Down from above and Distroy all the Toryes." These and other depositions gathered from women revealed their participation in the ongoing regional arguments about Marshfield's conservative outlook and imply women's similar but unrecorded involvement in other local episodes.

Faced with threats of mob action, residents of Marshfield and neighboring Scituate, including men who had been at the auction, addressed General Gage, asking him to send troops to protect them from the "many ill-disposed people who declare their intention of Assembling in great Numbers to Attack and destroy us." Gage obliged, quickly dispatching about one hundred soldiers. (One Marshfield resident observed sardonically that now a fellow townsman could "freely utter his thoughts, drink his tea, and kill his sheep as profusely as he pleases.") Gage forwarded the petition to Dartmouth, boasting that he had disproved one of the contentions of the "Faction," which was that no such aid would ever be available to the king's supporters, but rather that they would be left alone to defend themselves. He explained to the American secretary that the Marshfield pattern was a common one: "where the Majority in a Township has been averse to their Measures, the Faction has employed their Adherents in Neighbouring Towns to join and form Bodys sufficient to force them by Numbers to sign Recantations," with "Violence and ill Usage" a part of the strategy.

The arrival of British troops in their vicinity worried the selectmen of Plymouth and other towns near Marshfield, and early in February they sent Gage an address that can only be termed disingenuous in the extreme. They asserted that the fears expressed by Marshfield residents were "Entirely Groundless, that no design or Plan of Molestation was formed against them, or Existed but in their own Imaginations." They assured the governor that they had "Industriously and diligently" questioned unnamed Marshfield men of "unquestionable Veracity," and those men had never heard of any threats, nor had they observed their fellow townsmen behaving as though they anticipated an attack. The selectmen insisted that "the declarations of fear, were a Fallacious Pretext, Dictated by the Inveterate Enemies of our Constitution." The general, unsurprisingly, was unconvinced and failed to act on their request to remove the troops, nor did he change his mind later in March when others complained about the soldiers' misbehavior.

The Marshfield Loyalists had a very different reaction to the arrival of the soldiers in their midst. At a town meeting on February 20, which the record stressed was held legally under the Massachusetts Government Act (that is, with the governor's permission), they voted to thank Gage and Admiral Graves for the assistance they had received. They insisted that, whatever was said to the contrary, the presence of troops "preserved and promoted, not only the peace and tranquility of this Town in particular, but of the county in general." Affirming their loyalty to the king, they also expressed "utter detestation and abhorrence, of all assemblies and combinations of men (by whatever specious names they may call themselves) who have, or shall rebelliously attempt, to alter or oppose the wise constitution and government of Great Britain."

A few days later, though, a larger number of Marshfield residents protested that gathering, contending that they knew nothing of the request to the governor for permission to hold the meeting, "a thing so contrary to the general sense of the people in this Province." Moreover, the selectmen had called the meeting for an unusual site with only one day's notice. The purported formal statements from the town about political institutions had been "craftily drawn," making it seem as though Marshfield residents thought that congresses were illegal, whereas they were regarded as "both legal and necessary." Even a Loyalist-dominated town hosting a contingent of redcoat troops, then, had a sizable set of dissenting residents who did not hesitate to express their opinion.

Divisions arose too in the ranks of the one potentially widespread group that aligned itself with royal authority: the Quakers, centered on the middle colonies but with scattered adherents elsewhere. The pacifist sect formally tried "to steer a middle course," said Esther DeBerdt Reed, but ended up being "despised." In the fall of 1774, the Quaker Yearly Meeting in Philadelphia dispatched a letter recommending that members of the Society of Friends avoid involvement in current political controversies, a position that Ezra Stiles regarded as "subtil & artful . . . seemingly very innocent & harmless," but actually intended to "detatch the whole Quaker interest from the rest of America." In early January, Philadelphia Quakers met again, engaging in heated debates before adopting a convoluted statement advising Friends to forgo participation in any committees or other resistance activities and to adopt a posture of dutiful obedience to Britain.

After daily meetings during the following weeks, on January 24 a gathering of Quakers from Pennsylvania and New Jersey issued a more formal document, *The TESTIMONY of the People Called QUAKERS,* which offered what became semiofficial guidance to members of the Society of Friends in the coming months and years. Voicing their regret about the ongoing dispute with Britain, the Quaker leaders alluded to how "the Divine Principle of grace and truth which we profess" required them to behave peaceably and to "avoid every measure tending to excite disaffection to the king, as supreme magistrate, or to the legal authority of his government." Because that supremacy was currently being questioned, they believed it their duty to state their disapproval publicly. Citing the experience of their own sect with past monarchs, they expressed confidence that "decent and respectful addresses from those who are vested with legal authority" detailing the colonies' grievances would obtain relief. And so, they concluded, they opposed and would resist "every usurpation of power and authority" and "all combinations, insurrections, conspiracies and illegal assemblies."

The statement aroused such immediate antagonism from other colonists that its defenders tried to downplay or reinterpret its more inflammatory elements. One Virginian who received an explanation from a Quaker acquaintance declared that from his own reading of the *Testimony,* he had doubted its authors' concern for "public Liberty and the Rights of Mankind," but that his correspondent's arguments had changed his mind; unfortunately, those persuasive comments have not survived. An essayist insisted that the criticism of illegal assemblies did not refer to congresses or committees, and further that in any case the relatively small number of Friends who issued the statement lacked authority to speak publicly about politics on behalf of the larger Society. Another insisted unconvincingly that the Quakers only sought "to point out those rocks of licentiousness and outrage" that could be concealed by "the fairest pretensions" and that could be "fatal to the best of causes."

The responses revealed Quakers' difficulties in upholding their pacifist principles in the heated political atmosphere of the time, but even though some Friends quarreled with the message of the *Testimony,* one non-Quaker observed, "It is well known they never openly disagree, or divide from one another." In Virginia, Quakers steadfastly refused to sign the Continental Association, a crucial symbol of their adherence to the *Testimony.* James Madison explained that requiring such signatures was "used among us to distinguish friends from foes and to oblige the Common people to a more strict observance" of the Association. Unlike many of the New England associators, whose politics guided their actions, those with religious motivations thus seemed more likely to persist in resisting the pressures of rule by committees and congresses.

A WAR IN PRINT

In the early months of 1775, Americans seemed to be more interested in politics than ever, judging by the number of pamphlets and newspaper essays that aroused comments in their diaries, correspondence, and public statements. "I live here in a constant State of hot Debate," wrote a Philadelphian in late February. In New York three weeks later, a visitor penned in his journal, "Politics, Politics, Politics! There are numbers of Hand bills, Advertisements, Extracts of Letters on both sides daily & hourly printed, published, pasted up & handed about. Men, women, children, all ranks & professions mad with Politics." In Boston, he encountered the same. "All sorts of Political writings are bought up with amazing avidity," he observed. And he was one of those avid purchasers, recording that he bought pamphlets in both cities, including ones from Mills & Hicks in Boston and James Rivington in New York. He even had "much discourse" with Rivington on "the present state of Politics" and noted appreciatively that only Rivington could "furnish me with both sides of the question." Indeed, he planned to buy "a compleat set" of pamphlets from the printer before leaving town.

Men with access to such shops dispatched to others copies of publications they especially admired. For instance, in late December 1774 Richard Henry Lee forwarded a Pennsylvanian's "small but well written Pamphlet on the American dispute" to Landon Carter. Another Virginian who received a similar gift by a conservative writer replied in February 1775, "The Pamp[h]lett you was kind enough to send me, seems to be a sensible well wrote piece," but added that "the Author if he lived here wou'd undergo very severe discipl[in]e from our men in Authority." The next month, a conservative Connecticut lawyer living in Philadelphia sent his nephew in New Haven a copy of a pamphlet that "openly inveighs against the ruling party in the Congress," which he noted was attributed (accurately) to Joseph Galloway.

With the partial exception of Rivington and a few other printers, publishing had become wholly partisan and polarized. Even Rivington no longer included essays by critics of British policy in his newspaper, although he did continue to publish their pamphlets. Printers' alignments for or against resistance to Great Britain were now firm. From Norfolk, the Loyalist James Parker complained accurately that the three newspapers in Williamsburg were "all on one side" (not his). In Charleston, one paper supported the royal government while two did not. Christopher Gadsden, acting as the Bradfords' Carolina agent, signed up eighteen new subscribers there for *The Pennsylvania Journal.* In Philadelphia, conservatives unhappy with the *Journal* and other local papers persuaded a bookseller, James Humphreys, to begin a new paper with a decidedly loyal bent, *The Pennsylvania Ledger.* (Joseph Reed termed its backers "a little dirty despicable Party endeavouring to sow Dissension.") Farther north, most newspapers supported resistance, but the two Boston papers titled *The Massachusetts Gazette* (one published by Mills & Hicks, the other by Richard Draper) offered an outlet to conservative writers, as did Hugh Gaine and Rivington in New York.

Denied access to most, though not all, presses, Loyalist authors continued to complain bitterly about the absence of freedom of the press, which in mid-January Thomas Bradbury Chandler termed "one of the most sacred and invaluable rights of Englishmen, and consequently of the inhabitants of his Majesty's American colonies." On the first page of his new pamphlet, *What Think Ye of the Congress Now?*, he defined press freedom as the ability to discuss in print "all public transactions" relevant to government or religion, declaring that right to be part of an Englishman's property. "None can deprive him of it without his consent," Chandler insisted, thus cleverly analogizing to the familiar argument about taxation. He accused "*the Sons of Liberty,* of the lower and more illiberal classes," of failing to follow congressional recommendations to maintain order and of trying to intimidate "writers, and printers, and readers, and speakers, and thinkers, on the side of government." Citing pamphlets, his among them, that had been publicly dealt with in "the old popish way . . . by fire and faggot," he declared that such "burning zealots" should be known instead as the "Sons of Licentiousness." The clergyman thus advised "all writers of unpopular pieces to keep their own secrets" and "take care of themselves."

An essay in *Rivington's New-York Gazetteer,* almost certainly by James Rivington himself and signed "Anti-Tyrannicus," offered a robust defense of an "impartial Press," by which he meant the ability to critique those in authority—in this case, the committee of sixty, with which he was then embroiled in a dispute. "The liberty of the Press is a sacred privilege; it is the only means in the hands of the people, that can be safely used to check the growth of arbitrary power," the author asserted. If the very people who have identified themselves as "sentinels upon the watchtower of liberty" work to restrict that freedom, "will it not give the people cause to suspect that they themselves are about to establish a power more arbitrary and tyrannical than any thing we have hitherto complained of?" In effect, Anti-Tyrannicus declared, the committee of sixty was claiming that it was above all criticism. But "the peculiar excellency of the British Constitution," he observed, provided that "the proceedings of all publick bodies should be freely discussed." The committee of sixty, like Parliament or the New York assembly, was by definition subject to press scrutiny.

The key problem Loyalist authors faced in early 1775 was a vigorous campaign to suppress those conservative arguments that did manage to appear in print. Many local committees voted to prevent the sale or distribution of pamphlets from New York, which tended—as the committee of Fairfield, Connecticut, put it—"to lessen the weight and authority of the Congress, and to disunite the Colonies." A convention of committees in Worcester, Massachusetts, specifically criticized "*Rivington* and *Gaine,* of New-York, *Draper, Mills* and *Hicks,* of Boston," for distributing "scandalous Performances in their several News-Papers." The Worcester convention urged local residents to boycott those papers and instead to patronize some from "friendly" printers. And freeholders in Middlesex County, New Jersey, excoriated in purple prose "those insidious scribblers" who "skulk behind prostituted public printing presses" to spread "their pestilent compositions through the land under the show of friendship and a regard to the publick good."

Despite attempts to halt their distribution, Chandler's and Seabury's pamphlets made it at least as far south as the Chesapeake. An Annapolis merchant opined in late January that Chandler's latest, which had recently arrived, would "recover many here who have been misled by the loud unlettered Orators of the Republican tribe," because it "expresses the sentiments of all the true Loyalists." Two months later, in Orange County, Virginia, the local committee investigated the Reverend John Wingate, an Anglican cleric, for possessing Seabury's four pamphlets and one by Isaac Wilkins, all of which had reportedly been purchased at a Williamsburg shop. The committeemen pronounced the "execrable" publications "a collection of the most audacious insults" on the Continental Congress, composed of "the most imprudent falsehoods and malicious artifices to excite divisions among the friends of America." The committee then burned the pamphlets publicly in front of the local militia company and other residents. Further, they expressed "their ardent wishes for an opportunity of inflicting on the authors, publishers, and their abettors, the punishment due to their insufferable arrogance, and atrocious crimes."

Among the so-called Tory printers, Rivington attracted the most ire, perhaps because of his unmatched success in distributing his publications far and wide; those "execrable" pamphlets burned in Virginia in March 1775 were all produced at his press. As early as October 1774, the Massachusetts Provincial Congress expressed concern about the contents of both his newspaper and his pamphlets. In December, a self-styled group of New York "Friends of Liberty" referred to him as "a Pensiond Servile Wretch" whose recent pamphlets were designed "to Defeat the Salutary Intentions of the General Congress partly by Alarming the fears of the Timid & Stirring up the avarice of the Selfish." Further, the satirical poems he published (including the *Dialogue* by Mary V. V.) constituted "rascally" attempts "to Ridicule the United Councells of America." The men suggested that committees everywhere on the continent should vote to boycott Rivington's publications, linking such a policy to the Continental Association's call for ostracizing all noncomplying colonists. Concurrently, Rivington was advertising for sale the refutations of Chandler by Philip Livingston (which he had published) and Charles Lee (which he merely stocked), but his critics ignored his determination to print or sell pamphlets from both sides.

Just as the news of the Ruggles association buoyed Loyalists and British administrators, so too did the apparent increasing reach of such conservative publications. Governor Gage told Dartmouth in mid-January that in Boston the press was "more open to government than usual," which had been useful in exposing the "absurdity" of congressional resolutions. A North Carolinian wrote to Rivington that in his province "the loyalists are lifting up their heads," praising the writings of A. W. Farmer, and waiting impatiently to see *What Think Ye of the Congress Now?*, for which they had seen an announcement. A Philadelphian told him that "your pamphlets continue daily to change the minds of people," and Joseph Galloway too remarked that unnamed pamphlets sent from New York "have produced a happy effect" in Philadelphia, although most were not being formally sold or advertised there. Even James Warren wrote from Plymouth to inform John Adams that he thought an improved mood among the local "Tories" might be the result of the encouraging numbers of recent conservative publications.

Whether or not the author who published an essay as "A Converted Whig" in early March really was what he claimed to be, he attributed his political conversion in large part to reading Jonathan Boucher's *Letter from a Virginian* and Chandler's *Friendly Address,* along with articles in both *Massachusetts Gazette*s. Such essays, he wrote, exposed "the whole scene of our political errours and iniquities." He pronounced himself disappointed by the quality of the futile attempts to refute critiques of the congress. Responses were filled with "little more than scurrility and illiberal abuse," along with "invective and indecent railing." His former allies, the purported convert insisted, refused to allow the same freedom of thought to others that they claimed for themselves. How could such behavior be based on "good principles"? he asked. How could "a bad tree bring forth good fruit"?

From late December 1774 until mid-April 1775, the printers Mills & Hicks, Richard Draper, James Humphreys, Hugh Gaine, and James Rivington published in their newspapers numerous opinion pieces that could also have been read by the Converted Whig. Anonymous authors signing themselves "A Suffolk Yeoman," "Eugenio," "Conciliator," "America's Real Friend," "C," "Phileirene," and others published essays charging the Massachusetts Provincial Congress with treason, defending General Gage, attacking committee actions, dissecting congressional resolutions, or contending, as John Bullman had done in August, that ordinary folk should confine themselves to managing the affairs of their own families rather than meddling in politics. Additional pamphlet publications also continued into early 1775 the burst of criticisms of congressional actions that had begun in late 1774. Of those, the most important were Chandler's *What Think Ye of the Congress Now?* and Galloway's *Candid Examination,* both published by Rivington.

After Chandler opened his pamphlet with the remarks on press freedom quoted earlier, he posed a question he regarded as so important that he added it to the title of the pamphlet: *How Far the Americans Are Bound to Abide by, and Execute the Decisions of, the Late Congress?* If colonists *"lawfully"* authorized the congress, and if it acted in accordance with that authorization, he admitted, then its decisions were "undoubtedly binding upon us." But what if those conditions had not been met? Answering such queries led Chandler to analyze the summer meetings that elected and instructed the delegates as well as the results of the congressional session itself. He concluded that the del-

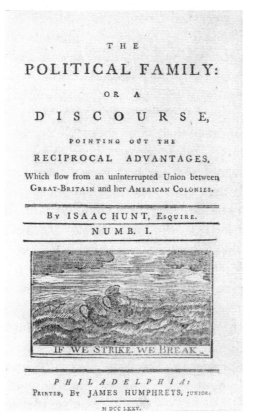

THE
POLITICAL FAMILY:
OR A
DISCOURSE,
POINTING OUT THE
RECIPROCAL ADVANTAGES,
Which flow from an uninterrupted Union between
GREAT-BRITAIN and her AMERICAN COLONIES.

By ISAAC HUNT, ESQUIRE.
NUMB. I.

IF WE STRIKE, WE BREAK.

PHILADELPHIA:
PRINTED, BY JAMES HUMPHREYS, JUNIOR.
M DCC LXXV.

The printer James Humphreys in Philadelphia published this pamphlet in early 1775. Its title page/frontispiece is the only such illustration in a Loyalist pamphlet, and the theme is opaque. Two jugs, presumably representing Britain and America, are adrift in a stormy sea; the caption reads, "If we strike, we break." The message seems to be that a clash would bring disaster.

egates exceeded their instructions, erred in rejecting Galloway's plan, and should have petitioned the Houses of Lords and Commons as well as the king. Accordingly, Americans did not owe obedience to the congress or the committees. Local bodies should be dissolved, though without recrimination for their members, and colonists should obey only "lawful authority," freeing themselves from the *"yoke"* of the congress and the *"fetters"* of the committees. The congress, he lamented, had "turned out to be a perfect monster—a *mad, blind* monster!"

The other significant Loyalist pamphlet of early 1775, Galloway's

Candid Examination, was completed by mid-February and served in large part to defend his Plan of Union and his role at the Continental Congress. He did not formally acknowledge his authorship of either the pamphlet or the plan but explained his detailed account of the congress as stemming from having "often conversed" with the plan's author. He assessed the current situation hyperbolically, describing "a lawless power established throughout the colonies, forming laws for the government of their conduct, depriving men of their natural rights, and inflicting penalties more severe than death itself, upon a disobedience to their edicts." Setting himself the task of reviewing the development of the controversy, Galloway reiterated at length the historical and theoretical narrative he had advanced in September 1774 about the colonies and their subordination to Britain. The contentions that Americans could be subject to the king and not to Parliament or that Parliament was not supreme in the empire, he argued, were absurd.

He insisted that the congressmen sought "absolute independence" and were leading Americans into "clear, palpable treason" that would cost them their property and even their lives. He went beyond Chandler in summoning up the specter of "undisciplined" and "unprincipled" American mobs that would wreak "havock and devastation" while "ravishing your wives and daughters, and afterwards plunging the dagger into their tender bosoms, while you are obliged to stand the speechless, the helpless spectators." But Galloway's major argument did not rest on such scary rhetoric; rather, he insisted that it was still possible for colonists to abandon "the licentious tyranny" of the congress and to turn instead to "your constitutional guardians," the assemblies, to draft "reasonable and just" petitions to Parliament and the king, requesting a redress of American grievances. Those would undoubtedly be successful, he assured his readers, citing the repeal of previous laws against which the colonies had protested. He ended with an expression of hope that Americans would know better than to exchange "the mild and equal rule of English customs and manners" for "calamitous consequences" and a "miserable fate."

The Chandler and Galloway pamphlets, along with the many newspaper essays penned by other Loyalists, placed Americans who supported the Continental Congress and resistance to Britain at something of a disadvantage in the contest in print, even if they retained their primacy in terms of political and military organizing. Accustomed to dominating discourse and setting the terms of debate in committees, congresses, and conventions, they found themselves on the defensive after the congress adjourned in late October and Chandler and Seabury produced their effective pamphlets. The same pattern continued well into 1775. For example, when John Dickinson and Charles Thomson responded in March to Galloway's *Candid Examination* in a lengthy newspaper essay in the Bradfords' *Pennsylvania Journal*, they focused on refuting his assertions—such as that about the structure of imperial authority—rather than advancing their own vision of an American future. They did, however, perpetuate the fiction that the pamphlet's author was not the congressman who proposed the plan, thus allowing them to slyly insult the author of the Plan of Union, terming him "a man of no principle or virtue."

If the attack on Galloway was shielded by nominal anonymity, that on his publisher was not. On April 13, the invective leveled at James Rivington reached a new height in a broadside titled *The Last Words, Dying Speech, and Confession of J——s R——g——n, P——t——r, who Was Executed at New Brunswick . . . Supposed to Be Written by Himself the Night Preceding the Day of His Execution.* The lengthy poem began, "The final period of my life is come, / I in the morn shall here receive a doom, / Which injured justice doth of right demand / For lies I've framed against this happy land." And it continued, in part,

> *My crimes, at length will fill each future page*
> *My name will be the curse of every age, . . .*
> *That tree on which my body hang'd will be,*
> *Which they once call'd by name of Liberty,*
> *A growing monument will there remain,*
> *Of my past, present, and my future shame. . . .*
> *My reverend friends! O Cooper! where are thou!*
> *No Seabury, Chandler, to assist me now! . . .*
> *In vain your aid, your friendship I implore,*
> *Old Satan has me now, for ever more.*

When Rivington began publishing conservative pamphlets in the fall of 1774, he surely did not anticipate being subjected to a symbolic hanging in New Jersey about six months later. But as early as the previous December, he had indicated to his Boston agent, Henry Knox, that he recognized the perils of an "impartial" printer's role. He forwarded to Knox three hundred copies of Philip Livingston's *Other Side of the Question* but explained to Knox that he would not send the publication it refuted, Chandler's *Friendly Address,* without a specific order. "My reason for not troubling you with these very warm, high seasoned pamphlets, is that your very numerous friends, on the patriot interest, may be greatly disgusted at your distributing them," he informed Knox. If the Boston bookseller wanted such items, "I will secure them for you from time to time," Rivington noted, but asked that Knox "explain [himself] on this head directly." He nevertheless went on to offer Knox a poem currently in press "in the Hudibrastic stile which will sell but I greatly fear you will not like I should send it to you." That poem, Bob Jingle's *Association,* a satire of the Continental Congress, does not appear to have appealed to Knox.

MASSACHUSETTENSIS VERSUS *NOVANGLUS*

The Boston equivalent of the Galloway and Chandler pamphlets was the newspaper series *Massachusettensis,* written jointly by the mandamus councillor Daniel Leonard and Attorney General Jonathan Sewall. Just as the contemporary importance of Chandler's *Friendly Address* was confirmed by the number of published attempts to refute it, so too the significance of the *Massachusettensis* essays was underscored by the reactions they provoked.

For example, Mercy Otis Warren's satirical play *The Group* prominently featured the series. The first scenes appeared in *The Boston Gazette* in late January 1775, presenting toadies linked to Rapatio (Thomas Hutchinson). They include Brigadier Hateall (Timothy Ruggles), Chief Justice Hazlerod (Peter Oliver), and Beau Trumps (Leonard). In a series of poetic exchanges, the men admit their venal motivations for betraying the Bay Colony as they seek wealth and position by cozying up to Rapatio and doing his bidding. The play opened with the characters appearing "attended by a swarm of court sycophants, hungry harpies, and unprincipled danglers . . . hovering over the stage in the shape of locusts, led by Massachusettensis in the form of a basilisk." Later in the play, Justice Hazlerod "retired to a corner to read Massachusettensis." Warren described Beau Trumps, whose authorship of the essays was suspected, thus: "I trim'd, and pimp'd, and veer'd, and wav'ring stood," until Rapatio "shew'd me my name among his chosen band, / And laugh'd at virtue dignify'd by fools, / Clear'd all my doubts, and bid me persevere."

Moreover, two congressmen, Robert Treat Paine (who did not complete a draft) and John Adams, writing as Novanglus, penned replies. The extended exchange between Massachusettensis and Novanglus appeared in Boston newspapers between December 12, 1774, and April 3, 1775. Leonard and Sewall published seventeen essays in *The Massachusetts Gazette, and the Boston Post-Boy,* Adams twelve in *The Boston Gazette.* Throughout the debate, Adams thought that he was disputing solely his old friend Jonathan Sewall (who was also writing as Phileirene at the time), rather than the younger Leonard. Leonard later explained that he undertook the task of writing the essays at the request of several "principal gentlemen" in Boston. His aim, he declared, was "to endeavour to trace the discontents of the people to their source, to point out the criminality and ruinous tendency of the opposition to the authority of parliament, and to convince the people of the justice of the measures of Administration."

The essays and responses appeared in an erratic order, in part because, as Adams explained in his first composition (published in late January), when he began to write he had access only to the third *Massachusettensis* essay, which had appeared a month earlier, and he had not yet seen the first and second entries in the series. Before Adams picked up his pen, Massachusettensis had already published six articles; the works were by then being read by Plymouth Loyalists "with more devotion & Esteem than Holy writ," according to James Warren, which surely helps to explain why his wife, Mercy, decided to highlight the essays' influence in her January satire. In order to clarify the nature of the debate, the narrative here will pair the essays by content, organized by the *Massachusettensis* chronology, rather than by the varied timing of Adams's responses.

One of the most direct exchanges dealt, appropriately enough, with the perpetual Loyalist topic of freedom of the press. In mid-December, Massachusettensis began his initial essay by describing the press, "when open to all parties and influenced by none," as necessary to a free state. But when one party gained control of the press either by government action or by arousing the people against certain printers and authors, the press became "an engine of oppression or licentiousness." That was precisely what had occurred in Boston during the current controversies with Britain, he charged. His goal was to correct the one-sided accounts people had been reading.

In *Novanglus,* Adams at first rebutted the accusation of suppression by naming the Boston newspapers that had been open to conservative authors and by referring to the "swarms of pamphlets" that attacked the Continental Congress. But two weeks later Massachusettensis reminded readers that the Worcester convention in January had called for a total boycott of those printers, thereby revealing "an illiberal, bigotted, arbitrary, malevolent disposition." Adams could not deny what the Worcester convention had done, so his second reply defended the silencing of some ideas, insisting that "the freedom of thinking was never yet extended to any country as far as . . . the abolition of the laws and constitution." Massachusettensis must have regarded that admission as a victory, because it fully confirmed his allegations about the deliberate quashing of Loyalist publications, and he did not raise the point again.

After the initial complaint about censorship, the first *Massachusettensis* essay began dramatically, not with a learned review of history, policies, and politics—that would come later—but rather with stunning questions: "Are not the bands of society cut asunder?" Was it not treason, he asked about the congresses and committees, for "men to assemble without being called by authority, and to pass governmental acts"?

War appeared inevitable if the colonies did not change their course, Massachusettensis warned, and no one could honestly believe that America could win such a contest. He reminded his readers that Britain had recently triumphed over both France and Spain and controlled the oceans besides. He discussed at length the colonies' vulnerabilities, including likely shortages of necessary supplies, persistence of internal disputes, and reliance on undisciplined militia. To him, the consequences were obvious: "We must be certain that, when ever the sword of civil war is unsheathed, the devastation will pass through our land like a whirlwind, our houses be burnt to ashes, our fair possessions laid waste, and he that falls by the sword will be happy in escaping a more ignominious death." And what was the cause of the impending disaster? He answered with a question. "Will not posterity be amazed," he asked, "when they are told that the present distraction took its rise from a three-penny duty on tea?" And could not current events be compared to the "frenzy" of witchcraft accusations in New England's past?

Adams's response to that essay did not appear for another two months. What he addressed and what he avoided were both equally telling. It was obvious to argue that not the tea duty but provisions of the Coercive Acts, including the Quebec Act's attack on the Protestant religion, had caused all the trouble. Likewise, he went point by point through the list of potential colonial vulnerabilities, rejecting them at every turn—for example, praising the readiness of militia units and denying the significance of political disagreements in the colonies. Although Britain controlled the seas, he pointed out, even the British navy had never been able to stop rampant smuggling, so Americans could always obtain supplies from abroad. Further, "in a land war," he asserted, "this continent might defend itself against all the world." Unlike his many predecessors, he indicated that he thought such a war might be imminent and could even be welcome. "Nip the shoots of arbitrary power in the bud, is the only maxim which can ever preserve the liberties of any people," he concluded, advocating quick action.

In a key passage, Adams cleverly turned the charge of "treason" on its head. "If the parliament had not a legal authority to overturn [the Bay Colony's] constitution, . . . every man, who accepts of any commission and takes any steps to carry those acts into execution, is guilty of overt acts of treason and rebellion against his majesty." (That numbered Leonard and Sewall among the treasonable actors.) Adams's insistence that Parliament had in the Massachusetts Government Act unconstitutionally altered the colony's charter placed the issue of constitutionality firmly in the foreground. Yet as he defended the committees and congresses, Adams failed to rebut directly the challenge to their own constitutionality. Instead, he merely stressed how those bodies revealed America's unified resistance to Britain. His omission revealed his unwillingness to claim, as had some Pennsylvanians, that freeholders' votes by themselves could provide constitutional legitimacy.

After the dramatic first essay laying out an apocalyptic vision of the current circumstances, Massachusettensis reverted in his second and third entries in the series to a more standard historical narrative with a conservative slant, summarizing events since 1763. He contended that the colonists should have been satisfied with the repeal of the Stamp Act and most of the Townshend duties, but, he claimed, a long-standing Whig party in Massachusetts "flattered the people with the idea of independence" and made accommodation impossible. Opponents had been intimidated into silence. Offering a detailed account of internal Bay Colony political struggles from the late 1760s on, he told readers that the nominal defenders of freedom had actually destroyed "real liberty, [and] subverted your charter constitution." The current government of the colony, he contended, was "a despotism, cruelly carried into execution by mobs and riots."

Adams challenged that account both in specific detail and in its general outlines. He disclaimed any interest in independence from the monarch. Again he adopted an aggressive approach that defended his position by reversing his opponent's accusations. Not the Whigs but their opponents had pursued a long-standing plan to deprive people of their liberty. He traced the Tories' "dark intrigues" back to the era of the Seven Years' War, naming those individuals he viewed as contributing to the conspiracy, including, among others, Thomas Hutchinson and Andrew Oliver. He blamed mobbing incidents on "the insults, provocations, and oppressions" the colonists had endured. No one had died or been seriously harmed on such occasions, but the other side had injured and killed New Englanders. To make such a case, Adams attributed the Boston Massacre to the "Tory" party and even cited the whippings the occupying army inflicted on disobedient soldiers as part of his complaint. That assertion stretched his argument to the breaking point and beyond.

In the fourth letter, published in early January 1775, Massachusettensis focused on the events of the past year, including the destruction of the tea. He observed that the dire impact of the Boston Port Act could have been avoided by compensating the EIC. He praised the "respectable persons" who had formally addressed Thomas Hutchinson before his departure and—in an inclusive gesture—also praised the "humane and benevolent" residents of other colonies who had contributed money and food to help the Boston poor while the port remained closed. He devoted considerable attention to criticizing the activities of local committees. In such bodies, the same men were "at once legislators, accusers, witnesses, judges and jurors, and the mob the executioners." The committees had abused officials, forcing resignations, recantations, and flight. "It is astonishing, my friends, that those, who are in pursuit of liberty, should ever suffer arbitrary power, in such an hideous form and squalid hue, to get a footing among them," he concluded.

In response, Adams offered a familiar story, a detailed account of Boston's reaction to the EIC ships. He charged that the tea had been sent "by the ministry in the name of the East India Company," because it wanted to establish the precedent for taxing the colonies. As had his cousin Samuel in December 1773, he insisted that the people of Massachusetts were not "so virtuous or so happy" as to be able or willing to abstain from their favorite hot beverage voluntarily. Therefore, the tea had to be destroyed to prevent it from being landed and sold. He reminded his readers that the Boston consignees had not resigned, unlike those in the other cities to which ships had been dispatched, and so sales remained possible had the tea been brought onshore. Adams devoted less space to defending the committees than Massachusettensis used to attack them, hinting once again at his possible discomfort in dealing with their legitimacy. Moreover, he stressed their communication rather than quasi-judicial functions. But he did remark that the committees' activities were justified by their targets: men with "some sinister private view." That line of argument was of a piece with his defense of the repression of Loyalist publications.

The fifth and sixth *Massachusettensis* essays, published on January 9 and 16, turned to the subject of the British constitution and in effect concluded the exchanges, because Adams then wrote about that topic alone at great length for the rest of his contributions to the debate (a total of six essays). Massachusettensis advanced a wholly conventional view: individual colonies were part of the empire, subject to "the checks, controul and regulation of the supreme authority [Parliament]," because "there is no possible medium between absolute independence and subjection." The arguments for colonial exemption from parliamentary rule were "specious," verging on treason and opening adherents to execution and confiscation of property. Once again, the Loyalist thus harped on the potentially dreadful consequences for individual colonists of persisting in opposition to Great Britain.

In his own seventh composition, the first of those six essays on the British constitution, Adams accused Massachusettensis of dealing deceptively with constitutional interpretation. Americans simply rejected Parliament's claim in the Declaratory Act of 1766 to rule America by right "in all cases whatsoever." Adams then embarked on the historical excursion that occupied the rest of his essays, discoursing learnedly and prolixly on English history; the charters of Virginia, Maryland, and Massachusetts; and the constitutional status of Ireland, Wales, Scotland, Guernsey, and Jersey. He concluded his seventh essay with the prediction that an attempt by Parliament to rule America would "infallibly" lead to armed resistance, but he did not wholly finish with the sixth *Massachusettensis* article until his last and thirteenth piece, which remained unpublished on April 19.

The later *Massachusettensis* essays, to which Adams never replied, developed some themes already introduced—for example, the dangers of treason and rebellion (letter 9, February 6) and the "fancied grievances" of the Whigs (letter 11, February 20)—but also moved on to new topics: the problems an independent American nation would face in a dangerous world (letter 8, January 30); the many benefits to America of the imperial connection (letters 14 and 15, March 13 and 20); and even a defense of the Massachusetts Government Act, a novel position for a New Englander to adopt (letter 10, February 13).

The most important of these essays was the penultimate one, published March 27, which discussed the First Continental Congress at length. It began with the assertion that a congress composed of representatives from the various colonies, "constitutionally appointed" by proper authorities and "amenable to and controlable" by them, could be "salutary" in many respects. (But Dartmouth's orders to governors to prevent assemblies from choosing delegates to the congress had made the appointment of such a body impossible.) A congress without authorization, Massachusettensis observed, was "an unlawful assembly, wholly incompatible with the constitution, and dangerous in the extreme." Still, even though numerous congressional delegates had irregular credentials, he pointed out accurately that many people viewed the Philadelphia congress "with an indulgent eye," and men of different political persuasions "bade the delegates God speed."

But, alas, the congress was dominated by men who had long practiced "hypocrisy, cunning and chicanery." Citing Galloway's *Candid Examination,* the author, most likely Leonard, argued that some members with "first rate abilities and characters" had been outmaneuvered by other delegates. Aware that the congress was "repugnant to, and inconsistent with, every idea of government," they set out to destroy that government through adopting the Suffolk Resolves. He charged that such congressmen had aimed at independence, evident in the way their resolves spoke "in the style of authority." In brief, he concluded, "had the delegates been appointed to devise means to irritate and enrage the inhabitants of the two countries"—note that phrasing—"against each other, beyond a possibility of reconciliation," they could not have done a more effective job. They had "united and consolidated" all the "disaffection, petulance, ingratitude and disloyalty" evident in America since 1765.

Abigail Adams, who termed *Massachusettensis* "execrable," and some of John Adams's friends, who praised *Novanglus* unreservedly, declared him the winner of the extended debate. Yet that partisan contemporary assessment must be tempered, because many of Leonard's points remained unanswered by mid-April 1775. Not only did Adams neglect all of the essays published after mid-January; he also failed to confront directly or at length Leonard's arguments about the legitimacy of committees and congresses, clearly *the* key current point of contention. He cleverly turned defense into offense by reversing some of Leonard's charges against the Whigs onto the Loyalists, but he also receded from his initial defense of a free press and ended up justifying occasionally brutal mob actions, as well as blaming Loyalists for the actions of British troops.

Even so, if John Adams and the other "disloyal" authors of early 1775 can be said to have lost the print war, their adherents were more successful off the printed page.

ADVICES FROM THE HAGUE,
BILBAO, LONDON, AND OFFSHORE

January 3, 1775. Sir Joseph Yorke writes from The Hague to assure the Earl of Suffolk that while waiting for ice to clear from navigation channels, he is working to see that all vessels leaving Amsterdam for the West Indies will be subjected to "the strictest Search" in order to stop the export of "Warlike Stores." Three days later, he reports that only one ship appears ready to sail: the *Catherine Elizabeth,* of New York, bound for Curaçao. It nominally carries a cargo of liquor and tea, but "certainly that is only a Mask." He notes pointedly that the vessel dared enter Amsterdam harbor only after the departure of the *Wells* cutter.

February 15. From Bilbao, Joseph Gardoqui informs Jeremiah Lee in Boston of progress in filling his orders for arms and ammunition. He has acquired about three hundred muskets and six hundred pistols, but they will have to be shipped "with a good deal of Caution" because the British ambassador to Spain "will look sharp in every port." He cannot ship any Spanish gunpowder, for that commodity is restricted to government use, but with adequate notice he can acquire some from Holland "on Reasonable Terms." He cautions Lee, "Should any of your vessels be taken in the Channel loaded with those articles, she should certainly be condemned."

February 17. The Earl of Suffolk informs Yorke that he has received seemingly reliable information about three Dutch ships loading at Texel, on the coast near Amsterdam, with "very considerable quantities of Arms, Powder & Lead," which have been packaged in "very small Parcels for the readier Conveyance by Hand." A sloop of war, the *Speedwell,* has been ordered to proceed to Texel with the *Wells* cutter to investigate the story. Four days later, urging Yorke to act, he adds an important observation: "The Situation of Affairs in North America, forbids all Delicacy in Matters of this serious Nature."

February 26. Captain Richard Pearson, of the *Speedwell*, stationed off Texel, expresses his concerns to Yorke about three ships in particular: one that is ready to sail for St. Eustatius; one from New York; and one from Bermuda that has reportedly already made five voyages to America "with powder and other warlike stores, since the commencement of the disturbances." He asks for the assignment of another vessel to help him interdict them.

March 1. Yorke reminds Captain Pearson about the difficulties they confront in dealing with Dutch ships at Texel. Dutch vessels have a "plausible pretence" when they claim to be sailing to the Dutch Caribbean colonies, "tho' we well know that their Colonies are a Magazine to furnish ours."

March 20. Pressed by Yorke to adopt such a policy, the States General of Holland formally ban the export of "Ammunition, Gunpowder, Guns, and Shot" aboard any vessels of the British dominions for a period of six months. Such items loaded onto any other ships must also receive specific clearance in writing.

April 8. Captain Pearson, who has returned to his regular station off Dover on the *Speedwell*, summarizes for the Admiralty what he has learned. At Texel, he encountered many American vessels, "going and coming there daily, and not one in ten ever clears in England." The Bermuda sloop loaded gunpowder and is nominally sailing to Lisbon. A Boston ship and a French vessel are both going to Portugal to load arms for America. Two Boston agents have been buying military supplies in Amsterdam; they are "exceedingly clamorous against the Prohibition of the States General." And a merchant smuggled over six thousand pounds of gunpowder on board the vessel bound for St. Eustatius. That ship was prevented from sailing, in part by contrary winds, but he does not know what happened to it after he was ordered to return to Dover on April 3.

CHAPTER 9

ALL OUR LIBERTIES AT STAKE

In early March 1775, Governor Jonathan Trumbull spoke to the Connecticut assembly, which he had summoned into session for the first time since the fall, to consider business of the "first Magnitude"—the "present unhappy and increasing Difference between Great Britain and the English Colonies in America." He warned that America's enemies, approaching their task with a "depraved, Malignant aviricious and haughty mind," were seeking to alter the charters of all the colonies, not just that of Massachusetts Bay. In particular, he feared a plan to create in each province a branch of government composed of nobility named by the king. As they all knew, those enemies had already succeeded in persuading Parliament "to claim a right and Authority to make Laws and Statutes . . . to bind the Colonies and people of America," and to tax them for the purpose of raising a revenue.

So he had called them together to discuss the issues at this critical time, "when our Freedom and all our Liberties are at Stake." He declared that "a manly Spirited defence of our just rights" was essential. Connecticut was fortunate, he added, that because of its charter the assembly itself could "without violence to [our constitution], lay hold on its power, wield it as you please . . . against those who by Force and Violence, seek our Ruin & Destruction." In Connecticut, he was reminding them, no provincial congress was required. The assemblymen themselves could act with "firmness, deliberation, moderation, union & Harmony."

No other source confirms that Trumbull correctly described a plan to designate an American nobility, but he was not the only colonist who feared the implications of the Massachusetts Government Act for other provinces with unusual political structures laid out in their charters. Nor, as has been seen, was he the only American political leader to sense that a crisis was approaching in the early months of 1775. That perception had heightened after colonists learned the contents of George III's speech to the opening session of the new Parliament on November 30, 1774.

THE KING'S SPEECH

A ship arrived in Marblehead on January 29 with London newspapers published in mid-December, carrying the text of the king's address, with answers from both Commons and Lords. A few days later a packet boat sailed into New York harbor with the same newspapers. Quickly the texts were rushed into print, and by early February people throughout the continent began to comment on the speech and the replies.

Henry Laurens waited anxiously in Charleston for information about the contents of the speech and the official responses. "These will be to me the Harbingers of good or Evil," he told a friend. Henry's son John, who remained in London, did not attend the speech, but another South Carolinian reported to him afterward that the king had referred to "dangerous Persons" who were "poisoning the Minds of his Majesty's Subjects." It seemed to him as though at that moment the king gestured at Josiah Quincy Jr., who was also present. After being thus singled out, Quincy himself predicted a "Civil War" to John Laurens, who informed his father that he nevertheless continued to pray for peace.

In the address, George III put an end to many colonists' hopes for reconciliation. He spoke of the "most daring spirit of resistance, and disobedience to the law" in Massachusetts and how "fresh violences" there had been "countenanced and encouraged" by the other colonies. The king declared that "unlawful combinations" were trying to obstruct imperial commerce and explained that he was taking steps to enforce the Coercive Acts. He assured the MPs of his "firm and stedfast resolutions to withstand every attempt to weaken or impair

For *The Royal American Magazine* in January 1775, Revere copied a British cartoon depicting George III plotting against America with his advisers. Lord North holds a bill labeled "for the total abolition of Civil & Religs liberty in America" and has in his pocket a treaty with France and Spain, while a cleric holds the Murder Act. On the left, an allegorical figure of Liberty looks to the heavens for assistance.

the supreme authority of this legislature over all the dominions of My crown." Both houses of Parliament responded in kind, largely parroting the king's own words in their praise of his words and actions.

John Carter, a Providence printer who published the speech in broadside format, added to it a brief account of dissenters in the House of Lords who asked for more information before agreeing to a response but were voted down. *"Thus it appears that the continued and anxious Suspence of the Colonies is at an End,"* he appended in a note to the parliamentary exchanges. *"Good GOD! What Spirit of Folly and Precipitation Persists in the British Councils!—The Dye seems to be cast. . . . May the united Colonies be directed to such Measures as will eventually terminate in the Defeat of Tyrants, and the Redemption of this devoted Country."*

Abigail Adams echoed Carter's words. "The die is cast," she told Mercy Warren in early February; the speech would mark the king's reign with "everlasting infamy." She predicted that "the most wicked and hostile measures" would follow and observed that "it seems to me the Sword is now our only, yet dreadful alternative." Indeed, given the option of submission, she concluded, "I had rather see the Sword drawn." The Loyalist Henry Pelham too used the same language in his description of the speech: "The Dye seems to be cast!" Yet not everyone agreed with him and Abigail Adams. Resistance leaders told Pelham that they had anticipated the speech's contents and discounted its importance. For his part, Henry Laurens too commented that "thinking Men" were treating it dismissively.

Following the speech, Americans such as Laurens, Thomas Cushing, and Richard Henry Lee all told correspondents in London that Americans were (in Cushing's words) "as firm and United as ever" or (in Lee's) "resolved to defend their liberties ad infinitum" or (in Laurens's) that they would never agree "to a tame Surrender of their just rights & Liberties." Even royal governors concurred in such assessments. Sir James Wright regretfully informed Dartmouth that Americans expressed such devotion to their "Ideas of Liberty" that "I do not Expect they will yet give up their Pretensions." And Governor Josiah Martin of North Carolina told him that in the aftermath of the king's speech the colonists' "seditious leaders . . . talk of resorting to violence instead of submission."

One of the most comprehensive letters sent to England in the wake of the king's speech was what became Joseph Reed's final communication with the American secretary. Reed assured Dartmouth that he always supported conciliatory measures "consistent with the Dignity & Interest of the Mother Country, and the Safety of this," but opposed policies that would "degrade me from the Rank of a Free Subject." Any move to effect reconciliation, he indicated, would have to be based on "those essential rights which we apprehend ought to distinguish an English Colonist from those [subjects] of an arbitrary State."

Still believing a settlement was attainable, Reed laid out his ideas for a compromise: Britain could insist on payment for the tea destroyed at Boston, but in return would repeal the Coercive Acts and the tea duty, in addition declaring "the Inexpediency of Taxation" (but not, implicitly, surrendering the "right" to tax). Such an arrangement could serve as the foundation for a new American constitution "upon reasonable Principles," with provisions for raising revenue to be negotiated.

If assemblies were encouraged to send representatives to Britain to work out such a deal, with the Coercive Acts being suspended in the interim, he thought the colonies would all agree. He concluded by cautioning Dartmouth that although the congress had some critics, they were too few for the British to rely upon. And his penultimate sentence contained a dire warning: "This Country will be deluged with Blood before it will submit to any other Taxation than by their own Assemblies."

Reed's advocacy of moderation, though, was becoming less and less acceptable to his fellow Americans, as was suggested by Abigail Adams's contrasting sense that the die had been cast and that only the "Sword" remained as an option. Moreover, another of Dartmouth's American correspondents warned him that the colonists disagreed not over principles but only about the best means of opposing the ministry, "though there is no great Difference even in that." Americans had also concluded, declared one New Englander, that the time had come "when different sentiments of the *mode* of opposition must not divide us in making opposition."

ENFORCING TRADE RESTRICTIONS, AMERICAN AND BRITISH

The Continental Association had decreed that after February 1 no items from Britain or the British West Indies could be imported into the colonies. Committees everywhere attempted to enforce that prohibition rigorously, without exception, even when it was clear that shippers and merchants had been unaware of the deadline. Thus a sloop that arrived from Bristol with rigging, sails, and other supplies for a ship under construction in Falmouth, Maine, was not allowed to unload. A ship with bales of goods from Glasgow was turned away from Maryland. A vessel from Antigua with cloth that had originated in Britain was ordered by a Virginia committee to return to the island. The Marblehead committee's seizure of candles intended for the private use of Admiral Samuel Graves led to a major confrontation between the British navy and the selectmen. And in Charleston, the local committee forced ships arriving with salt, coal, and potatoes from British ports to dump their cargoes overboard.

When a Norfolk trader was discovered trying to evade the Association's absolute prohibition on imports of slaves by concealing the presence of some enslaved people on a ship that arrived from Jamaica, the committee ordered his name published as an enemy. Also in Norfolk, James Parker reported that three ships ran afoul of the embargo and had to return whence they came: one from Barbados carrying salt, another from Liverpool with the same cargo, and one from Glasgow with goods he did not specify. "Such are the proceedings here & our Committe[emen] are said to be the most moderate in the Colony," he remarked. All the captains could do was protest and hope that eventually they would be able to recover damages from the committee members.

Such incidents caused little concern except for those individuals directly involved, but three others aroused considerable controversy among residents of Charleston and New York. William Henry Drayton later wrote at length about what happened in Charleston in March when a "respectable family" (which he did not name) that had been living in England returned home, bringing with them some furniture and horses. That set off a lengthy debate in the colony's general committee about whether the Association's restrictions should apply to such items.

Some members argued that used furniture and horses that would not be sold should be exempted from the ban on imports, whereas others contended that no exceptions should be made. In the initial tally of participating committeemen, the chair's vote in favor of the family provided a narrow margin of victory. That result "occasioned a ferment among the citizens," Drayton recalled, with many contending that the horses at least should be barred. Hundreds of people gathered to protest the decision, and further discussions were postponed so that more members of the large committee could take part. Three days later, many residents attended the rescheduled meeting. By then, according to Drayton, the town was in "universal commotion." Armed groups were asked to protect the horses if they were landed, whereas others declared that if the horses set foot on Carolina soil, they would be killed. Christopher Gadsden moved to reverse the previous decision. That led to a full-blown debate, with Edward Rutledge and his allies vehemently defending the committee and contending that admitting the items would accord with the spirit if not the letter of the Association.

Drayton recalled that he responded by stressing "our duty, to satisfy our constituents, as we were only servants of the public." At least according to his own account—as far as it may be trusted—Drayton asserted forcefully that "landing the horses, hazarded our union: for, the people were in commotion against it," and he reiterated that it was crucial to allow the people's voice to determine the outcome. After further debate, the committee reversed the original decision, again by a close vote. Drayton concluded with satisfaction, "This is the first instance of a point of importance and controversy, being carried against those; by whose opinions, the people had been long governed." Whether or not Drayton played the crucial role that he later claimed, his assessment was correct: the overriding of the general committee's vote to exempt a wealthy family from the Association's strictures did represent an important milestone in the evolution of South Carolina politics at that time.

In New York the previous month, two vessels, the *James* and the *Beulah,* provoked similar negative reactions from local residents. Both ships tried to evade the Association, the *James* openly, the *Beulah* by stealth. The *James* sailed into the harbor from Glasgow on February 2 with a cargo of coal and dry goods. The committee of sixty told the captain that he could not land any items from the ship, but he nonetheless sought to recruit workers for that task. People began to gather "in great numbers," reported John Holt; the captain then moved the ship a few miles away for safety, and when it returned to the harbor, it was placed under the protection of the *Kingfisher* sloop of war. This "greatly exasperated" the people, Holt recorded. A crowd seized the captain from his onshore lodging, paraded him through the streets, and put him in a small boat with oarsmen to take him to the *Kingfisher*. A few days later, the *James* sailed, reportedly bound for Jamaica, and the committee carefully monitored the ship until it passed Sandy Hook. Holt commented, "It must give real pleasure to every lover of his country, to observe, that the good people of this city, are determined to support the association of the general congress."

The *Beulah,* which arrived in mid-February, was not so easily or quickly handled, because its owners, the Quaker merchants Robert and John Murray, plotted to land some of its cargo clandestinely after they had failed to persuade other shippers to unite in unloading the vessel publicly. Cadwallader Colden offered the merchants protection from possible crowd action—an offer Thomas Gage commended—but the cargo's other owners, unwilling to confront the possible consequences to their business elsewhere, collectively decided to send the *Beulah* to Halifax. Colden told Dartmouth that their failure to accept his assistance "chagrined me a good deal."

The ship left New York in early March but, instead of sailing immediately for Nova Scotia, anchored off Sandy Hook for a night, during which a small boat hired by the Murrays removed the items they hoped to sell locally, along with some foodstuffs for their own use. But the city committee, suspicions aroused by the *Beulah's* lingering offshore, enlisted the aid of the Elizabethtown committee. The two groups cooperated in an extensive investigation, and they uncovered the malfeasance by questioning the New Jersey boatmen involved in the plot. The Murray brothers then confessed that they had knowingly violated the Association in order to partly offset their losses. They admitted that their "imprudent step" had been "unjustifiable" and provided the committees with a detailed inventory of the off-loaded goods. They also donated £200 to rebuild the New York hospital, which had recently burned down. Still, by the end of March, public pressure forced them to close their retail store, although a proposal to banish them formally from the city evidently failed.

Admiral Graves, reporting from Boston to the Admiralty in early March, expressed the hope that New York merchants, with assistance from naval vessels such as that offered to the *James* and the *Beulah,* "will I hope be induced to import as usual, notwithstanding any illegal Combinations to oppose it." The fate of the two ships dashed those hopes, and unfortunately from his perspective customs and naval officers did little better as they tried to interdict Americans' clandestine trade with other nations—commerce that colonial committees left unmolested. In mid-April, he admitted to the Admiralty that even with additional vessels he had hired, it was difficult to prevent smugglers from reaching Boston. Such ships frequently alleged "Distress, Ignorance [or] bringing provisions," he explained. Even though he had caught several vessels recently, he commented that smuggling was "so

3 9,

WHEREAS we the Subfcribers have broke the Affociation of the late Continental Congrefs, by unloading a Part of the Cargo from on board the Ship Beulah; we do declare that we are forry for the Offence we gave the Publick thereby, and that we will for the future ftrictly adhere to the faid Affociation, and to the further Orders of the Continental Congrefs, the Provincial Congrefs of the Colony of New-York, and the General Committee of Affociation for the City and County of New-York, faving to Robert Murray (who is one of the People called QUAKERS) his religious Principles. Dated at New-York, the 9th of June, 1775.

Robert Murray,
John Murray.

One of the many broadsides produced by the Murrays to apologize for violating the Continental Association in their attempt to unload cargo from the *Beulah* in secret in March 1775.

systematically followed" that his ships were required to be especially vigilant.

Graves and his naval vessels did have some success in deterring potential American smugglers of arms and ammunition. In February, a New London captain learned that gunpowder was available in St. Eustatius. Although he was warned about British ships lurking along the New England coast, the captain confidently predicted, "I shall Procure the Quantity Desir'd." Others were not so sure. A New Yorker observed that "the very strict watch" kept by customs officers and warships was preventing many merchants from dealing in arms. A Providence merchant cautioned Bostonians that because of the ships stationed between Long Island and Martha's Vineyard, "the getting any Warlike Stores into [Rhode Island] by Water, will be attended with almost an Impossibility." Even so, some ships successfully evaded the British. For example, Ezra Stiles learned in March that a Virginia vessel carrying "Powder, Arms, Field pieces & military stores" from France returned safely to its home province, "tho' pursued & fired at by the Man o' War & her Cutters."

If smugglers managed to elude royal ships on the seas and unload their cargoes, customs officers attempted to intercept them on land, but did not always succeed. For example, in February, a Savannah customs collector seized eight hogsheads of molasses and six of sugar, which had recently arrived clandestinely from the French Caribbean. He recruited several sailors from a king's schooner to join one of his subordinates in guarding the cargo onshore for the night. But, according to Governor Wright, the guards were attacked by "a large number of people, with their faces smutted and armed with Pistols and Cutlasses, in a very riotous and unlawful manner." They stripped the customs employee, tarred and feathered him, and then threw him and the other guards into the water, successfully carrying away the hogsheads. One sailor reportedly drowned. Also tarred and feathered that month was a customs informer in New York who had reputedly revealed the location of some smuggled hemp. Thomas Ellison Jr. witnessed the incident and reported that the informer "was Carted almost Round the town" before magistrates could rescue him. On that occasion, two members of the crowd were arrested and jailed.

The approaches to Philadelphia along the Delaware River appear to have posed a particularly difficult challenge to customs officers. A Marylander reported at length to the customs commissioners in Boston about an early March encounter on a road to Philadelphia with men driving two heavily loaded wagons filled with rum, sugar, coffee, and cloth. He attempted to seize the contents, but a crowd attacked him, threatened to tar and feather him, stole his gun and money, mounted him backward on a horse, and dragged him for several miles, repeatedly shouting, "Liberty," before he managed to escape.

On the river itself, in early February as a matter of routine a customs officer from Philadelphia boarded an unknown schooner reportedly from Maine that was anchored near the city. What happened to him next was not routine. The captain weighed anchor, turned the ship around, and headed downstream, "declaring he would go to St. Eustatia," taking the officer with him. Customs collectors in Philadelphia were convinced that the schooner was loaded with contraband, including "tea and War-like Stores from Holland." They sent a description of the vessel to other ports, but evidently after the captain dropped off the customs officer at the mouth of the Delaware, he simply turned around and sailed back to the city to unload his cargo, including tea and liquor in addition to dry goods and possibly the suspected arms as well. The kidnapped officer learned while being held that the vessel, the *Isabella,* was in fact from Portsmouth, New Hampshire, perhaps on a voyage from France. The uncertainty about the ship's identity, its contents, and the port whence it had come—not to mention its captain's actions—all pointed to an experienced smuggler, just as the customs service personnel suspected.

All in all, American committees' enforcement of the Association's prohibition on commerce from Britain and its possessions after February 1 was seemingly more effective than British officers' similar attempts to stop clandestine trade. In those early weeks and months of 1775, though, it was still an open question whether the ramshackle provincial governmental structures the colonists had started to build to replace or circumvent formal colonial institutions could achieve the same success as had local committees, or whether their efforts would be thwarted by governors and assemblies.

PENNSYLVANIA AND NEW YORK

When the 1775 session of the Pennsylvania assembly began in late February, the examples of William Franklin's actions in New Jersey the previous month and Cadwallader Colden's contemporaneous dealings with the New York assembly influenced Lieutenant Governor John Penn's approach to the political circumstances he faced. In his formal opening address, Penn advised the assemblymen that even though they had approved the resolutions of the First Continental Congress, they should revisit the idea of presenting a separate petition to George III. He insisted that "the only proper and constitutional Mode of applying for Redress was by way of humble petition from the legal Representatives of the People to his Majesty." But to Dartmouth he expressed pessimism about the assemblymen's reaction to that message. A majority, he predicted, would oppose "an Act which may have the Appearance of contravening the Proceedings of the General Congress."

Penn's prediction proved correct, but not before what Joseph Reed termed "warm Disputes" that consumed several weeks of the session and delayed a decision until mid-March. The debate centered on members' fear that approving such a petition would lead inevitably to further proposals to appeal to the Lords and Commons, which would be anathema because the congress rejected the right of Parliament to rule America. Reed identified the two major combatants as John Dickinson and Joseph Galloway. According to Reed, Dickinson "took a very decisive Part in the Debate agt Galloway who is now become the most violent & rancorous Opponent to the Congress I have ever met with." Galloway himself revealed to William Franklin that in the assembly he "censured and condemned the measures of the Congress in everything." Contradicting his earlier position, he argued for the necessity of parliamentary authority over the colonies "in all cases whatsoever." Despite intricate political maneuvers that Galloway detailed to Franklin, he failed to persuade the assembly to petition the king. After the session ended, he received a death threat in the form of a noose and a menacing letter in a wooden box. Still, he vowed, he would not be silent.

William Bradford voiced unhappiness about the assembly's lack of significant action to James Madison. It had adopted "a few harmless resolves," he reported, instead of taking necessary steps to organize militia companies. He observed that "we have Boston in the front & Virginia in the rear to defend us: we are placed where Cowards ought to be placed in the middle." Even so, Bradford mused that assembly petitions might have been helpful had they been drafted and adopted earlier. Such petitions might once have given Parliament a reason to comply with American requests, but now he thought that "our fate is already determined." Strictly following congressional guidelines was "the only means of safety," along with "Union among ourselves." Of Galloway, he memorably opined, "he can contract or dilate [his conscience] at pleasure," making it "strain at a Gnat or swallow a camel as best suits his purpose."

Even though Reed criticized Galloway's opposition to the Continental Congress, his own political position remained deliberately ambiguous in late February. He reported that he "studiously avoided" engaging in "personal Debates" and that the fact he chaired the Philadelphia committee was helpful, because he led the meetings and so did not participate directly in the committee's discussions. His wife, Esther, continued to hope for a compromise, telling her brother in mid-March that "this country wishes for nothing so much as dependency on the Mother State on proper terms, and to be secure of their liberties; and you may depend on it that the accounts given that this country is aiming at independence are false, and arise only from the enemies of both countries." The British-born Esther was undoubtedly sincere, but her own choice of words undercut her statement. Three times in one sentence she called the American colonies a "country," as though they constituted a separate unit, independent from another "country," Great Britain.

Perhaps the moderate opinions described by William Bradford and exemplified by Joseph and Esther Reed dominated Philadelphia. A visitor commented in March that there "people only minded their business." But not so New York: "here nothing is heard of but Politics," he wrote in his journal in mid-month. And more than that: "the People here are much divided, & Party spirit is very high."

As was recounted in chapter 7, in February the New York assembly rejected approval of the First Congress's resolutions and declined to name delegates to the second. Soon after the assembly's vote, the committee of sixty announced a citizens' meeting for March 6 to elect deputies to a provincial convention, the sole purpose of which would be to choose congressional delegates. That announcement set off a furious debate conducted in broadsides and in person. A group of merchants headed by John Thurman opposed a citywide election meeting, arguing that freeholders and freemen alone should be able to vote for deputies, and furthermore that it was important to avoid hasty decisions, so a formal poll should be postponed for several weeks. A broadside then charged that Thurman was being duplicitous, because he had been overheard to remark at the coffeehouse that he did not support sending delegates to the Second Congress. The author of one broadside, "Americanus," contended that it would be "dishonourable" and would open New York to sanctions if the colony did not elect representatives; the author of another, "A Citizen of New York," asserted that participating in the Second Congress would make "Our

Constitutional Assembly . . . a mere cypher" and lead to "rampant Republicanism."

Still, the meeting on March 6 proceeded as originally planned. According to a widely reprinted report from *The New-York Journal,* "A Union Flag, with a red field, was hoisted on the Liberty-pole," and men assembled under it. A Loyalist historian later charged that the leaders "marched round all the docks and wharves, with trumpets blowing, fifes playing, drums beating, and colours flying," to recruit "all the boys, sailors, negroes, New England and Jersey boatmen, that could be mustered." That group then marched to the meeting, "attended by musick," under a blue flag inscribed on one side GEORGE III. REX AND THE LIBERTIES OF AMERICA. NO POPERY and, on the other, THE UNION OF THE COLONIES, AND THE MEASURES OF THE CONGRESS. Thurman and his allies, including military and civilian officials, also attended but were outnumbered as the "vast concourse of people" voted to elect deputies to a provincial convention and authorized the committee of sixty to nominate a slate for city residents to consider. Following the meeting, the *Journal* reported, "the Friends of Freedom paraded through one of the principal Streets of the City, to the Liberty-pole, and there dispersed, in the most quiet and orderly Manner."

The committee of sixty scheduled the election—a poll by wards, as Thurman's group had advocated—for March 15. It also produced a slate of eleven deputies: the five delegates to the First Congress, Alexander McDougall, and five other men. Another flurry of broadsides appeared, among them one arguing for reelecting the previous delegates and eschewing a provincial convention. Thomas Ellison Jr., reporting these events to his father, observed that "our Streets abound with papers," in part because "the Parties for the Provincial Convention are Very Warm, in making all the Interest possible to Carry their Point." Indeed, the slate and the convention itself won overwhelmingly in the city vote, and the committee of sixty dispatched a circular letter to other New York counties, asking them also to choose deputies to an April 20 provincial convention.

That call stimulated debates elsewhere in the colony that mimicked those in the city. "A New-Town Freeholder" charged that only "hirelings and tools of state" opposed a provincial convention. "A Freeholder of Jamaica" supported reelecting the five delegates. A Hempstead town meeting declined to choose deputies because the sitting assemblymen were "our only legal and constitutional Representatives," but that decision was challenged by "A Freeholder of Hempstead." In Westchester County, the populace was so divided that residents met in two separate groups. One voted against deputies, but the other elected several. In the end, when the convention met, it reelected the five delegates from the First Congress to attend the second on New York's behalf.

While these debates consumed his province, Lieutenant Governor Colden watched from the sidelines. He explained to Dartmouth that he would have liked to halt the naming of delegates to the Second Congress by a convention, but he could not do so, because the measures were carried out "by individuals in their private characters and do not come within the energy of our laws." And that clearly described the crux of the challenge Colden and the other colonial governors faced in the first months of 1775: the extralegal committees and conventions established under the auspices of the First Continental Congress, for all their jerry-built nature, operated outside the official realm of government, and thus regular colonial officeholders had little leverage to employ to influence them. As Charles Carroll of Carrollton observed pointedly, "A Governor cannot dissipate [a convention] by his Fiat."

In that letter in early April, Colden informed Dartmouth about "a dangerous insurrection" that had occurred approximately two weeks earlier in northern New York, in what was then Cumberland County (which became part of Vermont), near the Massachusetts border. New York judges had attempted to hold a court session, but protesters wanted the courts closed, as they were in Massachusetts. Clashes ensued and a protester was killed by a New York sheriff's posse, with others wounded. Crowds then gathered, captured the responsible posse members, and carried them to jail in Northampton. There some posted bail and others eventually escaped. No one involved on either side seems to have been punished.

Colden omitted telling Dartmouth about another potentially dangerous plan for an "insurrection" in the Hudson valley about a month before those incidents on the Massachusetts border. John Holt and Hugh Gaine reported in their newspapers in early March about John Schoonmaker of Ulster County, who one night in mid-February overheard one of his slaves, York, talking with another enslaved man. The gist of their conversation disclosed a plot for slaves from nearby communities to gather a few nights later to set fire to houses and to kill people as they fled from the fires. One version of the story claimed that the enslaved men of African descent were going to combine with local Native Americans, but Gaine commented that there was no "good Foundation" for that part of the tale. Still, the authorities unearthed a hidden store of powder and shot and eventually arrested twenty men as participants. What happened to them is unknown, but Colden probably neglected to tell Dartmouth about the incident because the slaves' motive was reported to be "the Recovery of their Freedom" and it accordingly appeared to have little or no connection to current politics.

Had James Madison or Abigail Adams heard the story of the Ulster County slaves' plan, though, the possibility of a political link might not have been disregarded so readily. Months earlier, both Adams and Madison had heard rumors that enslaved people were plotting to aid the British in exchange for their freedom. In Boston, the reputed conspiracy took the form of a petition to Governor Gage "telling him they would fight for him provided he would arm them and engage to liberate them if he conquerd." In Virginia, Madison learned that slaves "chose a leader who was to conduct them when the English troops should arrive . . . & that by revolting to them they should be rewarded with their freedom." Neither account has been verified by other contemporary sources, but that such rumors existed and were believed demonstrated that Euro-Americans were attuned to the possibility that the people they held in actual bondage might seek assistance from the nation they claimed to be holding them in metaphorical enslavement.

VIRGINIA AND NORTH CAROLINA

In late March, Charles Yates, a Fredericksburg, Virginia, merchant, warned a friend, "We now seem very near a crisis in the affairs between great Brittain & the Colonys." Like others, he hoped for "conciliating measures" proposed by the British, for if good news did not arrive soon, "the consequences will indeed be bad to all concerned."

That assessment of the political situation came just as the second Virginia Provincial Convention was completing its work, the first such meeting in the colony since August 1774. Governor Dunmore's prolonged absence meant that the assembly session originally set for November had been prorogued until February and then prorogued again until early May. The repeated postponements left in abeyance the election of delegates to the Second Continental Congress and other business that might have been addressed by an assembly or a convention. So, after the second prorogation, the assembly Speaker, Peyton Randolph, summoned a provincial congress to meet in Richmond on March 20. Richard Henry Lee compared Dunmore to members of "the Tyrant Stewart race" who were afraid to meet with the people's representatives, with well-known consequences. "May we not hope that the same causes will produce similar effects and that ruin may recoil on the heads of the detestable contrivers of the present unjust and destructive system of Colony Administration?" he asked.

For his part, Dunmore predicted to Dartmouth that the convention's aim was to "confirm the power of Committees," to "establish the laws, as they are called, of their Continental Congress," and most likely "to provide for the arming and supporting of forces." Regardless of what else the convention accomplished, he wrote, the delegates planned "to erect their own body into the head which is to direct this new government which supersedes that of His Majesty in this colony and entirely subverts the constitution."

Yet the Provincial Convention was not as unified as Lee hoped or as Dunmore feared. It approved the resolutions of the First Congress and adopted provisions promoting home manufactures, encouraging the cultivation of hemp and flax, and forbidding the slaughter of sheep, along with following other congressional recommendations. It kept local courts closed to most cases, laid out a new plan for the militia, and named delegates to the May congress, ignoring Dunmore's solemn proclamation urging its members to "desist from such an unjustifiable Proceeding." But the members divided over taking on such government functions as appointing judges and collecting taxes, the very issues that bedeviled the Bay Colony's Provincial Convention. James Parker heard that the more conservative members intended only "to have errours rectified, & not to alter or destroy the Constitution." By contrast, Patrick Henry, the prime supporter of setting up a new government, was "infamously insolent," Parker reported in early April, relying on an unnamed acquaintance who attended the convention. Henry called the king "a Tyrant, a fool, a puppet & a tool to the ministry, said there was now no Englishman, nor Scots no Britons, but a Set of wretches sunk in Luxury, they had lost their native courage." He was, in short, "compleatly scurrilous."

Parker referred briefly to a concurrent meeting of the North Carolina assembly, but revealed that he had no news of what was happening in New Bern. Had he known, he would surely have been disheartened. In the neighboring colony, Governor Josiah Martin chose a tactic that differed from Dunmore's repeated prorogations. The new North Carolina assembly session was scheduled to begin on April 3. Directly challenging Martin, organizers of the Provincial Convention summoned a meeting for the same day, also in New Bern. The governor, pronouncing the timing "highly derogatory to the dignity of the Legislature," promulgated a lengthy proclamation against the convention, asserting that the assembly was "the only true and lawful representation of the people." Retaining April 3 as the date for the assembly session, he urged North Carolinians not to obey "the tyrannical and arbitrary Committees" and to refuse to elect delegates to the convention. In the end, the confrontation he invited by failing to retreat from the announced assembly schedule did not go well.

The day before the two bodies were to convene, Martin issued another proclamation, declaring that the convention was "highly offensive to The King and dishonorable to the General Assembly," and he forbade it to take place. In what must have been for Martin a maddening development, the convention achieved a quorum and began its meeting as scheduled, but the assembly lacked sufficient attendance and could not start until the fourth. When the convention defied the first proclamation, he circulated a second, ordering its members "to break up the said meeting and to desist from all such illegal unwarrantable and dangerous proceedings."

Succeeding events can only be deemed farcical, for membership in the assembly and the convention overlapped almost completely. The convention approved the Continental Association, and all but one of its members signed it. The delegates to the First Continental Congress received the thanks of the convention and were reelected to represent the colony at the Second Congress; funds were appropriated for their expenses. Notably, the convention insisted that the people had a right to petition the government, and thus that the governor's proclamations against it were "illegal, and an infringement of our just rights, and therefore ought to be disregarded as wanton and arbitrary exertions of power."

Martin's speech opening the assembly on April 4 railed against local committees, which he called "little unrestrained and arbitrary tribunals," and especially against the convention, never acknowledging that most of the men in his audience belonged simultaneously to both bodies. He told the assemblymen that supporting "your dignity and the just rights of the people" required them to oppose the meeting of the convention—that is, themselves in their other capacity. He continued,

> Are you not the only lawful Representatives of the people in this Country, and competent to every legal purpose? Will you, then, submit to see your constituents misled, to violate their dearest privileges by wounding your dignity, and setting up Representatives derogatory to your just power and authority? This, gentlemen, is an insult to you of so violent a nature that it appears to me to demand your every possible discouragement, for its evident tendency is to excite a belief in the people that they are capable of electing Representatives of superior powers to the Members of your House; which, if it can possibly obtain, must lead to obvious consequences, to the destruction of the essence, if not the very being of an Assembly in this Province, and finally to the utter dissolution and overthrow of its established happy Constitution.

He exhorted the assemblymen to "undeceive the people, to lead them back from the dangerous precipice to which all ill spirit of faction is urging them, to the paths of their duty." The example set by the assembly would then persuade the people to "gladly free themselves from that tyranny which ill-directed zeal and lawless ambition, by all the arts of misrepresentation and delusion," had subjected them.

When Martin dispatched a copy of his speech to Dartmouth, he explained that he hoped assembly members would "secede" from the convention in response to his urging, even though he knew that many of those listening to him served in the convention as well. That hope led him to agree to the choice of John Harvey as Speaker (which followed his selection as moderator of the convention), though "not without repugnance," in large part because the council advised him not to reject the assembly's choice. On April 5, far from separating themselves from the convention delegates, the assembly members formally joined with them to create a new body. That evening, Martin considered dissolving the assembly, for it "treated with utter neglect my most solemn exhortations to break up that illegal Meeting and to assert their own Rights." Yet a majority of the council, after a night to contemplate the options, advised him to let the assembly session continue "untill it should offend in its own Name, and Character." He reluctantly agreed. But then, while trying to conceal from him the actions they had taken, the assembly acting in that capacity approved the measures of the First Congress and confirmed the appointments of the same delegation to the second, among other offensive acts. On the night of April 7, the council at last concurred: he should dissolve the assembly. Martin issued a proclamation to that effect, which was published the next morning.

Reflecting on his frustrating experiences dealing with the assembly/ convention, he observed to the American secretary, "Government is here as absolutely prostrate, as impotent, and that nothing but the shadow of it is left. It is indeed alike the Case in every other Colony that I hear of except New York." He concluded disconsolately, "Unless effectual measures, such as British Spirit may dictate, are speedily taken, there will not long remain a trace of Britain's dominion over these colonies."

MASSACHUSETTS

"How much Longer sir do you think the political scale Can Hang in Equilibrium?" Mercy Otis Warren asked John Adams on January 30. "Will not justice and Freedom soon preponderate?" Then, as she often did, she added an acknowledgment of her gender identity to a political observation. "You will not think it strange that the timidity and tenderness of A Woman should Lead her to be anxious for the Consequences of Disputes which interrupt Almost Every Social Enjoyment and threaten to spread Ruin and Desolation over the Fairest possessions."

Yet in early 1775 the "social enjoyments" of Loyalists and British officers in occupied Boston do not seem to have been interrupted by the political quarrel. They attended dances, played cards, and called on the governor's wife at her weekly drawing room. Perhaps the partygoers concurred with the customs commissioner Henry Hulton, who thought that "the parade they make here of resistance is all a flash." The colonists lacked "order, and discipline, Officers and money, Military stores and places of defence." He foresaw little difficulty when British forces finally acted, nor did Major John Pitcairn, who told a superior that when the army moved against colonial militiamen, "they will soon be convinced that they are very insignificant when opposed to regular troops." For his part, Governor Gage revealed that he was "Impatiently" awaiting orders from England. He knew that maintaining order in Boston, which he had been doing successfully, was insufficient. He thought he had to act "Offensively," which meant that "the Troops must March into the Country."

Near the end of February, Gage accordingly did not hesitate to direct his men to march into the country when he learned about the presence of eight cannon at Salem from a man he regarded as a reliable source—probably Dr. Benjamin Church, member of the Boston committee, who had become a British spy. As Gage later told Dartmouth, he believed incorrectly that these were "brass Guns brought in from Holland," and so he dispatched two hundred men under Lieutenant Colonel Alexander Leslie to seize them. He reported that the troops "strictly searched" the places where they were said to be hidden, but the cannon could not be located. Subsequently, he learned that they were only old guns from a ship that had already been moved out of town.

But there was more to the story than the general revealed to the American secretary. He reported simply that "the People Assembled in great Numbers, with threats and abuse, but the Colonel pursued his orders, and returned to Marblehead, where he had first disembarked his detachment." That the troops traveled the short distance from Boston to Marblehead by sea rather than by land, and that they did not disembark in Salem itself, were important clues that the abortive raid was not as routine as Gage made it seem. On land, Gage foresaw, the soldiers might have encountered significant opposition from militiamen, so he ordered Leslie to use transport vessels and to go ashore at the smaller nearby community. A standoff then occurred at a Salem drawbridge, where militia under the command of Colonel Timothy Pickering raised the bridge and blocked the path of Leslie and his men. When the redcoats tried to cross the river on barges instead, the colonists scuttled the barges. The impasse continued until Leslie pledged that if the Americans would let him march over the bridge in a symbolic gesture, he would retreat. The compromise succeeded, and the confrontation ended. "The Country was alarmed, the News flew like Lightning," and men marched from other towns to Salem, Ezra Stiles recorded in his diary. He exulted that the people of Salem "shamefully out-generalled" Gage.

The context had changed dramatically since the powder alarm about six months earlier, although the events bore some resemblance to each other. Whereas in September 1774 many colonists hoped and expected the First Continental Congress to bring about a peaceful resolution of the dispute with Great Britain, in late February and early March 1775 their expectations differed significantly. The Reverend John Eliot of Cambridge, for example, told a friend that people would never be satisfied with less than "the security of our rights," even though "wading knee deep in maternal [British] blood or deluging the land with our own may be the consequence." Bostonians began reaching out to residents of Quebec and to the Mohawk Indians, requesting alliances in an anticipated conflict. And prominent men like Dr. Joseph Warren began writing openly about the prospect of independence. In late February, Warren mused to Arthur Lee that if General Gage used the army to enforce the Coercive Acts, "Great Britain may take her leave, at least of the New-England colonies, and, if I mistake not, of all America."

Dr. Warren had the opportunity to speak publicly when he delivered the annual Boston Massacre lecture on March 6 (the fifth was a Sunday), at the Old South Meeting House, to "a prodigious concourse of people." He used the event to review local history, arguing that New Englanders' ancestors had immigrated to North America to escape *"arbitrary government."* He asserted that the early settlers had purchased their land from Native peoples and initially owed nothing to England, until the colonists later negotiated a mutually beneficial relationship with the mother country. But then "the madness of an avaricious minister of state" (George Grenville) irrevocably altered British policy. Warren recounted a narrative of the massacre in pathetic terms, and he accused "traiterous" villains of persuading the king "to erect the hostile banner against a people ever affectionate and loyal to him." He referred to the "mutilation" of the Bay Colony's charter by the Massachusetts Government Act and insisted that "if Charters are not deemed sacred, how miserably precarious is every thing founded upon them." Although he indicated that he would prefer the dispute to be settled amicably, he like the Cambridge clergyman declared that if "the only way to safety, is thro' fields of blood," the people had to "press forward, until tyranny is trodden under foot."

Many army and naval officers attended the lecture, intending to disrupt it if Warren showed disrespect to the king. The physician, well aware of that intent, carefully directed his criticisms only at Parliament and successive ministries, describing his ideal vision as placing the "adored goddess LIBERTY, fast by a BRUNSWICK's side, on the American Throne." Samuel Adams, serving as chair, later explained that he deliberately treated the officers "with Civility, inviting them into convenient Seats &c that they might have no pretence to behave ill." One witness hostile to Warren recorded that the officers nevertheless interrupted the speech frequently, "laughing loudly at the most ludicrous parts, and coughing and hemming at the most seditious." When at the end of the lecture Adams called for the body to choose the orator for the following year's commemoration of the "bloody and horrid massacre," the officers erupted with shouts of *"fie! shame!"* and confusion ensued. Some members of the audience, including many women, jumped out of the windows, thinking the shouts were *"fire!"* But Adams managed to restore order, and the event ended without further incident.

Two days later, in Newburyport, the Reverend Oliver Noble struck similar notes in a sermon also delivered to commemorate the events of March 5, 1770. In the sermon, he relied on the story of Esther to create a clever parallel between the Persian king Ahasuerus and his evil adviser Haman, on the one hand, and George III and Thomas Hutchinson, on the other. Noble's account of New England's history echoed Warren's, emphasizing the early settlers' independence and their contracts first for land with the Natives and then for protection with the king. The violation of the contract with the king—the royal charter—had returned Massachusetts residents to the state of nature in which their enterprise began. Noble insisted that God would save New Englanders as he had saved Esther and the Jews; perhaps, indeed, God had allowed the massacre to occur in order to rouse people from their "lethargy" and lead them to "assert our invaded rights." He exhorted, "Awake! arise *Americans*! . . . by no means strike the first, but be ready to strike the second blow, to advantage. Had we not better *die* gloriously in the cause of GOD, of Liberty and our Country, than to dishonour *GOD* and human nature by submitting to *ignoble* slavery?"

The rising tensions evident in the public rhetoric of Joseph Warren and Oliver Noble were underscored by incidents in Boston during March—for example, when soldiers tarred and feathered "a poor simple Countryman" from Billerica after entangling him in a scam, or when the guards at Boston Neck stepped up their searches of cartloads of goods passing in and out of town and attacked, even "barbarously cut and mangled," some of the men who were operating the carts. A Bostonian complained that the soldiers seemed "insolent" and out of control, "a banditti of licensed free-booters, just let loose upon us, for the *innocent* and *laudable* purposes of robberies, rapes, and murders." Another charged that the soldiers were filling the town with "mock orations and songs," expressing sentiments that would "disgrace the most stupid and abandoned." They had created "a nest of filth and Billingsgate."

To whom could Bostonians turn for assistance? Not, evidently, to General Gage, who seemingly treated complaints that spring with indifference, after once having been more willing to impose discipline on the occupying troops. So in late March the Boston committee, in conjunction with committees from ten other nearby communities, addressed the Second Provincial Congress, which had initially convened in Cambridge in early February but had not met continuously. The committees wrote jointly of the need for "some immediate and effectual Measures . . . for the publick security," because they were subjected to "the Insults and Depredations of a lawless and hostile Band of armed Soldiers." The redcoats' acts of "wanton Cruelty and Mischief" were too numerous to detail. Bostonians could have been protected by law, they noted, "were the Constitution not unhinged thro' the Machinations of a tryannic [*sic*] Minister." They urgently needed assistance in restoring order.

The Provincial Congress had more than enough to handle without worrying about clashes in Boston. The deputies were fully occupied with basic governmental tasks involving preparations for the war every-one now expected: establishing a committee of safety to supervise the militia and a committee of supply to acquire arms and ammunition, warning people not to work for or sell supplies to the British army in Boston, gathering information on existing troops of regular militia or minutemen, encouraging certain manufactures, and designating another fast day (March 16) to beg God's *"Forgiveness and Blessings"* as they confronted the possible *"Evils of War."* They continued to urge towns to submit tax payments to Henry Gardner, their receiver gen-eral, with some—but not universal—success.

Finally, the deputies issued a formal address to the people of the Bay Colony, insisting that when freedom inherited from their ancestors was at risk, resistance to tyranny was the "Christian, and Social duty of each Individual." The security of men's lives and property depended on "this Constitution of Government," which ensured that property could be taken only by their own consent. Yet their money had been granted to others by a body in which they had no voice, and those funds used to support men who were trying to enforce the Coercive Acts. Fortunately, the other colonies, separately and through the First Continental Congress, had supported Massachusetts. "Though we depricate a rupture with the Mother State," the address continued, we must prepare for "your necessary defence." The deputies urged their constituents to obey resolutions of the Continental and Provincial Congresses, for "Misery" would "inevitably" result if they ignored "the plans, that have by your Authority, with that of the whole continent, been projected."

The language of the address was remarkable for three reasons. First, it forthrightly declared resistance to "Tyranny" to be a "Social duty."

Resistance was not merely *not* criminal, not merely a possible option, but positively *required* of all citizens in the current crisis. Second, it referred not to the hallowed British constitution, hitherto viewed as the foundation of colonists' rights, but rather to "this Constitution of Government." That deliberately vague phrase implied that the charter of Massachusetts had a role, possibly a primary one, in the ensuring of rights to individuals in the colony. Third, and perhaps most remarkable of all, it insisted that "your Authority, with that of the whole continent," had established "the Laws of the Land" they should obey. Just as Thomas Bradbury Chandler had warned months before, that was a statement of unvarnished republicanism. The Second Provincial Congress was proclaiming that current law in Massachusetts rested on the people's authority as embodied in congresses, not on the authority of the king or Parliament.

In spite of the apparent confidence displayed in such a bold statement, Thomas Gage's spy at the congress, Dr. Church, revealed that the deputies divided sharply over several issues. The leaders disagreed among themselves, and the members had "inadequate knowledge in conducting their novel enterprise." Some proposed reviving government under the old (1629) colonial charter, but that was rejected as precluding any possibility of peace. Others advocated establishing martial law under the committee of safety, but that was excluded because the First Continental Congress had not authorized such a move. The deputies, perhaps chastened by other colonies' reactions to steps considered at the First Provincial Congress, were wary of adopting any policies that might seem to violate a colonial consensus. So, in the absence of hostilities, all they could agree on was the preparations for defense in which they were engaged. Still, the spy reported, "a considerable sum" of money had been collected through the towns' payments to Henry Gardner. And, he predicted accurately, if war began, "the first opposition would be irregular, impetuous and incessant from the numerous bodies that would swarm to the place of action, and all actuated by an enthusiasm wild and ungovernable."

The provincial convention too had a spy, or rather a set of observers, who on March 20 submitted the results of "a minute inquiry" into the state of the British army in Boston—how many soldiers were there (about 2,850), where they were encamped, and the nature of the fortifications that guarded the town, both on the neck and elsewhere. But that report could not match the detailed information that Gage gained from his secret source: how deputies reacted to letters received from Benjamin Franklin, Arthur Lee, and Josiah Quincy Jr. in London; that finding waterproof fabric to make tents was proving difficult; that large quantities of foodstuffs were stored for potential use in Worcester and Concord; that several fieldpieces and gunpowder were to be moved from Concord to Leicester; and that in Concord such items had been cached in scattered locations.

In late March, Loyalists resident in Boston despaired, in contrast to their optimistic mood a few weeks earlier. The Reverend Henry Caner told the bishop of London that "it is hardly conceivable what a spirit of phrenzy reigns" in the Bay Colony. "England must either resign the Govmt of the Colonies or subdue them," he predicted. Likewise, Nathaniel Coffin described times "as bad as they well can be, we have no other prospect before us than that of a civil war," which he antici- pated would soon begin. Joseph Warren saw the same prospect, but for him it was positive: "We woud not boast, but we think united & prepared as we are, we have no reason to doubt of success, if we shoud be compell'd to the last appeal." Samuel Adams still held out hope for a peaceful solution, yet tellingly employed a military metaphor. "Let us like prudent Generals improve our Success, and push for perfect politi- cal Freedom," he exclaimed to his friend and ally Richard Henry Lee.

Early April then brought sensational news, indeed a bombshell, which one Bostonian commented had "almost as great an Effect on People in this Town, as the Arrival of the Port Bill produc'd. The Women are terrify'd by the Fears of Blood and Carnage." On the second, a ship sailed into Marblehead from England, bringing news- papers from mid-February. Parliament had declared the colonies to be in rebellion; the king had insisted that he would enforce the laws; large numbers of troops and ships of war were being dispatched; and Lord North had introduced a bill to deny New Englanders access to the Newfoundland fisheries, the basis of much of their export trade. Recently, the colonists had heard rumors that the Coercive Acts would be repealed in response to petitions from large groups of British mer- chants and the Continental Congress resolutions. Now they learned that exactly the opposite appeared to be the case.

As the news spread, in part because of the rapid production of broadsides with excerpted summaries of the parliamentary proceedings, a colonial consensus quickly emerged: a direct confrontation with Britain, even war, seemed a near certainty. Writing from the Second Provincial Congress, by then moved from Cambridge to Concord, James Warren told his wife, Mercy, that "all things wear a warlike appearance here. . . . The people are ready and determine to defend this Country Inch by Inch." In Cambridge, the Reverend John Eliot concluded that "it is now too late to think of any other method of obtaining redress than by the dint of the sword." In Newport, Ezra Stiles reported that "the Friends of Liberty . . . declare themselves ready for the Combat, & nothing is now talked of but immediately forming an American Army at Worcester & taking the Field with undaunted Resolution." And in Charleston, Henry Laurens did not doubt the colonists' bravery. Having heard "crude intelligence" of the information from England, he commented that "the Spirits will be tried—& the true distinguished from the Counterfeits," but he anticipated that "there will be very few found in the latter class."

On April 10, the Reverend John Winthrop, a Harvard professor and a direct descendant of the governor of the Bay Colony who had overseen the migration to North America, summed up New England opinion in a letter to Dr. Richard Price in London. Like Joseph Warren and Oliver Noble, he referred at length to the colonists' version of their own history. Their ancestors had "fled hither as to a safe retreat from tyrannical power 150 years ago" to settle "a perfect wilderness inhabited only by savages . . . *at their own expence.*" Their descendants had turned that wilderness into "a fruitful field" with "immense toil and danger." But now those descendants were being "treated like a parcel of slaves on a plantation, who are to work just as they are ordered by their masters, and the profit of whose labors is to be appropriated just as their masters please." How likely were such men to surrender "without a struggle" all that was "dear and valuable to them"?

Thus, Winthrop insisted, British officers were badly mistaken if they thought Americans would not stand up to regular troops. The militiamen of Massachusetts and neighboring colonies "will form an army which the General will not find it easy to subdue." New Englanders did not want to attack the British, but at least nineteen out of twenty were determined to defend themselves and their charter government. Indeed, he added, "their ardor is such that it is found difficult to restrain it within due bounds." War would be "ruinous" to Britain as well as to America, Winthrop foresaw, anticipating "a horrid carnage."

ADVICES FROM LONDON

January 27, 1775. Lord Dartmouth addresses General Gage in a letter labeled "secret," revealing that he now believes that Americans' actions "amount to actual revolt and show a determination in the people to commit themselves at all events in open rebellion." He announces he is sending reinforcements to Boston— seven hundred marines, three infantry regiments, and a regiment of light dragoons. He recommends that with this assistance Gage should "take a more active and determined part" and observes that "the only consideration that remains is in what manner the force under your command may be exerted to defend the constitution and to restore the vigour of government."

Then he presents his own assessment of the circumstances in the Bay Colony: "The violences committed . . . have appeared to me as the acts of a rude rabble, without plan, without concert and without conduct; therefore I think that a smaller force now, if put to the test, would be able to encounter them with greater probability of success than might be expected from a greater army if the people should be suffered to form themselves upon a more regular plan."

Accordingly, Dartmouth declares, Gage should first move to "arrest and imprison the principal actors and abettors in the Provincial Congress," forestalling opposition by keeping the plan secret as long as possible. Such a scheme could readily be carried out, even "perhaps . . . without bloodshed." Although Gage has warned that an attempt to arrest the resistance leaders would be viewed as "a signal for hostilities," Dartmouth asserts, "it will surely be better that the conflict should be brought on upon such ground than in a riper state of rebellion." Nevertheless, any plan "must be left to your own discretion to be executed or not as you . . . think most advisable."

Having just received Dartmouth's letter, General Gage issued orders of his own to Lieutenant Colonel Francis Smith on April 18, 1775:

Sir:

Having received Intelligence, that a Quantity of Ammunition, Provisions, Artillery, Tents and small Arms, have been collected at Concord, for the Avowed Purpose of raising and supporting a Rebellion against His Majesty, you will march with the Corps of Grenadiers and light Infantry, put under your Command with the utmost expedition and Secrecy to Concord, where you will Seize, and destroy all the Artillery, Ammunition, Provisions, Tents, Small Arms and all Military Stores whatever. But you will take care that the Soldiers do not plunder the Inhabitants, or hurt private property.

You have a Draught of Concord, on which is marked, the Houses, Barns, &c. which contain the above Military Stores. You will Order a Trunion [cannon mounting] to be knocked off each gun, but if it's found impracticable or any [sic], they must be spicked [spiked], and the Carriages distroyed. The Powder and flower, must be shook out of the Barrells into the River, the Tents burnt, Pork or beef destroyed in the best way you can devise, And the Men may put Balls or lead in their pockets, throwing them by degrees into Ponds, Ditches, &c. but no Quantity together, so that they may be recovered afterwards.

If you meet with any Brass Artillery, you will order their muzzles to be beat in so as to render them useless.

You will Observe by the Draught that it will be necessary to secure the two Bridges as soon as possible; you will therefore Order a party of the best Marchers, to go on with expedition for that purpose.

A small party on Horseback is ordered out to Stop all Advice of

your March getting to Concord before you, and a small number
of Artillery to go out in Chaises to wait for you on the Road, with
Sledge Hammers, Spikes, &c.

You will effect your business, and return with the Troops as
soon as possible, which I must leave to your own Judgment and
Discretion.

AFTERWORD

Having received his orders from Gage, Lieutenant Colonel Smith began moving his regiments out of Boston and toward Concord overnight on April 18–19. Bostonians learned of the troop movements and quickly dispatched three messengers, one of them Paul Revere, to warn the countryside. By the time the redcoats arrived at Lexington early on the morning of April 19, a group of about seventy minutemen had gathered on the common. The militia and the regulars confronted each other briefly, and the Americans began to withdraw under orders from their captain. A shot rang out: who fired first has never been definitively determined. The British soldiers fired several volleys, leaving eight Americans dead and ten others wounded.

The troops then continued to Concord, where local minutemen had mustered, augmented by men from nearby towns summoned by multiple messengers. At first the American militia units remained outside the town, but then—as smoke began to rise from fires—they advanced on British troops guarding the North Bridge. Redcoats and militiamen both fired; American muskets killed three regulars and wounded nine. The troops pulled back into Concord and eventually began to retreat toward Boston. Thousands of minutemen concealed themselves along the road and fired on the redcoats, who were reinforced by new regiments from Boston as they passed Lexington. By the end of the day, the British had suffered nearly three hundred casualties, seventy of them killed.

The news of the battles spread rapidly northeast, west, and south through the colonies, carried by land and sea, mimicking the routes taken by Israel Putnam's false information about the powder alarm eight months earlier. Initial accounts were often garbled and occasionally disbelieved. Some reports erroneously said that General Frederick Haldimand and Lord Percy had been killed. In Norfolk, James Parker expressed skepticism about the first description he heard of the encounter, pronouncing it "vague . . . a Yankee trick to alarm the other Colonies & to get all they possibly can involved in guilt with themselves." Elsewhere in Virginia, a merchant learned of the clash, but with no details he regarded as credible, so he declined to pass them on to a British correspondent. Yet this time there was no mistake.

Western Massachusetts, New Hampshire, Rhode Island, and Connecticut all learned of the battles by April 22; the news reached Manhattan a day later, causing "no little Tumult" in the city. By the twenty-fourth, Philadelphia and all of New Jersey had heard, although western Pennsylvania took longer; not until the second week of May was everyone there informed of the battles. The news was carried south along the shore of Maryland and Virginia; in Dumfries, south of Alexandria, a traveler heard the "dreadful news" at dinner on April 27. Williamsburg received word first on April 28 and then further details by express rider from Philadelphia late in the evening of May 2. Farther south, both messengers and ships brought the news. On May 8, a vessel from Salem arrived in Charleston with a copy of the April 25 *Essex Gazette*. Henry Laurens quickly penned a letter to his son John in London, though he did not yet have many details to convey.

Once convinced of the truth of the news from Massachusetts, colonists knew their world had changed. They now faced what the Boston merchant John Rowe termed "all the Miseries of a Civil War," which led a pious Connecticut farm woman to pray, "O god have mercy on our nation. . . . Alas it is a trying day with new england. I know if god doos by us as we deserve we shall all be distroyed in this affair." But when the Reverend Moses Mather completed a pamphlet he had begun drafting before April 19, he added an appendix titled "American Independance."

First, he defined what he meant: "Independance consists in being under obligation to acknowledge no superior power on earth." Then

he explained that George III, "by withdrawing his protection and levying war upon us, has discharged us of our allegiance, and of all obligations to obedience." The king had violated his compact with America,
and so colonists were released from it, and if the colonies had owed
obedience to Parliament (he inserted: "which we did not"), they were
"wholly discharged" from that obligation as well. So, "without our
act or choice," he asserted, "we are become necessarily independant."
Even prior to appending that discussion, Mather described Britain and
the American colonies as "two distinct countries, independent of each
other," language that could only have been employed in the wake of
the Americans' experiences in 1774.

By April 19, 1775, Americans had not yet formally adopted a Declaration of Independence, but their leaders had long since practiced
independence in thought and deed. The extralegal committees and
congresses, *unconstitutional* in traditional British understanding, had
assumed the mantle of governance. And throughout the colonies their
authority rested solely on election by local qualified voters. Even if the
members of those bodies did not fully comprehend the implications of
their deeds and governed hesitantly, royal authorities and their Loyalist supporters understood the meaning of the developments in 1774
altogether too well.

Although the centennial of American independence was celebrated
in 1876, not 1874—as that anonymous Philadelphian had speculated
after the First Congress adjourned—1774 was indeed "glorious," just
as a poem published in two different newspapers that summer insisted.

THE GLORIOUS SEVENTY FOUR
A NEW SONG
TUNE OF HEARTS OF OAK.

Come, come, my brave boys, from my song you shall hear,
That we'll crown Seventy-four, a most glorious year;
We'll convince Bute and Mansfield, and North, tho' they rave
Britons still like themselves, spurn the chains of a slave.
                                                                    CHORUS

Hearts of oak were our sires,
Hearts of oak are their sons,

Like them we are ready, as firm and as steady,
To fight for our freedom with swords and with guns.

Foolish elves to conjecture by crossing of mains,
That the true blood of freemen would change in our veins,
Let us scorch, let us freeze, from the line to the pole,
Britain's sons still retain all their freedom of soul.
   Hearts of oak were our sires, &c.

See—our rights to invade, Britain's dastardly foes,
Sending Hysons and Congoes, did vainly suppose,
That poor shallow pates, like themselves we were grown,
And our hearts were as servile and base as their own.
   Hearts of oak were our sires, &c.

Their tea still is driven away from our shores,
Or presented to neptune, or rots in our stores:—
But to awe, to divide, till we crouch to their sway,
On brave Boston, their vengeance—they fiercely display.
   Hearts of oak were our sires, &c.

How, unask'd, we unite, we agree to a man,
See our stores flow to Boston, from rear & from van;
Hark, the shout, how it flies, freedom's voice, how it sounds!
From each country, each clime; hark, the echo rebounds!
   Hearts of oak were our sires, &c.

Across the Atlantick,—so thund'ring the roar,
It has rous'd Britain's genius, who dos'd on his shore—
Who has injur'd my sons, my brave boys o'er the main'
Whose spirits to vigour it renews me again!
   Hearts of oak were our sires, &c.

With sons whom I foster'd and cherish'd of yore,
Fair freedom shall flourish till time is no more;
No tyrant shall rule them.—'tis Heaven's decree,
They shall never be slaves, while they dare to be free.
   Hearts of oak were our sires, &c.

NOTES

ABBREVIATIONS USED IN THE NOTES AND BIBLIOGRAPHY

Published Primary Sources (Correspondence and Other Documents)

AA 4: 1, 2   Force, ed., *American Archives*

AFC   Butterfield et al., eds., *Adams Family Correspondence*

"Andrews Letters"   Sargent, ed., "Letters of John Andrews"

BF Papers   Willcox et al., eds., *Papers of Benjamin Franklin*

Colls CHS   *Collections of the Connecticut Historical Society*

Colls MHS   *Collections of the Massachusetts Historical Society*

Colls NYHS   *Collections of the New-York Historical Society*

DAR   Davies, ed., *Documents of the American Revolution*

"Deane Correspondence"   "Correspondence of Silas Deane"

EAI   *Early American Imprints*

GW Papers: CS   Abbot et al., eds., *Papers of Washington: Colonial Series*

HL Papers   Rogers et al., eds., *Papers of Henry Laurens*

JA Diary   Butterfield et al., eds., *Diary of John Adams*

JA Papers   Taylor et al., eds., *Papers of John Adams*

JCC   Ford, ed., *Journals of the Continental Congress*

JM Papers   Hutchinson and Rachal, eds., *Papers of James Madison*

LOD   Smith et al., eds., *Letters of Delegates to Congress*

PIR   Wroth et al., eds., *Province in Rebellion*

"Price Letters"   "Letters to and from Dr. Richard Price"

Procs MHS   *Proceedings of the Massachusetts Historical Society*

Pubs CSM   *Publications of the Colonial Society of Massachusetts*

"Quincy Letters"   Howe, ed., "Letters to Josiah Quincy, Jr."

RevVa   Van Schreeven and Scribner, *Revolutionary Virginia*

Rowe Diary   Cunningham, ed., *Letters and Diary of John Rowe*
RTP Papers   Riley and Hanson, eds., *Papers of Robert Treat Paine*
SA Writings   Cushing, ed., *Writings of Samuel Adams*
Smith Memoirs   Sabine, ed., *Historical Memoirs of William Smith*
Stiles Diary   Dexter, ed., *Literary Diary of Ezra Stiles*
TJ Papers   Boyd et al., eds., *Papers of Thomas Jefferson*
"Wharton Letter-Books 33, 34"   "Selections from Letter-Books of Wharton"

Unpublished Manuscript Collections

AO   Audit Office, National Archives, Kew
BC   Bancroft Collection, New York Public Library
CO   Colonial Office, National Archives, Kew
Dartmouth Papers   American Papers of the Second Earl of Dartmouth
Russell Papers   James Russell Papers, Colonial Williamsburg
SA Papers   Samuel Adams Papers, BC
SP   State Papers, National Archives, Kew
Steuart Papers   Charles Steuart Papers, National Library of Scotland
T 1   Treasury letters received, National Archives, Kew

Colonial Newspapers

BEP   *Boston Evening-Post*
BG   *Boston Gazette*
CtC   *Connecticut Courant* (Hartford)
CtG   *Connecticut Gazette* (New London)
CtJ   *Connecticut Journal* (New Haven)
DPaPkt   *Dunlap's Pennsylvania Packet* (Philadelphia)
EG   *Essex Gazette* (Salem)
EJ   *Essex Journal* (Newburyport)
GaG   *Georgia Gazette* (Savannah)
MdG   *Maryland Gazette* (Annapolis)
MG&BNL   *Massachusetts Gazette & Boston News Letter*
MG&BPB   *Massachusetts Gazette & Boston Post-Boy*
MSpy   *Massachusetts Spy* (Boston)
NHG   *New-Hampshire Gazette* (Portsmouth)
NMerc   *Newport Mercury* (Rhode Island)
NPkt   *Norwich Packet* (Connecticut)
NYG   *New-York Gazette* (Hugh Gaine)
NYJ   *New-York Journal* (John Holt)
PaC   *Pennsylvania Chronicle* (Philadelphia)
PaG   *Pennsylvania Gazette* (Philadelphia)
PaJ   *Pennsylvania Journal* (Philadelphia)

PaL   *Pennsylvania Ledger* (Philadelphia)
ProvG   *Providence Gazette* (Rhode Island)
RNYG   *Rivington's New-York Gazetteer*
SCG (C)   *South Carolina Gazette & Country Journal* (Charles Crouch)
SCG (T)   *South Carolina Gazette* (Peter Timothy)
SCG (W)   *South Carolina & American General Gazette* (Robert Wells)
VaG (P&D)   *Virginia Gazette* (Purdie & Dixon) (later D&H, Dixon & Hunter)
VaG (R)   *Virginia Gazette* (Rind)

Historical Journals

EAS   *Early American Studies*
JAH   *Journal of American History*
JSH   *Journal of Southern History*
MdHM   *Maryland Historical Magazine*
NEHGR   *New England Historical and Genealogical Register*
NEQ   *New England Quarterly*
NYHSQ   *New-York Historical Society Quarterly*
PMHB   *Pennsylvania Magazine of History and Biography*
SCHM   *South Carolina Historical Magazine*
VMHB   *Virginia Magazine of History and Biography*
WMQ   *William & Mary Quarterly*

INTRODUCTION

xv   **"The year 1774":** Mary Beth Norton, *The British-Americans: The Loyalist Exiles in England, 1774–1789* (Boston: Little, Brown, 1972), 10.

xv   **phenomenon known as loyalism:** See ibid., 3–7. For an initial use of the term "Loyalist," see below, chapter 8. With this intense focus on events during "the long 1774," I am deliberately eschewing engagement with the debates over the long-term causes and consequences of the Revolution chronicled in such essays as Michael A. McDonnell and David Waldstreicher, "Revolution in the Quarterly? A Historiographical Analysis," *WMQ*, 3rd. ser., 74 (2017): 633–66, and others cited therein.

xvi   **Almost all historians:** For example, recent narrative histories of the Revolution by Patrick Griffin (*America's Revolution,* 2012) and Thomas P. Slaughter (*Independence,* 2014) fail to devote special attention to developments in 1774. Pauline Maier's exemplary and influential *From Resistance to Revolution* likewise devotes few pages primarily to events in 1774 (for example, 233–45).

xvi   **historians have concentrated:** See, for instance, Raphael, *First American Revolution,* and Bunker, *Empire on the Edge.* Breen, *American Insurgents,*

American Patriots, looks beyond Massachusetts, but his title reflects his focus on the revolutionaries to the near exclusion of Loyalists, and his narrative continues until the Declaration of Independence, including and occasionally conflating events in 1774 and 1775. Phillips, *1775,* takes a more comprehensive approach but obscures the importance of 1774 in his stress on the following year.

xvi **almost all scholars:** Well-known scholars of loyalism like Robert Calhoon and Wallace Brown, for example, along with other more recent authors like Philip Gould, have concentrated solely on Loyalists. Tellingly, the only book published prior to this one that focuses explicitly on 1774 is Neil R. Stout, *The Perfect Crisis: The Beginning of the Revolutionary War* (New York: New York University Press, 1976). Stout too arrived at his understanding of the importance of the year after having written about the opposition to revolution—in his case, *The Royal Navy in America, 1760–1775: A Study of Enforcement of British Colonial Policy in the Era of the American Revolution* (Annapolis, Md.: Naval Institute Press, 1973).

xviii **debates and disagreements:** For example, books that examine municipal political disputes in detail are Tiedemann, *Reluctant Revolutionaries,* and Ryerson, *Revolution Is Now Begun.* For similar state studies, see Larry R. Gerlach, *Prologue to Independence: New Jersey in the Coming of the American Revolution* (New Brunswick, N.J.: Rutgers University Press, 1976), and Anne M. Ousterhout, *A State Divided: Opposition in Pennsylvania to the American Revolution* (New York: Greenwood, 1987).

xix *A note on terminology:* I made the point about Americans' Whiggish views in my essay "The Loyalist Critique of the Revolution," in *The Development of a Revolutionary Mentality* (Washington, D.C.: Library of Congress, 1972), 126–48. A New Englander explained the terminology to a British friend thus: "The Government & AntiGovernment Subjects are now known by the old Names of W[h]ig & Tory—as they were in the End of Q. Anne's Reign" (James Murray to Charles Steuart, 18 Sept. 1774, reel 2, fol. 256, Steuart Papers).

xix **This book is firmly based:** As does, for example, Bunker, *Empire on the Edge.*

CHAPTER I THAT CURSED TEA

3 **stormy early morning:** For more on the shipwreck and its consequences, see the last section of this chapter and Norton, "Seventh Tea Ship."

3 **Boston Tea Party:** The earliest identified reference to the "tea party" came in a New York paper in 1826; see Lawrence Glickman, *Buying Power: A History of Consumer Activism in America* (Chicago: University of Chicago Press, 2009), 323n24. The books are Labaree, *Boston Tea Party,* and Carp,

Defiance of the Patriots. Bunker, *Empire on the Edge,* focuses almost exclusively on Boston's response to the EIC tea, considering events in New York and Philadelphia very briefly and those in Charleston not at all. Labaree, *Boston Tea Party,* 133, 150, and Carp, *Defiance of the Patriots,* 167, 175, mention the wreck of the *William;* other works do not.

4 **Neither American colonists:** Quotations: "ZYX" to Lord Dartmouth, ca. Jan. 1775, reel 12, no. 1126, Dartmouth Papers; Drake, *Tea Leaves,* 192. Carole Shammas concluded that two pounds of tea a year would equal consumption of one cup a day per capita; see *Pre-industrial Consumer,* 84. Useful discussions of the consumption and significance of tea are Merritt, *Trouble with Tea;* Carp, *Defiance of the Patriots,* chap. 3; and David S. Shields, *Civil Tongues and Polite Letters in British America,* chap. 4 (Chapel Hill: University of North Carolina Press, 1997). See also Norton, *Separated by Sex,* 164–71, on women and tea drinking.

4 **Calculating the quantity of tea:** See Drake, *Tea Leaves,* 191–201; Jeffrey Amherst to Lord Dartmouth, 9 March 1774, reel 10, no. 852, Dartmouth Papers; and Sir Joseph Yorke, "Report Concerning the Trade Between Great Britain & the United Provinces in 1774," 30 Dec. 1774, SP 84/543. See also Victor Enthoven, " 'That Abominable Nest of Pirates': St. Eustatius and the North Americans, 1680–1780," *EAS* 10 (2012): 239–301; Merritt, *Trouble with Tea,* especially 52–60, 72–75; and Peter Andreas, *Smuggler Nation: How Illicit Trade Made America* (New York: Oxford University Press, 2013), chaps. 1, 2. Complaints about smuggling from St. Eustatius were legion; see, for example, Sir Joseph Yorke to the Earl of Suffolk, 20 Sept. 1774, SP 84/543; and Caleb Wheaton to Thomas Gage, 28 Sept. 1774, in *PIR,* 623.

5 **A rare surviving set:** Vernon and Vernon to Tanner, 2 March 1774, William and Samuel Vernon Letter (see also an early draft, 28 Feb., William and Samuel Vernon Letters, South Caroliniana Library, Columbia). Admiral Samuel Graves complained of "the prodigious Smugling [*sic*] carrying on [in Newport] with Impunity"; see Graves to Philip Stephens, 30 Oct. 1774, CO 5/121, fol. 3.

6 **most revealing aspects:** Another letter implicating St. Croix in smuggling is Mr. Delaval to Earl of Suffolk, 1 Nov. 1774, CO 5/138, fol. 430; and see Scott & Fraser (Gothenburg) to Aaron Lopez (Newport), 29 Oct., for a link between the tea trade in the two ports (*Commerce of Rhode Island* 69:519–20).

6 **Such covert tactics continued:** Colden to Lord Dartmouth, 2 Nov. 1774, in *DAR* 8:224; Hulton to ——, 14 Aug., in York, *Henry Hulton,* 307. Hulton and two other customs officials forwarded reports about smuggling in the vicinity of Manhattan to the Lords of the Treasury in August; see

T 1/505, fols. 322–29. And see the report of the seizure of a vessel smuggling tea from Portugal, captured "off the Capes of Philadelphia": James Ayscough to John Tabor Kempe, 13 Oct., box 116, folder 13, Sedgwick Papers (Kempe Papers).

6 **The clandestine nature of such activities:** Quotations: John Patterson to James Duane, 20 Feb. 1774, James Duane Papers; Eliza Farmar to Jack, [ca. early 1774], "Letters of Farmar," 200. Estimates of legal tea consumed: Shammas, *Pre-industrial Consumer,* 83 (25 percent); Schlesinger, *Colonial Merchants,* 249 (10 percent in 1771). Customs figures: "An Account of the Tea That Has Been Imported into the Several Ports Under the Management of the Board . . . ," n.d., T 1/505, fol. 156. The observer was an informant of Jeffrey Amherst, who wrote on 9 March 1774 to Lord Dartmouth, reel 10, no. 852, Dartmouth Papers.

7 **Judging by customs records:** Massachusetts total tea consumption in 1771: Drake, *Tea Leaves,* 192–93 (see also 303–4). A *BG* author claimed on 1 November 1773 that most of the Dutch tea consumed in the province came via "southern" (that is, middle) colonies; a similar observation is in Drake, *Tea Leaves,* 261–62. For speculations about why Bostonians were less likely to drink smuggled tea: Tyler, *Smugglers & Patriots,* 189; Shammas, *Pre-industrial Consumer,* 86.

7 **Such illegal tea:** Quotation: Rivington to Knox, 28 July 1774, in "Knox and the London Book-Store," 296–97. The tea had been acquired by an "adventurers Vessel" from an EIC ship encountered near Ascension Island in the South Atlantic, Rivington explained; a captain in the Royal Welsh Fusiliers carried it to Boston. See also same to same, 15 Aug., in ibid., 299, for more on the shipment.

7 **Knox responded:** Knox to Rivington, 4 Aug., 22 Aug. 1774, 6 Feb. 1775, Knox Papers II. See also Knox to Rivington, 19 Sept., 10 Oct., 4 Nov., Knox Papers II, describing his efforts to find buyers. He also warned Rivington that people might suspect that this tea came from the wreck of the *William* (4 Aug., Knox Papers II).

8 **Colonists disagreed over the relative:** Quotation: Drake, *Tea Leaves,* 191; lack of serious risk, ibid., 194; on the EIC's potentially gaining a greater share of the colonial market, ibid., 197–98. The relative merits of EIC and Dutch tea came up in the debates over the Poplicola broadsides in New York in November 1773; see below. Price comparisons vary, but smuggled tea seems to have sold for about 1 shilling, 8 pennies (20d.) or 2 shillings (24d.) per pound and taxed tea for 3 or more shillings; see Drake, *Tea Leaves,* 191–92; Tyler, *Smugglers & Patriots,* 192; and Bunker, *Empire on the Edge,* 396–97n15.

8 **Its first major attempt:** These events are discussed in many books; see,

for example, Maier, *From Resistance to Revolution;* Schlesinger, *Colonial Merchants;* Jensen, *Founding of a Nation;* and Edmund S. Morgan and Helen M. Morgan, *The Stamp Act Crisis: Prologue to Revolution,* rev. ed. (New York: Collier Books, 1963).

8 **But Great Britain:** Quotation: Reed to Lord Dartmouth, 22 Dec. 1773, reel 1, no. 923, Dartmouth Papers. Samuel Adams regarded the Bostonians' willingness to buy legal tea as a source of "Shame and Scandal"; see Upton, "Proceedings of Ye Body," 296. On the continuing impact of nonimportation in the middle colonies, see Schlesinger, *Colonial Merchants,* 190–94, 246–48. Boston's imports of tea in the early 1770s were sufficiently controversial that in late 1774 Philadelphians raised the issue with John Adams when he attended the First Continental Congress (see *LOD,* 1:87). On opposition to the Townshend Acts, see the Jensen, Maier, and Schlesinger books cited in previous note.

9 **The retained tea tax:** For discussions of the origins of the Tea Act and its initial implementation, see Labaree, *Boston Tea Party,* chap. 4; Bunker, *Empire on the Edge,* chaps. 6, 7, 9; Merritt, *Trouble with Tea,* chap. 4; and Thomas, *Tea Party to Independence,* chap. 1. London merchants decided not to send private orders of tea to North America in the summer of 1773, assuming that EIC tea would dominate the market because of its cheapness; see *Commerce of Rhode Island* 69:451. See also Benjamin Franklin to Thomas Cushing, 4 June 1773, in *BF Papers,* 20:228.

9 **Although the ministry:** Benjamin Hallowell to John Pownall, 29 Sept. 1773, in *Facsimiles of Manuscripts in European Archives Relating to America, 1773–1783,* comp. B. F. Stevens (London: Maltby & Sons, 1895), 24:2029.

10 **August 1773:** Drake, *Tea Leaves,* 241–42, 245.

11 **Even given the common delays:** See Tyler, *Smugglers & Patriots,* 199, for North's mistake. Also, Labaree, *Boston Tea Party,* 88, for early, incomplete brief notices of the act in the colonial press that governors could have read or, more likely, missed. See Schlesinger, *Prelude to Independence,* chap. 8, for another account of the published attacks on EIC tea in fall 1773.

11 **ocean voyages:** First published in *PaG,* 11 Aug., 1773; reprints were headed "Philadelphia, Aug. 11. Extract of a Letter from London, May 26." Labaree, *Boston Tea Party,* 88–89, identified Pigou as the author.

12 **A New York newspaper:** For the Tea Act, see *NYG,* 6 Sept. 1773; it was published in Boston, Philadelphia, and Charleston by early November. The first Poplicola broadside (see below) misinterpreted the language about taxation; it was corrected by a critic calling himself "A Student of Law" (*EAI,* no. 12765). The first report that tea was headed to Charleston appeared in Philadelphia on 13 October, preceded on 4 October by news of shipments to the middle colonies. On 15 November, the *SCG*

(T) revealed to South Carolina readers that a tea ship was en route to Charleston. The EIC Court of Directors finalized plans for shipments to the northern ports by 4 August but did not finish the contracts for Charleston until 15 September; see minutes, India Office Records, B/89, fols. 330, 389.

12 **As the news arrived:** For example, Thomas Hutchinson did not receive official notification of the act from Dartmouth until 4 November, after the initial attacks on the Boston consignees (see below).

12 **The adoption of the Tea Act:** Benjamin Carp addresses clandestine traders' involvement in opposing EIC tea in "Did Dutch Smugglers Provoke the Boston Tea Party?," *EAS* 10 (2012): 335–59. For a contemporary's charge that traders in Dutch tea instigated the attacks on the EIC, see Seabury, *View of the Controversy,* 20. The EIC's decision to sell some of its tea through consignees would not have by itself put a halt to the regular method of legal tea sales, in which colonial merchants purchased tea through British wholesalers, but consignees could potentially charge lower prices because they would avoid paying middlemen.

12 **Americans' first published attacks:** Boston: essays by "A Consistent Patriot" and "Joshua the Son of Nun" appeared in *MSpy,* 14 Oct. 1773. New York: Hampden [Alexander McDougall], *The Alarm,* published as five broadsides, starting on 6 Oct., followed by others on 9, 15, 19, 27 Oct. (*DAR,* 4:403). See *Smith Memoirs,* 1:156. Tiedemann identifies the *Alarm* author as McDougall, in *Reluctant Revolutionaries,* 176. Russ Castronovo stresses the significance of McDougall's charges against the EIC in *Propaganda 1776,* chap. 3, esp. 88.

13 **Other tactical suggestions:** Scaevola [Thomas Mifflin], *To the Commissioners Appointed by the East-India Company . . . ,* first published as a broadside on 9 Oct., as noted in "Extract of a Letter from a Gentleman in Philadelphia," *VaG* (R), 11 Nov. 1773; reprinted in, for example, *BG,* 25 Oct.; *SCG* (C), 23 Nov. A copy arrived in New York on 12 Oct.; see *Smith Memoirs,* 1:156.

13 **Then, two days later:** Hamden [Benjamin Rush], "On Patriotism," *DPaPkt,* 11 Oct. 1773, later reprinted in Boston, Williamsburg, and Charleston newspapers. See Butterfield, *Letters of Rush,* 1:82, for Rush's admission that he was "Hamden" and Mifflin was "Scaevola." The alias chosen by Rush and McDougall linked them to John Hampden, an English Parliamentarian opposed to Charles I in the 1640s.

13 **John Dickinson:** Both statements by Dickinson are reprinted in Stillé, *Life of Dickinson,* 455–63. Thomas, *Tea Party to Independence,* 14, and Merritt, *Trouble with Tea,* 91–93, both point out that New York and Philadelphia took the lead in opposing the EIC tea and that Boston lagged behind.

14 **Philadelphians chose to follow:** The Philadelphians' resolutions, first
published in the *PaG* on 20 Oct. 1773, were reprinted in northern papers
later that month and in Virginia and South Carolina by mid-November.
For "*first* rank": Thomas Wharton to Thomas Walpole, 30 Oct., in Drake,
Tea Leaves, 276. On 15 October, New York merchants met to thank the
captains of the city's London trading ships for refusing to carry the East
India Company's tea in their vessels, but they adopted no other resolutions and did not address the tea duty in general. (A report of that meeting
in *NYJ,* 21 Oct., was widely reprinted.)

14 **A letter sent to England:** Quotation and comparison: "Extract of Two
Letters from Philadelphia Dated October 3 and October 20 1773," CO
5/133, fol. 51c. See also extracts from New York in early November, CO
5/133, fols. 50c–d.

14 **In Boston, by contrast, resistance:** Hutchinson to Lord Dartmouth,
4 Nov. 1773, in *DAR,* 6:240; "Extract of a Letter Dated Boston
18th October 1773," CO 5/133, fol. 50b. The *BG* reprinted Mifflin's essay
on 25 October; the article signed "A Merchant" appeared in *MSpy* on
28 October. For the ultimatum to the consignees and subsequent events
in November, see Labaree, *Boston Tea Party,* 109–25. As Labaree points
out, ibid., 105–6, even the Massachusetts committee of correspondence
seemed unconcerned about the implications of the Tea Act as late as
21 October (see *SA Writings,* 3:63–67).

15 **At the appointed hour:** Quotations: William Gordon to Lord Dartmouth, 11 Dec. 1773, reel 9, no. 754, Dartmouth Papers; Thomas Hutchinson to Lord Dartmouth, 4 Nov., in *DAR,* 6:240–41; "Resolutions of the
Town of Boston, November 5, 1773," in *SA Writings,* 3:67. The "daringly
effrontive" phrase appeared in newspaper accounts of the town meeting;
for example, *PaG,* 24 Nov. On these events, see also letters in Drake, *Tea
Leaves,* 280–94 (with a comment by Clarke on the impact of the Scaevola
and *Alarm* broadsides); Joseph Green's narrative, in *DAR,* 6:239–40; and
Rowe Diary, 252–54. Gordon claimed that at this early juncture the protesters would have been willing to accept the consignees' pledge to store
the tea at Castle William until they received instructions from the EIC,
rather than their resignations. See Gordon to Dartmouth, 11 Dec., reel 9,
no. 754, Dartmouth Papers.

15 **Thomas Hutchinson:** Bailyn, *Ordeal of Hutchinson,* 238–58, discusses the
letters affair. See also Bernard Bailyn, "Thomas Hutchinson in Context:
The Ordeal Revisited," in *Sometimes an Art: Nine Essays on History* (New
York: Alfred A. Knopf, 2015), 147–70. On 17 December 1773, Samuel
Cooper admitted to Benjamin Franklin that Boston had lagged in oppos-
ing the tea shipments; see *BF Papers,* 20:503.

16 **Philadelphians, who led the opposition:** Wharton to Thomas Walpole,
    30 Oct. 1773, in Drake, *Tea Leaves,* 277; James & Drinker to EIC, 28 Dec.,
    enclosing their resignation statement of 2 Dec., CO 5/133, fols. 38d, 38c.
    The demand for their resignation, same date, is CO 5/1285, fol. 10, printed
    in Drake, *Tea Leaves,* 389. See also Labaree, *Boston Tea Party,* 97–101, and
    Ryerson, *Revolution Is Now Begun,* 34–37.

16 **From New York:** Tryon to Dartmouth, and Haldimand to Dartmouth,
    both 3 Nov. 1773, in *DAR,* 6:238–39. Tryon enclosed the five *Alarm* essays
    (and others) with his letter; see ibid., 4:403. Other predictions of the likely
    reception of the tea in New York accorded with Tryon's and Haldimand's:
    see *Smith Memoirs,* 1:157; and Abraham Lott to William Kelly, 5 Nov., in
    Drake, *Tea Leaves,* 269. Kelly (a consignee then in London) was burned in
    effigy in Manhattan on 5 November because of a purported role in urging
    the EIC to send the tea to North America (*RNYG,* 11 Nov.).

16 **To combat that sedition:** When he testified before the Loyalist Claims
    Commission in London in 1784, Vardill revealed that he wrote the "Popli-
    cola" broadsides. See AO 12/20, fol. 15. For a similar article instigated by
    the Boston consignees, see essay by "Z," *BEP,* 25 Oct. 1773 (attribution
    by Richard Clarke in Drake, *Tea Leaves,* 281).

17 **In addition to defending:** Poplicola, "To the Worthy Inhabitants of the
    City of New-York," *RNYG,* 18 Nov. 1773, dated 12 Nov., also published
    as a broadside (*EAI,* no. 12956).

17 **One of the broadside replies:** A Mechanic, *To the Worthy Inhabitants of
    New-York,* [Nov. 1773], broadside (*EAI,* no. 13042). For other replies to
    Vardill, see A Student of Law, *Fellow Citizens, Friends of Liberty and Equal
    Commerce,* 19 Nov., broadside (*EAI,* no. 12765); A Tradesman, *To the Free-
    Holders and Free-Men, of the City, and Province of New York,* broadside
    (*EAI,* no. 13040). *NPkt* reprinted the first Poplicola essay, along with A
    Tradesman's and A Student of Law's responses; see issues of 2, 16 Dec.

18 **The clergyman, by contrast:** Poplicola, *To the Worthy Inhabitants of the
    City of New-York,* [Nov. 1773], broadside (*EAI,* no. 12957); see also a broad-
    side with the same title but different content (no. 12955). The Philadel-
    phia quotation: "Queries," *PaG,* 8 Dec. 1773. A purportedly female poet,
    "Marcia," satirized Poplicola in *NYJ,* 23 Dec. Her lengthy verse read, in
    part, "Men . . . against their Appetites must struggle, / Because it is a sin
    to smuggle, / So *Poplicola* says, but he / Shall not make Creeds, or Laws
    for me."

18 **residents of Charleston finally learned:** Quotations: *SCG* (T), 15 Nov.
    1773; *NYJ,* 9 Dec. The 15 November story was reprinted, for example, in
    DPaPkt, 20 Dec.; and *PaG,* 22 Dec. For Charleston newspapers carrying
    tea information and essays reprinted from the northern press, see, for

example, *SCG* (C), 16, 23, 30 Nov., 7 Dec.; *SCG* (T), 22, 29 Nov.; *SCG* (W), 24 Dec. The lieutenant governor of the colony reported that these accounts affected local opinion; see *DAR,* 6:265–66.

19 **On November 22:** *SCG* (T), 22 Nov. 1773; "Junius Brutus" and "Cassius," *SCG* (T), 29 Nov. The "Cassius" essay originally appeared in *PaJ,* 13 Oct. See also Junius Brutus's own call for a meeting in Charleston about the "stampt Tea" titled "To the Freemen of South-Carolina," dated 29 Nov., printed in *DPaPkt,* 20 Dec. 1773.

19 **Tensions rose in the three:** On these events, see Clarke et al. to the governor and council, [19 Nov. 1773], in *Bowdoin and Temple Papers,* 321–22; "Proceedings of the Council of Massachusetts," 27 Nov., in ibid., 323–26; Thomas Hutchinson to Lord Dartmouth, 2 Dec., in *DAR,* 6:248–49; *Rowe Diary,* 254–55. Colonial newspapers elsewhere carried accounts of the Boston violence; see, for example, *VaG* (P&D), 16 Dec. For the departure of the ships from England, see, for example, *PaJ* and *PaG,* both 1 Dec.

20 **In Philadelphia, the organizers:** Quotation: Reed to Lord Dartmouth, 22 Dec. 1773, reel 1, no. 923, Dartmouth Papers. See Frederick D. Stone, "How the Landing of the Tea Was Opposed in Philadelphia by Colonel William Bradford and Others in 1773," *PMHB* 15 (1891): 385–93. On the importance of the pilots: Simon Finger, " 'A Flag of Defyance at the Masthead': The Delaware River Pilots and the Sinews of Philadelphia's Atlantic World in the Eighteenth Century," *EAS* 8 (2010): 386–409.

20 **In New York, the tea agents:** *Smith Memoirs,* 1:157–58. The tea agents' resignation: Henry White et al. to EIC Court of Directors, 1 Dec. 1773, CO 5/133, fols. 35b–c. On McDougall and other "Liberty Boys," see Roger Champagne, "Liberty Boys and Mechanics of New York City, 1764–1774," *Labor History* 8, no. 2 (Spring 1967): 115–37; Roger Champagne, *Alexander McDougall and the American Revolution in New York* (Schenectady, N.Y.: Union College Press, 1975); and Bernard Friedman, "The Shaping of Radical Consciousness in Provincial New York," *JAH* 56 (1970): 781–801.

20 **an anonymous New Yorker:** After appearing on 9 December in *NYJ* (source of quotations in next two paragraphs) and *RNYG,* the unsigned essay was republished in Philadelphia (*DPaPkt,* 13 Dec.), Connecticut (*NPkt,* 16 Dec., and *CtC,* 21 Dec.), Williamsburg (*VaG* [P&D], 30 Dec.), Boston (*BEP,* 3 Jan. 1774, and *MSpy,* 27 Jan.), and Providence (*ProvG,* 8 Jan.).

21 **On November 28:** Labaree, *Boston Tea Party,* 127–33, describes the arrival of the tea ships in Boston and, on 150–59, briefly summarizes the arrival and fate of the others. See also Carp, *Defiance of the Patriots,* 108–9. The *Beaver* had smallpox on board when it arrived and was quarantined until 15 December, when it joined the other vessels at the wharf. A tally of the tea shipped to each port is in Drake, *Tea Leaves,* 245.

22 **Because of the dates:** See Labaree, *Boston Tea Party,* 126–27, for a succinct statement of the law.

22 **The nearly simultaneous events:** Mifflin's Scaevola broadside was reprinted in Boston on 25 October and in Charleston on 23 November; Rush's Hamden essay was reprinted in Boston on 8 November and in Charleston on 29 November.

23 **The *Dartmouth*'s arrival in Boston:** Broadside reprinted in *MG&BNL,* 2 Dec. 1773, and many other newspapers. For more comprehensive accounts of subsequent events, see Labaree, *Boston Tea Party,* 118–45; and Carp, *Defiance of the Patriots,* 95–140.

23 **Accounts of the ensuing:** Quotations: "Diary of Thomas Newell," 345 (entry of 30 Nov. 1773); Hutchinson to Dartmouth, 2 Dec., in *DAR,* 6:249. Reports of the meeting appear in, for example, *MSpy,* 2 Dec.; *SCG* (W), 24 Dec.; *VaG* (P&D), 30 Dec. See also Upton, "Proceedings of Ye Body," 289–96; "An Impartial Observer," *NHG,* 14 Dec. 1773; and the contemporary Loyalist account in Leonard and Sewall, *Massachusettensis,* 29–31. Rotch and Hall recounted their experiences at the meeting to the Privy Council on 19 February 1774 (*DAR,* 8:51–54). Tyler, *Smugglers & Patriots,* argues, 199, that the Boston mercantile community was more divided over the question of landing the tea than has commonly been recognized. If so, that is not evident in the accounts of the general meetings in November–December 1773, although vocal dissenters did appear at the town meetings of late June 1774 (see chapter 3, below).

23 **Captain Curling arrived in Charleston:** *SCG* (T), 6 Dec. 1773; story reprinted, for example, in *VaG* (P&D), 13 Jan. 1774. The northern newspaper stories were attributed to information from a Captain Hunt, who arrived in New York on 23 December, "15 days from Charlestown." (See, for example, *NYG,* 27 Dec.) The most comprehensive study of the Charleston events is Rogers, "Charleston Tea Party"; see also the brief accounts in Carp, *Defiance of the Patriots,* 165–66; Labaree, *Boston Tea Party,* 152–54; and Schlesinger, *Colonial Merchants,* 295–98.

24 **Timothy, who had advance information:** Quotation: William Bull to Lord Dartmouth, 10 March 1774, in *DAR,* 8:64. On all the Charleston printers, see Thomas, *History of Printing,* 566–82 (esp. 568–69 and 579–81 on Timothy and his paper). On the clash of Timothy's politics and the ideal of an "open press," see Jeffery A. Smith, "Impartiality and Revolutionary Ideology: Editorial Policies of the *South-Carolina Gazette, 1732–1775,*" *JSH* 49 (1983): 511–26. For the most conservative of the three papers, see Christopher Gould, "Robert Wells, Colonial Charleston Printer," *SCHM* 79 (1978): 27–49.

25 **In the newspaper:** *SCG* (T), 6 Dec. 1773. Timothy peppered his printed account with phrases in capital letters obviously designed to gain his readers' attention, for example, "EXPRESS PURPOSE OF RAISING A REVENUE ON AMERICA, WITHOUT OUR CONSENT."

25 **not the only contemporary account:** Drayton, *Memoirs,* 1:98; Bull to Dartmouth, 24 Dec. 1773, in *DAR,* 6:265. See also James Laurens to Henry Laurens, 2 Dec. (addition of 4 Dec.), in *HL Papers,* 9:190–91; and Captain Hunt's report of debates at the meeting: *RNYG,* 23 Dec.; *NYG,* 27 Dec. On Drayton in this period: Keith Krawczynski, *William Henry Drayton: South Carolina Revolutionary Patriot* (Baton Rouge: Louisiana State University Press, 2001), 86–119.

25 **The meeting did achieve consensus:** Northern newspapers reprinted Timothy's story in whole or in part at the end of the month; see, for example, *DPaPkt,* 27 Dec. 1773; *CtJ,* 31 Dec. "Threats and flattery" was Bull's assessment: see Bull to Dartmouth, 24 Dec., in *DAR,* 6:265. Presumably Hunt carried a copy of the *SCG* (T) of 6 December with him to New York; the story reached Philadelphia in time to appear in the 22 December issue of *PaG.* See also *SCG* (C), 7 Dec., which published a rumor that there would be an attempt to land the tea.

26 **Junius Brutus:** Junius Brutus, "My friends & countrymen," *SCG* (T), 6 Dec. 1773.

27 **On November 29:** Quotations: Henry Bromfield to [Thomas Bromfield], 12 Dec. 1773, Bromfield Letterbooks, 5:88; Copley to his wife, Susanna, 22 July 1775, Copley Papers, a letter also recalling sardonically, with respect to the "unhappy & miserable . . . Reached [wretched]" Bostonians, "with how little Judgment did I then seem to speak, in the wise Judgment of those people." The events are recounted in *Rowe Diary,* 255–57; and York, *Henry Hulton,* 155–57, 286–97. On the consignees: *NMerc,* 20 Dec. 1773; *CtC,* 21 Dec. Copley's efforts were detailed in a letter to his brothers-in-law, Jonathan and Isaac W. Clarke, [1 Dec.], in *Letters of Copley and Pelham,* 211–13. For Hutchinson's position: Hutchinson to Dartmouth, 15 Dec., in *DAR,* 6:251–52; and Bailyn, *Ordeal of Thomas Hutchinson,* 259–63.

27 **While the governor:** Adams to Warren, 5 Dec. 1773, in *AFC,* 1:88–89; reports of Lexington town meeting in *BG* (supp.), 20 Dec.; *RNYG,* 23 Dec. For similar resolves adopted in Portsmouth, New Hampshire, see John Wentworth to Lord Dartmouth, 17 Dec., in *DAR,* 6:256–57; and *NHG,* 24 Dec.

28 **But not everyone agreed:** "The Following Is a Protest of Some of the Inhabitants of the Town of Plymouth," *MG&BNL,* 23 Dec. 1773, with forty signatures, printed after a copy of the original resolutions; Benja-

min Hallowell to Israel Mauduit, 5 Dec., box 6, Boylston Family Papers. For comments on the Plymouth dissenters, see, for example, "An Old Colonist," *MSpy,* 30 Dec.; "Cornelius Nepos," *BG,* 10 Jan. 1774; Hannah Winthrop to Mercy Warren, 1 Jan., Winthrop-Warren Correspondence; and James Warren to John Adams, 3 Jan., in *JA Papers,* 2:6.

28 **Despite Timothy's apparently definitive narrative:** Drayton, *Memoirs,* 1:97; Smith, Leger, and Greenwood to P. Mitchell, 4 Dec. 1773, CO 5/133, fol. 40d.

29 **According to the ex-consignees:** Quotations: Smith, Leger, and Greenwood to P. Mitchell, 18 Dec. 1773, CO 5/133, fol. 40d; *Rules of the Charlestown Chamber of Commerce* (Charleston, S.C.: Robert Wells, 1774), 4. Report on the founding: *SCG* (T), 13 Dec. 1773. For Timothy's oblique admission that Charleston residents were smuggling from the "Dutch, Danes," and others: *SCG* (T), 27 Dec.

29 **Brief notices published:** *SCG* (T), 13, 20 Dec. 1773; John Morris to Corbyn Morris, 22 Dec., in Drake, *Tea Leaves,* 342.

30 **In Benjamin Hallowell's Boston:** See Labaree, *Boston Tea Party,* 126–45; Carp, *Defiance of the Patriots,* 117–60; and Carp's appendix for his identification of the participants, who kept their involvement secret for many years. For Hutchinson's description, see *DAR,* 6:256; for Samuel Adams's, see *SA Writings,* 3:73–76; for Loyalists' accounts, Thomas Danforth to Lord Dartmouth, 28 Dec., reel 9, no. 758, Dartmouth Papers; and Adair and Schutz, *Peter Oliver's Origin & Progress,* 102–3. For the town's, which was reprinted numerous times, see, for example, *EG,* 21 Dec. According to a Virginian, it was "universally known" that "some of the principal leading Men" of Boston had ships in St. Eustatius purchasing smuggled tea at the time of the attack on the EIC tea (William Wiatt to Francis Wiatt, 3 July 1774, Wiatt Papers).

30 **Despite the protection:** For the attack on Hutchinson's house, see Hoerder, *Crowd Action,* 101–10. Hutchinson received compensation equivalent to more than £2,200 sterling, less than one-third the value of the destroyed tea. (Thanks to John Tyler for this information.)

31 **Before many weeks:** Samuel Cooper to Benjamin Franklin, 17 Dec. 1773, in *BF Papers,* 20:504; Hutchinson to Israel Williams, 23 Dec., Israel Williams Papers; Hutchinson to Lord Dartmouth, 18 Dec., reel 1, no. 919, Dartmouth Papers; Massachusetts committee of correspondence to Franklin, 21 Dec., in *BF Papers,* 20:512; Hannah Winthrop to Mercy Warren, 1 Jan. 1774, Winthrop-Warren Correspondence; Henry Bromfield to Flight & Halliday, 17 Dec. 1773, Bromfield Letterbooks, 5:90.

31 **In Charleston, a second general meeting:** *SCG* (T), 20 Dec. 1773. Timothy specified that this meeting occurred "under the Exchange," suggesting

that the reports of problems with the "main beams" at the session on 3 December might have been accurate. Pauline Maier speculated that the emphasis on maintaining "good order" in the Charleston meetings reflected the participants' concern about possibly rebellious enslaved people in their midst; see "The Charleston Mob and the Evolution of Popular Politics in Revolutionary South Carolina, 1765–1784," *Perspectives in American History* 4 (1970): 176–81.

32 **This time the gathering:** Quotations: *SCG* (T), 20 Dec. 1773. Smith, Leger, and Greenwood to P. Mitchell, 4 Dec., CO 5/133, fol. 40d, noted the merchants' stress on consistency. On 17 December, a vessel arrived from the North, bringing news of tea-related events in Philadelphia (to 9 December), New York (to 3 December), and Boston (through 29 November). It is unknown whether the meeting's participants learned this information while they were in session (between 10:00 and 3:00). In Boston, tea merchants rather than a general meeting dealt with the issue of smuggled versus duty-paying tea; a week after the tea was destroyed, they reached essentially the same conclusion as the Charleston meeting on the seventeenth, but not every merchant agreed. See Tyler, *Smugglers & Patriots*, 206.

32 **The ex-consignees' report to the EIC:** Smith, Leger, and Greenwood to P. Mitchell, 18 Dec. 1773, CO 5/133, fol. 40d. In his *Novanglus* essay of 27 February 1775, John Adams described the decision to seize and store the tea in Charleston as collusive; see *JA Papers*, 2:295. Perhaps he based that assessment on conversations with South Carolina delegates to the First Continental Congress in the fall of 1774.

32 **Lieutenant Governor William Bull:** Drayton, *Memoirs*, 1:115–17; Bull to Dartmouth, 24 Dec. 1773, in *DAR*, 6:266.

33 **Peter Timothy:** *SCG* (T), 27 Dec. 1773; John Morris to Corbyn Morris, 22 Dec., in Drake, *Tea Leaves*, 342. Haliday's and Morris's official account of the seizure, 24 Dec., is T1/505, fol. 61. The Charleston customs collector was ordered to keep the tea safely stored until he received further orders (*DAR*, 7:38). "Extract of a Letter from a Gentleman in Charles-Town, South Carolina to His Friend in New-York," *PaJ*, 16 March 1774 (also in *MG&BNL*, 24 March), reported that the tea had deteriorated in the damp conditions of the Exchange cellar, but cf. Bull to Dartmouth, 25 May 1774, CO 5/396, fol. 36, implying that the tea's condition was still satisfactory. The good tea remaining was sold in October 1776; see *SCG* (W), 9 Oct. (thanks to James Fichter for the reference to the sale).

33 **Between November 28:** The Boston consignees finally resigned in early January 1774; see *DAR*, 7:16.

33 **Adams declared publicly:** Quotation from Adams: Upton, "Proceedings

of Ye Body," 299. See also Samuel Cooper to Benjamin Franklin, 17 Dec. 1773, in *BF Papers,* 20:502; Cooper too thought that his fellow townsmen would find the tea, if landed, an "almost invincible Temptation." John Adams agreed; see his 27 Feb. 1775 *Novanglus* essay, in *JA Papers,* 2:297–98.

34 **On the morning:** Boston committee of correspondence to other committees, 17 Dec. 1773, in *SA Writings,* 3:72. *PaC,* 27 Dec., contained news of the *Polly*'s arrival and of events in Charleston and Boston. The Philadelphia and New York papers quickly published the news from Boston; see, for example, *RNYG,* 23 Dec.; *PaG,* 24 Dec. ("postscript"). The story also made it soon to Williamsburg, where it was published in *VaG* (P&D), 6 Jan. 1774.

35 **Before the *Polly:*** The narrative in this paragraph and the next two is based on the nearly identical accounts published in *PaG,* 29 Dec. 1773, and *PaC,* 3 Jan. 1774. See reprints in whole or in part in, for example, *NYJ,* 6 Jan., and *NMerc,* 17 Jan. The New York printer John Holt published a lengthy account as a broadside (*EAI,* no. 13487). Wharton's comment: Thomas Wharton to Samuel Wharton, 30 Nov. 1773, in "Wharton Letter-Books 33," 319–20; the "custody" phrase: John Patterson and Zachariah Hood to American Board of Customs Commissioners, 28 Dec. 1773, T 1/505, fol. 69. For a brief summary that identifies the committeemen: Ryerson, *Revolution Is Now Begun,* 36–37. The consignees' account: Thomas & Isaac Wharton et al. to EIC Court of Directors, 28 Dec. 1773, CO 5/133, fol. 38b.

36 **The meeting also approved:** George Clymer and Thomas Mifflin to Adams, 27 Dec. 1773, SA Papers; Wharton to Thomas Walpole, 2 May 1774, in "Wharton Letter-Books 33," 329. Wharton thought that Pennsylvania should compensate the EIC for the *Polly*'s shipping costs (ibid., 328). See also Wharton to Samuel Wharton, 1 Jan. 1774, in ibid., 323. One Loyalist later recalled that he took his "first . . . steps in a political character" at the Philadelphia meeting when he opposed approving Boston's conduct; see Phineas Bond's testimony on behalf of his postwar claim for compensation, AO 12/38.

36 **Some commentators applauded:** Reed to Lord Dartmouth, 27 Dec. 1773, reel 1, no. 926, Dartmouth Papers; Madison to Bradford, 24 Jan. 1774, in *JM Papers,* 1:105.

37 **John Penn's role:** Wharton to Samuel Wharton, 30 Nov. 1773, in "Wharton Letter-Books 33," 320; Penn to Juliana Penn, 31 May 1774, in "Letters of Governor Penn," 233–34. See Dartmouth to Penn, 5 Feb. 1774, in *DAR,* 8:45–46; and vice versa, 3 May, in ibid., 103.

37 **New Yorkers:** For a more detailed description of New York's reaction to tea, with specific attention to local political alignments, see Tiedemann, *Reluctant Revolutionaries,* 175–83.

37 **Unsurprisingly, they imitated Philadelphia:** Tryon to Dartmouth, 1 Dec. 1773, in *DAR*, 6:248; Brutus, untitled narrative, *RNYG*, 12 May 1774 (printed in *AA* 4, 1:253–55). New York's "general voice" was embodied in a formal association circulated for signatures in early December, declaring the tea duty unconstitutional and committing its signers to boycotting both EIC tea and anyone dealing in it.

38 **Governor Tryon sent the mayor:** *Smith Memoirs*, 1:159–62. Accounts of the meeting suggesting more agreement than Smith reported were published in newspapers in other colonies; see, for example, *PaG*, 22 Dec. 1773; *NHG*, 7 Jan. 1774.

38 **news of the tea destruction:** *Smith Memoirs*, 1:166 (see 163–65); Henry White et al. to EIC Court of Directors, 27 Dec. 1773, CO 5/133, fol. 41b; Tryon to Dartmouth, 3 Jan. 1774, in *Letters of Colden*, 200; "Extract of a Letter from New-York, Dated January 7, 1774," *SCG* (C), 2 Feb. 1774. See Frederick Haldimand to Dartmouth, 28 Dec. 1773, reel 1, no. 927, Dartmouth Papers. William Palfrey, a Bostonian visiting New York, reported the decision to return the tea to his wife, Susannah, on 28 December (Palfrey Papers). See also the accounts in *NYG*, 27 Dec. 1773; and *BEP*, 3 Jan. 1774.

38 **Throughout January, colonial newspapers:** On the agreement of the Liberty Boys and the ex-consignees: *Smith Memoirs*, 1:173. For reports of the *Nancy*, see, for example, *NYJ*, 6 Jan. 1774; *BG*, 31 Jan. On 10 March, *RNYG* published the news that the ship had wintered in Antigua, which was then reprinted in other papers. Lockyer's letter, 15 February, was published in various papers between late March (*NPkt*, 31 March) and mid-April (*EG*, 12 April).

39 **The hard-luck *Nancy:*** The *Nancy*'s arrival was announced in broadsides, 19 and 21 April 1774 (*EAI*, nos. 13671, 13672). Quotations: *NYG*, 25 April.

39 **Narratives of the East India Company:** For a more detailed account of the wreck and its consequences, see Norton, "Seventh Tea Ship."

40 **The news of the *William*'s wreck:** *MG&BNL*, 16 Dec. 1773. John Rowe recorded that news of the mishap arrived on the evening of 15 December; see *Rowe Diary*, 257. Based on Captain Joseph Loring's description of the circumstances of the wreck, it seems likely that the *William* was driven ashore on the Peaked Hill sandbars, now within the Cape Cod National Seashore. (Thanks to the National Park Service employees who took me to the site in June 2015 and to Heather Huyck for arranging that expedition.) See Joseph Loring, deposition, 7 Jan. 1774, Price Notarial Records, 6:169–71.

40 **Commentary in newspapers:** *EG*, 21 Dec. 1773; Henry Bromfield to Flight & Halliday, 17 Dec., Bromfield Letterbooks, 5:91; Adams to James

Warren, 22 Dec., in *JA Papers,* 2:3, 5. Brief accounts of the shipwreck appeared in many northern newspapers during the last two weeks of December; see, for example, *RNYG,* 23 Dec.; *PaG,* 24 Dec.; *NPkt,* 30 Dec.

40 **Yet such confidence turned out:** Depositions of Joseph Loring, 7, 21 Jan. 1774, Price Notarial Records, 6:171–72, 180. Jonathan Clarke's report to the other consignees on salvaging the tea, 31 Dec. 1773, is in Misc. MSS Bound. For paying the workers in tea, see Freeman, *History of Cape Cod,* 2:668. On board the *William* were twenty-eight chests of black, or Bohea, tea (350 pounds each) and thirty chests of green tea (70 pounds each); the damaged chests all contained Bohea. See "An Account of the Tea . . . ," CO 5/133, fol. 49b. For amount saved: T 1/505, fol. 89.

40 **Shortly after the unloading:** Samuel Adams to James Warren, 10 Jan. 1774, in Winthrop, "Tea-Party Anniversary," 205. Thomas Hutchinson said that Clarke left the Castle on 16 December; see Hutchinson to Dartmouth, 20 Dec. 1773, reel 1, no. 920, Dartmouth Papers.

41 **Clarke and Greenough knew:** Greenough obtained the two vessels to carry the other cargo to Boston; see Freeman, *History of Cape Cod,* 2:667–68; and, for other residents and ships, ibid., 2:563.

41 **After the fifty-four chests:** *EG,* 25 Jan. 1774; *NYJ,* 13 Jan., story datelined Boston, 6 Jan.; *ProvG,* 22 Jan., story datelined Salem, 11 Jan. The account of the "Indians" and their proposed attack on Bickford first appeared in *BEP,* 17 Jan. For the tea's arrival at Castle William: *DAR,* 7:16. James Fichter has discovered that it was sold by the consignees in August 1775; see his "The Tea That Survived the Boston Tea Party," in the online *Journal of the American Revolution*: https://allthingsliberty.com/2019/06/the-tea-that-survived-the-boston-tea-party/. Thanks to him for this information, received while this book was in the editing process.

42 **Initially, disputes centered on:** Truro men: Freeman, *History of Cape Cod,* 2:561; elderly man: *MSpy,* 17 Feb. 1774; searching Provincetown for tea: Greenough to Richard Clarke & Sons, 26 March, draft, John Greenough Papers.

42 **Another raid in Provincetown:** Greenough to Richard Clarke & Sons, 26 March 1774, Misc. MSS Bound; *CtJ,* 18 Feb., 25 March. The peddler claimed he had purchased the tea in Newport, clearly implying it was smuggled rather than from the Cape. And see a possibly related scam in Maine, reported in *BG,* 31 Jan.

43 **That left one damaged chest:** David Stoddard Greenough to John Greenough, 4 Jan. 1774, John Greenough Papers.

43 **The presence of EIC tea:** This paragraph and the next are based on a copy of the Eastham town meeting records for January, February, and March

1774; and on John Greenough to Thomas Greenough, draft, 22 March, all in John Greenough Papers. A record of the February meeting was published in the *BEP,* 4 April, confirming the accuracy of the handwritten copy.

44 **defend himself verbally:** John Greenough to "Gentn," draft, ca. 21–25 Jan. 1774, John Greenough Papers. The comment on "Ruffains": his letter to Richard Clarke & Sons, draft, 26 March, John Greenough Papers.

44 **Wellfleet men voted to place:** William Cooper to Wellfleet committee, 24 March 1774, Boston committee of correspondence minute books, 7:740. On his tea sales, see Greenough to Richard Clarke & Sons, 2 June, Misc. MSS Bound (the quotation); and also to Jonathan Clarke, draft, 7 May, John Greenough Papers. For the Wellfleet letter, see Freeman, *History of Cape Cod,* 2:666–68.

46 **Greenough's family was divided:** Quotations: John Greenough to Thomas Greenough, 22 March, 1 March 1774, drafts, John Greenough Papers.

CHAPTER 2 DIVIDED SENTIMENTS

47 **Eleven days after:** Israel Holly, *God Brings About His Holy and Wise Purpose or Decree, Concerning Many Particular Events . . . a Sermon Preached at Suffield, December 27, 1773 . . .* (Hartford, Conn.: Eben Watson, 1774), 15.

47 **Given his strong language:** *JA Diary,* 2:85–86 (entry of 17 Dec. 1773). A Maine Anglican priest put the opposite vision into verse, predicting British retaliation for the tea's destruction: "The daring Indians then shall fall in swarms / And dying curse the Wretch that call'd to Arms / . . . Their Blood shall crimson oer the flowing sea / And mix promiscuous with the sunken tea." Printed in James S. Leamon, *The Reverend Jacob Bailey, Maine Loyalist: For God, King, Country, and Self* (Amherst: University of Massachusetts Press, 2012), 105.

47 **Holly's reaction to the events:** Holly, *God Brings About His Holy and Wise Purpose,* 19, 22, 23.

48 **Holly's congregation seems to have:** Ibid., 22n. Because the sermon with "some Enlargements," described as such on the title page, lacks any reference to the Boston Port Act, it was probably revised and published before mid-May. Holly's appears to be the sole sermon published in the immediate aftermath of the destruction of the tea.

49 **News of the destruction:** The *Nancy,* of course, did not arrive off New York until April. In Williamsburg, Purdie & Dixon's *VG* first published the news from Boston on 6 January 1774, as did Peter Timothy's paper

in Charleston; see also *MdG* of the same date, reprinting the Boston story from a New York paper. Short accounts of the wreck of the *William* appeared in many newspapers from late December through early February (for example, *CtG,* 7 Jan.; and *SCG* [C], 1 Feb.); that information was conveyed to London in the letters that also carried news of the Mohawks' action. For Savannah, see *GaG,* 26 Jan. (notice dated 20 Jan., including the shipwreck); for London: *HL Papers,* 9:243 (Boston) and 9:258 (Charleston and Philadelphia). New Yorkers learned of the seizure in Charleston on 2 January (see letter of 7 Jan. in *SCG* [C], 1 Feb.), but that news was not published in Williamsburg until late in the month (*VaG* [P&D], 27 Jan.).

49 **Bostonians weighed in quickly:** *MSpy,* 13 Jan. 1774; *BG,* 17 Jan. See also *BEP,* 17, 24 Jan.

50 **Benjamin Franklin:** Franklin to assembly committee of correspondence, 2 Feb. 1774, in *BF Papers,* 21:76–77. See also ibid., 152–53, 178–80. Franklin did not alter his opinion until September 1774, when he wrote that reimbursing the EIC would be a bad idea because of ambiguities in the Port Act (ibid., 287).

50 **Laurens, who on initially hearing:** Laurens to his son John, 21 Jan. 1774, in *HL Papers,* 9:244; Laurens to George Appleby, 15 Feb., in ibid., 9:277–78; see also Laurens to James Air, 25 Feb., and to John Lewis Gervais, 9 April, in ibid., 9:314, 391–92.

50 **In that assessment:** "Tacitus" and unsigned in *NYJ,* 6 Jan. 1774, also reprinted elsewhere: for example, *ProvG,* 22 Jan.; *VaG* (R), 27 Jan. In Philadelphia, Thomas Wharton heard that Carolinians feared losing trade preferences for indigo and rice, and so decided to "receive the tea"; see Wharton to Samuel Wharton, 4 Jan., in "Wharton Letter-Books 33," 325. As late as 31 December, Ezra Stiles, a resident of Newport, believed that Charleston had sent the tea ship back, but by 10 January he knew the true story; see *Stiles Diary,* 1:427, 431.

51 **By the time he prepared:** "Charles-Town," *SCG* (T), 17 Jan. 1774; "Extract of a Letter from New-York, Dated January 7, 1774," *SCG* (C), 1 Feb.

51 **The dissension in Charleston:** See Christopher Gadsden to Samuel Adams, 23 May 1774, in Walsh, *Writings of Gadsden,* 93. The issues discussed are evident in the *SCG* (T) reports of the third "general meeting" held on 16 March, which were published on 21 and 28 March 1774.

52 **Charlestonians moved once more:** *SCG* (T), 24 Jan., 21, 28 March 1774. Henry Laurens disagreed with the substance of these tea resolutions (*HL Papers,* 9:428).

52 **Despite the seeming unanimity:** Gadsden to Adams, 23 May 1774, in Walsh, *Writings of Gadsden,* 93.

53 **Commentary in places outside:** Farish, *Journal of Fithian,* 59; Calhoon, "Sorrowful Spectator"; William Wiatt to his mother, and to his brother (2 letters), 3 July 1774, Wiatt Papers; Henry Tucker Jr. to St. George Tucker, 21 March 1774, box 2, folder 8, Tucker-Coleman Papers.

53 **Virginia newspapers echoed:** *VaG* (R), 17 Feb. 1774 (see *VaG* [P&D], 10 Feb., for a prior rejection of the same essay); *VaG* (P&D), 20 Jan., 3 March 1774. Presumably "L.H." was the same author who earlier signed himself "Landon Honduras" and expressed the same sentiments; see *VaG* (P&D), 25 Nov. 1773.

54 **In New England:** Marshfield: 31 Jan. 1774, town meeting, record printed in Lysander Salmon Richards, *History of Marshfield* (Plymouth [Mass.]: Memorial Press, 1901), 1:102. Two weeks later, some residents dissented, but even they criticized "riotous and disorderly conduct," an obvious reference to the Mohawks; see ibid., 121. Freetown: town meeting record, 17 and 26 Jan., *MG&BNL,* 10 Feb. 1774. Only two of eighty Massachusetts towns explicitly praised Boston; see Brown, *Revolutionary Politics,* 167–68.

54 **Other towns in the region:** *NHG,* 7 Jan. 1774 (Exeter), 14 Jan. (Dover), 21 Jan. (Greenland), 4 Feb. (Rochester), 18 Feb. (Stratham), 25 Feb. (Barrington), 4 March (Hampton, Falmouth). Quotations: Falmouth, Greenland. Dover did vote to approve "the general Exertions, and noble Struggles" against tea imports in the "opulent COLONIES." Hinsdale, a conservative town, satirized these resolutions; see Jere Daniell, "Reason and Ridicule: Tea Act Resolutions in New Hampshire," *Historical New Hampshire* 20, no. 4 (1965): 23–26.

54 **Of eight town meetings:** Town meeting records, in Bartlett, *Records of Rhode Island,* 7:272–80 (quotation, Richmond, 276). For Newport, 12 Jan., see *At a Meeting Held at NEWPORT . . . ,* broadside (*EAI,* no. 13498); for Little Compton, *NMerc,* 14 Feb. The resolutions from Newport and Providence largely copied Philadelphia's from October 1773.

54 **The silences were significant:** Bartlett, *Records of Rhode Island,* 7:275.

55 **In February:** Quotations in this and the next paragraph come from John Greenough to Thomas Greenough, draft, 1 March 1774, John Greenough Papers. John referred to three February missives from his father. In the draft, "outragious Cruelty" replaced the original word "Bloodshed."

56 **Thomas Greenough did not let:** Thomas to John Greenough, 28 March 1774, HM 70282, Greenough Family Papers.

57 **In the spring of 1774:** Not all such shipments were destroyed. For a cargo that was landed but reshipped from Portsmouth, New Hampshire, to Halifax, Nova Scotia, in June, see *AA* 4, 1:499; *PIR,* 575–78; *DAR,* 8:138–40; and George Meserve and Robert Traill to American Board of Customs Commissioners, 30 June 1774, T 1/505, fols. 316–17. In Portsmouth, a

committee of local "gentlemen" prevented a crowd from attacking the ship and the tea.

58 **The first vessel with new:** Quotation: Hutchinson to Dartmouth, 9 March 1774, in *DAR*, 8:63. Gorham left England on 9 January, about two weeks before the news of the December tea incidents started to arrive (Nathaniel Taylor to Isaac Clarke, 8 March, Misc. MSS Bound). Accounts of the destruction of the tea in the *Fortune*'s cargo: T 1/505, fols. 117–24 (Boston customs' officers reports); and statements of sailors and owners, Price Notarial Records, 6:186–99. See also the usefully detailed report headed Boston, March 10, in *VaG* (R), 7 April.

58 **The next new shipment:** The account in this paragraph and the next is based on reports that appeared in numerous newspapers, reprinted from stories first published in *NYG*, 25 April 1774, and *RNYG*, 28 April (see also 12 May). See, for example, *VaG* (P&D), 5 May. See *Smith Memoirs*, entry of 22 April, 1:184–85.

59 **The shipowners then publicly:** Quotations: "Extract of a Letter from New-York, April 25, 1774," *SCG* (T), 16 May 1774 (reprinted from a Philadelphia paper); Colden to Dartmouth, 4 May, in *DAR*, 8:108. "Persons of reputation" from *NYG*, 25 April.

59 **The Boston-style destruction:** *RNYG*, 28 April 1774, printed in *AA* 4, 1:251; Brutus, "To the Printer of the New-York Gazetteer," *RNYG*, 12 May, printed in *AA* 4, 1:251–58.

59 **Yet others who contemplated:** Reed to Dennis DeBerdt, 4 May 1774, in Reed, *Life of Joseph Reed*, 1:60.

60 **In the midst of such discussions:** *EJ*, 19 Jan. 1774; Mentor, *NMerc*, 14 Feb.; A Batchelor, *NPkt*, 13 Jan.

60 **So the commodity:** Quotations: James Parker to Charles Steuart, 17 May 1774, reel 2, fol. 201, Steuart Papers; John Adams to Abigail Adams, 6 July, in *AFC*, 1:129–30. In Falmouth, a "Committee for Tarring and Feathering" publicly warned residents against consuming tea (*MG&BPB*, 14 Feb.). An anecdote in which "No American, but a Lover of Liberty" supposedly convinced an innkeeper that he was a "Tory" and could be served tea appeared in *MG&BPB*, 24 Jan. Some continued to drink tea, of course; see Riley, *Journal of Harrower*, 49.

61 **Essayists and clergymen:** "Needless" tea: Peter Whitney, *The Transgression of a Land Punished by a Multitude of Rulers* . . . (Boston: John Boyle, 1774), 41; "Balsam": Miller and Riggs, *Romance, Remedies, and Revolution*, 188 (entry of 26 March 1775). Drinking sage tea: William Reynolds to Samuel Rogers, 16 Aug. 1774, Reynolds Letterbook. Growing tea: *CtJ*, 28 Jan. The Ellisons: Thomas Ellison Jr. to his father, Thomas, 3, 11 June, Ellison Family Papers.

61 **Newspaper editors frequently:** Quotations: "Diary of Newell," 347 (entry for 31 Dec. 1773); *BG* (supp.), 20 Dec. A Boston Common bonfire: *Rowe Diary,* 259 (entry for 1 Jan. 1774); *NYJ,* 13 Jan. Another incident in which tea was destroyed in Charlestown involved self-described "friends to liberty" who were secretly transporting twenty-six pounds of tea for an acquaintance and were outraged when it was destroyed. See *EJ,* 19 Jan.; and the exchange of five letters among the Woburn and Charlestown committees, and Loammi and Cyrus Baldwin, from 24 Jan. to 1 Feb., Misc. MSS Bound.

61 **Students and teachers:** Princeton: *VaG* (P&D), 31 March 1774. Boston: *NMerc,* 27 Dec. 1773; *GaG,* 3 Feb. 1774. See Newport stories in, for example, *NMerc,* 20, 27 Dec. 1773; *VaG* (R), 16 Dec. 1773, 27 Jan. 1774; *SCG* (W), 24 Dec. 1773; *CtJ,* 7 Jan. 1774. Some stories stressed that only a small number of imported tea chests in Rhode Island had paid duty (*EG,* 1 Feb. 1774, referring to Providence), thus implying that most of the tea consumed there was smuggled.

62 **Because women were especially associated:** William Wiatt to Francis Wiatt, 3 July 1774, Wiatt Papers; A Mechanic, *To the Worthy Inhabitants of New York,* [Oct. 1773], broadside (*EAI,* no. 13042); Junius Brutus, "My Friends and Countrymen," *SCG* (T), 6 Dec. 1773. Attention to women and tea dated back to the earlier boycotts; see, for example, *The Female Patriot, No. I, Addressed to the Tea-Drinking Ladies of New-York,* 10 May 1770, broadside (*EAI,* no. 11653).

62 **The anonymous author:** *A Sermon on Tea* (Lancaster, Pa.: Francis Bailey, [1774]), 4–8. See also untitled poem, *NHG,* 22 July, describing tea as putting forth "Noxious Effluvia," some of it "tinctur'd with the Filth / Of Carcases embalm'd." The *Sermon's* author regarded women's political role negatively. Instead of attempting to enlist them in the movement, he accused some of "high treason," remarking that "here and there a silly Eve, regardless of her countries call, stretches forth her unthinking hand, and receives the accursed herb" (*Sermon,* 6).

62 **Such "scare crow stories":** A Woman, "For the Massachusetts Spy," *MSpy,* 23 Dec. 1773; T[homas] Young, "To the Lady, Who in No. 151 of This Paper Signs a WOMAN," *MSpy,* 30 Dec. See also the essay signed "Frugality," *NMerc,* 28 Feb. 1774.

63 **two anti-tea essays:** A Planter's Wife, "To the Ladies of South-Carolina," *SCG* (C), 19 July 1774; Margaret Homespun, "To the Ladies of This Province," *GaG,* 18 Jan. 1775. Issues of newspapers containing these essays were sent by Governor James Wright of Georgia to Lord Dartmouth; I read them in CO 5/663, fol. 138, and CO 5/664, fol. 56, respectively. William Tennent III, writing as "the husband of the planter's wife" in *SCG* (C)

on 2 August 1774, echoed his nominal wife's political themes but added a reference to tea's "time consuming Poison" and its negative effects on the health of women and their children. His "To the Ladies of South Carolina" is reprinted in *Journal of Presbyterian History* 52 (1974): 370–72.

63 **In the same vein:** Version 1 (unrhymed): *VaG* (P&D), 20 Jan. 1774 (reprinted four times in northern papers between February and September); version 2, *EJ*, 2 March; reprinted in *CtG*, 14 Oct. See also "Virginia Banishing Tea. By a Lady," *PaJ*, 21 Sept.; and a poem supposedly composed by the women of Bedford, Massachusetts, which ended, we'll "bid adieu to India Stuff, / Before we'll lose our Liberty," *VaG* (P&D), 17 March; with a related article about the Bedford "daughters of liberty," *NMerc*, 7 Feb. Mercy Otis Warren's elaborate poem about the events in Boston on 16 December 1773, much admired by John Adams and published at his instigation in the *BG* on 21 March 1774, was not reprinted anywhere. See *JA Papers*, 2:3, 82; *AFC*, 1:93, 99–103.

64 **Women's prominence in the anti-tea:** The most elaborate was a series of essays by Philo Justiciae, personifying "Lady Tea," titled "To the Essex Journal, &c., Messrs Printers," *EJ*, 12, 19, 26 Jan.; 2, 9 Feb. 1774, including exchanges with critics, 16, 23 Feb.; 2, 16, 30 March; and 6 April.

64 **The most famous satire:** *CtC*, 15 Feb. 1774; Susanna Spindle, *NHG*, 18 Feb., reprinted in Daniell, "Reason and Ridicule," 26–28. On the Edenton meeting and Philip Dawe's cartoon, see Don Higginbotham, *Papers of Iredell*, 1:282–86. The association the women signed in October 1774 supported the deputies of the North Carolina Provincial Congress in their plan to boycott British goods generally; it is printed in *AA* 4, 1:891. For more on the cartoon: Norton, *Liberty's Daughters*, 161–63.

66 **Given the paucity of evidence:** Stephen Salisbury to Samuel Salisbury, 6 Jan. 1774, Salisbury Family Papers, American Antiquarian Society, Worcester, Mass.; Rhoda Barber, Journal-Memoir, ca. 1830. James Fichter's forthcoming book on the tea trade and consumption in the revolutionary era examines tea advertisements in detail; thanks to James Fichter for information about his findings.

66 **January 29, 1774:** See Sheila L. Skemp, *The Making of a Patriot: Benjamin Franklin at the Cockpit* (New York: Oxford University Press, 2013); Kenneth L. Penegar, *The Political Trial of Benjamin Franklin: A Prelude to the American Revolution* (New York: Algora, 2011); or, more briefly, Bunker, *Empire on the Edge*, 241–45. See also observers' accounts of Franklin's humiliating experience in *Bowdoin and Temple Papers*, 335–39; *HL Papers*, 9:266–67; and Franklin's own narrative of his ordeal in *BF Papers*, 21:86–96.

67 **January 31:** Barkley to EIC Court of Directors, 31 Jan. 1774, India Office

Records, E/1, 58, fols. 65–66 (noted on verso, not accepted, 2 Feb.). See EIC Court of Directors to Lords of Treasury, 16 Feb., India Office Records, E/1, 217, fol. 76; same to Lord Dartmouth, 22 March, India Office Records, E/1, 217, fol. 99; and same to same, 10 March, CO5/115, fol. 37. See also their memorial to the Treasury about the tea seized in Charleston, 16 Feb., T 1/509, fols. 174–75.

67 **February 5:** Dartmouth to Law Lords, 5 Feb. 1774, in *DAR*, 8:37–42; and vice versa, 11 Feb., in ibid., 47–48; Dartmouth to Bull, 5 Feb., CO 5/396, fol. 5; Dartmouth to six governors and General Frederick Haldimand, 5 Feb., in *DAR*, 7:35–37. The Massachusetts attorney general, Jonathan Sewall, decided that the destruction of the tea constituted burglary, not treason; see *JA Papers*, 2:3.

68 **March 14 and 31:** Quotation: Simmons and Thomas, *Proceedings and Debates*, 4:59 (see 56–64). For accounts of the meetings and copies of the Americans' petitions: *HL Papers*, 9:366–76 (see also Laurens's comments on the Port Bill, in ibid., 9:360, 364); for the agent's opinion: *AA* 4, 1:235. A recent description of the ministry's deliberations and decisions is Bunker, *Empire on the Edge*, chaps. 11, 12.

68 **April 9:** Dartmouth to Gage, 9 April 1774, in *PIR*, 1–7 (quotations 3, 5, 6); also in *DAR*, 8:86–90.

69 **In early April:** Reed to Dartmouth, 4 April 1774, reel 1, no. 965.a, Dartmouth Papers; Reed to DeBerdt, 4 May, in Reed, *Life of Joseph Reed*, 1:59. All but two of the letters Reed wrote to Dartmouth over the next year were published in this volume from Reed's letterbook copy (not always precisely the same as the versions Dartmouth received); see ibid., xv–xvi, 51–96. The 1773 letters were quoted in chapter 1; see above. The letters must have made a positive impression on Dartmouth, for he did not customarily encourage correspondence from non-office-holding Americans.

69 **Reed, a graduate of the College:** For a brief biography, see G. S. Rowe, "Reed, Joseph," in *American National Biography*, ed. John A. Garraty and Mark C. Carnes (New York: Oxford University Press, 1999), 18:270–72. On the relationship of DeBerdt and Dartmouth, see Michael G. Kammen, *A Rope of Sand: The Colonial Agents, British Politics, and the American Revolution* (Ithaca, N.Y.: Cornell University Press, 1968), 30.

70 **The colonists had detested:** On William Legge, Lord Dartmouth, see Bunker, *Empire on the Edge*, 115–23.

70 **So in April, having been:** Reed to Dartmouth, 4 April 1774, reel 1, no. 965.a, Dartmouth Papers. On the post office, proposed by William Goddard in early 1774, see *AA* 4, 1:500–504; letters from Dr. Thomas Young (18 March) and Paul Revere (28 March) in Lamb Papers; and Breen, *American Insurgents, American Patriots*, 105–10.

70 **No Bostonian actively involved:** Adams to Arthur Lee, 4 April 1774 (addendum), in *SA Writings,* 3:104; Nathaniel Coffin to Charles Steuart, 29 April, reel 2, fol. 188, Steuart Papers. See also Matthew Brickdale to Dartmouth, 4 April, reel 10, no. 878, Dartmouth Papers.

72 **John Malcom, a customs officer:** The narrative: *MG&BPB,* 31 Jan. 1774. Quotations: Hutchinson to Dartmouth, 28 Jan., in *DAR,* 8:26; and *Rowe Diary* (entry of 25 Jan.), 261. Accounts in York, *Henry Hulton,* 158, 297, revealed even more brutality than described in the newspapers. The injured tradesman was George Robert Twelves Hewes, one of the destroyers of the tea; see Alfred F. Young, *The Shoemaker and the Tea Party: Memory and the American Revolution* (Boston: Beacon Press, 1999), 46–51. See also Frank W. C. Hersey, "Tar and Feathers: The Adventures of Captain John Malcolm," *Pubs CSM* 34 (1941): 429–73; and Benjamin H. Irvin, "Tar, Feathers, and the Enemies of American Liberties, 1768–1776," *NEQ* 76 (2003): 197–238, esp. 210–13.

72 **The next month:** For Hutchinson's comments on the impeachment attempt: *DAR,* 8:50, 62; for Samuel Adams's, *SA Writings,* 3:97–99; for the Massachusetts committee of correspondence, *BF Papers,* 21:161–68; for Oliver's own account, Adair and Schutz, *Peter Oliver's Origin & Progress,* 107–11.

72 **Andrew Oliver:** Quotations: *Stiles Diary,* 1:437 (entry of 12 March 1774); Adair and Schutz, *Oliver's Origin & Progress,* 112. The description in this paragraph draws on both accounts.

73 **Marblehead smallpox hospital:** Quotations in this and the next paragraph: Samuel Adams to Elbridge Gerry, 25 March 1774, in *SA Writings,* 3:83 (also, 94–97). See Andrew M. Wehrman, "The Siege of 'Castle Pox': A Medical Revolution in Marblehead, Massachusetts, 1764–1777," *NEQ* 82 (2009): 385–429.

74 **Referring to the attempts:** Hannah Winthrop to Mercy Warren, 1 April 1774, Winthrop-Warren Correspondence; Benjamin Hallowell to Ward N. Boylston, 5 Feb., box 6, Boylston Family Papers; Lechmere to Lane, Son & Fraser, 14 Feb., 28 March, both in Misc. MSS Bound, MHS; Caner to John Wentworth, 28 Feb., 14 March, both in *Letterbook of Caner.*

74 **In that context:** Adams to John Dickinson, 21 April 1774, in *SA Writings,* 3:104; *JA Diary* (entry of 5 March), 2:89–90; *Rowe Diary* (entry of 5 March), 264; Hannah Winthrop to Mercy Warren, 1 April, Winthrop-Warren Correspondence. Also present was Thomas Newell; see "Diary of Newell" (entry of 5 March), 349. John Andrews, who did not attend, noted that the oration was "asserted to be *his own* production." See Andrews to William Barrell, 14 April, in "Andrews Letters," 327. By contrast, Henry

Hulton complained of Hancock's "violent invectives against Government" (York, *Henry Hulton,* 160).

74 **Hancock drew such praise:** Quotations in this and the next two paragraphs from John Hancock, *An Oration; Delivered March 5, 1774 . . . to Commemorate the Bloody Tragedy of the Fifth of March 1770* (Boston: Edes & Gill, 1774), 9, 15, 16–18. The address was published almost immediately, being advertised for sale in Boston papers before the end of the month. The only published attack on the oration, by "Phileleutheros," appeared in *RNYG,* 21 April; its author, who claimed to have attended the trial in 1770, challenged Hancock's description of the "massacre," pointing out accurately that all the soldiers but one were acquitted of any crime. Rivington apologized for being "under a necessity" of printing the "Controversial peice," explaining that he did not want to "risque . . . disobliging the Colonel [Hancock]" and offering the chance to respond (but no one did). See Rivington to Henry Knox, 20 April, in "Knox and the London Book-Store," 281, enclosing the critical essay, 281–85.

76 **establishment of an intercolonial congress:** For Virginia's call for colony-wide committees: *RevVa,* 1:89–91. For 1754, see Timothy Shannon, *Indians and Colonists at the Crossroads of Empire: The Albany Congress of 1754* (Ithaca, N.Y.: Cornell University Press, 2000); and for 1765, C. A. Weslager, *The Stamp Act Congress* (Newark: University of Delaware Press, 1976). "Americanus" in the *NYJ,* reprinted in *VaG* (R), 10 March 1774, proposed an annual congress composed of delegates from the committees, which would make recommendations for action to colonial assemblies.

77 **Before the tea was destroyed:** W.T. to Samuel Adams, 16 Dec. 1773, SA Papers; Andrews to William Barrell, 18 Dec., in "Andrews Letters," 325; John Adams to James Warren, 17 Dec., in *JA Papers,* 2:1–2; Van Schaack to John Vardill, 14 Feb., Van Schaack Family Papers.

77 **Late in March:** Quotation: *VaG* (P&D), 7 April 1774, story datelined New York, 28 March, attributed to a ship just arrived after a two-month voyage from London. For reports of warships and troops dated in late January, see, for example, *VaG* (P&D), 14 April; *SCG* (T), 11 April; *SCG* (C), 19 April, with reports from early February as well.

77 **In early April:** Adams to James Warren, 9 April 1774, in *JA Papers,* 2:83; *SCG* (T), 16 May, quoting a letter from London, 17 Feb.; "Extract of a Letter from London, Feb. 19, 1774," reprinted in *NPkt,* 28 April, and *SCG* (C), 30 April; "Extract of a Letter from London, Dated March 4," *SCG* (T), 16 May, reprinted from a New York paper, 28 April. Hutchinson's letter to his son William, 30 April, is in Egerton Manuscripts 2661, fol. 3.

78 **All that changed:** Hutchinson to ———, 2 May 1774, Egerton Manuscripts

2661, fol. 25; *BEP* and *MG&BPB*, both 2 May, carried the brief report of North's speech.

78 **Three days later:** Quotation: John to Abigail Adams, 12 May 1774, in *AFC*, 1:107. Newport date: *Stiles Diary* (entry of 5 May), 1:440; New York dates: Alexander McDougall, "Political Memorandums Relative to the Conduct of the Citizens on the Boston Port Bill," 11, 12 May 1774, Alexander McDougall Papers; Boston dates: *Rowe Diary* (entry of 10 May), 269; Boston committee of correspondence (hereafter for this chapter BCC) to neighboring towns, 11 May 1774, *PIR*, 91. The complete text was published in Philadelphia on 16 May (in *DPaPkt*); summarized in *VaG* (P&D), 19 May; printed in *SCG* (T), 3 June, and in *GaG*, 8 June. Many New England papers published the act in full between 14 May (*ProvG*) and 18 May (*EJ*).

78 **On May 12:** BCC, minutes, 12 May 1774, in *PIR*, 85–86; untitled broadside, Boston, 12 May 1774, addressed to "Gentlemen" (*EAI*, no. 42562).

78 **Stressing Bostonians' unity:** BCC, circular letter to other colonies, 13 May 1774, in *PIR*, 92–93. Even Thomas Hutchinson thought the act "severe and distressing" and privately denied ever recommending any such measure (Hutchinson to Israel Williams, 14 May, Israel Williams Papers).

80 **boycott of all trade with Britain:** The fullest examination of this theme is Breen, *Marketplace of Revolution.*

80 **Men crowded into the town meeting:** Quotations: *BG*, 16 May 1774; Town Meeting Record, 13 May, in *PIR*, 74–78.

81 **Dr. Thomas Young:** Young to John Lamb, 13 May 1774, Lamb Papers. See also Samuel Adams's reflections on the Port Act and the meeting in his letter to James Warren, 14 May, in *SA Writings*, 3:111–14.

81 **official minutes recorded:** Boston town meeting record, 18 May 1774, in *PIR*, 78–79; John Andrews to William Barrell, 18 May, in "Andrews Letters," 329.

81 **Harrison Gray:** Gray, *Few Remarks*, 5–6. Possibly Gray erred in his recollection, and the specific debate he described took place at the contentious town meeting of late June 1774 (see below, chapter 3), or perhaps he conflated different discussions at the two gatherings. He attended the later meeting as well; see *Rowe Diary*, 276. One remark he recounted seems to date to May, whereas the content of another would have been more likely offered in late June, if he reported them accurately.

82 **Josiah Quincy Jr.:** Quincy's works have been conveniently collected in Coquillette and York, *Portrait of a Patriot.*

82 **The pamphlet's contents revealed:** Quincy, *Observations,* unpaginated preface. The first twenty-seven pages focused on the Port Act; the next forty-five, on standing armies and history; and the final ten (especially the

last three) on threats to New England, historic and current. Peter Shaw's assessment of Quincy in his *American Patriots and the Rituals of Revolution* (Cambridge, Mass.: Harvard University Press, 1981), 153–74, emphasized his emotional style and noted that he rarely made a sustained argument.

82 **With respect to the "astonishing" statute:** Quotations: Quincy, *Observations*, 14, 15, 25, 81–82.

83 **respond to the urgent pleas:** The requests to other colonies, approved by the town meeting, had cover letters signed by Samuel Adams, as the meeting's moderator (*PIR*, 96–97; *SA Writings*, 3:106–11). Governor Gage reported to Dartmouth on 19 May that he had heard that the act "staggered the most presumptuous" Bostonians; see *DAR*, 8:116.

CHAPTER 3 THIS BARBAROUS EDICT

84 **arrival in mid-May:** Lee to his brother Arthur, 26 June 1774, in Ballagh, *Letters of Lee*, 1:114; Washington to George William Fairfax, 10 June, in *GW Papers: CS*, 10:96; Carroll to Wallace, Davidson, and Johnson, 5 June, in Hoffman, *Dear Papa*, 2:720–21.

85 **Boston town meeting:** Adams to Arthur Lee, 18 May 1774, in *SA Writings*, 3:118; Boston town meeting record, 13, 18 May, in *PIR*, 77–78; merchants' agreement, 21 May, with signatures, in ibid., 97–98. For a firm that countermanded existing orders, see Nathaniel and Joseph Cranch to Edward Moody, and to James Elworthy (two letters), May, Cranch Papers. Merchants considered themselves freed from this obligation when the other provinces refused to adopt immediate nonimportation; see Nathaniel Coffin to Charles Steuart, 6 July, reel 2, fol. 226, Steuart Papers; and *MG&BPB*, 27 June.

85 **positive responses poured in:** Quotation: Young to John Lamb, 18 May 1774, Lamb Papers. For Providence, Newport, Westerly, and Portsmouth, see *AA* 4, 1:333–34, 343–44, 336–37; for Salem, Gloucester, and Newburyport, see *PIR*, 107, 113, 474n58.

86 **evident in correspondence:** Gerry to Samuel Adams, 20 May 177[4], HM 41595, Huntington Library [misdated 1772, which *PIR*, 90, corrects]; Gerry to Boston committee of correspondence, 24 May, in *PIR*, 114–15. See also ibid., 109–10, for the same men's exchange of letters on 22 May.

86 **Despite the majority:** Richard Lechmere to Lane, Son, and Fraser, 30 May 1774, Misc. MSS Bound; Coffin to Charles Steuart, 30 May, reel 2, fol. 204, Steuart Papers; Hulton to John ———, 24 May, in York, *Henry Hulton*, 300.

86 **men also repeated them publicly:** Quotation: *AA* 4, 1:363 (29 May). For the other addresses to Hutchinson, see ibid., 346 ("Address of the Episcopal Ministers . . . in Boston," 23 May); 358 ("Address . . . by Sundry

Gentlemen of Marblehead," 25 May); 361–62 ("Address of Merchants and Others," 28 May); 364–65 ("Address from the Magistrates of the County of Middlesex," 30 May). For Samuel Adams's predictably acid comments on the Addressers of Hutchinson, see *SA Writings*, 3:124; and see Marblehead's formal statement repudiating the address from its merchants, 3 June, in *PIR*, 462–65. James Warren described the drafting of addresses to Hutchinson and Gage in Plymouth to Samuel Adams, 10 July, SA Papers.

87 **Other similar, overlapping groups:** Quotations: merchants' address to Gage, [8 June 1774], in *PIR*, 425–26. See also other addresses: ibid., 61–62 (Episcopal Clergy, 20 May); 62–63 (Suffolk County Justices, 24 May); 429–30 (Harvard Corporation, 9 June); 430–32 (Salem Merchants, 10 June).

88 **Collectively, the men:** Hulton quotations: York, *Henry Hulton*, 161. The "PROTEST of the Merchants and Traders of This Town," dated 24 May, was published as one component of a lengthy broadside, *Addresses &c to the Late Governor Hutchinson*, 30 May (*EAI*, no. 42546); protest also in *AA* 4, 1:362. On the drafting of the protest, see *PIR*, 444, 445n15. For the undated alphabetical list with commentary, see *A List of the Addressers to the Late Gov. Hutchinson*, broadside (*EAI*, no. 13379), probably the "*New* Catalogue of the names of the Addressors and protestors" to which John Andrews later referred; see Andrews to William Barrell, 10 Oct., in "Andrews Letters," 375. The quotations, in order, described James Anderson, Dr. Silvester Gardiner, and John Taylor. Examples of "murmurs": *PIR*, 492, 950. William Hunting Howell, "Entering the Lists: The Politics of Ephemera in Eastern Massachusetts, 1774," *EAS* 9 (2011): 187–217, discusses the coercion of merchants and Addressers.

88 **Bostonians expressed varying opinions:** And in other Bay Colony towns; see, for example, *PIR*, 485–86; and the summary in Brown, *Revolutionary Politics*, 185–208.

89 **Residents of Manhattan:** See *AA* 4, 1:289, for the ship *Samson*'s arrival with copies of the act on May 12; sending the act north on May 15: Alexander McDougall, "Political Memorandums Relative to the Conduct of the Citizens on the Boston Port Bill . . . ," 15 May, Alexander McDougall Papers; ibid., 17 May, for Revere's arrival. McDougall recorded the first news of the act's passage in ibid., 11 May.

89 **New Yorkers thus knew:** Haldimand to Dartmouth, 15 May 1774, in *DAR*, 8:112; Van Schaack to John Vardill, 13 May (draft), box 4, Van Schaack Family Papers; McDougall, "Political Memorandums," 14 May, McDougall Papers. The political struggles in New York during the following week are discussed in greater detail in Roger Champagne, "New York and the Intolerable Acts, 1774," *NYHSQ* 45 (1961): 195–207.

90 **John Holt:** The "Extracts" and the essay from Gaine's *Gazette* are reprinted in *AA* 4, 1:289–91, including assertions that the April letters from London were genuine, not forged. Haldimand on 15 May (*DAR*, 8:112) said the broadside, probably *EAI*, no. 13273, was distributed *"gratis."*

90 **At the scheduled meeting:** McDougall's account: "Political Memorandums," 16 May 1774, McDougall Papers; Colden to Dartmouth, 1 June, in *DAR*, 8:121. A broadside, *At a Meeting at the Exchange* (*EAI*, no. 13125), 16 May, announced the vote in favor of a larger committee.

90 **After a citywide meeting:** A broadside titled *To the Public* and dated both 17 and 18 May announced the two meetings (*EAI*, no. 13669). See *A Committee of Twenty-Five*, broadside (*EAI*, no. 13474); A Citizen, *To the Worthy Inhabitants of the City and County of New-York*, 19 May, broadside (*EAI*, no. 13684). The other quotations and arrival of Revere on the evening of 17 May: McDougall, "Political Memorandums," 17, 18 May, McDougall Papers; *Smith Memoirs*, 1:186.

91 **Many merchants attended:** These events are recounted in *Smith Memoirs*, 1:187 (entries of 19, 20 May 1774); McDougall, "Political Memorandums," 19, 20 May, McDougall Papers; *AA* 4, 1:293–95 (Low quotation, 294); Peter Van Schaack to Peter Silvester, 21 May, in Van Schaack, *Life of Peter Van Schaack*, 16 ("irreparably"); and Haldimand to Dartmouth, 1 June, in *DAR*, 8:120 (quotations). Low, who later went into exile as a Loyalist, was criticized by other New York Loyalists for his role as "a speaker at all popular assemblies" in 1774; see the testimony on his claim by William Smith Jr. (quotation), AO 12/21, fol. 120, and others (ibid., 126–28).

91 **Outvoted and outmaneuvered:** For the procedures, see *AA* 4, 1:298–99. The committee arranged for the printing of a brief form to summon its members, with blanks to be filled in with appropriate meeting times (*EAI*, no. 42650). Extracts from the member Peter Van Schaack's notes of meetings between May and November 1774 are in box 5, Van Schaack Family Papers. For Gouverneur Morris's acerbic and cynical account of the process through which ordinary people were "trick[ed] . . . handsomely" in order to select a "Committee of patricians," see *AA* 4, 1:342–43.

91 **The crucial first meeting:** *AA* 4, 1:295–98 (quotations 297–98). For divisions in the committee: McDougall, "Political Memorandums," 23 May 1774, McDougall Papers. See also ibid., 21, 25 May. An anonymous New York pamphleteer writing in late May recommended the adoption of nonimportation; see *A Serious Address to the Inhabitants of the Colony of New-York* . . . (New York: John Holt, 1774). The copy at the Huntington Library has what seem to be the author's handwritten corrections.

92 **The day before that meeting:** For these exchanges, see *PIR*, 444–46, 451n21; *AA* 4, 1:302–3, 344.

92 **In Philadelphia too:** Reed to Dennis DeBerdt, 14 May 1774, in Reed, *Life of Esther Reed,* 193–94; Richard Reeve to Dartmouth, 17 June, enclosing an extract of a letter from a Philadelphia customs officer, 15 May, reel 10, no. 910, Dartmouth Papers; Wharton to Samuel Wharton, 17 May, in "Wharton Letter-Books, 33," 334–35. See also "To the Freemen of America," *PaG,* 18 May 1774 (reprint in *AA* 4, 1:335–36).

93 **Revere rode into town:** The account in this paragraph and the next three is based on three sources: *AA* 4, 1:340–42, a semiofficial narrative of the meeting; and two versions of events, one by Joseph Reed and one by Charles Thomson, which differ in some details but concur on the major points. Both appear in "[Charles] Thomson Papers," 269–73 (Reed), 274–79 (Thomson).

93 **In 1767–1768, Dickinson:** See generally David J. Jacobson, *John Dickinson and the Revolution in Pennsylvania, 1764–1776* (Berkeley: University of California Press, 1965). Dickinson's reputation for moderation was such that a rumor spread in New York to the effect that at the 20 May meeting he "declared that the Boston Port Act was a Constitutional Law," which Alexander McDougall regarded as a "Calumny" and urged its refutation. See McDougall to Charles Thomson, 1 June 1774 (draft), McDougall Papers.

93 **the plan worked perfectly:** Wharton's account: Wharton to Thomas Walpole, 31 May 1774, in "Wharton Letter-Books 33," 336–38. Another, similar account, Edward Tilghman to his father, 26 May, is printed in Stillé, *Life of Dickinson,* 107–8.

94 **The three plotters correctly predicted:** On 31 May 1774, Penn informed Dartmouth about the City Tavern meeting, assuring him that he would not summon the assembly (*DAR,* 8:119); he explained his interpretation of the participants' aims in a personal letter of the same date in "Letters of Governor Penn," 234–35. The colony's council formally rejected the call for an assembly meeting on 7 June (*AA* 4, 1:391–92). Reed's remark is in "[Charles] Thomson Papers," 272.

94 **The Philadelphia committee's letter to Boston:** Philadelphia Committee to Boston, 21 May 1774, in *RevVa,* 2:76–77, accompanying the committee's letter to Peyton Randolph of the same date. See above, on Revere's ride back to New York and thence to Boston.

94 **Philadelphian characterized:** "Extract of a Letter Received at New-York," 4 June 1774, in *AA* 4, 1:386; Daniel Dulany Jr. to Arthur Lee, May, in ibid., 354; Thomson to Adams, 3 June, SA Papers. After receiving the 21 May letter from Philadelphia, Adams wrote to Thomson on 30 May, continuing to argue for immediate nonimportation (*SA Writings,* 3:122–24). The

New Castle, Delaware, committee, under Pennsylvania's jurisdiction, was more forthright than the Philadelphians; see *RevVa*, 2:82–83.

95 **Also writing a private letter:** Reed to Dartmouth, 30 May 1774; and Dartmouth to Reed, 11 July, reel 2, nos. 980, 991, Dartmouth Papers.

95 **Philadelphia balked at signing:** See accounts in *AA* 4, 1:365; Duane, *Extracts from Diary of Marshall*, 5–6 (entries for 30 May, 1 June); undated German-language broadside (*EAI*, no. 13114), translated in Oswald Seidensticker, *The First Century of German Printing in America, 1728–1830* (Philadelphia: Schaefer & Koradi, 1893), 89.

96 **two copies of the Port Act:** Charles Steuart sent copies of the act from London to two Norfolk merchants, who each acknowledged their receipt; see William Aitchison to Steuart, 16 May 1774; and James Parker to Steuart, 17 May, reel 2, fols. 198, 200, Steuart Papers. On the routes of the documents from Philadelphia, see *RevVa*, 2:73–74.

96 **On May 19:** Quotation: Lee to Samuel Adams, 23 June 1774, in Ballagh, *Letters of Lee*, 1:111 (see also Lee to his brother Arthur, 26 June, in ibid., 1:114–17). See *VaG* (P&D), 19 May; and *RevVa*, 1:93.

96 **On May 24:** *Tuesday, the 24th of May, 14 Geo. III. 1774*, broadside proclamation of the fast day (*EAI*, no. 13746). See George Mason to Martin Cockburn, 26 May, for the mistaken expectation that the burgesses would continue to meet until late June, in Rutland, *Papers of Mason*, 1:190–91.

96 **Their caution went for naught:** For these events, see *AA* 4, 1:350–51; *RevVa*, 1:96–98, 2:84–85. Dunmore reported the developments to Dartmouth on 29 May (*DAR*, 7:110–11). Because the burgesses could not act, several Virginia counties and towns adopted resolutions of their own about the Port Act (*RevVa*, 1:152–53, 2:87, 92–97, 111). All sympathized with Boston's plight but neither defended the tea destruction nor agreed on the appropriate response.

97 **Two days later:** Quotation: Lee to Adams, 23 June 1774, in Ballagh, *Letters of Lee*, 1:113. See *RevVa*, 1:99–100, for the rump burgesses' session. According to the Baltimore committee of correspondence in mid-June, such actions fell "far short of that Spirit & Zeal" expected of Virginians; see Baltimore committee to committee of Norfolk and Portsmouth, 17 June, Purviance Papers.

97 **Marylanders acted more decisively:** The record of the Annapolis meeting is published in *RevVa*, 2:79–81; and *AA* 4, 1:352–54, including the "protest," with signatures. See also *At a Meeting of the Inhabitants of the City of Annapolis*, 25 May, broadside (*EAI*, no. 13119). William Eddis, a British official in Maryland, claimed that those who supported honorably paying their debts were seen as "inimical" to American liberty (Eddis, *Letters from*

America, 88). One Annapolis lawyer who opposed the lawsuit resolution was the future Loyalist Daniel Dulany Jr., who described the meeting in his claims memorial and testimony, AO 12/6. Residents of the larger Anne Arundel County adopted the same resolution on 4 June (*AA* 4, 1:384–86).

98 **Baltimore meeting held at the courthouse:** Quotations: Chalmers, claims memorial, 14 Oct. 1783, and undated testimony, AO 12/6. He also testified that "there had been a plot concerted to throw him out of the Court house Window" if he had spoken publicly at the meeting and claimed that he had later remained active behind the scenes by supplying "the Loyal with Arguments to enable them to support the Cause of Britain, as they used to apply to him when they were at a difficulty to answer the Arguments of their Opponents." The broadside announcing the meeting, *To the Freeholders and Gentlemen of Baltimore County,* 27 May, noted an invitation to Annapolis "Gentlemen" to attend as well (*EAI,* no. 42549). The report of the meeting is *At a General Meeting of the Freeholders,* 31 May, broadside (*EAI,* no. 13130); also *AA* 4, 1:366. Resolutions from other Maryland counties: ibid., 366, 379, 384–86, 409. The Baltimore letter pleased Dr. Joseph Warren; see his letter to Samuel Adams, 15 June, SA Papers.

98 **merchants occasionally added political comments:** Alexander Hamilton to James Brown & Co., 30 May 1774, in McMaster and Skaggs, "Letterbooks of Alexander Hamilton," 162 (see also 164); James Parker to Charles Steuart, 17 May, reel 2, fol. 201 (the Norfolk quotations), Steuart Papers.

98 **Scot in Virginia:** James Robinson to W. Cunninghame & Co., 7 June 1774, in Devine, *Scottish Firm in Virginia,* 142–43; William Reynolds to George Norton, 3 June, William Reynolds Letterbook. See also William Carr to James Russell, 26 May, bundle 2, Russell Papers; Harry Piper to Dixon & Littledale, 9 June, Harry Piper Letterbook.

99 **Virginia planters' comments:** Greene, *Diary of Landon Carter,* 2:817–19, 821 (entries for 2, 3, 8 June 1774); Gill and Curtis, *Man Apart,* 11; Farish, *Journal of Fithian,* 110, 111, 113 (entries of 29, 31 May; and to Andrew Hunter, 3 June) (see also 116, 117, 122). And see John Harrower to his wife, 14 June, in Riley, *Journal of Harrower,* 56.

99 **first news of the Port Act:** *SCG* (T), 23 May; 3, 6 June 1774; *GaG,* 8 June. See *AA* 4, 1:370, for the notice of the arrival of the Philadelphia packet of materials.

100 **Immediate reactions in South Carolina:** James Laurens to Henry, 3 June 1774, in *HL Papers,* 9:464; Gadsden to Adams, 5 June, in Walsh, *Writings of Gadsden,* 94–95 (see also 97); "Extract of a Letter Received at Philadelphia," 14 June, in *AA* 4, 1:408–9. In London in April, Henry Laurens had assumed that the tea should be paid for and offered to share the cost but

also called for a trade boycott of Britain and the West Indies (*HL Papers,* 9:387–88, 392–93).

100   **Carolinians (and Georgians):** Gadsden to Adams, 23 May, 5 June 1774, in Walsh, *Writings of Gadsden,* 93, 94; Drayton, *Memoirs,* 1:113.

101   **Coffin accordingly reported:** Coffin to Charles Steuart, 6 July 1774, reel 2, fol. 226, Steuart Papers.

101   **April 15, 1774:** For a brief account of the act's passage, see Jensen, *Founding of a Nation,* 456–60; for the exact timing of votes: *HL Papers,* 9:415n5. For the extensive debates: Simmons and Thomas, *Proceedings and Debates,* 4:158–78, 262–81, 285–95, 299–317, 329–83.

101   **April 21:** For "Murther Bill," see William Lee to Thomas Cushing, 1 June 1774, CO 5/118; and "Murder Act," Samuel Adams to Arthur Lee, 29 Jan. 1775, in *SA Writings,* 3:170. See Simmons and Thomas, *Proceedings and Debates,* 4:260–61, 283–85, 384–405, 431–35.

102   **April 16–May 11:** Laurens to John Lewis Gervais, 16 April 1774, in *HL Papers,* 9:415; Franklin to Thomas Cushing, 16 April, in *BF Papers,* 21:192. The 11 May petition has been published in both *HL Papers,* 9:445–48 (see also a 19 May petition to the king, ibid., 458–59), and *BF Papers,* 21:214–16. For two colonial agents' reports on their futile attempts to oppose the acts, see William Bollan to the Massachusetts council, 30 April, Misc. MSS Bound; and same to same, 12 May, *Bowdoin and Temple Papers,* 367–71; and Charles Garth to South Carolina assembly committee of correspondence, 21, 30 April, 12 May, all in Charles Garth (Committee of Correspondence) Papers. For Massachusetts's reply to Bollan, 10 June: *PIR,* 392–94.

102   **May 7:** Laurens to James, 7 May 1774, in *HL Papers,* 9:434–35.

102   **May 20:** See above, April 15, 21.

103   **June 3:** Dartmouth to Gage, 3 June 1774, in *DAR,* 8:122–25, not received until 6 Aug. Also published in *PIR,* 502–5, and *AA* 4, 1:380–82.

103   **Bostonians had heard rumors:** The rumors, which began arriving in late April in a private letter to Samuel Adams and which started appearing in print in early May, are traced in *PIR,* 448n21. The "extracts" from the London letters of early April, published as a broadside by John Holt in New York on 14 May (see above), which mentioned a possible "extraordinary" new law "more general in its operation" than the Port Act, were reprinted in *BG* on 23 May.

103   **implementation of the Port Act:** Quotations: John Andrews to William Barrell, 18 May 1774, in "Andrews Letters," 328; Gage to Dartmouth, 19 May, in Carter, *Correspondence of Gage,* 1:355. See also *Rowe Diary,* 270–71 (entries of 10, 14, 17 May); and *PIR,* 56–57.

103 **newly elected assembly:** *PIR,* 159, 162–63, events reported without comment in the Boston newspapers of 30 May 1774. The assembly asked Gage to declare a fast day, but he refused; see *PIR,* 169, 245; and Gage to Dartmouth, 31 May, in *DAR,* 8:117–18.

104 **Massachusetts ritual:** This and the next two paragraphs are based on *PIR,* 299–322 (quotations 299n, 300, 312, 317–18, 321). Gad Hitchcock, *A Sermon Preached Before His Excellency Thomas Gage, Esq.; Governor: . . . May 25th 1774,* was published in Boston by Edes & Gill, 1774. On the origins of the election sermon tradition, see T. H. Breen, *The Character of the Good Ruler: A Study of Puritan Political Ideas in New England, 1630–1730* (New Haven, Conn.: Yale University Press, 1970).

104 **"high Discourse suitable to his Party":** *Rowe Diary,* 271 (entry of 25 May 1774).

105 **In that note:** John Lathrop, *A Sermon Preached to the Ancient and Honorable Artillery-Company in Boston . . . June 6th 1774* (Boston: Kneeland and Davis, 1774), 21n–22n. Unlike Israel Holly, then, he did not retreat when questioned by a listener about his political statements.

105 **The theme of the sermon:** Ibid., quotations: 26–28.

106 **Lathrop made it clear:** Ibid., 35n.

106 **usually sure-footed Samuel Adams:** In her superb short study of Adams, included in *Old Revolutionaries,* 20, Pauline Maier commented that at this juncture Adams made one of the few serious mistakes of his long career. Brown, *Revolutionary Politics,* 191, also noted a "tactical blunder." Neither author suggested a reason why Adams and the committee erred.

106 **identified the key problem:** Chauncy to Richard Price, 30 May 1774, in "Price Letters," 267. See also Chauncy's anonymously published pamphlet, which, although dated 30 May, contained material added after 1 June: *A Letter to a Friend. Giving a Concise, but Just, Representation of the Hardships and Sufferings the Town of Boston Is Exposed To . . .* (Boston: Greenleaf, 1774).

106 **The committee made its reasoning:** The letter to Colrain (a town in northwestern Massachusetts), 18 July 1774: *PIR,* 745. For Adams's 1773 statement, see chapter 1, above.

107 **need to act swiftly:** See *Rowe Diary,* 273–74 (entry of 2 June); *RevVa,* 2:113; and Bouton, *Documents of New-Hampshire,* 7:406.

107 **At a town meeting:** Quotations: "Extract of a Letter Received in Philadelphia," 2 June 1774, in *AA* 4, 1:380; Coffin to Charles Steuart, 6 July, reel 2, fol. 226, Steuart Papers. The 30 May meeting: *PIR,* 438; the drafting of the Covenant and the origins of the title: Brown, *Revolutionary Politics,* 190–91. The published statement: "To the Free and Brave Americans," *MSpy,* 9 June. John Andrews later explained that he did not see the Covenant "till

near a month after it had been circulated through the country" (Andrews to William Barrell, 22 July, in "Andrews Letters," 330).

107 **The Covenant itself described:** The Solemn League and Covenant: *PIR*, 458–59, 499–501; the circular letter, ibid., 453–55. Two major versions of the agreement circulated in the colony, along with other variants. See, for instance, a brief one, *EG*, 26 July 1774; and a longer agreement drafted in Berkshire County, 8 July, with twenty-eight signatures, including two from women, in oversize box, Sedgwick Papers. Scholars disagree about which widely circulated version was Boston's and which was produced a few days later in Worcester; one version contained an oath (*EAI*, no. 13163), the other a second deadline of 1 October (*EAI*, no. 13427), after which signers pledged not to purchase items imported before 31 August as well. See the discussions in *PIR*, 456–57n37; Albert Matthews, "The Solemn League and Covenant, 1774," *Pubs CSM* 18 (1915–1916): 103–22; and Brown, *Revolutionary Politics*, 191–93, 205–6.

109 **Most Bay Colony towns:** The second circular letter, 10 June, appeared as a broadside (*EAI*, no. 42756), also in *PIR*, 459–60. Summaries of towns' reactions: Brown, *Revolutionary Politics*, 200–209; Matthews, "Solemn League," 109, 112, 118–21. For contemporary comments, pro and con: *PIR*, 564–65, 567–69, 589, 709–12, 714–30, 734–37, 746–49, 754, 763, 774–75; Gray, *Few Remarks*, 7–8. For a later negative assessment of the Covenant, see Adair and Schutz, *Peter Oliver's Origin & Progress*, 103–5.

109 **In early July:** Coffin to Charles Steuart, 6 July 1774, reel 2, fol. 227, Steuart Papers. Coffin's letters to Steuart provide detailed summaries of events in Boston during the summer of 1774 from a conservative perspective, but historians have used them infrequently. See, though, Colin Nicolson, " 'McIntosh, Otis, and Adams Are Our Demagogues': Nathaniel Coffin and the Loyalist Interpretation of the Origins of the American Revolution," *Procs MHS* 108 (1996): 72–114, a study of all his extant letters to Steuart.

109 **"man of influence":** Quotations and information in this and the next two paragraphs are from Belknap's statement, 28 June 1774, and related documents in *Procs MHS* 22 (1885–1886): 481–86. He was responding to a copy of the Covenant distributed by the committee of Portsmouth, New Hampshire, which mimicked Boston's (probably *EAI*, no. 42748). The clergyman also raised a series of practical objections, among them that the Covenant's wording was too vague; that it was likely to fail unless other colonies agreed; that it would harm patriotic merchants who would not have time to countermand orders for the fall; and that it would unnecessarily create "animosities" within colonial communities.

110 **Shortly after Belknap:** They were not the only contemporaries to voice

such views. See, for example, *PIR,* 717, 734–35; and Brown, *Revolutionary Politics,* 200–209. Norton, "Seventh Tea Ship," 698, 702–4, presents a more detailed account of Greenough's concerns about "private men" and their actions on Cape Cod.

110 **Representatives created controversy:** Quotations: Gage to Dartmouth, 26 June 1774, in *DAR,* 8:136; Gage's reply to the Council, 14 June, in *PIR,* 273. See *PIR,* 179–81, 184–86, 255–57, on the beginnings of the legislative session.

110 **deliberately deceptive:** Robert Treat Paine, "Narrative of Proceedings of General Court, 1774," ca. 1795, in *RTP Papers,* 2:544–46.

111 **proposals for a congress:** Deane to Samuel H. Parsons, 13 April [that is, June] 1774, in "Deane Correspondence," 130, 129; Deane to Boston committee of correspondence, 13 June 1774, in Ford, *Correspondence of Webb,* 1:28. For his 13 June letter to Virginia's committee: *RevVa,* 2:115; the Rhode Island assembly also supported a congress at the same time (ibid., 2:120–21). Although still promoting immediate nonimportation, Samuel Adams admitted when answering a Deane letter of 26 May that a congress would be necessary; see *SA Writings,* 3:125–26.

111 **marathon closed-door session:** The 17 June records are in *PIR,* 223–33, 293–95; Deane letter from early June is in *AA* 4, 1:304–5. The motion for the congress was adopted by a vote of 128–12. The delegates elected were James Bowdoin, Thomas Cushing, Samuel and John Adams, and Robert Treat Paine. For details of the pretense, see Paine's narrative, cited above.

111 **flurry of resolutions:** For the circumstances of the dissolution: *PIR,* 232–34, 296.

112 **Boston, meanwhile, was dealing:** *Rowe Diary,* 275 (entry of 12 June 1774); John Andrews to William Barrell, 12 June, in "Andrews Letters," 330; Coffin to Charles Steuart, 6 July, reel 2, fol. 226, Steuart Papers; Henry Caner to John Wentworth, 16 June, in *Letterbook of Caner.* See also "Diary of Newell," 353 (entry of 15 June).

112 **cope with changes:** See, on these points, *PIR,* 423, 435; American Board of Customs Commissioners to Attorney General Jonathan Sewall, 30 June 1774, enclosing questions, T 1/505, fols. 248–68; Thomas Greenough, Ledger ("An Acct of what moneys I have or may recive [*sic*] from the Charity Meeting in Fanueil Hall began June 5th 1774"), HM 70285, Greenough Family Papers. On 6 June, he recorded his first outlays, a total of £13.16 given to eight women, five of whom he identified as widows.

112 **Debates roiled the blockaded town:** Andrews to William Barrell, 12 June 1774, in "Andrews Letters," 329; Warren to Hannah Q. Lincoln, 12 June, in Richards and Harris, *Warren Letters,* 30.

112 **Many Bostonians took:** Coffin to Charles Steuart, 6 July 1774, reel 2, fol.

226, Steuart Papers; William Greenough to Thomas Greenough, 22 June, John Greenough Papers.

113 **So on June 15:** Coffin to Charles Steuart, 6 July 1774, reel 2, fol. 226, Steuart Papers; Young to John Lamb, 19 June, Lamb Papers; Warren to Adams, 15 June, SA Papers ("Altercations"); *Rowe Diary,* 275 (entry of 15 June); Gray, *Few Remarks,* 6.

113 **Newspapers were filled with debates:** Cincinnatus, "For the Massachusetts Spy," *MSpy,* 16 June 1774, responding to Mercator, quoted internally. Cincinnatus defended the tea's destruction yet was willing to contemplate the prospect of paying for it.

113 **Other authors acknowledged:** *MG&BNL,* 16 June 1774. Gage was heartened by the public efforts to persuade the town to comply with the act; see Gage to Dartmouth, 26 June, *DAR,* 8:137.

114 **June 17 town meeting:** The official town meeting record: *PIR,* 439–40; a brief newspaper report, *BG* (supp.), 20 June 1774. Young's comments: Young to John Lamb, 19 June 1774, Lamb Papers. An edited version of Young's letter was published in *NYJ,* 30 June, and reprinted in *AA* 4, 1:429–30. The Sandemanians composed a small religious sect with unusual beliefs; many eventually ended up as Loyalists.

114 **After the meeting:** Young to John Lamb, 26 June 1774, Lamb Papers. See Nathaniel Coffin to Charles Steuart, 6 July, reel 2, fol. 226, Steuart Papers; and Henry Hulton to ———, 19 June, in York, *Henry Hulton,* 303, on the merchants' plans. Plymouth conservatives expected the committee's critics to win (James Warren to Samuel Adams, 10 July 1774, SA Papers).

115 **The newspaper debates continued:** Y.Z., untitled essay addressed to the printers, *MG&BPB,* 20 June 1774; two untitled and unsigned essays in *MG&BNL,* 23 June. For one town's concerns about possible internal divisions caused by nonsigners of the Covenant: *PIR,* 783.

115 **defense of the committee:** *SA Writings,* 3:130–33, reprinting essay from *BG,* 27 June 1774.

117 **The town meeting convened:** Quotations: *PIR,* 674n67, quoting from the committee's letters; Jonathan Williams to John Adams, 28 June 1774, in *JA Papers,* 2:102–4; John Andrews to William Barrell, 22 July, in "Andrews Letters," 331. The succinct official record is in *PIR,* 627–30; and *AA* 4, 1:489–90. See also the accounts of this critical meeting in Brown, *Revolutionary Politics,* 196–99; and of the May–June debates in general in Stephen E. Patterson, *Political Parties in Revolutionary Massachusetts* (Madison: University of Wisconsin Press, 1973), 74–90.

117 **The debate raged on until dark:** Jonathan Williams to John Adams, 28 June 1774, in *JA Papers,* 2:102–4; *Rowe Diary,* 276 (entry of 27 June listing some of the debaters). On Erving's role, see Henry Hulton to ———,

19 June, in York, *Henry Hulton,* 303. The committee itself described the debate as "very fair & free"; see its letter to Silas Deane, 28 June, in Ford, *Correspondence of Webb,* 1:35. John Adams was attending court sessions elsewhere in Massachusetts.

118 **wrote John Andrews proudly:** Andrews to William Barrell, 22 July 1774, in "Andrews Letters," 331–32.

118 **When the debate finally ended:** Town meeting record, 28 June 1774, in *PIR,* 630; Coffin to Charles Steuart, 6 July, reel 2, fol. 227, Steuart Papers. See Andrews to William Barrell, 22 July, in "Andrews Letters," 331. John Rowe aligned himself with the committee's opponents; see *Rowe Diary,* 276–77 (entry of 28 June, counting the majority as four to one against his position).

119 **The mercantile minority:** John Adams to Abigail Adams, 1 July 1774, in *AFC* 1:118, quoting Dr. Silvester Gardiner; "Protest Against the Proceedings of the Town Meeting in Boston, on the 27th of June, 1774," *MG&BNL,* 7 July 1774, printed in *AA* 4, 1:490, with 129 signatures. One contemporary, the Reverend William Clarke, noted that some of the signers "have heretofore been high in Liberty Schemes"; see Crary, *Price of Loyalty,* 26. A new broadside appeared, listing both the Addressers and these "Protesters"; see *Procs MHS* 11 (1869–1870): 392–95.

119 **Eight other dissidents:** Untitled statement, *BEP,* 4 July 1774; also in *MG&BNL,* 7 July. Signed by Edward Payne, Caleb Blanchard, Frederick William Geyer, and Samuel Bradstreet in addition to those mentioned in the text; none of the signers of this document also signed the other one.

119 **Fifty-two residents of Worcester:** Untitled statement, *BG,* 4 July 1774; *EG,* 5 July. See Raphael, *First American Revolution,* 43–45.

120 **his enraged, though delayed, reaction:** Thomas Gage, "Proclamation Against Illegal Combinations," 29 June 1774, in *PIR,* 545–46 (also published in *AA* 4, 1:491–92); Gage to Dartmouth, 5 July, in *DAR,* 8:140. Justices of the peace in Pittsfield explained to Gage on 15 July that they could not enforce the proclamation without lessening their authority, as well as the governor's (*PIR,* 579–80).

120 **No one ever seems to have been arrested:** Samuel Goodwin, memorial to Thomas Gage, 10 Aug. 1774, in *PIR,* 598; Warren to Adams, 10 July, SA Papers; Coffin to Charles Steuart, 6 July, reel 2, fol. 227, Steuart Papers. "Extract of a Letter Received in New-York, Dated Boston, July 3, 1774," claimed the same—that the effect of the proclamation was "quite contrary to the design of it" (*AA* 4, 1:505, from *NYJ,* 14 July), as did Henry Knox to James Rivington, 18 July, Bookseller Letterbook, Knox Papers II.

121 **Covenant failed:** *PIR,* 567 (Easton), 564 (Pownalborough), 589 (Bowdoinham), 789 (Palmer). For an exception (by Gloucester, of items needed

for the fisheries): ibid., 810. In one town, the Covenant was rumored to be a "Trick" by Boston merchants to enable them to sell their current stock of goods at "an exorbitant Rate" by halting further imports; see *SA Writings*, 3:145.

121 **debates in Boston persisted:** B, "To Mr. Edward Payne and the Seven Other Protesters Against the Proceedings of the Town at Their Late Meeting," *BEP,* 18 July 1774. For a defense of destroying the tea, see "A Farmer," *BG,* 4 July; on behalf of paying for it, a purported letter from a member of the New York committee of fifty-one, ibid.; for an attack on the Covenant, see a front-page unsigned essay directed to "Mess'rs Printers," *MG&BNL,* 7 July (also in *BEP,* 4 July).

121 **Newspaper coverage:** Copies of the protest: *NPkt,* 7 July 1774; *NYG,* 11 July; *PaG,* 20 July (postscript); *SCG* (W), 26 Aug. The report charging "virulent abuse" of the committee: *NPkt,* 7 July; *CtJ,* 8 July; *SCG* (T), 26 Sept. Connecticut newspapers tended to print the minutes of the 27–28 June meeting and the Covenant, sometimes along with pro-Covenant commentary (for example, *NPkt,* 7 July). Coverage was rare in the New York papers, but *NYJ* printed Gage's proclamation, 7 July; and *NYG* printed the Covenant with negative commentary, 11 July. *VaG* (P&D), 21 July, conflated reports of the two town meetings of June, making it seem as though there was no dissent, and on 4 August claimed the Covenant had "scarce a Dissentient in many Towns." *VaG* (R) carried a story to the same effect on 11 August. The three Charleston papers had varied coverage: *SCG* (C), 16 Aug., printed Gage's proclamation but not the Covenant, along with a very brief account of the town meeting; *SCG* (T), 26 Sept., published the minutes and pro-Covenant comments; and *SCG* (W), the most conservative of the three, printed the Covenant, the cover letter, and Gage's proclamation (12 Aug.), followed by the minutes and the long protest on 26 August.

122 **the message conveyed:** Samuel Adams too did not disclose negative reactions to the Covenant when he wrote to allies in other colonies; see Adams to Christopher Gadsden, 18 July 1774, in *SA Writings*, 3:144.

CHAPTER 4 TIMES OF PERPLEXITY, DANGER, AND DISTRESS

123 **From late June through mid-July:** Quotations, in order: John to Abigail, 29 June 1774, in *AFC,* 1:110; same to same, 5, 6 July, in ibid., 124, 126–27. Adams was referring to events of 1765 (the destruction of Thomas Hutchinson's house) and 1770 (the death of a young boy, shot by Ebenezer Richardson, and the Boston Massacre). See Hoerder, *Crowd Action,* 101–10, 220–34. For his reports of other political conversations in Maine: *AFC,* 1:118, 120, 128, 130–31.

124 "These private Mobs": Quotations in this paragraph and the next: John to Abigail, 7 July 1774, in *AFC,* 1:132.

124 **While on his journey:** John to Abigail, 2 July 1774, in *AFC,* 1:121; John to Joseph Hawley, 27 June, in *JA Papers,* 2:101; John to Abigail, 6 July, in *AFC,* 1:129, 127. See also *JA Papers,* 2:99. In mid-July, the Reverend Charles Chauncy noted that other colonies had accepted the time and place for the congress designated by the Massachusetts assembly before Gage dissolved it; see Chauncy to Richard Price, 18 July, in "Price Letters," 269.

125 **other Americans' conversations:** For other accounts of events in the summer of 1774, see Ammerman, *Common Cause,* chaps. 2, 3; Rakove, *Beginnings of National Politics,* chap. 2.

125 **"We have been almost stunn'd":** Observator to Mr. Draper, *MG&BNL,* 25 Feb. 1773 (supp.). See also Publicus, "To the Good People of Pennsylvania," *DPaPkt,* 11 Jan. 1773 (supp.), asking for a definition of "unconstitutional."

125 **rise of a neologism:** This statement rests on my keyword search for "unconstitutional" in the America's Historical Newspapers (hereafter AHN) database, accessed on several days in February 2013. Examples of usage before 1765 include a quotation from Ireland in *BEP,* 3 June 1754, and a comment from the House of Commons about the Jamaica assembly in *NYG,* 17 Sept. 1757. Such searches are incomplete because the database does not include all colonial newspapers and because the search engine occasionally errs, but they do expose general patterns and trends.

125 **began to deem those statutes:** According to *The Oxford English Dictionary* (*OED*) in an entry unrevised since 1921, the word first appeared in English in 1734. Unfortunately, the definition of its obvious counterpart, "constitutional" in a political sense, remains unrevised since the first edition in 1893 and so its usage cannot be traced accurately (personal communication from the editors, Feb. 2013; confirmed as an unrevised entry in *OED* online, June 2019). For American colonists' understanding of "constitutional," see Jack P. Greene, *The Constitutional Origins of the American Revolution* (New York: Cambridge University Press, 2011).

125 **Colonial authors:** My 2013 keyword search in the AHN database produced high numbers of 56 examples in 1765, 82 in 1769, 68 in 1773, and 162 in 1774. The word was used rarely in *EAI* publications throughout the period.

126 **resist the Tea Act:** For a few examples, among many others, see "By the Eastern Mail," *CtG,* 4 Feb. 1774; "At a Meeting of the Freeholders and Others . . . of the County of Chesterfield," *VaG* (R), 21 July; "At a Provincial Meeting of Delegates [Philadelphia]," *NYJ,* 28 July; and "A Constitutional Catechism," repeatedly reprinted and cited in chapter 1, above.

126 **mused about the validity:** Drinker, *Observations on the Late Popular Measures,* 21.

126 **Colonial representatives:** But keyword searches in AHN for 1774 produced no associations of the congresses of 1754 and 1765 with that of 1774 (accessed 13 July 2016 and 13 Jan. 2018). For a useful discussion of Americans' earlier experiences with congresses, see Rakove, *Beginnings of National Politics,* chap. 1. For the choice of delegates to the Stamp Act Congress, see C. A. Weslager, *The Stamp Act Congress* (Newark: University of Delaware Press, 1976), chap. 2.

127 **"late burgesses":** For Virginia, see chapter 3, above.

127 **informal gathering:** *To the Representatives of the Freemen of the Counties of Chester, Bucks, and Philadelphia . . . ,* 9 May 1774, broadside (*EAI,* no. 13678). The authors of this broadside, who signed themselves "A Great Number of Your Constituents," were concerned about another political matter, not a potential congress, but the same reasoning applied.

127 **governors clearly understood:** Franklin to Dartmouth, 31 May 1774, in *DAR,* 8:118–19; Wentworth to same, 8 June, in ibid., 129; Colden to same, 1 June, in ibid., 122. See also Sir James Wright to same, 24 Aug., in ibid., 162, in which Wright referred to the dangers posed by "private" men calling others to meetings he could not prevent. By late June, Franklin had decided that a "properly authorized" congress composed of governors and representatives from each colony might be useful in effecting reconciliation (Franklin to Dartmouth, 28 June, in ibid., 8:138).

128 **The novel issue forced colonists:** A Friend to G[eorgia], *To the Worthy Freeholders, and Others, Inhabitants of the Province of Georgia,* Savannah, 25 July 1774, broadside (*EAI,* no. 42721); "To the Inhabitants of the British Colonies in America," *RNYG,* 7 July. See also Wells, *Few Political Reflections,* 59; and Drinker, *Observations on the Late Popular Measures,* 22–23.

128 **Philadelphia tradesmen:** *To the Manufacturers and Mechanics of Philadelphia . . . ,* New York, 8 June 1774, broadside (*EAI,* no. 13664); *AA* 4, 1:406, reprinting an account from *VaG* (R), 23 June. The New York artisans were obviously trying to circumvent the more conservative committee of fifty-one, and remarkably they referred to Bostonians as their "countrymen," a term usually employed for men from the same colony. For the more common usage of "countrymen," see the statement adopted by the "late burgesses" of Virginia on 26 May, in which the term obviously designated Virginians. That statement was widely reprinted in the colonies (for example, *DPaPkt,* 6 June). See also Charles S. Olton, "Philadelphia's Mechanics in the First Decade of Revolution, 1765–1775," *JAH* 59 (1972): 311–26, esp. 323–25.

128 **"respectable Inhabitants":** *At a Meeting at the Philosophical Society's*

Hall... (10–11 June 1774), broadside (*EAI*, no. 13534). Thomas Wharton took part; see his letter to his brother Samuel, 5 July, in "Wharton Letter-Books 33," 436–37. See also Joseph Reed to Lord Dartmouth, 10 June, in Reed, *Life of Joseph Reed*, 1:69; and Duane, *Extracts from Diary of Marshall*, 7 (entries of 9, 10 June).

128 **results of the men's deliberations:** *Meeting at the Philosophical Society's Hall*..., broadside (*EAI*, no. 13534); *AA* 4, 1:405. A brief broadside headed *Philadelphia (Saturday), June 18, 1774* (*EAI*, no. 42670), indicated that only voters "qualified by Law" would be welcome. See also Duane, *Extracts from Diary of Marshall*, 7 (entry of 22 June); Penn to Lord Dartmouth, 5 July, in *DAR*, 8:141–43; and "Letters of Governor Penn," 235–37 (letter of 24 June).

129 **Thomas Willing and John Dickinson:** "The Speech of the Reverend William Smith, D.D., Provost of the College of Philadelphia, at the Very Numerous Meeting of the Freeholders and Freemen . . . ," 18 June 1774, in *AA* 4, 1:427; "At a Very Large and Respectable Meeting . . . ," 18 June, in ibid., 426 (also broadside, *EAI*, no. 42666). For comments on methods of choosing delegates, see untitled essay, Philadelphia, 22 June, in *AA* 4, 1:441; a dispute involving Galloway, in ibid., 485–86; [Thomson Mason], "The British American, no. V," 30 June, in *RevVa*, 1:177; and *RevVa*, 2:125 (North Carolina committee of correspondence, 21 June).

129 **The committee of forty-four:** See Isaac Howell to John Lamb, 29 June 1774, Lamb Papers. After the Philadelphia meeting, John Dickinson, Thomas Mifflin, and Charles Thomson, "under colour of an excursion of pleasure," traveled to several frontier counties populated by German settlers to learn their political views prior to the July meetings. See "[Charles] Thomson Papers," 279; and, in general, John B. Frantz and William Pencak, eds., *Beyond Philadelphia: The American Revolution in the Pennsylvania Hinterland* (University Park: Pennsylvania State University Press, 1998).

130 **June 22, 1774:** Parliament debated the Quebec Act at length in May and June; see Simmons and Thomas, *Proceedings and Debates*, 4:442–75, 484–501; 5:3–233. The king's statement on the act, 22 June, is 5:233–34.

130 **July 6:** Dartmouth to Gage, 6 July 1774, in *DAR*, 8:143.

131 **July 25:** Lee to Adams, 25 July 1774, SA Papers. A version of this letter is in *AA* 4, 1:701. See also William's brother Arthur to a third brother, Richard Henry Lee, 30 July 1774, Lee Family Papers, 1, box 4, Brock Collection, on current opinions in England about the controversies.

131 **August 3:** Dartmouth to Gage, 3 Aug. 1774, reel 2, no. 1001, Dartmouth Papers.

132 **two additional statutes:** See "Advices from London," chap. 3, above. For

"Murder Act," see, for example, Thomas Nelson Jr. to Thomas & Rowland Hunt, 7 Aug. 1774, Thomas and William Nelson Letterbook; Marblehead committee to Boston committee, 28 July, in *PIR,* 758.

132 **Information about the two statutes' provisions:** Baltimore committee to committee of Norfolk-Portsmouth, 17 June 1774, Samuel Purviance Papers; John Winthrop to Richard Price, 20 Sept., in "Price Letters," 272–73. Samuel Adams, though, at first expressed uncertainty about how the other colonies would interpret the two laws; see Adams to Richard Henry Lee, 15 July, in *SA Writings,* 3:137–38.

133 **negative consensus on the acts:** *Stiles Diary,* 1:443 (entry of 15 June 1774; see also entries for 9, 14 July, 448–49); George Clymer to Josiah Quincy Jr., 13 June, in *AA* 4, 1:407; *Smith Memoirs,* 1:188 (entry of 4 June, quoting John Watts).

134 **Likewise, an Alexandria, Virginia, merchant:** Harry Piper to Dixon & Littledale, 25 July 1774, Harry Piper Letterbook; Adam Stephen to Richard Henry Lee, 27 Aug., in Hoffman, *Lee Family Papers,* reel 2, frame 1234; Gage to Dartmouth, 20 Sept., in *DAR,* 8:198. See also a letter from Maryland, 31 Aug., forwarded to Lord Dartmouth by William Molleson, reel 11, no. 953, Dartmouth Papers. As late as 1 August, Bostonians still did not have official confirmation of the acts' adoption; see John Andrews to William Barrell on that date, in "Andrews Letters," 333.

134 **New Castle, Delaware, committeemen:** "To the Gentlemen, Freeholders, and Others, in the County of New-Castle, upon Delaware . . . ," 17 June 1774, in *AA* 4, 1:419; Hopkinson, *Pretty Story,* 32, for quotation.

134 **local meetings convened in colonies:** Jerrilyn Marston compiled a list of 99 such local meetings, starting with a few in New England in mid- to late May and ending with some in North Carolina in late August. South Carolinians and Georgians met only in general congresses in Charleston (July) and Savannah (August). Most of the meetings occurred in July. See Marston, *King and Congress,* 313–17 (app.), with a total of 108, including 9 provincial conventions excluded from my count of 99 local meetings.

135 **a mix of common elements:** Copies of many sets of these resolves are in *AA* 4, 1:402 (Harford County, Md., 11 June)–618 (Wilmington, N.C., 21 July). August resolutions from North Carolina are in Saunders, *Colonial Records,* 9:1031–38. One Virginia county, Dunmore, uniquely copied the resolves of another (Frederick); see *AA* 4, 1:392, 417; *RevVa,* 1:122–23, 135–36. Almost all the known Virginia resolves are published in *RevVa,* 1:109–68.

135 **One Philadelphian:** Thomas Fisher to Miers Fisher, 2 July 1774, Fisher Family Collection. For a good brief introduction to the situation in Virginia in June and July, see *RevVa,* 1:105–8; see also *AA* 4, 1:523.

135 **resolves adopted in those Virginia meetings:** The resolves tabulated here are those published in *RevVa*, vol. 1, with the exception of resolves from Isle of Wight County not included in that volume or in *AA* 4, vol. 1. That document is located in box 258, Brock Collection. Prince George resolves, including comments about encouraging manufacturing and raising sheep and flax to compensate for the loss of imports: *RevVa*, 1:150–52; Chesterfield County: ibid., 1:116–18; Fairfax County: ibid., 1:127–33. Some counties immediately began collecting the promised aid (for example, *AA* 4, 1:517–18, 593).

136 **youthful but politically savvy:** Madison to William Bradford, 1 July 1774, in *JM Papers,* 1:115.

136 **Even more fundamental disagreements:** Essex: *RevVa*, 1:125–27; Middlesex: ibid., 143–45; Hanover: ibid., 139–41; Dinwiddie: ibid., 120–22; Norfolk, *AA* 4, 1:518; Parker to Charles Steuart, 17 June 1774, reel 2, fol. 206, Steuart Papers. Edmund Pendleton agreed with the Middlesex County position; see his letter to Joseph Chew, 20 June (David John Mays, ed., *The Letters and Papers of Edmund Pendleton 1734–1803* [Charlottesville: University Press of Virginia, 1967], 1:93). A few counties (for example, Isle of Wight) proposed a nonconsumption agreement for tea and other EIC items (box 258, Brock Collection).

137 **Scots schoolteacher:** Quotations: "Extract of a Letter from a Gentleman in Westmoreland County," in *RevVa*, 2:135–36; Dr. Walter Jones to Landon Carter, 17 June 1774, in Hoffman et al., *Carter Family Papers,* reel 1, frame 1789; Parker to Charles Steuart, 16 July, reel 2, fol. 231, Steuart Papers; John Saunders: *RevVa*, 2:222–23.

137 **Robert Beverley:** Beverley to Carter, 28 Aug. 1774, enclosing a copy of his resolutions, Robert Beverley Letters. In a note on the page, Carter indicated that he found the delegation idea "weak." Cf. the Essex resolves as adopted, in *RevVa*, 1:125–27. See also Beverley's earlier comments on the drafting and reception of his resolutions in a letter to Carter, 27 July, in Hoffman et al., *Carter Family Papers,* reel 1, frames 1799–1800; and his later letter to a London correspondent advocating a delegation to the king, 6 Sept., Robert Beverley Letterbook. See Robert M. Calhoon, " 'Unhinging Former Intimacies': Robert Beverley's Perception of the Prerevolutionary Controversy, 1761–1775," in Calhoon et al., *Tory Insurgents,* 89–108.

138 **exchange of letters:** The Fairfax resolves are printed in both *GW Papers: CS,* 10:119–27 (see also ibid., 112); and Rutland, *Papers of Mason,* 1:201–9. Rutland believes that Mason was the principal author (see notes, ibid., 1:199–201, 209–20).

138 **Bryan Fairfax:** Fairfax to Washington, 17 July 1774, in *GW Papers: CS,*

10:114–18 (quotations 116, 117–18). John Dickinson too favored a petition to the king before any other option was pursued; see Thomas Mifflin to Samuel Adams, 30 July, SA Papers.

139 **Washington insisted:** Washington to Fairfax, 20 July 1774, in *GW Papers: CS,* 10:129–30; Fairfax to Washington, 5 Aug., in ibid., 144. Fairfax's long letter, covering pp. 143–50, continued the dialogue, explaining his position further, expressing his concern that people found his ideas "repugnant," and adding another account of dissent—in the Middlesex County meeting (145–46). Washington replied curtly on 24 August (ibid., 154–56).

139 **Not all the dissidents:** Alexander Hamilton to James Brown & Co., 6 Aug. 1774, in McMaster and Skaggs, "Letterbooks of Alexander Hamilton," 312. The Albemarle resolutions are in *RevVa,* 1:112–13. See also a brief reference to a like discussion in Anne Arundel County, Maryland, in *AA* 4, 1:385.

139 **veneer of unanimity:** Quotation: John Pringle to William Tilghman, 30 July 1774, Preston Davie Papers. On agreement about taxation, see, for example, the Georgia broadside of 25 July cited above, *To the Worthy Freeholders . . .* (*EAI,* no. 42721), which criticized "outrages" against the property of the EIC, yet also adopted the "British Parliament" terminology and declared that Britain could not tax the colonies. James Parker, a future Loyalist, agreed; see Parker to Charles Steuart, 17 June, reel 2, fols. 206–7, Steuart Papers.

140 **opinions continued to differ:** William Franklin to his father, 3 July 1774, in *BF Papers,* 21:238; Benjamin to William, 7 Sept., in ibid., 287 (see also 323); Wells, *Few Political Reflections,* 11; Yet a Free Citizen, "To the People of Pennsylvania," *PaJ,* 20 July; untitled essay from New Jersey, 25 July, in *AA* 4, 1:636–37. One of Henry Laurens's correspondents mimicked Benjamin, changing from supporting payment to opposing it (*HL Papers,* 9:533). William Franklin privately approved the Port Act (*BF Papers,* 21:314–15). For Benjamin's original position, see above, chapter 2. Robert Beverley predictably critiqued both the Bostonians, whom he declared had acted "imprudently & unjustly," and the ministry, which had responded "tyrannically & oppressively" (Beverley to Landon Carter, 9 June, Beverley Letters, a-16).

140 **major debate erupted:** Both pamphlets have been conveniently reprinted in *RevVa,* vol. 1. For Randolph, see 204–18 (quotations, 212–13); for Nicholas's *Considerations on the Present State of Virginia Examined,* 257–85 (quotations, 261, 271, 273). Randolph wrote after 1 June and probably before Dunmore's departure on 10 July; Nicholas wrote before the 1 August meeting of the Virginia convention (see ibid., 277), but the pamphlet was not advertised for sale until 25 August. Both were published anonymously,

but the authorship was widely known. Only Nicholas mentioned (briefly) the two later Coercive Acts; at the time both men penned their pamphlets, the news of their final approval by the king had not yet arrived in the colonies.

141 **brig *Mary and Jane:*** For the *Mary and Jane: AA* 4, 1:703–5, 727–28. For the tea in Salem: *PIR,* 694, 829. And for New Hampshire's insistence in mid-September that thirty chests on board the ship *Fox* be sent to Halifax: *DAR,* 8:196.

141 ***Magna Charta:*** Bull to Dartmouth, 3 July 1774, in *DAR,* 8:154; Drayton, *Memoirs,* 1:134 (see 132–35).

141 **Richard Maitland's difficulties:** James Laurens to Henry Laurens, 22 July 1774, in *HL Papers,* 9:526 (see 524–27).

142 **Laurens thus pointed:** For examples of the discussion in print of the relative merits of nonimportation alone, or with the addition of nonexportation, see *AA* 4, 1:508–12, 620–24, 647, 753–54; Brutus, *To the Free and Loyal Inhabitants of the City and Colony of New-York,* broadside (*EAI,* no. 13180); and Wells, *Few Political Reflections,* 6–11, 18–27, 52–57, 62–74. For comments in personal correspondence: James Laurens to Henry Laurens, 21 June 1774, in *HL Papers,* 9:477; William Hooper to James Iredell, 21 June, in Higginbotham, *Papers of Iredell,* 1:240; Robert Beverley to Landon Carter, 18 June, Beverley Letters, a-17; Joseph Reed to Lord Dartmouth, 26 July, reel 2, no. 1000, Dartmouth Papers.

142 **Only in Georgia:** Elsewhere, colonists could only read attacks on the laws in newspapers and pamphlets. See, for example, *AA* 4, 1:410–15, 430–33, 658–61. The most extended treatment was by the Reverend Ebenezer Baldwin of Danbury, Connecticut, in his *Appendix* to Samuel Sherwood, *A Sermon Containing Scriptural Instructions to Civil Rulers . . . Delivered on the Public FAST, August 31, 1774* (New Haven, Conn.: T. & S. Green, [1775]), 43–81.

142 **James Johnston:** Anonymous, "The Case Stated," and A Georgian, "To the Freemen of the Province of Georgia," both in *GaG,* 27 July 1774. On Johnston, a Scot who had been in Savannah since 1762, see Thomas, *History of Printing in America,* 584–85. In publishing all sides, Johnston adopted the traditional role of printers; see Botein, " 'Mere Mechanics' and an Open Press," 127–225.

142 **flurry of responses:** A True Friend to Georgia, "To the Publick," *GaG,* 3 Aug. 1774; A Friend to Moderation, *To the Public,* Savannah, 3 Aug., broadside (*EAI,* no. 42718); untitled, unsigned broadside, [Savannah, 1774], (*EAI,* no. 42717). No copy of the broadside by the "Religious and Faithful Friend of Georgia" appears to have survived, but the quotations are from an unsigned reply to it, "To the Worthy Freeholders and Other

Inhabitants of the Province of Georgia," *GaG*, 3 Aug. That essay also challenged the remarks about the danger Indians posed to the colony.

143 **the Reverend Haddon Smith:** Mercurius, untitled essay, *GaG*, 10 Aug. 1774; A Freeholder, "To the Publick," and Mercurius, untitled essay, *GaG*, 17 Aug. See also Mercurius's further comments in response to Freeholder, *GaG*, 31 Aug. and 21, 28 Sept. Freeholder contributed other essays to *GaG* on 14, 21, 28 Sept., 12 Oct. Smith revealed his identity as Mercurius in a letter to Bishop Terrick, 4 April 1776, in *Fulham Papers in the Lambeth Palace Library: American Colonial Section Calendar and Indexes,* comp. William Wilson Manross (Oxford: Clarendon Press, 1965), 20. (I owe this reference to Betty Wood.)

144 **two other Church of England clergymen:** Smith's letter to Terrick, cited above, disclosed that he had to flee once his authorship was discovered. Bullman included biographical details in his claims memorial, AO 12/48, fols. 57–60. For Peters, see Charles Mampoteng, "The Reverend Samuel Peters, M.A.: Missionary at Hebron, Connecticut, 1760–1774," *Historical Magazine of the Protestant Episcopal Church* 5 (1936): 73–91.

144 **Bullman's offense:** All material in this and the next three paragraphs comes from vestry minutes, 15, 18 Aug. 1774, box 20, St. Michael's Church records; and Drayton, *Memoirs,* 1:142–45.

145 **The controversy did not end:** Quotations: Drayton, *Memoirs,* 1:144–45; Bull to Dartmouth, 15 March 1775, reel 2, no. 1107, Dartmouth Papers. Details of the controversy that emerged after Bullman's dismissal can be traced in vestry minutes of 27 August and 5 December 1774 and 8 May 1775, all in box 20, St. Michael's Church records. See also John Pringle to William Tilghman, 15 Sept. 1774, folder 59, Preston Davie Papers, for a comment that Bullman was "the best [preacher] in the Province."

146 **In Hebron:** Quotations, in order: Jonathan Trumbull, "A General State of the Transactions Relative to the Revd Samuel Peters of Hebron . . . ," n.d., Trumbull Papers, 20:89a; Statement of John Grou and John Peters, *NYG*, 5 Sept. 1774, reprinted in *AA* 4, 1:711. The story of the confrontations between Peters and his neighbors in August and September can be followed in *AA* 4, 1:711–18, which reprints many relevant documents and newspaper accounts (but not one from *PaJ*, 26 Oct.). The narrative here relies on the materials in *AA* 4, vol. 1, and Trumbull's "General State." Footnotes in the next six paragraphs specify the origin of all quotations. Peters later claimed that he had persuaded his fellow residents of Hebron not to contribute funds for the relief of Boston and that his success led to the difficulties; see Kenneth W. Cameron, ed., *The Works of Samuel Peters, of Hebron, Connecticut* (Hartford: Transcendental Books, 1967), 79.

146 **Peters apparently survived:** "Mr. Peters's Resolves," in *AA* 4, 1:713–14.

146 **After the resolves appeared:** Statement of Hezekiah Huntington et al., 6 Dec. 1774, in *AA* 4, 1:717–18; *NPkt*, 8 Sept. (Peters's statement on 6 Sept., not reprinted in *AA* 4, vol. 1). While Peters was talking with the crowd outside, someone fired a gun from inside his house, which led the men to search it and to confiscate several guns, some swords, and two dozen clubs.

147 **Peters sought assistance:** Trumbull, "General State," Trumbull Papers, 20:89c, 89d. See also Trumbull to Joseph Spencer, Trumbull Papers, 20:90; and *BEP*, 20 Oct. 1774, story datelined Pomfret. For a similar opinion about the negative impact on the "General Cause" of "so much petty mobbing" as that aimed at Peters, see Simon Deane to Silas Deane, 15 Oct., in "Deane Correspondence," 191.

147 **Once in the garrisoned city:** For the story of how the letters were intercepted, see *AA* 4, 1:715; the letters themselves are printed in ibid., 715–16. For reprints in newspapers, see, for example, *CtG*, 14 Oct. 1774; *DPaPkt*, 24 Oct.; *BEP*, 24 Oct. The *BEP*, like many other papers, added its own preface excoriating Peters: it pronounced him "the most unnatural Monster, diabolical Incendiary & detestable Parricide to his Country that ever appeared in America, or disgraced Humanity." The other clergymen's disavowals were also reprinted; see *DPaPkt*, 24 Oct.; *BEP*, 14 Nov. Stiles's statement: *Stiles Diary*, 1:467. The publication of the indiscreet letters seems to have made others skittish; Joseph Reed, for one, started signing letters with his initials only (*AA* 4, 1:892, 964).

147 **Peters's departure from the colonies:** His departure from Portsmouth: John Wentworth to T. W. Waldron, 25 Oct. 1774, in *Belknap Papers*, 56–57; the letter criticizing him: "Extract of a Letter from Connecticut," [Sept. 1774], reel 11, no. 974, Dartmouth Papers (see also Peters's letter to Dartmouth, 14 March 1775, reel 12, no. 1188, Dartmouth Papers); intercepted letter to Auchmuty, 25 Feb. 1775, *NPkt*, 8 June 1775. He did carry a letter of introduction to the bishop of London from the Reverend Henry Caner of Boston and two other clerics, 7 Oct. 1774, in *Letterbook of Caner*.

148 **provincial-level gatherings:** Gage to Dartmouth, 17 Feb. 1775, in *DAR*, 9:51–52.

149 **Dartmouth ordered:** See, for example, Dartmouth to Dunmore, 3 Aug. 1774, in *DAR*, 7:149.

149 **At five of the conventions:** Wentworth's proclamation, 6 July 1774: Bouton, *Documents of New-Hampshire*, 7:400 (see also 399–408; *DAR*, 8:146–50; and *EAI*, no. 42644, the broadside summoning the convention); Martin to Dartmouth, 1 Sept., in *DAR*, 8:174–77 (quotations, 175). (See also, on North Carolina, *AA* 4, 1:705–7, 733–37.) For Maryland: *AA* 4,

1:438–40; New Jersey: ibid., 624–25, 657–58; Delaware: ibid., 663–68. Maryland had no resident governor at the time; William Franklin knew he could not stop the New Jersey meeting; and John Penn was the governor of Delaware as well as of Pennsylvania. Because he would not convene the assembly, the convention ignored him, meeting on 2 August and electing three delegates to the congress. In "their private Capacity," some members of the Maryland convention asked Daniel Dulany, author of an influential pamphlet against the Stamp Act in 1765, if he would accept an appointment to the congressional delegation; he declined. See Daniel Dulany to his son Daniel, 3 Aug. 1784, in E. Alfred Jones, *American Members of the Inns of Court* (London: St. Catherine Press, 1924), 70.

149 **Rhode Island and Connecticut:** Bartlett, *Records of Rhode Island,* 7:246–47; the Connecticut selection process: *AA* 4, 1:554–55; quotation: Johnson to B. LaTrobe, 25 July 1774, William Samuel Johnson Papers. Eliphalet Dyer and Silas Deane, the other two initially elected, served in congress, along with Roger Sherman. Deane believed Johnson's public explanation but cautioned that others thought he dissembled. He suggested that Johnson make a public statement refuting the "groundless" rumors, but Johnson failed to do so, probably because the rumors were accurate. See Deane to Johnson, 1 Aug., Connecticut Papers, BC; and Deane to Thomas Mumford, 1 Aug., in Ford, *Correspondence of Webb,* 1:37–38. Elizabeth McCaughey, *From Loyalist to Founding Father: The Political Odyssey of William Samuel Johnson* (New York: Columbia University Press, 1980), 163–72, discusses his political neutrality.

150 **Virginia delegates:** Norfolk committee to Baltimore committee, 3 Aug. 1774, Purviance Papers; Virginia Association, 6 Aug., in *RevVa,* 1:230–35 (quotation, 231); see also ibid., 219–28, and the instructions to the delegates, in ibid., 236–38. James Parker learned about the "secret" closure decision; see Parker to Charles Steuart, 14 Aug., reel 2, fol. 242, Steuart Papers. Thomson Mason, George Mason's brother, who thought nonimportation would be ineffective (see chapter 5), refused to sign the Association, which was, however, said to have been adopted "unanimously." See Greene, *Diary of Landon Carter,* 2:848 (entry of 11 Aug.). Thomas Jefferson, who did not attend the convention, was also dissatisfied with the Association (*TJ Papers,* 1:143).

150 **one hundred South Carolinians:** Edward Rutledge to Ralph Izard, 21 July 1774, in Deas, *Correspondence of Ralph Izard,* 1:2–5 (quotation, 3). See Drayton, *Memoirs,* 1:126–30, for a detailed account of the meeting.

151 **South Carolina's congressional delegation:** Quotations: "Extract of a Letter Received in Boston, Dated Charlestown, S.C., July 11, 1774," in *AA* 4, 1:531–32. See also ibid., 525–26, 534; John Pringle, then studying

law with John Rutledge, described the five delegates selected in a letter to William Tilghman, 30 July, folder 59, Preston Davie Papers.

151   **two additional steps:** Drayton, *Memoirs,* 1:131.

151   **legitimize the appointment of congressional delegates:** Ibid., 1:137–41; Bull to Dartmouth, 3 Aug. 1774, in *DAR,* 8:158. Other accounts of the 2 August meeting are in *AA* 4, 1:671–72; and Henry Laurens to Ralph Izard, 20 Sept., in *HL Papers,* 9:567.

152   **Another was Pennsylvania:** Reed to Charles Pettit, 16 July 1774, Joseph Reed Papers; "Pennsylvania Convention," in *AA* 4, 1:555–57. John Dickinson himself reportedly strongly opposed nonimportation at the convention, favoring "a Decent & firm" petition instead; see Jared Ingersoll to Jonathan Ingersoll, 22 Feb. 1775, in Dexter, *Jared Ingersoll Correspondence,* 450.

152   **The convention members established:** "Pennsylvania Convention," in *AA* 4, 1:557–64 (quotations 561, 562). Dickinson included a lengthy treatise the convention ordered removed from the basic text. This, the "Argumentative Part," appeared as a separate publication, *Essay on the Constitutional Power of Great Britain.* A correspondent speculated to Dartmouth that the "instructions" were created by "many of the ablest Men" of Pennsylvania and that they formed "a Model, or ground plan" for congressional resolutions. See T. Webb to Dartmouth, 8 Sept., CO 5/1285, fol. 66. But Josiah Quincy Sr. complained that Dickinson had conceded too much to Britain; see his letter to his son Josiah Junior [26 Oct.], in "Quincy Letters," 480–81.

153   **resolutions on the Coercive Acts:** Reed to Dartmouth, 18 July 1774, reel 2, no. 998, Dartmouth Papers; Madison to William Bradford, 23 Aug., in *JM Papers,* 1:121. Thomas Wharton, another convention member, argued for softening some of the language; see Wharton to Thomas Walpole, 2 Aug., in "Wharton Letter-Books 33," 439. For a positive assessment of the resolutions and instructions, see Devine, *Scottish Firm in Virginia,* 151–52.

153   **One of the potential enemies:** *Advices from Philadelphia, July 23, 1774,* New York, broadside (*EAI,* no. 13096), reprints the Freeman essay, terming it "the production of a masterly pen." Ryerson, *Revolution Is Now Begun,* 61, suggests that Joseph Galloway was "A Freeman." The essay was also published in *RNYG,* 28 July 1774; it duplicates views Galloway later expressed about the importance of assembly elections for congressional delegates.

154   **they declared unanimously:** "Assembly of Pennsylvania," in *AA* 4, 1:602–10 (quotation, 606). Galloway later asserted that he had personally drafted the assembly's instructions to himself and the other delegates; see his Loyalist claims memorial, n.d. [ca. 1783], AO 12/38, fol. 21. After Dickinson

was elected to the assembly in September, he was added to Pennsylvania's congressional delegation, and he helped to draft some of the addresses produced near the end of the meeting. Both John Penn (30 July, in *DAR*, 8:153) and Joseph Reed (26 July, reel 2, no. 1000, Dartmouth Papers) assessed the assembly meeting for Dartmouth.

154 **"virulence" of political struggles:** Deane to his wife, Elizabeth, 29 Aug. 1774, in *Deane Papers*, 7; Rivington to Henry Knox, 25 July, in "Henry Knox and the London Book-Store," 296.

154 **The committee of fifty-one:** Quotations: Peter Van Schaack, Notes on Committee of 51, n.d. [ca. 4 July 1774], box 6, Van Schaack Family Papers. The committee of correspondence decision: *AA* 4, 1:306; the committee of fifty-one's actions: ibid., 307–9, and announcement, 5 July, broadside (*EAI*, no. 13094). See also a broadside misdated 5 June (*EAI*, no. 13661), which explicitly mentioned the hope to avoid the *"turbulent tempers"* that had previously promoted a committee of twenty-five. The mechanics' slate considered by the committee of fifty-one included Livingston, Low, and Jay but replaced Duane and Alsop with McDougall and John Morin Scott (see *AA* 4, 1:308). Low later defended his decision to accept appointment as a delegate "when a Congress became unavoidable" because of his desire to see "lenient and conciliatory Measures" adopted (Low, claims memorial, n.d. [1784], AO 12/21, fol. 90).

154 **mechanics summoned residents:** The meeting in the fields: *NYJ*, 7 July 1774; the committee of fifty-one's censure: *AA* 4, 1:311 (see 311–13); Sears and McDougall to Samuel Adams, 25 July, SA Papers. See also two broadsides (*EAI*, nos. 13093, 13095).

155 **Attendees at a wider city meeting:** This dispute over New York's delegate slate can be traced in multiple broadsides published between 7 and 11 July: *EAI*, nos. 13389, 13475, 13476, 13655, 13683, and 42713. See also *AA* 4, 1:313–15. McDougall was publicly criticized by "Agricola"; see a broadside (*EAI*, no. 13097); *NYJ*, 4 Aug.; and a copy of a document signed Agricola, 15 July, McDougall Papers.

155 **resolutions prepared by its subcommittee:** The committee's resolutions were published as *Proceedings of the Committee of Correspondence in New-York*, 13 July, broadside (*EAI*, no. 13477). Quotations: McDougall and Sears to Samuel Adams, 25 July, SA Papers ("indirect Censure"); *Smith Memoirs*, 1:189 (entry for 20 July 1774). See also the broadside call to the 19 July meeting (*EAI*, no. 13478). The coffeehouse meeting was later described to John Adams; see *JA Diary*, 20 Aug., 2:103.

155 **committeemen with a dilemma:** Quotation: Sears and McDougall to Samuel Adams, 25 July 1774, SA Papers. For these developments and the revised resolves, see *Proceedings of the Committee of Correspondence*, 19 July,

broadside (*EAI*, no. 13479) (also in *AA* 4, 1:315–17); untitled broadside, headed New York, 19 [that is, 20] July (*EAI*, no. 13480) (the revised resolutions). The amended resolves did not meet with universal approval; see *Remarks upon the Resolves of the New Committee*, 22 July, broadside (*EAI*, no. 13244), and a late-breaking amendment to the third resolve published 25 July in *NYG* (see *AA* 4, 1:318). See also *To the Respectable Publick*, 20 July (*EAI*, no. 13681), a broadside signed by Isaac Low, John Jay, and two others, objecting to the appointment of the new subcommittee; and a broadside (*EAI*, no. 13680), 20 July, signed by Low, Jay, and John Alsop, expressing uncertainty about their election as delegates.

155 **citywide poll for July 28:** Quotation: An Honest American, *To the Respectable Public*, 25 July 1774, broadside (*EAI*, no. 13679). Voters do not seem to have considered any resolutions on 28 July. Tiedemann, *Reluctant Revolutionaries*, 193–97, also describes the confusing sequence of meetings and counter-meetings. The broadsides announcing the poll and the results are *EAI*, nos. 13481 and 42648. Unsurprisingly, the events provoked satirical broadsides, for example: *At a Meeting of the True Sons of Liberty*, 27 July (*EAI*, no. 13126). See also the committee's minutes, 27–29 July, in *AA* 4, 1:319–21. Although New Yorkers had rejected the committee's resolution that nothing but "dire necessity" should lead to the adoption of nonimportation, the committee stressed that very point to the congressional delegates on 22 August (see *AA* 4, 1:324).

155 **additional matters:** *AA* 4, 1:318–23. Albany County decided to name its own delegate, Philip Schuyler, but he declined the appointment for health reasons, so it accepted the city representatives. See minutes of the Albany committee of correspondence, 13–30 Aug. 1774, box 5, Van Schaack Family Papers.

155 **Colden wrote three times:** Colden to Dartmouth, 6 July 1774, in *DAR*, 8:147 ("considerable merchants"); same to same, 2 Aug., in ibid., 155–56 ("moderate," "violent," "prudent"); same to same, 7 Sept., CO 5/1105, fol. 342 ("Demagogues" and following quotations).

156 **In Georgia, the governor:** Wright to Dartmouth, 25 July 1774, CO 5/663, fol. 133; *By His Excellency Sir James Wright, Baronet . . . a Proclamation*, Savannah, 5 Aug., broadside (*EAI*, no. 42607). See the call to the meeting on 27 July, broadside (*EAI*, no. 42694), and for an account of it, revealing that attendees signed a nonimportation agreement as individuals as well as scheduling the larger gathering, see *AA* 4, 1:638–39.

156 **men gathered at a Savannah tavern:** *Resolutions Entered Into at Savannah in Georgia . . .* , 10 Aug. 1774, broadside (*EAI*, no. 42695) (also printed in *AA* 4, 1:700–701; and *RevVa*, 2:157–58); *GaG*, 7 Sept.

157 **Haddon Smith:** Mercurius, untitled essay, *GaG*, 24 Aug. 1774, copy in

CO 5/663, fol. 160, enclosed in Wright to Dartmouth, 24 Aug. (see *DAR*, 7:156). As he had before, Smith cited the possibility of an Indian war as a reason to avoid angering Great Britain.

157 **Wright took steps:** Wright to Dartmouth, 13 Aug. 1774, CO 5/663, fol. 146; *GaG*, 21, 28 Sept., 12 Oct., all in CO 5/664, enclosures included with Wright to Dartmouth, 13 Oct., fols. 1, 5–9. For the 30 August meeting convened by Wright at Savannah, see *AA* 4, 1:766–67. One account of Wright's actions, composed in the early nineteenth century, claimed that some of the signers of the statements he solicited were bribed and that other signatures were forged. See Charles C. Jones, *The History of Georgia* (Boston: Houghton Mifflin, 1883), 2:155–57, relying on an account by Hugh McCall published in 1811.

157 **Summing up his efforts:** Wright to Dartmouth, 24 Aug. 1774, in *DAR*, 8:162–63.

158 **Massachusetts House:** The fast-day call: *PIR*, 233. John Rowe wrote in his diary on 14 July 1774 that he would prefer people to "Recommend Payment for the Tea instead of losing a Day by fasting" (*Rowe Diary*, 278). Because the governor did not order the fast day, it was not observed by Anglican clergy; see William Clarke to William Fisher, 6 August, in Crary, *Price of Loyalty*, 26. An anonymous letter addressed to Governor Gage on 14 July warned him of possible violence that night; see *PIR*, 573.

158 **six sermons delivered that day:** Quotation: Peter Whitney, *The Transgression of a Land Punished by a Multitude of Rulers: Considered in Two Discourses, Delivered July 14, 1774 . . . a Day of Fasting and Prayer . . .* (Boston: John Boyle, 1774), 60. For a report of the arrest rumors, see John Andrews to William Barrell, 22 July, in "Andrews Letters," 332. Samuel Webster, *The Misery and Duty of an Oppress'd and Enslav'd People, Represented in a Sermon Delivered at Salisbury, July 14, 1774 . . .* (Boston: Edes & Gill, 1774), 26–27, also alluded to the rumors of impending arrests of "our best friends."

158 **The six ministers lamented:** Whitney, *Transgression*, 41–44; Nathan Fiske, *The Importance of Righteousness to the Happiness, and the Tendency of Oppression, to the Misery of a People Illustrated, in Two Discourses Delivered at Brookfield, July [1]4, 1774 . . .* (Boston: John Kneeland, 1774), 33. Three who spoke about sin generally or in traditional terms were Thaddeus Maccarty, *Reformation of Manners, of Absolute Necessity . . . in Times of Public Evil and Distress . . . Shewn in Two Sermons, Preached at Worcester, . . . July 14th, 1774* (Boston: William M'Alpine, 1774), 32; Timothy Hilliard, *The Duty of a People Under the Oppression of Man, to Seek Deliverance from God . . . Delivered at Barnstable, July 14th, 1774 . . .* (Boston: Greenleaf, 1774), 16; and Webster, *Misery and Duty*, 10, 14.

159 **John Allen:** [John Allen], *The Watchman's Alarm to Lord N——H; or, The British Parliamentary Boston Port-Bill Unwraped* . . . (Salem: E. Russell, 1774), 25–28. In a footnote, Allen named and lauded men who had manumitted their enslaved servants, urging his listeners to follow their example. Although Allen's title did not explicitly reveal that he preached this sermon on July 14, a reference on the final unnumbered page of his introduction to "the peculiar solemnities of this day . . . by the public consent of the churches" indicates that he did so then. See also Levi Hart, *Liberty Described and Recommended, in a Sermon . . . on September 20, 1774* . . . (Hartford, Conn.: Eben Watson, 1775); and the antislavery essays by "A Son of Africa," *MSpy*, 10 Feb. 1774; Caesar Sarter, *EJ*, 17 August; Bristol Lambee, *ProvG*, 22 Oct.; and cf. Wells, *Few Political Reflections*, 79–84. Wells criticized slavery but proposed stopping imports of enslaved people rather than abolishing the institution outright. For other 1774 proposals to halt the slave trade, see, for example, *PIR*, 285, 409–11; Bartlett, *Records of Rhode Island*, 7:251–53. A useful modern compilation is Bruns, *Am I Not a Man and a Brother*, esp. for this period, 293–385. David Waldstreicher, "Ancients, Moderns, and Africans: Phillis Wheatley and the Politics of Empire and Slavery in the American Revolution," *Journal of the Early Republic* 37 (2017): 701–33, discusses an antislavery letter from Wheatley reprinted widely in newspapers in 1774.

159 **The Massachusetts clergymen who preached:** Maccarty, *Reformation of Manners*, unpaginated "advertisement"; Hilliard, *Duty of a People*, 24 (see 22–25). Maccarty, who saw Britain's actions as a "secondary" cause of the colony's circumstances, used the "advertisement" to defend his decision to avoid politics, citing the desire of his congregation that the sermon be published as evidence for its suitability on the fast day. He also defended the observance itself, even though the governor had not authorized it in a proclamation. See Maccarty, *Reformation of Manners*, 26, 34n–35n.

159 **The other four emphasized:** Quotations: Allen, *Watchman's Alarm*, 16; Webster, *Misery and Duty*, 23–24; Fiske, *Importance of Righteousness*, 28, 40; Whitney, *Transgression*, 16, 55, 54. Whitney came close to suggesting that the unruly behavior of Massachusetts residents might have brought the Government Act on themselves (see *Transgression*, 55–59).

160 **Peter Whitney and Nathan Fiske:** For "patriotic terror," see James S. Leamon, *The Reverend Jacob Bailey, Maine Loyalist: For God, King, Country, and for Self* (Amherst: University of Massachusetts Press, 2012), 107. Another attack two weeks later on an Addresser, David Ingersoll of Great Barrington, also involved a crowd from Connecticut; see "Declaration of David Ingersoll," [Aug. 1774], in *PIR*, 606–9; and *AA* 4, 1:724–25.

161 **Boston newspaper reprinted a story:** See *MG&BPB*, 11 July 1774, and

MG&BNL, 14 July, both reprinting from *NPkt,* 7 July; Francis Green, affidavit, 20 July, in *AA* 4, 1:631 (see 629–33 for more details of his confrontations with the crowds). A brief account of the incident was published as far away as Charleston, *SCG* (C), 23 Aug.

161   **Governor Gage alerted:** Gage to Dartmouth, 5 July 1774, in *DAR,* 8:141; Colonel James Robertson to J.M., 5 July, reel 11, no. 950, Dartmouth Papers; Ann Hulton to Elizabeth Lightbody, 8 July, in York, *Henry Hulton,* 305. One of those intimidated by the crowds was Thomas Hutchinson Jr., a tea consignee, who feared coming to Boston to fulfill his duties as a judge. See Gage to Hutchinson Junior, 14 July, in *PIR,* 578. Nathaniel Coffin claimed that only Salem contained "Gentlemen of Fortune & sense" who would publicly support the government in early July; see Coffin to Charles Steuart, 6 July, reel 2, fol. 227, Steuart Papers.

162   **assistance from other colonies:** Thomas Newell recorded the aid arriving between early July and early December in "Diary of Newell," 354–63. Greenough's ledger recording his relief distributions is HM 70285, Greenough Family Papers. For employing the poor, see Boston town meeting minutes, 19 July–30 Aug., in *PIR,* 634, 642–43, 646, 648, 659; *Notification* (of town meeting), 23 July, broadside (*EAI,* no. 42563). *EG,* 19 July, and *MG&BPB,* 11 July, summarized rumors. "A Friend to Boston," *NYJ,* 15 Sept. (also in part in *AA* 4, 1:743–44), defended Bostonians' practice of hiring the poor against charges of profiteering. See, too, William Cooper's defense of that use for donations, 12 Sept., in *AA* 4, 1:784–85.

162   **the presence of so many troops:** Quotation: Graves to Philip Stephens, 8 Aug. 1774, in *DAR,* 8:159 (see also 7:182), but the last ship was finished in Boston about six weeks later (see *JA Papers,* 2:174), so the loophole thereafter closed. On the economic benefits of the occupation for some New Englanders, see Nathaniel Coffin to Charles Steuart, Aug.–Sept. 1774 [20 Aug. section], reel 2, fol. 261, Steuart Papers. Some tradesmen made axes and hoes that were shipped for sale to Charleston; see Samuel Adams to Peter Timothy, 27 July, in *SA Writings,* 3:147–48.

162   **Boston residents commented:** Mary Cranch to Abigail Adams, 20 Aug., in *AFC,* 1:143–44. Addressers were expelled from their social clubs, as Joseph Warren wrote to Samuel Adams, 4 Sept. (Frothingham, *Life of Warren,* 358). For observations on conditions in Boston: Ann Hulton to Elizabeth Lightbody, 8 July 1774, in York, *Henry Hulton,* 305; Henry Knox to James Rivington, 18 July, Henry Knox Papers II; John Andrews to William Barrell, 1, 20 Aug., in "Andrews Letters," 335–37, 343; Henry Caner to John Wentworth, 8 Aug., in *Letterbook of Caner.* See also an unsigned and untitled report from *BEP,* 1 Aug., which was republished throughout

the colonies between 2 Aug. (*EG*) and 3 Oct. (*SCG* [T]). Despite the difficult conditions, Boston's resistance leaders stressed their unity: see *AA* 4, 1:646–47; and Samuel Cooper to Benjamin Franklin, 15 Aug., in *BF Papers,* 21:274–76.

163 **Bostonians apprehensively awaited:** Coffin to Charles Steuart, 6 July 1774, reel 2, fol. 227, Steuart Papers; Warren to Abigail Adams, 9 Aug., in *AFC,* 1:138. Gage also anticipated attempts to intimidate the new councillors and other officeholders, but he discounted their impact; see Gage to Dartmouth, 27 July, in *DAR,* 8:151–52; and Gage to Lord Barrington, 18 July, in Carter, *Correspondence of Gage,* 2:649. The text of the Massachusetts Government Act is in *PIR,* 506–19; John Andrews noted its arrival in a letter to William Barrell on 6 August: "Andrews Letters," 337.

163 **Gage tendered the oath:** Quotation: Young to Samuel Adams, 19 Aug. 1774, SA Papers. For the oaths of office and the first meeting: *PIR,* 522–24. For refusals: Gage to Dartmouth, 25 Aug., in Carter, *Correspondence of Gage,* 1:364. See also Gage to Dartmouth, 27 Aug., in *DAR,* 8:163–64. Raphael, *First American Revolution,* chap. 3, details the events following the implementation of the act.

164 **Timothy Ruggles of Hardwick:** Many of the attacks are described in Albert Matthews, "Documents Relating to the Last Meetings of the Massachusetts Royal Council, 1774–1776," *Pubs CSM* 32 (1933–1937): 460–507, but see also, on examples mentioned here, Nathaniel Coffin to Charles Steuart, Aug.–Sept. 1774, reel 2, fols. 262–63, Steuart Papers (Ruggles, Leonard); *PIR,* 534–35 (Leonard); *AA* 4, 1:731–32 (Willard); *DAR,* 8:166–70, and *PIR,* 528–31, 537–39 (Paine, Loring); *PIR,* 525–27, 532 (Oliver, Hutchinson). And see "Articles Alledg'd Against the Honble Israel Williams Esq.," 26 Aug., a rare surviving set of formal charges produced by a crowd against an appointed councillor, along with Williams's undated recollection of the incident, Israel Williams Papers.

164 **Gage informed Dartmouth:** Gage to Dartmouth, 2 Sept. 1774, in *DAR,* 8:180–81. The enclosures are listed in ibid., 7:163–65.

165 **courts too could no longer function:** Gage to Dartmouth, 2 Sept. 1774, in *DAR,* 8:182; Warren to Norwich, Connecticut, committee, 27 Aug., HM 8143, Huntington Library. A detailed account of the failed Superior Court session in *MSpy,* 1 Sept., was widely and rapidly reprinted, even reaching Charleston by 23 Sept., *SCG* (W); also see *AA* 4, 1:747–49. Courts in both Berkshire and Hampshire Counties in western Massachusetts were prevented from holding sessions in mid- to late August. For Berkshire, see *AA* 4, 1:724; and Nathaniel Coffin to Charles Steuart, Aug.–Sept. [20 Aug.] 1774, reel 2, fol. 263, Steuart Papers. For Hampshire:

PIR, 883–85; and Thomas Eliot Andrews, ed., "The Diary of Elizabeth (Porter) Phelps," *NEHGR* 118 (1964): 221.

165 **citizens also brazenly refused:** Boston: selectmen's minutes, 13 Aug. 1774, in *PIR*, 662; and Nathaniel Coffin to Charles Steuart, Aug.–Sept., reel 2, fol. 262, Steuart Papers. Salem: Salem committee to Boston committee, 25 Aug., in *PIR*, 816; Gage to Judge Peter Frye, 27 Aug., in ibid., 605; "Salem Town Meeting," 24 Aug., in *AA* 4, 1:730 (quotation); and Octavius Pickering, *The Life of Timothy Pickering* (Boston: Little, Brown, 1867), 1:54–58.

166 **Various ad hoc bodies:** Middlesex County Convention Proceedings, 30–31 Aug. 1774, in *PIR*, 889–94 (quotation, 891); minutes, Boston committee et al., 26 Aug., in ibid., 691; Worcester County Convention, resolves, 30–31 Aug., in ibid., 895. The Middlesex Proceedings were published in a broadside (*EAI*, no. 13439).

166 **implications of the statements:** Benjamin Akin, for the Dartmouth committee, to Samuel Adams, 29 July 1774, in *PIR*, 764.

166 **One Bostonian predicted:** "Extract of a Letter Dated Boston, August 29, 1774," in *AA* 4, 1:744–45; Dickinson to Quincy, 20 June, in ibid., 434; Quincy to Dickinson, 20 Aug., in ibid., 725; John Gerry, for Marblehead committee, to Boston committee, 31 Aug., in *PIR*, 825 (see also ibid., 758–60, 782, and *JA Papers*, 2:128–29, for similar sentiments). On 28 October, Dickinson explained to Quincy that he wrote his June letter "in Agonies of Mind," fearing that "something might have happened, . . . which might have been eagerly & basely seiz'd by others, as a Pretence for deserting" Bostonians; see *LOD*, 1:252.

167 **Massachusetts delegation to the Continental Congress:** Andrews to William Barrell, 10 Aug. 1774, in "Andrews Letters," 339; Abigail to John Adams, 19 Aug., in *AFC*, 1:142.

CHAPTER 5 EXPECTING GREAT THINGS

168 **Nathaniel Coffin disdained:** Coffin to Charles Steuart, Aug.–Sept. 1774 [20 Aug. section], reel 2, fol. 261, Steuart Papers; Greenleaf to Paine, 13 Sept., in *RTP Papers*, 3:1.

168 **The respectful attention:** *JA Diary*, 2:97–114 (entries for 10–29 Aug. 1774); quotations, 100–101 (New Haven); 110 (Holt); 112 (Witherspoon); 114 (arrival in Philadelphia). See also Adams to William Tudor, 28 Aug., in *JA Papers*, 2:133.

169 **Adams, Paine, and the others:** Deborah Cushing to Thomas Cushing, n.d. [Aug. 1774], Cushing Family II Papers; Warren to Samuel Adams, 21 (quotation), 29 Aug., SA Papers; Hawley to John Adams, n.d. [Aug.],

in *JA Papers,* 2:135 (also, same to same, 25 July, in ibid., 2:117). See also William Tudor to John Adams, 21, 29 Aug., in ibid., 2:132, 134. A correspondent in late August also told Richard Henry Lee that the congress should focus on acquiring arms and ammunition (*AA* 4, 1:740).

169 **More than two months earlier:** *JA Diary,* 2:96, 97 (entries for 20, 25 June 1774).

170 **As the summer weeks passed:** Mason's essays are reprinted in *RevVa,* 1:169–203. The New Jersey essays are reprinted in *AA* 4, 1:642–43, 634–37. The latter, signed B.N., originally appeared in *NYJ,* 4 Aug. 1774. "Juba" was published in *RNYG,* 2 Sept.

170 **As the publications multiplied:** Drinker, *Observations on the Late Popular Measures . . . by a Tradesman,* 3, 13–14. See also an untitled broadside signed "A Tradesman" and presumably by Drinker, dated 1 September, complaining that "moderate Men" were being inaccurately "stigmatized" as advocating submission to Parliament (*EAI,* no. 13545).

171 **Bradfords published the first:** Editors' note at end of A Tradesman, "To the People of Pennsylvania," *PaJ* (supp.), 17 Aug. 1774. The first Tradesman essay was reprinted in both *NYG,* 22 Aug., and *RNYG,* 25 Aug., but I located no separate printings of the second one, which seems to have been included only in the pamphlet.

171 **In his pamphlet:** Drinker, *Observations on the Late Popular Measures,* 3–4. For a complaint about poorly written pamphlets that could have applied to Drinker's prolix prose style, see John Pringle to William Tilghman, 15 Sept. 1774, folder 59, Preston Davie Papers. Among other contemporary complaints about anti-British bias in the colonial press are [Robert Prescott], *A Letter from a Veteran to the Officers of the Army Encamped at Boston* (America [New York: Hugh Gaine], 1774), 3; and Adair and Schutz, *Peter Oliver's Origin & Progress,* 105–6. John Adams instead complained about the "ministerial" press; see his remarks to Abigail in early July in *AFC,* 1:122–23, 127.

171 **This dialogue between Drinker and the Bradfords:** See Martin, *Free and Open Press.* On printers' traditional way of operating, see Botein, " 'Mere Mechanics' and an Open Press." Rivington first added the phrase to his masthead on 5 May 1774, continuing to use it through 17 August 1775. On 7 June 1774, Eben Watson, the editor of Hartford's *Connecticut Courant,* likewise began running on his masthead, "Open to all PARTIES, but not under the Influence of ANY," a phrase he retained through 3 April 1775 but then discarded. The conservative newspapers were *GaG, SCG* (W), *NYG, MG&BNL,* and *MG&BPB,* along with, increasingly, *RNYG.* My understanding of Rivington throughout this book has been influenced by Anne Powell, "Printing at His Peril: James Rivington and a Free Press

in Revolutionary New York, 1773–1775" (senior honors thesis, Cornell University, 2016).

172 **four Americans wrote pamphlets:** Jefferson's *Summary View* was evidently printed by John Pinkney, then in charge of Clementina Rind's press; it has been reprinted in both *RevVa*, 1:243–56, and *TJ Papers*, 1:121–37, with Julian Boyd's extensive note on publication 1:669–76. Peter Timothy published Drayton's *Letter from Freeman.*

172 **The other two criticized:** No publication information appeared on the title page of *Letter from a Virginian,* but a brief note in *NYJ,* 8 Sept. 1774, identified Hugh Gaine as the printer. Thomas R. Adams rejected the attribution to Boucher because the clergyman later failed to claim authorship; see *American Independence,* 98. Boucher's biographer, though, has persuasively argued for Boucher on the basis of content and language; see Anne Y. Zimmer, *Jonathan Boucher: Loyalist in Exile* (Detroit: Wayne State University Press, 1978), 333–36.

172 *American Querist:* For Chandler's authorship of *American Querist* and other pamphlets initially attributed to the Reverend Myles Cooper, see Clarence Vance, "Myles Cooper," *Columbia University Quarterly* 32 (1930): 261–86. John Tabor Kempe, a prominent New York lawyer and later Loyalist, was another man accused of writing the *Querist;* see James Duane to Kempe, 11 Oct. 1774, in *LOD,* 1:174.

172 **Jefferson's *Summary View:*** Thomas Jefferson, *A Summary View of the Rights of British America,* in *RevVa,* 1:243–44, 247, 255 (quotations). It was reprinted in Philadelphia (1774) and London (1775). James Wilson's *Considerations on the Nature and the Extent of the Legislative Authority of the British Parliament,* published in late September, also denied parliamentary power over the colonies. Eric Nelson, in *The Royalist Revolution,* esp. chaps. 1, 2, argues for the significance in the revolutionary movement of "patriot royalism" such as that in the works by Wilson and Jefferson.

173 **Jefferson ended his proposed instructions:** Jefferson, *Summary View,* in *RevVa,* 1:256.

173 **William Henry Drayton's *Letter:*** Drayton, *Letter from Freeman of South-Carolina,* 7, 47 (quotations). Drayton's pamphlet elicited a reply published the following month, *Some Fugitive Thoughts on a Letter Signed Freeman . . .* ([Charleston], S.C., 1774), challenging Drayton's interpretations of British law and declaring his ideas about American autonomy within the empire "incongruous" and "absurd" (3–4). For a detailed comment about the author of *Some Fugitive Thoughts,* see John Pringle to William Tilghman, 1 Nov., folder 59, Preston Davie Papers. The *Freeman* pamphlet led to Drayton's removal from the South Carolina Council in March

1775. The controversy can be followed in letters from William Bull and Drayton himself to Dartmouth, in CO 5/396, fols. 61, 88, 122, 126–30; in CO 5/380, fols. 136–42; and in Drayton, *Memoirs,* 1:149–53, 158–60. Many of the documents are published in R. W. Gibbes, ed., *Documentary History of the American Revolution, . . . Chiefly in South Carolina* (New York: D. Appleton, 1855), 1:39–85. Henry Laurens read the pamphlet in London in October, approving its message (*HL Papers,* 9:599).

173 **Boucher's *Letter:*** [Boucher], *Letter from a Virginian,* 4, 5, 9.

174 **Boucher turned to history:** Ibid., 21, 29.

174 **The other pamphlet:** A copy of Chandler's *American Querist* without publication information is no. 106656 at the Huntington Library; it has Captain John Montresor's name as the owner, and thus was probably produced in New York, where he was stationed as a British officer in August (although he was in Boston by late October). This could have been the edition burned; Adams attributes that printing to Rivington (see *American Independence,* 82). The Huntington copy of the "eleventh edition" (no. 12085) is the one cited in this book; pagination differs in the various printings. The Boston Athenaeum has two copies of the "tenth edition" (one once owned by Thomas Jones, a New York Loyalist; another seemingly owned serially by Sir James Wright and William Franklin); and a copy of the Boston edition. Such information suggests a wide distribution and readership for the pamphlet, as do the many surviving copies listed in the English Short Title Catalogue and by Adams, *American Independence,* 82–83. An unspecified Rivington edition was advertised for sale in *DPaPkt* on 17 October 1774.

175 **A brief comment:** Untitled comment beginning "POPLICOLA and Company," *NYJ,* 8 Sept. 1774, 2. No newspaper report of any burning of the pamphlet has been discovered.

176 **Chandler's initial seven queries:** Chandler, *American Querist,* 5–8 (quotations: 5, 8). L. F. S. Upton pointed out that in the *Querist* Chandler drew on "the full range of argumentation available to him" in his one hundred questions. See Upton, "Dilemma of Loyalist Pamphleteers," 80. In *Ideological Origins,* Bailyn placed special emphasis on Chandler's thirteenth question (see 313–14).

176 **The clergyman next posed:** Chandler, *American Querist,* 9–22 (quotations: 9, 10, 22).

176 **Query 74 echoed:** Quotations: ibid., 25, 26, 29, 30, 32.

177 **Chandler's remarks:** So the eventual Loyalist Peter Van Schaack told his friend James Duane, one of the New York delegates, "It must be the Wish of every good Member of the Community that every thing might remain suspended till the Result of yr Deliberations are known. Are we

not otherwise in Danger of defeating the Prospect we might have from the Wisdom of your Measures?" (Van Schaack to Duane, draft, n.d. [Sept. 1774], box 4, Van Schaack Family Papers). General Frederick Haldimand too expressed the hope that the congress would prove to be "more moderate"; see his letter to Dartmouth, 7 Sept., in *DAR*, 8:193.

177 **Most of the congressmen:** *JA Diary*, 2:119–21, 156 (entries for 1, 2, 3 Sept., 24 Oct. 1774). For other initial impressions, see Joseph Galloway to William Franklin, 3 Sept., in *DAR*, 8:184–85. Some delegates carried letters of introduction to prominent Philadelphians from mutual friends. For examples introducing the Virginia delegation, see Thomson Mason to John Dickinson, 25 Aug., box 1, folder 9, R. R. Logan Collection; and Robert Pleasants to Anthony Benezet, and to William Fisher, 20 Aug., Robert Pleasants Letterbook. Conversely, some correspondents warned delegates against others: John Adams was cautioned not to trust Joseph Galloway (*LOD*, 1:3, 6–7), and Samuel Adams was warned about Silas Deane (William Williams to Adams, 30 July, SA Papers). Washington recorded many dinners with Philadelphians but no personal observations: Jackson, *Diaries of George Washington*, 3:275–87.

178 **congressmen immediately confronted:** James Duane, Notes of Debates, 5 Sept. 1774, in *LOD*, 1:25; *JCC*, 1:27; William Bradford to James Madison, 17 Oct., in *JM Papers*, 1:126 (quoting the librarian). North Carolina's delegates did not arrive until 7 Sept. (*JCC*, 1:28).

178 **rebuke to Galloway:** Galloway to William Franklin, 5 Sept., in *LOD*, 1:27, also in *DAR*, 8:185–86. Franklin forwarded this letter to Dartmouth, adding that Thomson was "one of the most violent *Sons of Liberty* (so called) in America." See also James Duane, Notes of Debates, 5 Sept. 1774, in *LOD*, 1:25.

178 **Congressional rules:** *JCC*, 1:25–26 (also *LOD*, 1:31). On Duché, see Clarke Garrett, "The Spiritual Journey of Jacob Duché," *Proceedings of the American Philosophical Society* 119, no. 2 (April 1975): 143–55. Duché had to defend his role at the congress when he applied to the British government for compensation after the war; see his claims memorial, 28 Oct. 1783; and testimony, 14 Sept. 1784, AO 12/38.

179 **decision to keep the content:** For comments on the delegates' secrecy rule, see Charles Carroll of Carrollton to Charles Carroll of Annapolis, 7 Sept., in Hoffman, *Dear Papa*, 2:733 (see also same to same, 9, 12 Sept., 735, 737); Samuel Wharton to [Thomas Walpole], 23 Sept., in "Wharton Letter-Books 33," 446; and William Bradford to James Madison, 17 Oct. 1774, in *JM Papers*, 1:126. After the congress adjourned, some detailed information about the debates was forwarded to Dartmouth by third parties who had received reports from delegates (for example, William

Knox to Dartmouth, 15 Nov., reel 11, no. 994; William Molleson to same, 17 Dec., reel 11, no. 1023; ZYX to same, 8 Jan. 1775, reel 12, no. 1093, Dartmouth Papers).

179 **Two of the three most informative:** William Franklin to Dartmouth, 6 Sept. 1774, in *DAR*, 8:191–92, enclosing Galloway's letters of 3 and 5 Sept., in ibid., 184–86 (see account of congressional organizing above for information from these letters). The calendar in *DAR*, 7:167, indicates that Dartmouth received Franklin's letter on 11 October 1774. Franklin belatedly advised Dartmouth that secrecy was important because his sources would not know that he was passing on information to the ministry, and they might not continue communication with him if they knew (Franklin to Dartmouth, 3 April 1775, in Ricord and Nelson, *Documents Relating to the Colonial History of the State of New Jersey*, 10:570–71).

179 **Franklin and others in London:** Benjamin Franklin to Galloway, 25 Feb. 1775, in *BF Papers*, 21:508. For the third such letter: William Knox to Dartmouth, 15 Nov. 1774, reel 11, no. 994, Dartmouth Papers (forwarding information from Colden, see below). On Jay, see William Lee to Richard Henry Lee, 25 Feb. 1775, in Ford, *Letters of William Lee*, 1:127–28; Stephen Sayre to Samuel Adams, 4 April 1775, SA Papers; William Lee to Adams, 10 April, SA Papers. In the letters to Adams, Jay's name has been crossed out but is still legible; Lee rendered Galloway's as "Mr. G———y." Jay could have been suspected in part because of his friendship and continuing correspondence with John Vardill (Poplicola). See Jay to Vardill (in London), 24 Sept. 1774, in *LOD*, 1:95, in which Jay remarked that he had to be "very reserved" in his comments because of "the Injunction of Secrecy laid on all Members of the Congress." Later, Galloway claimed that he had described the "secret proceedings" of the congress to William Franklin, who concurred; see Galloway's claims memorial, n.d. [1783], and Franklin's testimony, 18 Feb. 1784, AO 12/38, fols. 22, 94–95. But whether he referred to more than those early letters is unknown.

180 **The first session:** John Adams, Notes of Debates, 6 Sept. 1774, in *LOD*, 1:29; John Witherspoon, "Thoughts on American Liberty," reprinted in Gerlach, *New Jersey in the American Revolution*, 85–87. This appears to have been the unnamed pamphlet that one of Dartmouth's correspondents indicated was distributed on the evening of Sept. 3; see T. Webb to Dartmouth, 8 Sept., CO 5/1285, fol. 66.

180 **congress's deliberations:** Zachariah Hood to James Russell, 10 Sept. 1774, bundle 8, Russell Papers; *JA Diary*, 2:124 (entry of 6 Sept.). See also Eliza Farmar to Jack, 19 Sept., in "Letters of Farmar," 201; Charles Carroll of Carrollton to Charles Carroll of Annapolis, 7 Sept., in Hoffman, *Dear Papa*, 2:733.

181 **A congressman later recounted:** Samuel Ward to Samuel Ward Jr., 24 Sept. 1774, in *LOD*, 1:98 (see also ibid., 85); *JCC* 1:28 (for committee appointments); *JA Diary*, 2:127 (entry of 8 Sept.).

181 **the powder alarm:** Deborah to Thomas Cushing, 14 Sept. 1774, Cushing Family II Papers; Farish, *Journal of Fithian*, 191–92, 194 (diary entries of 17, 18, 22 Sept.). The story reached the senior Charles Carroll in Annapolis on the eleventh (Hoffman, *Dear Papa*, 2:739) and Alexandria, Virginia, on the fourteenth (Harry Piper to Dixon & Littledale, 14 Sept., Harry Piper Letterbook). For an expression of skepticism in Maryland, see Thomas Ringgold to Samuel Galloway, 11 Sept., Galloway Maxcy Markoe Papers, 13:10248. Accurate but incomplete accounts of the Boston-area events were finally published in Philadelphia papers in mid-September (*PaG* [supp.], 16 Sept.; *DPaPkt*, 12, 19 Sept.).

181 **The powder alarm began:** *The Following Is a Copy of a Letter, Said to Be Wrote by Gen. Brattle, to the Commander in Chief*, Cambridge, 29 Aug. 1774, broadside (*EAI*, no. 13176), also printed in *PIR*, 603–4. On 2 September, Brattle published a broadside, *To the Public*, defending his conduct (*EAI*, no. 42567). John Rowe termed it "a Flimsey Recantation" (*Rowe Diary*, 283; entry of 2 Sept.). Richmond, *Powder Alarm 1774*, chap. 4, has a good brief description of the manufacture and storage of gunpowder in the eighteenth century.

181 **That move, undertaken by a large number:** See Raphael, *First American Revolution*, 112–30, for another account of these events; for "boys and negroes," *BG* (supp.), 5 Sept. 1774. A version of the story that passed through Hartford attributed the purported deaths to guards protecting Brattle's house in Cambridge; see Titus Hosmer to Silas Deane, n.d. [ca. 4 Sept.], in "Deane Correspondence," 154.

182 **Ezra Stiles of Newport:** The narrative in this paragraph and the next is based on *Stiles Diary*, 1:476–85, esp. 477, 482–84 (entry of 17 Nov. 1774). Months later, Stiles was still so interested in the story that he copied into his diary details about Putnam's missive that appeared in a London newspaper; ibid., 509–11 (entry of 25 Jan. 1775).

182 **a letter Putnam dispatched:** Ibid., 1:483, quoting Putnam's words; William Cooper to Putnam, 7 Sept. 1774, in *AA* 4, 1:783 (see also ibid., 325). Gurdon Saltonstall, Silas Deane's father-in-law, expressed skepticism about Putnam's story from the outset, thinking it "improbable." He reported Keyes's denial of responsibility for the tale to Deane on 5 September, in "Deane Correspondence," 150–51. In early October, Putnam published a defense of his conduct in the *New London Gazette*, seeking to correct "unfavourable impressions"; it was reprinted in several newspapers, including *NMerc*, 17 Oct., and *NYJ*, 27 Oct. A satirist attributed

the circulation of the false story to men plotting to distract the congress from its work; see Mulford, *John Leacock's First Book,* 54.

182 **in Cambridge on September 2:** Quotation: Samuel Cooper to Benjamin Franklin, 9 Sept. 1774, in *BF Papers,* 21:299. For general accounts of these events: Thomas Oliver to Dartmouth, 3 Sept., in *DAR,* 8:182–84; and *Stiles Diary,* 1:478–85 (entry of 17 Nov.). One of Stiles's sources was a man who described women's patriotic ardor during the crisis. He said he saw them making bullets, gathering supplies, and urging their husbands and sons to "fight courageously & manfully & behave themselves bravely for liberty" (ibid., 480).

183 **All seemed likely to end:** Hallowell to Gage, 8 Sept. 1774, in *PIR,* 611 (see 609–12); Hallowell to Grey Cooper, 5 Sept., in *DAR,* 8:189–91.

183 **Colonists who favored:** Abigail to John, 2 Sept. 1774, in *AFC* 1:147; Revere to John Lamb, 4 Sept., John Lamb Papers; Warren to Samuel Adams, Sept., SA Papers; *Stiles Diary,* 1:457 (entry of 25 Sept.). Mercy Otis Warren and her friend Hannah Quincy Lincoln disagreed about these events; see Warren to Lincoln, 3 Sept., in Richards and Harris, *Warren Letters,* 33–35.

183 **Henry Hulton and Nathaniel Coffin:** Hulton to two unnamed correspondents, 13, 8 Sept. 1774, in York, *Henry Hulton,* 309, and Hulton's retrospective account, 169; Coffin to Charles Steuart, Aug.–Sept. [27 Sept.], reel 2, fol. 263, Steuart Papers; Elizabeth Adams to her husband, 18 Sept., SA Papers. See also Robert McKenzie to George Washington, 13 Sept., in *GW Papers: CS,* 10:161, and vice versa, 4 Oct., ibid., 171–72; and John Andrews to William Barrell, 9 Sept., in "Andrews Letters," 357–58.

184 **Talk about attacking:** William Read, untitled statement, 15 Sept. 1774, Israel Williams Papers; Seth Tubbs, untitled, undated statement, Israel Williams Papers. See Gregory H. Nobles, *Divisions Throughout the Whole: Politics and Society in Hampshire County, Massachusetts, 1740–1775* (Cambridge, U.K.: Cambridge University Press, 1983), 171–76, for a somewhat different interpretation of this incident and for a more complete discussion of its context. Another incident in which a crowd was composed of men from "Neighbouring Towns" is described in *PIR,* 1228.

185 **The potential recruits:** James Hunt, untitled statement, 15 Sept. 1774, and Benjamin Read, untitled statement, 15 Sept., Israel Williams Papers. The other two towns that supplied men for the crowd were Chesterfield and Number 5 (now Cummington).

185 **Early on the morning:** Miller and Riggs, *Romance, Remedies, and Revolution,* 115–17 (entries for 6–8 Sept. 1774). See Bruce G. Merritt, "Loyalism and Social Conflict in Revolutionary Deerfield, Massachusetts," *JAH* 57 (1970): 277–89, for more on the Williams and Ashley families; and, on the

region in general, Robert J. Taylor, *Western Massachusetts in the Revolution* (1954; New York: Kraus Reprint, 1967); and Lee Nathaniel Newcomer, *The Embattled Farmers: A Massachusetts Countryside in the American Revolution* (New York: Columbia University Press, 1953).

185 **The recorded exchanges:** Miller and Riggs, *Romance, Remedies, and Revolution,* 116n365, points out that Israel Williams was not in town on the fast day and that the purported violator of it was instead his son, Israel Williams Jr.

185 **They characterized their targets:** Smith, *Freedoms We Lost,* chap. 3, offers insights into the dynamics of small communities coping with divisive disputes between elite and ordinary residents.

186 **had not elected a provincial congress:** Quotation: Adams to Joseph Warren, Sept. 1774, in *SA Writings,* 3:157. For example, the Worcester convention requested, and received, the resignation of judges who had signed the welcoming address to Gage, but retained in office other justices, along with sheriffs and some local officials, until a provincial congress could decide on additional steps. See *PIR,* 904–10 (6–7 Sept.). Other records of county meetings: ibid., 898–904 (Essex County, meeting in Ipswich, 6–7 Sept.); 922–24 (Middlesex, meeting in Concord, 13 Sept.), 941–47 (Plymouth County, meeting in Plimpton and Plymouth, 26–27 Sept.); and 958–63 (Bristol County, meeting in Taunton, 28–29 Sept.). A county meeting in Worcester in August, by contrast, had focused on protest, not governance (ibid., 877–80).

187 **The most important convention:** This paragraph and the next four are based on *At a Meeting of the Delegates of Every Town and District in the County of Suffolk* . . . [9 Sept. 1774], broadside (*EAI,* no. 13646), also in *PIR,* 914–20. An earlier draft, which differs considerably, is in ibid., 910–14. Benjamin Kent to Samuel Adams, 20 Aug., SA Papers, described the initial stages of organizing the Suffolk convention; see also *PIR,* 647, 682–84, 794–95, 882.

188 **Employing the word "manly":** Eunice Paine to Robert Treat Paine, 16 Sept. 1774, in *RTP Papers,* 3:5. For similar terminology, see also records of Cumberland County convention, 21–22 Sept., in *PIR,* 935 (which did not copy Suffolk County); and Hampshire County convention, 22–23 Sept., in *PIR,* 940 (which adopted the exact Suffolk language). See also items reprinted in *AA* 4, 1:510, 626, 685 ("every power of manhood"), 756; and the comments of Wells, in *Few Political Reflections,* for example, 33: "The day of independant manhood is at hand—we *feel* our strength." Two congressional delegates used "manly" as Eunice Paine did, to indicate steady but not provocative conduct (*LOD,* 1:97, 247).

189 **The fervent prose of the Suffolk Resolves:** The convention also addressed

Gage to complain about new fortifications on Boston Neck; the delegates' letter, his reply, and their further response are all printed in *PIR*, 612–18. The exchanges ended with Gage's statement that he "could not see that any further Argumentation upon the Subject would be to any good Purpose" (ibid., 618n117).

189 **The leaders of the Suffolk convention:** *JCC*, 1:31–39, indicates a discussion on Saturday, 17 September 1774, only. For Galloway's comment: *LOD*, 1:121. See also Thomas Cushing to Richard Devens and Isaac Foster Jr., 19 Sept., Misc. MSS Bound.

189 **Thomson immediately released:** See *DPaPkt*, 19 Sept. 1774, a report reprinted in *RNYG*, 22 Sept.; *MG&BPB*, 26 Sept., and many other papers. The congressman was Philip Livingston; see his *Other Side of the Question*, 26. Other quotations: Adams, diary entry of 17 Sept., in *LOD*, 1:75; Coffin to Charles Steuart, Aug.–Sept. [27 Sept. section], reel 2, fol. 264, Steuart Papers.

190 **September 10, 1774:** William Lee to Richard Henry Lee, 10 Sept. 1774, in Ford, *Letters of William Lee*, 1:87–91.

190 **September 15:** Vardill to Duane, 15 Sept. 1774, James Duane Papers. See also Vardill to Peter Van Schaack, 15 Sept., box 4, Van Schaack Family Papers. Dartmouth repeated essentially the same comment in correspondence with colonial governors; see, for example, his letter to John Penn, 7 Sept., in *DAR*, 8:193, which also remarked that there could be "much doubt" about the "propriety and legality" of the congress.

191 **September 24:** Hutchinson to Williams, 24 Sept. 1774, Israel Williams Papers.

191 **October 8:** DeBerdt to Reed, 8 Oct. 1774, fol. 88, Joseph Reed Papers.

191 **October 17:** Dartmouth to Gage, 17 Oct. 1774, in *DAR*, 8:211–12.

191 **October 29:** Laurens to John Petrie and to Laurens Theodore Gronovius, both 29 Oct. 1774, in *HL Papers*, 9:607 ("dismal Gloom"), 608–9 ("Deep Distress," "Felicitie"). Note that Laurens's "country" was still South Carolina. He had been absent from North America for several years, and the change in usage had not yet affected him.

192 **delegates to the congress began:** But according to a Rhode Island delegate, some congressmen would have permitted Parliament "the general Regulation of Trade" (*Stiles Diary*, 1:475; entry of 8 Nov. 1774). See Beeman, *Our Lives, Our Fortunes*, 41–197, for a recent work on the congress. For discussions in earlier books, see Ammerman, *Common Cause*, chaps. 4–7; Rakove, *Beginnings of National Politics*, chap. 3; and Marston, *King and Congress*, chaps. 3, 4. For local context: Robert F. Oaks, "Philadelphia Merchants and the First Continental Congress," *Pennsylvania History* 40 (1973): 146–66.

192 **myriad familiar topics:** The year 1763 as a divide: *JCC,* 1:42; William
Henry Drayton later indicated that the Virginians had insisted on the
limitation to post-1763 legislation (Drayton, *Memoirs,* 1:167–68). No compensation for tea: Silas Deane, diary entry, 1 Oct. 1774, in *LOD,* 1:133; and
Isaac Low's testimony to the Loyalist Claims Commission, ca. 1785, AO
12/21, fol. 106, stating that he and Jay supported reimbursement. Massachusetts government: Joseph Warren to Samuel Adams, 12 Sept. 1774,
SA Papers; William Tudor to John Adams, 3 Sept., and Adams to Tudor,
7 Oct., in *JA Papers,* 2:138–39, 157; John Adams to Abigail Adams,
29 Sept., in *LOD,* 1:128; *JCC,* 1:59–60. Raise and arm a militia: Silas
Deane, diary entries, 1, 3 Oct., in *LOD,* 1:133, 138–39.

193 **Jay succinctly laid out:** John Adams, Notes of Debates, Sept. 1774, in
LOD, 1:105 (Jay's options); Adams to William Tudor, 7 Oct., in ibid., 157;
JCC, 1:40, 43, 77; *Philadelphia. In Congress. Thursday, September 22, 1774,*
broadside (*EAI,* nos. 42733, 13702). Thomas Wharton, who expected "the
principal part of Congress" to dine with him on the twenty-eighth, knew
that day about the 27 September vote for nonimportation; see "Wharton
Letter-Books 33," 451. Despite accepting at least one invitation to dine
with Wharton, Silas Deane did not trust the Quaker merchant, declaring
that he had "as much of the Serpent, as the Dove in his Composition"
(Deane to his wife, Elizabeth, 10–11 Sept., in *LOD,* 1:62).

193 **congress's deliberations:** William Knox to Dartmouth, 15 Nov. 1774,
reel 11, no. 994, Dartmouth Papers, conveying information included in
a confidential letter probably written in late September by a congressman (possibly John Jay) to Colden. Also in late September, Joseph Reed
gave Dartmouth inaccurate details about the proposed agreements. Either
his information was incorrect, or he described a version that was later
amended (Reed to Dartmouth, 25 Sept., reel 2, no. 1023, Dartmouth
Papers).

194 **The debates over nonexportation:** See Adams's and Deane's notes on
these debates in *LOD,* 1:103–5, 145–46, 151–54 (quotation, 103); Eliphalet
Dyer et al. to Trumbull, 10 Oct. 1774, in ibid., 169. See also Samuel Ward
to Governor Joseph Wanton (R.I.), 3 Oct., in ibid., 141, for a comment
similar to that of the Connecticut delegates. Another report on the nonexportation debates, Edward Rutledge to Ralph Izard, 29 Oct., is in Deas,
Correspondence of Ralph Izard, 1:21–25.

194 **had only the partial information:** Reed to Dartmouth, 25 Sept. 1774, reel
2, no. 1023, Dartmouth Papers. John Adams's diary detailed his association
with Reed (*JA Diary,* 2:122, 131–32), as did Esther Reed in a letter to her
brother Dennis, 2 Nov., in Reed, *Life of Esther Reed,* 202. Joseph wrote
again to Dartmouth a month later, once more underscoring colonial unity

and Americans' willingness to carry out the congress's resolutions (Reed to Dartmouth, 24 Oct., reel 2, no. 1054, Dartmouth Papers).

195 **In their sessions, congressmen wrestled:** Some colonists mused about possibilities for imperial reorganization in the preceding months: "a Viceroy a Parliament composed of Delegates from the different Colonies, a Council with hereditary Honors" (Peter Van Schaack to John Vardill, draft, 13 May 1774, box 4, Van Schaack Family Papers); "a supreme magistrate . . . on this continent, . . . with a fixed number from each House of Assembly" (Thomas Wharton to Samuel Wharton, 5 July, in "Wharton Letter-Books 33," 436). But these, like most such ideas, focused only on structures, not on the divisions of authority that intrigued Galloway. Cf. Drayton, *Letter from Freeman,* 15–16, which did lay out such a division based on taxing powers.

195 **Galloway, the experienced Pennsylvania lawyer:** For Galloway's early career and his 1774 illness and depression, see Ferling, *Loyalist Mind,* 7–24. See also Benjamin H. Newcomb, *Franklin and Galloway: A Political Partnership* (New Haven, Conn.: Yale University Press, 1972). His political stance in the 1760s was defended in [Jabez Fisher], *Americanus Examined, and His Principles Compared with Those of the Approved Advocates for America. By a Pennsylvanian* (n.p., 1774). Galloway's claims memorial inaccurately declared that he had actively opposed "rising Sedition" from "early in the year 1774," one of his later distortions of his record (AO 12/38, fol. 20).

195 **Galloway informed a British:** Galloway to Richard Jackson, 10 Aug. 1774, in *Colonies to Nation: 1763–1789,* ed. Jack P. Greene (New York: McGraw-Hill, 1967), 240–41. The pamphlet was titled *Arguments on Both Sides in the Dispute Between Great-Britain and Her Colonies . . . by a Sincere Friend to Both Countries,* published in Ricord and Nelson, *Documents Relating to the Colonial History of the State of New Jersey,* 10:478–92; he enclosed it in his 5 September letter to William Franklin (see above). Adams's notes of debates for 8 September show that Galloway repeated some of the arguments from the pamphlet in the congress that day (*LOD,* 1:47–48).

196 **Galloway later explained:** Galloway, *Candid Examination,* 51. He later indicated that one of those possible additional ideas was to have a council with two branches; see William Franklin to Galloway, 12 March 1775, in *DAR,* 9:79; and Galloway to Franklin, 26 March, in ibid., 9:87.

196 **Pennsylvanian introduced his plan:** "Mr. Galloway's introductory Resolve, proposed with his Plan, to the Congress at Philadelphia," enclosed in Cadwallader Colden to Lord Dartmouth, 7 Dec. 1774, CO 5/1106, fol. 4; and "Introductory Resolves prepared by Mr. Galloway but not carried into the Congress," CO 5/1106, fol. 6. Galloway person-

ally gave these documents to Colden when he visited New York in early December. See Smith's useful editorial note in *LOD*, 1:112–13. For Colden's letter to Dartmouth, 7 Dec.: *DAR*, 8:238.

196 **His Plan of Union applied:** "Joseph Galloway's Plan of Union," in *LOD*, 1:117–18 (also printed elsewhere). Dartmouth replied that the "Idea of Union" was "very just" and possibly "attainable." See Dartmouth to Colden, 7 Jan. 1775, in *Letters of Colden*, 259. The most detailed examination of Galloway's thinking at this time is Robert M. Calhoon, "'I Have Deduced Your Rights': Joseph Galloway's Concept of His Role, 1774–1775," in Calhoon et al., *Tory Insurgents*, 70–88. See Julian Boyd, *Anglo-American Union: Joseph Galloway's Plans to Preserve the British Empire, 1774–1788* (Philadelphia: University of Pennsylvania Press, 1941), esp. chap. 3.

197 **Galloway asserted at the outset:** John Adams, Notes of Debates, 28 Sept. 1774, in *LOD*, 1:109–12.

198 **Other delegates reportedly seconded:** Galloway, *Candid Examination*, 56–57, added information to Adams's record. See Duane to Chase, 29 Dec. 1774; and Chase to Duane, 5 Feb. 1775, in *LOD*, 1:278–80, 304–6. Ferling assesses Galloway's role at the congress in *Loyalist Mind*, 26–34.

198 **Galloway on several occasions:** Galloway, claims memorial, n.d. [1783], AO 12/38, fol. 22 (assembly/convention distinction, "civil War") (see also fols. 20, 39); Galloway, *Candid Examination*, 56 ("secret"); Galloway, speech to congress as reconstructed in 1780, in *LOD*, 1:119 ("connexion"); *The Examination of Joseph Galloway, Esq. . . . Before the House of Commons*, 2nd ed. (London: J. Wilkie, 1780), 52 ("gentlemen"). Galloway's 1780 version of the speech omitted his explicit criticism of the Stamp Act recorded by Adams, among other discreet modifications (*LOD*, 1:119–27). Ammerman convincingly rejects Galloway's characterization of such a division at the congress (*Common Cause*, chap. 7). Duane, Jay, and Isaac Low all supported Galloway's plan; on Low, see his testimony to the Loyalist Claims Commission, ca. 1785, AO 12/21, fol. 106.

198 **misrepresented the reception:** [Dickinson and Thomson], "To the Author of a Pamphlet, Entitled, 'A Candid Examination . . . ,'" *PaJ*, 8 March 1775; Duane to Thomas Johnson, 29 Dec. 1774, in *LOD*, 1:281. A delegate, though, later told Ezra Stiles that the plan was "almost universally rejected" (*Stiles Diary*, 1:475). For Galloway's accounts of what happened: *Candid Examination*, 52; *Examination of Galloway*, 53; [Galloway], *A Reply to an Address*, 33–35. See editorial notes by Paul Smith (*LOD*, 1:113, 116) and Worthington C. Ford (*JCC*, 1:43). The divided colony appears to have been Rhode Island (*LOD*, 1:234). Galloway also charged that Thomson "expunged" the plan from the minutes, but Bernhard Knol-

lenberg points out that Thomson omitted all failed resolutions from the published record, so no explicit action was necessary to "expunge" Galloway's plan. See Knollenberg, *Growth of the American Revolution, 1766–1775* (New York: Free Press, 1975), 246.

199 **option of utilizing commercial weapons:** The most comprehensive study of the colonists' conclusions about commerce, and the policies they instituted as a result, is Breen, *Marketplace of Revolution.*

199 **The decision they made:** Deane to Trumbull, 22 Oct. 1774, in *LOD,* 1:227; Eliphalet Dyer et al. to Trumbull, 10 Oct., in ibid., 1:168; John Sullivan and Nathaniel Folsom to Meshech Weare, 12 Oct., in ibid., 181. See *JCC,* 1:57, 62–63, 75, 80–81, for the uninformative minutes about the debates on the Association.

200 **The Association itself:** Continental Association, 20 Oct. 1774, in *JCC,* 1:77–81, esp. 77–79. Galloway explained his signature as purely formulaic, not accurately reflecting his opposition to the Association, both in print (Galloway, *Reply to an Address,* 39–40) and in his testimony before the Loyalist Claims Commission in London, 12 Feb. 1784, AO 12/38, fols. 40–41. For "too warm & indiscreet," see Galloway to Thomas Nickleson, 1 Nov. 1774, in *LOD,* 1:255. James Duane's position on the Association is unclear: he told Colden he too dissented from the final congressional proceedings (see Colden to Dartmouth, 7 Dec., in *DAR,* 8:238), but Henry White reported that same day that Duane was "the most violent [of the New York delegates] for supporting the Congress" ([Henry White] to William Tryon, 7 Dec., reel 11, no. 1011, Dartmouth Papers). Isaac Low reportedly disapproved; see Ebenezer Hazard to Silas Deane, 1 Feb. 1775, in "Deane Correspondence," 194.

202 **controversies over the salvaged EIC tea:** See chapter 1, above; and, for more detail about mobbing on the Cape, Norton, "Seventh Tea Ship," 694–702.

202 **social and economic punishment:** For the sorts of random violent or coercive acts in September that the Association was designed to prevent, see, for example, Joseph Spencer to Jonathan Trumbull, 14 Sept. 1774, in *AA* 4, 1:787; Abigail to John Adams, 14 Sept., in *AFC,* 1:151–52; Henry Pelham to John Singleton Copley, 16 Feb. 1775 (reporting an incident in September 1774), in *Letters of Copley and Pelham,* 290–92; and the statements and depositions relating to a purported attempt to assassinate a Dr. Russell, 15–20 Sept., Misc. MSS Bound.

203 **Just as the congress was finishing:** But not all North American British colonies uniformly rejected EIC tea in the fall of 1774, although it was not necessarily greeted warmly. See Governor Francis Legge (Nova Scotia) to Lord Dartmouth, 20 Sept., 18 Oct. 1774, in *DAR,* 8:199, 7:191.

203 **The brig *Peggy Stewart*:** Statements of Jackson and Stewart, 17 Oct. 1774, reprinted in Eddis, *Letters from America,* 91–95 (quotation, 93); "To the Public, Messrs's Vindication," *NYJ,* 8 Dec. 1774. The customs collector told a different and dubious story, informing a crowd that Stewart forced him "against his Inclination" to accept payment of the tea duty. See Richard Jackson, affidavit, 10 March 1777, in Fisher, "Burning of the 'Peggy Stewart,'" 239. The fallout from the affair also involved Thomas Charles Williams, the nominal head of the firm, in New York; see two broadsides, both titled *To the Public,* 27 Oct., 21 Nov. 1774 (*EAI,* nos. 13675, 13676), the latter calling him a "most daring, insolent, and flagitious Criminal."

203 **a disastrous mistake:** Narrative in this paragraph and the next based on memorial of Anthony Stewart and Thomas Charles Williams to Lords of Treasury, 10 March 1777, in Fisher, "Burning of the 'Peggy Stewart,'" 235–38 ("Fury," 236); Richard Jackson, affidavit, 10 March 1777, in ibid., 239–41; John Galloway to Samuel Galloway, 20 Oct. 1774, in Kelly, "'Tulip Hill,'" 373–75 ("clamorous," 373); and Eddis, *Letters from America,* 91–97. *The Brig* Peggy Stewart, *Captain Jackson, from London . . . ,* 20 Oct. 1774, broadside (*EAI,* no. 13120), reprints the statement the men signed. James Parker to Charles Steuart, 26 Oct. 1774, reel 2, fol. 273, Steuart Papers, included the information that the other cargo had been unloaded from the ship. The Williams brothers blamed Stewart and complained that they should not have had to apologize; they also described Hammond's role ("To the Public," *RNYG,* 10 Nov. 1774; *NYJ,* 8 Dec.). For another account of the incident, see Hoffman, *Spirit of Dissension,* 133–37.

204 **He was not the only one:** John Galloway to Samuel Galloway, 20 Oct. 1774, in Kelly, "'Tulip Hill,'" 373–74.

205 **Galloway assumed:** Ibid., 374–75 (see also Thomas Ringgold to Samuel Galloway, 25 Oct. 1774, in ibid., 375–76). *The Brig* Peggy Stewart . . . , 20 Oct., broadside (*EAI,* no. 13120), was reprinted more or less verbatim in many newspapers; see, for example, *PaJ,* 26 Oct.; *BG,* 7 Nov.; *NPkt,* 24 Nov. Only the New York papers, *RNYG,* 10 Nov., and *NYJ,* 8 Dec. (following Holt's printing of the broadside on 26 Oct.), published additional information—statements supplied by the Annapolis merchants. A Bostonian compared the burning of the ship to the equally involuntary resignations of the mandamus councillors; see James Lovell to Josiah Quincy Jr., 3 Nov., in "Quincy Letters," 473.

205 **Maryland merchant:** Alexander Hamilton to James Brown & Co., 31 Oct. 1774, in McMaster and Skaggs, "Letterbooks of Alexander Hamilton," 319; "Extract of a Letter from a Gentleman at Bladensburg, Md . . . ," 1 Nov., in *AA* 4, 1:953.

205 **Americans' opinion appeared divided:** Reed to Quincy, 26 Oct. 1774, in

AA 4, 1:892; Carroll of Annapolis to Carroll of Carrollton, 21 Oct. 1774, in Hoffman, *Dear Papa,* 2:749; Lee to Stewart, 4 Jan. 1775, in Ford, *Letters of William Lee,* 1:106. For more opinions, see *AA* 4, 2:309–11; Harry Piper to Samuel Martin, 26 Oct. 1774, Piper Letterbook; and James Parker to Charles Steuart, 26 Oct., 1, 5 Nov. 1774, reel 2, fols. 273–74, 278, Steuart Papers. A letter published in London did reveal the vote against destroying the ship (Willard, *Letters on the American Revolution,* 5).

206 **It is unclear what message Americans:** James Parker included, then corrected, the gallows story in his letters to Charles Steuart, 1, 5 Nov. 1774, reel 2, fols. 274, 278, Steuart Papers.

206 **Webb wrote from New Haven:** Webb to Deane, 10 Oct. 1774, in "Deane Correspondence," 187.

CHAPTER 6 A FERMENT THROUGHOUT THE CONTINENT

207 **few reliable sources:** Samuel Swift to Cushing, 2 Oct. 1774, in *Belknap Papers,* 55; Warren to Adams, 29 Sept., SA Papers. The extracts appeared in *MSpy* on 29 September, conveying the congress's approval of the Suffolk Resolves. Eagerly awaited newspapers so infrequently reached Robert Carter's Virginia plantation that "it is said that the Post Men are bribed & give away the News papers." See Farish, *Journal of Fithian,* 203 (entry of 10 Oct., with Fithian's complaint about "no intelligence of the carryings on of the Congress").

207 **Intense interest and comments:** John Pringle to William Tilghman, 15 Sept. 1774, folder 59, Preston Davie Papers; Parker to Charles Steuart, 26 Sept., reel 2, fol. 259, Steuart Papers; Simon Deane to Silas Deane, 15 Oct., in "Deane Correspondence," 191; Jared Ingersoll to Jonathan Ingersoll, 24 Oct. 1774, in Dexter, *Correspondence of Jared Ingersoll,* 449. Rumors nevertheless abounded. For an accurate story, see William Fitzhugh to James Russell, 18 Oct., bundle 6, Russell Papers; for an inaccurate one, see Thomas Gage to Lord Barrington, 25 Sept., in Carter, *Correspondence of Gage,* 2:654.

207 **Governors, too, knew little:** Bull to Dartmouth, 12 Oct. 1774, CO 5/396, fol. 92. He continued to report that nothing much was happening in South Carolina with respect to the "American discontents" through 19 December (CO 5/396, fol. 98). For routine business, see Sir James Wright to Dartmouth, 1 Oct.; Cadwallader Colden to same, 2 Oct.; John Penn to same, 4 Nov., in *DAR,* 8:202–4, 228–29.

208 **the uncertainty finally ended:** James Allen to Ralph Izard, 29 Oct. 1774, in Deas, *Correspondence of Ralph Izard,* 1:28; Van Schaack to John Vardill, 3 Jan. 1775, draft, box 4, Van Schaack Family Papers; Z, "To the People of New Jersey," *RNYG,* 1 Dec. 1774, reprinted in *AA* 4, 1:987–89, without

the signature. A reply to Z by Y appeared in *NYJ*, 12 Jan. 1775, reprinted in *AA* 4, 1:1096–97.

208 **"the utmost Unanimity"**: Reed to Dartmouth, 6 Nov. 1774, reel 2, no. 1068, Dartmouth Papers.

209 **Unnerved by the crowd action**: Gage to Boston selectmen, 6 Sept. 1774, in *PIR*, 666 (see also the further exchange on 9 Sept., in ibid., 666–67). John Andrews told William Barrell about the placement of the cannon, 9 September, in "Andrews Letters," 358. Both Joseph Warren and Benjamin Church described the fortifications and the guards' actions to Samuel Adams in separate letters dated 29 September, SA Papers. The selectmen later enlisted the Continental Congress to complain to Gage about the fortifications; an exchange of letters in October is printed in *PIR*, 1216–18, 1224–25.

209 **Gage took steps**: "Diary of Newell," 358. In New York, resistance to Gage's orders soon surfaced. A broadside published in Manhattan commended "those worthy citizens, who have, to their immortal honour," refused to allow their ships to be employed in transporting soldiers and matériel to New England. See *A Card*, New York, 9 Sept. 1774, broadside (*EAI*, no. 13184). For Philadelphia: *To the Public*, New York, 28 Sept., broadside (*EAI*, no. 13667). See also James Lovell to Josiah Quincy Jr., 3 Nov., in "Quincy Letters," 474, for pressures on Rhode Islanders and Marylanders who were supplying the troops. Richard Lechmere commented that because he was an Addresser and allowed the troops to be housed in his distillery, he had become "one of the most obnoxious of all the friends of Government" (Lechmere to Lane, Son & Fraser, 28 Sept., Misc. MSS Bound).

209 **Bostonians probably welcomed**: Minutes, selectmen and Boston committee of correspondence (hereafter BCC), 24, 26 Sept. 1774, in *PIR*, 701–3; Andrews to William Barrell, 25 Sept., in "Andrews Letters," 368 ("country brethren"); minutes, BCC, 27 Sept., in *PIR*, 704–6. The untitled broadside in which the joint committees urged withholding all supplies from the troops, 29 Sept., is *EAI*, no. 13162. One of the first recorded expressions of "uneasiness" came from the Medford committee of correspondence, after the barrack master asked the town to supply bricks. See Medford committee to Charlestown committee, 21 Sept., Misc. MSS Bound; and Samuel Locke, for several town committees, to BCC, 26 Sept., in *PIR*, 842.

210 **The directive had immediate consequences**: Summary based on Andrews's letters to William Barrell, 26 Sept. to 26 Nov. 1774, in "Andrews Letters," 368–87 (quotations, in order, 372, 379, 386–87). See also Joseph Warren to Samuel Adams, 29 Sept., SA Papers; and, on the Portsmouth

carpenters, John Wentworth to T. W. Waldron, 25 Oct., in *Belknap Papers,* 57; and to Dartmouth, 15 Nov., in Bouton, *Documents of New-Hampshire,* 7:417–18. For the quartermaster's account of the same events, see "Extract of a Letter from Colonel Robinson . . . ," 3 Nov., reel 12, no. 1094, Dartmouth Papers. Officers, though, continued to live in houses scattered through the city; see Jane Mecom to Benjamin Franklin, 5–15 Dec., in *BF Papers,* 21:371; and *AA* 4, 1:980 (also 991). For Maine, see two reports to Gage in late October, in *PIR,* 1225–28. The epidemic is chronicled in Elizabeth Fenn, *Pox Americana: The Great Smallpox Epidemic of 1775–82* (New York: Hill and Wang, 2001).

210 **Gage wrote regularly:** Gage to Dartmouth, 20 Sept. 1774, in *DAR,* 8:197–98; same to same, 25 Sept., in ibid., 201; same to same, 30 Oct., in ibid., 222–23. His order dissolving the new assembly: 28 Sept., in *PIR,* 554. See also Gage to Dartmouth, 17 Oct., in *DAR,* 8:212–13; and Gage to Lord Barrington, 3, 17 Oct., in Carter, *Correspondence of Gage,* 2:656.

210 **friends and relatives:** For example, William Tudor to John Adams, 17 Sept. 1774, in *JA Papers,* 2:167; Joseph Greenleaf to Robert Treat Paine, 16 Oct., in *RTP Papers,* 3:11; Samuel Swift to Thomas Cushing, 2 Oct., in *Belknap Papers,* 55. Events in Boston during this period were satirized in a popular series of broadsides published in Philadelphia between October 1774 and February 1775 and republished as a pamphlet. See Mulford, *John Leacock's First Book.* One of those interested in reading Leacock's satires was David Greenough in Wellfleet; see David to Thomas Greenough, 4 Feb. 1775, HM 70286, Greenough Family Papers. On the pamphlet's popularity, see Slauter, "Reading and Radicalization," 14, 40.

211 **Young revealed that his wife:** Young to Samuel Adams, [20 Sept. 1774], SA Papers; Deborah to Thomas Cushing, 19, 21 Sept., Cushing Family II Papers; Thomas to Deborah Cushing, 4 Oct., in *LOD,* 1:142. Similarly, Silas Deane praised the "daughters of liberty" he met in Philadelphia, including Esther DeBerdt Reed; see *LOD,* 1:61, 92. On Young, see Maier, *Old Revolutionaries,* 101–38, esp. 110, on his sudden move to Newport.

212 **Massachusetts delegates' wives:** Quotation: Abigail Greenleaf to Paine, 8 Oct. 1774, in *RTP Papers,* 3:9 (see also 15, 16). For Abigail Adams: *AFC,* 1:161, 172–73. For women's reluctance to discuss politics, see Norton, *Liberty's Daughters,* chap. 6; and for the origins of that hesitancy, with special reference to *The Spectator,* Norton, *Separated by Their Sex,* chap. 4.

213 **commentaries in letters to each other:** Winthrop to Warren, 27 Sept. 1774, in *Warren-Adams Letters,* 33 ("Horrors"); Winthrop to Warren, 27 Oct., Winthrop-Warren Correspondence ("perplext"); Warren to Winthrop, Sept. [*sic;* probably Oct.], ibid. For the differences in the content of

women's letters to each other, as opposed to their letters to male relatives, see Norton, *Separated by Their Sex*, 179.

213 **instruct her younger cousin:** Cranch to Smith, 15 Oct. 1774, in *AFC*, 1:171–72.

213 **Isaac resisted Mary's message:** Smith to Cranch, 20 Oct. 1774, in ibid., 174–76. Isaac went into exile in England as a Loyalist but maintained cordial ties to his extended family.

214 **Isaac Smith's concerns:** Elizabeth Smith to John Adams, 14 Oct. 1774, in *AFC*, 1:169, 168; Greenleaf to Paine, 8 Oct., in *RTP Papers*, 3:9. For the attack on Leonard's house in August, see chapter 4, above.

214 **provincial congress could provide:** Town meeting minutes, Boston, 21 Sept. 1774, in *PIR*, 650–53; several town committees to BCC, 26 Sept., in ibid., 841 (see also 846, 847, 1295, 1305, 1307); "Resolutions of Members Attending the General Court," 7 Oct., in ibid., 1074–76, 1091. For Boston's attempts to preempt disturbances, see Boston town meeting, minutes, 7 Nov. 1774, in *PIR*, 1238. The town's leaders had earlier thwarted the sort of attack that concerned them; see accounts of what happened to the ironmonger and Addresser Joseph Scott, who in late September angered Bostonians by selling cannon and cannonballs to the British army: Joseph Greenleaf to Robert Treat Paine, 27 Sept. 1774, in *RTP Papers*, 3:7; Joseph Warren to Samuel Adams, 29 Sept., SA Papers; and BCC to First Continental Congress, 29 Sept., in *AA* 4, 1:810.

215 **The new congress then had to confront:** Church to Adams, 29 Sept. 1774, SA Papers; Andrews to William Barrell, 5 Oct., in "Andrews Letters," 373; Worcester, Instructions to Timothy Bigelow, 4 Oct., in *PIR*, 1312–13. Raphael first recognized that those instructions in effect declared independence; see *First American Revolution*, 159. On the prevention of court sessions: *PIR*, 947–54 (Barnstable), 1215–16, 1314–17 (Plymouth).

215 **Most members of the Provincial Congress:** Warren to John Adams, 16 Oct. 1774, in *JA Papers* 2:191; Provincial Congress, minutes, 27, 29 Oct., in *PIR*, 1123–24, 1129. For an observation resembling Warren's, see also Elbridge Gerry to Samuel Adams, 15 Oct., SA Papers.

216 **limited agenda:** Provincial Congress, minutes, 13 Oct. 1774, in *PIR*, 1094–95; Gage to Dartmouth, 17 Oct., in *DAR*, 8:212; Provincial Congress, minutes, 17, 27, 29 Oct., in *PIR*, 1100, 1123, 1132–37 ("grievance," 1133). Gage's 17 October response to "a committee to wait on his Excellency," "said to be ordered in a provincial Congress," was published with other documents in Salem in an untitled broadside (*EAI*, no. 42731). Gage employed the same tactic when he replied to a letter from the Continental Congress about the fortifications, writing to Peyton Randolph as an individual rather than as

the presiding officer of the congress; see his report to Dartmouth, 30 Oct., in *DAR*, 8:223.

216 **could not avoid addressing:** The following references are from Provincial Congress, minutes, 21–28 Oct. 1774. Tea: *PIR*, 1106, 1108. Nonconsumption agreement: ibid., 1106, 1109, 1112, 1129–30. Straw for troops: ibid., 1109. Criminals: ibid., 1131 (see also petitions on this point, ibid., 1185, 1186, and 1218–19, about a specific case; and the proceedings of the Barnstable County congress, ibid., 1325). Slaves: ibid., 1112. Abigail Adams agreed with the gist of the motion about enslavement; see her letter to John, 22 Sept. 1774, in *AFC*, 1:162.

217 **receiver general of taxes:** This important issue can be followed in Provincial Congress, minutes, 14–28 Oct. 1774, in *PIR*, 1097, 1103, 1123–28; and in town meeting records, 24 Oct.–6 Dec., ibid., 1292–93, 1297–98, 1301, 1302, 1330, 1332. The town of Concord, 11 Nov. (1298), and Dukes County, 9 Nov. (1319), ordered money paid to Gardner; the others did not. Gray's orders of 31 October and 2 November: ibid., 1207–8; the proclamation, ibid., 2009–10 (broadside, *EAI*, no. 13414).

217 **delegates boldly considered:** Provincial Congress, minutes, 20–27 Oct. 1774, in *PIR*, 1103, 1108, 1111, 1115–25 (quotations, 1103, 1111, 1116, 1118). Final quotation from *In Provincial Congress, Cambridge, October 26, 1774*, broadside (*EAI*, no. 13416). For forced resignations of previous officers, see, for example, *PIR*, 1223, 1228–29. Rhode Island and Connecticut had already adopted similar measures with respect to their militia units; see Bartlett, *Records of Rhode Island*, 7:247, 255, 257, 260; letters to Silas Deane in August and September 1774, in "Deane Correspondence," 140–42, 157–61; and *At a Meeting of Delegates of the Towns in the Counties of New-London and Windham . . .* , 8 Sept., broadside (*EAI*, no. 42660). To Silas Deane, the choice of proper officers was crucial; see Deane to Thomas Mumford, 16 Oct., in *LOD*, 1:203.

217 **troops would need arms:** Provincial Congress, minutes, 22, 25, 28 Oct. 1774, in *PIR*, 1111–14, 1130; Gerry to Adams, 15 Oct., SA Papers (also, same to same, 19 Dec., ibid.); Gerry to [Henry?] Gibbs, 7 Nov., carton 1, Gerry Papers (Billias Collection); "private & confidential" note from New York to William Tryon, 5 Oct., enclosed in Tryon to Dartmouth, 19 Nov., reel 11, no. 997, Dartmouth Papers. Silas Deane's stepson bought arms in New York to carry to New England; see Samuel Webb to Deane, 10 Oct., in "Deane Correspondence," 188. Gerry argued for augmenting the militia much earlier; see Gerry to BCC, 4 April 1774, carton 1, Gerry Papers (Billias Collection). In October, access to arms and ammunition became an issue in South Carolina; see *AA* 4, 1:857, for the policy of the Charleston general committee on that topic.

218 **After the congress adjourned:** Gage to Dartmouth, 30 Oct., in *DAR*, 8:220–21. For contrasting comments on the first session of the Provincial Congress, cf. Joseph Warren to Josiah Quincy Jr., 21 Nov. 1774, in Frothingham, *Life of Joseph Warren*, 394; and John Andrews to William Barrell, 29 Oct., in "Andrews Letters," 380–81 (see also 1, 2, 19 Nov., 382, 385–86). Gage's accurate assessment of the congressmen's tentative approach to governance—despite that body's injunction of secrecy—suggests that he might have had a confidential source among them then, as he did later (see chapter 9).

219 **frequent confrontations:** Mecom to Franklin, 3 Nov. 1774, in *BF Papers*, 21:347; Andrews to William Barrell, 9 Nov., in "Andrews Letters," 383. See also James Lovell to Josiah Quincy Jr., 3 Nov., in "Quincy Letters," 472, for attempts by military and civil authorities to deal with "a little snarl."

219 **The outlook appeared bleak:** James Lovell to Josiah Quincy Jr., 25 Nov. 1774, in "Quincy Letters," 477; James Murray to Charles Steuart, 17 Nov., reel 2, fol. 281, Steuart Papers; Samuel Stillman to Patience Wright, 13 Nov., in "Quincy Letters," 475. See also "Extract of a Letter from Boston," 8 Nov., in Willard, *Letters on the American Revolution*, 5.

219 **New Yorkers were more "moderate":** Colden to Dartmouth, 5 Oct. 1774, in *DAR*, 8:206–7; "Private & Confidential" anonymous note to William Tryon, 5 Oct., enclosed in Tryon to Dartmouth, 19 Nov., reel 11, no. 997, Dartmouth Papers. After two weeks in the city, the visiting governor of North Carolina, Josiah Martin, too concurred that "the spirit of loyalty runs higher here than in any other colony of the continent" (Martin to Dartmouth, 4 Nov., in *DAR*, 8:226). See also "Extract of a Letter from New York," 7 Nov., reel 11, no. 991, Dartmouth Papers, reporting that "the Proceedings of the Congress are very Generally and greatly disliked in this place" and that New York is "the most Moderate & the most Peaceable of any [colony] on the Continent."

220 **from his new base:** Young to John Lamb, 4 Oct. 1774, John Lamb Papers.

220 **nearly constant political battles:** Quotations: *To the Publick*, 1 Oct. 1774, broadside (*EAI*, no. 13484); Colden to Dartmouth, 5 Oct., in *DAR*, 8:207. See the preceding competing broadsides, The Free Citizens, *To the Public*, 14 Sept. (*EAI*, no. 13668); and *To the Worthy Inhabitants of the CITY OF NEW-YORK*, 16 Sept. (*EAI*, no. 13100). See also reprints of additional material in *AA* 4, 1:782, 803–4, 809; and Tiedemann, *Reluctant Revolutionaries*, 200–201.

220 **Complex political alignments:** Humanus, *To the Inhabitants of New-York*, 29 Sept. 1774, broadside (*EAI*, no. 13342), with a handwritten notation that it was published by John Holt. Sears's response: *To the Publick*, 1 Oct., broadside (*EAI*, no. 13484).

220 **Other groups intervened:** Joseph Totten, *To the Respectable Body of Gentlemen Nominated by the Publick Voice . . .* , 29–30 Sept. 1774, broadside (*EAI*, no. 13483), including a reply from Henry Remsen, chairing the committee in the absence of Isaac Low and agreeing to meet on the thirtieth with "our Fellow-Citizens." Because Totten's name appeared alone on the broadside, it is not clear how many "citizens" he represented.

220 **remaining members of the city committee:** *It Was Resolved Unanimously, That the Following Narrative of the Proceedings of the Committee, Be Published,* 30 Sept. 1774, broadside (*EAI*, no. 13482); Colden to Dartmouth, 5 Oct., in *DAR,* 8:207. See also the committee minutes, 30 Sept., in *AA* 4, 1:326–27. After the meetings, Sears reportedly engaged in a physical altercation with "a sturdy Hibernian captain," which ended with his "very severe drubbing." See Peter Van Schaack to John Jay, 12 Oct., in Van Schaack, *Life of Peter Van Schaack,* 21; and the "private & Confidential" note dated 5 Oct., forwarded to Dartmouth by William Tryon, 19 Nov., reel 11, no. 997, Dartmouth Papers.

221 **The victory of the rump committee:** Philo-Libertas, "To the Worthy Merchants and Citizens of New-York," *RNYG,* 20 Oct. 1774; *To the Freeholders, Freemen, and Inhabitants of the City of New-York, and Particularly to Our Steady Friends and Associates, the Children and Negroes of the Said City,* n.d. [after 30 Sept.], broadside (*EAI*, no. 13656).

221 **progenitor of public Loyalism:** Scholars disagree about the chronology of the emergence of a "Loyalist press." Philip Gould, *Writing the Rebellion,* begins his book with the Stamp Act crisis of 1765–1766, whereas Janice Potter and Robert M. Calhoon, "The Character and Coherence of the Loyalist Press," in Bailyn and Hench, *Press & Revolution,* 229–72, concur with me that the fall of 1774 is the appropriate date, as does Upton, "Dilemma of Loyalist Pamphleteers."

222 **In his memorial:** Charles Inglis, claims memorial, n.d. [ca. 1783], AO 12/20. In his claims memorial, Seabury referred to the same agreement (AO 12/19, fol. 356). Rhoden, *Revolutionary Anglicanism,* discusses the three men, among others. See also Bruce Steiner, *Samuel Seabury, 1729–1796: A Study in the High Church Tradition* (Athens: Ohio University Press, 1971); and Ross N. Hebb, *Samuel Seabury and Charles Inglis: Two Bishops, Two Churches* (Madison, N.J.: Fairleigh Dickinson University Press, 2010). There is no full biography of Chandler, but he is used as a counterpoint in S. Scott Rohrer, *Jacob Green's Revolution: Radical Religion and Reform in a Revolutionary Age* (University Park: Pennsylvania State University Press, 2014).

222 **Two printers willing to open:** Stephen Botein, "Printers and the American Revolution," in Bailyn and Hench, *Press & Revolution,* 36–38, points

to the importance of New York as a center of "Tory" publishing because of Gaine and Rivington. G. Thomas Tanselle's geographic analysis of Loyalist imprints, "Some Statistics on American Printing, 1764–1783," in ibid., 356 (table 7D), reveals that many more Loyalist pamphlets, broadsides, and replies to them were published in New York in 1774 than in any other colonial locale (42 percent of Loyalist-related broadsides, or 21 of 50, and 46.5 percent of Loyalist-related pamphlets, 20 of 43; the next highest percentages came from Boston: 20 percent of broadsides and 18.6 percent of pamphlets). Colden recognized the dominance of New York in this respect; see his letter to Dartmouth, 5 Oct. 1774, in *DAR*, 8:207.

222 **Gaine, Irish-born:** For Gaine, see Alfred Lawrence Lorenz, *Hugh Gaine: A Colonial Printer-Editor's Odyssey to Loyalism* (Carbondale: Southern Illinois University Press, 1972). Nothing of comparable length has been written about Holt, but see Thomas, *History of Printing in America*, 474–75, 503–5; and the brief account of Holt's life by Kevin J. Hayes in *American National Biography*, available in print and online.

222 **James Rivington:** There is no full biography of Rivington, but my discussion of him relies in part on Anne Powell, "Printing at His Peril: James Rivington and a Free Press in Revolutionary New York, 1773–1775" (senior honors thesis, Cornell University, 2016). See Thomas, *History of Printing*, 478–80, 508–11; Robert M. Ours, "James Rivington: Another Viewpoint," in *Newsletters to Newspapers: Eighteenth-Century Journalism,* ed. Donovan H. Bond and W. Reynolds McLeod (Morgantown, W.Va.: School of Journalism, 1977), 219–33; and Catherine Snell Crary, "The Tory and the Spy: The Double Life of James Rivington," *WMQ,* 3rd ser., 16 (1959): 61–72. Joseph Adelman examines the large cohort of immigrant printers, including Gaine and Rivington, in "Trans-Atlantic Migration and the Printing Trade."

222 **Rivington published numerous Loyalist pamphlets:** Rivington's boast: *RNYG,* 6 Oct. 1774. He advertised nine political pamphlets on 8 December and thirteen on the final pages of one printing of Seabury's *View of the Controversy* (a copy is located at Huntington Library, no. 149080), offering discounts for bulk purchases. When in late 1774 he published an edition of Captain James Cook's journal of his first voyage to the South Pacific (*EAI,* no. 13324), subscribers' names consumed eighteen pages of front matter, many identified as residing outside the New York–New Jersey region. Although not all of them would have subscribed to the newspaper, their places of origin revealed his publication network: Philadelphia (including William Franklin, Joseph Reed, and Joseph Galloway), New Bern (North Carolina), Jamaica, Antigua, Dominica, Quebec, Boston (including John Adams), Connecticut (including Silas Deane), the Nine Partners pat-

ent on the Hudson, Savannah, and West Florida. Holt did not appear to have a distribution network comparable to Rivington's, for Thomas Young complained that he could not find Holt's pamphlets in Boston; see Young to John Lamb, 4 Oct. 1774, Lamb Papers. By comparison, the Bradfords in Philadelphia had about seventeen hundred subscribers to their *Pennsylvania Journal* in 1774, with a geographic reach comparable to Rivington's. See Robert G. Parkinson, *The Common Cause: Creating Race and Nation in the American Revolution* (Chapel Hill: University of North Carolina Press, 2016), 44–77.

223   **New Yorkers eagerly snapped up:** Quotations: Clarke to Joe [Jekyll], 10 Sept. 1774, Charity Clarke Moore and Clement Clarke Moore Papers. For Rodney and Adams, see *LOD,* 1:66, 152. The "intended speech," which criticized British colonial policy but did not support the colonies' claims to exemption from parliamentary power, was reprinted in *MSpy,* 15 Sept., and *NYJ,* 22 Sept., among other newspapers. Pamphlet editions appeared in both Britain and America; see Adams, *American Independence,* 110–13, esp. 112. According to Slauter, "Reading and Radicalization," 40, Shipley's pamphlet was second only to Paine's *Common Sense* in the number of American reprints (twelve editions in eight cities) in the revolutionary era.

223   **letter he wrote to Thomas and William Bradford:** Rivington to "Gentm" (the Bradfords), 4 Nov. 1774, EM 16, Emmet Collection; Rivington to Knox, 2 Oct., in "Henry Knox and the London Book-Store," 300. An anonymous poet, whose defense of Rivington's "impartial" political stance appeared in *RNYG* on 8 December, asserted, "He gives you H[an]-c[oc]k, S[hi]p[le]y too," thus implying sales if not reprinting. For Dickinson's pamphlet, see chapter 4, above. In unpaginated front matter of his *Considerations,* Wilson explained that he had written it "during the late Non-Importation Agreement," but because the agreement ended before he completed it, he regarded publication as "unseasonable" at that time. Rivington advertised Wilson's pamphlet for sale in late 1774 (see above, for the location of the list). Because he offered to supply multiple copies, he might have reprinted it, but Adams, *American Independence,* 116, does not list such a reprint.

224   **stereotyped by Silas Deane:** Deane to Thomas Mumford, 16 Oct. 1774, in *LOD,* 1:202; Mercator, "To Mr. Rivington," *RNYG,* 11 Aug.; "The Printer to the Public," *NYJ,* 18 Aug., 1 Sept. Holt also addressed Rivington in a broadside (*EAI,* no. 13335), 12 August, accusing him of publishing "an abusive piece of Scurrility against me." See Holt's defender, "Reprobator," *NYJ,* 18 Aug. Booth revealed his identity as "Mercator" to Holt in a note dated 17 August and published in *NYJ,* 1 Sept.

224   **When Joseph Reed referred:** Reed to Quincy, 6 Nov., in *AA* 4, 1:964.

For more invective directed at Rivington and the Loyalist authors he published, see Mulford, *Leacock's First Book*, 65–66; and James Madison to William Bradford, [early March 1775], in *JM Papers*, 1:141. But in May 1773, when Quincy and two other men had stopped at Rivington's bookstore in New York, and Rivington asked them about a possible Boston correspondent, they recommended Henry Knox, who became Rivington's agent. See "Henry Knox and the London Book-Store," 226–303, and Knox's unpublished bookseller letterbook, for frequent business correspondence between the two men.

224 **articles to which Reed referred:** Charles Inglis, claims memorial, n.d., AO 12/20; Inglis, "To the Inhabitants of North-America," *NYG*, 12, 26 Sept., 10 Oct. 1774. Other essays in the series appeared on 19 September and 3 October. In his memorial, Inglis recalled his pseudonym incorrectly as "A New York Farmer." A lengthy refutation of his first two essays, dated 6 October, is printed in *AA* 4, 1:821–27.

225 **most extended and influential response:** Chandler's lengthy title continued: *In Which the Necessary Consequences of Violently Opposing the King's Troops, and of a General Non-importation Are Fairly Stated.* See detailed publication information in Adams, *American Independence*, 83–84. Jocular quotations: *RNYG*, 17 Nov. 1774; public burning in Elizabethtown, *AA* 4, 1:1013. On the Philadelphia sales ban, see William Hooper to James Duane, 22 Nov., in *LOD*, 1:263; on Norfolk and burning in Maryland, see James Parker to Charles Steuart, 6 Dec., reel 2, fol. 291, Steuart Papers; on rural New York, see Willard, *Letters on the American Revolution*, 74. Also burned in Elizabethtown on 1 December was Samuel Seabury's *Free Thoughts* . . . (see below for that pamphlet).

226 **The contents of the *Friendly Address:*** Chandler referred to the congress's statement on the Suffolk Resolves, and the latest internal date in the pamphlet is 16 October, so he drafted it between mid-September and mid-October. He noted on page 3 of the abridged version, cited below, that he decided not to add new material after the congress ended. In addition to Rivington's original and abridged versions, Mills & Hicks published a full Boston edition, also without title-page identification of the printer, and full editions followed in London, Dublin, and Cork. See Adams, *American Independence*, 83–84. Authorship of the *Friendly Address* was erroneously attributed to the Reverend Myles Cooper.

226 **supporters of resistance:** Hooper to James Duane, 22 Nov. 1774, in *LOD*, 1:263; Madison to William Bradford, [early March 1775], in *JM Papers*, 1:141 (see also vice versa, in ibid., 132); Nathaniel Walker to Dartmouth, 12 Jan. 1775, reel 12, no. 1101, Dartmouth Papers. Washington's purchasing agent sent him a copy from Philadelphia despite the reported ban on sales

there; see William Milnor to Washington, 29 Nov. 1774, in *GW Papers: CS*, 10:189; and he eventually owned the 1774 London edition, a copy now in the Boston Athenaeum. Like Hooper, "Nimrod" recommended ignoring the pamphlet: "For the *Pennsylvania Packet*," DPaPkt, 28 Nov. 1774. See also *AA* 4, 1:1011, 2:18.

226 **surviving evidence points to:** According to the English Short Title Catalogue, thirty-one copies of the original New York edition are in twenty-six libraries; eighteen copies of the Boston edition in fifteen libraries; and eleven copies of the later abridged edition in ten libraries. Fourteen copies of the London edition can be found in American repositories today, along with five of the Dublin and three of the Cork editions. Two copies of the London edition are in Canadian libraries. Ownership was clearly widely dispersed, yet a later defender of Chandler lamented what he saw as the inadequate circulation of *Friendly Address*. See [Henry Barry], *The General Attacked by a Subaltern; or, The Strictures on the Friendly Address Examined, and a Refutation of His Principles Attempted* (New York: James Rivington, [1775]), 3.

226 **Chandler began:** Chandler, *Friendly Address*, 3–24 (quotations 5, 14, 24). All quotations come from this edition, no. 120822 at Huntington Library.

226 **Chandler abridged:** Ibid., 25–45 (quotations 29–30n, 32–34). See also Chandler, *The Friendly Address to All Reasonable Americans . . . Carefully Abridged* (New York: [James Rivington], 1774).

227 **So what did Chandler recommend:** Chandler, *Friendly Address*, 45–46, 47.

227 **number of refutations:** John Adams, "A Reasonable Americans Answer to, The Friendly Address to Him on the Subject of Our Political Confusions," in *JA Papers*, 2:193–96 (quotation 196); Charles Lee, *Strictures on "A Friendly Address,"* 6. James Madison pronounced Lee's *Strictures* "very sensible," finding it written with "much Spirit & Vivacity" (Madison to William Bradford, [early March 1775], in *JM Papers*, 1:141). Lee's pamphlet was reprinted many times both in newspapers and as a pamphlet; see Adams, *American Independence*, 94–97. It received a refutation of its own early in 1775: [Barry], *General Attacked by a Subaltern*, and was satirized by "Protector, OLIVER," in an essay addressed to "People of America," *RNYG*, 9 Feb. 1775. According to John Andrews, Henry Knox thought Barry's "rather a weak performance" and refused to publish it in Boston; see Andrews to William Barrell, 15 Jan. 1775, in "Andrews Letters," 394 (also, 398).

228 **comprehensive attack:** Livingston, *Other Side of the Question*, quotations 4, 26. See Adams, *American Independence*, 99. William Bradford sent a copy to Madison (Bradford to Madison, 4 April 1775, in *JM Papers*, 1:143). This might be the refutation of *Friendly Address* that was forwarded to Benjamin Franklin in London on 11 [Jan. 1775?], in *BF Papers*, 21:376.

228 **perhaps the most convincing:** A Friend *to his* Country, "A Few Remarks on a Pamphlet Lately Published, Entitled *A Friendly Address to All Considerate Americans*," *DPaPkt*, 19 Dec. 1774, in part in the supplement.

228 **New Yorkers were preparing:** Minutes of city committee, 7, 14, 15 Nov. 1774, in *AA* 4, 1:328–30. The members of the new committee of sixty, elected on 22 November, are listed in ibid., 330. See also the broadsides announcing mechanics' committee meetings, 13, 18 Nov. 1774 (*EAI*, nos. 42653, 13435), and that naming the hundred nominees, 17 Nov. (*EAI*, no. 13485). For contemporary comments: William Smith to Philip Schuyler, 22 Nov. 1774, in *Smith Memoirs*, 1:203; Smith to William Tryon, 25 Nov., reel 11, no. 1002, Dartmouth Papers; William Hooper to James Duane, 22 Nov., in *LOD*, 1:262–63; Henry White to Tryon, 8 Nov., reel 11, no. 992, Dartmouth Papers; and White's assessment of current politics, which differed somewhat from Smith's, in his letter to Tryon, 7 Dec., reel 11, no. 1011, Dartmouth Papers. See also Tiedemann, *Reluctant Revolutionaries*, 202–3, on these events.

229 **New Yorkers remained less enthusiastic:** Reed to Josiah Quincy Jr., 6 Nov. 1774, in Reed, *Life of Joseph Reed*, 1:86; "To the Publick," from the Philadelphia committee, 30 Nov., in *AA* 4, 1:1010 (also 1026–27); Drayton, *Memoirs*, 1:154–56. See also, on the Philadelphia committee elections, *AA* 4, 1:956–57, 965–67; and a broadside, 11 Nov., *EAI*, no. 13537.

229 **burst of Loyalist pamphlets:** Quotations in this and the next paragraph from Mary V. V., *Dialogue, Between a Southern Delegate, and His Spouse*, 7–8, 10–13. I read V.V. as meaning "vice versa," or signaling a critique of the congress. Although once again he included no identifying information on the title page, Rivington advertised it in December 1774 (see above). For Bradford's comment: his letter to James Madison, 4 Jan. 1775, in *JM Papers*, 1:132. For other discussions of this poem, see my "History on the Diagonal," *AHR* 124 (2019): 15–17; and Benjamin H. Irvin, "Of Eloquence 'Manly' and 'Monstrous': The Henpecked Husband in Revolutionary Political Debate, 1774–1775," in *New Men: Manliness in Early America*, ed. Thomas A. Foster (New York: New York University Press, 2011), 195–216, especially 206–11.

230 **Whatever Mary V. V.'s identity:** *Dialogue*, 12. Immediately following the quoted passage, Mary wrote, "I am distracted by fear." Other references to fears are on 9, 10. For rhetorical femininity, see Osell, "Tatling Women in the Public Sphere," 283–99; and the discussion of American uses in Norton, *Separated by Sex*, 127–35, 144–46, 153–61. Other satirical poems about the congress are Bob Jingle, *The Association*; and *The Poor Man's Advice to His Poor Neighbours: A Ballad to the Tune of Chevy-Chace* (New York: [James Rivington], 1774). Rivington advertised *The Association* in

RNYG on 8 December and *Poor Man's Advice* in *View of the Controversy* later in December (see above).

231 **The new emphasis continued:** The full title of *Free Thoughts* continued: *Wherein Their Errors Are Exhibited, Their Reasonings Confuted, and the Fatal Tendency of Their Non-importation, Non-exportation, and Non-consumption Measures, Are Laid Open to the Plainest Understandings; and the Only Means Pointed Out for Preserving and Securing Our Present Happy Constitution.* Rivington's initial advertisement for *Congress Canvassed,* on 8 December in *RNYG,* called it simply *An Examination into the Conduct of the Delegates.* For publication information on both pamphlets, see Adams, *American Independence,* 105–7. Steiner, *Samuel Seabury,* discusses all of Seabury's pamphlets, 132–54.

231 **Seabury focused:** Seabury, *Free Thoughts,* quotations 15, 17, 19, 22. In a postscript on p. 24, dated 16 November, he added that most of the New York congressional delegates opposed the Association, but reluctantly signed it because they had agreed to nominal unity early in the session. Rivington printed two editions, one of which had twenty-four pages (the one cited here), and another with thirty-one. According to the English Short Title Catalogue, twenty-six libraries in the United States have copies of the twenty-four-page edition and eight have the thirty-one-page edition, so, like Chandler's work, Seabury's was widely distributed. (The twenty-four-page edition owned by Washington is in the Boston Athenaeum.) It was publicly burned in several places in Ulster County, New York, in January 1775 (*AA* 4, 1:1100, 1183, 1191, 1201) and was tarred and feathered in Freehold, New Jersey, in early March (*AA* 4, 2:35).

232 **Seabury's message:** Seabury, *Congress Canvassed,* quotations 20, 12, 14, 16, 24–26. An essay, "To the Publick," ca. 26 Jan. 1775, in *AA* 4, 1:1188–89, defended the New York congressional delegates' election as legitimate. The Short Title Catalogue shows only one printing of this pamphlet, now available in twenty-eight American libraries. Cook's first journal was published in England in 1771. Starting in February 1774, Rivington began advertising for subscribers to support an American edition of a version of Cook's journal edited by John Hawkesworth, which he published before the end of the year (*EAI,* no. 13324). Seabury was not listed among the subscribers, but both Inglis and Chandler were. (See above.)

232 **response from a newcomer:** The rest of the long title of Hamilton's pamphlet read thus: *Whereby His Sophistry Is Exposed, His Cavils Confuted, His Artifices Detected, and His Wit Ridiculed; in a General Address to the Inhabitants of America, and a Particular Address to the Farmers of the Province of New-York.* Adams, *American Independence,* 88, notes only one printing and that it was advertised in *RNYG* on 15 December. Seabury's

16 December postscript indicated that he had seen Hamilton's response to *Free Thoughts* (presumably Rivington showed it to him, because he printed both pamphlets) and that he had not changed his mind, nor was he "disconcerted" by its content (*Congress Canvassed,* 28).

232 **Hamilton began by asking:** Hamilton, *Full Vindication,* 3–13 (quotations 3–6, 13).

234 **Hamilton devoted several pages:** Ibid., 15–35 (quotations, 23–24, 34–35).

234 **Seabury replied to Hamilton:** Seabury, *View of the Controversy,* 36; Hamilton, *Farmer Refuted, . . . in Answer to a Letter from A. W. Farmer,* quotations from unpaginated front matter. On these pamphlets, see Adams, *American Independence,* 107, 131. In late December 1774–early January 1775, debates over the results of the Continental Congress likewise reignited in the pages of *The Georgia Gazette.* See the essays by A Georgian and A Freeman, 14 Dec.; and several essays, especially the one by Hugh Simple, 18 Jan. Critics of the congress charged that it erred in supporting Massachusetts, whereas Hugh Simple held up Quebec as a possible malign model for how all colonies might be treated in the future.

235 **anonymous Philadelphia author:** "Political Observations, Without Order, Addressed to the People of America," *DPaPkt,* 14 Nov. 1774, soon reprinted in many other newspapers, for example, *NYJ,* 24 Nov.; *MG&BPB,* 28 Nov.; *RNYG,* 1 Dec. See Adams to [Edward Biddle], 12 Dec. 1774, in *JA Papers,* 2:200. The author is unknown; the essay appeared before Thomas Paine arrived in Philadelphia, so he did not write it.

235 **Commentators employed terms:** "Anti-tormentor," *DPaPkt,* 21 Nov. 1774 ("extraordinary"); "To the Printer," *RNYG,* 1 Dec. ("audacious"), "Nestor," ibid. ("Republican," "fabrick"); "M," ibid. ("companies," "vile," "visage"). *AA* 4, 1:976–79, reprints the original essay, Nestor, and M, but not the other writings cited in this note.

236 **October 11, 1774:** Yorke to Suffolk, 11 Oct. 1774, SP 84/543. Because "smack" designates a type of small ship, it is possible that this was not the vessel's name, but it is always called the *Smack* in the correspondence. This was not the first such statement of concern about colonists smuggling arms and ammunition, but it initiated a flurry of exchanges, as previous letters on the same topic did not. See also same to same, 5, 26 Aug., SP 84/543, about a Nantucket ship and a cargo of gunpowder; Admiral Samuel Graves to Philip Stephens, 31 Aug., CO 5/120, fol. 260; Dartmouth to Colden, 10 Sept., in *Letters of Colden,* 249. Some but not all of the exchanges in this section are also available in the Holland Transcripts.

236 **October 14 (Hamburg):** Mathias to Suffolk, 14 Oct. 1774, CO 5/138, fol. 410.

236 **October 14 (Bath):** Barrington to Dartmouth, 14 Oct. 1774, reel 11, no. 979, Dartmouth Papers.

237 **October 17:** Suffolk to Yorke, 17 Oct. 1774, SP 84/543.

237 **October 18:** Dartmouth to Lords of Admiralty, 18 Oct. 1774, in *DAR,* 8:213–14. See William Eden to John Pownall, 18 Oct., reel 11, no. 983, with a note from Pownall, no. 984, both Dartmouth Papers, describing internal discussions in the Colonial Office.

237 **October 19:** George III, order in council, in *DAR,* 8:214. For Dartmouth's circular letter to American governors conveying this order: ibid., 7:192.

237 **October 21–November 18:** Yorke to Suffolk, 21, 24, 25, 28 Oct., 1, 8, 11, 15, 18 Nov. 1774, and a document headed "Dysart 5 November 1774," all in SP 84/543. Some replies from Suffolk are in the same volume. See also Yorke to Suffolk, 15 Nov., in *DAR,* 8:234–35; Yorke to William Eden, 4 Nov., CO 5/138, fol. 422; Lieutenant Walton, captain of the *Wells,* to Philip Stephens, 1, 11 Nov., 6 Dec., CO 5/120, fols. 308, 310, 312. For an account of the affair published in America, see "Extract from a Gentleman in Amsterdam to His Friend in Philadelphia, Dated November 15, 1774," in *AA* 4, 1:979.

238 **November 1, 22:** Mathias to Suffolk, 1, 22 Nov. 1774, CO 5/138, fols. 424, 448. See "Extract of a Letter from Mr. Mathias to the Earl of Suffolk," 15 Nov., reel 11, no. 995, Dartmouth Papers, reporting that the *Flora* had forty tea chests in its cargo as well as arms.

238 **November 2:** Dartmouth to Colden, 2 Nov. 1774, in *Letters of Colden,* 254.

238 **November 22, 25, December 2:** Yorke to Suffolk, 22, 25 Nov., 2 Dec. 1774, SP 84/543.

238 **December 9:** Suffolk to Yorke, 9 Dec. 1774; and Yorke to Suffolk, 20 Dec., both in SP 84/543. See also Yorke to Suffolk, 16 Dec., SP 84/543.

239 **When Peter Oliver:** Adair and Schutz, *Peter Oliver's Origin & Progress,* 116. Elbridge Gerry ordered gunpowder from Rhode Island, a smuggling center, as well as from New York; see Gerry to [illeg.] Gibbs, 7 Nov. 1774, Gerry Papers (Billias Collection).

CHAPTER 7 THE BRINK OF A PRECIPICE

240 **day of thanksgiving:** Provincial Congress, Minutes, 22 Oct. 1774, in *PIR,* 1109–10. Ezra Stiles, in Newport, recorded that some Massachusetts churches did not observe the holiday; *Stiles Diary,* 1:502. Some Boston shopkeepers also purportedly opened for business on that day; see *AA* 4, 1:1210.

240 **sermons on December 15:** Isaac Story, *The Love of Our Country Recommended and Enforced in a Sermon . . . December 15, 1774* (Boston: John Boyle, 1775), 18; William Gordon, *A Discourse Preached December 15th*

1774 . . . (Boston: Thomas Leverett, 1775), 7. See also Samuel Williams, *A Discourse on the Love of Our Country* . . . (Salem: Samuel & Ebenezer Hall, 1775). Gordon's rousing sermon attracted two published responses: [Harrison Gray], *Observations on the Reverend Pastor (Rev. William Gordon) of Roxbury's Thanksgiving Discourse* (Boston: [Mills & Hicks?], 1775); and *Remarks upon a Discourse Preached December 15th 1774 . . . by William Gordon* (n.p.: 1775). Gray's pamphlet was in turn derided by a reader in Truro (Samuel Adams to Samuel Adams, 20 Feb. 1775, SA Papers).

241 **so-called friends:** Gad Hitchcock, *A Sermon Preached at Plymouth December 22d, 1774 Being the Anniversary Thanksgiving* . . . (Boston: Edes & Gill, 1775), quotations, in order: 39, 40, 42, 44.

241 **footnote listed all the British regiments:** John Lathrop, *A Discourse Preached, December 15th 1774 Being the Day Recommended by the Provincial Congress* . . . (Boston: D. Kneeland, 1774), quotations, in order: 38, 18, 14; footnote on troops and ships, 13. He also forcefully defended the Boston committee distributing relief to the poor against the *"false* and *malicious"* charges that they were taking some of the contributions for themselves (21).

242 **"Gutters of Sedition":** Adair and Schutz, *Peter Oliver's Origin & Progress,* 105.

242 **one North Carolina critic:** Archibald Neilson to James Iredell, 4 Feb. 1775, in Higginbotham, *Papers of Iredell,* 1:287.

242 **John Murray, Lord Dunmore:** A succinct account of the military and political situation on the frontier in the summer and fall of 1774 is David, *Dunmore's New World,* chap. 3. See also Reuben Gold Thwaites and Louise Phelps Kellogg, eds., *Documentary History of Dunmore's War, 1774* (Madison: Wisconsin Historical Society, 1905); and broadside proclamations by Dunmore, 25 April 1774 (*EAI,* no. 42742), and John Penn, 12 Oct. (*EAI,* no. 13521).

243 **skepticism about Dunmore's mission:** Madison to William Bradford, 23 Aug. 1774, in *JM Papers,* 1:120; Parker to Charles Steuart, 26 Sept., 1 Nov., reel 2, fols. 259, 274, Steuart Papers; Richard Henry Lee to William Lee, 15 Dec., in Hoffman, *Lee Family Papers,* reel 2, frame 1257. For an account of the campaign and the battle, see [Parker] to Steuart, 27 Nov., reel 2, fol. 288, Steuart Papers; and same to same, 6 Dec., reel 2, fol. 291, Steuart Papers, on the "high estimation" for Dunmore among the "back people," but expressing doubt about whether the governor "will meet with a proper return for his Service here."

243 **Dunmore's return with a victory:** The addresses of Williamsburg and the faculty appeared in *VaG* (P&D), 8 Dec. 1774, and that of the council, *VaG* (P&D), 22 Dec.; Lee to John Dickinson, 7 April 1775, in *LOD,* 1:328. In

late January 1775, freeholders of the western Fincastle County also formally thanked Dunmore; see *RevVa*, 2:255. According to one witness, the four Native hostages were "genteely entertained" by Norfolk "gentlemen" (Willard, *Letters on the American Revolution*, 58).

243 **Dunmore waited for almost three weeks:** Dunmore's letter, dated 24 December 1774, is one of the longest contemporary reports (if not *the* longest) from a colonial governor to the ministry; it covers seventeen pages in *DAR*, 8 (252–68); quotation, 262.

244 **Dunmore revealed that county committees:** This paragraph and the next are based on ibid., 265–67.

245 **other governors too described:** Wright to Dartmouth, 13, 20 Dec. 1774, CO 5/664, fols. 28, 39; Wentworth to Dartmouth, 20 Dec., in *DAR*, 8:248; same to same, 2 Dec., in Bouton, *Documents of New-Hampshire*, 7:419. In a third letter in December, Wentworth attributed the trouble in New Hampshire to the "unlimited influence" of Boston's leaders (Wentworth to Dartmouth, 28 Dec., CO 5/939, fol. 30).

245 **William Franklin:** Franklin to Dartmouth, 6 Dec. 1774, in Ricord and Nelson, *Documents Relating to the Colonial History of the State of New Jersey*, 10:503–4. Governor Robert Eden of Maryland informed the Colonial Office in late December that his province was "tolerably quiet," although Marylanders seemed determined to resist parliamentary taxation and would accordingly adhere to "their Non Importation & Non-Exportation Experiments in spite of every Inconvenience . . . & the total Ruin of their Trade." See Robert Eden to William Eden, 30 Dec., in Clark et al., *Naval Documents*, 1:45. See also Thomas Gage to Dartmouth, 15 Dec., in *DAR*, 8:241–42; and John Penn to same, 31 Dec., CO 5/1286, fol. 7.

245 **others joined the governors:** Reed to Dartmouth, 24 Dec. 1774, reel 2, no. 1089, Dartmouth Papers (see also same to same, 10 Dec., reel 2, no. 1087, Dartmouth Papers); and Reed to Dennis DeBerdt, 24 Dec., in Reed, *Life of Joseph Reed*, 1:89.

246 **Reed was proceeding:** Reed to DeBerdt, 24 Dec. 1774, in Reed, *Life of Joseph Reed*, 1:89; Reed to [Charles Pettit], 31 Jan. 1775, fol. 96, Joseph Reed Papers. Another of Dartmouth's correspondents who conveyed information about America asked the minister to burn his letter after reading it, because he did not want colonists to regard him as an "Informer"; see Nathaniel Walker to Dartmouth, 12 Jan. 1775, reel 12, no. 1101, Dartmouth Papers. Reed enclosed the letters to Dartmouth in some addressed to DeBerdt, in a later letter indicating that this was his "usual" practice. Such enclosures concealed the correspondence from prying eyes on both sides of the Atlantic. See Reed to DeBerdt, 13 Feb. 1775, in Reed, *Life of Joseph Reed*, 1:97.

246 **urgent missives across the Atlantic:** In no other two-month period during the time covered by this book did I locate so many surviving letters from America to Britain, which I regard as a rough indication of how many must have been written during those weeks. All citations in this and the next two paragraphs are from colonists' letters to correspondents in Britain. The few letters advocating concessions on both sides included William Fitzhugh to James Russell, 17 Dec. 1774, bundle 6, Russell Papers; Thomas Wharton to Thomas Walpole, 18 Jan. 1775, in "Wharton Letter-Books 33," 453; and Reed to DeBerdt, 24 Dec. 1774, in Reed, *Life of Joseph Reed,* 1:88.

247 **"civil War":** John Adams to James Burgh, 28 Dec. 1774, in *JA Papers,* 2:205–6; Abigail Adams to Macaulay, ca. late 1774, in *AFC,* 1:177; Warren to Macaulay, 29 Dec., in Richards and Harris, *Warren Letters,* 39; Reynolds to Mrs. Courtney Norton, 24 Dec., William Reynolds Letterbook. See also James Lovell to Josiah Quincy Jr., 9 Dec., in "Quincy Letters," 484.

247 **Some letter writers held out hope:** Carroll of Annapolis to William Graves, 29 Dec. 1774, in Hoffman, *Dear Papa,* 2:770; Laurens to his son John, 12 Dec., in *HL Papers,* 10:3; Laurens to William Manning, 4 Jan. 1775, in ibid., 20; Laurens to Richard Oswald, 4 Jan., in ibid., 22. For hopes that Parliament would repeal the Coercive Acts: William Carr to James Russell, 10 Dec. 1774, bundle 2, Russell Papers; Samuel Galloway and Stephen Steward to Russell, 13 Dec., bundle 7, Russell Papers.

247 **October order in council:** Quotations: *ProvG,* 10 Dec. 1774, reprinted in *BG,* 12 Dec., and other newspapers; Cushing to Josiah Quincy Jr., 30 Dec., in *AA* 4, 1:1080. For Trumbull's rhetorical question, see his letter to William Samuel Johnson, 17 Dec., Connecticut Papers, 174, fol. 403, BC. Arrival of the news on 8 December ("last Thursday"): Nathaniel Wales Jr. et al. to Governor Trumbull, 10 Dec., Misc. MSS Bound.

248 **arrival of a vessel carrying guns:** Quotation: "Extract of a Letter to Mr. Williames Dated New York Jany 6th 1775," reel 12, no. 1092, Dartmouth Papers. Narrative in this and the next paragraph is based on ibid.; Colden to Dartmouth, 4 Jan., CO 5/1106, fol. 16; and *AA* 4, 1:1070–72, a widely reprinted account first published in *RNYG,* 5 Jan. A broadside headed *To the PUBLIC,* 30 Dec. 1774 (*EAI,* no. 13666), and signed "A Number of Citizens," included a deposition from the *Lady Gage*'s captain, claiming that the ship sailed from Gravesend on 18 October and that such armaments were usually designated as "hardware" on manifests—and thus that no deception was intended.

248 **The seizure of the disputed cargo:** Quotations: Andrew Elliot, certificate for Isaac Low, 26 Oct. 1785, AO 12/21, fol. 104; Dartmouth to Colden, 1 Feb. 1775, CO 5/1106, fol. 18. See also Plain English, *To the Inhabitants of NEW-YORK,* n.d., broadside (*EAI,* no. 13658), also in *AA* 4, 1:1071; A

Number of Citizens, *To the Publick,* 15 Dec. 1774, broadside (*EAI,* no. 42719).

249 **Rhode Island General Assembly:** The assembly's order to remove the cannon: Bartlett, *Records of Rhode Island,* 7:262. For accounts of these events, see *Stiles Diary,* 1:499–500 (entries for 9, 10, 11 Dec.); James Wallace to Admiral Samuel Graves, 15 Dec. 1774, in *DAR,* 8:247–48; Graves to Philip Stephens, 8 Jan. 1775, CO 5/121, fol. 41. The assemblymen also authorized the establishment of several new local militia units; see Bartlett, *Records of Rhode Island,* 7:262–71.

249 *Rose* **man-of-war:** Wallace to Graves, 12 Dec. 1774, in Clark et al., *Naval Documents,* 1:15; "Extract of a Letter to a Gentleman in New-York, Dated Newport, Rhode Island, December 14, 1774," in *AA* 4, 1:1041. (When a mob threatened to tar and feather both Wallace and a local customs officer, Wanton replied to Wallace's request for protection by admitting that he feared an attack on himself and therefore could not offer assistance. "So much for Governor Wanton," Wallace told Graves dismissively in that 12 December letter.)

249 **New London residents:** G[urdon] Saltonstall to Jonathan Trumbull, 15 Dec. 1774, Misc. MSS Bound; Nathaniel Wales Jr. et al. to Trumbull, 20 Dec., Misc. MSS Bound. See also same to same, 10 Dec., Misc. MSS Bound, warning of a possible attack from Boston on Providence.

250 **determined to thwart any attack:** The narrative in this and the next three paragraphs is based on Wentworth to Dartmouth, 20 Dec. 1774, in *DAR,* 8:249–50; and "From a Gentleman in Boston, to Mr. Rivington, in New-York," 20 Dec., in *AA* 4, 1:1053–54, along with additional sources listed below.

250 **The local committee met:** Quotations: "From a Gentleman in Boston, to Mr. Rivington, in New-York," 20 Dec., in *AA* 4, 1:1054; Wentworth to Dartmouth, 20 Dec. 1774, in *DAR,* 8:249. The fort's captain John Cochran's account of the attack is in *AA* 4, 1:1042.

250 **Describing the assault to General Gage:** Wentworth to Gage, 14 Dec. 1774, in *AA* 4, 1:1041–42; "Extracts of Letters to Gentlemen in New-York," Portsmouth, 16 Dec., in *AA* 4, 1:1043 ("property and note"); Captain John Dennet, report to Major Theodore Atkinson, 15 Dec., in Bouton, *Documents of New-Hampshire,* 7:421; Wentworth to Dartmouth, 20 Dec., in *DAR,* 8:249–50. See also "From a Gentleman in Boston, to Mr. Rivington, in New-York," 20 Dec., in *AA* 4, 1:1054.

251 **town was still full:** Wentworth to Gage, 16 Dec. 1774, in *AA* 4, 1:1042; Wentworth to Dartmouth, 20 Dec., in *DAR,* 8:249. See also Graves to Philip Stephens, 8 Jan. 1775, CO 5/121, fol. 41, and Wentworth to Graves, 30 Dec. 1774, CO 5/121, fol. 51.

251 **defended the crowd action:** A Watchman, "To the Inhabitations of British America," New Hampshire, 24 Dec. 1774, in *AA* 4, 1:1065; "From a
Gentleman in Boston, to Mr. Rivington, in New-York," 20 Dec., in *AA*
4, 1:1054. See also, "A Lover of Order," Portsmouth, 23 Dec., in Clark et
al., *Naval Documents*, 1:40; and an untitled essay, 17 Feb. 1775, in *AA* 4,
1:1246–47, for other commentaries.

252 **decried not only the attack:** Wentworth to Dartmouth, 20 Dec. 1774, in
DAR, 8:250–51; Wentworth to Thomas Waldron, 30 Dec. 1774, in *Belknap
Papers*, 70; *Province of New-Hampshire. A Proclamation by the Governor,*
26 Dec., broadside (*EAI*, no. 42642). Early in 1775, Wentworth decided
that the fort's attackers should be charged with treason. He collected
evidence and dispatched large packets of documents to Dartmouth; see
his communications of 14 Jan. and 15 Feb., CO 5/939, fols. 38–108, and
esp. a copy of his letter to Gage, 13 Feb., CO 5/939, fol. 93. Three relevant
documents have been published: the New Hampshire attorney general's
opinion that the conduct was treasonous (*DAR*, 9:28); and letters from
Gage to Dartmouth, 23 Feb., in *PIR*, 2038–39; and to Wentworth, 23 Feb.,
in *DAR*, 9:57.

252 **alarmed ordinary colonists:** Stephen Collins to Robert Treat Paine,
14 Jan. 1775, in *RTP Papers*, 3:31; Duane to Johnson, 29 Dec. 1774, in
LOD, 1:281–82. Paine replied to Collins on 23 February 1775, arguing that
New Englanders who seized the guns were relying on "the natural inherent
principle of Self preservation"; see ibid., 316–17.

253 **Maryland Provincial Convention:** Duane to Chase, 29 Dec. 1774, in
LOD, 1:277–78. For the Maryland militia resolution, adopted at a meeting
of 8 to 12 December, along with resolves implementing the Continental
Association, see *Proceedings of the Conventions of the Province of Maryland*
(Annapolis: Frederick Green, [1775]), 7. But Charles Lee heartily approved
Maryland's action; see Lee to Benjamin Rush, 15 Dec., *Colls NYHS* 4
(1871):143; so too did John Adams and James Warren (see their exchange
of letters in *JA Papers*, 2:208, 213).

253 **Johnson and Chase remained staunch supporters:** Annapolis committee and Anne Arundel County meeting records: 23 Dec. 1774, in *AA* 4,
1:1061–62, and 16 Jan. 1775, in ibid., 1140–41; Baltimore County meeting
record, 16 Jan. 1775, in ibid., 1142–43. On the dissension in Baltimore,
see [Samuel Purviance] to John Dickinson, 19 Jan. 1775, box 1, folder 10,
R. R. Logan Collection. Johnson supported the militia plan in a letter
to George Washington, 24 Jan., in *GW Papers: CS*, 10:243; for Chase, see
William Fitzhugh to James Russell, 25 Jan., bundle 6, Russell Papers.

253 **refused to give any money:** "To the Printers of the *Maryland Gazette*,"
19 Jan. 1775, in *AA* 4, 1:1141. For Chalmers, see his Loyalist claims memo-

rial, 14 Oct. 1783, AO 12/6; for Johnson, his letter to Samuel Purviance, 23 Jan. 1775, in *LOD*, 1:299–300. A handbill dated 29 December 1774 was sent to London; it is in CO 5/1286, fol. 183, with a notation that it was presented to Parliament in February 1775. The militia vote is fol. 184.

254 **the events in New Hampshire:** Van Schaack to John Vardill, draft, 3 Jan. 1775, box 4, Van Schaack Family Papers; Fitzhugh to James Russell, 6 Jan., bundle 6, Russell Papers. For Rhode Island's actions in early December: Bartlett, *Records of Rhode Island*, 7:262–71.

255 **Connecticut assembly had authorized:** Correspondence about Connecticut's militia has been published in *AA* 4, 1:1077, 1133–35, 1139, 1173, 1177. Three of Governor Trumbull's letters appointing officers, all dated 10 Jan. 1775, are in Misc. MSS Bound. See also *Stiles Diary*, 1:498.

255 **In Virginia, individual counties:** Quotation: Mason to Washington, 8 March 1775, in Rutland, *Papers of Mason*, 1:225 (see also 220–24). The Fairfax committee of safety's endorsement of the Maryland resolution, 17 Jan., is in ibid., 212. See also Jackson et al., *Diaries of Washington*, 3:291 and n., 303 (entries for 13 Nov. 1774, 16 Jan. 1775); and correspondence between 3 January and 21 February about outfitting such companies with uniforms, muskets, and other equipment purchased in Philadelphia, *GW Papers: CS*, 10:224, 240–41, 259, 270.

255 **Notable for its absence:** Provincial Congress, minutes, in *PIR*, 1156 (election of delegates); 1157–58, 1165–68, 1204 (enforcement); 1159–61 (aid for Boston); 1171–72, 1195–99 (Baptists); 1172–73 (opposition); 1169–70 (paying taxes). From mid-December into January, though, towns did start to order taxes paid to Gardner; see ibid., 1402, 1408, 1412, 1416, 1419, 1423, 1425, 1428 (but cf. Barnstable, 1092). The dissolution and election for a second congress were announced in a broadside, 10 Dec. 1774 (*EAI*, no. 13421). See also the congress's address to the people of the colony, 10 Dec., in *PIR*, 1173–76 (broadside, *EAI*, no. 13422). Some towns did organize militia units (for example, Braintree: Abigail Adams to Mercy Warren, [25 Jan. 1775], in *AFC*, 1:180).

256 **discussions of military or governance:** "Extracts of Letters to Govr Hutchinson": Oliver to Hutchinson, 10 Dec. 1774; Flucker to same, 15 Dec., both in reel 11, no. 1020, Dartmouth Papers. In the same "extracts" that Hutchinson forwarded to Dartmouth, a Colonel Brown on 10 December termed the Provincial Congress a "heterogeneous Gathering" that was "much divided and embarrassed," filled with men "actuated by different Motives, agitated by different Passions." See also *AA* 4, 1:1039.

256 **most detailed narrative of events:** Coffin to Charles Steuart, 10–15 Dec. 1774, reel 2, fols. 293, 295, Steuart Papers. Henry Caner told Hutchinson about Hancock's near election, 22 Dec., in *Letterbook of Caner*. Among

those agitating for a new government were James and Mercy Otis Warren; see James to John Adams, 15 Jan. 1775, in *JA Papers*, 2:213; and Mercy to Catharine Macaulay, 29 Dec. 1774, in Richards and Harris, *Warren Letters*, 38.

256 **A brief notice of the heated:** *RNYG* reported the dissension about the militia (not the governor) in the Provincial Congress under the heading "Extract of a Letter from Boston," 29 Dec. 1774. This paragraph and the next are based on Purviance to Cushing, 20 Jan. 1775, CO 5/118, fols. 99–100, a volume of letters confiscated from Cushing's house by British troops. Purviance's letter confirms the wide reach of *RNYG* by demonstrating that it was read carefully in Baltimore by a resistance leader. In Newport, Ezra Stiles too read *RNYG* and was annoyed by a satire that included him as "Dr. Magpie"; see *Stiles Diary*, 1:528, 531–33 (entries of 20 March, 7 April 1775). For the satire, see the first page of *RNYG*, 30 March.

257 **Dickinson quickly followed up:** Dickinson to Cushing, 26 Jan. 1775, in *LOD*, 1:301–2 (original in CO 5/118, fol. 101). It is unknown whether Mifflin did as Purviance asked. An account of disagreements between Cushing and Samuel Adams in the Massachusetts congress arrived in Philadelphia before Purviance wrote to Dickinson. See Stephen Collins to Robert Treat Paine, 14 Jan., in *RTP Papers*, 3:31–32; Paine to Collins, 25 Feb., in *LOD*, 1:317–18; and Samuel Adams to Collins, 31 Jan., in *SA Writings*, 3:173: "Any Difference between Mr Cushing & me is of very little consequence to the public cause," a statement that tellingly did not deny the dispute, but instead argued for its insignificance.

258 **Johnson also drafted:** Johnson to Purviance, 23 Jan. 1775, in *LOD*, 1:298–99.

258 **Cushing replied:** Cushing to Dickinson, 13 Feb. 1775, in ibid., 310–11. See also Cushing to Purviance, 13 Feb., in ibid., 312 (see facsimile 351, Huntington Library). Purviance's fears were assuaged by Cushing's reply, which Cushing shared with Samuel Adams (Purviance to Cushing, 4 March, SA Papers). The lack of a functioning court system was a repeated theme in John Adams's correspondence in December 1774; see his letters to Edward Biddle, 12 Dec.; and James Burgh, 28 Dec., in *LOD*, 1:265, 276. Hannah Winthrop reported that the "Torys . . . say the stopping the Courts of Justice will opperate more in their Favor than any thing that has happned, for in a little time we shall be ready to fall on one another" (Winthrop to Mercy Warren, 3 Jan. 1775, Winthrop-Warren Correspondence).

258 **Dartmouth forwarded the record:** Dartmouth to attorney general and solicitor general, 20 Jan. 1775, and vice versa, 2 Feb., in *DAR*, 7:247–48, 259.

259 **September 28, 1774:** Josiah Quincy Sr. to his son Josiah Junior, [26 Oct.

1774], in "Quincy Letters," 480, summarized the speculations about motives. Even Josiah Junior's brother, the future Loyalist Samuel Quincy, was unfamiliar with his aims (Samuel to Thomas Hutchinson, 12 Dec., reel 11, no. 1020, Dartmouth Papers). John Andrews to William Barrell, 29 Sept., in "Andrews Letters," 370, gave Quincy's departure date and speculated about his purpose. Quincy told the Reverend Charles Chauncy that he was seeking "to exert himself in serving his Country" (Chauncy to Samuel Adams, 26 Aug., SA Papers), and informed Joseph Reed that he traveled "at the earnest solicitation of a number of warm friends to my Country & me" (Quincy to Reed, 20 Aug., Reed Papers). He carried letters of introduction from James Bowdoin to both Benjamin Franklin (*BF Papers*, 21:282–83) and the Bay Colony's agent, William Bollan (*Bowdoin and Temple Papers*, 371–73); and from Chauncy and the Reverend John Winthrop to Richard Price, a London cleric sympathetic to the American cause. See "Price Letters," 270, 272–73. Before he sailed, he wrote to Samuel Adams asking for letters of introduction from congressmen (Quincy to Adams, 20 Aug., SA Papers).

260　**November 17:** Coquillette and York, *Portrait of a Patriot*, 1:228.

260　**November 19:** Ibid., 231–32.

260　**November 22:** Ibid., 234.

261　**November 29:** Ibid., 237.

261　**December 12:** Ibid., 240–41.

261　**December 17:** Josiah Quincy Jr. to Joseph Reed, 17 Dec. 1774, Reed Papers.

262　**"An independent authority virtually arose":** Drayton, *Memoirs,* 1:175. In some colonies, including Virginia and North Carolina, such contests were delayed by local circumstances until after January; those are discussed in chapter 9.

262　**Governor Wentworth, who had dissolved:** Provincial Convention record, Exeter, N.H., 25 Jan. 1775, in *AA* 4, 1:1180–82; Wentworth to Thomas Waldron, 27 Jan., in *Belknap Papers,* 73. See also Wentworth to Dartmouth, 10 March, in *DAR*, 9:70, and, on the failed assembly session of March, see Jere Daniell, *Experiment in Republicanism: New Hampshire Politics and the American Revolution, 1741–1794* (Cambridge, Mass.: Harvard University Press, 1970), 86–89. In January, Dartmouth dispatched a circular letter to the colonial governors, directing them not to approve assemblies' elections of delegates to the Second Congress (*DAR*, 9:24). Not only did the order arrive in America so late (March) as to be irrelevant, but it also could not be employed when the voting body was a convention, not an assembly under a governor's jurisdiction. On such points, see William Bull to Dartmouth, 28 March, in *DAR*, 9:88.

263 **William Franklin tried without success:** New Jersey assembly proceedings, 11 Jan.–3 Feb. 1775, in *AA* 4, 1:1121–27, and petition to the king, 13 Feb., in ibid., 1132–34; Franklin to Dartmouth, 1 Feb., in Ricord and Nelson, *Documents Relating to the Colonial History of the State of New Jersey,* 10:537 (quotations), with copies of his speech and the assembly's reply, 538–45. Franklin described the politics of the session to Galloway, 12 March; see *DAR,* 9:76–77.

263 **assemblies and provincial congresses roughly coincided:** Pennsylvania assembly record, 5 Dec. 1774, and convention record, 23–28 Jan. 1775, in *AA* 4, 1:1023–25, 1169–71. Quotations: Dickinson to Samuel Ward, 29 Jan. 1775, in *LOD,* 1:303; Thomson to William Henry Drayton, n.d., in "[Charles] Thomson Papers," 282. See Wharton to Samuel Wharton, 31 Jan., in "Wharton Letter-Books 34," 43. Reed was not a radical; he still advocated "some middle Line" of mutual concessions in a letter to Charles Pettit, 31 Jan., Reed Papers. At the assembly session, Joseph Galloway was elected as a delegate to the Second Congress but refused to serve. See *LOD,* 1:295–96.

263 **in South Carolina a provincial congress:** Drayton, *Memoirs,* 1:214–15 (see 205–15); Eliza Pinckney to Harriott Horry, 17 Feb. 1775, Pinckney Family Papers. See also Charles Pinckney to the committee of sixty, New York, 1 March 1775, in *AA* 4, 2:1; Bull to Dartmouth, 4 Jan. 1775, CO 5/396, fol. 106; and William E. Hemphill and Wylma Wates, eds., *Extracts from the Journals of the Provincial Congresses of South Carolina, 1775–1776* (Columbia: South Carolina Archives Department, 1960), 11–30. For Bull's comments on the congress, Bull to Dartmouth, 20 Jan., in *DAR,* 9:30–31; and on the assembly: same to same, 28 Jan., CO 5/396, fol. 112, and 22 Feb., in *DAR,* 9:55–56.

264 **record of the Provincial Congress:** Laurens to his son John, 8 Jan. 1775, in *HL Papers,* 10:25–26. For Drayton's account of the congress: Drayton, *Memoirs,* 1:166–79. Laurens also described a geographic split in the congress between "frontier Inhabitants" and "Sea Coast Inhabitants"; see Laurens to his son John, 22 Jan., in *HL Papers,* 10:39–40.

264 **many participants in the convention expressed:** Laurens to his son John, 18 Jan. 1775, in *HL Papers,* 10:27–31 (quotation, 28). Drayton detailed the compensation plans, *Memoirs,* 1:176. Thomas Middleton, the other congressional delegate, did not participate in the convention.

265 **closure of the civil courts:** Laurens to his son John, 27, 22 Jan. 1775, in *HL Papers,* 10:43, 41. See also same to John Delagaye, 25 Jan., in ibid., 48. Laurens was so uncomfortable about the committee's role that he declined to participate further after his second meeting. Bull took the same approach to communications with the congress as Gage had, treat-

ing it as a group of respectable, propertied men, not as an entity with legal standing. See "To the Honorable William Bull Esquire," with response, 17 Jan. 1775, CO 5/396, fol. 110; and Bull to Dartmouth, 20 Jan., in *DAR*, 9:30–31. For Laurens's opinion: his letter to his son John, 18 Jan., in *HL Papers*, 10:30–31.

265 **Georgia sent no delegates:** See, in addition to sources cited below, Charles C. Jones, *The History of Georgia* (Boston: Houghton Mifflin, 1883), 2:159–72, a summary that serves as background for my discussion. The fourteenth clause of the Continental Association forbade any "Trade, Commerce, Dealings, or Intercourse whatsoever" with non-associating colonies.

266 **that official meeting began:** Wright, address to assembly, 18 Jan. 1775, CO 5/664, fol. 47; assembly to Wright, 20 Jan., CO 5/664, fol. 54; council to Wright, 20 Jan., CO 5/664, fol. 50; Wright to Dartmouth, 1 Feb., in *DAR*, 9:42. The addresses are printed in *AA* 4, 1:1152–56.

266 **The assembly and the convention met:** Quotations: Wright to Dartmouth, 1 Feb. 1775, in *DAR*, 9:42–43. For the Georgia association and the record of the assembly, see *AA* 4, 1:1157–60, and for the Georgia delegates' letter to Peyton Randolph, 6 April, explaining why they were not attending the Second Congress: *LOD*, 1:326–27. A letter written in Savannah on 9 December 1774 attributed Georgians' compliance to their fear of losing their trade with South Carolina rather than coercion from that colony (*AA* 4, 1:1033). Wright later proudly informed Dartmouth that he had prevented the convention from publishing its proceedings (Wright to Dartmouth, 24 April 1775, CO 5/664, fol. 86).

267 **neither the assembly nor the convention:** Quotation: Andrew Wells to Samuel Adams, 18 March 1775, SA Papers. Documents detailing St. John's Parish's efforts are in *AA* 4, 1:1161–63; see also Drayton, *Memoirs*, 1:180–81. Wright attributed the attempt to break away to St. John's planters' descent from New England migrants and retaining "Republican or Oliverian Principles" from their ancestors (Wright to Dartmouth, 24 April 1775, CO 5/664, fol. 87). The one Georgian who attended the Second Continental Congress, Lyman Hall, represented only St. John's Parish.

267 **Some residents of St. Andrew's:** "Darien (Georgia) Resolutions," 13 Jan. 1775, in *AA* 4, 1:1135–37 (quotations, 1136). See Wood, *Slavery in Colonial Georgia*, 201–3.

268 **Colden summoned the assembly:** Colden to Dartmouth, 7 Dec. 1774, in *DAR*, 8:238. For other comments on the upcoming assembly meeting, see William Smith to William Tryon, 6 Dec., reel 11, no. 1008, Dartmouth Papers; James Duane to Thomas Johnson, 29 Dec., in *LOD*, 1:280–81.

268 **newly published pamphlet:** Wilkins, *Short Advice,* quotations, 13–15
(advertised by Rivington on 1 Dec. 1774); Samuel Seabury, *Alarm to the
Legislature,* quotations, 4, 7, 9, 12, 13 (advertised 19 Jan. 1775), which was
distributed at least as far south as Annapolis within a month (see *AA* 4,
1:1208).

268 **celebrate the outcome:** Quotations: Ebenezer Hazard to Deane, 18 Feb.
1775, in "Deane Correspondence," 199 (also same to same, 1 Feb., in ibid.,
192–93); McDougall to Josiah Quincy Jr., 6 April 1775, draft, McDougall
Papers. The record of the assembly session, 10 Jan. to 3 April 1775, is in
AA 4, 1:1282–324. The assembly voted against discussing congressional
resolutions on 26 January (ibid., 1286–87); and against naming delegates
to the Second Congress on 23 February (ibid., 1290). The final texts of the
addresses are printed, in ibid., 1313–21. See also Colden's opening speech
to the assembly, 13 Jan., broadside (*EAI,* no. 14293); a broadside opposing
the assembly's actions, 19 Jan. (*EAI,* no. 14170); positive reports by Colden
to Dartmouth, 21 Jan., CO 5/1106, fol. 64, and 1 Feb., in *DAR,* 9:43–44; a
statement about "the joy that fills the breasts of all the friends to Government," 30 Jan., in *AA* 4, 1:1203; and [Crean Brush], *Speech of a Member
of the General Assembly of New York . . .* (New York: [James Rivington?],
1775). A few local meetings did approve the actions of the Continental
Congress; see *AA* 4, 1:1027–28, 1166–67; and Henry Van Schaack to Peter
Van Schaack, 16 Jan., in Van Schaack, *Memoirs of Henry Van Schaack,* 33.

269 **claims of authority:** See chapter 8 for the discussion of these topics after
late 1774 and early 1775.

269 **appointment of committees:** Quotation: James Lovell to Josiah Quincy
Jr., 9 Dec. 1774, in "Quincy Letters," 484. The Boston town meeting had
voted to establish local committees two days earlier; see *PIR,* 1242–45.
For four localities that refused to establish committees, see *AA* 4, 1:1076–
77 (Oyster Bay, Long Island), 1165 (Shrewsbury, N.J.), 1202 (Ridgefield,
Conn.), and Van Schaack, *Memoirs of Henry Van Schaack,* 35 (Kinder-
hook, N.Y.); and for two objecting to local committees as self-selected
and unrepresentative, *AA* 4, 1:1191–92 (Jamaica, N.Y.); and *RNYG,* 12 Jan.
(White Plains, N.Y.). For committee elections in Maryland, for example,
see *AA* 4, 1:972, 975, 982–83, 985–86. On the committees, see Ammerman, *Common Cause,* chap. 8; Marston, *King and Congress,* chap. 4; and
William B. Warner, *Protocols of Liberty: Communication, Innovation, and
the American Revolution* (Chicago: University of Chicago Press, 2013).

270 **vague and potentially wide-ranging:** Copies of the Association, on which
this paragraph and the next two are based, are widely available. One of
the earliest printings, *The Whole Proceedings of the American Continental*

Congress . . . (New York: John Holt, 1775), includes the eleventh clause on 16–17. Not all the Association's obligations fell on the committees; for example, merchants were to tell their British correspondents not to ship any more goods, and shipowners were to tell captains not to receive such goods. On committee activities, see Wellenreuther, *Revolution of the People.*

271 **frugality would be encouraged:** On aspects of the Association and the revolution related to "virtuous" conduct, see Withington, *Toward a More Perfect Union.*

271 **the ship *Virginia:*** Descriptions of the ship's arrival and the committees' statements are printed in *RevVa,* 2:163–64, 166, 175–76, as well as in part in *AA* 4, 1:964–65; the initial account, later republished in other colonies, appeared in *VaG* (R), 24 Nov. 1774. [James Parker] to Charles Steuart, 27 Nov., reel 2, fol. 287, Steuart Papers, gives additional details, including the fact that Williamsburg men wanted to burn the vessel. An inaccurate satirical report appeared in Mulford, *John Leacock's First Book,* 75. Other incidents involving arriving tea imports in late 1774 and early 1775 are detailed in *RevVa,* 2:162, 172–73, 200, 206, 231; *AA* 4, 1:1009; and Drayton, *Memoirs,* 1:153.

272 **That recommendation, potentially devastating:** Quotations: Reynolds to George Norton, 24 Dec. 1774 ("amazes," "hate the name"), Reynolds to Norton & Sons, 24 Dec. ("unjust reports"), William Reynolds Letterbook (see also similar letters, 16, 25 May 1775); and Reynolds to Norton & Sons, 4 June 1774, in Mason, *John Norton & Sons,* 370–71. Comments by others: Charles Yates to Gale Fearon & Co., 2 Dec. 1774, Charles Yates Letterbook; and James Parker to Charles Steuart, 28 Dec. 1774, reel 2, fol. 301, Steuart Papers, reporting the cargo of staves. Open letters from Norton & Sons to Virginians, offering excuses for the shipment, 5, 16 Jan. 1775, are printed in *RevVa,* 2:218–19, 238–39.

272 **Another incident in Virginia:** [James Parker] to Charles Steuart, 27 Nov. 1774, reel 2, fol. 287, Steuart Papers. The letter is unusual in that the writer's signature and his place of residence (Norfolk) have been crossed out, but it is recognizably Parker's handwriting. These circumstances suggest that Steuart concealed the name of his source when he passed the letter on to someone else, perhaps Philip Dawe, the artist who drew the cartoon. Another account of the same incident is reprinted in Crary, *Price of Loyalty,* 58–59.

273 **Parker tried to avoid trouble:** Parker to Charles Steuart, 27 Nov. 1774 ("almost every body," "American Constitution," "determined enmity"), 6 Dec. ("vile," "perjury"), reel 2, fols. 287–88, 291–92, Steuart Papers; same to same, 11 Feb. 1775, reel 3, fol. 21, Steuart Papers.

274 **Parker nevertheless complained:** Parker to Charles Steuart, 27 Jan. 1775, reel 3, fol. 14, Steuart Papers; Daniel Horsmanden to William Tryon, 3 Dec. 1774, reel 11, no. 1005, Dartmouth Papers; Charles Startin to Henry Pelham, 3 Dec. 1774, in *Letters of Copley and Pelham,* 276–77.

274 **Local committees had remarkably full agendas:** See, in order, "Epsom (New-Hampshire) Resolves," in *AA* 4, 1:1105; *In Committee, December 14, 1774* [Philadelphia], broadside (*EAI,* no. 13539); *The Committee, Taking into Consideration the Tenth Article of the Association . . . ,* [Philadelphia], 6 Dec., broadside (*EAI,* no. 13538); Virginia committees and prices: *RevVa,* 2:211–12, 215, 217–20, 235, 262–64, 281–82, 196. For the ban on balls and directions to farmers, see *AA* 4, 1:1031, 1034; and for bans on gambling and other entertainments, *AA* 4, 2:300, 337. Charleston too banned balls; see William Palfrey to his wife, Susannah, 1 Jan. 1775, Palfrey Papers. The Annapolis woman's letter, dated 2 December 1774, was published in London on 1 February 1775 and is reprinted in Willard, *Letters on the American Revolution,* 22. The Virginia merchant William Carr described committees seeking access to information about past sales "if any suspicion should arise of their selling Goods higher than they had for 12 Months Preceding" the congress; see his letter to James Russell, 24 Jan. 1775, bundle 2, Russell Papers.

275 **Some committees policed speech:** "Candid Confession and Declaration of Paul Thilman," 12 Nov. 1774, in *RevVa,* 2:169–70; "Hearty Sorrow of Malcolm Hart," 15 Dec., in ibid., 2:180–81; "Westmoreland County (Virginia) Committee," 3 Nov., in ibid., 2:165, 179–80. See also ibid., 2:160–61, for another, similar case. See Isaac, "Dramatizing the Ideology of Revolution," 357–85.

275 **cargoes that arrived after December 1:** Parker to Charles Steuart, 28 Dec. 1774, reel 2, fol. 301, Steuart Papers; Penn to Dartmouth, 31 Dec. 1774, CO 5/1286, fol. 7; Laurens to his son John, 4 Jan. 1775, in *HL Papers,* 10:18. A report of the New York City committee on such sales, 17 April 1775, is printed in *AA* 4, 2:342–43. For Thomas Jefferson's problems with goods arriving after the deadline, see Jefferson to Archibald Cary and Benjamin Harrison, 9 Dec. 1774, in *TJ Papers,* 1:154–55. For elections and auctions in Virginia in general, see *RevVa,* 2:168–246, but cf. Charles Yates to Samuel Martin, 6 Feb. 1775, fol. 128, Charles Yates Letterbook, about a different practice in Fredericksburg.

276 **rumors spread in January:** Samuel Adams, for the committee, *To the Publick,* Boston, 20 Jan. 1775, broadside (*EAI,* no. 42777), printed in *SA Writings,* 3:167–69. Greenough's account book, begun 17 January 1775, listed some dates, the names of over 150 individuals and families he had assisted and their sizes, and sometimes items he had given them: for example,

"Widow Goodwin & Daugr," "Walter Piper 6 famy," "Ann Solen Widow Huckster 4 famy," "Jerh Taylor supd [supplied] with sund[ry] and wood," "John How suppd 40/ [shillings] & 6 foot wood." Presumably, those he listed without specific items received a standard allowance. See the ledger, HM 70285, Greenough Family Papers. The "scandelous" rumors were heard on the Cape, but David Greenough assured his father that they were not believed; see David to Thomas, 4 Feb., HM 70286, Greenough Family Papers. An example of payments: John Brown sent £16 currency for profits from sales of goods in Providence, Rhode Island, on 27 February, SA Papers.

276 **The need to interpret:** Baltimore committee: Clark et al., *Naval Documents,* 1:36–37 (for the saga of a "Damnd Salt" shipment intended for Baltimore in early 1775: ibid., 87–88, 118, 143, 154, 167); Norfolk committee: *RevVa,* 2:258–59, 270, 272, 278; New York: *To the Freeholders, Freemen, and Inhabitants of the City and County of New-York,* [ca. 2 Feb.], broadside (*EAI,* no. 14497).

276 **dispute arose between James Duane:** McDougall to Samuel Adams, 29 Jan. 1775, draft, Alexander McDougall Papers. James Fichter, who is completing a study of the tea trade and consumption in the colonies, confirms that many ads for tea continued to appear in mid-Atlantic and New England newspapers between 1 December 1774 and 1 March 1775 (personal communication, 2 April 2017). Surely all or at least most of that tea had been smuggled, as must have been the case with tea that Thomas Ellison Jr. planned to dispatch to his father from Manhattan; see Ellison to Colonel Thomas Ellison, 28 Nov. 1774, Ellison Family Papers.

276 **Colden correctly predicted:** Colden to Dartmouth, 7 Dec. 1774, in *DAR,* 8:237 (see also Colden to William Tryon, 7 Dec., reel 11, no. 1009, Dartmouth Papers); letter from Boston, 8 Dec. 1774, in Willard, *Letters on the American Revolution,* 26; "Proceedings of the Inhabitants of Cumberland County . . . ," 22 Dec. 1774, in Ricord and Nelson, *Documents Relating to the Colonial History of the State of New Jersey,* 10:531–32.

277 **regardless of the rules:** Peter Van Schaack to his brother Henry, 25 Feb. 1775, in Van Schaack, *Memoirs of Henry Van Schaack,* 36; Gill and Curtis, *Man Apart,* 35 (entry of 28 Feb.); report from Providence, 4 March, in *AA* 4, 2:15; Andrews, *Journal of a Lady of Quality,* 155 (composite entry, dated 22 March).

277 **same female English visitor:** Andrews, *Journal of a Lady of Quality,* 147; Duane, *Extracts from Diary of Marshall,* 14 (entry of 1 March 1775).

277 **his obituary was premature:** James Ireland to Dartmouth, 30 Sept. 1774, reel 11, no. 973, Dartmouth Papers (see also John Vardill to same, 21 Oct.,

reel II, no. 986, Dartmouth Papers); Massachusetts Provincial Congress, resolution on peddlers, 15 Feb. 1775, in *PIR,* 1482; Padelford, *Colonial Panorama,* 37 (entry of 16 March); case of Thomas Lilly, 25 March, in *AA* 4, 2:234.

278 **The problems of enforcement:** Committee of Cumberland County, N.J., 6 March, II May, in *AA* 4, 2:34–35; Committee of Ulster County, N.Y., 7 April, in ibid., 298; Miller and Riggs, *Romance, Remedies, and Revolution,* 181–82 (entry of 14 March), 197 (entry of 13 April). Ashley had recorded that the town of Worthington was "very much divided" on whether to enforce the Provincial Congress's injunction against tea drinking (161, entry of 23 Jan.), so many residents of the area rejected the scheme. See also *RevVa,* 2:300, on a Pittsylvania man who defied the local committee in February by continuing to drink tea and whose name was accordingly published in the *VaG* (Purdie), 7 July 1775.

278 **London newspaper recounted the experience:** "Extract of a Letter from . . . New York," 10 April 1775, in Willard, *Letters on the American Revolution,* 73–74; Minutes, Baltimore committee, 13 March, in *AA* 4, 2:124.

279 **surviving scraps of paper:** Williams to Chester, 16 June 1775, HM 70292; same to same, 10 June, HM 70291; same to same, 12 Aug., HM 70295, all in Huntington Library. See also HM 70294, 70296, 70300, for similar notes. Also in Wethersfield, Silas Deane's wife, referred to as a "Daughter of Liberty," seems to have hesitated to drink tea when she was ill in February 1775. See Dr. Benjamin Gale to Deane, 27 Feb., in "Deane Correspondence," 202.

279 **"The Laws of [the Continental Congress]":** Adams to Arthur Lee, 4 March 1775, in *SA Writings,* 3:196.

CHAPTER 8 A CONSTANT STATE OF HOT DEBATE

282 **introduction of the locution "Loyalist":** The earliest reference to "American Loyalists" that I have located is Jonathan Sewall to Thomas Hutchinson, II Dec. 1774, included in "Extracts of Letters to Govr Hutchinson," reel II, no. 1020, Dartmouth Papers (Sewall advocated "manly" steps by Britain, because "Temporizing Measures will be fatal to all American Loyalists immediately, and to all America finally").

283 **brave, or possibly foolhardy:** Nansemond County committee, 6 March 1775, in *RevVa,* 2:314–15; King George County committee, 8 March, in ibid., 2:317–18, 337–38. Both men went into exile in England as Loyalists, but Brockenbrough eventually returned to the United States.

283 **group of about twenty Scots traders:** This paragraph and the next are

based on Richard Henry Lee, Legal Opinion on the Application of the 11th Article of the Association, n.d. [ca. Feb. 1775], in Hoffman, *Lee Family Papers,* reel 2, frame 1305; and William Allason to Thomas B. Martin, 6–13 Feb. 1775, William Allason Letterbook. Allason predicted to Martin on 31 January, ibid., that he and his allies would suffer "very harsh" treatment by the county committee.

284 **some groups signed statements:** See, for example, the statement by the "Freeholders and Inhabitants" of Rye, New York, 24 Sept. 1774, including a retraction by some, 17 Oct., in *AA* 4, 1:802–3; the "Frances Town Resolves," New Hampshire, 21 Oct., in ibid., 888; and statement by "Inhabitants" of Hackensack, New Jersey, 14 March 1775, in *AA* 4, 2:130–31. But some signers of a petition circulated by Benjamin Floyd on Long Island in February and March later withdrew their support, claiming they had been duped about its meaning. See ibid., 36–37, 117–18.

284 **The grand jury and magistrates:** "Declaration of the Grand Jury and Magistrates . . . at Joba's-Town, March the 16th, 1775," *RNYG,* 6 April 1775; "Address of the Inhabitants of Anson County, North Carolina, to the Governour," [March 1775], in *AA* 4, 2:115–17, with shorter but similar statements from Rowan, Surry, and Guilford Counties, and a recorded total of more than five hundred signatures.

284 **began to form counter-associations:** Chalmers, claims memorial, 14 Oct. 1783, and testimony, n.d., AO 12/6. In the 1780s in London, Chalmers published *Political Annals of the Present United Colonies, An Introduction to the History of the Revolt of the American Colonies,* and other works on American history.

285 **greatest success:** This paragraph and the next are based on Timothy Ruggles, "To the Printers of the Boston Newspapers," 22 Dec. 1774, published in *BEP* and *MG&BPB,* both on 26 Dec.; reprinted in *AA* 4, 1:1057–58. Carol Berkin found a copy of this association in Jonathan Sewall's handwriting in his papers at the Public Archives of Canada, so possibly he drafted or contributed to writing it. See Berkin, *Jonathan Sewall,* 107. An association from Dutchess County, New York, dated 18 January 1775, is nearly an exact copy of Ruggles's (*AA* 4, 1:1164); see also one from Portsmouth, New Hampshire, 17 Jan., in *AA* 4, 2:251–52; and one from Reading and Fairfield County, Connecticut, 23 Feb., *AA* 4, 1:1259–60. For references to Ruggles in Virginia, see James Parker to Charles Steuart, 27 Jan., reel 3, fol. 14, Steuart Papers; and Richard Henry Lee to Samuel Adams, 4 Feb., in Ballagh, *Letters of Richard Henry Lee,* 1:129.

285 **threat posed by Ruggles:** Statement by Joseph Root, Montague, *MG&BPB,* 16 Jan. 1775; "Proceedings of the Town of Petersham," 2 Jan., broadside (*EAI,* no. 49293); item datelined "Boston, March 17," *PaL,*

25 March. See *PIR*, 1172–73, on the Provincial Congress and the town of Hardwick, 9–10 Dec. 1774; and document headed "Wrentham Jan. 16 1775," Misc. MSS Bound, for the Ruggles association in those towns.

286 **The news of Ruggles's association:** Quotation: Coffin to Charles Steuart, 10 Dec. 1774, reel 2, fol. 294, Steuart Papers; on Weston: *PIR*, 1430–32; on Williams: Miller and Riggs, *Romance, Remedies, and Revolution*, 155–56, 164–66. See also optimistic reports about Ruggles's association in Willard, *Letters on the American Revolution*, 54; and "Extract of a Letter Received in Edinburgh, . . . Dated Boston, December 26, 1774," in *AA* 4, 1:1068.

286 **fate of Colonel Thomas Gilbert:** The tale of Gilbert and his men in Freetown can most easily be traced in Clark et al., *Naval Documents*, 1:130, 144, 159–60, 167; and *Stiles Diary*, 1:533–34. Quotations: Massachusetts Provincial Congress to Bristol County, 6 April 1775, in *PIR*, 1521 ("enemy"); Bristol County committee of inspection to John Hancock, 4 April, in ibid., 1556 ("knot"); Clark et al., *Naval Documents*, 1:160 ("wretches"); *AA* 4, 2:340 ("humble").

287 **Ruggles association began circulating in Marshfield:** Narrative about the auction in this and the next paragraph is based on seven depositions from men who attended it, dated 13–20 February 1775, in *PIR*, 1999–2011. Two depositions, in ibid., 1997–98, described a young man signing the association on 20 January, even though his father was a "minnit Man." Depositions detailing threats of large mobs descending on Marshfield from nearby towns are in ibid., 1351, 2004, 2008–10.

287 **crowd confronted several Marshfield residents:** Quotations from Lot Keen, deposition, 17 Feb., in ibid., 2007–8.

287 **debate over the Ruggles association:** Elizabeth White, deposition, 15 Feb. 1775, in ibid., 1998; Ruth Baker, deposition, 15 Feb., in ibid., 2002; Huldah Wright, deposition, 16 Feb., in ibid., 2004. See also depositions by Sarah Garnett, 16 Feb., in ibid., 2003; Rodah Trouant, 17 Feb., in ibid., 2005; and Ruth Wales, 17 Feb., in ibid.

288 **threats of mob action:** Petition to Gage from Marshfield and Scituate, [20] Jan. 1775, in ibid., 1352 (also in *DAR*, 9:41); Gage to Dartmouth, 27 Jan., in *PIR*, 1351–52; "Extract of a Letter from Marshfield, to a Gentleman at Boston," 24 Jan., *RNYG*, 9 Feb. (also in *AA* 4, 1:1177) ("freely utter"). For contemporary comments, see John Andrews to William Barrell, 24 Jan., in "Andrews Letters," 396; and *AA* 4, 1:1178.

288 **The arrival of British troops:** Remonstrance of Selectmen of Plymouth and Other Towns, 3 Feb. 1775, in *PIR*, 1961–62. For later complaints and exchanges: ibid., 1963–64, 2045–46.

289 **very different reaction:** Marshfield, address to Gage, [20 Feb. 1775], in

ibid., 1957–58; town meeting record, 20 Feb., in *AA* 4, 1:1249. See also ibid., 1250–51.

289 **larger number of Marshfield residents:** Protest of Marshfield residents, n.d., in *AA* 4, 1:1249–50.

290 **Divisions arose too in the ranks:** Reed to Dennis DeBerdt, 13 Feb. 1775, in Reed, *Life of Esther Reed,* 207; *Stiles Diary,* 1:492 (entry of 3 Dec. 1774); Duane, *Extracts from Diary of Marshall,* 12 (entry of 2 Jan. 1775). The statement Quakers issued on 5 January is in *AA* 4, 1:1093.

290 **more formal document:** *The TESTIMONY of the People Called QUAKERS, Given Forth by a Meeting of the Representatives of Said People, in PENNSYLVANIA and NEW-JERSEY . . . ,* 24 Jan. 1775, broadside (*EAI,* no. 14052); also in *AA* 4, 1:1176–77. See also Duane, *Extracts from Diary of Marshall,* 13 (entry of 24 Jan.). The Quaker merchant Thomas Wharton approved the statement and forwarded it to his brother in England; see Thomas to Samuel Wharton, 31 Jan., in "Wharton Letter-Books 34," 41.

290 **statement aroused such immediate antagonism:** Robert Bolling Jr. to Robert Pleasants, 26 Feb. 1775, Pleasants Family Papers, 1 (box 12, Brock Collection); the essayist was "Amicus Veritatis," conveying an essay by B.L. to *PaG,* from *PaJ,* 8 March, in *AA* 4, 2:80–81 (source of the final quotations).

291 **Quakers' difficulties in upholding their pacifist principles:** Jared Ingersoll to Jonathan Ingersoll, 11 Feb. 1775, in Dexter, *Correspondence of Jared Ingersoll,* 451; Madison to William Bradford, 20 Jan., in *JM Papers,* 1:135.

291 **pamphlets and newspaper essays:** Edward Biddle to Jonathan Potts, 25 Feb. 1775, in *LOD,* 1:316; Padelford, *Colonial Panorama,* 31–32 ("Politics," "both sides,"), 58 ("avidity"), 69 ("discourse") (entries for 13, 31 March, 15 April 1775), see also ibid., 54, 67–70. William Franklin's large collection of prerevolutionary pamphlets is now at the Boston Athenaeum, but the library has no record of how or when they were acquired (personal communication). See Schlesinger, *Prelude to Independence,* for another account of publications in these months.

292 **Men with access to such shops:** Lee to Carter, 20 Dec. 1774, in Ballagh, *Letters of Richard Henry Lee,* 1:127, probably enclosing James Wilson's *Considerations on the Nature and Extent of the Legislative Authority of the British Parliament,* published by the Bradfords in September 1774; William Allason to Andrew Sproule, 26 Feb. 1775, William Allason Letter-book, perhaps referring to Thomas Bradbury Chandler's *What Think Ye of the Congress Now?,* which was available in Virginia at the time; Jared Ingersoll to Jonathan Ingersoll, 10 March, in Dexter, *Correspondence of Ingersoll,* 454. For the Chandler and Galloway pamphlets, see below.

292 **publishing had become wholly partisan:** Quotations: Parker to Charles

Steuart, 6 Dec. 1774, reel 2, fol. 291, Steuart Papers; Reed to [Charles Pettit], 31 Jan. 1775 (see also same to same, 14 Jan.), Joseph Reed Papers. See Gadsden to [Thomas and William Bradford], 28 March 1775, in Walsh, *Writings of Gadsden,* 101–4. Humphreys testified to the Loyalist Claims Commission that a group of Philadelphians urged him to start the paper to support the government and that local committees "frequently" questioned him to learn the identity of the authors whose essays he published. See Humphreys, claims testimony, 15 June 1785, AO 12/38, fol. 104. A study of the *BEP* concluded that it managed to maintain neutrality longer than most papers; see Sandra Nevelsen Cleary, "Of No Party: The Independent Newspaper and the Rhetoric of Revolution, 1765–1775," *Communication Studies* 44 (1993): 157–67.

293 **Loyalist authors continued to complain:** Chandler, *What Think Ye of the Congress Now?,* 3–4. For other complaints about a lack of press freedom, see Philo Patriae, "To His Excellency General Gage," *MG&BNL,* 22 Dec. 1774; Benjamin Floyd to Smithtown, L.I., committee, 6 March 1775, in *AA* 4, 2:37.

293 **An essay in *Rivington's:*** Anti-Tyrannicus, "To the Committee of Inspection for the City and County of New York," *RNYG,* 23 March 1775 (also printed in *AA* 4, 2:213–14).

294 **vigorous campaign to suppress:** "Fairfield (Connecticut) Committee," 29 Dec. 1774, in *AA* 4, 1:1076; At a *CONVENTION OF COMMITTEES . . . ,* Worcester, 27 Jan. 1775, broadside (*EAI,* no. 42988); "Middlesex County (New-Jersey) Resolutions," 16 Jan., in *AA* 4, 1:1084–85. "Plainheart," writing in the *MG&BNL,* 2 March, accused the Worcester men of "tyranny" for suggesting that people not read such newspapers, comparing them to "the crafty Roman-catholic priests" who tried to prevent ordinary folk from reading the Bible, "the key to knowledge."

294 **Chandler's and Seabury's pamphlets:** Annapolis merchant to a friend in Philadelphia, 28 Jan. 1775, in *AA* 4, 1:1194; Proceedings of Orange County committee, 25, 28 March, in *RevVa,* 2:377, 386. James Parker sent Charles Steuart a copy of Seabury's *Congress Canvassed* from Norfolk; see Parker to Steuart, 11 Feb., reel 3, fol. 21, Steuart Papers.

294 **Rivington attracted the most ire:** Quotations: Friends of Liberty to Silas Deane, 15 Dec. 1774, in Ford, *Correspondence of Webb,* 1:45–46. For the Provincial Congress, see its minutes, 21 Oct. 1774, in *PIR,* 1105–7. The *RNYG* advertisement on 8 December, to which the "Friends" letter referred, mentioned both Mary V. V.'s *Dialogue* and Bob Jingle's *Association,* in addition to the Lee and Livingston pamphlets, among others. Charles Lee himself called Rivington a "miscreant" and expressed astonishment that he was "suffer'd to heap insult upon insult on the Congress

with impunity"; see Lee to Benjamin Rush, 15 Dec. 1774, *Colls NYHS* 4 (1871): 143–44. Attacks on Rivington and his pamphlets were especially fierce in New Jersey. For examples, see *AA* 4, 1:1029–30, 1051–52, 1103, 1106; *AA* 4, 2:35; and for other references to Rivington's publications, see *AA* 4, 1:1257; *AA* 4, 2:12–13, 50, 111, 132–34.

295 **increasing reach of such conservative publications:** Gage to Dartmouth, 18 Jan. 1775, in *DAR*, 9:29–30; *RNYG*, 2 March, column headed "New-York, March 2"; extract of letter from Philadelphia to Rivington, 4 Feb., in *AA* 4, 1:1211; Galloway to [Samuel Verplanck], 14 Feb., in "Some Letters of Joseph Galloway," 480; Warren to Adams, 15 Jan., in *JA Papers*, 2:214. Despite his praise for the New York pamphlets, Galloway faulted them for not acknowledging "the rights of the American Subject" and failing to propose "a Constitutional Remedy."

295 **attributed his political conversion:** "A Converted Whig," *MG&BPB*, 6 March 1775 (included with incorrect date in *AA* 4, 2:103–6). One commentator, 24 March, remarked that readers thought the Converted Whig was "a fiction of some Tory" (*AA* 4, 2:230).

296 **numerous opinion pieces:** Suffolk Yeoman: *MG&BNL*, 29 Dec. 1774; Eugenio: *PaL*, 28 Jan. 1775; Conciliator: *MG&BPB*, 6 Feb.; America's Real Friend: *RNYG*, 16 Feb.; C: *MG&BNL*, 16 Feb.; Phileirene: *MG&BNL*, 12, 26 Jan.; 9 Feb.; 2, 9, 30 March; 6, 13 April. Phileirene has been identified as Jonathan Sewall. Philadelphians' replies to Phileirene are reprinted in *AA* 4, 2:8–10, 81–85. I have concluded that "C," who repeated Bullman's argument, was the Reverend Henry Caner, who on 16 January 1775 informed Thomas Hutchinson that he was writing in support of the government "(tho' incog)." Like C in that February essay, Caner frequently included Latin quotations in his writings. See *Letterbook of Caner.*

296 **Additional pamphlet publications:** In addition to the Chandler and Galloway pamphlets, discussed below, see Wells, *Middle Line;* Hunt, *Political Family;* and Gray, *Few Remarks.*

296 **Chandler opened his pamphlet:** Advertised by Rivington on 12 January 1775, with just one edition noted by Adams, *American Independence,* 123–24. According to the English Short Title Catalogue, twenty-nine U.S. and four U.K. libraries today own copies of this edition; three U.K. libraries, six U.S., and two Canadian libraries have copies of a U.K. reprint, also published in 1775. Washington's copy of the New York printing is now in the Boston Athenaeum.

296 **analyze the summer meetings:** Chandler, *What Think Ye of the Congress Now?,* quotations, 7, 42, 48.

297 **Galloway's *Candid Examination:*** See 51 for the "often conversed" comment. In mid-February, he explained that the pamphlet's composition had

been delayed by illness and reported that it was "now in the Press in New York"; see Galloway to [Samuel Verplanck], 14 Feb. 1775, in "Some Letters of Galloway," 480. In sending this pamphlet to Dartmouth, Colden described it as "one of the best" of the recent "good political pieces"; see Colden to Dartmouth, 1 March 1775, in *DAR*, 9:60. For a critique of it as "speciously written," see Ebenezer Hazard to Silas Deane, 7 April, in "Deane Correspondence," 211–12. According to the English Short Title Catalogue, this printing, the only American one, is today owned by six U.K., one Canadian, and thirty-four U.S. libraries; a U.K. reprint, published 1780, is in five U.K., one Canadian, and twenty-five U.S. libraries. William Franklin's copy of the 1775 New York edition is in the Boston Athenaeum.

298 **assessed the current situation hyperbolically:** Galloway, *Candid Examination*, 1 (quotation); see 2–26. In his 27 March 1775 *Novanglus* essay, John Adams replied to Galloway's arguments about colonial subjection to the king but not to Parliament (*JA Papers*, 2:346–54). William Franklin told Galloway in mid-March that his pamphlet was "much admired by all whom I have heard speak of it" (Franklin to Galloway, 12 March, enclosed in Franklin to Dartmouth, 3 April, in *DAR*, 9:77). For some of that praise, see James Robertson to [Francis Legge?], 4 March, reel 12, no. 1180, Dartmouth Papers. Galloway told Franklin immodestly that "from all quarters it is universally applauded by men of candour and abilities" (to Franklin, 26 March, in *LOD*, 1:324; also enclosed to Dartmouth, 3 April, in *DAR*, 9:87).

298 **congressmen sought "absolute independence":** Galloway, *Candid Examination*, quotations 61, 27, 31, 33, 59.

299 **John Dickinson and Charles Thomson responded:** [Dickinson and Thomson], "To the Author of a Pamphlet, Entitled, 'A Candid Examination . . . ,'" *PaJ*, 8 March 1775. Galloway quickly responded in *Reply to an Address,* accusing Dickinson and Thomson of "low chicanery" and of being "destitute of candor and honour," among other reciprocal insults (quotations, 3). On 26 March, he told William Franklin that he had completed this reply (*LOD*, 1:322); he knew his critics were Dickinson and Thomson and feared he had responded with "too much acrimony, and yet I think they deserve it" (Galloway to [Samuel Verplanck], 1 April, in "Some Letters of Galloway," 481–82). See also C.E. [Joseph Galloway], "To the Public," *PaG*, 26 April 1775, replying to criticism that his Plan of Union in effect plagiarized Benjamin Franklin's 1754 plan, developed just prior to the Seven Years' War.

299 **invective leveled at James Rivington:** *The Last Words, Dying Speech, and Confession* . . . , New Brunswick, N.J., 13 April 1775, broadside (*EAI*,

no. 14041). If the author of the poem had known that about a week earlier John Pownall wrote from the Colonial Office to Rivington to appoint him king's printer for New York with an annual stipend of £100, the invective would presumably have been worse. See Pownall to Rivington, 5 April, CO 5/1106, fol. 78. That same day Pownall wrote to Chandler and to Myles Cooper, president of King's College (the Cooper of the poem), who was erroneously thought to have written some of the pamphlets, to offer them £200 a year (CO 5/1106, fol. 80). Confusion resulting from the contemporary attribution to Cooper led to some difficulties in Barnstable; see John Andrews to William Barrell, 29 Jan., in "Andrews Letters," 398.

300 **surely did not anticipate:** Rivington to Knox, 1 Dec. 1774, in "Henry Knox and the London Book-Store," 303. Rivington protected Chandler's anonymity as a New York–region author from Knox by claiming, 302, that the manuscript of *Friendly Address* had been sent to him by Boston's Mills & Hicks. For Bob Jingle's poem, *The Association,* see chapter 6, above. Knox's bookseller's correspondence volume, MHS, containing some of his replies to Rivington, does not include an order for the poem or for *Friendly Address.*

300 **newspaper series *Massachusettensis:*** A recent article has attributed some of the essays and the series as a whole to joint authorship on the basis of statistical analyses of style and content, although Leonard alone later claimed responsibility. At the time and for some years afterward, Sewall was usually thought to be the sole author (on these points, see below). See Colin Nicolson et al., "A Case of Identity: *Massachusettensis* and John Adams," *NEQ* 91 (2018): 651–82. Hereafter cited as "Case of Identity," with final attributions of authorship on 682.

300 **Mercy Otis Warren's satirical play:** Quotations: *The Group,* in Franklin, *Plays of Warren,* unpag. front matter, 7, 9. The characters in the play are identified through contemporary notations by Worthington C. Ford, in "Mrs. Warren's 'The Group,'" *Procs MHS* 62 (1928–1929): 15–19. On Leonard as Massachusettensis: John Eliot to Jeremy Belknap, 11 April 1775, in *Belknap Papers,* 86. For correspondence among Mercy and James Warren and John and Abigail Adams about *The Group,* see *JA Papers,* 2:214, 389–90, 394, 406, 408; and *AFC,* 1:185–86. On Warren's plays in general, see Castronovo, *Propaganda 1776,* 71–78.

301 **Robert Treat Paine:** Paine left a response unfinished and unpublished; see "To Massachusettensis," in *RTP Papers,* 3:21–30. For an anonymous set of responses, see below.

301 **John Adams, writing as Novanglus:** The editions cited here are, for *Novanglus,* the version in *JA Papers,* 2; and the complete, 118-page 1776 London edition of *Massachusettensis,* which has become the standard ver-

sion of the essays. This is one of several editions the Short Title Catalogue indicates J. Mathews printed in that year; numerous copies of these editions survive in the United States and the U.K. Mathews reprinted a Mills & Hicks 1775 Boston edition, also with 118 pages, of which the Short Title Catalogue lists nine surviving copies, eight in the United States. A 1776 Dublin edition appeared with different pagination. In mid-March 1775, Rivington published an 86-page pamphlet containing the first eight essays, titled *The Origin of the American Contest with Great-Britain . . . Published at Boston, Under the Signature of Massachusettensis. . . .* Twenty copies of the Rivington compilation are recorded in the United States; it promised a continuation, which never appeared.

301 **Leonard later explained:** Leonard to Sir Grey Cooper, 28 June 1779, AO 13/74, fol. 517. Early collected editions of the exchanges listed Adams and Sewall as the authors. For Sewall's Phileirene essays, see above. Adams wrote a thirteenth essay, but it remained unpublished on 19 April 1775 and was not printed at that time. Samuel Adams too thought Sewall was Massachusettensis; see Adams to Arthur Lee, 4 March 1775, in *SA Writings,* 3:197.

301 **The essays and responses appeared:** *JA Papers,* 2:226, on initial timing; Warren to Samuel Adams, 1 Jan. 1775, SA Papers. The Adams Papers editors observe that John Adams only stepped forward to refute Massachusettensis when others failed to act, so that perhaps explains the tardy appearance of his replies. See the useful editorial note to the *Novanglus* essays, in *JA Papers,* 2:216–26.

301 **One of the most direct exchanges:** *Massachusettensis,* 1–2 (12 Dec. 1774, no. 1). "Case of Identity" assigns this first essay to Sewall.

302 **Adams at first rebutted:** *JA Papers,* 2:243–46 (6 Feb. 1775, *Novanglus* 3; quotation, 245); *Massachusettensis,* 76 (20 Feb., no. 11); *JA Papers,* 2:305 (27 Feb., *Novanglus* 6). "Plainheart," writing in the *MG&BNL,* 16 Feb., told his readers that Adams's initial position was "an insult upon your common sense." For the Worcester convention, see above.

302 **After the initial complaint:** *Massachusettensis,* 2–3 (12 Dec. 1774, no. 1).

302 **War appeared inevitable:** Ibid., 5, 7.

303 **Adams's response to that essay:** *JA Papers,* 2:252–55, quotations, 253, 255 (6 Feb. 1775, *Novanglus* 3).

303 **In a key passage:** *JA Papers,* 2:246–47 (6 Feb. 1775, *Novanglus* 3).

304 **After the dramatic first essay:** Quotations: *Massachusettensis,* 12 (19 Dec. 1774, no. 2), 24 (26 Dec., no. 3); see 8–24. "Case of Identity" assigns the second essay to Leonard alone, or Leonard and Sewall together; and the third to Sewall.

304 **Adams challenged that account:** Adams's replies to the second and third

Massachusettensis essays consumed four of his: *Novanglus* 4 (13 Feb. 1775) replied to the second; *Novanglus* 1, 2, and 5 (23, 30 Jan.; 20 Feb.) replied to the third. For these: *JA Papers*, 2:226–33 (*Novanglus* 1), 233–42 (*Novanglus* 2), 256–68 (*Novanglus* 4), and 269–87 (*Novanglus* 5). Quotations: 233, 267. Massachusettensis defended Hutchinson and others against Adams's attack in his thirteenth letter, 6 March, but did not address the conflation of British soldiers and local "Tories"; see *Massachusettensis*, 85–91. "Case of Identity" does not attribute that letter definitively to either author.

304 **focused on the events of the past year:** Quotations: *Massachusettensis*, 33, 35, 36 (2 Jan. 1775, no. 4); see 31–37. Assigned to Sewall in "Case of Identity."

305 **Adams offered a familiar story:** Quotations: *JA Papers*, 2:288, 305 (27 Feb. 1775, *Novanglus* 6); see 288–305.

305 **British constitution:** *Massachusettensis*, 40, 41, 45 (9, 16 Jan. 1775, nos. 5, 6); see 37–51. Both assigned to Leonard by "Case of Identity."

306 **six essays on the British constitution:** *JA Papers*, 2:307, 326 (6 March, *Novanglus* 7), and 307–85. In the last paragraph of the unpublished final article (385), he pronounced the 16 January essay as "the feeblest, the most frivolous, the weakest, the most absurd, Effort that ever was made." (Yet he devoted six essays to refuting it.) An author signing himself "From the County of Hampshire," possibly Joseph Hawley, who replied to Massachusettensis in a series of nine essays—in *MSpy*, from 9 February through 13 April—also devoted a great deal of space to arguing about interpretations of the British constitution.

306 **Adams never replied:** For these, see *Massachusettensis*, 59–63 (letter 8), 63–69 (letter 9), 70–74 (letter 10), 74–79 (letter 11), 93–97 (letter 14), 98–104 (letter 15). The methods used in "Case of Identity" attribute the last two possibly to Sewall but gave divided results on the others.

306 **The most important of these essays:** This paragraph and the next: ibid., 105–7, 110, 113–14 (letter 16, 105–14). Most likely by Leonard, according to "Case of Identity."

307 **praised *Novanglus* unreservedly:** See Abigail to Mercy Otis Warren, [25 Jan. 1775], in *AFC*, 1:180; James Warren to John Adams, 20 Feb., in *JA Papers*, 2:293; and Samuel Swift to Adams, 13 March, in ibid., 403.

308 **January 3, 1775:** Yorke to the Earl of Suffolk, 3, 6 Jan. 1775, SP 84/546.

308 **February 15:** Gardoqui to Lee, 15 Feb. 1775, in Clark et al., *Naval Documents*, 1:401. This volume contains many excerpts from correspondence and newspapers about smuggling in general and acquiring arms and ammunition in particular. The potential sources mentioned include St. Eustatius, Hamburg, Stockholm and Gothenburg in Sweden, and ports in France, as well as Holland. See esp. 393–439, for January through

March 1775. On the importance of the fisheries trade to later commerce in arms, see Christopher P. Magra, *The Fisherman's Cause: Atlantic Commerce and Maritime Dimensions of the American Revolution* (New York: Cambridge University Press, 2009), 161–76.

308 **February 17:** Suffolk to Yorke, 17, 21 Feb. 1775, SP 84/546. The information was deemed sufficiently serious to warrant attention from Lord Dartmouth. See Paul Wentworth to Dartmouth, 18 Feb., reel 12, no. 1151, Dartmouth Papers; and same to same, 11 March, reel 12, no. 1185, Dartmouth Papers.

309 **February 26:** Pearson to Yorke, 26 Feb. 1775, Holland Transcripts, 247, BC.

309 **March 1:** Yorke to Pearson, 1 March 1775, SP 84/546.

309 **March 20:** Proclamation of the States General, 20 March 1775, in *AA* 4, 2:277. See Yorke to Suffolk, 14 March, Holland Transcripts, describing his efforts to persuade the States General to adopt such a policy.

309 **April 8:** Pearson to Philip Stephens, 8 April 1775, Holland Transcripts. For more on the Americans' search for munitions in Europe in 1775 and thereafter, see Phillips, *1775*, 295–313.

CHAPTER 9 ALL OUR LIBERTIES AT STAKE

310 **Governor Jonathan Trumbull spoke:** This paragraph and the next are based on Trumbull, Address to the Connecticut House and Council, draft, March 1775, Jonathan Trumbull Papers, 20:101a–c.

310 **So he had called them together:** The assembly then proceeded to deal with the militia, among other topics. See *AA* 4, 2:107, 110–11.

311 **A ship arrived in Marblehead:** The speech was published in most colonial newspapers; the earliest was *EG,* 31 Jan. 1775, followed by, for example, *RNYG,* 2 Feb., *VaG* (D&H), 4 Feb., and *PaJ,* 4 Feb. There were two broadside publications, one by John Carter in Providence, datelined Boston, 30 Jan. 1775 (*EAI,* no. 14083), and one by John Dunlap in Philadelphia, dated in that city 3 Feb. (*EAI,* no. 14082). The newspapers and the former included Parliament's responses; the latter did not. Lord Dartmouth dispatched copies of the speech and the responses in a circular letter to all American governors dated 10 Dec. 1774 (*DAR,* 7:218–19).

311 **Henry Laurens waited anxiously:** Henry Laurens to William Manning, 21 Jan. 1775, in *HL Papers,* 10:38; John Laurens to Henry Laurens, 3–4 Dec. 1774, in ibid., 9:646–47, 649. Other Americans who heard the speech included William Bollan, agent for Massachusetts, and the Virginian Arthur Lee, who rushed back from a trip to Rome to attend. Both also reported pessimistic reactions to its content. See Bollan to James

Bowdoin, 6 Dec. 1774, in *Bowdoin and Temple Papers*, 379–81; and Lee to Thomas Cushing, 6 Dec., CO 5/118, fols. 92–93.

311 **George III put an end:** *The King's Speech, &c*, broadside, Providence (*EAI*, no. 14083). The king did not receive the communications from the Continental Congress until January, so the speech was based on prior information.

312 **John Carter, a Providence printer:** Ibid.

312 **Abigail Adams echoed Carter's words:** Adams to Warren, [3 Feb. 1775], in *AFC*, 1:183–84; Pelham to Charles Startin, 31 Jan., in *Letters of Copley and Pelham*, 288; Laurens to his son John, 6 Feb., in *HL Papers*, 10:60.

313 **told correspondents in London:** Cushing to Benjamin Franklin, 20 Feb. 1775, in *BF Papers*, 21:503; Lee to Arthur Lee, 24 Feb., in *LOD*, 1:313; Laurens to Thomas Denham, 7 Feb., in *HL Papers*, 10:63. See also *Stiles Diary*, 1:514 (entry of 3 Feb.). But cf. "Extract of a Letter from a Gentleman at Boston, to His Friend at New-York," *RNYG*, 23 Feb.; and Willard, *Letters on the American Revolution*, 70–71.

313 **royal governors concurred:** Wright to Dartmouth, 13 Feb. 1775, CO 5/664, fol. 62; Martin to Dartmouth, 10 March, in *DAR*, 9:71. See also John Wentworth to Dartmouth, 16 March, CO 5/939, fol. 116. Jonathan Trumbull's response to the speech, dated 10 March (*DAR*, 9:74–76), was amended and formally approved by the Connecticut assembly; see *AA 4*, 2:110–11, 113.

313 **Reed's final communication:** This and the next paragraph are based on Reed to Dartmouth, 14 Feb. 1775, reel 2, no. 1097, Dartmouth Papers. At nearly the same time, George Washington and Charles Carroll of Carrollton also expressed some hope that the ministry might change course; see Washington to John Connolly [?], 25 Feb., in *GW Papers: CS*, 10:273; and Carroll to Wallace, Davidson, and Johnson, 17 Feb., in Hoffman, *Dear Papa*, 2:792.

313 **settlement was attainable:** Reed was not alone in early 1775 when he asserted that almost all Americans were united in opposition to taxation by Parliament. See, for example, Charles Yates to Henry Fletcher, 16 Feb. 1775, Charles Yates Letterbook, declaring that "not one in fifty" supported it; and Eddis, *Letters from America*, 104, a letter dated 13 March, explaining that if in a published essay he had failed to reject parliamentary taxation, readers would have paid no attention to his criticisms of congressional rule.

314 **colonists disagreed not over principles:** "Extract of a Letter from the Revd. Dr. John Rodgers (Dated New York, 17th Feb. 1775) to J.T. Esq.," reel 2, no. 1101, Dartmouth Papers; Benjamin Gale to Silas Deane, 27 Feb., in "Deane Correspondence," 202.

314 **Committees everywhere attempted to enforce:** Falmouth: Samuel Freeman to Samuel Adams, 5 March 1775, SA Papers; Talbot County, Maryland, committee, 21 March, in *AA* 4, 2:175–76; Essex County, Virginia,
committee, 2 March, in *RevVa*, 2:306 (the cloth was much traveled; it had
initially failed to sell in Virginia two years earlier); Marblehead: "A Private
Letter from a Gentleman at Boston," 19 Feb., in Willard, *Letters on the
American Revolution*, 65–66; Charleston: Henry Laurens to John Laurens,
18 Feb., in *HL Papers*, 10:72. Laurens was relieved when a ship filled with
goods he was importing arrived in port late on the evening of 31 January;
see his letters on the subject, 4, 6, 7 Feb., in ibid., 10:51–54, 62.

315 **Norfolk trader was discovered:** Statement of Norfolk committee,
6 March 1775, in *RevVa*, 2:307–8; Parker to Charles Steuart, 24 March,
reel 3, fol. 36, Steuart Papers. In the same letter, Parker thanked Steuart
discreetly for "two small parcells" that "highly Pleased the partys Concerned," which probably contained tea.

315 **controversy among residents of Charleston:** The account in this and the
next two paragraphs is based on Drayton, *Memoirs*, 1:181–87.

316 **Drayton recalled that he responded:** I follow Drayton's account, which
has details not available elsewhere, for although he misremembered some
of the specifics and might well have exaggerated his own role, he accurately described the outcome and its significance. According to William
Bull's much shorter report, a man had traveled from London via Antigua
to Charleston. The first committee vote would have let him land with
his horses, but local mechanics raised "much clamour," leading to several "private meetings" of the committee not mentioned by Drayton. A
compromise was reached (the details of which Bull did not describe),
but it lost by two votes in the full committee. The man then had to sail
for Jamaica with his horses. So, as Drayton recounted, the Charleston
populace prevailed, although he said it was by a positive committee vote,
rather than by the failure to adopt a negotiated settlement. See Bull to
Dartmouth, 28 March 1775, in *DAR*, 9:89.

316 **The *James* sailed into the harbor:** The *NYJ* account, 14 Feb. 1775, is
reprinted in Clark et al., *Naval Documents*, 1:89–91. Ezra Stiles summarized the story on 21 February; see *Stiles Diary*, 1:519. Alexander McDougall told Dr. Thomas Young that he hoped New York's handling of the
challenge presented by the *James* would convince others that "the City is
in earnest." (McDougall to Young, 16 Feb., SA Papers.)

316 **The *Beulah*, which arrived:** Quotation: Colden to Dartmouth, 1 March
1775, in *DAR*, 9:59. See Gage to Colden, 26 Feb., in *Letters of Colden*,
267; and James Robertson to [Francis Legge?], 4 March, reel 12, no. 1180,
Dartmouth Papers. The *Beulah*'s arrival and the Murrays' meeting with

the other owners are described in Peter R. Livingston to Robert Livingston, 19 Feb., Livingston-Redmond Papers.

317   **The ship left New York:** Summary based on voluminous documentation, much of it from *NYJ*, reprinted in Ricord and Nelson, *Documents Relating to the Colonial History of the State of New Jersey*, 10:561–69 (quotations, 563), and in Clark et al., *Naval Documents*, 1:92, 94, 99–100, 105. Multiple broadsides, not included in the reprinted material and some by the Murrays, addressed aspects of the *Beulah* affair (*EAI*, nos. 14031, 14266, 14267, 14496, 14513, 14514, 14516). Alexander McDougall was deeply involved, as was Isaac Sears; see McDougall's draft letters to Thadd[e]us Burr, 26 Feb., and Josiah Quincy Jr., 2 March and 6 April; and his political notes dated 20 Feb., 13, 15, 20 March, all in Alexander McDougall Papers. Ezra Stiles followed developments closely; see *Stiles Diary*, 1:519, 524, 525, 528 (entries of 23 Feb., 11, 13, 24 March). See also *AA* 4, 2:48.

317   **Admiral Graves, reporting from Boston:** Graves to Philip Stephens, 4 March 1775, in Clark et al., *Naval Documents*, 1:124; Graves to Stephens, 11 April, in ibid., 1:178.

318   **New London captain:** Nathaniel Shaw to David Trumbull, 21 Feb. 1775, Misc. MSS Bound; Samuel Broome to Silas Deane, 13 April, in "Deane Correspondence," 213–14; John Brown to Boston Committee for Donations, 27 Feb., SA Papers; *Stiles Diary*, 1:527 (entry of 18 March).

319   **customs officers attempted to intercept:** Sir James Wright, Proclamation, 21 Feb. 1775, in *AA* 4, 1:1253; Thomas Ellison Jr. to Thomas Ellison Sr., 6 Feb., Ellison Family Papers. Wright reported the Savannah incident to Dartmouth, 24 Feb., CO 5/664, fol. 66, enclosing depositions about the attack, fols. 68–74, and a copy of his proclamation (fol. 76).

319   **Delaware River:** Robert Byrne to customs commissioners, 10, 17 March 1775, in Clark et al., *Naval Documents*, 1:132–36 (enclosing a deposition), 151–52. Byrne claimed in the second letter to be the first customs officer who tried to stop the "prodigious Counterband Trade" between Maryland and Pennsylvania.

319   **customs officer from Philadelphia:** Quotations: John Patterson and Zach[ariah] Hood to customs collector, Newport, R.I., 3 Feb. 1775, in *Commerce of Rhode Island*, 70:5. See also Francis Welsh to Philadelphia customshouse, 8 Feb., in Clark et al., *Naval Documents*, 1:83–84, 87, 92. For another smuggling incident in the region in March: ibid., 1:142, 161, 189–90.

320   **Pennsylvania assembly:** Penn to Dartmouth, 28 Feb. 1775, CO 5/1286, fol. 44. See fols. 50, 52, for his address to the assembly and its response. Joseph Galloway informed William Franklin that Penn had been influenced by Franklin's and Colden's actions; see Galloway to Franklin,

26 March, in *DAR,* 9:85. For the official record of the assembly session, 20 Feb.–15 March: *AA* 4, 1:1277–82. Delaware's assembly, which met 13–29 March, was somewhat more conciliatory; see *AA* 4, 2:126–29.

321 **"warm Disputes" that consumed several weeks:** Reed to [Charles Pettit], 25 Feb. 1775, Joseph Reed Papers; Galloway to Franklin, 28 Feb., in *DAR,* 9:58. He described his maneuvers in greater detail and the death threat in his letter to Franklin of 26 March, in ibid., 9:84–88 (also in *LOD,* 1:322–25; the letter of 28 Feb. is in *LOD,* 1:318–20).

321 **Bradford voiced unhappiness:** Bradford to Madison, [3–6 March 1775], in *JM Papers,* 1:139.

321 **political position remained deliberately ambiguous:** Joseph Reed to [Charles Pettit], 25 Feb. 1775, Reed Papers; Esther Reed to Dennis DeBerdt, 14 March, in Reed, *Life of Esther Reed,* 209. On the evolution of both Reeds' political views, see Owen S. Ireland, "Esther DeBerdt Reed and Female Political Subjectivity in Revolutionary Pennsylvania: Identity, Agency, and Alienation in 1775," in Pencak, *Pennsylvania's Revolution,* 168–91. Other Philadelphians were stronger supporters of American resistance; see two letters printed in English newspapers, one from a man (31 March) and one from a woman (3 April), in Willard, *Letters on the American Revolution,* 71, 72.

322 **But not so New York:** Padelford, *Colonial Panorama,* 29 (entry of 11 March 1775). Robert R. Livingston expressed concern lest New Yorkers would "ruin all ourselves & Continent by our divisions" (Livingston to James Duane, 8 March, James Duane Papers).

322 **declined to name delegates:** Quotations: Americanus, *To the Freeholders and Freemen of the City of NEW-YORK,* 4 March 1775, broadside (*EAI,* no. 13809); A Citizen of New-York, "To the Respectable Inhabitants of the City of New-York," 6 March, in *AA* 4, 2:45–46. For Thurman's group, see untitled account by "Impartial," 8 March, in *AA* 4, 2:49; for the charge that he was being deceptive, *To the FRIENDS of AMERICAN LIBERTY,* 4 March (*EAI,* no. 14502). See also broadside *EAI,* no. 14518 (signed "A Tory"), and statements dated 6 and 7 March, reprinted in *AA* 4, 2:44, 46–47.

323 **meeting on March 6 proceeded:** Quotations: untitled account, *NYJ,* 9 March 1775 (reprinted in *AA* 4, 2:48, with slightly different punctuation and capitalization); Thomas Jones, *History of New York During the Revolutionary War . . . ,* ed. Edward Floyd de Lancey (1879; New York: Arno Press, 1968), 1:38. For a contemporary reprint, see *MG&BPB,* 13 March.

323 **committee of sixty scheduled:** Quotation: Thomas Ellison Jr. to Thomas Ellison Sr., 14 March 1775, Ellison Papers. See committee of sixty, minutes, 15 March, and related documents, 16 March, in *AA* 4, 2:137–39, on

the vote and its immediate aftermath, including the circular letter. An untitled, undated broadside (*EAI*, no. 42902) listed the eleven nominees; another read in its entirety, "No Provincial Convention. Let us choose for ourselves The old Five Delegates. No Deputies" (*EAI*, no. 14350). Other broadsides produced in this period are *EAI*, nos. 14167, 14319, 14399, 14491, 14494, 14511, and 42945. Ezra Stiles recorded the vote tally, 18 March: *Stiles Diary*, 1:527.

323 **stimulated debates elsewhere:** Quotations: *To the Free-Holders of New-Town*, 3 April 1775, broadside (*EAI*, no. 14498); Resolutions, Hempstead, 4 April, followed by "To the Publick" from the Hempstead freeholder, in *AA* 4, 2:273–74. See also *To the Freeholders of the Town of Jamaica*, 28 March, broadside (*EAI*, no. 14499); accounts from Westchester County, in *AA* 4, 2:314, 321–24; and untitled report from Staten Island, 14 April, in ibid., 313.

324 **Colden watched from the sidelines:** Colden to Dartmouth, 5 April 1775, in *DAR*, 9:91; Carroll to William Graves, 10 Feb., in Hoffman, *Dear Papa*, 2:788.

324 **"a dangerous insurrection":** Colden to Dartmouth, 5 April 1775, in *DAR*, 9:91. For more information, see Reuben Jones, "A Relation of the Proceedings of the People of the County of Cumberland, and Province of New-York," 23 March, in *AA* 4, 2:218–21; and Miller and Riggs, *Romance, Remedies, and Revolution*, 184, 187, 192 (entries of 21, 25 March, 6 April). What happened to the officials or the rioters is unclear.

324 **another potentially dangerous plan:** *NYG*, 6 March 1775 (quotations); *NYJ*, 2 March. *RNYG*, 2 March, had just one sentence about the story. See Michael E. Groth, "Black Loyalists and African American Allegiance in the Mid–Hudson Valley," in *The Other Loyalists*, ed. Tiedemann et al., 85–86.

325 **enslaved people were plotting:** Abigail to John Adams, 22 Sept. 1774, in *AFC*, 1:162; Madison to William Bradford, 26 Nov., in *JM Papers*, 1:130 (and Bradford's reply, 132). After the war, a South Carolina Loyalist asserted that revolutionaries had used rumors of the need to combat a slave rebellion to enlist men in their ranks (Thomas Knox Gordon, claims memorial, n.d., AO 12/51, fols. 289–91). See Peter H. Wood, " 'Liberty Is Sweet': African-American Freedom Struggles in the Years Before White Independence," in *Beyond the American Revolution*, ed. Young, 149–84; and Frey, *Water from the Rock*, 49–55. After fighting began, the feared alliance did take shape when Lord Dunmore offered freedom to revolutionaries' slaves. See, among other works, Alan Gilbert, *Black Patriots and Loyalists: Fighting for Emancipation in the War for Independence* (Chicago: University of Chicago Press, 2012).

325 **"We now seem very near":** Yates to John Lewthwait, 29 March 1775, Charles Yates Letterbook.

325 **second Virginia Provincial Convention:** Lee to Adams, 4 Feb. 1775, in Ballagh, *Letters of Richard Henry Lee,* 1:127–28. For a more moderate position that might or might not have been presented at the convention, see "Instructions Drawn Up for the Delegates to the Convention at Richmond, the 20th of March, from a[n Alleged] Certain County in Virginia," in *RevVa,* 2:349–50. A response from "Americanus," 8 April, appeared in *VG* (Purdie), 21 April, and is reprinted in *AA* 4, 2:300–301, indicating that the "instructions" appeared in print only after the convention ended.

326 **Dunmore predicted:** Dunmore to Dartmouth, 14 March 1775, in *DAR,* 9:78–79, 82.

326 **as unified as Lee hoped:** Quotations: *By His Excellency the Right Honourable John Earl of Dunmore . . . a Proclamation,* 28 March 1775, broadside (*EAI,* no. 42975); Parker to Charles Steuart, 6 April, reel 3, fol. 39, Steuart Papers. The records of the Provincial Convention are printed in *RevVa,* 2:361–86. Jefferson prepared the plan for the militia, 24 March (*TJ Papers,* 1:160–61). He also drafted a resolution to investigate whether New Yorkers had "deserted the Union" by failing to endorse the First Congress's actions (ibid., 159–60).

327 **Josiah Martin chose:** Minutes, Council, New Bern, N.C., 1 March 1775, in *AA* 4, 2:7–8, including the text of the proclamation. Martin learned about the plans for the convention when he saw broadsides announcing elections for it; see, for example, *Advertisement, Perquimans County, Feb. 11, 1775,* broadside (*EAI,* no. 42761). Ekirch, *Poor Carolina,* 203–11, treats Martin sympathetically.

327 **The day before the two bodies:** Martin's proclamations, CO 5/318, fols. 89, 91 (see also *AA* 4, 2:253).

327 **Succeeding events can only be deemed:** North Carolina Provincial Convention, minutes, 3–7 April 1775, in *AA* 4, 2:266–67 (see 265–66 for assembly votes). The council removed Harvey from his post as a justice of the peace in Perquimans County because of his role in the convention (ibid., 273). For details about Thomas Macknight, the man who did not sign the Association (and a later Loyalist exile in England), see *At a Convention of the Delegates . . . Held at Newbern the 6th Day of April, 1775,* broadside (*EAI,* no. 42912).

328 **Martin's speech:** Assembly record, North Carolina, 4 April 1775, in *AA* 4, 2:258–59.

328 **Martin dispatched a copy:** Quotations: Martin to Dartmouth, 7 April 1775, CO 5/318, fols. 85–86. The assembly actions on 6–7 April are in their records, in *AA* 4, 2:265–66. Martin sent his letter to Dartmouth before

he saw the full minutes from 6–7 April; he reported his reaction and his subsequent dissolution of the assembly to Dartmouth, 20 April, reel 12, no. 1227, Dartmouth Papers.

329 **frustrating experiences:** Martin to Dartmouth, 7 April 1775, CO 5/318, fol. 89. On New England, see Martin to Dartmouth, 23 March, CO 5/318, fol. 70.

329 **"How much Longer sir":** Warren to Adams, 30 Jan. 1775, in *JA Papers,* 2:390.

330 **"social enjoyments":** Henry Hulton to ——, Feb. 1775, in York, *Henry Hulton,* 311; Pitcairn to Lord Sandwich, in Clark et al., *Naval Documents,* 1:89; Gage to Lord Barrington, 10 Feb., in Carter, *Correspondence of Gage,* 2:669. For a description of the socializing, see [James Murray] to Charles Steuart, 16 Feb., reel 3, fol. 23, Steuart Papers.

330 **Gage accordingly did not hesitate:** Gage to Dartmouth, 4 March 1775, reel 12, no. 1179, Dartmouth Papers. For a succinct assessment of Church as a spy, see John Kenneth Rowland, "General Thomas Gage, the Eighteenth-Century Literature of Military Intelligence, and the Transition from Peace to Revolutionary War, 1774 to 1775," *Historical Reflections/ Reflexions Historiques* 32 (2006): 503–21, esp. 506–7.

330 **more to the story:** Gage to Dartmouth, 4 March 1775, reel 12, no. 1179, Dartmouth Papers; *Stiles Diary,* 1:522–24 (entry of 7 March). See also Octavius Pickering, *The Life of Timothy Pickering* (Boston: Little, Brown, 1867), 1:60–63; and Samuel Adams to Arthur Lee, 4 March, in *SA Writings,* 3:194. The only detailed study of the incident is Hoffer, *Salem Gunpowder Raid.*

331 **context had changed dramatically:** Quotations: Eliot to Jeremy Belknap, 28 Feb. 1775, in *Belknap Papers,* 84; Warren to Lee, 20 Feb., in Frothingham, *Life of Joseph Warren,* 418 (also in *AA* 4, 1:1252). For the approach to Quebec, see John Brown to Samuel Adams, 15 Feb., SA Papers; and Boston committee of correspondence to the inhabitants of Quebec, 21 Feb., in *SA Writings,* 3:182–88. "Address of Massachusetts to Mohawk Indians," [March 1775], is in ibid., 211–13.

331 **Warren had the opportunity:** Joseph Warren, *An Oration, Delivered March Sixth, 1775, at the Request of the Inhabitants of the Town of Boston . . .* (Boston: Edes & Gill, 1775), quotations: 6, 11, 17, 20, 22. For "prodigious concourse": "Extract of a Letter from Boston to a Gentleman in New-York," 12 March, in *AA* 4, 2:120. For a satirical response: Dr. Thomas Bolton, *An Oration Delivered March Fifteenth 1775 at the Request of a Number of the Inhabitants of the Town of Boston* ([Boston], 1775) (*EAI,* no. 13840).

332 **army and naval officers attended:** Quotations: Warren, *Oration,* 22;

Adams to Richard Henry Lee, [21] March 1775, in *SA Writings*, 3:206 (see also ibid., 195, 199–200, for more comments on Warren's speech); "Extract of a Letter to Mr. Rivington, in New-York," 9 March, in *AA* 4, 2:106 (also ibid., 120).

332 **Two days later:** Oliver Noble, *Some Strictures upon the Sacred Story Recorded in the Book of Esther . . . in a Discourse in Commemoration of the Massacre at Boston . . . March 8th, 1775* (Newburyport: E. Lunt & H. W. Tinges, 1775), quotations: 28, 30.

333 **The rising tensions evident:** For the experience of the Billerica man, Thomas Ditson, see *PIR*, 1964–65, 1975, 2013–15, 2139–40; *AA* 4, 2:93–94, 120–21, 153; and Samuel Adams to Richard Henry Lee, [21] March 1775, in *SA Writings*, 3:207 ("countryman"), 200. On carters' problems: "Letter from Boston to Newport, Rhode-Island," 20 March, in *AA* 4, 2:173 (quotations); ibid., 211; and John Andrews to William Barrell, 18 March, in "Andrews Letters," 401; Robert Pierpoint, statement, 20 March, SA Papers. Final quotation: "The following letters were received by a very respectable gentleman here, from his friend at Boston," in Willard, *Letters on the American Revolution*, 79.

333 **To whom could Bostonians turn:** Boston committee and other towns to Provincial Congress, 31 March 1775, in *PIR*, 2130–31. Gage told Dartmouth that he had tried to prevent "any thing of Consequence" from being instigated by "Trifles and idle Quarrells"; see his letter, 28 March, CO 5/92, fol. 123. According to Samuel Adams, the case of Ditson left people "universally enragd," in part because of Gage's inaction. See Adams to Richard Henry Lee, [21] March 1775, in *SA Writings*, 3:208.

334 **more than enough to handle:** Second Provincial Congress, minutes, 4 Feb. to 15 April 1775 (with a hiatus from 16 Feb. to 22 March), are available in *PIR*, 1459–542, along with committee of safety records from 3 Feb. to 18 April, 1830–43. See the untitled broadsides requesting information on militiamen and supplies, 16 Feb. (*EAI*, no. 14216), and proclaiming the fast day (quotations), 16 Feb. (*EAI*, no. 14217). On 7 February, the congress issued the order not to cooperate with the army, *PIR*, 1461, followed up by the Boston committee, 25 Feb., in a broadside (*EAI*, no. 14193); and on 31 March they directed towns yet again to pay taxes to Gardner, *PIR*, 1496. (For a few records of towns' varied responses: ibid., 2153–54, 2167, 2174, 2180.) Hulton heard that the congress discussed paying for the tea, but that story could well have been false, because it referred to a name not listed as a member; York, *Henry Hulton*, 184. The congress does not seem to have considered a 23 February petition on behalf of the many victims of crowd action who had taken refuge in Boston (*AA* 4, 1:1260–63).

334 **deputies issued a formal address:** Provincial Congress, minutes, 9 Feb.

1775, in *PIR*, 1467–69 (address printed in a pamphlet also containing resolutions from the First Provincial Congress, *EAI*, no. 14215), including the brief quotations in the next paragraph as well.

335 **Thomas Gage's spy at the congress:** "Intelligence Reports of Military Preparations in Massachusetts," enclosed in Gage to Dartmouth, 4 March 1775, in *DAR*, 9:63–65 ("first opposition," 65); also in *PIR*, 1970–73, 3 March, in slightly different form ("executive power," "inadequate," "sum," 1971–72). Gage first revealed information obtained from the spy to Dartmouth, 20 Feb., in *DAR*, 9:52. Church's reports continued until 24 May; see *PIR*, 1967–93. Only the final report can be definitively identified as by him because of an internal reference. Church's reports led Gage to conclude, perhaps correctly, that the congressmen were "much puzzled how to act" (Gage to Josiah Martin, 12 April, in Clark et al., *Naval Documents*, 1:180).

335 **set of observers:** "Intelligence of Provincial Congress of Massachusetts," 8, 21, 26 March 1775, enclosed in Gage to Dartmouth, 28 March, in *DAR*, 9:68–70 (quotation, 69); also in *PIR*, 1974–76. The report on the army in Boston is in the papers of William Heath, *Procs MHS* 4 (1860): 292–94.

336 **Loyalists resident in Boston:** Caner to the bishop of London, 27 March 1775, in *Letterbook of Caner;* James Parker to Charles Steuart, 11 April, quoting letter from Coffin to Parker, 20 March, reel 3, fol. 45, Steuart Papers; Warren to Arthur Lee, 3 April, in Hoffman, *Lee Family Papers*, reel 2, frames 1360–61; Adams to R. H. Lee, [21] March, in *SA Writings*, 3:209. When Warren's letter was published in *AA* 4, 2:255, and in Frothingham, *Life of Joseph Warren*, 447, it included two sentences preceding the sentence quoted above and absent from the original, which I suspect were added later: "America must and will be free. The contest may be severe—the end will be glorious."

336 **Early April then brought sensational news:** Quotation: William Tudor to John Adams, 4 April 1775, in *JA Papers*, 2:42. Cf., for example, the optimism expressed by Ezra Stiles on 15 March with his comments on 4 April (*Stiles Diary*, 1:525, 530). Or see Elihu Ashley's remarks on 5 April (Miller and Riggs, *Romance, Remedies, Revolution*, 191) or James Warren to Mercy Warren, 6 April (*Warren-Adams Letters*, 44). Both commented that what were thought to be recent positive developments had changed dramatically for the worse because of the news that arrived on 2 April.

337 **colonial consensus quickly emerged:** James Warren to Mercy Warren, 6 April 1775, in *Warren-Adams Letters*, 45; Eliot to Jeremy Belknap, 11 April, in *Belknap Papers*, 86; *Stiles Diary*, 1:530 (entry of 4 April); Laurens to George Appleby, 10 April, in *HL Papers*, 10:98. See also Joseph Greenleaf to Robert Treat Paine, 16 April, in *RTP Papers*, 3:42. Thomas

Ellison Jr. sent his father "hand Bills" printed in New York with the news; see his letter to Thomas senior, 12 April, Ellison Papers. The broadsides included one printed in Newport, 5 April, by Solomon Southwick (*EAI,* no. 42854), and one in Philadelphia, undated, by John Dunlap (*EAI,* no. 14075). In mid-April, ships arrived with more positive news dispatched in late February: that North had proposed to suspend the operation of parliamentary tax laws in those colonies willing to voluntarily contribute adequate amounts for imperial defense, but that information was quickly overtaken by the news from Lexington and Concord. Thomas and John Fleet, in Boston (*EAI,* no. 42856), and John Carter, in Providence (*EAI,* no. 42855), issued undated broadsides with the February "advices."

337 **Reverend John Winthrop:** This and the next paragraph are based on Winthrop to Price, 10 April 1775, in "Price Letters," 285–86.

338 **January 27, 1775:** This paragraph and the next two are based on Dartmouth to Gage, 27 Jan. 1775, in *DAR,* 9:37–39.

339 **Gage issued orders:** Transcript of Gage to Smith, 18 April 1775, in *PIR,* 2054–56.

AFTERWORD

341 **Smith began moving:** Many published accounts describe the events of 19 April. See, for example, Gross, *Minutemen and Their World;* Fischer, *Paul Revere's Ride;* Nathaniel Philbrick, *Bunker Hill: A City, a Siege, a Revolution* (New York: Viking Press, 2013); and Walter R. Borneman, *American Spring: Lexington, Concord, and the Road to Revolution* (Boston: Little, Brown, and Co., 2014).

342 **The news of the battles:** Fischer, *Paul Revere's Ride,* 272, has a map showing the progress of the news, with dates, which I largely follow in this paragraph and the next, although at least one is incorrect (Dumfries, Virginia; the date on the map is 30 April; for the accurate date, see below).

342 **Initial accounts were often garbled:** Quotation: Parker to Charles Steuart, 6 May 1775, reel 3, fol. 49, Steuart Papers. For the other points: Percy and Haldimand deaths: Eliza Farmar to Jack, 28 April, in "Letters of Farmar," 203, and William Carr to James Russell, 16 April–1 May, bundle 2, Russell Papers. The skeptical merchant: William Fitzhugh to same, 6 May, bundle 6, Russell Papers.

342 **news reached Manhattan:** Quotations: Richard Yates to Lord Dartmouth, 1 May 1775, reel 12, no. 1240, Dartmouth Papers; Padelford, *Colonial Panorama,* 77 (entry of 27 April). See Henry to John Laurens, 9 May, in *HL Papers,* 10:115–16.

342 **their world had changed:** *Rowe Diary,* 292 (entry of 19 April); Lacey, *World of Hannah Heaton,* 159 (entry of 22 April).

342 **Mather completed a pamphlet:** Quotations in this paragraph and the next from Mather, *America's Appeal to the Impartial World,* 68–69, 47. Precisely dating the composition of this pamphlet is difficult, but most of the contents seem to precede the beginning of armed conflict, whereas the last few pages of the main text (for example, 61) and the appendix refer to warfare. Mather explained at the beginning of the appendix that the pamphlet was written "some time past," but with publication delayed "for want of paper" (65). Despite the 1775 date on the title page, it was possibly not printed until 1776, but it does not mention the Declaration of Independence.

343 **The Glorious Seventy Four:** *NYJ,* 18 Aug. 1774; reprinted in *MSpy,* 1 Sept.

BIBLIOGRAPHY

(For newspapers, see list of abbreviations)

FREQUENTLY CITED PRIMARY SOURCES

Unpublished Manuscript Collections National Archives, Kew, U.K.

Audit Office files
Colonial Office files
State Papers files
Treasury Letters Received

Other U.K. Repositories

American Papers of the Second Earl of Dartmouth, Staffordshire Record Office
    (microfilm)
Egerton Manuscripts 2661, British Library
India Office Records, British Library
Charles Steuart Papers, MSS 5028, National Library of Scotland, Edinburgh
    (microfilm)

Massachusetts Historical Society, Boston

Boylston Family Papers
Cushing Family II Papers
Elbridge Gerry Papers (Billias Collection)
John Greenough Papers
Henry Knox Papers II (Bookseller Letterbook)
Miscellaneous Manuscripts Bound
Sedgwick Papers, including John Tabor Kempe Papers

Israel Williams Papers
Winthrop-Warren Correspondence

Other Boston-Area Repositories

Bromfield Letterbooks, New England Historic Genealogical Society
Cranch Papers, New England Historic Genealogical Society
William Palfrey Papers, Houghton Library, Harvard University
Ezekiel Price Notarial Records, Boston Athenaeum

Hartford, Connecticut, Repositories

William Samuel Johnson Papers, Connecticut Historical Society
Jonathan Trumbull Papers, Connecticut State Library

Columbia University Library

Charity Clarke Moore and Clement Clarke Moore Papers
Van Schaack Family Papers

New-York Historical Society

James Duane Papers
Ellison Family Papers
John Lamb Papers
Livingston-Redmond Papers
Alexander McDougall Papers
Joseph Reed Papers

New York Public Library; Astor, Lenox, and Tilden Foundations

Samuel Adams Papers
Bancroft Collection
Boston Committee of Correspondence, Minute Books
Connecticut Papers
Holland Transcripts

Historical Society of Pennsylvania, Philadelphia

Rhoda Barber, Journal-Memoir
Cox-Parrish-Wharton Papers
Fisher Family Collection
R. R. Logan Collection

South Carolina Historical Society, Charleston

Charles Garth (Committee of Correspondence) Papers, Collection 11/150
Pinckney Family Papers, Collection 38/23

Records of St. Michael's Church
William and Samuel Vernon Letter, Collection 43/718

University of North Carolina-Chapel Hill
Preston Davie Papers, no. 3406

Maryland Historical Society, Baltimore
Samuel Purviance Papers, MSS 1394

Colonial Williamsburg
James Russell Papers, Coutts & Company (microfilm)

Earl Gregg Swem Library, College of William & Mary, Williamsburg
Robert Pleasants Letterbook
William Reynolds Letterbook
Tucker-Coleman Papers
William Wiatt Papers

Alderman Library, University of Virginia
Thomas and William Nelson Letterbook, film 1204
Harry Piper Letterbook, Alexandria Papers, acc. 2981
Charles Yates Letterbook, acc. 3807

Richmond, Virginia, Repositories
William Allason Letterbook, film 389, Library of Virginia
Robert Beverley Letters (MSS 1 C2462), Virginia Historical Society
Charles Steuart Papers, film 3703, Library of Virginia

Library of Congress Manuscript Division
Robert Beverley Letterbook
John Singleton Copley Papers
Galloway Maxcy Markoe Papers

Huntington Library, San Marino, California
Brock Collection, including Lee Family Papers; Pleasants Family Papers
Emmet Collection
Greenough Family Papers
Individual documents not in specific collections

PUBLISHED LETTERS AND DOCUMENTS

Abbot, W. W., et al., eds. *The Papers of George Washington: Colonial Series.* 10 vols. Charlottesville: University Press of Virginia, 1983–1995.

Adair, Douglass, and John A. Schutz, eds. *Peter Oliver's Origin & Progress of the American Rebellion: A Tory View.* Stanford, Calif.: Stanford University Press, 1961.

Andrews, Evangeline Walker, ed. *Journal of a Lady of Quality . . . in the Years 1774 to 1776.* New Haven, Conn.: Yale University Press, 1921.

Ballagh, James C., ed. *The Letters of Richard Henry Lee.* 2 vols. New York: Macmillan, 1911, 1914.

Bartlett, John Russell, ed. *Records of the Colony of Rhode Island and Providence Plantation in New England.* 10 vols. Providence: A. Crawford Greene, 1856–1865.

Belknap Papers. Colls MHS 54 (1891).

Bouton, Nathaniel, ed. *Documents and Records Relating to the Province of New-Hampshire. . . .* 7 vols. Nashua, N.H.: Orren C. Moore, 1873.

Bowdoin and Temple Papers. Colls MHS 59 (1897).

Boyd, Julian P., et al., eds. *The Papers of Thomas Jefferson.* 42 vols. Princeton, N.J.: Princeton University Press, 1950–.

Bruns, Roger, ed. *Am I Not a Man and a Brother: The Antislavery Crusade of Revolutionary America, 1688–1788.* New York: Chelsea House, 1977.

Butterfield, L. H., ed. *Letters of Benjamin Rush.* Princeton, N.J.: Princeton University Press, 1951.

Butterfield, L. H., et al., eds. *Adams Family Correspondence.* 13 vols. Cambridge, Mass.: Harvard University Press, 1963–.

Butterfield, L. H., et al., eds. *Diary and Autobiography of John Adams.* 4 vols. Cambridge, Mass.: Harvard University Press, 1961.

Calhoon, Robert M., ed. " 'A Sorrowful Spectator of These Tumultuous Times': Robert Beverley Describes the Coming of the Revolution." *VMHB* 73 (1965): 41–55.

Carter, Clarence C., ed. *The Correspondence of General Thomas Gage . . . 1763–1775.* 2 vols. New Haven, Conn.: Yale University Press, 1931.

"The [Charles] Thomson Papers." *Colls NYHS* 11 (1878).

Clark, William Bell, et al., eds. *Naval Documents of the American Revolution.* 12 vols. Washington, D.C.: Government Printing Office, 1964–2013.

Commerce of Rhode Island, 1726–1800. Colls MHS 69, 70 (1914, 1915).

Coquillette, Daniel R., and Neil L. York, eds. *Portrait of a Patriot: The Major Political and Legal Papers of Josiah Quincy, Junior.* 6 vols. Boston: Colonial Society of Massachusetts, 2006–2014.

"Correspondence of Silas Deane, . . . 1774–1776." *Colls CHS* 2 (1870): 127–368.

Crary, Catherine S., ed. *The Price of Loyalty: Tory Writings from the Revolutionary Era*. New York: McGraw-Hill, 1973.

Cunningham, Anne Rowe, ed. *Letters and Diary of John Rowe, Boston Merchant*. Boston: W. B. Clarke, 1903.

Cushing, Harry Alonzo, ed. *The Writings of Samuel Adams*. 4 vols. New York: G. P. Putnam's Sons, 1904–1908.

Davies, K. G., ed. *Documents of the American Revolution, 1770–1783*. 21 vols. Shannon: Irish Universities Press, 1972–1981.

The Deane Papers. Vol. 1. *Colls NYHS* 19 (1886).

Deas, Anne Izard, ed. *Correspondence of Mr. Ralph Izard, of South Carolina*. . . . 2 vols. New York: Charles S. Francis, 1844.

Devine, T. M., ed. *A Scottish Firm in Virginia, 1767–1777*. Edinburgh: Clark Constable, 1984.

Dexter, Franklin B., ed. *The Literary Diary of Ezra Stiles, D.D., LL.D.* 3 vols. New York: Charles Scribner's Sons, 1901.

———. *A Selection from the Correspondence . . . of Jared Ingersoll*. Papers of the *New Haven Colony Historical Society* 9 (1918): 201–472.

"Diary for 1773 to the End of 1774 of Mr. Thomas Newell, of Boston." *Procs MHS* 15 (1876–1877): 335–63.

Drake, Francis S., ed. *Tea Leaves*. . . . Boston: A. O. Crane, 1884.

Drayton, John. *Memoirs of the American Revolution*. 2 vols. Charleston, S.C.: A. E. Miller, 1821.

Duane, William, ed. *Extracts from the Diary of Christopher Marshall*. Albany, N.Y.: Joel Munsell, 1877.

Early American Imprints. [New Canaan, Conn.: Readex, 2002–]. Broadsides and pamphlets.

Eddis, William. *Letters from America*. Edited by Aubrey C. Land. Cambridge, Mass.: Harvard University Press, 1969.

Farish, Hunter Dickinson, ed. *Journal & Letters of Philip Vickers Fithian, 1773–1774: A Plantation Tutor of the Old Dominion*. Williamsburg, Va.: Colonial Williamsburg, 1957.

Fisher, Richard D., ed. "The Burning of the 'Peggy Stewart.' " *MdHM* 5 (1910): 235–45.

Force, Peter, ed. *American Archives*. 4th ser. Vols. 1–2. Washington, D.C.: Peter Force and M. St. Clair Clarke, 1839.

Ford, Worthington Chauncey, ed. *Correspondence and Journals of Samuel Blachley Webb*. 3 vols. Lancaster, Pa.: Wickersham Press, 1893.

———. *Letters of William Lee, 1766–1783*. 3 vols. 1891. New York: Burt Franklin, 1968.

Ford, Worthington Chauncey, et al., eds. *Journals of the Continental Con-*

gress, 1774–1789. 34 vols. Washington, D.C.: Government Printing Office, 1904–1937.

Franklin, Benjamin, V, comp. *The Plays and Poems of Mercy Otis Warren*. Delmar, N.Y.: Scholars' Facsimiles and Reprints, 1980.

Frothingham, Richard. *Life and Times of Joseph Warren*. Boston: Little, Brown, 1865.

Gerlach, Larry, ed. *New Jersey in the American Revolution, 1763–1783: A Documentary History*. Trenton: New Jersey Historical Commission, 1975.

Gill, Harold B., and George M. Curtis III, eds. *A Man Apart: The Journal of Nicholas Cresswell, 1774–1781*. Lanham, Md.: Rowman & Littlefield, 2009.

Greene, Jack P., ed. *The Diary of Colonel Landon Carter of Sabine Hall, 1752–1778*. 2 vols. Charlottesville: University Press of Virginia, 1965.

"Henry Knox and the London Book-Store at Boston, 1771–1774." *Procs MHS* 61 (1928): 226–303.

Higginbotham, Don, ed. *The Papers of James Iredell*. 3 vols. Raleigh, N.C.: Division of Archives and History, 1976–2003.

Hoffman, Paul P., ed. *Lee Family Papers*. Charlottesville: University of Virginia Library, 1966 (microfilm).

Hoffman, Paul P., et al., eds. *The Carter Family Papers, 1659–1797, in the Sabine Hall Collection*. Charlottesville: University of Virginia Library, 1967 (microfilm).

Hoffman, Ronald, et al., eds. *Dear Papa, Dear Charley*. 3 vols. Chapel Hill: University of North Carolina Press, 2001.

Howe, Mark DeWolfe, ed. "Letters to Josiah Quincy, Jr." *Procs MHS* 50 (1916–1917): 471–96.

Hutchinson, William T., and William M. E. Rachal, eds. *The Papers of James Madison*. 17 vols. Chicago: University of Chicago Press, 1962–1991.

Jackson, Donald, and Dorothy Twohig, eds. *The Diaries of George Washington*. 6 vols. Charlottesville: University Press of Virginia, 1976.

Kelly, J. Reaney, ed. "'Tulip Hill': Its History and Its People." *MdHM* 60 (1965): 349–403.

Lacey, Barbara E., ed. *The World of Hannah Heaton: The Diary of an Eighteenth-Century New England Farm Woman*. DeKalb: Northern Illinois University Press, 2003.

Letterbook of the Rev. Henry Caner, 1728–1778. East Ardsley, U.K.: Microform Academic Publishers, 2000 (microfilm).

Letters and Papers of Cadwallader Colden. Colls NYHS 56 (1923).

Letters and Papers of John Singleton Copley and Henry Pelham, 1739–1776. Colls MHS 71 (1914).

"Letters of Eliza Farmar to Her Nephew." *PMHB* 40 (1916): 199–207.

"Letters of Governor John Penn to Lady Juliana Penn, 1774." *PMHB* 31 (1907): 232–38.

"Letters to and from Dr. Richard Price." *Procs MHS* 37 (1903): 262–382.

Mason, Frances Norton, ed. *John Norton & Sons: Merchants of London and Virginia*. Newton Abbot: David & Charles, 1968.

McMaster, Richard K., and David C. Skaggs, eds. "The Letterbooks of Alexander Hamilton, Piscataway Factor, Part 1, 1774; Part 2, 1774–1775." *MdHM* 61 (1966): 146–66, 305–28.

Miller, Amelia F., and A. R. Riggs, eds. *Romance, Remedies, and Revolution: The Journal of Dr. Elihu Ashley of Deerfield, Massachusetts, 1773–1775*. Amherst: University of Massachusetts Press, 2007.

Mulford, Carla, ed. *John Leacock's "The First Book of the American Chronicles of the Times," 1774–1775*. Newark: University of Delaware Press, 1987.

Padelford, Philip, ed. *Colonial Panorama, 1775: Dr. Robert Honyman's Journal for March and April*. San Marino, Calif.: Huntington Library, 1939.

Reed, William B. *Life and Correspondence of Joseph Reed*. 2 vols. Philadelphia: Lindsay and Blakiston, 1847.

———. *The Life of Esther De Berdt, Afterwards Esther Reed*. Philadelphia: C. Sherman, 1853.

Richards, Jeffrey H., and Sharon M. Harris, eds. *Mercy Otis Warren: Selected Letters*. Athens: University of Georgia Press, 2009.

Ricord, Frederick, and William Nelson, eds. *Documents Relating to the Colonial History of the State of New Jersey*. Vols. 9–10. Newark, N.J.: Daily Journal, 1880.

Riley, Edward M., ed. *The Journal of John Harrower*. New York: Holt, Rinehart and Winston, 1953.

Riley, Stephen T., and Edward W. Hanson, eds. *The Papers of Robert Treat Paine*. 3 vols. Boston: Massachusetts Historical Society, 1992–2005 (*Colls MHS* 87–89).

Rogers, George C., et al., eds. *The Papers of Henry Laurens*. 16 vols. Columbia: University of South Carolina Press, 1968–2003.

Rutland, Robert A., ed. *The Papers of George Mason, 1725–1792*. 3 vols. Chapel Hill: University of North Carolina Press, 1970.

Sabine, William H. W., ed. *Historical Memoirs of William Smith. . . .* 3 vols. New York: Colburn & Tegg, 1956.

Sargent, Winthrop, ed. "Letters of John Andrews, Esq., of Boston." *Procs MHS* 8 (1864–1865): 316–412.

Saunders, William S., ed. *The Colonial Records of North Carolina*. 10 vols. Raleigh, N.C.: Josephus Daniels, 1886–1890.

"Selections from the Letter-Books of Thomas Wharton, of Philadelphia, 1773–1783." *PMHB* 33 (1909): 319–39, 432–53; 34 (1910): 41–61.

Simmons, R. C., and P. D. G. Thomas, eds. *Proceedings and Debates of the British Parliament Respecting North America, 1754–1783*. 6 vols. White Plains, N.Y.: Kraus International Publications, 1982–1987.

Smith, Paul H., et al., eds. *Letters of Delegates to Congress, 1774–1789*. 26 vols. Washington, D.C.: Library of Congress, 1976–2000.

"Some Letters of Joseph Galloway, 1774–1775." *PMHB* 21 (1897): 477–84.

Stillé, Charles J. *The Life and Times of John Dickinson, 1732–1808*. Philadelphia: Historical Society of Pennsylvania, 1891.

Taylor, Robert J., et al., eds. *Papers of John Adams*. 18 vols. Cambridge, Mass.: Harvard University Press, 1977–.

Upton, L. F. S., ed. "Proceedings of Ye Body Respecting the Tea." *WMQ*, 3rd ser., 22 (1965): 289–96.

Van Schaack, Henry C. *The Life of Peter Van Schaack, LL.D.* New York: D. Appleton, 1842.

———. *Memoirs of the Life of Henry Van Schaack*. Chicago: A. C. McClurg, 1892.

Van Schreeven, William J., and Robert L. Scribner, eds. *Revolutionary Virginia: The Road to Independence*. 7 vols. Charlottesville: University Press of Virginia, 1973–1983.

Walsh, Richard, ed. *The Writings of Christopher Gadsden*. Columbia: University of South Carolina Press, 1966.

Warren-Adams Letters. Colls MHS 72 (1917).

Wellenreuther, Hermann, ed. *The Revolution of the People: Thoughts and Documents on the Revolutionary Process in North America, 1774–1776*. Göttingen: Universitätsverlag Göttingen, 2006.

Willard, Margaret Wheeler, ed. *Letters on the American Revolution, 1774–1776*. Boston: Houghton Mifflin, 1925.

Willcox, William B., et al., eds. *The Papers of Benjamin Franklin*. 41 vols. New Haven, Conn.: Yale University Press, 1959–.

Winthrop, Robert C., et al., eds. "Tea-Party Anniversary." *Procs MHS* 13 (1873–1875): 151–216.

Wroth, L. Kinvin, et al., eds. *Province in Rebellion: A Documentary History of the Founding of the Commonwealth of Massachusetts, 1774–1775*. Cambridge, Mass.: Harvard University Press, 1975 (microfiche).

York, Neil Longley, ed. *Henry Hulton and the American Revolution: An Outsider's Inside View*. Boston: Colonial Society of Massachusetts, 2010.

POLITICAL PAMPHLETS
(EXCLUDING PUBLISHED SERMONS AND ORATIONS)

Adams, John. *Novanglus*. Reprinted in *JA Papers*, 2:216–385.

[Boucher, Jonathan]. *A Letter from a Virginian, to the Members of the Congress to Be Held at Philadelphia, on the First of September, 1774*. [New York: Hugh Gaine], 1774.

Chandler, Thomas Bradbury. *The American Querist; or, Some Questions Proposed Relative to the Present Disputes Between Great Britain, and Her American Colonies*. New York: James Rivington, 1774.

————. *A Friendly Address to All Reasonable Americans*. . . . New York: [James Rivington], 1774.

————. *What Think Ye of the Congress Now?* . . . New York: James Rivington, 1775.

Dickinson, John. *An Essay on the Constitutional Power of Great Britain over the Colonies in America*. . . . Philadelphia: William and Thomas Bradford, 1774.

Drayton, William Henry. *A Letter from Freeman of South-Carolina, to the Deputies of North-America, Assembled in the High Court of Congress*. Charleston, S.C.: Peter Timothy, 1774.

Drinker, John, Jr. *Observations on the Late Popular Measures*. . . . Philadelphia: printed for A Tradesman, 1774.

Galloway, Joseph. *A Candid Examination of the Mutual Claims of Great Britain and the Colonies, with a Plan of Accommodation, on Constitutional Principles*. New York: James Rivington, 1775.

————. *A Reply to an Address to the Author of a Pamphlet, Entitled, "A Candid Examination*. . . ." New York: James Rivington, 1775.

Gray, Harrison. *A Few Remarks upon . . . the Continental Congress . . . and the Provincial Congress*. Boston, 1775 (republished in New York by James Rivington as *The Two Congresses Cut Up*).

Hamilton, Alexander. *The Farmer Refuted . . . Intended as a Further Vindication of the Congress*. . . . New York: James Rivington, 1775.

————. *A Full Vindication of the Measures of the Congress . . . in Answer to a Letter, Under the Signature of A. W. Farmer*. . . . New York: James Rivington, 1774.

Hopkinson, Francis. *A Pretty Story Written in the Year of Our Lord 2774, by Peter Grievous*. 2nd ed. Philadelphia: John Dunlap, 1774.

Hunt, Isaac. *The Political Family; or, A Discourse Pointing Out the Reciprocal Advantages, Which Flow from an Uninterrupted Union Between Great-Britain and Her American Colonies*. Philadelphia: James Humphreys, 1775.

Jefferson, Thomas. *A Summary View of the Rights of British America* (1774). Reprinted in *RevVa*, vol. 1.

Jingle, Bob. *The Association, &c. of the Delegates of the Colonies, at the Grand Congress*. . . . [New York: James Rivington], 1774.

Lee, Charles. *Strictures on a Pamphlet, Entitled, "A Friendly Address*. . . ." Philadelphia: Thomas and William Bradford, 1774.

Leonard, Daniel, and Jonathan Sewall. *Massachusettensis; or, A Series of Letters*. . . . London: J. Mathews, 1776.

Livingston, Philip. *The Other Side of the Question . . . in Answer to a Late Friendly Address*. . . . New York: James Rivington, 1774.

Mather, Moses. *America's Appeal to the Impartial World*. . . . Hartford: Ebenezer Watson, 1775.

Nicholas, Robert Carter. *Considerations on the Present State of Virginia Examined*. Reprinted in *RevVa*, vol. 1.

The Poor Man's Advice to His Poor Neighbours. . . . [New York: James Rivington], 1774.

Quincy, Josiah, Jr. *Observations on the Act of Parliament Commonly Called the Boston Port-Bill*. . . . Boston: Edes & Gill, 1774.

Randolph, John. *Considerations on the Present State of Virginia*. Reprinted in *RevVa*, vol. 1.

Seabury, Samuel. *An Alarm to the Legislature of the Province of New-York*. . . . New York: James Rivington, 1775.

Seabury, Samuel [A. W. Farmer]. *The Congress Canvassed; or, An Examination into the Conduct of the Delegates at Their Grand Convention*. New York: James Rivington, 1774.

———. *Free Thoughts, on the Proceedings of the Continental Congress*. . . . New York: James Rivington, 1774.

———. *A View of the Controversy Between Great-Britain and Her Colonies . . . in a Letter to the Author of A Full Vindication*. . . . New York: James Rivington, 1774.

Shipley, Jonathan. *A Speech Intended to Have Been Spoken on the Bill for Altering the Charters of the Colony of Massachusetts Bay*. London: Goadby and Berry, 1774 (with many American reprints, including by Edes & Gill, Boston).

V., Mary V. *A Dialogue, Between a Southern Delegate and His Spouse, on His Return from the Grand Continental Congress*. . . . [New York: James Rivington], 1774.

Wells, Richard. *A Few Political Reflections Submitted to the Consideration of the British Colonies by a Citizen of Philadelphia*. Philadelphia: John Dunlap, 1774.

———. *The Middle Line; or, An Attempt to Furnish Some Hints for Ending the Differences Subsisting Between Great-Britain and the Colonies*. Philadelphia: Joseph Crukshank, 1775.

Wilkins, Isaac. *Short Advice to the Counties of New-York, by a Country Gentleman*. New York: James Rivington, 1774.

Wilson, James. *Considerations on the Nature and Extent of the Legislative Authority of the British Parliament*. Philadelphia: Thomas and William Bradford, 1774.

SELECTED SECONDARY SOURCES

Adams, Thomas R., ed. *American Independence: The Growth of an Idea*. Providence: Brown University Press, 1965.

Adelman, Joseph A. "Trans-Atlantic Migration and the Printing Trade in Revolutionary America." *EAS* 11 (2013): 526–44.

Ammerman, David. *In the Common Cause: American Response to the Coercive Acts of 1774*. New York: W. W. Norton, 1975.

Bailyn, Bernard. *The Ideological Origins of the American Revolution*. Cambridge, Mass.: Harvard University Press, 1967.

———. *The Ordeal of Thomas Hutchinson*. Cambridge, Mass.: Harvard University Press, 1974.

Bailyn, Bernard, and John Hench, eds. *The Press & the American Revolution*. Worcester, Mass.: American Antiquarian Society, 1980.

Beeman, Richard R. *Our Lives, Our Fortunes, and Our Sacred Honor: The Forging of American Independence*. New York: Basic Books, 2013.

Berkin, Carol. *Jonathan Sewall: Odyssey of an American Loyalist*. New York: Columbia University Press, 1974.

Botein, Stephen. "'Mere Mechanics' and an Open Press: The Business and Political Strategies of Colonial American Printers." *Perspectives in American History* 9 (1975): 127–225.

Boyd, Julian. *Anglo-American Union: Joseph Galloway's Plans to Preserve the British Empire, 1774–1788*. Philadelphia: University of Pennsylvania Press, 1941.

Breen, T. H. *American Insurgents, American Patriots: The Revolution of the People*. New York: Hill and Wang, 2010.

———. *The Marketplace of Revolution: How Consumer Politics Shaped American Independence*. New York: Oxford University Press, 2004.

Brown, Richard D. *Revolutionary Politics in Massachusetts: The Boston Committee of Correspondence and the Towns, 1772–1774*. New York: W. W. Norton, 1976.

Bunker, Nick. *An Empire on the Edge: How Britain Came to Fight America*. New York: Alfred A. Knopf, 2014.

Calhoon, Robert M., et al., eds. *Tory Insurgents: The Loyalist Perception and Other Essays*. Rev. ed. Columbia: University of South Carolina Press, 2010.

Carp, Benjamin L. *Defiance of the Patriots: The Boston Tea Party & the Making of America*. New Haven, Conn.: Yale University Press, 2010.

Castronovo, Russ. *Propaganda 1776: Secrets, Leaks, and Revolutionary Communications in Early America*. New York: Oxford University Press, 2014.

David, James Corbett. *Dunmore's New World*. Charlottesville: University of Virginia Press, 2013.

Ekirch, A. Roger. *"Poor Carolina": Politics and Society in Colonial North Carolina, 1727–1776*. Chapel Hill: University of North Carolina Press, 1981.

Ferling, John F. *The Loyalist Mind: Joseph Galloway and the American Revolution.* University Park: Pennsylvania State University Press, 1977.

Fischer, David Hackett. *Paul Revere's Ride.* New York: Oxford University Press, 1994.

Freeman, Frederick. *The History of Cape Cod: Annals of the Thirteen Towns of Barnstable County.* Boston: W. H. Piper, 1869.

Frey, Sylvia. *Water from the Rock: Black Resistance in a Revolutionary Age.* Princeton, N.J.: Princeton University Press, 1991.

Gould, Philip. *Writing the Rebellion: Loyalists and the Literature of Politics in British America.* New York: Oxford University Press, 2013.

Griffin, Patrick. *America's Revolution.* New York: Oxford University Press, 2012.

Gross, Robert. *The Minutemen and Their World.* New York: Hill and Wang, 1976.

Hoerder, Dirk. *Crowd Action in Revolutionary Massachusetts, 1765–1780.* New York: Academic Press, 1977.

Hoffer, Peter Charles. *The Salem Gunpowder Raid of 1775.* Baltimore: Johns Hopkins University Press, 2013.

Hoffman, Ronald. *A Spirit of Dissension: Economics, Politics, and the Revolution in Maryland.* Baltimore: Johns Hopkins University Press, 1973.

Isaac, Rhys. "Dramatizing the Ideology of Revolution: Popular Mobilization in Virginia, 1774–1776." *WMQ,* 3rd ser., 33 (1976): 357–85.

Jensen, Merrill. *The Founding of a Nation: A History of the American Revolution, 1763–1776.* New York: Oxford University Press, 1968.

Labaree, Benjamin Woods. *The Boston Tea Party.* New York: Oxford University Press, 1964.

Maier, Pauline. *From Resistance to Revolution: Colonial Radicals and the Development of American Opposition to Great Britain, 1765–1776.* New York: Alfred A. Knopf, 1972.

———. *The Old Revolutionaries: Political Lives in the Age of Samuel Adams.* New York: Vintage Books, 1982.

Marston, Jerrilyn Greene. *King and Congress: The Transfer of Political Legitimacy, 1774–1776.* Princeton, N.J.: Princeton University Press, 1987.

Martin, Robert W. T. *The Free and Open Press: The Founding of American Democratic Press Liberty, 1640–1800.* New York: New York University Press, 2001.

Merritt, Jane T. *The Trouble with Tea: The Politics of Consumption in the Eighteenth-Century Global Economy.* Baltimore: Johns Hopkins University Press, 2017.

Nelson, Eric. *The Royalist Revolution: Monarchy and the American Founding.* Cambridge, Mass.: Harvard University Press, 2014.

Norton, Mary Beth. *Liberty's Daughters: The Revolutionary Experience of American Women, 1750–1800.* Boston: Little, Brown, 1980.

———. *Separated by Their Sex: Women in Public and Private in the Colonial Atlantic World.* Ithaca, N.Y.: Cornell University Press, 2011.

———. "The Seventh Tea Ship." *WMQ,* 3rd ser., 73 (2016): 681–710.

Osell, Tedra. "Tatling Women in the Public Sphere: Rhetorical Femininity and the English Essay Periodical." *Eighteenth-Century Studies* 38 (2005): 283–99.

Parkinson, Robert G. *The Common Cause: Creating Race and Nation in the American Revolution.* Chapel Hill: University of North Carolina Press, 2016.

Pencak, William, ed. *Pennsylvania's Revolution.* University Park: Pennsylvania State University Press, 2010.

Phillips, Kevin. *1775: A Good Year for Revolution.* New York: Viking Press, 2012.

Rakove, Jack. *The Beginnings of National Politics: An Interpretive History of the Continental Congress.* Baltimore: Johns Hopkins University Press, 1979.

Raphael, Ray. *The First American Revolution: Before Lexington and Concord.* New York: New Press, 1990.

Rhoden, Nancy L. *Revolutionary Anglicanism: The Colonial Church of England Clergy During the American Revolution.* New York: New York University Press, 1999.

Richmond, Robert P. *Powder Alarm 1774.* Princeton, N.J.: Auerbach, 1971.

Rogers, George C., Jr. "The Charleston Tea Party: The Significance of December 3, 1773." *SCHM* 75 (1974): 153–68.

Ryerson, Richard. *The Revolution Is Now Begun: The Radical Committees of Philadelphia, 1765–1776.* Philadelphia: University of Pennsylvania Press, 1978.

Schlesinger, Arthur M. *The Colonial Merchants and the American Revolution, 1763–1776.* 1918. New York: Athenaeum, 1968.

———. *Prelude to Independence: The Newspaper War on Britain, 1764–1776.* New York: Alfred A. Knopf, 1958.

Shammas, Carole. *The Pre-industrial Consumer in England and America.* Oxford: Clarendon Press, 1990.

Slaughter, Thomas P. *Independence: The Tangled Roots of the American Revolution.* New York: Hill and Wang, 2014.

Slauter, Eric. "Reading and Radicalization: Print, Politics, and the American Revolution." *EAS* 8 (2010): 5–40.

Smith, Barbara Clark. *The Freedoms We Lost: Consent and Resistance in Revolutionary America.* New York: New Press, 2010.

Thomas, Isaiah. *The History of Printing in America,* ed. Marcus McCorison. 1810. Barre, Mass.: Imprint Society, 1970.

Thomas, Peter D. G. *Tea Party to Independence: The Third Phase of the American Revolution, 1773–1776.* Oxford: Clarendon Press, 1991.

Tiedemann, Joseph S. *Reluctant Revolutionaries: New York City and the Road to Independence, 1763–1776.* Ithaca, N.Y.: Cornell University Press, 1997.

Tiedemann, Joseph S., et al., eds. *The Other Loyalists: Ordinary People, Royalism, and the Revolution in the Middle Colonies, 1763–1787*. Albany: State University of New York Press, 2009.

Tyler, John W. *Smugglers & Patriots: Boston Merchants and the Advent of the American Revolution*. Boston: Northeastern University Press, 1986.

Upton, L. F. S. "The Dilemma of the Loyalist Pamphleteers," *Studies in Burke and His Time* 18, no. 1 (winter 1977): 71–84.

Warner, William B. *Protocols of Liberty: Communication, Innovation, and the American Revolution*. Chicago: University of Chicago Press, 2013.

Withington, Ann Fairfax. *Toward a More Perfect Union: Virtue and the Formation of American Republics*. New York: Oxford University Press, 1991.

Wood, Betty. *Slavery in Colonial Georgia*. Athens: University of Georgia Press, 1984.

Young, Alfred, ed. *Beyond the American Revolution: Explorations in the History of American Radicalism*. DeKalb: Northern Illinois University Press, 1993.

INDEX

Page numbers in *italics* refer to illustrations.

ILLUSTRATION CREDITS

A NOTE ON THE TYPE

This book was set in Adobe Garamond. Designed for the Adobe Corporation by Robert Slimbach, the fonts are based on types first cut by Claude
Garamond (ca. 1480–1561). Garamond was a pupil of Geoffroy Tory and
is believed to have followed the Venetian models, although he introduced
a number of important differences, and it is to him that we owe the letter
we now know as "old style." He gave to his letters a certain elegance and
feeling of movement that won their creator an immediate reputation and
the patronage of Francis I of France.

Composed by North Market Street Graphics,
Lancaster, Pennsylvania

Printed and bound by Berryville Graphics,
Berryville, Virginia

Designed by Betty Lew

THE REAL LOLITA

ALSO BY SARAH WEINMAN

Women Crime Writers:
Eight Suspense Novels of the 1940s & 50s

Troubled Daughters, Twisted Wives:
Stories from the Trailblazers of Domestic Suspense

THE

REAL LOLITA

*The Kidnapping of Sally Horner
and the Novel That Scandalized the World*

SARAH WEINMAN

An Imprint of HarperCollins *Publishers*

Pages 291–93 constitute a continuation of this copyright page.

THE REAL LOLITA. Copyright © 2018 by Sarah Weinman. All rights reserved. Printed in the United States of America. No part of this book
may be used or reproduced in any manner whatsoever without written permission except in the case of brief quotations embodied in
critical articles and reviews. For information, address HarperCollins
Publishers, 195 Broadway, New York, NY 10007.

HarperCollins books may be purchased for educational, business,
or sales promotional use. For information, please email the Special
Markets Department at SPsales@harpercollins.com.

FIRST EDITION

Designed by Suet Yee Chong

Library of Congress Cataloging-in-Publication Data

Names: Weinman, Sarah, author.
Title: The real Lolita : the kidnapping of Sally Horner and the novel that
scandalized the world / [by Sarah Weinman].
Description: First edition. | New York, NY : HarperCollins Publishers, 2018.
| Includes bibliographical references and index.
Identifiers: LCCN 2018006366 (print) | LCCN 2018021107 (ebook) | ISBN
9780062661944 (ebook) | ISBN 9780062861184 | ISBN 9780062661951 | ISBN
9780062661920 | ISBN 9780062661937
Subjects: LCSH: Horner, Sally. | Kidnapping—United States—Case studies. |
Child abuse—United States—Case studies. | Captivity—United States—Case
studies.
Classification: LCC HV6603.H67 (ebook) | LCC HV6603.H67 W45 2018 (print) |
DDC 362.88092 [B] —dc23
LC record available at https://lccn.loc.gov/2018006366

ISBN 978-0-06-266192-0

18 19 20 21 22 LSC 10 9 8 7 6 5 4 3 2 1

For my mother

You have to be an artist and a madman, a creature of infinite melancholy, with a bubble of hot poison in your loins and a super-voluptuous flame permanently aglow in your subtle spine (oh, how you have to cringe and hide!), in order to discern at once, by ineffable signs—the slightly feline outline of a cheekbone, the slenderness of a downy limb, and other indices which despair and shame and tears of tenderness forbid me to tabulate—the little deadly demon among the wholesome children; *she* stands unrecognized by them and unconscious herself of her fantastic power.

—Vladimir Nabokov, *Lolita*

I want to go home as soon as I can.

—Sally Horner, March 21, 1950

CONTENTS

THE REAL LOLITA

"Had I Done to Her . . . ?"

"Had I done to Dolly, perhaps, what Frank Lasalle,
a fifty-year-old mechanic, had done to eleven-year-old
Sally Horner in 1948?"

—Vladimir Nabokov, *Lolita*

A couple of years before her life changed course forever, Sally Horner posed for a photograph. Nine years old at the time, she stands in front of the back fence of her house, a thin, leafless tree disappearing into the top right-hand corner of the frame. Tendrils of Sally's hair brush her face and the top shoulder of her coat. She looks straight ahead at the photographer, her sister's husband, trust and love for him evident in her expression. The photo has a ghostly quality, enhanced by the sepia color and the blurred focus.

This wasn't the first photograph of Sally Horner that I saw, and I've seen a great many more since. But this is the one I think of the most. Because it's the only photo where Sally has

Florence "Sally" Horner, age nine.

a child's utter lack of guile, without any idea of what horrors lie ahead. Here was evidence of one future she might have had. Sally didn't have a chance to live that one out.

FLORENCE "SALLY" HORNER disappeared from Camden, New Jersey, in mid-June 1948, in the company of a man calling himself Frank La Salle. Twenty-one months later, in March 1950, with the help of a concerned neighbor, Sally telephoned her family from San Jose, California, begging for someone to send the FBI to rescue her. Sensational coverage and La Salle's hasty guilty plea ensued, and the man spent the remainder of his life in prison.

Sally Horner, however, had only two more years to live. And when she died, in mid-August 1952, news of her death reached Vladimir Nabokov at a critical time in the creation of his novel-in-progress—a book he had struggled with, in various forms, for more than a decade, and one that would transform his personal and professional life far beyond his imaginings.

Sally Horner's story buttressed the second half of *Lolita.* Instead of pitching the manuscript into the fire—Nabokov had come close twice, prevented only by the quick actions of his wife, Véra—he set to finish it, borrowing details from the real-life case as needed. Both Sally Horner and Nabokov's fictional creation Dolores Haze were brunette daughters of widowed mothers, fated to be captives of much older predators for nearly two years.

Lolita, when published, was infamous, then famous, always controversial, always a topic of discussion. It has sold more than sixty million copies worldwide in its sixty-plus years of life. Sally Horner, however, was largely forgotten, except by her immediate family members and close friends. They would not even learn of the connection to *Lolita* until just a few years ago. A curious reporter had drawn a line between the real girl and the fictional character in the early 1960s, only to be scoffed at by the Nabokovs. Then, around the novel's fiftieth anniversary, a well-versed Nabokov scholar explored the link between *Lolita* and Sally, showing just how deeply Nabokov embedded the true story into his fiction.

But neither of those men—the journalist or the academic—thought to look more closely at the brief life of Sally Horner. A life that at first resembled a hardscrabble American childhood, then became something extraordinary, then uplifting, and, last of all, tragic. A life that reverberated through the culture, and irrevocably changed the course of twentieth-century literature.

I TELL CRIME STORIES for a living. That means I read a great deal about, and immerse myself in, bad things happening to people, good or otherwise. Crime stories grapple with what causes people to topple over from sanity to madness, from decency to psychopathy, from love to rage. They ignite within me the twinned sense of obsession and compulsion. If these feelings persist, I know the story is mine to tell.

Some stories, I've learned over time, work best in short form. Others break loose from the artificial constraints of a magazine article. Without structure I cannot tell the story, but without a sense of emotional investment and mission, I cannot do justice to the people whose lives I attempt to re-create for readers.

Several years ago I stumbled upon what happened to Sally Horner while looking for a new story to tell. It was my habit then, and remains so now, to plumb obscure corners of the Internet for ideas. I gravitate toward the mid-twentieth century because that period is well documented by newspapers, radio, even early television, yet just outside the bounds of memory. Court records still exist, but require extra rounds of effort to uncover. There are people still alive who remember what happened, but few enough that their recollections are on the cusp of vanishing. Here, in that liminal space where the contemporary meets the past, are stories crying out for greater context and understanding.

Sally Horner caught my attention with particular urgency. Here was a young girl, victimized over a twenty-one-month odyssey from New Jersey to California, by an opportunistic child molester. Here was a girl who figured out a way to survive away from home against her will, who acted in ways that baffled her friends and relatives at the time. We better comprehend those means of survival now because of more recent accounts of girls and women in captivity. Here was a girl who survived her ordeal when so many others, snatched away from their lives, do not. Then for her to die so soon after her rescue, her story subsumed by a novel, one of the most iconic, important works of the twentieth century? Sally Horner got under my skin in a way that few stories ever have.

I dug for the details of Sally's life and its connections to *Lolita* throughout 2014 for a feature published that fall by the Canadian online magazine *Hazlitt*. Even after chasing down court documents, talking to family members, visiting some of the places she had lived—and some of the places where La Salle took her—and writing the piece, I knew I wasn't finished with Sally Horner. Or, more accurately, she was not finished with me.

What drove me then and galls me now is that Sally's abduction defined her entire short life. She never had a chance to grow up, pursue a career, marry, have children, grow old, be happy. She never got to build on the fierce intelligence so evident to her best friend that, nearly seven decades later, she spoke to me of Sally not as a peer, but as a mentor. After Sally died, her family rarely mentioned her or what had happened. They didn't speak of her with awe, or pity, or scorn. She was only an absence.

For decades Sally's claim to immortality was as an incidental reference in *Lolita,* one of the many utterances by the predatory narrator, Humbert Humbert, that allows him to control the narrative and, of course, to control Dolores Haze. Like Lolita, Sally Horner was no "little deadly demon among the wholesome children." Both girls, fictional and real, *were* wholesome children. Contrary to Humbert Humbert's assertions, Sally, like Lolita, was no seductress, "unconscious herself of her fantastic power."

The fantastic power both girls possessed was the capacity to haunt.

I FIRST READ *LOLITA* at sixteen, as a high school junior whose intellectual curiosity far exceeded her emotional maturity. It was something of a self-imposed dare. Only a few months earlier I'd breezed through *One Day in the Life of Ivan Denisovich* by Alexander Solzhenitsyn. Some months later I'd reckon with *Portnoy's Complaint* by Philip Roth. I thought I could handle what transpired between Dolores Haze and Humbert Humbert.

I thought I could appreciate the language and not be affected by the story. I pretended I was ready for *Lolita*, but I was nowhere close.

Those iconic opening lines, "Lolita, light of my life, fire of my loins. My sin, my soul. Lo-lee-ta," sent a frisson down my adolescent spine. I didn't like that feeling, but I wasn't supposed to. I was soon in thrall to Humbert Humbert's voice, the silken veneer barely concealing a loathsome predilection.

I kept reading, hoping there might be some salvation for Dolores, even though I should have known from the foreword, supplied by the fictional narrator John Ray, Jr., PhD, that it does not arrive for a long time. And when she finally escapes from Humbert's clutches to embrace her own life, her freedom is short-lived.

I realized, though I could not properly articulate it, that Vladimir Nabokov had pulled off something remarkable. *Lolita* was my first encounter with an unreliable narrator, one who must be regarded with suspicion. The whole book relies upon the mounting tension between what Humbert Humbert wants the reader to know and what the reader can discern. It is all too easy to be seduced by his sophisticated narration, his panoramic descriptions of America, circa 1947, and his observations of the girl he nicknames Lolita. Those who love language and literature are rewarded richly, but also duped. If you're not being careful, you lose sight of the fact that Humbert raped a twelve-year-old child repeatedly over the course of nearly two years, and got away with it.

It happened to the writer Mikita Brottman, who in *The Maximum Security Book Club* described her own cognitive dissonance discussing *Lolita* with the discussion group she led at a Maryland maximum-security prison. Brottman, reading the novel in advance, had "immediately fallen in love with the narrator," so much so that Humbert Humbert's "style, humor, and sophistication blind[ed] me to his faults." Brottman knew she shouldn't sympathize with a pedophile, but she couldn't help being mesmerized.

The prisoners in her book club were nowhere near so enchanted. An hour into the discussion, one of them looked up at Brottman and cried, "He's just an old pedo!" A second prisoner added: "It's all bullshit, all his long, fancy words. I can see through it. It's all a cover-up. I know what he wants to do with her." A third prisoner drove home the point that *Lolita* "isn't a *love story.* Get rid of all the fancy language, bring it down to the lower [*sic*] common denominator, and it's a grown man molesting a little girl."

Brottman, grappling with the prisoners' blunt responses, realized her foolishness. She wasn't the first, nor the last, to be seduced by style or manipulated by language. Millions of readers missed how *Lolita* folded in the story of a girl who experienced in real life what Dolores Haze suffered on the page. The appreciation of art can make a sucker out of those who forget the darkness of real life.

Knowing about Sally Horner does not diminish *Lolita*'s brilliance, or Nabokov's audacious inventiveness, but it does augment the horror he also captured in the novel.

WRITING ABOUT VLADIMIR NABOKOV daunted me, and still does. Reading his work and researching in his archives was like coming up against an electrified fence designed to keep me away from the truth. Clues would present themselves and then evaporate. Letters and diary entries would hint at larger meanings without supporting evidence. My central quest with respect to Nabokov was to figure out what he knew about Sally

Horner and when he knew it. Through a lifetime, and afterlife, of denials and omissions about the sources of his fiction, he made my pursuit as difficult as possible.

Nabokov loathed people scavenging for biographical details that would explain his work. "I hate tampering with the precious lives of great writers and I hate Tom-peeping over the fence of those lives," he once declared in a lecture about Russian literature to his students at Cornell University, where he taught from 1948 through 1959. "I hate the vulgarity of 'human interest,' I hate the rustle of skirts and giggles in the corridors of time—and no biographer will ever catch a glimpse of my private life."

He made his public distaste for the literal mapping of fiction to real life known as early as 1944, in his idiosyncratic, highly selective, and sharply critical biography of the Russian writer Nikolai Gogol. "It is strange, the morbid inclination we have to derive satisfaction from the fact (generally false and always irrelevant) that a work of art is traceable to a 'true story,'" Nabokov chided. "Is it because we begin to respect ourselves more when we learn that the writer, just like ourselves, was not clever enough to make up a story himself?"

The Gogol biography was more a window into Nabokov's own thinking than a treatise on the Russian master. With respect to his own work, Nabokov did not want critics, academics, students, and readers to look for literal meanings or real-life influences. Whatever source material he'd relied on was grist for his own literary mill, to be used as only he saw fit. His insistence on the utter command of his craft served Nabokov well as his reputation and fame grew after the American publication of *Lolita* in 1958. Scores of interviewers, whether they wrote him letters, interrogated him on television, or visited him at his house, abided by his rules of engagement. They handed over their questions in advance and accepted his answers, written at leisure, cobbling them together to mimic spontaneous conversation.

Nabokov erected roadblocks barring access to his private life for deeper, more complex reasons than to protect his inalienable right to tell stories. He kept family secrets, quotidian and gargantuan, that he did not wish anyone to air in public. And no wonder, when you consider what he lived through: the Russian Revolution, multiple emigrations, the rise of the Nazis, and the fruits of international bestselling success. After he immigrated to the United States in 1940, Nabokov also abandoned Russian, the language of the first half of his literary career, for English. He equated losing his mother tongue to losing a limb, even though, in terms of style and syntax, his English dazzled beyond the imagination of most native speakers.

Always by his side, aiding Nabokov with his lifelong quest to keep nosy people at bay, was his wife, Véra. She took on all of the tasks Nabokov wouldn't or couldn't do: assistant, chief letter writer, first reader, driver, subsidiary rights agent, and many other less-defined roles. She subsumed herself, willingly, for his art, and anyone who poked too deeply at her undying devotion looking for contrary feelings was rewarded with fierce denials, stonewalling, or outright untruths.

Yet this book exists in part because the Nabokovs' roadblocks eventually crumbled. Other people did gain access to his private life. There were three increasingly tendentious biographies by Andrew Field, whose relationship with his subject began in harmony but curdled into acrimony well before Nabokov died in 1977. A two-part definitive study by Brian Boyd is still the biographical standard, a quarter century after its publication, with which any Nabokov scholar must reckon. And

Stacy Schiff's 1999 portrayal of Véra Nabokov illuminated so much about their partnership and teased out the fragments of Véra's inner life.

We've also learned more about what made Nabokov tick since the Library of Congress lifted its fifty-year restriction upon his papers in 2009, opening the entire collection to the public. The more substantive trove at the New York Public Library's Berg Collection still has some restrictions, but I was able to immerse myself in Nabokov's work, his notes, his manuscripts, and also the ephemera—newspaper clippings, letters, photographs, diaries.

A strange thing happened as I looked for clues in his published work and his archives: Nabokov grew less knowable. Such is the paradox of a writer whose work is so filled with metaphor and allusion, so dissected by literary scholars and ordinary readers. Even Boyd claimed, more than a decade and a half after writing his biography of Nabokov, that he still did not fully understand *Lolita*.

What helped me grapple with the book was to reread it, again and again. Sometimes like a potboiler, in a single gulp, and other times slowing down to cross-check each sentence. No one could get every reference and recursion on the first try; the novel rewards repeated reading. Nabokov himself believed the only novels worth reading are the ones that demand to be read on multiple occasions. Once you grasp it, the contradictions of *Lolita*'s narrative and plot structure reveal a logic true to itself.

During one *Lolita* reread, I was reminded of the narrator of an earlier Nabokov story, "Spring in Fialta": "Personally, I never could understand the good of thinking up books, of penning things that had not really happened in some way or other . . .

were I a writer, I should allow only my heart to have imagination, and for the rest to rely upon memory, that long-drawn sunset shadow of one's personal truth."

Nabokov himself never openly admitted to such an attitude himself. But the clues are all there in his work. Particularly so in *Lolita*, with its careful attention to popular culture, the habits of preadolescent girls, and the banalities of then-modern American life. Searching out these signs of real-life happenings was no easy task. I found myself probing absence as much as presence, relying on inference and informed speculation as much as fact.

Some cases drop all the direct evidence into your lap. Some cases are more circumstantial. The case for what Vladimir Nabokov knew of Sally Horner and when he knew it falls squarely into the latter category. Investigating it, and how he incorporated Sally's story into *Lolita*, led me to uncover deeper ties between reality and fiction, and to the thematic compulsion Nabokov spent more than two decades exploring, in fits and starts, before finding full fruition in *Lolita*.

Lolita's narrative, it turns out, depended more on a real-life crime than Nabokov would ever admit.

OVER THE FOUR OR SO YEARS I spent working on this book project, I spoke with a great many people about *Lolita*. For some it was their favorite novel, or one of their favorites. Others had never read the book but ventured an opinion nonetheless. Some loathed it, or the idea of it. No one was neutral. Considering the subject matter, this was not a surprise. Not a single person, when I quoted the passage about Sally Horner, remembered it.

I can't say Nabokov designed the book to hide Sally from the reader. Given that the story moves so quickly, perhaps an homage to the highways Humbert and Dolores traverse over many thousands of miles in their cross-country odyssey, it's easy to miss a lot as you go. But I would argue that even casual readers of *Lolita*, who number in the tens of millions, plus the many more millions with some awareness of the novel, the two film versions, or its place in the culture these past six decades, should pay attention to the story of Sally Horner because it is the story of so many girls and women, not just in America, but everywhere. So many of these stories seem like everyday injustices—young women denied opportunity to advance, tethered to marriage and motherhood. Others are more horrific, girls and women abused, brutalized, kidnapped, or worse.

Yet Sally Horner's plight is also uniquely American, unfolding in the shadows of the Second World War, after victory had created a solid, prosperous middle class that could not compensate for terrible future decline. Her abduction is woven into the fabric of her hometown of Camden, New Jersey, which at the time believed itself to be at the apex of the American Dream. Wandering its streets today, as I did on several occasions, was a stark reminder of how Camden has changed for the worse. Sally should have been able to travel America of her own volition, a culmination of the Dream. Instead she was taken against her will, and the road trip became a nightmare.

Sally's life ended too soon. But her story helped inspire a novel people are still discussing and debating more than sixty years after its initial publication. Vladimir Nabokov, through his use of language and formal invention, gave fictional authority to a pedophile and charmed and revolted millions of readers in the process. By exploring the life of Sally Horner, I reveal the truth behind the curtain of fiction. What Humbert

Humbert did to Dolores Haze is, in fact, what Frank La Salle did to Sally Horner in 1948.

With this book, Sally Horner takes precedence. Like the butterflies that Vladimir Nabokov so loved, she emerges from the cage of both fiction and fact, ready to fly free.

ONE

The Five-and-Dime

Sally Horner walked into the Woolworth's on Broadway and Federal in Camden, New Jersey, to steal a five-cent notebook. She'd been dared to by the clique of girls she desperately wanted to join. Sally had never stolen anything in her life; usually she went to that particular five-and-dime for school supplies and her favorite candy. The clique told her it would be easy. Nobody would suspect a girl like Sally, a fifth-grade honor pupil and president of the Junior Red Cross Club at Northeast School, to be a thief. Despite her mounting dread at breaking the law, she believed them. She had no idea a simple act of shoplifting on a March afternoon in 1948 would destroy her life.

Once inside Woolworth's, Sally reached for the first notebook she spied on the gleaming white nickel counter. She stuffed it into her bag and walked away, careful to look straight ahead to the exit door. Before she could cross the threshold to freedom, she felt a hand grab her arm.

Sally looked up. A slender, hawk-faced man loomed above her, iron-gray hair underneath a wide-brimmed fedora, eyes shifting between blue and gray. A scar sliced his cheek by the right side of his nose, while his shirt collar shrouded another mark on his throat. The hand gripping Sally's arm bore the traces of an even older, half-moon stamp forged by fire. Any adult would have sized him up as middle-aged, but to ten-year-old Sally, he looked positively ancient.

"I am an FBI agent," the man said to Sally. "And you are under arrest."

Sally did what many young girls would have done in a similar situation: She cried. She cowered. She felt immediately ashamed.

The man's low voice and steely gaze froze her in place. He pointed across the way to City Hall, the tallest building in Camden. That's where girls like her would be dealt with, he said. Sally didn't understand his meaning at first. Then he explained: to punish her for stealing, she would be sent to the reformatory.

Sally didn't know that much about reform school, but what she knew was not good. She kept crying.

Then his stern manner brightened. It was a lucky break for a little girl like her, he said, that he was the one who caught her and not some other FBI agent. If she agreed to report to him from time to time, he would let her go. Spare her the worst. Show some mercy.

Sally stopped crying. He was going to let her go. She wouldn't have to call her mother from jail—her poor, overworked mother, Ella, still struggling with the consequences of the suicide of her alcoholic husband, Sally's father, five years earlier; still tethered to her seamstress job, which meant that Sally, too often, went home to an empty house after school.

But she couldn't think about that. Not when she was about to escape real punishment. Any desire she felt about joining the girls' club fell away, overcome by relief she wouldn't face a much larger fear.

Sally did not know the reprieve had an expiration date. One that would come due at any time, without warning.

MONTHS PASSED WITHOUT further word from the FBI man. As the spring of 1948 inched its way to summer, Sally finished up fifth grade at Northeast School. She kept up her marks and remained on the honor roll. She also stuck with the Junior Red Cross and continued to volunteer at local hospitals. Her homeroom teacher, Sarah Hanlin, singled Sally out as "a perfectly lovely girl. . . . [A] better than average pupil, intelligent and well behaved." Sally had had a major escape. She must have been grateful for each successive day of freedom.

The Camden of Sally's girlhood was far removed from the Camden of today. Emma DiRenzo, one of Sally's classmates, remembered it as a "marvelous" place to grow up in. "Everything about Camden back then was wonderful," she said. "When you tell people now, they look at you with big eyes." There were pep rallies at City Hall and social events at the YMCA. Girls jumped rope on the sidewalks, near houses adorned with marble steps. Camden residents took pride in their neighborhoods and communities, whether they were among the Italians in South Camden, the Irish in the city's North Side, the Germans in the East Side neighborhood of

Cramer Hill, or the Polish living along Mt. Ephraim Avenue, lining up to buy homemade kielbasa at Jaskolski's or fresh bread at the Morton Bakery. They didn't dream of suburban flight because there was no reason to leave.

Sally lived at 944 Linden Street, between Ninth and Tenth Streets. Cornelius Martin Park lay a few blocks east, and the city's main downtown was within walking distance to the west, and the Ben Franklin Bridge connecting Camden to Philadelphia was minutes away. The neighborhood was quiet but within reach of Camden's bustling core. Now it isn't a neighborhood at all. The town house where Sally grew up was demolished decades ago. What houses remain across the street are decrepit, with boarded-up windows and doors.

Sally's life in Camden was not idyllic. Despite outward appearances, she was lonely. Sally knew how to take care of herself but she wished she didn't have to. She didn't want to come home to an empty house after school because her mother was working late. Sally couldn't help comparing her life with those of her classmates, who had both mother and father. She confided her frustrations to Hanlin, her teacher, who often walked home with her at the end of a school day.

It's not clear if Sally had close friends her age. Perhaps her desire to be accepted by the popular girls stemmed from a lack of companionship. Her father, Russell, had died three weeks before Sally's sixth birthday, and she'd hardly seen him much before then. Her mother, Ella, worked long hours, and was tired and distant when she was at home. Her sister, Susan, was pregnant with her first child. Sally looked forward to becoming an aunt, whatever being an aunt meant, but it made the eleven-year age gap between the sisters all the more unbridgeable. Sally was still a little girl. Susan was not only an adult, but about to be a mother.

SALLY HORNER WAS WALKING home from Northeast School by herself after the last bell on a mid-June day in 1948. The route from North Seventh and Vine to her house took ten minutes by foot. Somewhere along the way, Sally was intercepted by the man from Woolworth's. Sally had dared to think he'd forgotten about her. Seeing him again was a shock.

Keep in mind that Sally had just turned eleven. She believed he was an FBI agent. She felt his power and feared it, even though it was false. She was convinced if she didn't do what he said that she would be sent to the reformatory and be subject to its horrors, as well as worse ones conjured up in her imagination. No matter how he did it, the man convinced Sally that she must go with him to Atlantic City—the government insisted.

But how would she persuade her mother? This would be no easy task, despite Ella's general state of apathy and exhaustion. The man had an answer for that, too. Sally was to tell her mother that he was the father of two school friends who had invited her to a seashore vacation after school ended for the year. He would take care of the rest with a phone call to her mother. Sally wasn't to worry—he would never let on that she was in trouble with the law. He sent the girl on her way.

At home, Sally waited for her mother to return from work, then parroted the FBI man's story. Ella was uneasy, and let it show. Sally sounded sincere in her desire to go to the Jersey Shore for a week's vacation with friends, but who were these people? Ella had never heard Sally mention the names of these two girls before, nor that of their father, Frank Warner. Or if she had, Ella didn't recall.

The telephone rang. The man on the other end of the line told Ella he was Mr. Warner, father to Sally's school friends. His manner was affable, polite. He seemed courteous, even

charming. Sally stayed by her mother as the conversation unfolded. "Warner" told Ella that he and his wife had "plenty of
room" in their five-room apartment in Atlantic City to put Sally
up for the week.

Under the force of his persuasion, Ella let her concerns
slide. "It was a chance for Sally to get a little vacation," she said
weeks later. "I couldn't afford to give her one." She did wonder
why Sally didn't seem to be all that excited about the vacation.
It was out of character. Normally her bright little girl loved to
go places.

On June 14, 1948, Ella took Sally to the Camden bus depot. She kissed her daughter goodbye and watched her climb
aboard an express bus to Atlantic City. She spied the outlines
of a middle-aged man, the one she took to be "Warner," next
to Sally, but he did not come out to greet her. Ella also did not
see anyone else with the man, neither wife nor children. Still,
she tamped down her suspicions. She wanted so badly for her
daughter to enjoy herself. And it seemed, from the first few letters Sally sent her from Atlantic City, that the girl was having
a good time.

Ella Horner never dreamed that, within weeks, her girl
would become a ghost. By sending Sally off on that bus to
Atlantic City, she had consigned her daughter to the stuff of
nightmares that would rip any mother apart.

A Trip to the Beach

R obert and Jean Pfeffer were newlyweds who couldn't afford a honeymoon. So the couple, both twenty-two, settled on a day trip with their family, which included Robert's mother, Emily, his seventeen-year-old sister, also named Emily, his nine-year-old younger sister, Barbara, and four other relatives whose names have been lost to time. The sea-cooled Brigantine Beach, a small town east of Atlantic City, was far enough away from their North Philadelphia neighborhood of Nicetown to feel like a treat, but close enough to get back home by nightfall.

Robert, Jean, Emily senior and junior, and Barbara piled into Robert's car on a weekend morning in July 1948 and set out for the beach. (The other four relatives had their own car.) Somewhere along Route 40, a tire blew out. Robert's car went off the road and landed on its side.

The Pfeffers climbed out, shaken and in shock. No one was hurt, thank goodness, but the car was far too damaged to continue. As Robert stood there, wondering how much it would cost to get the car towed and fixed, a station wagon pulled up. A middle-aged man got out of the front seat, and a girl he introduced as his daughter stepped out from the passenger side.

From there the story Robert Pfeffer told both the *Philadelphia Inquirer* and the Camden *Courier-Post* turns strange, riddled with unsolvable inconsistencies. People turn up where they shouldn't. Chronologies bend out of shape. What's clear is that he was so disturbed by what happened that July morning that he alerted law enforcement and, when they didn't listen, the newspapers.

The man told the Pfeffers his name was Frank and that his daughter's name was Sally. (Robert later recalled the man used La Salle as a last name, but it's unclear if that was really the case.) La Salle offered to take the young couple to get help. Robert and Jean agreed. They got into the back of La Salle's station wagon, and La Salle, with Sally beside him, drove them to the nearest roadside phone. Robert called his father and told him about the accident and the Good Samaritan who had come to their aid. He also asked his father to come pick up his wife and daughters.

There was a hamburger joint at the rest stop, and La Salle, Sally, Robert, and Jean stopped for a quick bite to eat. The waitress seemed to be familiar with Frank and Sally, addressing them by name. Robert figured they must be regulars. After the meal, everyone returned to the wreck and La Salle offered to drive the entire family to Brigantine Beach so their day trip wouldn't be spoiled. He also said he would take care of towing and fixing the car. The Pfeffers accepted.

Sally and Barbara, only two years apart in age, hit it off right away. They went swimming together and played on the beach. La Salle told the Pfeffers that he operated a gas station and garage in Atlantic City, that he was divorced, and that Sally lived with him on summer vacations. Sally behaved as if nothing was amiss. She referred to Frank as "Daddy" and treated him with affection. "She told us how good he had been to her," Pfeffer said.

Later that day, Sally suggested that her "dad" could drive her and Barbara back to their place to clean themselves up. They lived on Pacific Avenue in Atlantic City, just ten minutes away by car.

The minutes passed, then became an hour, then an hour and a half. The Pfeffers, waiting at the beach, started to worry. What was taking so long? Robert's father had arrived, and he offered to squeeze everyone into his car and drive into Atlantic City to see what was going on. Why had they let Barbara go off with strangers, even if one of those strangers was a friendly, blue-eyed little girl? Minutes into the drive, they saw La Salle's station wagon coming toward them, with Sally and Barbara sitting together in the backseat.

They headed back to the wrecked car, which La Salle attached to the back of his station wagon. The group, divided between La Salle's vehicle and Robert's father's car, drove to the Atlantic City garage where La Salle claimed he worked and dropped off the damaged vehicle to be fixed. The body shop, Robert noted, was across the street from a New Jersey State Police station.

Before the Pfeffers went back to Philadelphia, Sally invited Barbara to come stay with her for a weekend. La Salle said they'd love to have the girl visit. The family did not take them up on the invite.

Several days later, the Pfeffers would have even more reason to remember their extended encounter with the middle-aged man and the girl he claimed was his daughter.

EVERY TIME ELLA HORNER began to wonder if she had done the right thing in sending Sally off to Atlantic City, a letter or a call—always from a pay phone—arrived to assuage her guilt and soothe her mind. Sally seemed to be having a swell time, or so Ella convinced herself. Perhaps she felt some relief, too, at having a reprieve from the expense of feeding and entertaining her little girl, which stretched her puny paycheck beyond its limits.

At the end of her first week away, Sally told her mother she wanted to stay longer so she could see the Ice Follies. Ella reluctantly gave permission. After two weeks, Sally's excuses for staying in Atlantic City grew more vague, but Ella thought her daughter still sounded well. Then, at the three-week mark, the phone calls stopped. Ella's letters to her daughter came back with "return to sender" stamped on the front.

On July 31, 1948, Ella was relieved to receive another letter. Sally wrote to say she was leaving Atlantic City and going on to Baltimore with Mr. Warner. Though she promised to return home to Camden by the end of the week, she added, "I don't want to write anymore."

At last, something woke up inside Ella's mind. "I don't think my little girl has stayed with that man all this time of her own accord." Her sister, Susan, was days away from giving birth. Would Sally really choose to stay away when she was about to become an aunt? Ella finally understood the horrible truth. She called the police.

After Detective Joseph Schultz spoke with Ella, he sent

two other Camden detectives, William Marter and Marshall Thompson, to look for Sally in Atlantic City. On August 4, they arrived at the lodging house on 203 Pacific Avenue that Sally gave as the return address on her letters. There they learned from the landlady, Mrs. McCord, that Warner had been living there, and he'd been posing as Sally's father. There were no other daughters, nor was there a wife. Just one little girl, Sally.

The police also learned the man Ella knew as "Mr. Warner" worked at a gas station, and adopted the alias of "Frank Robinson." When the cops went to the gas station, he wasn't there. He'd failed to show up for work and hadn't even bothered to pick up his final paycheck. "Robinson" had disappeared, and so had Sally. Two suitcases remained in their room, as did several unsent postcards from Sally to her mother. "He didn't take any of his or the girl's clothes, either," Thompson told the *Philadelphia Inquirer*. "He didn't even stop long enough to get his hat."

Among the items left behind in the rooming house was a photograph, one that Ella had never seen before. In it, Sally sat on a swing, feet dangling just above the ground, staring directly at the camera. She wore a cream-colored dress, white socks, and black patent

Photograph of Sally discovered at the Atlantic City boardinghouse in August 1948, six weeks after her disappearance.

shoes, and her honey-streaked light brown hair was pulled away from her face. Her eyes conveyed a mixture of fear and a bottomless desire to please. She looked like she wanted to get this moment right, but didn't know what "right" was supposed to be, when everything was so wrong.

It seemed likely that Sally's kidnapper was the photographer. She was only three months past her eleventh birthday.

Marshall Thompson led the search for Sally in Atlantic City. When that search turned up empty, he took the photo of her back to Camden police headquarters to be sent out on the teletypes. He had to find Sally, the sooner, the better, because police now knew who they were dealing with.

For Sally's mother, it was awful enough that the Camden police had failed to bring her daughter home. Far worse was the news they broke to Ella: the man who had called himself "Warner" was well-known to local law enforcement. They knew him as Frank La Salle. And only six months before he'd abducted Sally, he had been released from prison after serving a sentence for the statutory rape of five girls between the ages of twelve and fourteen.

THREE

From Wellesley to Cornell

The year 1948 was a pivotal one for Vladimir Nabokov. He had spent six years in Cambridge, Massachusetts, teaching literature to Wellesley College undergraduates and, in his spare time, indulging his passion for studying butterflies at Harvard's Museum of Comparative Zoology. After eight years in the United States, the tumult and trauma of emigration had receded. English, Nabokov said many times, was the first language he remembered learning, and the lure of America had sustained him as he fled the Russian Revolution for Germany, and then from the Nazis to Paris—a necessary step when married to a woman who was proud and unafraid to be Jewish.

The United States, and particularly the Boston area, proved a generally happy environment for Nabokov, Véra, and their son, Dmitri, who was fourteen years old in 1948. Since they'd found a haven there, Nabokov had worked on a book about Nikolai Gogol, about whom he had decidedly mixed feelings; published a novel, *Bend Sinister;* and begun the version of his autobiography that would appear as *Conclusive Evidence* a couple of years later. (He would later rewrite it and publish it under the title *Speak, Memory.*)

Nabokov had also traveled across America three times, in the summers of 1941, 1943, and 1947. (He would repeat the cross-country trip four more times.) He never drove, entrusting the task to his wife, Véra, or a graduate student. The first time, Dorothy Leuthold, a middle-aged student in his language class, had spirited the Nabokovs from New York City in a brand-new Pontiac (dubbed Pon'ka, the Russian word for "pony") all the way to Palo Alto, California.

The trio stayed in motor courts and budget hotels and other cheap lodgings that wouldn't break the bank. The America Nabokov witnessed on these trips was eventually immortalized as the "lovely, trustful, dreamy, enormous country" that Humbert Humbert comments on in *Lolita:* "Beyond the tilled plain . . . there would be a slow suffusion of inutile loveliness, a low sun in a platinum haze with a warm, peeled-peach tinge pervading the upper edge of a two-dimensional, dove-gray cloud." Though his marriage to Véra was once again stable, an affair had nearly derailed it a decade earlier, when she had gone on to Paris before him. Perhaps news of his romantic attentions to at least one Wellesley student had not reached Véra—or if it had, she did not view the dalliance as anything serious.

Nabokov had been ill for much of the first half of 1948. He suffered a litany of lung troubles during the spring that no doctor could adequately diagnose. They thought it might be tuberculosis because of the alarming quantities of blood Nabokov coughed up. It wasn't. The next guess was cancer. That, too, proved untrue. When doctors put a vulcanized rubber tube down his windpipe under local anesthetic to inspect his ailing lungs, all they found was a single ruptured blood vessel. Nabokov himself figured his body was "ridding itself of the damage caused by thirty years of heavy smoking." Bedridden, he had enough energy to write, but not to teach, so Véra stood in for him as lecturer.

After these summer trips, Nabokov was always glad to return to Cambridge. Wellesley, his academic and personal refuge, had turned down his multiple entreaties for a full-time professorship. Nor could he find full-time work at Harvard, where he'd made a quixotic bid to turn his butterfly-hunting hobby into a proper profession. But the Nabokovs' fortunes were about to change thanks to Morris Bishop, a romance literature professor at Cornell who would remain a close friend to both Vladimir and Véra. Bishop lobbied Cornell to appoint Nabokov a professor of Russian literature, and it worked. On July 1, the Nabokovs moved to Ithaca, New York, finding solace in a "quiet summer in green surroundings." By August, they had rented a large house on 802 East Seneca Street, one far bigger than their "wrinkled-dwarf Cambridge flatlet"—and future inspiration for the house where a man named Humbert Humbert would discover the object of his obsession.

The summer also brought Nabokov a formative book, thanks to the literary critic Edmund Wilson, who sent Nabokov a copy of Havelock Ellis's *Studies in the Psychology of Sex*. He drew attention to one appendix that contained the late-nineteenth-century confession of an unnamed engineer of Ukrainian descent. The man had first had sex at age twelve with another child, found the experience so intoxicating he repeated it, and eventually destroyed his marriage by sleeping with child prostitutes. From there the man went further downhill, to the point where he

flashed young girls in public. The confession, as Nabokov related in a later interview, "ends with a feeling of hopelessness,
of a life ruined by hunger beyond control."

Nabokov appreciated Wilson's gift and wrote him after
reading the case histories. "I enjoyed the Russian's love-life
hugely. It is wonderfully funny. As a boy, he seems to have
been quite extraordinarily lucky in coming across [willing
girls]. . . . The end is rather bathetic." Nabokov also directly
acknowledged the impact of Ellis to his first biographer. "I was
always interested in psychology," he told Andrew Field. "I knew
my Havelock Ellis rather well. . . ."

He was, by this point, five years from finishing the manuscript for *Lolita*, and a decade from its triumphant American
publication. But Nabokov was also nearly twenty years into his
efforts to wrestle a thematic compulsion into its final form: the
character who became Humbert Humbert.

SKIP PAST THE OFT-QUOTED opening paragraph of *Lolita*'s
first chapter. Chances are, even if you've never read the novel,
you probably know it by heart, or some version of it. Move
directly to paragraph two: "She was Lo, plain Lo, in the morning, standing four feet ten in one sock. She was Lola in slacks.
She was Dolly at school. She was Dolores on the dotted line."

In Humbert Humbert's eyes, the girl named Dolores Haze
is a canvas blank enough to project whatever he, and by virtue
of his narration, the reader, sees or desires—"But in my arms
she was always Lolita." She is never allowed to be herself. Not
in Humbert's telling.

When the reader meets her, Dolores Haze is just shy of
twelve years old, born around the first of the year in 1935, making her two years and three months older than Sally Horner.

She is an inch shorter than Sally and, at seventy-eight pounds, a good twenty pounds lighter than her real-life counterpart. There aren't other facts and figures available for Sally, but Humbert measures every physical aspect of Dolores: twenty-seven-inch chest, twenty-three-inch waist, twenty-nine-inch hips, while her thigh, calf, and neck circumferences were seventeen, eleven, and eleven, respectively.

Dolores's mother, the former Charlotte Becker, and her father, Harold Haze, were living in Pisky, a town somewhere in the Midwest best known for producing hogs, corn, and coal, when their daughter was born. Conception, however, took place in Veracruz, Mexico, during the Hazes' honeymoon. Another child followed in 1937, the year of Sally's birth, but that offspring, a blond-haired boy, died at two. Sometime thereafter—Humbert is vague on details—Harold also perished, leaving Charlotte a widowed single mother. She and Dolores move east to Ramsdale, and set up house at 342 Lawn Street, where both mother and daughter will encounter a man who will alter their lives irrevocably and with monumental consequences.

When he first sees her, Humbert Humbert describes Dolores in poetic terms: "frail, honey-hued shoulders . . . silky supple bare back . . . chestnut head of hair" and wearing "a polka-dotted black kerchief tied around her chest" that shields her breasts from Humbert's "aging ape eyes."

Humbert confides to the reader that when he was nine, he met a girl named Annabel Leigh, also nine. They embarked on a friendship with strong romantic overtones and multiple rendezvous by the beach. Then Annabel fell ill and died prematurely, the idyll forever cut short. Her death imprinted a type, and a predilection, upon Humbert for the rest of his days. Girls who fall between the ages of nine and fourteen. Girls whose "true nature," according to Humbert, bore little resemblance to real life. Girls he characterized as "little deadly demons." Girls immortalized, forevermore, by him as well as his creator, as nymphets.

Humbert Humbert was describing a compulsion. Vladimir Nabokov set out to create an archetype. But the real little girls who fit this idea of the mythical nymphet end up getting lost in the need for artistic license. The abuse that Sally Horner, and other girls like her, endured should not be subsumed by dazzling prose, no matter how brilliant.

FOUR

Sally, at First

The seeds of Sally Horner's kidnapping grew out of choices made by her mother. Ella kept secrets about the circumstances of her daughters' births and the death of Sally's father. Sally never knew of them. Susan may have, but if so she never spoke of them to her family. Digging up these secrets transformed me into an accidental forensic genealogical detective. I spent so many months stuck on Sally's origin story and the clash between what was reported and what really happened because I thought it would help me better understand Ella's behavior.

Her decisions, with respect to Sally's disappearance, hold her up to severe scrutiny by the modern world. She let her daughter go off with a stranger she'd only spoken to by telephone. She grew more distant, perhaps more baffling, to her family, let alone to neighbors. She fit the pejorative "difficult" bill so often affixed to women who don't fit within neat little boxes. But in 1948, with little money and fewer resources available to Ella as a single mother, she functioned within her own limited framework. Her best was not good enough for Sally, but it was all she knew based on the life she'd lived up until she saw her daughter off at the Camden bus depot.

SALLY WAS HER NICKNAME. No one is alive to remember why, or who used it first, or how it stuck. Her legal name, listed on the certificate announcing her birth at Trenton Hospital on April 18, 1937, was Florence, no middle name, Horner. Her mother, the former Ella Katherine Goff, took the baby back to the home she shared with Russell Horner in Roebling, New Jersey. The house at 238 Fourth Avenue is long gone, replaced by a more modern town house a stone's throw from the River Line train station to the east, and several blocks south of the Delaware River.

Ella's older daughter, Susan, also lived with the Horners, though Russell was not her father. Eleven years earlier, at the age of nineteen, Ella had had some sort of relationship with an older man of about thirty. When the subject came up, Ella told her family that she and Susan's birth father, whom she never named, were married, but that he passed away. Susan knew her father's real name, William Ralph Swain, because she listed it on her marriage license. She likely knew little else.

Ella had good reason to keep Swain's existence a secret, and never mention him by name. Records indicate he was married to someone else when Susan was born, contrary to the "yes" ticked off on Susan's birth certificate, indicating her legitimate status. Nor could I find any existing marriage record between Swain and Ella, though one may turn up in the future—vital records are irregularly stored from city to city, state by state. To confuse matters further, the 1930 census listed Ella's last name as Albara, which she used for at least a half dozen more years. The census record also listed her as being married, but I could not track down any marriage record between Ella and a man named Albara.

Ella raised Susan on her own, with occasional help from her parents, Job and Susannah Goff. One subject they all fretted about was how long it took Susan to learn to speak. She'd had some sort of head injury as a baby, and did not begin talking in earnest until she was five, by which time she and her mother had moved to Prospertown to be closer to Ella's parents, who were growing older and more infirm.

That's where Ella met Russell Horner, a widower with a son, also named Russell. Horner began to court her, and some of their meetings were recorded by the local papers, as was the custom of the day. On December 9, 1935, the *Asbury Park Press* noted that Ella and Russell were "recent visitors to friends in Lakehurst." The paper also reported on June 8, 1936, that Ella and Susan visited Russell and his son (both names were spelled as "Russel") in New Egypt, and noted a solo visit by Ella to the town on August 8. Ella and Russell were not husband and wife, though. It seems Ella had repeated the pattern begun with Swain. While Russell's first wife, the mother of his son, had died, he had married a second time and never bothered to divorce the woman. By the end of 1937, Russell and Ella were living as husband and wife at the Fourth Avenue house in Roebling.

As for Russell Junior, he married two months before Sally Horner's birth. Sally never knew of her half brother's existence. Neither her mother nor Susan mentioned him.

Ella and Russell's domestic arrangement was as short-lived

as their earlier relationships. By the time Sally was about three, the situation had grown volatile. Russell had a drinking problem, which did not mix well with his job as a crane operator, and he could be abusive to his wife and her daughters. Susan remembered the beatings her stepfather gave her mother, memories she did not allow herself to think about until close to the end of her own life. Sally, much younger when her parents split up, may have been spared the worst of these memories.

Eventually, Ella fled her relationship. She took Susan and Sally to Camden, where they moved into the town house at 944 Linden Street. Russell became itinerant, drifting from town to town around southern New Jersey, looking for and not finding work. He lost his driver's license when caught taking a short-cut along some railroad tracks. By the beginning of 1943, he was living at his parents' farm in Cassville. On March 24, he hanged himself from the rafters of the garage. Horner left a note for his mother in the kitchen, directing her where to find his body. According to the state police, he "had been despondent over ill health for some time."

Police told the *Asbury Park Press* that Russell had been married twice and was "estranged from his current wife," though they did not say whether the wife in question was Ella. But the address listed on Russell's death certificate was the address where he'd lived with Ella and the girls in Roebling. And the name of his daughter, "Florence," is handwritten just below the address line.

Sally was not quite six years old when her father committed suicide. It isn't clear how much she knew of her father's history and manner of death. Later, when it became necessary to clarify her parentage, she said, "My real daddy died when I was six and I remember what he looks like."

After Russell killed himself, Ella, already living as a single mother, was truly on her own. Her mother, Susannah, had passed away in 1939, while her father, Job, died in January 1943, just two months before Russell killed himself. Ella had to go to work as a seamstress.

Susan, by now sixteen, had left school and was working a factory job. That summer, Susan met Alvin Panaro, a sailor on leave, at a friend's party. Though Al was three years older, he was immediately smitten, but the Second World War was on and they were too young to marry. Al hailed from Florence, near the same part of town where Susan and Sally had once lived. His parents owned a greenhouse, and planned for Al to take over responsibility running it once he was finished with the navy, once he was home for good. It was also understood he might not get that chance; even the navy carried a high casualty risk.

When Susan turned eighteen, they decided not to wait any longer. On his next furlough, she and Al wed in Florence on February 17, 1945. When the war ended, Al received his honorable discharge and he and Susan began married life in earnest, running the greenhouse together. They wanted children, but Susan's initial pregnancies ended in early miscarriages. Then their luck turned.

In June 1948, Susan and Al Panaro were two months away from the birth of their daughter, Diana, Ella's first grandchild. But when the baby girl arrived that August, celebration was the furthest thing from the minds of her parents and grandmother. Sally had disappeared and they knew who had taken her. They also now knew what sort of man he was.

FIVE

The Search for Sally

An eight-state police search for Sally Horner began on August 5, 1948. By then she had been gone from Camden for six weeks. The news wires picked up the story of her abduction, as well as Ella's delay in reporting her daughter missing. The picture of Sally on the swing went out across the country, appearing in wire reports published from Salt Lake City, Utah, to Rochester, New York, and in local papers like the Camden *Courier-Post* and the *Philadelphia Inquirer*.

Robert and Jean Pfeffer were among those who read the news about Sally Horner's disappearance. How strange, the couple thought. "If [Sally] had wanted to warn us about anything she had every opportunity, but never did so." Robert picked up the phone, called the Camden police, and told the officer who answered about their encounter in Brigantine Beach. Robert also mentioned his little sister Barbara's visit to

La Salle's apartment, which had stretched to ninety agonizing minutes of waiting. Perhaps reading about La Salle's prior incarceration made him wonder what, exactly, might have happened to Barbara during those ninety minutes. He never heard a word back from the police.

The shock of the news about Sally, combined with mundane family matters, delayed Pfeffer from making the two-and-a-half-hour round trip back to Atlantic City to pick up their car for several weeks. He never learned whether La Salle himself or some other mechanic restored it to good working order.

Sally and La Salle, however, were long gone from Atlantic City. Camden police now knew, with queasy certainty, why Sally's family had ample reason to be fearful of what Frank La Salle might do to their little girl.

AT FIRST MARSHALL THOMPSON worked the Sally Horner case with other Camden police officers. But when the summer of 1948 gave way to fall, he took on the investigation full-time and never stopped. As the months wore on, his colleagues weren't shy about voicing their opinions. The girl had to be dead. She couldn't up and vanish like this, no trace, no word, when they knew who had her, what they both looked like, and that they were posing as father and daughter.

Thompson felt otherwise. Sally must be alive. He figured it was likely she was still near enough to Camden. And even if she wasn't, he would find her. It was his job as detective to care about every case, but the plight of a missing girl really got to him.

He had been promoted to detective only the year before, nearly two decades into his time on the force. Thompson's appointment in March 1928 happened the same year his only daughter, Caroline, was born, and not long after he and his wife, Emma, moved to the Cramer Hill neighborhood in Northeast Camden. The young couple had long-standing Camden roots, Thompson in particular. His father, George, had served as justice of the peace, and his grandfather John Reeve Thompson was a member of Camden's first city council.

Tangles with "local pugilists," raids on illegal speakeasies, breaking up home gambling dens, and other minor crimes littered Thompson's stretch as a Camden cop. Most of the time he worked with Sergeant Nathan Petit; their names often appeared together in the local papers' accounts of various notable arrests.

Off duty, Thompson entertained family and friends by playing classical piano, which his mother, Harriette, taught him as a child. His musical ability was called out with hyperbolic flourish by a *Courier-Post* columnist in 1939: "Marshall Thompson, one of Camden's finest, is a talented pianist. He never took a music lesson."

Thompson's innate tenacity made him the perfect choice to look for Sally Horner and Frank La Salle. Over the course of his investigation Thompson learned much about Sally's abductor, from his choice of haircut to the "quantity of sugar and cream he desired when drinking coffee." He chased every lead and followed up on every tip. One phone call came in to say La Salle was holed up in a house on Trenton Avenue and Washington Street in downtown Camden. A state police teletype arrived placing La Salle at a residence on Third and Sumner Avenue in Florence, the same town where Sally lived as a little girl. Neither tip panned out.

Once Thompson was on the case full-time, he let it dictate his entire waking life. He got in touch, in person and by telephone, with the FBI; state and city police at Columbus,

Newton, Riverton, and Langhorne, Pennsylvania; state parole offices at Trenton and Camden; detective divisions in Philadelphia; and the Trenton post office. Several months into Sally's disappearance, Thompson received reports of La Salle being spotted in Philadelphia, northern New Jersey, South Jersey Shore resorts, and at a restaurant in Haddonfield, observed by a waitress working there. He followed each lead to no avail.

Thompson also cast his net farther and deeper in the surrounding states. He checked in regularly with state and city police in Absecon, Pleasantville, Maple Shade, Newark, Orange, and Paterson, New Jersey; parole offices in Atlantic City and the state prison farm in Leesburg; and the Compensation Bureau in Trenton, in case La Salle drew or cashed a paycheck in the state.

There were periods where he worked twenty-four hours or more without taking a break. Finding Sally Horner was more important than sleep. Thompson tracked down La Salle's first wife in Portland, Maine, but she knew nothing of his whereabouts. The detective also contacted La Salle's second wife, now living in Delaware Township with her daughter, her new husband, and their baby son. The woman gave Thompson an earful about her wayward, criminal ex-husband's habits and history, including the dramatic beginning of their marriage and its equally explosive end.

Thompson used his holidays to travel for the case. On one six-day "vacation," Thompson went to the Trenton State Fair. Each morning, he stood outside the entrance to the grounds, hoping that La Salle might turn up to apply for a job. Or perhaps he would bring Sally with him.

None of the leads amounted to anything. Nor did tips from numerous anonymous phone calls and letters. All had to be followed up on, but none yielded the answer Detective Marshall Thompson craved: the whereabouts of Sally Horner.

It was the nature of a detective's job to get hopes up and have them crushed. So many of his colleagues believed the girl was dead. But not Thompson. He could not give up. He knew in his bones that he would, someday, find Sally alive and bring her back to Camden, to her mother, her family.

And that he would find Frank La Salle and see justice done.

SIX

Seeds of Compulsion

Vladimir Nabokov holding a butterfly, 1947, at Harvard's
Museum of Comparative Zoology, where he was a fellow.

A s Marshall Thompson continued to track Frank La
Salle's whereabouts without results, Vladimir Nabokov remained on a quest to plumb the fictional mind
of a man with a similar appetite for young girls. So far, he had
not been successful. He could have, and tried to, abandon it
altogether—there were plenty of other literary projects for

Nabokov to pursue. But the drive to get this story right went beyond formal exercise. Otherwise, why did Nabokov explore this same topic, over and over, for more than twenty years? At almost every stage of his literary career, Nabokov was preoccupied with the idea of the middle-aged man's obsession with a young girl.

As Martin Amis wrote in a 2011 essay for the *Times Literary Supplement,* "Of the nineteen fictions, no fewer than six wholly or partly concern themselves with the sexuality of prepubescent girls. . . . [T]o be clear as one can be: the unignorable infestation of nymphets . . . is not a matter of morality; it is a matter of aesthetics. There are just too many of them."

"Aesthetics" is one way to phrase it. Robert Roper, in his 2015 book *Nabokov in America,* suggested a more likely culprit: compulsion—"a literary equivalent of the persistent impulse of a pedophile." Over and over, scholars and biographers have searched for direct connections between Nabokov and young children, and failed to find them. What impulses he possessed were literary, not literal, in the manner of the "well-adjusted" writer who persists in writing about the worst sort of crimes. We generally don't bear the same suspicions of writers who turn serial killers into folk heroes. No one, for example, thinks Thomas Harris capable of the terrible deeds of Hannibal Lecter, even though he invented them with chilling psychological insight.

Nabokov likely realized how often this theme persisted in his work. That would explain why he was quick to deny connections between *Lolita* and real-life figures, or to later claim the novel's inspiration emerged from, of all things, a brief article in a French newspaper about "an ape in the Jardin des Plantes who, after months of coaxing by a scientist, produced the first drawing ever charcoaled by an animal: this sketch showed the bars of the poor creature's cage."

But there is no getting around the deep-seated compulsion that recurs again and again in Nabokov's work. I read through his earlier Russian-language novels, as well as more contemporary accounts by literary critics, to figure out why this awful subject held such allure for him.

NABOKOV'S INITIAL EXPLORATION of an older man's unnatural desire for a preteen girl was published in 1926, within the first year of his career as a prose writer. Before then, he devoted himself exclusively to poetry. Did prose free Nabokov up to wrestle with the darkness and tumult that already surrounded him? His father, the jurist and journalist Vladimir D. Nabokov, had been assassinated four years earlier, and he was a year into his marriage to Véra Slonim, a fellow émigré he met while both lived in Berlin among the community of other Russians who'd fled the Revolution. Neither particularly cared for the city, but they stayed in Berlin for fifteen years, Nabokov supplementing his writing income and growing literary reputation by teaching tennis, boxing, and foreign languages to students.

Nabokov published his first novel, *Mashen'ka (Mary)*, in 1926, under the pseudonym of V. Sirin, which he would use for all of his poetry and prose published before he moved to America. That same year Nabokov, as Sirin, published "A Nursery Tale." The short story includes a section on a fourteen-year-old girl clad in a grown-up cocktail dress designed to show off her cleavage, though it isn't clear that the narrator, Erwin, immediately notices that aspect:

"There was something odd about that face, odd was the flitting glance of her much too shiny eyes, and if she were not just a little girl—the old man's granddaughter, no doubt—one might suspect her lips were touched up with rouge. She walked swinging her hips very, very slightly, her legs moved closer to-gether, she was asking her companion something in a ringing voice—and although Erwin gave no command mentally, he knew that his swift secret wish had been fulfilled."

Erwin's "swift secret wish" is his inappropriate desire for the girl.

Two years later, in 1928, Nabokov tackled the subject in po-etry. "Lilith" also strongly features the so-called demonic effect of a little girl, of her "russet armpit" and a "green eye over her shoulder" upon an older man: "She had a water lily in her curls and was as graceful as a woman." The poem continues:

> And how enticing, and how merry,
> her upturned face! And with a wild
> lunge of my loins I penetrated
> into an unforgotten child.
> Snake within snake, vessel in vessel
> smooth-fitting part, I moved in her,
> through the ascending itch forefeeling
> unutterable pleasure stir.

But this illicit coupling is the man's ruin. Lilith closed her-self off to him and forced him out, and as he shouts, "let me in!" his fate is sealed: "The door stayed silent, and for all to see / writhing with agony I spilled my seed / and knew abruptly that I was in Hell." Two and a half decades before *Lolita*, Nabokov anticipated Humbert Humbert's remark that he was "perfectly capable of intercourse with Eve, but it was Lilith he longed for."

Another proto-nymphet appears in *Laughter in the Dark*, though this one, Margot, is a little older: eighteen in the origi-nal version published in Russian, *Camera Obscura* (1932), and sixteen in the heavily revised and retitled edition Nabokov released six years later. (Nabokov rewrote the novel a third time in the 1960s.) Margot attracts the attention of the much-older, wealthy art critic Albert Albinus,* whose name foreshadows Humbert Humbert.

We only see Margot's actions and personality filtered through Albinus's eyes. He depicts her as capricious, whimsical, and full of manipulation. Just as in *Lolita,* when Humbert's plans are upended by the arrival of Clare Quilty, an interloper foils the relationship between Albinus and Margot. Axel Rex's affair with Margot in *Laughter in the Dark* serves a more mercenary purpose—gaining access to Albinus's status and fortune—while Quilty is after Dolores for the same illicit reasons as Humbert Humbert.

Except for Margot, who is a proper character, the early precursors to Dolores Haze are merely images that tempt and torment Nabokov's male protagonists. The image grows in substance in tandem with Nabokov's artistic growth. A paragraph in *Dar,* written between 1935 and 1937 but not published until 1952 (the English translation, published as *The Gift,* appeared a decade later), all but summarizes the future plot of *Lolita.* "What a novel I would whip off!" declares a secondary character, contemplating his much, much younger stepdaughter:

> Imagine this kind of thing: an old dog—but still in his prime, fiery, thirsting for happiness—gets to know a widow, and she has a daughter, still quite a little girl—you know what I mean—when nothing is formed yet but she has a way of walking that drives you out of

---

* In the original Russian, Albinus was called Bruno Kretchmar, while Margot's name was Magda.

your mind—A slip of a girl, very fair, pale with blue under the eyes—and of course she doesn't even look at the old goat. What to do? Well, not long [after] he ups and marries the widow. Okay. They settle down, the three of them. Here you can go on indefinitely—the temptation, the torment, the itch, the mad hopes . . .

Nabokov did not exactly "whip off" the novel that became *Lolita*. There was one more abortive attempt written in his mother tongue, *Volshebnik,* which was the last piece of fiction he wrote in Russian. He worked on it at a critical point in his life, while waiting to see if he and his family would be able to flee Europe and immigrate to America. But *Volshebnik* would not see publication until almost a decade after his death.

WHEN GERMANY DECLARED WAR on Poland in September 1939, plunging the rest of the world into global battle, Vladimir Nabokov was under considerable stress. He had reunited with his wife, Véra, and their son, Dmitri, in Paris, after an extended separation stranded them in Germany. He had broken off his affair with fellow émigré Irina Guadanini to join his family, but Paris was no safe haven anymore, as the Vichy regime became increasingly close with the Nazis. Véra was Jewish, and so was Dmitri, and if they could not get out of France, they might be bound for concentration camps.

The personal stakes were never higher, and Nabokov's health suffered. That fall, or perhaps in the early winter of 1940, he was "laid up with a severe attack of intercostal neuralgia," a mysterious ailment of damage to nerves running between the ribs that would plague him off and on for the rest of his life. He could not do much more than read and write, and he retreated into the refuge of his imagination. What emerged was *Volshebnik,* the fifty-five-page novella that most closely mirrored the future novel.

Unlike Humbert Humbert, the narrator of *Volshebnik* is nameless (though Nabokov once referred to him as "Arthur"). He does not have Humbert's artful insolence. Instead he is in torment from the first sentence, "How can I come to terms with myself?" A jeweler by trade, he moves back and forth between being open about his attraction to underage girls and his resolve to do nothing about it, coupling his inner torment to overweening self-justification. "I'm no ravisher," he declares. "I am a pickpocket, not a burglar." Humbert would sneer at the hypocrisy of this declaration.

Nabokov was not the artist he would later become, and it shows in the prose: "I'm not attracted to every schoolgirl that comes along, far from it—how many one sees, on a gray morning street that are husky, or skinny, or have a necklace of pimples or wear spectacles—*those* kinds interest me as little, in the amorous sense, as a lumpy female acquaintance might interest someone else." He doesn't have the wherewithal to describe his chosen prey, whom he first sees roller-skating in a park, as a nymphet. Such a word isn't in his vocabulary because it wasn't yet in Nabokov's.

Still there are glimpses of *Lolita*'s formidable style, as when *Volshebnik*'s narrator comments on "the radiance of [one girl's] large, slightly vacuous eyes, somehow suggesting translucent gooseberries" or "the summery tint of her bare arms with the sleek little foxlike hairs running along the forearms." Not quite up to the level and the hypnotic rhythm of Humbert's rhapsodizing about Dolores Haze ("The soot-black lashes of her pale-gray vacant eyes . . . I might say her hair is auburn, and her lips as red as licked candy"), but the disquiet is present, waiting to spring like a trapdoor.

As in the later novel, Nabokov's narrator preys upon his underage quarry through her mother. She is more broadly cast than Charlotte Haze, whose rages against and aspirations for her daughter make her an interesting figure. The mother here is little more than a cipher, a plot device to engineer the man and girl toward their fates.

Volshebnik's narrator may be tormented by his unnatural tastes, but he knows he is about to entice his chosen girl to cross a chasm that cannot be uncrossed. Namely, she is innocent now, but she won't be after he has his way with her. Humbert Humbert would never be so obvious. He has the "fancy prose style" at his disposal to couch or deflect his intentions. So when he does state the obvious—as he will, again and again— the reader is essentially magicked into believing Dolores is as much the pursuer as the pursuee.

Both men's plans are the same: "He knew he would make no attempt on her virginity in the tightest and pinkest sense of the term until the evolution of their caresses had ascended a certain invisible step," says *Volshebnik*'s narrator. He also sets the same stage for his seduction, in a faraway hotel, away from knowing, prying eyes, or so he thinks. The hotel, in Europe, is less shabby than Humbert's choice of The Enchanted Hunters, but serves the same purpose: allowing the narrator to watch over the sleeping girl and make his move against her will.

The outcome differs from *Lolita*. The narrator is consumed by the girl lying supine on the bed, robe half-open, and begins "little by little to cast his spell . . . passing his magic wand above her body," measuring her "with an enchanted yardstick." Here, again, Humbert Humbert would sneer. But then he did not have the girl look "wild-eyed at his rearing nudity," caught out like the pedophile he is. Nor does Humbert become "deafened by his own horror" when the girl begins to scream at his rejected advances. Humbert is all about self-justification; *Volshebnik*'s narrator suffers no such delusion about his quarry.

He tries to soothe the girl—"be quiet, it's nothing bad, it's just a kind of game, it happens sometimes, just be quiet"—but she will not be placated. And when two old women burst into the room, he flees, only to be hit by a truck, the ensuing gory mess described as "an instantaneous cinema of dismemberment." The narrator's fate is awful and inevitable. He is the predator hunted, captured, taken down. The girl's big bad wolf is punished by a passing truck.

Nabokov did not publish *Volshebnik* during his lifetime because he knew, as was clear to me upon reading it, that the story was not a stand-alone work but source material. It is more straightforward and less sophisticated than *Lolita*. As the scholar Simon Karlinsky wrote when *Volshebnik* was finally published in English as *The Enchanter* in 1986, the novella's pleasure is "comparable to the one afforded by studying Beethoven's published sketchbooks: seeing the murky and unpromising material out of which the writer and the composer were later able to fashion an incandescent masterpiece."

In other words, the story carries equal value to the creation of *Lolita* as did the story of Sally Horner. One was fiction; the other was truth. But art is fickle and merciless, as Nabokov explained repeatedly throughout his life. *Volshebnik* possesses a powerful engine of its own. It does not possess *Lolita*'s literary trickery and mastery of obfuscation, which continue to make moral mincemeat out of the novel's wider readership. Here, instead, is a more prosaic depiction of deviant compulsion and tragic consequences.

TWO OTHER WORKS are notable influences upon *Lolita*. Annabel Leigh, Humbert Humbert's first love, is named in homage to Edgar Allan Poe's poem "Annabel Lee." The novel's working title, *The Kingdom by the Sea,* is a quote from that poem, and Humbert's memories of his Annabel, dead of typhus four months after their seaside near-consummation, echo many more of Poe's lines. (Nabokov: "I was a child and she was a child." Poe: "I was a child and she was a child.")

Lolita also owes a great deal to an influence never explicitly referenced in the text, but one Nabokov knew well from translating into Russian in his early twenties: *Alice's Adventures in Wonderland,* by Lewis Carroll. As he later explained to the literary critic Alfred Appel:

"[Carroll] has a pathetic affinity with Humbert Humbert but some odd scruple prevented me from alluding in *Lolita* to his wretched perversion and to those ambiguous photographs he took in dim rooms. He got away with it, as so many Victorians got away with pederasty and nympholepsy. His were sad scrawny little nymphets, bedraggled and half-undressed, or rather semi-undraped, as if participating in some dusty and dreadful charade."

Perhaps a similar "odd scruple" may explain why Nabokov was quick to deny any connection between *Lolita* and a real-life figure he knew early on in his American tenure. Henry Lanz was a Stanford professor of motley European stock, "of Finnish descent, son of a naturalized American father, born in Moscow and educated there and in Germany." He was fluent in many languages, an avid chess player. By World War I Lanz was in London, married, at the age of thirty, to a fourteen-year-old.

Not long after the Nabokovs immigrated to America in May 1940, arriving in New York on the SS *Champlain*, Lanz arranged for Nabokov to teach at Stanford. Their friendship grew over regular chess games; Nabokov beat Lanz more than two hundred times. Over these jousts Lanz revealed his predilections—specifically, that he most enjoyed seducing young girls and he loved to watch them urinate. Four years later, Lanz was dead of a heart attack at the age of fifty-nine.

Nabokov's first biographer, Andrew Field, suggested that Lanz was a prototype for Humbert Humbert. Nabokov, however, denied it: "No, no, no. I may have had [Lanz] in the back of my mind. He himself was what is called a fountainist, like Bloom in *Ulysses*. First of all, this is the commonest thing. In Swiss papers they always call them un triste individuel."

Such a denial makes sense, in light of other future denials of real-life influence. Yet the months Nabokov spent being peppered with stories from a known pederast could not help but inform his fiction—and further bolster his involuntary, unconscious need to unspool *this* particular, horrible narrative.

SEVEN

Frank, in Shadow

U nlike Humbert Humbert, there was nothing erudite about Frank La Salle. His prison writings are unreliable, lacking the silky sheen that is *Lolita*'s narrative hallmark; grammatical mistakes pepper La Salle's rambling and incoherent oral and typewritten declamations. When he was employed, irregularly at best, he worked blue-collar jobs, a far cry from teaching foreign languages.

La Salle was a crude, slippery figure, who lied so much in middle age that it was impossible for me to verify the facts of the first four decades of his life. One pseudonym dead-ended into another. Calls and emails to helpful, friendly archivists around the country bore no fruit, save for commiseration over my extended, failed, quest.

Without knowing the substance of his childhood and upbringing, and whether or not his predilections asserted themselves early on, it was difficult for me to determine where he came by his long-running desire for young girls. La Salle behaved as a pedophile, but it's hard to say whether that was his orientation—compulsion spurring opportunity—or he impulsively seized on opportunity as a means of asserting power. Whatever he was is dwarfed by what he did.

A likely birth date is May 27, 1895, give or take a year, somewhere in the Midwest. Frank La Salle was probably not his birth name. Once, he said that his parents were Frank Patterson and Nora LaPlante. Another time he wrote down their names as Frank La Salle and Nora Johnson. He hailed from Indianapolis, or perhaps Chicago. He said he served four years at the Leavenworth, Kansas, federal prison between 1924 and 1928 on a bootlegging charge, but the prison has no record of him being there during those years. He needed a new origin story every time he changed aliases, among them Patterson, Johnson, LaPlante, and O'Keefe. As far as I could find out, the first name almost never varied.

For someone who shrouded his life in secrecy, it seems fitting that one of his most notorious aliases was that of Frank Fogg.

It is as Fogg that a sharper picture forms of the man later known as La Salle. In the summer of 1937, Fogg had a wife and a nine-year-old son. They lived in a trailer in Maple Shade, New Jersey. He claimed that his wife took their son and ran away with a mechanic. It's possible that might be true. By July 14 they were gone, and just over a week later Fogg himself would become a fugitive, with a new wife in tow.

He met her at a carnival: Dorothy Dare, not quite eighteen, with brown curly hair that framed an openhearted, bespectacled face. Born in Philadelphia, the oldest of six, Dorothy lived with her family in Merchantville, a ten-minute car trip from

Maple Shade, and had graduated high school just the month before. Fights with her father over his strict parenting had grown so tense that Dorothy looked for every chance to escape. At the carnival, she found it in the man calling himself Frank Fogg.

He was more than twice as old as Dorothy, but she didn't mind the age difference. He wanted to marry her and she thought it was a terrific idea to elope. Which they did, only a few days after meeting, to Elkton, Maryland, the "Gretna Green of the United States," where weddings happened fast with few questions asked.

Dorothy's father, David Dare, was livid. Though they fought, he knew Dorothy was fundamentally a good girl. Even if she was not, technically, a minor, she was young, and this Fogg fellow was clearly not. When Dare discovered that Fogg was using a fake name, and was actually married, he got local police to swear out an eight-state warrant for the man's arrest on kidnapping and statutory rape charges on July 22, 1937. He claimed that Dorothy was fifteen, and thus a minor. The law caught up with the couple ten days later.

Cops arrested La Salle, still using the Fogg alias, in Roxborough, Pennsylvania, where he'd found a job, and took him to jail in Haddonfield, New Jersey. The charge: enticing a minor. Bail: withheld. Police simultaneously picked up Dorothy in the Philadelphia neighborhood of Wissahickon, where the couple had rented a room, and also brought her to jail. The two had a surprise for the arresting officers: Dorothy was not a minor, their Elkton marriage was legit, and Frank had the certificate, dated July 31, to prove it.

"He told me the truth," Dorothy cried, nervously fingering the shiny gold ring on her left hand. "I know he did. He couldn't have been married before. But if he did—oh, I'd just want to die!" Not long after uttering those words, Dorothy was released from jail, and slipped away from her parents, not yet ready to give up on her new husband, Frank.

The next morning, La Salle appeared in Delaware Township court. Dorothy was not there; nor did anyone know her whereabouts. Her father, however, was very much present. When he spotted La Salle, he punched the other man in the jaw. Dare grew even more furious when the presiding judge, Ralph King, dismissed the charges against La Salle, after the man testified that Dorothy had gone with him of her own will, and that they were lawfully married.

"I'll lock you up if you aren't careful," King warned Dare after he raised his voice in court one too many times demanding La Salle be held. But in the end, Dare got his wish, because the court wasn't done with Frank.

A day after the eight-state warrant had gone out on the wire, there was a hit-and-run accident near Marlton. A car resembling the one La Salle drove collided with a car owned by a man named Curt Scheffler. The driver of the first car fled the scene. La Salle, in court, denied he had been the driver. Justice of the Peace Oliver Bowen disagreed. On August 11, 1937, La Salle was fined fifty dollars and sentenced to fifteen days in jail. He also received an additional thirty days' sentence after failing to pay a two-hundred-dollar fine for giving false information. When he got out of jail, Dorothy was waiting. They picked up their marriage where it had been interrupted, and, apparently, the next few years were happy ones.

Dorothy and Frank, who cast off the Fogg alias and was La Salle once more, moved to Atlantic City. Their daughter, Madeline (not her real name), was born in 1939, and the young family were living at 203 Pacific Avenue when the Census came knocking a year later. So, too, did police, who this time arrested

La Salle on bigamy charges. Few details are available—was it the earlier wife or a different woman?—save that La Salle wriggled out of it with an acquittal.

Two years later, when Madeline was three, Dorothy sued Frank for desertion and nonpayment of child support. Dare family lore had it that Dorothy discovered her husband in a car with another woman, and grew so enraged she hit the other woman over the head with her shoe.

What was passed down as a dark but amusing family story turned out to hide a more sinister truth. What Dorothy Dare discovered about her husband first came to light in the wee hours of March 10, 1942.

THREE CAMDEN POLICE OFFICERS walked into a restaurant on Broadway near the corner of Penn and spotted a girl sitting alone in a booth. Women sitting by themselves in public at three in the morning still stand out. Imagine what the cops thought in the early 1940s when they stumbled across a twelve-year-old girl all on her own so late in the night.

When acting sergeant Edward Shapiro and patrolmen Thomas Carroll and Donald Watson asked the girl what she was up to, "being out alone at such an hour," she evaded their questioning. So the policemen took her back to headquarters, where a city detective would ask the questions.

Under gentle coaxing by police sergeant John V. Wilkie, the girl opened up. She admitted she'd been out that night because she "had a date with a man about 40 years old." The man's name, she said, was Frank La Salle. He'd given her a card with the phone number and address of the Philadelphia auto body shop where he worked.

In his report, Wilkie wrote that the girl said La Salle had

"forced her into intimacies." The girl almost certainly used plainer language. She also told Wilkie that La Salle made her introduce him to four of her friends by threatening to tell her mother what she had done with him.

The five girls were Loretta, Margaret, Sarah, Erma, and Virginia.* From the available records, it's not clear which of them was the one in the diner, but based on their birth dates, it was likely Loretta or Margaret. (Sarah, the oldest, had just turned fifteen.) All of them lived in Camden County, either in the city or in nearby Pennsauken. All of them were named in a 1944 divorce petition by Dorothy Dare as having "committed adultery" with her husband.

When police brought the other girls in to be questioned, Wilkie reported, each of them also told of "how they had been raped by La Salle."

SERGEANT WILKIE SWORE OUT a warrant for Frank La Salle's arrest, alerting police in Philadelphia of the twelve-year-old girl's sickening allegation. But when police showed up at La Salle's workplace, he wasn't there. They didn't find him at his last known address, either. Who knows how La Salle learned the police were coming for him, but he had fled. What's more, police learned, he'd gone back to his earlier alias of Fogg. They dug up an address in Maple Shade, then received word that he, Dorothy, and Madeline had moved back to Camden.

Police got a tip La Salle and his family now lived at a house on the 1000 block on Cooper Street. They kept the place under

---

* I am withholding their last names to protect the privacy of their families, and because of the difficulty in locating descendants to verify the details.

constant surveillance, hoping he might turn up. On the evening of March 15, a car pulled up in front of the house. The car had a license number linked to La Salle.

Detectives rushed into the house. They found and arrested a nineteen-year-old man who claimed he was La Salle's brother-in-law. But no La Salle. "We found out later," Wilkie said, "that as detectives walked up the front steps, La Salle made his escape out the back door."

For nearly a year, La Salle eluded the law. An official indictment for the statutory rape of the five girls came down on September 4, 1942. Tips streamed into Camden and Philadelphia police placing him in New Jersey, and sometimes in Pennsylvania, but nothing panned out—not until the beginning of February 1943, when cops got a tip that La Salle now lived at 1414 Euclid Avenue in Philadelphia, in the heart of where Temple University stands today.

On February 2, police descended upon the house and found La Salle, alone. They arrested him, taking him back to Camden to be arraigned. The Camden city court judge who signed the indictment and oversaw the February 10 hearing was a man named Mitchell Cohen. The two men would meet again, seven years later, in even more explosive circumstances.

La Salle pleaded not guilty to the multiple rape indictments from the Camden grand jury, but on March 22, 1943, he changed his plea to *non vult*, or no contest. The presiding judge, Bartholomew Sheehan, sentenced La Salle to two and a half years on each rape charge, to be served concurrently at Trenton State Prison.

WHILE LA SALLE was incarcerated, Dorothy and Madeline had moved back to Merchantville to be closer to Dorothy's parents.

Mug shot of Frank La Salle taken upon the start of his prison sentence for the statutory rape of five girls, 1943.

She moved quickly to divorce him, filing a petition on January 11, 1944, stating that La Salle had "committed adultery" with the five girls beginning on March 9, 1942—the night the first girl reported her rape to police—and "at various times" between that date and February 1943, when La Salle was finally arrested. Frank wrote her frequently from prison—a habit he would repeat later in life—but if he meant to persuade Dorothy to stay married to him, he was not successful.

La Salle was paroled on June 18, 1944, after fourteen months in prison. He took a room at the YMCA on Broadway and Federal, registered for the draft, and got his Social Security card. He also had to register with the city as a convicted criminal; a blurry photo from June 29, 1944, shows a middle-aged man with gray hair, blue eyes, high cheekbones, and a squint. He wore a more subdued expression than in the prison intake photo from March 1943, where he'd smirked at the camera, seemingly free from worry or care.

La Salle found work as a car mechanic in Philadelphia, but found himself in repeated trouble with the law. An indecent assault charge was dropped on Halloween, but the following August, he got caught at Camden's Third National Bank trying to pass off a forged $110 check. He was indicted the following month and swiftly convicted for "obtaining money under false pretenses." His divorce from Dorothy also moved toward completion that same month. The family court judge awarded full custody of Madeline to her mother on August 21. The divorce was final on November 23.

La Salle returned to Trenton State Prison on March 18, 1946, to serve eighteen months to five years on the new charges. The clock also began again on the balance of the statutory rape sentence. La Salle finished up both those sentences in January 1948, and was paroled again on the fifteenth of that month.

Now that he was back on the streets, it seems likely La Salle went to the downtown Camden YMCA for a cheap place to stay. It was across the street from Woolworth's, where weeks later, on a crisp March afternoon, he would spy a ten-year-old girl attempting to steal a five-cent notebook.

EIGHT

"A Lonely Mother Waits"

The more months that slipped by without answers, the greater the existential toll on Sally Horner's family. Ella bore the brunt of it. Sally was her daughter. She'd let the girl go off with a stranger because he'd said he was the father of school friends, who were waiting for her down by the Jersey Shore. She believed the lies the man forced her daughter to tell, and now the girl was gone.

Perhaps Ella entertained fleeting thoughts that Sally was dead, but she never admitted it in public. She'd found work as a seamstress for Quartermaster Depot, so at least there was enough money coming in to keep the lights on in the house, as well as the telephone in operation. Sally hadn't called home again, but if she ever chose to, it would be a disaster if the line was disconnected.

Ella aired her anguish in a December 10, 1948, article published by the *Philadelphia Inquirer*, headlined "A Christmas Tree Glows, a Lonely Mother Waits." Sally had been missing for nearly half a year by that point. Ella kept a figurative candle burning for the time when her daughter would return home safe. And with Christmas a little more than two weeks away, the tree Ella set up was, according to the unbylined reporter, "freighted with memories of other and happier Christmases," a means of multiplying the "candle's tiny gleam." Ella could think of no better way to express her faith that Sally would come back to her.

When that happened—Ella could not allow herself to think "if," only "when"—Sally would have to contend with one very big change to the family. Her niece, Diana, was five months old when the article appeared in the *Inquirer*. But Diana's arrival couldn't help but be bittersweet for her grandmother, Susan, and her husband, as long as they had no clue to Sally's whereabouts. Sally had so looked forward to being an aunt.

The young couple buried their uncertainty and despair in the daily care of their new baby. Changing diapers, rocking her to sleep, trying to get much-needed rest in small bursts. They also had the family greenhouse to look after—the flowers and plants wouldn't grow themselves.

Ella was thrilled to be a grandmother. But her joy was always tempered so long as Sally wasn't here with her. And as she told the *Inquirer*, the moment Sally walked back through the front door at 944 Linden Street, she would not be punished in any way. "Whatever she has done, I can forgive her for it. If I can just have her back again."

SALLY HORNER'S TWELFTH BIRTHDAY, on April 18, 1949, came and went with no news. Had she vanished into the ether?

Would her body turn up? Or was Sally out there, ready to be found, hoping that she would come home again? Camden police kept the case open, and Marshall Thompson tracked every lead.

The case had taken on added urgency a month earlier, on March 17, when the Camden County prosecutor's office added a second, more serious, indictment of kidnapping to the existing charge against La Salle. Where abduction carried a maximum prison sentence of only a few years, a kidnapping conviction upped the ante to between thirty and thirty-five years—effectively, for someone of Frank La Salle's age, a life sentence.

No documents have survived to explain the more serious charge. Perhaps the prosecutor, or the Camden Police Department, had received a credible tip to La Salle's whereabouts and hoped that news of the new indictment might flush him out. Or perhaps there were concerns about the statute of limitations on the original abduction charge if Sally stayed missing for a long time, or even forever.

The media moved on from covering the story. No one marked the first anniversary of her disappearance. At Christmas 1949, they did not publicize appeals for Sally's safe return. Other sensational local crimes pushed her out of the papers, including a mass shooting on Camden's East Side and another mysterious disappearance: that of the wife of Jules Forstein, a Philadelphia magistrate.

Dorothy Forstein's disappearance baffled investigators. She had spent the previous four years in a state of anxiety after an unknown assailant nearly killed her just outside her front door. On the evening of October 18, 1949, Dorothy's husband, Jules, attended a party on his own. He said he asked Dorothy to come with him, but she insisted she'd rather stay home with the children, stepdaughter Marcy, nine, and their seven-year-old, Edward.

When Jules got home at 11:30 P.M. Dorothy was gone and the children were frantic. They claimed a stranger had come into the house, knocked their mother unconscious, and then hefted the five-foot-two, 125-pound woman, clad in pajamas and red slippers, over his shoulder, carrying her out and locking the door behind them. Before he left, he patted Marcy on the head and told her, "Go back to sleep." Marcy recalled that he was wearing a brown cap and "something brown in his shirt."

Jules said he did not report Dorothy missing right away because he thought Marcy was telling a fib, and believed—oddly, considering her near-agoraphobia—that his wife must still be in the neighborhood. He called police four and a half hours later, just before 4:00 A.M. The police also brushed off Marcy's story as fantasy. Then a female psychiatrist was called in to question the little girl, and after several lengthy conversations, the psychiatrist concluded Marcy was telling the truth about what happened that night.

Over the next few days, people reported sightings of the missing woman all over the Philadelphia area. Camden also figured in the initial investigation. The Friday night after Dorothy vanished, Camden patrolman Edward Shapiro noticed a blond woman hovering around the corner of Broadway and Fourth Street. Shapiro told Philadelphia detectives he first saw the woman coming out of a telephone booth next to a candy store. She seemed startled to see him, and he was himself startled by how much she resembled Dorothy Forstein. Shapiro followed her to a tavern, where she ordered a beer, but when the woman noticed him again, she split.

The following night, Shapiro saw the woman again on the same corner, and overheard her speaking with a male companion. "I've only got one arm," he heard the woman say. This statement caused detectives to perk up. One of Dorothy's lingering injuries from her earlier attack was a recurrent dislocated shoulder that landed her in the hospital for treatment several times a year. Detectives were certain Dorothy, even under a false name, might turn up at a hospital to have her shoulder reset again. She did not. A thousand-dollar reward offered by Jules Forstein yielded no new leads. Dorothy was declared legally dead eight years later, in 1957, a year after her husband had died of a heart attack at home.

SALLY'S FAMILY took the waning public interest as a sign that it was better not to speak of her disappearance, even among themselves. Her absence was a low thrum, ever-present but unacknowledged. Of course they worried. Of course they feared for her safety. But no news meant no answers, and her fate was beyond their control. It was better to carry on with life.

Baby Diana turned one in August 1949. She was, by her parents' account and her own later recollection, a happy little girl, eager and talkative, who loved eating Grape-Nuts and drinking apple juice. Al ran the greenhouse, and Susan stopped in when she was up to it. Ella remained at 944 Linden Street, but living there was like a nightmare. "It was so different when Sally was here," she later recalled. "She was so cheerful and full of life."

Ella had difficulty sleeping. Many times in the night she would leave her room and go to Sally's. She would take out her daughter's toys and games and "just sit there and look at them." Ella washed and rewashed Sally's clothes "so they would be ready for her when she came back."

As the months wore on, she lost jobs and found others.

Sometimes she couldn't pay her bills for weeks. Sometimes the phone got disconnected, or the electricity was shut off. Periodically, Ella would go to Florence to stay with Susan and look after her granddaughter. Otherwise, Ella was alone. Alone to contemplate again and again the ways in which she held herself responsible for Sally's disappearance.

NINE

The Prosecutor

S ally Horner disappeared a few months after Mitchell Cohen was appointed as prosecutor for Camden County, a
ten-year term that would last until 1958. He was already
on the way to becoming the pivotal law enforcement figure in
the city, a status that saw his name emblazoned, decades later,
on the downtown federal courthouse. Taking on the prosecutor
gig only bolstered his reputation. In the late 1940s, Camden
County did not have enough major crime to justify a full-time
prosecutor. So Cohen worked in spurts, spending the rest of
his time on Republican party politics. He was so successful at
it that he became the state party's de facto leader, allied closely
with the New Jersey governor of the day, Alfred Driscoll.

Cohen's term as prosecutor was one of many jobs he held
in law enforcement over a long legal career that stretched from
early private practice with local law firms all the way to chief

judge for the federal district court of New Jersey. He moved smoothly between prosecuting criminals and delivering judgments. Cohen wasn't one to bask in career glories, though. He was far too busy working to spend much time reflecting on the past.

Cohen did, however, take the time to dress the part of a bigshot lawyer. In his bespoke suits, he cut a figure that landed somewhere between David Niven and Fred Astaire. One lawyer told Cohen's son, Fred, "Whenever I appeared in front of your father, I felt I wanted to wear a white tie and tails and be at the top of my game because he was a classy guy."

Any resemblance Cohen bore to famous actors was, perhaps, intentional. He caught the bug for theater early in life, making trips up to New York to see Broadway shows a priority. In his younger years, Cohen spent his Saturday nights in line for concerts and stage performances at Philadelphia's Academy of Music, angling for a twenty-five-cent seat in the gallery. Once established in his legal career, he could afford to split a box seat with a friend.

He'd met Herman Levin at South Philadelphia High; they remained pals even after Cohen's family moved to Camden just before his senior year. The boys made a point of seeing every play in Philadelphia—long a city where Broadway-bound shows worked out problems and test-ran productions on audiences—on opening night. Levin ended up producing musicals like *Gentlemen Prefer Blondes, Destry Rides Again*, and *My Fair Lady*. Before the latter show opened in 1956, Levin told Cohen to "hock everything he had in the world" to invest in the production. Cohen did, and reaped the benefits as *My Fair Lady* smashed box-office records. Cohen also became a theatrical producer himself, cochairing the short-lived Camden County Music Circus during the summers of 1956 and 1957.

But Cohen's fashion sense, his theatrical interests, and even his political machinations did not overshadow his commitment to jurisprudence. Cohen cared about the law and about being fair. He believed it was as important to know when *not* to prosecute a case as when to prosecute. In 1938, early in his tenure as acting judge for the city of Camden, a husband and wife appeared together in his courtroom after she had attempted suicide by poison—back then a punishable crime.

"We had a quarrel, and I thought he didn't love me anymore," the twenty-eight-year-old woman told Cohen.

"Do you?" Cohen asked her husband, who was twenty-nine.

"I sure do."

"Then go home and forget about it."

Cohen didn't seek out notorious cases. They found him. When he won a trial, he didn't dwell upon the details. Those cases, and how Cohen approached them, are an important window into 1940s Camden, as well as the forces that set the city up for great societal changes.

WHEN MITCHELL COHEN set out to prosecute the men responsible for the murder of Wanda Dworecki in the fall of 1939, he had never worked on a capital case before, even though he'd been appointed city prosecutor for Camden three years earlier. Murders were rare then, a far cry from the statistics that designated the city as America's murder capital as recently as 2012. The strangulation of a girl a month shy of her eighteenth birthday stood out in its singular brutality.

Wanda's body was discovered on the morning of August 8, 1939, in an area near Camden High School frequently used as a lovers' lane. A corsage of red and white roses adorned her neck. The killer strangled her so forcefully that he broke her collarbone and breastbone. Then he dropped a rock onto her head, fracturing her skull.

Police working on the case weren't all that surprised Wanda had died so violently. Four months before her murder, in April 1939, two men had accosted Wanda on the street and thrown her into their car. They beat her up—a near-fatal assault—and tossed her out into a field in a desolate part of Salem County, just south of Camden. She spent weeks recovering in the hospital.

That beating wasn't Wanda's first brush with violence. In late 1938, she and a friend had been out walking in the neighborhood when several men tried to kidnap them. Police were convinced—or at least, this is what they said—that Wanda was "destined to be murdered." What they would soon learn is how much one man manipulated things so that destiny would become reality.

Wanda's father, Walter Dworecki, who had emigrated from Poland in 1913, appeared to be an upstanding figure. He preached at the First Polish Baptist Church, a congregation he'd founded when the family moved to Camden from rural Pennsylvania. His teenage daughter troubled him, especially after her mother, Theresa, collapsed at the breakfast table and died in 1938. He brooded over Wanda's fondness for the opposite sex, lecturing her about preserving her virtue, verbally abusing her in such a way to make an example of her to her younger siblings, Mildred and Alfred.

Respectable appearances can hide awful secrets, and Dworecki had plenty. Like being out on bail for setting fire to a house in Chester, Pennsylvania, in a scheme to collect insurance. Or having been sentenced to five years' probation for passing counterfeit money. Like getting so angry at a neighborhood boy that he allegedly fractured the teen's jaw with a broomstick. Or taking out a $2,500 life insurance policy (nearly

$45,000 in 2018 dollars) on his wife, Theresa, whose cause of death was officially "lobar pneumonia"—the same cause of death listed for a number of victims of a murder-for-insurance scheme in Philadelphia whose culprits had some connections to the preacher.

The secret Walter Dworecki should have tried harder to keep was his fondness for hanging around Philadelphia dives, looking for men who might be willing and able to kill his daughter.

Immediately after Wanda's murder, Dworecki slipped into the role of grieving father. He cried, "My poor Wanda!" when he saw his daughter's body at the morgue, and then fainted. He had an alibi for the time of her death, but his grief-stricken act cracked quickly once police started to investigate.

A witness had seen Wanda with a "large blond gentleman" the night before she was murdered, who turned out to be twenty-year-old Peter Shewchuk, who boarded at the Dworeckis' and romanced Wanda every now and then. When Shewchuk learned he was wanted for questioning, he fled Camden for his boyhood home in rural Pennsylvania. Police caught up to him on August 27, after his father turned him in.

In the interview room, all it took was the offer of a single cigarette for Shewchuk to open up. He told the detectives that he and Dworecki had met up in Philadelphia earlier in the evening of August 7. "He gave me 50 cents to cover my expenses and then went to conduct his religious services. I met Wanda and we strolled down the street." Walking past the lovers' lane, Shewchuk said he "suddenly felt the urge to kill" Wanda the way her father had told him to: "Choke her, hit her with a rock, twist her neck." Dworecki was supposed to pay Shewchuk a hundred dollars for the murder, but after Wanda was dead, he reneged on the deal.

Armed with Shewchuk's confession, Camden police brought in the preacher. It turned out Dworecki had taken out a life insurance policy on Wanda around the same time as he had taken one out on her mother. He had hired three men, including Shewchuk, to kidnap and kill Wanda back in April. When she survived the failed attempt, Dworecki upped the policy on his daughter to nearly $2,700, with a double indemnity clause should she die in an accident, and got ready to try again.

Dworecki eventually confessed in a statement that ran to nearly thirty pages. The preacher admitted to being aggrieved by Wanda's behavior, but he claimed the idea to kill Wanda originated with two men, Joe Rock and John Popolo, whom he'd met in Philadelphia. Dworecki said they urged him to kill his daughter to collect the insurance money and pressed him again as time went on. He roped Shewchuk into the murder plot after learning the younger man had bragged about sleeping with Wanda. Shewchuk denied it, but Dworecki sensed an opportunity to manipulate the boy into carrying out his murderous scheme.

Both men entered guilty pleas in Camden County Court on August 29, 1939. Dworecki refused to look at anyone. Shewchuk chose the opposite tack, smiling whenever someone caught his eye. Then Mitchell Cohen, the city prosecutor, explained to the assembled crowd, including the surprised defendants and their lawyers, why the guilty pleas had to be thrown out. New Jersey state law at the time stipulated that one was not allowed to be sentenced to death if he pleaded guilty. Capital cases, and murder certainly counted, required that the defendants face a full trial, verdict, and sentencing.

Cohen voided the pleas, then bound the cases over to the county court, where Samuel Orlando (whom Cohen would succeed a few years later) would prosecute them. Cohen's work was done, but he paid attention to what happened in the county courtroom. Orlando cross-examined both Shewchuk and Dworecki with extra vigor. Shewchuk received a life sentence in exchange for being the primary witness against Dworecki. The preacher's confession was admitted into evidence, despite his lawyer protesting it should be kept out. The jury found him guilty after swift deliberations.

Shewchuk was paroled in 1959 after surviving his own near-fatal beating in prison; he died in the late 1980s. Dworecki was put to death by electric chair on March 28, 1940. Before his execution, he implored his surviving children, Mildred and Alfred, to lead pious lives and asked that "God have mercy on their souls." Dworecki's grave lies next to that of the daughter he murdered.

UNLIKE THE DWORECKI CASE, where Cohen did not have to work to establish the defendants' guilt, he played a larger role in a subsequent murder trial that garnered a great deal of media attention. This case concerned the death of twenty-three-year-old Margaret McDade (Rita to her friends) on August 14, 1945, as Philadelphia, Camden, and the entire country celebrated V-J Day. That night, Rita's best friend and fellow waitress Ann Rust saw her in the arms of a stranger, dancing to a Johnny Mercer tune. Five days later, Rita was found naked and dead at the bottom of a cistern near a sewage disposal plant. An autopsy determined that she had been raped, beaten bloody, and tossed into the cistern alive. She died of suffocation.

Not long after, police arrested the stranger Rita had danced with on the last night she was seen alive. Howard Auld was a former army paratrooper, recently discharged. When police found him, Auld gave them a fake name ("George Jackson") and claimed to be innocent. Discharge papers he carried caught him out on the first lie. Careful interrogation spurred Auld to confess to McDade's murder.

Auld recounted an all-too-familiar, all-too-horrible story: after the dance, he had made a move on Rita that she turned down. He got angry, punched her in the face, and choked her until she passed out. Auld claimed he felt for a pulse and, when he found none, dumped her into the cistern. (Never mind that she was still alive and he omitted mention of the rape.) Auld's time in the army also included repeated stints in a mental hospital and various bouts of violent behavior, which his lawyer, a court-appointed defense attorney named Rocco Palese, would use as a mitigating circumstance in the trial.

Auld was sentenced to death for Rita McDade's murder in 1946, but the conviction was tossed out on appeal several months later. The presiding judge, Bartholomew Sheehan, had failed to tell the jury that they could recommend mercy—meaning, a verdict other than death—in finding Auld guilty of first-degree murder. The Camden County prosecutor's office moved quickly to try Auld again, but proceedings did not begin until 1948, after Mitchell Cohen's appointment as top prosecutor.

Sheehan was also the judge for the second trial. Cohen asked for the death penalty, in accordance with New Jersey state law. Auld's new court-appointed attorney, John Morrissey—Palese had since been appointed as a judge—implored the jury to be lenient toward his client, "a feeble-minded boy," and deliver a not-guilty verdict by reason of insanity. But Cohen prevailed with the jury. Morrissey indicated he would appeal, and did, several times over, delaying the execution date a half dozen times. Howard Auld did not die in New Jersey's "Old Smokey" until March 27, 1951. His final words were "Jesus, have mercy on me."

BY THE END OF 1949, Mitchell Cohen had established his bona fides as Camden County prosecutor. He had tried one capital case directly and worked on another, even though he was deeply conflicted about the death penalty. Decades later his son, Fred, recalled Cohen becoming "very emotional" when the subject came up, so much so that they did not discuss it again. Cohen did his duty, whether asking for the harshest sentence as a prosecutor or delivering the sentence as a judge. But he did not have to like it and, with that single exception, took care not to bring his feelings home to the Rittenhouse Square town house he shared with his family.

He would also vault onto the national stage with his handling of a case that would shake the city to its foundation, and foreshadow similar massacres in the decades to come. But he did not close the books on Sally Horner's abduction. To his knowledge, the new kidnapping charge had not flushed out Frank La Salle. Sally was still missing. And the more time passed, the less likely the outcome would be a good one.

TEN

Baltimore

H ere's the point in the narrative where I would like to tell you everything that happened to Sally Horner after Frank La Salle spirited her away from Atlantic City to Baltimore, and the eight months they lived in the city, from August 1948 through April 1949. The trouble is, I didn't find out all that much. A scattershot list of addresses and court documents can't bring to life what a little girl thought or felt. Visiting the neighborhood where Sally lived, and walking by the school she attended, can't adequately bridge the decades. The neighborhood has changed, demographically and socio-economically. Sally, were she still alive today, would barely recognize it.

The meager paper trail frustrated me. My patience frayed as I ran up against dead end after dead end, record search after fruitless record search, to try to build up a picture of the months Sally lived in Baltimore. If she made friends, or had someone she felt she could trust, I couldn't find them. If there are people still living who knew her at the time, I could not track them down. If she kept a journal during her captivity, it did not survive. She did go to school in Baltimore—a Catholic school—but if any of its records remain, they are buried under decades of detritus no one has the inclination to sift through.

But I needed to understand what Sally was thinking and feeling—or at least approximate an understanding—so I read as many accounts as I could find by girls, born one or two generations after her, who survived years or decades of abuse by their kidnappers. I also examined kidnappings from the decade or so before Sally was taken.

Stranger abductions are rare now and were, perhaps, even rarer when Sally vanished. That's why the kidnapping of Charles Lindbergh, Jr., in 1932 caught America's attention and held it for weeks. The celebrity of the boy's parents, superstar pilot Charles Lindbergh and his wife, Anne Morrow Lindbergh, certainly helped, but the boy's snatching felt like the manifestation of every parent's worst fear—that their child might be stolen in the middle of the night from his bedroom by strangers—and kept the country gripped until the baby's body was discovered weeks later.

Abductions where the child is held for a significant period of time before being rescued alive occur with even lesser frequency. That's why, fourteen years before Sally Horner's abduction, the kidnapping of six-year-old June Robles, the daughter of a well-to-do Tucson, Arizona, family, stood out. A man driving a Ford sedan waited for June after school on April 25, 1934, and enticed her to get into his car. Several ransom notes arrived at the Robles household. The first demanded fifteen thousand dollars; the second, ten thousand. Days passed with false sightings and near-arrests, until a Chicago-postmarked letter delivered to Arizona governor B. B. Moeur's residence described where June was being held. A search in the Tucson desert turned up a metal box buried three feet underground. June, chained, malnourished, and covered in ant bites, was found alive inside.

For someone held captive in a tiny box for nineteen days, the girl was in remarkably good spirits. Several days after her rescue, June appeared at a press conference filmed by Pathé studios. (Reporters did not ask her questions, though, allowing her father, Fernando, to steer June through the session.) The little girl seemed poised, her answers sounding rehearsed. She said she was looking forward to going back to school that Friday. It was the last interview Robles ever gave. She never spoke to the media again.

As June's public silence stretched, so did the investigation. Leads proved false, no arrests were made, a grand jury failed to indict anyone, and the FBI eventually gave up, privately agreeing with the grand jury's conclusion of "alleged kidnapping." June stayed in Tucson, where she married and had children and grandchildren. By the time she died in 2014, in such obscurity that it took the press three years to connect her to her childhood ordeal, authorities still had no proper answer about who kidnapped her. It remains a mystery, as does the effect the kidnapping had upon June and her family.

Captivity narratives, such as the recent "found alive" stories of young women including Elizabeth Smart, Jaycee Dugard, Natascha Kampusch, and the trio Ariel Castro held prisoner in Cleveland, opened up a psychological trapdoor into Sally's probable state of mind. They also allowed me to understand how kidnappers were able to subject these girls and women to years of sexual, physical, and psychological abuse.

Smart, Dugard, and Colleen Stan—the "Girl in the Box" under her tormentors' sway for seven years—left their abductors' homes, shopped at supermarkets, and even traveled (Stan visited her parents while she was a captive) without asking anyone for help. They survived by adjusting their mental maps so that brutality could be endured, but never entirely accepted as normal. Every day, every hour, their kidnappers told these women that their families had forgotten all about them. Year after year, their only experience of "love" came from those who abused, raped, and tortured them, creating a cognitive dissonance impossible to escape.

Dugard's eighteen-year bond with her abductor resulted in her bearing two children by him. The fear of losing her daughters, no matter how squalid her situation, caused her to deny her real identity to the police at first, revealing the truth only when she felt secure that she was safe from her kidnappers. Smart, too, needed the same foundation of trust to tell law enforcement who she really was.

We know how these girls coped and felt because several of them published books about their extended ordeals. Smart, Dugard, and the Cleveland three—Amanda Berry and Gina DeJesus together, and Michelle Knight on her own—were able to tell their stories the way they wished and when they chose. In doing so they sought to make something meaningful of their lives.

Sally Horner did not have the chance to tell her story to the world, unlike the women and girls of later generations. She also didn't have the choice of keeping her account wholly private, unlike June Robles. What remains of her time on the road with Frank La Salle are bits and pieces cobbled together from court documents and corroborated by city records. Absence is as telling as substance. Inference will have to stand in for confidence. Imagination will have to fill in the rest.

THE SUMMER'S GREAT HEAT WAVE was some weeks away, but it still sweltered plenty on the Baltimore-bound bus. Frank La Salle and Sally Horner had taken a taxicab to the bus depot in Philadelphia. Perhaps Sally wondered why they were going so far out of the way if they were headed south. Maybe she asked why they had to leave Atlantic City so quickly, or where the station wagon had gone, or why they had to leave their clothes and photos behind. Most likely, she kept any complaints or questions to herself.

She had to keep remembering the script, that La Salle was her father. His word was law. She had to stick to the story to avoid punishment. She had to endure his daily torments. She had to retreat to her own mind to escape the void of her current situation.

The cab pulled up in front of the Philadelphia station. Frank and Sally made their way to the Greyhound bus bound for Baltimore before it pulled away at 11:00 A.M. He bought their tickets, Sally squeaking under the wire for the half-price fare. They settled in their seats for the three-hour trip. They may not have been alone. Sally later said that a woman she knew as "Miss Robinson" had joined them. La Salle had told her the woman was some sort of assistant or secretary. She was perhaps twenty-five, though an eleven-year-old girl's sense of how old people are can be skewed.

The Philadelphia Greyhound made one stop along the way, either in Wilmington or in Oxford, Delaware. After the short break, the bus moved over to Route 40, which turned into the

Pulaski Highway. Was Sally impressed by the wider lanes and speeding cars on the still-new highway? What did she allow herself to dream over the three-hour trip before the bus pulled into the downtown depot in Baltimore? Did she hope for a chance of escape, or had she resigned herself to being trapped by La Salle's new vision of her life?

They arrived in Baltimore just after 2:15 in the afternoon. "Miss Robinson," if she existed, vanished from the picture, perhaps as soon as they got off the bus, collected their luggage, and looked for a cab or local transit to take them to their lodgings. Most likely they ended up staying downtown that first evening and for the next few days, around West Franklin Street in the neighborhood of Mount Vernon. Blocks away lay the city's most prized landmarks, including City Hall, the Museum of Art, and the original Washington Monument. Testaments to Baltimore's beauty and power, but also a refuge out of Sally's grasp.

La Salle needed to find work right away. The Belvedere Hotel, a place so swanky that Woodrow Wilson, Theodore Roosevelt, and King Edward VIII and Wallis Simpson stayed there, may have hired him. It was less than a mile's walk from West Franklin Street. It would explain why La Salle listed a hotel bellman named Anthony Janney as a reference in later court documents. And what better place for a fugitive to hide than among hotel staff serving the toniest, richest guests in a Beaux Arts building nestled within Baltimore's most prominent neighborhood?

I was also struck, while walking around the district, by how close Sally was to the Enoch Pratt Free Library. It's a wonderful place for researchers, and a safe harbor for bookish types of all kinds. Sally loved to read; were books a way for her to imagine herself in different worlds she could control, or was the library yet another place she couldn't go, somewhere she fantasized about as a refuge from Frank La Salle's relentless assaults?

Because in Baltimore, something changed in their relationship. Publicly, they kept up the pose of father and daughter. In private, the power imbalance between them grew more noxious. It was in Baltimore, according to Sally, that rape became a regular occurrence. It was the place where Frank La Salle subjugated her totally to his will psychologically and physically. The outside world never had a clue, even after La Salle sent his "daughter" to school.

There was no way he could have kept her home if he wanted to maintain the illusion of normalcy. The summer was over and an eleven-year-old girl, shut away at home or loose on the streets while he was at work, would draw attention— and questions. La Salle couldn't control her every thought and move while she was at school, true. But by this point he'd broken her down enough, between the threats and the rapes, and the apologies and the treats, that he must have felt a measure of confidence that Sally would do exactly what he said, at all times.

To enroll Sally at Saint Ann's Catholic School, they had to leave West Franklin Street. So in September 1948, they moved to Barclay, a neighborhood on Baltimore's east side. There La Salle and Sally settled in an apartment around East Twentieth Street between Barclay and Greenmount Avenues, a block up from the local cemetery. At the time, the neighborhood was a middle-class enclave of brick town houses, where neighbors mingled freely if they wished, or kept to themselves if they did not. Over the next eight months, Sally got used to the new name Frank had given her: Madeline LaPlante.

Here's how I imagine Sally Horner's days during the 1948–1949 school year. She'd wake up, get dressed, act the part of daughter to her "daddy," and shove from her mind the fact that her current life was the opposite of normal. He probably took Sally to school for the first week, just to be sure she wouldn't do anything rash like speak out or run away. Afterward, he trusted Sally to go by herself. She knew he had to be at work early in a different part of town. She did not want to disappoint him. She resolved she never would.

She'd smile and nod to their landlady—Mary or Ann Troy; she got the two confused even though she'd been told over and over that they weren't related—and other neighbors as they headed off to work. Then, she'd walk west along East Twentieth Street. At the end of the block was the Diamond, the diner where she and La Salle took many of their meals, since he didn't have the time or the patience to cook, and she was still learning how. Sally usually skipped breakfast, waiting to eat until after morning prayers. Perhaps on some days, the waitress, Marie Farrell, packed up a piping-hot fried egg sandwich for her and put it on Frank's tab.

Breakfast in hand, Sally would turn right at the end of the block, walking up Greenmount Avenue until she reached the corner of Twenty-Second Street. There was Saint Ann's, an extension of a Roman Catholic church that had been in Barclay for more than a century. The schedule was strict. All students had to attend mass first thing in the morning. Sally sat with her classmates on uncomfortable pews as Monsignor Quinn, Saint Ann's pastor and principal, intoned the daily prayers in Latin and English. She kept an eagle eye out for Mother Superior Cornellous—the older woman did not tolerate her students fidgeting or misbehaving.

Then, if she had remembered to fast, Sally took Communion. The priest placed the host on her tongue. As it melted, Sally knelt and prayed for her eternal soul. Was the possibility of escape part of her prayers? Did she pray that someone would see behind the calm facade of Madeline LaPlante to the captive Sally Horner? Did she wonder if the things Frank asked her to do, which he said were "perfectly natural," were, in fact, a mortal sin? Or did she pray for things to stay as they were because they might get even worse?

When Communion ended, Sally went back to her pew. Mass was over, so it was time for the fried egg sandwich, now cool enough to eat, and then for her classes. So many hours in the day stretched ahead where all she had to think about was her studies. She had to do well and keep up her grades or else there would be more punishment at home, and so she likely did. But Sally also didn't want to draw undue attention to herself, in case someone—especially the Monsignor or the Mother Superior—grew suspicious and started asking too many questions. Better to embrace the invisibility. Better not to stand out.

When the last school bell rang and it was time to go home, Sally reversed her morning walk. But if there was time, or if she felt a smidgen bolder, perhaps she ventured up a block to Mund Park. The park was a place where the mind could roam and think of freedom. Where the green grass grew just like it did in Camden. Where she could think of her real home, and wonder if she would ever see it again.

I DON'T KNOW WHY La Salle chose to enroll Sally in Catholic schools, both in Baltimore and elsewhere. No one remembered him being a churchgoer or having any religious leanings. Before her abduction, Sally likely attended a Protestant church. One possible reason is that a parochial school did not have to conform to the same rules and regulations as public schools.

Catholic institutions were less likely to ask questions of a new student arriving later in the school year, under a false name, with dubious documentation at best. Instead of viewing a girl like Sally with suspicion, some opposite effect, like sympathy, may have prevailed.

But I suspect La Salle gravitated toward Catholic institutions because they were a good place to hide in plain sight. The Church, as we now know from decades' worth of scandal, hid generations of abused victims, and moved pedophile priests from parish to parish because covering up their crimes protected the Church's carefully crafted image. Perhaps La Salle saw parochial schools for what they were: a place for complicity and enabling to flourish. A place where no one would ask Sally Horner if something terrible was happening to her.

ELEVEN

Walks of Death

Back in Camden, Sally Horner's plight had been consigned to the same purgatory that befalls every long-term missing child investigation. The city hadn't moved on, but her fate was no longer the highest priority. Camden residents wanted to embrace progress, to bask in fortunes they believed would last forever. There was little warning of the outsized event that would bewilder them and foreshadow the precipitous decline in the city's near-future.

In the fall of 1949, Camden believed in its own prosperity. It had weathered the Great Depression and near-bankruptcy in 1936, the result of financial mismanagement by the local government. Private industry still thrived. The New York Shipbuilding Corporation still had contracts from the navy and the Maritime Administration. Smaller shipbuilding companies, like John Mathis & Company, had doubled their workforce during the Second World War and seemed primed to expand. Manufacturing jobs in the region were a year away from an all-time peak of 43,267. Campbell's Soup still employed thousands of workers at its local headquarters.

No company represented Camden's sense that the future was theirs for the taking more than RCA Victor, the phonograph company. In June 1949, it had introduced the "45," a smaller, faster alternative to Columbia's "LP" record format. RCA Victor also began producing technology for television, making equipment required by broadcast studios as well as for television sets regular home-buyers could acquire.

A great many forces underlay Camden's eventual negative transformation. But Sally Horner's abduction wasn't the spark. Rather, the morning of September 6, 1949, seems to me like the inflection point between progress and backlash, hope and despair, promise and decline. The scope of the crime seemed an unfathomable one-off, but its grotesque repetition in the decades to come demonstrates how a singular evil can become all too mundane.

AT EIGHT O'CLOCK that morning, a mother woke up her son for breakfast. He'd been out late the night before, sitting and stewing in a movie theater on Market Street in Philadelphia, waiting for a date who never showed. The son's homosexuality wasn't quite a secret, but nor could he flaunt it when sex between men was still very much against the law.

That his date, a man with whom he'd been in the midst of a weeks-long affair, stood him up was indignity enough. Then he'd returned to his home in Cramer Hill to find the fence he built to separate his house from his neighbors' home had been torn down.

The man drank a glass of milk and ate the fried eggs his mother, Freda, prepared. Then he went into the basement, whose walls were covered in memorabilia from the war he'd fought in, and where he had written down meticulous notes on each enemy soldier he'd killed. He regarded his nine-millimeter pistol, a Luger Po8, for which he had two full clips and thirty-three loose cartridges, and thought about the list of people—neighbors, shopkeepers, even his mother—he wanted to wipe off the face of the earth.

He grabbed a wrench and went back to the kitchen. He raised it, threatening Freda. "What do you want to do that for, Howard?" she cried. When he didn't answer, she repeated the question as she backed away from him, then ran out of the house to a neighbor's. He retrieved his Luger and ammunition from the basement, as well as a six-inch knife and a five-inch pen-like weapon tricked up to hold six shells. Then he cut through the backyard and shot at the first person he saw: a bread deliveryman sitting in his truck.

Howard Unruh missed his first target, but he wouldn't miss many more. Twenty minutes. Thirteen dead. And a neighborhood, a city, and a nation forever marked by his "Walk of Death."

FOR MARSHALL THOMPSON, Unruh's murderous spree hit too close for comfort. He and his family lived around the corner from Unruh and his mother, at 943 North Thirty-Second Street. Most of those who died or were injured on the morning of September 6 were Unruh's neighbors on River Road, which was the main thoroughfare of East Camden.

Thompson might have gotten his hair cut at Clark Hoover's barbershop a few feet down River Road. That awful morning, the barber took a fatal shot, as did six-year-old Orris Smith, perched on a hobbyhorse inside the shop. If Thompson needed his shoes repaired and shined, he likely got it done at the repair shop next door, where Unruh killed the cobbler, John Pilarchik. Down the street was the tailor shop, owned by Thomas Zegrino. He was out when Unruh arrived, but Zegrino's new wife, Helen, was not, and she paid the price.

Unruh then shot Alvin Day, the television repairman. James Hutton, the insurance agent, made the dreadful mistake of running out of the drugstore to see what the commotion was all about, and also died. So, too, did a mother and daughter, Emma Matlack, sixty-six, and Helen Matlack Wilson, who'd driven in from Pennsauken for the day and failed to comprehend the massacre unfolding. Unruh shot them dead, and Helen's twelve-year-old son, John, took a bullet in the neck. He died the next day in the hospital.

Others were injured. Like Madeline Harrie, caught in the arm by a bullet after Unruh's first two missed, and her son, Armand, who tried vainly to tackle Unruh when he invaded their home.

Unruh moved on to his worst grudge late in the rampage, hunting down his next-door neighbor, Maurice Cohen, owner of the drugstore, to make him pay for the business with the fence as well as other perceived grievances. Not spotting him in the store, Unruh went upstairs to the family apartment. As Maurice climbed onto the roof, his wife, Rose, shoved their son, twelve-year-old Charles, into a closet, and then hid in a separate one. Unruh searched the apartment and then went out on the roof, where he caught a glimpse of Maurice running away. Unruh fired into the druggist's back. The shot jerked Maurice off the roof and he was dead before hitting the street.

Unruh went back inside and fired his Luger several times into the closet where Rose was hiding. She died instantly. Maurice's mother, Minnie, was in the bedroom, in a frantic state as she tried to get police on the phone, when Unruh caught up to her. He shot her in the head and body. She fell back on the bed and died there.

Charles stayed hidden until it was utterly quiet. When officers finally found him, he would not be comforted—he'd heard everything. Charles leaned halfway out his apartment window and screamed, "He's going to kill me. He's killing everybody."

Howard Unruh had walked down the stairs and made his way to the Harries' place. There he discovered he was out of ammunition. Hearing the police sirens, he doubled back to his mother's house to await his fate.

IN A LARGER CITY, where officers didn't walk the beats where they lived, Marshall Thompson might not have taken part in police efforts to apprehend Howard Unruh. But it's unlikely Thompson could have begged off even if he wished. One of Thompson's colleagues on the Camden detective squad, John Ferry, also lived in Unruh's Cramer Hill neighborhood. The summer before, Ferry had tried to help Unruh find a job as a favor to the man's uncle, a deputy fire chief.

Ferry had just finished up a midnight-to-eight shift. He was on his way home when he saw his insurance man dead in the street, as well as other victims. "When the other cops started arriving I went home and came back with my shotgun," Ferry recalled in 1974, the twenty-fifth anniversary of the massacre. With the body count rising and ambulances blaring to and from Cooper Hospital, Thompson was one of more than four dozen cops who descended upon Cramer Hill that morning.

Howard Unruh had barricaded himself in his home. It was up to a group of policemen led by Detective Russ Maurer to figure out how to coax him out. Maurer sidled up to the front of the house. A throng of cops, including Thompson, covered Maurer, poised to throw tear gas through the window if Unruh acted rashly. As *Courier-Post* columnist Charley Humes observed, "Russ [Maurer] could have paid with his life, because the killer seldom missed. That was a brave act."

John Ferry was crouched with several other policemen in Unruh's backyard, awaiting any sign of the man. When Unruh appeared in the window, Ferry turned to James Mulligan, his supervisor on the detective unit, and asked, "Jim, should I take his head off?"

"No," replied Mulligan. "There has been plenty of killing."

Unruh later told police he "could have killed Johnny Ferry . . . any time I wanted." Ferry's past attempt to find Unruh a job may well have saved his life, and perhaps the others. Unruh made his decision. "Okay. I give up, I'm coming down," he shouted to the cops down below.

"Where's that gun?" a sergeant yelled.

"It's on my desk, up here in the room," Unruh said, then repeated: "I'm coming down."

Unruh opened the back door and came out with his hands up. More than two dozen officers trained their guns upon him. One yelled, "What's the matter with you? You a psycho?"

"I'm no psycho," said Unruh. "I've got a good mind."

MITCHELL COHEN, THE Camden County prosecutor, had just returned from a summer vacation at the Jersey Shore. He expected his office would be its usual bustling self the morning after Labor Day, and that he would be faced with a fresh round

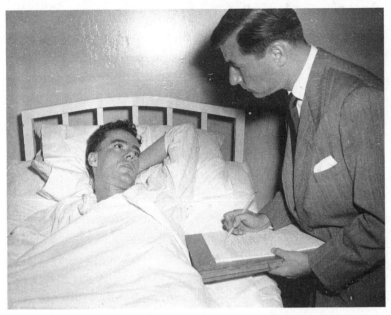

Mitchell Cohen questions Howard Unruh in a hospital bed,
September 7, 1949.

of indictable crimes, from gambling rackets, to robberies, to teens illegally buying beer.

The office was the opposite of bustling. None of the detectives were around, and the quiet cast a strange pall over the place. Then the phone rang. Larry Doran, chief of detectives, was on the line. He told Cohen that a local man had gone "berserk on River Road and was shooting people," which was why every police officer was out of the office. He also told Cohen that Unruh was alive and in custody after his twenty-minute rampage.

Cohen walked over to the police station to interview the mass shooter and found him cooperative. "It was a horrible, revolting narrative," Cohen recalled in a 1974 interview. "He really gave it cold, cut-and-dry. There was no attempt to conceal or be furtive. He didn't seem to experience the normal relief of getting it off his chest. There was no remorse, no tears. There was a lack of all emotion."

Over the two or so hours he spoke with Cohen, Unruh was concealing something. When Cohen realized what it was, he was stunned. "What really convinced me that [Unruh] was terribly insane was when he got up after two hours and his chair was covered with blood. . . . He had been shot and wasn't even aware of it." Unruh was sent to a nearby hospital to recuperate, and Cohen interrogated him further upon his recovery from the bullet wound.

One month after the massacre, Cohen released the psychiatric reports he'd ordered on Unruh to the public. Unruh had been ruled clinically insane, and therefore not competent to stand trial. And so the deaths of thirteen people and the injuries of many more were never properly accounted for in court. Unruh didn't go free. He would spend the rest of his life in mental institutions in and around Trenton. But for those who survived the massacre, who attended hearing after hearing to ensure Unruh was never released, it did not seem like proper justice. He died in 2009 at the age of eighty-eight, just one month after Charles Cohen, the last survivor of the massacre, died.

Unruh's "Walk of Death" also seemed to foreshadow Camden's deeper decline. "It's something you never really forget. . . . You take extra precautions to protect your family and your property," Paul Schopp, a former director of the Camden County Historical Society, said in an interview to mark the sixtieth anniversary of the mass shooting. "He didn't just rob them of their lives. He robbed them of their essence." The trauma of a mass shooting, and a collective desire to forget, seems like the true beginning of Camden's downward slope.

TWELVE

Across America by Oldsmobile

Vladimir Nabokov finished the 1948–1949 academic year at Cornell University in a state of irritation. He hadn't found much time to write. He fumed over cuts and changes made without his permission by the *New York Times Book Review* to his review of Jean-Paul Sartre's *La Nausée*, which he had submitted in March. His finances were depleted: Nabokov hadn't budgeted for unexpected housing costs and the added expense of Social Security (what he termed "old-age insurance") taken out of his monthly salary. And he was exhausted from teaching a full load of English and Russian literature undergraduate classes, exacerbated by the extra work he'd inflicted upon himself by translating a pivotal Russian poetic masterpiece, "The Song of Igor's Campaign," for one of those classes.

Nabokov had, at least, completed another two chapters

of his memoir, *Conclusive Evidence*, both of which were published later that year in the *New Yorker*. He did love teaching, and Cornell proved to be more amenable to his idiosyncrasies than Wellesley. But he couldn't resist complaining: "I have always more to do than I can fit into the most elastic time, even with the most careful packing," he wrote his friend Mstislav Dobuzhinsky in the spring of 1949. "At the moment I am surrounded by the scaffoldings of several large structures on which I have to work by fits and starts and very slowly."

Lolita, which he still thought of as *The Kingdom by the Sea*, was less a work in progress than a seed in Nabokov's mind, one that wasn't quite ready to germinate. Perhaps he would make a beautiful work on his summer trip—another cross-country jaunt with Véra and Dmitri. They said goodbye to the Plymouth that had carried them all the way to Palo Alto, California, in 1941, and hello to a used black 1946 Oldsmobile. Dorothy Leuthold, who had shared the driving with Véra eight years earlier, wasn't available, and neither were two other friends, Andree Bruel and Vladimir Zenzinov. But one of Nabokov's Russian literature students, Richard Buxbaum, volunteered, and the Nabokovs picked him up at Canandaigua on June 22.

Their first destination was Salt Lake City, where Nabokov was to take part in a ten-day writers' conference at the University of Utah starting on July 5. But their westward journey almost ended a few miles from Canandaigua, when Véra changed lanes on the highway and narrowly missed plowing into an oncoming truck. Pulling over, she turned to Buxbaum and said: "Perhaps you'd better drive."

With Buxbaum now behind the wheel, the group traveled south of the Great Lakes and across Iowa and Nebraska. The Nabokovs spoke Russian and encouraged Buxbaum to do the same, chiding him when he lapsed into English. Vladimir was never without his notebook, ready to record all observations, however minuscule, of quotidian American life on the road, be it overheard conversation at a restaurant or vivid impressions of the landscape. They arrived in Salt Lake City on July 3, two days before the conference's start, and were lodged at a sorority house, Alpha Delta Phi, where the Nabokovs had a room with a private bath—a pivotal part of his participation agreement.

The conference introduced Nabokov to writers he might not have otherwise met, including John Crowe Ransom, the poet and critic who founded and edited the *Kenyon Review;* and Ted Geisel, a few years away from children's book superstardom as Dr. Seuss, whom Nabokov recalled as "a charming man, one of the most gifted people on this list." He also got reacquainted with Wallace Stegner, whom he'd first met at Stanford. Nabokov and Stegner spent the conference debating each other in the novel workshops and in the off-hours playing doubles on the tennis courts, with their sons as partners.

Nabokov did not have much time to idle, though. He taught three workshops on the novel, one on the short story, and another on biography. He took part in a reading with several poets, and repurposed an old lecture on Russian literature under a new title, "The Government, the Critic, and the Reader." When the conference ended on July 16, he, Véra, Dmitri, and Richard Buxbaum headed north to the Grand Tetons in Wyoming.

Nabokov, once more, was game to hunt more butterflies. But Véra was worried. The Teton Range, she had heard, was a haven for grizzly bears. How would Vladimir protect himself against them carrying a mere butterfly net? Nabokov wrote to the lepidopterist Alexander Klots for advice; Klots assured him that Grand Teton was "just another damned touristed-out National Park." Any danger would come from clueless visitors, not ravenous bears.

Nabokov re-creating the process of writing Lolita *on note cards.*

From there the quartet headed to Jackson Hole, where Nabokov wanted to look for a particularly elusive subspecies of butterfly, *Lycaeides argyrognomon longinus.* On the way the Oldsmobile blew a tire. As Dmitri and Richard started changing it, Nabokov said, "I'm no use to you," and spent the next hour catching butterflies. They arrived the following day, around July 19. For the next month and a half, the Nabokovs' home base was the Teton Pass Ranch, at the foot of the mountain range. Nabokov's hunt for his coveted butterfly subspecies proved successful.

The six-week stay was not without rough moments, though. Dmitri and Richard Buxbaum decided to try climbing Disappointment Peak, next to the Grand Tetons' East Ridge. The climb to the top, seven thousand feet above base level, was straightforward at first. Then Dmitri, with the overconfidence befitting a fifteen-year-old boy, decided they should switch to a more difficult path, one that required extra equipment they lacked. Realizing they would get stuck up there if they carried on, they turned around, but hours passed—and the sun nearly set—by the time they made it back to Vladimir and Véra, who were understandably frantic.

Buxbaum hitchhiked home at the end of August. The Nabokovs, with Véra now driving, ventured northeast to Minnesota, then up to northern Ontario, for more butterfly collecting, before they finally arrived in Ithaca on September 4. Nabokov had three courses to teach that fall, but had attracted only twenty-one students, combined, a workload greeted with suspicion by his fellow professors. Even so, Nabokov wanted more money.

Cornell's head of the Literature Department, David Daiches, received Nabokov's request and offered a deal: he would approve a salary raise if Nabokov took over teaching the European fiction course, Literature 311-12. Nabokov could shape the curriculum as he saw fit and pick the authors he liked most. Nabokov said yes. He began right away, scribbling notes on the back of Daiches's letter for the course that would define his Cornell career for the next decade.

And in spare moments, Nabokov began at last to shape the novel that had lived in his head for so long.

NABOKOV'S RAMSDALE IS not Camden. The made-up town where Humbert Humbert insinuates himself into the lives of Charlotte and Dolores Haze is most likely located in New England, which is why Dolores is deposited in a school in the Berkshires, and why both older man and younger girl seem to know the area well. Nabokov gleaned this knowledge during his

years living in Cambridge, Massachusetts. But the names of
the towns are similar, as is the Linden Street of Sally Horner's
childhood home and the Lawn Street where the Haze women
live. Both towns shared a white, middle-class bucolic atmosphere. As would happen again and again, the Sally Horner
story parallels *Lolita* in all sorts of surprising ways.

Humbert Humbert came to Ramsdale by design, but moved
into the Haze home at 342 Lawn Street by accident. He meant
to stay nearby with the McCoos, parents to "two little daughters, one a baby the other a girl of twelve." Lodging there, he
assumed, would allow him to "coach in French and fondle in
Humbertish." But when Humbert gets there, he finds out that
the McCoos' house has burned down, and he must find some-
place else to live.

He is not pleased to be shuffled off to a "white-frame horror . . . looking dingy and old, more gray than white—the kind
of place you know will have a rubber tube affixable to the tub
faucet in lieu of a shower." Humbert is further irked upon overhearing Charlotte Haze's contralto voice ask a friend if "Mon-
sieur Humbert" has arrived.

Then she comes down the steps—"sandals, maroon slacks,
yellow silk blouse, squarish face, in that order"—tapping her
cigarette with her index finger. In Humbert's estimation,
Charlotte isn't much: "the poor lady was in her middle thirties,
she had a shiny forehead, plucked eyebrows and quite simple
but not unattractive features of a type that may be defined as
a weak solution of Marlene Dietrich." Then he spies Dolores,
and it is as if he saw his "Riviera love peering at me over dark
glasses," two and a half decades after his prepubescent romance with Annabel, as if the years "tapered to a palpitating
point, and vanished." Now that the true object of Humbert's

obsession has revealed herself, Charlotte becomes a nuisance to be manipulated and endured.

When Charlotte sends Humbert a letter, confessing she is "a passionate and lonely woman and you are the love of my life," he senses opportunity: marry Charlotte to gain access to Dolores. Another line in Charlotte's letter stands out: that if Humbert were to take advantage of her, "then you would be a criminal—worse than a kidnapper who rapes a child." Charlotte, bafflingly, concludes that if he showed no sign of romantic interest in her, and remained in her home, then she would take it that he was "ready to link up your life with mine forever and ever and be a father to my little girl." (Since we're always in Humbert's head, we only have his word that Charlotte wrote this.)

The American widow and the European widower marry in haste while Dolores is away at summer camp. It is, suffice to say, a bad match. What galls Humbert the most is what he describes as Charlotte's vituperative attitude toward her daughter. The words Charlotte underlined in her copy of *A Guide to Your Child's Development* to mark her daughter's twelfth birthday: "aggressive, boisterous, critical, distrustful, impatient, irritable, inquisitive, listless, negativistic (underlined twice) and obstinate."

Humbert has already decided to murder Charlotte and stage it as an accident, perhaps at a thinly populated beach they visited ("The setting was really perfect for a brisk bubbling murder"). His simmering rage boils over when Charlotte informs him that she intends to send Dolores to boarding school at Beardsley, so that the two of them can take a trip to England. He resists. They argue. Then she reveals to him that she has read his notes, and knows the truth about him: "You're a monster. You're a detestable, abominable, criminal fraud. If you come near—I'll scream out the window. Get back!"

Humbert exits the house. He notes that Charlotte's face is "disfigured by her emotion" and remains calm. He goes back into the house. He opens a bottle of Scotch. Then, quietly, he begins to gaslight her. "You are ruining my life and yours. Let us be civilized people. It is all your hallucination. You are crazy, Charlotte. The notes you found were fragments of a novel."

Charlotte runs back to her room, claiming she has a letter to write. Humbert makes her a drink—or so he says—while she is gone. He realizes she is not, in fact, in her room. The telephone rings. "Mrs. Humbert, sir, has been run over and you'd better come quick." Fate has played a trick. Instead of becoming the potential savior of her daughter's virtue, Charlotte ends up dead. It's also played a fast one upon Humbert: he was all set to become a murderer.

THE DESCRIPTION OF CHARLOTTE HAZE as Dietrich-lite sounds a jarringly familiar bell when I look at pictures of Ella Horner from when her daughter disappeared in 1948. She was forty-one and often wore her hair pulled back, sometimes in a bun (a "bronze-brown bun"), and plucked her eyebrows over eyes that tended to disappear into their creases. Her other facial features—strong jawline, prominent nose, pronounced cheekbones—were reminiscent of Marlene Dietrich before she emigrated from Germany and became a Hollywood star. Based on the photographs of her that I've seen from before and after Sally's kidnapping, I imagine when Ella smiled, it didn't often reach her eyes. (Humbert on Charlotte: "Her smile was but a quizzical jerk of one eyebrow.")

There is another similarity, coincidence or otherwise, that

ties Charlotte Haze to Ella Horner: the device of marriage to gain access to their daughter. For the fictional Humbert Humbert it was a real gambit. For Frank La Salle, it was a delusion he created to explain why he took Sally away from her mother. It was a ruse Sally had to live by in order to survive being with him in Atlantic City and Baltimore, and she would have to endure it for quite a while longer.

THIRTEEN

Dallas

Frank La Salle took Sally Horner aside one day in March 1949 and broke the news that they were leaving Baltimore. He told her that the FBI had assigned him a new case, one that required him to move southwest to investigate. By then she'd been with him for nine months. Sally did not know, and could not know, that the real reason they were leaving Baltimore was that Camden County prosecutor Mitchell Cohen had indicted La Salle on the more serious charge of kidnapping on March 17. The new indictment meant La Salle could face between thirty and thirty-five years for taking Sally. Police had not located the pair, but this charge, on top of the original indictment, promised greater scrutiny, more resources for the hunt, and a better probability of arrest. Baltimore was no longer safe, nor was the entire East Coast. Instead of flushing La Salle out, the new charge caused him to run.

The journey from Baltimore to Dallas is approximately 1,366 miles. Today, by car, it would take about twenty hours to drive, on I-81 and I-40. Neither of those highways existed in 1949. La Salle and Sally likely drove south on U.S. 11, traveling all the way to the highway's end in New Orleans, Louisiana, before switching over to U.S. 80, arriving in Dallas less than two hundred miles later. However they traveled, Sally and La Salle got to Dallas around April 22, 1949. For the next eleven months, she and Frank continued to play father and daughter, sticking to the cover story that he had taken Sally away from her wayward mother to provide her with a more stable upbringing. None of their new neighbors seemed to question this. At least, not right away.

They moved into a quiet, well-kept trailer park on West Commerce Street, about four hundred feet from Dallas's bustling downtown core. The park was designed like a horseshoe, with trailers—including one that La Salle bought on the premises—dotted all along the curve. The park could hold as many as a hundred motor homes. The mothers mostly stayed home and the fathers worked as farmhands, for steel companies, or at gas stations. Neighbors were closer in the trailer park than they had been in Baltimore. They could pay more attention to the pair, and get to know Sally—or think they did.

La Salle had changed their names again. Sally was no longer known as Madeline LaPlante, but as Florence Planette. Oddly, it isn't clear whether La Salle also used the "Planette" alias. One of their new neighbors, Dale Kagamaster, who ended up working with La Salle, knew him as LaPlante. Frank also told people that he was widowed, a change from the divorced father cover story he used in Atlantic City and Baltimore.

The trailer park was owned by Nelrose and Charles Pfeil, who'd bought it a year earlier, after moving to Dallas from Akron, Ohio, with their three sons. Tom, the eldest, was nine years old when Frank and Sally arrived at the trailer park. He did not recall the name "LaPlante," but thought "La Salle" seemed familiar. He also remembered "Florence's" father as aloof, cold, standoffish. "I understand why, now," Pfeil told me. "He had to be suspicious of everyone around him." Tom had dim memories of Sally. "I don't know if I could tell you I remember much of her except for talking a time or two. I was nine. I just wanted to play ball."

As in Baltimore, La Salle got a job as a mechanic, but kept Sally in the dark about what he was really doing all day. He also enrolled Sally in another Catholic school. This time it was Our Lady of Good Counsel Academy at 210 Marsalis Avenue in the neighborhood of Oak Cliff, about a seven-minute drive away from West Commerce Street. Like Saint Ann's in Baltimore, Our Lady of Good Counsel no longer exists, having been absorbed into Bishop Dunne Catholic School in 1961. None of its records have survived. And also like Saint Ann's, the school was in a predominantly white, middle-class neighborhood that is no longer so, thanks to suburban migration, systemic inequality, and poverty.

Sally likely kept to a routine similar to the one she had in Baltimore. A bus ride to Our Lady of Good Counsel, where she began the day with morning prayers. Schoolwork wasn't a breeze, but her grades were generally good: a copy of Sally's report card from between September 1949 and February 1950, which La Salle kept after she brought it home, showed she received primarily As and A-minuses, with the occasional B, in geography and writing. The only time she received a lower grade—a C-plus, in languages—was in her final month at the school.

At first their Commerce Street neighbors didn't see anything amiss. Sally appeared to be a typical twelve-year-old living with her widowed father, albeit one he never let out of his sight except to go to school. Sally never displayed despair or asked for help. La Salle wouldn't let her.

Her neighbors thought Sally seemed to enjoy taking care of her home. She would bake every once in a while. She had a dog, one she apparently spoiled. La Salle provided her with a generous allowance for clothes and sweets. She would go shopping, swimming, and to her neighbors' trailers for dinner— sometimes with La Salle, and other times by herself, when he told her he was working the case for the FBI.

Dale Kagamaster's wife, Josephine, thought Sally was a well-adjusted girl. "There were several times we noticed the need for the love and care of a mother but we both felt that the father was doing a good job of providing better living conditions for [her]." The consensus about Sally and her "father" was that they "seemed happy and entirely devoted to each other." Maude Smillie, who was living in a nearby trailer, seemed bewildered by the idea that Sally had been a virtual prisoner: "[Sally] spent one day at the beauty parlor with me. I gave her a permanent and she never mentioned a thing. She should have known she could have confided in me."

Nelrose Pfeil was quoted in a court document several years later saying something similar: "Sally was in my home many times a day and she had access to several phones should she choose to use one. Sally had plenty of time to talk to me about being kidnaped [sic] if she had wanted to and I am sure she knew me well enough to know if she had said anything like that I would have helped her." The only time La Salle kept Sally from playing with other children, according to Pfeil's statement, "was when the person's character was in question."

It appears the Pfeils, the Kagamasters, and other neighbors

bought La Salle's cover story about Sally. They did not notice anything amiss, even for the ten-day period when Sally dropped off the radar and didn't attend school. She'd suffered an appendicitis attack, one that required her to undergo an operation and spend three nights at the Texas Crippled Children's Hospital (now the Texas Scottish Rite Hospital for Children). The other seven days, presumably, she spent at home, recuperating.

Something did change in Sally, though, after the operation. She grew more pensive. Josephine Kagamaster observed that the girl did not move like a "healthy, light-hearted youngster." She'd heard La Salle say the girl "walks like an old woman."

ON THE SURFACE, Sally acted as free as she had been in Camden, before Frank La Salle took her away from everyone she loved. She might have been left alone for long stretches at a time, stayed late at a neighbor's house watching television, and been on her own in the hospital for several nights. But if she told the truth, who would believe her story? Who would believe she had been abducted when, to all appearances, Frank La Salle was her father, and a loving one at that? And even if someone *did* believe her, could they help, or would they put Sally in greater peril?

Later, Josephine Kagamaster, Nelrose Pfeil, Maude Smillie, and others said they would have helped Sally had she chosen to confide in them. But they made such declarations with the benefit of hindsight, months or years after Frank La Salle's diabolical crimes were exposed to the public. At the time, they were living ordinary and happy lives. The idea that a young girl and an older man would be in a cruel parody of a father-daughter relationship seemed inconceivable, unimaginable. And no matter what they believed about what they would have done, Sally did not confide in these neighbors. She did not feel she could trust them.

But Sally did talk to someone, a woman named Ruth Janisch, and she believed what the girl had to say. Though Ruth's motivations were more complex than anyone knew, her belief in the girl eventually emboldened Sally to make the most important decision of her life.

FOURTEEN

The Neighbor

R uth Janisch and her family arrived at the Commerce Street trailer park around December 1948. They had spent most of the 1940s traveling a particular geographic loop, following the employment her husband, George, found repairing televisions or working in bowling alleys. It began in San Jose, where Ruth and George met and married, then moved up to Washington, where she'd grown up, tracked east to Minnesota, the home of George's parents, and finally on to Texas, situated more or less in between. The Janisches bought a caravan somewhere along the way and made it the family home.

Periodically, the trailer ran into trouble. On Thanksgiving 1948, it broke down on the way to Dallas, somewhere in the desert. New Mexico, perhaps, or Arizona. George and his elder stepson, Pat, went looking for help, leaving the rest of the

family stranded by the road. Ruth and her other children—
another boy from an earlier marriage, and two girls sired by
George—figured that if they were stuck by the road, they
might as well have Thanksgiving dinner while they waited.

They fetched chairs from a closet in the trailer and set up
outside. Ruth cooked up an impromptu meal of pancakes and
beans, which she served inside the broken-down trailer. The
children lined up to get their meal and then ate outside in the
baking desert sun. Ruth warned the children not to stay outside for too long. She was nervous that rattlesnakes might bite
them if the kids lingered.

Eventually George and Pat returned with the part they
needed to fix the trailer, and they drove on to Dallas, setting up
camp at the Commerce Street site. A few months later, in April
1949, a man in his fifties and a girl he said was his daughter
moved into the trailer next door. The Janisch girls immediately
took to the girl, who introduced herself as Florence Planette.
She was twelve, practically grown up, but she was willing
to give them her attention. The little girls were five, six, and
seven, and regarded her with a mixture of awe and envy.

Ruth may well have regarded the girl's father with extramarital interest. That's her children's theory now. Whatever
her motives, Ruth noticed something askew in the relationship
between Sally Horner and Frank La Salle that had eluded everyone else who interacted with them. What Ruth saw between
the older man and the young girl spurred her to the single
gesture that defined her as a decent human being, an act she
would relive for the rest of her days and memorialize in scrap-
books. That act did not make her a heroine in the eyes of her
children. But it would bring her a level of attention she spent
the rest of her life trying to find again.

Ruth Janisch may have been suspicious of Frank La Salle

because she wasn't in the habit of trusting people. She craved love she never found. She got pregnant so often she was in a perpetual state of exhaustion, dealing with babies and children. George always found work, but the money he brought in was hardly enough for an ever-expanding family. When her children misbehaved, it was all too easy for Ruth to fall back into the patterns she learned as a child, berating them the way her mother had berated her, telling them they were worthless, useless, or worse.

Ruth Janisch, ca. 1940s.

Her bitter outlook took hold upon leaving Washington State to marry her second husband, Everett Findley. (Ruth later said her first marriage, at sixteen to a man whose name she failed to remember, didn't count.) The former Ruth Douglass was eager to flee her mother, Myrtle, whose cuts were always unkind, and her father, Frank, whom her children later grew fond of but whom Ruth, in her cups, recalled as being "not so innocent." The children were never sure if Ruth was referring to her father's penchant for drink or something uglier.

After their marriage, Ruth had followed Findley, a man more than twice her age, to San Jose, and bore him two sons. She met husband number three, George Janisch, sometime after the dissolution of her marriage to Findley. George hailed from Minneapolis; he was short and slight, and his blond hair and fair appearance befitted his Scandinavian heritage.

He'd moved west for work and to escape the harsh Minnesota winter.

George and Ruth ran off to Carson City, Nevada, to wed on October 24, 1940. Perhaps they married for love. Not long before he died, George confided in one of his daughters that before their wedding, Ruth was a "good girl." But afterward, according to George, she changed, and he admitted that it was his fault.

It wasn't enough for George to sleep with his wife. He had to sleep with other men's wives, too. Ruth herself had taken up with him while he was married. Since George was fine if Ruth slept with the leftover husbands, she wasn't about to say no. The fact was that Ruth had a craving for men that would persist for the rest of her life.

The extramarital doings damaged the already tenuous bond between the Janisches, which had been frayed by having three daughters in quick succession. The couple seemed to bring out the worst in each other. One particularly clever, or insidious, way Ruth and George tested each other was with the naming of every new child. Each baby received a first name either spouse liked. The middle names, however, were those of former lovers. Nine children later, Ruth and George split up. He would marry twice more; she married ten times in total, with lovers scattered in between.

By 1949, Ruth was thirty-three (though would only admit to thirty-one) with a husband she couldn't help needling and at the mercy of that perpetual pregnancy-birth cycle. She still had most of her looks, with dark hair curling about her face, full, pointed breasts, a strong nose and wide-lipped mouth. Every new child added another dose of bitterness at her lot in life, and the family's poverty.

But there was something about Sally Horner that Ruth

could see clearly. The way the girl shuffled after coming home from an extended hospital stay after an appendectomy. The way Sally's smile didn't reach her eyes. The closeness between Sally and Frank that did not strike the right note. "He never let Sally out of his sight, except when she was at school," Ruth later recounted. "She never had any friends her own age. She never went any place, just stayed with La Salle in the trailer." She thought La Salle seemed "abnormally possessive" of the girl he said was his daughter. Ruth tried to cajole Sally, still recovering from her appendectomy, to tell her the "true story" of her relationship with La Salle. Sally wouldn't open up.

In early 1950, the Janisches packed up their trailer and drove west. Work had dried up for George in Dallas, and he figured he might have better luck in San Jose, which had proven lucky in the past. Once the family, larger by two more children, landed at the El Cortez Motor Inn—perhaps at their exact prior parking space—Ruth wrote to Frank saying that he and Sally should follow them to California. There's work to be had here, she said. He and Sally could be their neighbors again.

La Salle agreed. Perhaps he had some other pressing reason to abandon Dallas. Maybe he sensed that Sally was distancing herself from him and another move might keep her closer. Whatever the reason, La Salle pulled Sally out of school in February 1950 and they drove the house trailer attached to his car from Dallas to San Jose. Just as in Baltimore, and Atlantic City before it, La Salle had decided he and Sally needed to be on the move. And just as before, Sally had no say in the decision. She did what Frank La Salle told her to do. But his mood was different on the day they headed west. This time they were running toward opportunity, not running from the law.

Sally and La Salle's journey to San Jose took at least a week, if not more. He drove the trailer through Texas, going around the border of Oklahoma, then through New Mexico, Arizona, and Southern California, before moving up the South Bay to their final destination, the farthest Sally had ever been from Camden. She would never venture this far again. Sally had been La Salle's captive for nearly two years, since she was just eleven. She felt his presence at every turn, even when she was alone and seemingly free to do what she pleased. How trapped she must have felt to be in such close quarters to him as they spent that week or ten days on the road.

If Sally had allowed herself to let her mind roam, she might have given in to feelings of despair, or to anger over what La Salle had taken away from her. Or perhaps she was focused on how vital it was for her to survive. After days in the car and nights in the trailer parked at a rest stop, eating at diners, one after another, the emotional toll on her must have been considerable.

On the West Coast, Northern California in particular, palm trees lined broad boulevards where cars had room to move instead of getting jammed up like they did back home. Police in uniform shorts patrolled the streets on motorcycles. The air was far less humid than in Dallas, or even on the East Coast. But the prospects of betterment that had enticed La Salle, and so many others before him, were not on Sally's mind. She had a great many other things to think about.

By the time Frank La Salle pulled the house trailer into the El Cortez Motor Inn on Saturday, March 18, Sally Horner felt able to reckon with the changes roiling inside her. She'd already made a significant first step. Before leaving Dallas, she'd mustered up the courage to tell a friend at school that her relationship with her "father" involved sexual intercourse. The friend told Sally her behavior was "wrong" and that "she ought to stop," as Sally later explained. As her friend's admonishment sank in, Sally began refusing La Salle's advances, but kept up the illusion he was her dad.

For so long she felt she had to stay silent, or to accept what the man posing as her father said was the natural thing to do between them. All this time she opted to give in because it seemed the surest path to survival. Now Sally felt freer in a small way. Not free—she was still in La Salle's clutches, and could not see a way to escape. But she could say no now, and he didn't punish her like he had in the old days. Perhaps he looked at Sally, a month shy of her thirteenth birthday, and saw a girl aging out of his tastes. Or perhaps he trusted that Sally belonged to him so completely he no longer needed to use rape as a means of physical and psychological control.

What she knew now was that her relationship with Frank La Salle was the opposite of natural. It was against nature. It was wrong.

FRANK LA SALLE needed to find work. Several days after landing at the trailer park, La Salle abandoned his car—perhaps it needed repairs after so many days on bumpy, unevenly paved highway roads—and took the bus two miles into town to look for a job. Sally was already enrolled in school, and may have attended as many as four days of classes. She did not attend class that morning, though. By staying away, Sally changed the course her life had traveled on for the past twenty-one months.

FIFTEEN

San Jose

On the morning of March 21, 1950, Ruth Janisch invited Sally Horner over to her trailer. She knew Frank La Salle wouldn't return from his job search for several more hours, and sensed the girl might open up to her. All it would take was the right push at the right time. If Ruth didn't seize the opportunity now, she never would. Gently, she coaxed more honesty out of the young girl. Before, in Dallas, Sally wouldn't budge. This time, in San Jose, she did.

Sally confirmed Ruth's suspicion that Frank La Salle was not, in fact, her father, and that he'd forced her to stay with him for nearly two years. She said she missed her mother, Ella, and her older sister, Susan. Sally told Ruth she wanted to go home.

Ruth absorbed what the girl told her. Though she had been suspicious of the relationship, she never imagined that La Salle had kidnapped Sally. Then she sprang into action. She beckoned Sally over to the telephone and showed her how to make a long-distance phone call. Sally had never done so before.

Sally dialed her mother's number first, but the line was disconnected; Ella had lost her seamstress job in January and, while unemployed, could not afford to pay the bill. Next, she tried her sister, Susan, in Florence. No one answered the house phone, so Sally tried the greenhouse next.

Her brother-in-law, Al Panaro, picked up.

"Will you accept a collect call from Sally Horner in San Jose, California?" the operator asked.

"You bet I will," Panaro replied.

"Hello, Al, this is Sally. May I speak to Susan?"

He could barely contain his excitement. "Where are you at? Give me your exact location."

"I'm with a lady friend in California. Send the FBI after me, please! Tell Mother I'm okay, and don't worry. I want to come home. I've been afraid to call before."

The connection was poor, and Al had a hard time hearing his sister-in-law. But he heard enough to get the trailer park address down on paper, and to assure Sally he would call the FBI. She just had to stay exactly where she was.

Then Panaro passed the phone over to Susan, who was with him in the greenhouse. She was flabbergasted that her younger sister was alive, and on the telephone line. She also urged Sally to stay put and wait for the police.

After Sally hung up, she turned to Ruth, her face drained of color. She looked ready to collapse. She kept saying, over and over, "What will Frank do when he finds out what I have done?"

Ruth spent the next little while keeping Sally calm, hoping the FBI, or even the local police, would show up soon and arrest Frank. Sally, anxious, thought she should go back to her own trailer to wait for the police. Ruth let her go, hoping it would not be for too long.

AFTER SPEAKING with his sister-in-law for the first time in nearly two years, Al Panaro immediately called the Camden County Police Department. He asked for Detective Marshall Thompson, the man who'd been investigating Sally's disappearance exclusively for more than a year. But Thompson worked the night shift and was home in bed when Panaro's call came in. William Marter, another detective, answered.

Marter was the one who relayed Sally's whereabouts to the New York FBI office. He warned them to proceed with caution around La Salle. He had eluded capture before, and they needed to be certain he would not escape again. Then the FBI rang the sheriff's office in Santa Clara County. Sheriff Howard Hornbuckle picked up, and soon learned that a girl abducted almost two years earlier was alive and well and in his jurisdiction.

Hornbuckle had been elected sheriff three years earlier. He was a local boy, a graduate of San Jose High School, and had attended the state college before he joined the police department in 1931. He had spent fourteen years on the force, as a detective and later a captain. He'd also moonlighted as a traffic safety instructor in his spare time, where he stressed the danger of cars and how too many young people died while at the wheel. A cautionary slogan he coined—"Death Begins at 40"—even got picked up by the wire services and circulated nationally for a while.

Santa Clara County had its fair share of crime. Hornbuckle's own predecessor was indicted on gambling and bribery charges, and more recently the brutal murder of a high school girl had garnered headlines. But this situation was extraordinary. While many in local law enforcement got their hackles up when the FBI called, Hornbuckle did not. The case of a young girl so far from home was no time to get your nose out of joint. The FBI and the sheriff's office would work together on this.

When Hornbuckle sent his deputies to the trailer park on Monterey Road, federal agents were already on their way. The fleet of cops, local and national, sped to the El Cortez Motor Inn. Three men from the sheriff's office, Lieutenant John Gibbons and Officers Frank Leva and Douglas Logan, found Sally, alone, in La Salle's trailer.

"Please get me away from here before he gets back from town," she said, terror winning out over relief for the moment. What if he returned before she could get away from the trailer park? What if he tried to take her again? And if he did, what if he did things to her she didn't want to think about?

But this time she was in the hands of the real police and the real FBI, not the pretend agent, Frank La Salle. These cops promised Sally she was safe. La Salle would not be able to take her or touch her again. Three deputies whisked her to a detention center in the city, run by Matron Lillian Nelson. Once she was settled there, the remaining local and federal police waited for La Salle to return.

Lieutenant Gibbons at first held back from questioning Sally. "She's too shaken up," he told reporters a few hours later when they pressed him for details. But when Sally calmed down, Sheriff Hornbuckle led her into an interview room where she told him what had happened, and where she had been all this time. Hornbuckle listened, with patience, as Sally told him the whole terrible story. At first she gasped, sobbed, and cried. The hysterics were understandable, and the sheriff did not hurry her.

Then, at last, Sally found her voice. She started at the beginning, describing how La Salle caught her trying to steal a notebook on a dare at the five-and-dime. How he said he was an FBI agent and that she was "under arrest." How scared she was, and then how relieved when he let her go. How he found her again several months later, coming home from school. And how he told her she could avoid reform school only if she went away to Atlantic City with him, telling her mother he was the father to her friends, "because the government insisted I go there."

Sally confirmed that she and La Salle had lived in Baltimore for eight months before moving on to Dallas, and had only just arrived in San Jose. The entire time he held on to her, La Salle told Sally "that if I went back home, or they sent for me, or I ran away, I'd go to prison. The government ordered him to keep me and take care of me, that's what he said."

Hornbuckle then had to ask Sally the toughest question: whether La Salle had forced her to have sex with him during their nearly two years on the road. He phrased it delicately, asking if Sally had "been intimate" with La Salle. She denied it. But later, after a doctor's examination, she confessed the truth. "The first time was in Baltimore right after we got there. And ever since, too." And then in Dallas, she said a "school chum of mine" told her that what she was doing with Frank was "wrong, and I ought to stop. I did stop, too."

She said La Salle was "mean and scolded me a little, but the rest of the time he treated me like a father." Sally also said he had carried a gun for a time, in keeping with his pose as an FBI agent, but she thought La Salle had left it behind in Baltimore.

Sally was emphatic that La Salle was not her father. "My real daddy died when I was six and I remember what he looks like. I never saw [La Salle] before that day in the dime store."

Once she began to talk, she could not stop. Until finally, pausing for breath, she said, "I want to go home as soon as I can."

IT'S NOT CLEAR if Frank La Salle found gainful employment that morning in San Jose. When he stepped off the bus and walked back to the trailer just after one o'clock in the afternoon, dozens of police officers surrounded him before he could reach his front door. They'd been hiding behind other trailers. Deputies from the sheriff's office. FBI agents. Local San Jose cops. All present because of a chain of events that began as soon as Sally Horner hung up the phone. La Salle did not fight, but instead surrendered quietly.

At the San Jose jail, La Salle grew more animated. He denied abducting Sally. He insisted he was her father and that her mother "has known where I am and where the girl is every day since I've been gone." La Salle elaborated his alternate reality. "I took her when she was a little thing. . . . I am the father of six kids, three by this wife (Mrs. Horner) and three by another wife. I didn't take [Sally] from Camden but from New York. It was four years ago, not two. She kept house for me and she had money and freedom." The authorities, La Salle claimed, could have found him "at any time." He had a business in Dallas, after all, and "always had cars registered in my name." When he was done protesting his innocence, La Salle refused to speak further.

"He's a tough, vicious character," said Lieutenant Gibbons.

ELLA HORNER WAS OVERJOYED and overcome by the news that her daughter was alive and had been found. So much so that at first, she could hardly speak. When she composed herself, she told the large crowd of reporters and photographers who had descended upon 944 Linden Street that she was chiefly concerned with Sally's safety. "I just want her back and to see her again. I am very thankful, and I will be a whole lot more thankful when I really see Sally."

She also repeated the sentiment she'd expressed to the press—and, perhaps, countless other times in private—back in December 1948, while Sally was still missing. "Whatever she has done, I can forgive her."

Later that day, a Camden *Courier-Post* reporter, Jacob Weiner, found Ella clutching a photo of Sally, the one that had been recovered from the Atlantic City boardinghouse in August 1948. "It seems so long ago, Sally, so long ago," Ella murmured, gazing at the picture of her daughter. In a stronger tone, but with her voice still shaking, Ella said: "I'm so relieved."

Ella repeated that Sally had been gone for nearly two years. "That's a long time," she said. "During that time, I didn't hear from her. No word. No postcard. No news of any kind."

About that June day when she allowed Sally to accompany Frank La Salle for a seashore vacation, she said, "I must have been very foolish . . . at least I know it now." She picked up the picture of Sally again. "Anyway, I let her go. I haven't seen her since. . . ."

Weiner asked Ella if she ever gave up hope that Sally would be found alive. There were times, Ella said, where she felt "pretty hopeless" because "I always knew she had enough sense to call me or drop me a line." And yet Sally hadn't.

What did Ella think about Frank La Salle? "That man . . . ," she began, but her voice broke.

Susan was sitting with her mother during Weiner's interview, and picked up the thread. "I hope that man La Salle is properly punished. He should receive life imprisonment . . . or the electric chair."

Then Susan turned her thoughts to a second telephone conversation she'd just had with her younger sister. "I couldn't believe it was Sally I was talking to. It was wonderful." Her eyes filled with tears. "I can't wait to see her."

Sally had asked Susan how their mother was faring. She also asked after Susan's daughter, Diana, now nineteen months old.

"She looks just like you," Susan said, and Sally burst into tears.

TELEPHONES ARE A recurring motif in *Lolita*. The incessant ringing of the "machina telephonica and its sudden god" interrupts the narrative, as Humbert Humbert's psyche begins to fissure—the monster underneath waging war with the amiable surface personality he presents to the world. Telephones are also the means through which Humbert discovers Charlotte's accidental death, since he is too preoccupied with fixing her a drink to notice that she has left the house.

Sally on the telephone to her family in the hours after her rescue.

With Charlotte permanently out of the picture, he

goes to pick up Dolores at Camp Q to break the news of her mother's death in his own special way—"all a-jitter lest delay might give her the opportunity of some idle telephone call to Ramsdale." After he picks her up, he takes Dolores to the Enchanted Hunters hotel, where he rapes her for the first time. The following morning, the telephone plays a pivotal role in binding the older man and girl together. Humbert had told Dolores that he was taking her to Charlotte, who he said was in the hospital in Lepingville. At a rest stop, Dolores asks: "Give me some dimes and nickels. I want to call mother in the hospital. What's the number?"

Humbert says, "You can't call that number."

"Why?" cries Dolores. "Why can't I call my mother if I want to?"

"Because," he says, "your mother is dead."

It is the news that totally breaks Lolita and puts her in Humbert Humbert's power. He knows it, too: "At the hotel we had separate rooms, but in the middle of the night she came sobbing into mine, and we made it up very gently. You see, she had absolutely nowhere else to go."

From there Humbert and Dolores begin their road trip, a journey that would take them thousands of miles across the United States. Deep into their trip, Humbert's paranoia grows as he suspects Dolores has confided the truth about him to Mona, a school friend suspicious of the relationship between the so-called father and daughter: "the stealthy thought . . . that perhaps after all Mona was right, and she, orphan Lo, could expose [Humbert] without getting penalized herself."

Dolores's first escape, after she yells "unprintable things" and accuses Humbert of murdering her mother and violating her, occurs as the phone rings and she breaks free of his grip on her wrist (in part echoing La Salle's grip upon Sally's arm at the Camden five-and-dime). That escape lasts only a few hours, and Humbert finds her "some ten paces away, through the glass of a telephone booth (membranous god still with us)."

After that, Dolores asserts her will as to where they should go next. And then, though the reader is not privy to it, she makes a final, mysterious call, presumably to Clare Quilty, to help her escape. Telephones, Humbert concludes, "happened to be, for reasons unfathomable, the points where my destiny was liable to catch." For Dolores, telephones are the means for her to find freedom from the abuser who has engulfed her life—just as a telephone call was for Sally Horner.

SIXTEEN

After the Rescue

Though Frank La Salle was in jail, it wasn't clear which law enforcement agency would have jurisdiction over him. There were the outstanding warrants for kidnapping and abduction from Camden County. But because La Salle had transported Sally across several states, it became a federal case. La Salle was charged with violating the Mann Act, for "allegedly taking the girl across state lines for immoral purposes."

On the morning of March 22, Camden County prosecutor Mitchell Cohen spoke with the San Jose police, including Sheriff Hornbuckle. After the thirty-minute call, he told reporters in Camden that he would convene a grand jury to indict La Salle on the outstanding warrants, and start extradition proceedings immediately.

La Salle seemed ready to fight his extradition to Camden,

but Cohen was undeterred. "Regardless of what La Salle says he will do about returning here, I am taking no chances," Cohen said. "I will start formal proceedings at once and get him back here as soon as possible." But the prosecutor had to wait on New Jersey governor Alfred Driscoll's approval, and there was a delay because Driscoll was out of town on a business trip.

That afternoon, in California, Commissioner Marshall Hall presided over La Salle's arraignment on the Mann Act charges. He set a $10,000 bond and scheduled a hearing for the following morning. La Salle retained Manny Gomez as his attorney, while Frank Hennessy was the federal prosecutor.

The hearing began at 10:30 A.M. on March 23. There Hennessy revealed that La Salle's birth name was Frank La Plante; if true, then at various points during Sally's captivity, she'd attended school using the first name of La Salle's biological daughter and his own real last name.

When police officers attempted to lead Sally into the courtroom, she resisted at first, frantic at the thought of seeing La Salle: "I'm afraid, I'm afraid," she cried.

May Smothers, a juvenile court matron, had accompanied the girl to court, and calmed her down. Sally finally entered the courtroom clutching Smothers's hand. She took a seat only four feet away from La Salle and stole furtive glances at him throughout the proceedings, looking away whenever she came close to breaking down. La Salle stared at her, impassive, saying nothing.

When Sally began her testimony, Commissioner Hall asked, "Are you afraid of anything? Is there anything you want?"

"I want to go home!"

"He can't hurt you," said Hall.

And so, once more, Sally described her ordeal, starting with the Camden five-and-dime and ending with the San Jose trailer park. She told the court how La Salle had forced her to have sex with him, the abuse only ending in Dallas. La Salle told his story again, too, continuing to insist that he was Sally's real father.

Commissioner Hall affirmed the $10,000 bond, and ordered La Salle transferred to the county jail in San Francisco.

The hearing also decided La Salle's jurisdictional fate. Hennessy told the court that the federal charges would eventually be dropped because the New Jersey state kidnapping charges took precedence. But for the time being, La Salle would sit tight. Even if he raised the full $10,000 bond, federal authorities "were confident they could hold [La Salle] on other charges until he could be extradited," reported the *Courier-Post*.

Sally returned to the San Jose detention center. At first, she was so anxious about La Salle possibly going free that she could hardly eat. Matron Smothers told the papers that Sally also "fretted a lot about whether her folks would want her after what happened." Sally was kept apart from the other detained juveniles because, an unnamed sheriff's official told the *Courier-Post*, "We have some pretty hardened kids here and we don't want Sally to come in contact with them."

Over the next few days, Sally grew more secure in the detention center. Matron Smothers took her shopping for new clothes, because in her estimation, Sally's old ones did not measure up: "The clothes she had at the [trailer park] were neat but shabby and very inadequate." Smothers said that Sally had also stopped worrying about whether her family would welcome her back. "All she's thinking about is getting home and what she'll do when she gets there."

The detention center felt "responsible for Sally's well-being until New Jersey's authorities arrive to take her home," said an unnamed sheriff's official. "We've had a number of offers from people in San Jose to take care of Sally until she's ready to go home, but we are positive no harm can come to her where she is now."

BACK IN CAMDEN, police continued to investigate another dangling thread: the mysterious "Miss Robinson" Sally said had accompanied her and Frank La Salle on the bus to Baltimore, after which she disappeared. Camden police tried to reconcile Sally's statement to Sheriff Hornbuckle with what they found in their own initial investigations. They had proof, after all, that Sally and La Salle had spent time in Atlantic City, in the form of unsent letters, photographs, clothing, and other material abandoned at 203 Pacific Avenue. Proof bolstered by the recollections of Robert and Jean Pfeffer, the young Philadelphia couple who had reported spending a summer day with Sally and La Salle.

No trace of the woman known as "Miss Robinson" was ever discovered by law enforcement. It remains another of the unresolved mysteries of Sally's captivity. I believe the woman existed, because I believe Sally. Just because police did not track the woman down, and that decades later I also could not find her, does not mean Sally made her up.

A CAMDEN GRAND JURY indicted La Salle for kidnapping and abduction at 2:20 P.M. on March 23, the same day as the hearing in San Francisco. Ella Horner testified in front of the grand jury. There's no record of what she said, but she was likely asked about why she put Sally on the bus to Atlantic City and whether La Salle was her daughter's biological father, as he claimed.

Mitchell Cohen sent a copy of the grand jury indictment

to the New Jersey governor to start the extradition process. A second copy of the proceedings, signed by Judge Rocco Palese, was airmailed to California to reinforce La Salle's detention. Cohen also received permission to bring both Sally and La Salle—separately—back to Camden, and to cover their travel expenses, as well as those of Camden city detective Marshall Thompson and county detective Wilfred Dube.

Cohen, Dube, and Thompson flew into San Francisco on Sunday, March 26. Over the next few days, Cohen received approval to extradite La Salle from Governor Driscoll in New Jersey as well as his California counterpart (and future chief justice of the Supreme Court) Earl Warren. Cohen also interviewed various residents of the trailer park. One was Ruth Janisch, who told Cohen she was willing to testify at La Salle's trial.

On Thursday, Sally was released from the San Jose detention center into Cohen's custody. Just after 8:40 A.M. Pacific time on Friday, March 31, Sally and Cohen boarded a United Airlines flight headed for Philadelphia. Sally wore a navy-blue suit, polka-dot blouse, black shoes, a red coat, and a straw Easter bonnet for her first-ever plane trip. She told Cohen how much she looked forward to seeing her family. She threw up only once, when the plane ran into turbulence just outside of Chicago.

Sally Horner and Mitchell Cohen board a Philadelphia-bound United Airlines flight, March 31, 1950.

Ella waited at the airport in the backseat of Assistant

Camden County Prosecutor (and future New Jersey governor) William Cahill's car. The rest of Sally's family, including Susan, Al, and their baby, Diana, arrived separately. Several other planes landed first, each one lifting Ella's spirits before crushing them again. "Why doesn't it come," Ella said, her face pressed against the car window. Sally's plane finally landed just after midnight, just over an hour late.

From the plane, Sally spotted her brother-in-law in the crowd. Sally wanted to get out right away, but Cohen told her to wait for the other passengers to leave first. Then she spotted her mother. "I want to see Mama!" she cried.

"All right, Sally," said Cohen. "Let's go."

Sally stood at the doorway for a moment, looking around. Then she spotted her mother running toward her, holding out her arms. Sally raced down the steps, her face lit up with joy and washed in tears.

Sally sees her mother, Ella Horner, for the first time in twenty-one months.

She and her mother clung to each other for several minutes, oblivious to the myriad flash-bulbs popping at them. At first, they were weeping too hard to speak. Then Sally said: "I want to go home. I just want to go home."

When they were safely in Assistant Prosecutor Cahill's car, Ella explained to Sally that she couldn't go home just yet. Instead, the authorities would take her to the Camden County Children's Shelter in nearby Pennsauken, New Jersey, where she had to stay "until the trial is over."

Sally leans on her mother's shoulder minutes after they are reunited.

After a short drive, their car arrived at the center, the Pan-aros following closely behind in a separate vehicle. Susan got out of the car at the same time as Sally.

"Susan!" Sally cried upon spotting her older sibling. Sally had been so overwhelmed by the sight of her mother, the photographers, and so many well-wishers that she hadn't realized her sister was part of the crowd.

"I kissed you at the airport but you didn't recognize me!" Susan said.

Then Sally realized her sister was holding a little girl in her arms. Sally reached for Diana, the niece she'd never met, and hugged her tightly. "Gee, she looks like pictures of me taken when I was a baby!"

Cohen, exhausted from the trip, gently informed the family that Sally needed to get some sleep.

In the days that followed, Ella was the only family member allowed to visit Sally at the Children's Shelter, to ensure the girl stayed in a calm frame of mind before and during the trial. Fortunately, Sally got along well with the matron. She also attended Palm Sunday mass with six other children from the shelter the day before her first scheduled court appearance, and that offered some solace. No one knew how long La Salle's trial would last, and they tried not to bring the subject up with Sally, lest she get upset. The place she really wanted to be, after all, was home.

Thanks to an unexpected development, Sally's stay at the center didn't last long at all.

SEVENTEEN

A Guilty Plea

F rank La Salle wasn't allowed to travel from California to Camden by plane. Airline regulations at the time did not allow for passengers to be shackled, and Mitchell Cohen wasn't about to take any chances that the man would escape. "It is possible he could be a docile prisoner," Cohen remarked. "On the other hand, he could cause trouble."

The solution was to transport La Salle by train. Doing so would increase the travel time from hours to days, but on the train he could stay handcuffed to an officer for the entire duration. Marshall Thompson got stuck with being shackled to the prisoner for the cross-country trip, hardly a reward for all of his dogged investigative efforts. Wilfred Dube took the berth next door to Thompson and La Salle, staying as close as possible to the two men. (While it would have made sense for the two detectives to trade off being handcuffed to La Salle, I couldn't find any evidence that they did.)

Mitchell Cohen was at the train station to see La Salle and the detectives off. Before La Salle boarded, he asked Cohen why he and Sally Horner weren't getting on the same train. Cohen explained the two were due to fly later on in the day.

"Well, take good care of Sally," said La Salle.

"I'll take better care of her than you did," Cohen replied.

The train trip took two nights and two days. La Salle, Detective Thompson, and Detective Dube left San Francisco at 5:00 P.M. Pacific time on the *City of San Francisco*. Overnight the train passed through Sacramento, Salt Lake City, Cheyenne, Omaha, and Council Bluffs and reached Chicago early Saturday morning, where the trio changed trains to the New York–bound *General*. Thompson had no relief or privacy, shackled to the man he'd been chasing for nearly two years. Just as La Salle could not escape the law, so could the law not escape La Salle.

The *General* pulled into North Philadelphia Station at six minutes before seven in the morning on April 1. To the surprise of waiting reporters and photographers, the trio of men were not on board. To avoid the scrum, they'd gotten off at an earlier stop in Paoli, met there at 6:30 A.M. by Assistant Prosecutor William Cahill and Camden County Police Captain James Mulligan.

They took La Salle directly to the prosecutor's office. Then Thompson went home, no doubt relieved to be free of the man. Dube, Mulligan, and Cahill stuck around for Cohen's interrogation of La Salle, which lasted about four hours. At 1:00 P.M., La Salle was taken to the Camden County jail.

Mitchell Cohen told the press later on Sunday that he expected the case to go before the jury no earlier than June. Early on the morning of April 3, 1950, the day La Salle was due to be arraigned on the abduction and kidnapping charges, Cohen received a phone call from the county jail. The accused wanted to talk.

Cohen arrived at the jail at 9:45 A.M. and discovered La Salle by himself in a waiting room. He still lacked a lawyer—he hadn't been able to keep on Manuel Gomez because Gomez was not licensed to practice outside of California.

Cohen reminded La Salle of his right to an attorney. If he couldn't afford one, the court would appoint a lawyer for him.

"I don't need any counsel," La Salle replied. "I am guilty, and I am willing to go in and plead guilty. The sooner the better. I want to get it off my chest, and I want my time to commence to run."

When Cohen asked him why he wanted to plead guilty, La Salle said, "I want to avoid this girl [receiving] any further unfavorable publicity."

Cohen told him that court was already in session, and he could immediately enter his plea.

"Then I want to get it over with now," said La Salle.

Cohen left the Camden County jail and went straight to the courthouse for the arraignment. The courtroom was packed with onlookers. Sally Horner took her seat at the back next to a detective assigned to guard her. She wore a blue suit, pink blouse, straw hat, and patent leather Mary Jane shoes.

At ten minutes to noon, La Salle filed in, wearing a navy-blue suit, white collared shirt, and tie.

As Judge Rocco Palese entered, the room rose to attention. Like Mitchell Cohen, the judge had tangled with La Salle before. Palese, then a lawyer, had worked on Dorothy Dare's divorce petition against La Salle in 1944, even filling in for Dorothy's main lawyer, Bruce Wallace, at one of the hearings while La Salle was still serving time for statutory rape.

Palese, to the best of anyone's knowledge, never disclosed this prior association with the defendant. Perhaps he did not remember. Perhaps he didn't see a conflict because he had never engaged La Salle directly in court. Camden County's legal world was so small that defense attorneys became prosecutors who then became judges, everyone working with everyone else. What mattered was that, right now, Frank La Salle was in Judge Palese's courtroom.

When the gallery took their seats again, Palese called on Cohen to begin.

The prosecutor first outlined the story of Sally's kidnapping and confinement. How La Salle "persuaded and enticed her" to leave her mother in mid-June 1948, and told her that his repeated rapes of her were "natural." How Ruth Janisch "broke La Salle's spell" in San Jose, and Sally made the fateful phone call to the Panaros. How La Salle's long criminal record and his deviant behavior toward Sally made him, in Cohen's estimation, "a menace to society—a depraved man and a moral leper."

Cohen addressed both the judge and the crowd with his final words: "Mothers throughout the country will give a sigh of relief to know that a man of this type is safely in prison. That La Salle is somewhere safe, unable to harm anyone else."

Judge Palese asked Cohen if he had anything further. He did.

"If the Court please, at this time I propose to take pleas from this defendant, Frank La Salle, but before doing so I want the Court to know that I have discussed this case quite at length with this defendant, I have advised him of his right to be represented by counsel, and to have the benefit of the advice of counsel. I have warned him of the seriousness of these charges, and the length of the sentences which these charges impose.

"Being in Court is not an unfamiliar subject to this defendant and he understands, and he has told me so, the contents of both indictments. He understands the seriousness of them and the sentences, the minimum sentences, which the Court can impose, and he has advised me he does not desire to obtain counsel either on his own or appointed by the Court. I do, however, feel, in order that this defendant may properly understand the situation that it may be best for the Court to repeat to him his rights before I take the pleas."

Judge Palese then addressed Frank La Salle. "Mr. La Salle, you have just heard the prosecutor advise the Court that he has talked to you and explained to you the two indictments that have been returned against you by the Grand Jury of our County, and he has indicated to the Court that you do not desire to be represented by counsel and you desire to proceed in the matter without representation, is that correct?"

La Salle replied, "Yes."

"You understand the seriousness of the two indictments that have been returned against you by our Grand Jury?" Palese asked.

"Yes, sir."

"And that they carry with them rather serious sentences?"

Again, La Salle replied, "Yes, sir."

Judge Palese asked how La Salle would plead.

"Guilty," he said, in a voice barely audible.

The judge asked if there was anything more La Salle wished to say before he handed down the sentence.

La Salle said, his voice still weak: "I don't want any more publicity for the children." (Cohen later explained to reporters that La Salle was likely nervous and meant to say "child.")

Just like that, the proceeding was over. The whole matter took perhaps twenty minutes, ending just after noon. But not before Palese decided upon a sentence for Frank La Salle. The judge ordered Sally's abductor to spend no less than thirty and no more than thirty-five years in prison for the kidnapping charge. He would have to serve at least three-quarters of the full sentence before being eligible for parole. Palese also added a two- to three-year sentence for the original abduction charge, as well as an additional two to three years for violating his parole.

Two days later, just after noon on April 5, La Salle began his sentence at Trenton State Prison.

Frank La Salle, after pleading guilty.

BECAUSE FRANK LA SALLE pleaded guilty, Sally did not get to testify against him. In Mitchell Cohen's office after the hearing, she asked, once more, letting go of the earlier courtroom stoicism and blinking back tears, when she could go home. With the case finished, and Frank La Salle going to prison, surely she could return to her mother right away?

Cohen sympathized with Sally, and told her so. There seemed no reason to keep her in the state's custody when the case was finished and La Salle incarcerated, but the wheels of bureaucracy turned at their own pace, not his. Judge Palese was the one who would have to decide when she could be released into Ella's custody again. Palese did so the very next day.

At noon on April 4, 1950, Cohen summoned Sally and Ella to his office for what he later told the press was a "lengthy conference" in which he delivered the news both of them wanted to hear the most. He also offered mother and daughter some advice. They were free, of course, to return to 944 Linden Street, but he thought it best they "went away from this area, changed their names and began life anew."

The extensive media coverage meant all of Camden, and much of Philadelphia and the surrounding towns, knew what had happened to Sally. Cohen worried the girl might be judged harshly for the forcible loss of her virtue, even if that reaction was in no way warranted. Cohen also urged Ella to seek the advice of the Reverend Alfred Jass, director of the Bureau of Catholic Charities, "in directing Sally's return to a normal life." Ella was a Protestant, but clergy was still clergy, and Sally's recent attendance at Catholic schools may have influenced Cohen's choice of religious advisor.

Sally and Ella got home at 1:45 P.M. Waiting reporters and photographers shouted questions and snapped pictures as they walked through the front door, Ella shielding her daughter. Ignoring the shouts, she shut the door firmly behind them.

From that afternoon on, the Horner women were private citizens. They were no longer at the mercy of the legal system, or the national press. The rest of the world could leave them alone.

In some fashion, it worked out that way, but their new-found calm did not last for long.

EIGHTEEN

When Nabokov (Really) Learned About Sally

Vladimir Nabokov spent the morning of March 22, 1950, much as he would every morning for the next month: bedridden and pain-plagued from the same neurological malady that had afflicted him a decade earlier, in the months leading up to his arrival in America. "I have followed your example and am in bed with a temperature above 102 degrees," Nabokov wrote Katharine White, his editor at the *New Yorker,* on March 24. "No bronchitis but grippe with me is invariably accompanied by the hideous pain of intercostal neuralgia."

White had also been ill and advised Nabokov to prize rest above work. Nabokov rested, but did not stop working. Just as he had written *The Enchanter* while bedridden a decade earlier, so now did he complete two late chapters of *Conclusive*

Evidence, the first version of the autobiography that became *Speak, Memory.* But as Nabokov told James Laughlin, his editor at New Directions, a month later, he did not "get back to normal conditions" for weeks. That summer, he and Véra did not travel across America to hunt butterflies, as they had done the previous year and on three earlier occasions. Not enough time, not nearly enough money, and too many deadlines loomed as his health slowly mended.

It's easy to imagine that, as he was laid up in bed at home in Ithaca with limited capacity to work, Nabokov picked up a copy of the local newspaper and came across the news of a kidnapped girl rescued in California after almost two years of cross-country captivity. It is not difficult to believe Nabokov, whom Véra described in their diary as being fascinated by true crime, paid avid attention from his sickbed as each day brought fresh news about Sally's rescue and Frank La Salle's crimes.

Here, in newspaper accounts of Sally Horner's plight, was a possible solution to a long-standing problem with the manuscript that would become *Lolita:* how to create the necessary scaffolding for all of the ideas rattling around in his mind, the decades of compulsion, and the games he wished to play with the reader.

Robert Roper, the author of *Nabokov in America,* was certainly convinced that Nabokov "read newspaper reports of a sensational crime" around the time of Sally's rescue. He told me, "I think reading about Sally was momentous for [Nabokov]. He was on the verge of abandoning his project when the March 1950 stories appeared, and it was as if the world were providing him with justification and template for writing his daring little sex novel. He cribbed so much from the story."

Yet there is no direct proof that Vladimir Nabokov learned of Sally Horner's abduction and rescue in March 1950. There was no story in the papers he was most likely to read—the *Cornell Daily Sun*, the college newspaper, or the *New York Times*. Similarly, there's no direct proof he glanced at the Camden or Philadelphia papers, the ones that carried the best details and the most vivid photos. Neither his archives at the New York Public Library nor those at the Library of Congress contain newspaper clippings about Sally. Any connection dances just outside the frame.

However, there is plenty of indirect proof that Nabokov knew about Sally Horner and her rescue. The circumstantial evidence is there in *Lolita*. And I believe he would never have fully realized the character of Dolores Haze without knowing of Sally's real-life plight.

LET'S FIRST CONSIDER HOW, roughly at the halfway point of *Lolita*, Humbert Humbert threatens Dolores into complying with him. He tells her that if he is arrested or if she reveals the true nature of their relationship, she "will be given a choice of varying dwelling places, all more or less the same, the correctional school, the reformatory, the juvenile detention home. . . ." Humbert's ultimatum echoes La Salle's repeated threats to Sally Horner, reported in the newspapers in March 1950, that if she did not do what he said, she would be bound for juvenile hall.

But earlier in the same scene, the comparison between Humbert and Frank La Salle is even more explicit: "Only the other day we read in the newspapers some bunkum about a middle-aged morals offender who pleaded guilty to the violation of the Mann Act and to transporting a nine-year-old girl across state lines for immoral purposes, whatever they are. Dolores darling! You are not nine but almost thirteen, and I would not advise you to consider yourself my cross-country slave. . . . I am your father, and I am speaking English, and I love you."

As Nabokov scholar Alexander Dolinin pointed out in his 2005 essay linking Sally Horner to *Lolita,* Nabokov fiddled with the case chronology. The cross-country journey in *Lolita* begins in 1947, an entire year before Sally Horner's abduction. At that time, Sally would have been nine going on ten, matching the age Humbert cites to his Lolita instead of the age she was when Frank La Salle abducted her. It is clear to Dolinin that "the legal formulae used by [Humbert Humbert] as well as his implying that he, in contrast to La Salle, is really Lolita's father, leave no doubt that the passage refers to the newspaper reports of 1950. . . ." In other words, the circumstantial evidence is right there in the text that Nabokov did, in fact, read about Sally Horner in March 1950, rather than retroactively inserting her story into *Lolita* several years after the fact.

To throw off the scent, or perhaps to amuse himself, Nabokov assigned details of La Salle to other characters. Dolores's eventual husband and the father of her child, Dick Schiller, is a mechanic. Meanwhile, Vivian Darkbloom—an anagram for Vladimir Nabokov—has a "hawk face," a phrase akin to the description of La Salle as a "hawk-faced man" in the March 1950 coverage of Sally's rescue. And as Dolinin underscored, references to Dolores's "Florentine hands" and "Florentine breasts" seem to point as much to Sally Horner's legal first name of Florence as they do to Botticelli.

Sally's captivity lasted twenty-one months, from June 1948 to March 1950. At the twenty-first month mark of their connection, Lolita and Humbert land at Beardsley, where Humbert realizes that he no longer has the same hold on the girl he once possessed. He worries Dolores has confided the true nature of her relationship with her "stepfather" to her school friend, Mona. And that in doing so, she might be cherishing "the stealthy thought . . . that perhaps after all Mona was right, and she, orphan Lo, could expose [Humbert] without getting penalized herself."

Dolores's potential confession to Mona echoes Sally's actual confession of her abuse at Frank La Salle's hands, first to the unnamed school friend, and later to Ruth Janisch. And just as Sally's escape comes about because of her long-distance phone call to her family, so, too, does Dolores make a mysterious phone call—immediately after fighting with Humbert—and then announces, "A great decision has been made." She doesn't flee him for another month, but the setup is already in place.

Then there is Humbert's aside in *Lolita*'s final chapter. He states that he would have given himself "at least thirty-five years for rape, and dismissed the rest of the charges." The exact sentence Frank La Salle received.

NINETEEN

Rebuilding a Life

S ally Horner was only two months past her eleventh birthday when Frank La Salle spirited her away from Camden. She returned home less than two weeks before turning thirteen on April 18. "When she went away she was a little girl," Ella murmured on the day she was finally reunited with her daughter. "Now she is practically a young lady." Sally had seen the country and how different so many other places were from Camden. She had been forced to grow up in the cruelest way possible, knowledge foisted upon her that could not be suppressed.

How the family marked her birthday isn't known, since no one, aside from Sally's niece, Diana, is alive to recall—and Diana was only twenty months old at the time. But a family outing to the Philadelphia Zoo, captured on a minute-long film clip shot by Sally's brother-in-law, Al Panaro, appears to provide a possible answer. It is the only known surviving footage of Sally.

In it, Sally seems dressed for spring, wearing the same outfit that she had on the plane from California, as well as to court the day that Frank La Salle pleaded guilty to her kidnapping. Her sister, Susan, has on a cream or white coat covering a pale blouse and dark skirt, while Diana is dressed in a pink two-piece suit.

Sally walks, shoulders hunched, beside Susan. At one point she pushes her niece in a white-handled stroller. She moves slowly, with hesitation, but it's not clear whether that's how she really moved or if the film clip was preserved at a slower speed.

In a close-up, Sally's face is angled to the left. Her expression is tentative, suggesting she still feels vulnerable out in public. That even though she is among her family, among those she loves, she isn't ready to let down her guard.

She does not look at the camera once.

THERE WERE OTHER PRESSING MATTERS as Sally Horner readjusted to life with her family, in Camden and elsewhere. She had been taken at the tail end of sixth grade; in the fall she would start eighth grade at Clara S. Burrough Junior High School, and was eager for what promised to be a fresh start. When she had gone to school during her captivity period, her energy was focused on surviving each day with Frank La Salle instead of dreaming about what she might want to be when she grew up. Now that Sally was free, she could think of what she wanted, for her own future. "She has a definite ambition," the San Jose detention center matron had said a few days after Sally's dramatic rescue. "She wants to be a doctor."

Ella, who had been out of work, needed to find a new job to support not only herself, but also a daughter who, through no fault of her own, was far closer to womanhood than any thirteen-year-old was supposed to be. Ella's repetition to the press of the phrase "whatever Sally has done, I can forgive her" points to her discomfort about the abuse Sally suffered, or even her lack of comprehension.

There was no vocabulary, in 1950, to describe the mechanism or the impact of Sally's victimization, where the violence was psychological manipulation, not necessarily brute force. Where the innocent-seeming facade of the father-daughter dynamic masked repeated rapes, unbeknownst to almost everyone around her. For Ella, who was struggling to pay the bills, put food on the table, and keep the lights on in the house, the details of Sally's captivity may have been too much to bear. As was the idea of starting over where no one knew what had happened to her. The stigma they knew must have seemed a better choice than the uncertainty of what they didn't know.

Taking Cohen's advice under consideration, Ella opted for a compromise: Sally would spend the summer of 1950 with the Panaros in Florence, while Ella remained in Camden. No one changed their names, and no one would discuss what happened to Sally for decades.

Over the summer of 1950, Sally Horner allowed herself to feel safe. She looked after Diana when Susan and Al Panaro had to work in the greenhouse, and sometimes Sally tended to the flowers and herbs as well. One family photo shows Sally in the greenhouse next to Susan, wearing dungarees, a white shirt, and a dark cardigan, her curly hair tousled around her face and chin, her mouth open as she is caught in mid-conversation with her sister.

Sally Horner and her older sister, Susan Panaro,
in the family greenhouse.

Other photographs from the same time suggest that living at the Panaros did Sally some good. One shows Sally standing by herself, clad in an elaborate pale-hued frock suitable for going to church or an afternoon social event. She's smiling at the camera, though her eyes carry remnants of the shyness she displayed while being filmed at the Philadelphia Zoo.

Sally's smile is wider in a second photo of her in a different fancy dress. Here she poses with a dark-haired young man wearing a suit at least two sizes too large. The boy is her apparent date, for a school dance or a church social. His name, and how the evening went, is lost to time—as is whether he was aware of what had happened to Sally.

By Sally's fourteenth birthday in April 1951, she looked like the typical American teenager of that period, the type to be wowed by Perry Como or Tony Bennett or Doris Day or other popular singers of the time. (In *Lolita*, Nabokov dutifully listed the soundtrack of Dolores and Humbert's road trip, including Eddie Fisher's "Wish You Were Here," Peggy Lee's "Forgive Me," and Tony Bennett's "Sleepless" and "Here in My Heart.")

One candid photo, likely taken by Al Panaro, hints at more complicated undercurrents in her than in a "bobby-soxer," as Sally was sometimes referred to in the press coverage of her rescue. She wears jeans again, as she did in the greenhouse photo with Susan, but now her shirt is dark, and her curly hair is pulled back. Her lipstick looks near-black in the black-and-white photo, which suggests she is wearing a ruby-red shade. The camera has captured Sally as she emerged from her bedroom, newspaper in her right hand, expression quizzical, as if she'd been interrupted while reading the funnies. She seems to be in need of sleep, caffeine, or a combination of the two.

A candid shot of Sally holding a newspaper.

Though Sally adopted a mask of good-natured resilience, Al recalled his sister-in-law drifting into melancholic moods. She would be in the moment, then gone. A light would shine, and then flicker out. "She never said she was sad and depressed," Al told me in 2014, "but you knew something was wrong." The family discouraged discussion about her ordeal, and she almost never spoke of what happened with anyone. There were no heart-to-hearts. She underwent no psychological examinations; nor did she see a therapist. There was only Before, and After.

At Burrough Junior High, located on the corner of Haddon and Newton Avenues, Sally, once more, excelled on the academic side. Al recalled his sister-in-law being "very smart, an A student," and said that "it seemed like she knew a subject before it was taught." She graduated in June 1952 with honors.

Despite the photo of Sally with a date, her social life did not open up. She'd had trouble making friends before her abduction; afterward it became even more difficult. Classmates whispered and gossiped about her time with La Salle. Boys, emboldened and entitled, peppered her with unwanted remarks and propositions. As her classmate Carol Taylor—née Carol Starts—remembered, "they looked at her as a total whore." Emma DiRenzo, whom Sally knew as Emma Annibale, agreed. "She had a little bit of a rough time at first. Not everyone was very nice. I think some people didn't believe her."

It didn't matter to Sally's classmates that she had been abducted and raped. That she was not a virgin was enough to taint her. Nice girls were supposed to be pure until marriage. "No matter how you looked at it, she was a slut," Carol said. "That's the way it was in those days."

Carol met Sally in eighth-grade homeroom. Carol had street smarts; Sally did, too, but she wanted to close the door on how she got them, and escaped into the land of books. Carol lived two blocks away from the junior high while Sally had a longer daily walk of four to five blocks. Carol came from a large family—she was one of ten siblings, a far cry from Sally's smaller pool of immediate relatives. Carol had some other friends. Sally had no one but Carol, who didn't care a whit what anyone else thought of Sally. Carol said she was oblivious about Sally's supposedly sullied reputation, but it's as likely Carol chose not to behave the same way as her classmates, and not to judge Sally so harshly. Carol admired Sally's manners, her love of books, and sophisti-